# COGNITIVE NEUROPSYCHOLOGY AND COGNITIVE REHABILITATION

# Cognitive Neuropsychology and Cognitive Rehabilitation

Edited by

M. Jane Riddoch

*and*

G. W. Humphreys

*School of Psychology*
*University of Birmingham, UK*



LAWRENCE ERLBAUM ASSOCIATES, PUBLISHERS
Hove (UK) Hillsdale (USA)

Lawrence Erlbaum Associates Ltd., Publishers
27 Palmeira Mansions
Church Road
Hove
East Sussex, BN3 2FA
UK

**British Library Cataloguing in Publication Data**

Cognitive Neuropsychology and Cognitive Rehabiliation
I. Riddoch, M. Jane II. Humphreys, Glyn W.

153.4

ISBN 0-86377-291-9



Printed and bound in the United Kingdom by BPC Wheatons Ltd., Exeter

# Contents

# List of Contributors

**Anderson, M.**
Department of Psychology, University of St. Andrews, St. Andrews, Fife KY16 9JU, UK

**Bartolomeo, P.**
Istituto di Neurologia, Università Cattolica S. Cuore, Largo A. Gemelli 8, 00168 Roma, Italy

**Bates, A.**
School of Behavioural Sciences, Macquarie University, Sydney, New South Wales, 2109 Australia

**Berndt, R.**
Department of Neurology, University of Maryland School of Medicine, 22 S. Greene Street, Box 175, Baltimore, Maryland 21201-1595, USA

**Brouwer, W.H.**
Traffic Research Centre and Department of Neurology of the University Hospital, University of Groningen, Rijksstraatweg 76, P.O. Box 69, 9750 AB Haren (Gr.), The Netherlands

**Bunce, F.**
Department of Psychology, The University of Dundee, Dundee DD1 4HN, UK

**Butters, M.**
The Amnesia and Cognition Unit, Department of Psychology, The University of Arizona, Tucson, Arizona 85721, USA

**Campbell, R.**
Department of Psychology, Goldsmiths' College, University of London, New Cross, London SE14 6NW, UK

**Caramazza, A.**
Cognitive Science Centre, Johns Hopkins University, Baltimore, Maryland 21218, USA

**Carlomagno, S.**
Istituto di Scienze Neurologiche, Università di Napoli, Via Pansini 5, 80131 Napoli, Italy

**Castles, A.**
School of Behavioural Sciences, Macquarie University, Sydney, New South Wales, 2109 Australia

**Colombo, A.**
Istituto di Scienze Neurologiche, Università di Napoli, Via Pansini 5, 80131 Napoli, Italy

**Coltheart, M.**
School of Behavioural Sciences, Macquarie University, Sydney, New South Wales, 2109 Australia

**Crerar, A.**
Department of Computer Studies, Napier College and Department of Speech Pathology and Therapy, Queen Margaret Polytechnic, Edinburgh, UK

**Decety, J.**
Vision et Motricité, INSERM U94, 16 avenue du Doyen Lepine, 69500 Bron, France

**De Haan, E.H.F.**
Cognitive Neuropsychology Division, Department of Psychonomics, University of Utrecht, Postbus 180.140, 3508 TU Utrecht, The Netherlands

**D'Erme, P.**
Istituto di Neurologia, Università Cattolica S. Cuore, Largo A. Gemelli 8, 00168 Roma, Italy

**Duncan, L.G.**
Department of Psychology, University of St. Andrews, St. Andrews, Fife KY16 9JU, UK

**Ellis, A.W.**
Department of Psychology, University of York, York, YO1 5DD, UK

**Franklin, S.**
Department of Psychology, University of York, York, YO1 5DD, UK

**Gade, A.**
Psychological Laboratory, Copenhagen University, Njalsgade 88, DK-2300 Copenhagen S, Denmark

**Gainotti, G.**
Istituto di Neurologia, Università Cattolica S. Cuore, Largo A. Gemelli 8, 00168 Roma, Italy

**Glisky, E.L.**
The Amnesia and Cognition Unit, Department of Psychology, The University of Arizona, Tucson, Arizona 85721, USA

**Hillis, A.E.**
Cognitive Science Center, Johns Hopkins University, Baltimore, Maryland 21218, USA

**Humphreys, G.W.**
Cognitive Science Research Centre, School of Psychology, University of Birmingham, Edgbaston, Birmingham, B15 2TT, UK

**Iavarone, A.**
Istituto di Scienze Neurologiche, Università di Napoli, Via Pansini 5, 80131 Napoli, Italy

**Jeannerod, M.**
Vision et Motricité, INSERM U94, 16, avenue du Doyen Lepine, 69500 Bron, France

**Job, R.**
Dipartimento di Psicologia Generale, Università di Padova, Piazza Capitaniato 3, 35139 Padova, Italy

**Johnston, R.S.**
Department of Psychology, University of St. Andrews, St. Andrews, Fife KY16 9JU, UK

**Kamsma, Y.P.T.**
Traffic Research Centre and Department of Neurology of the University Hospital, University of Groningen, Rijksstraatweg 76, P.O. Box 69, 9750 AB Haren (Gr.), The Netherlands

**Lakke, J.P.W.F.**
Traffic Research Centre and Department of Neurology of the University Hospital, University of Groningen, Rijksstraatweg 76, P.O. Box 69, 9750 AB Haren (Gr.), The Netherlands

**Làdavas, E.**
Dipartimento di Psicologia, Università di Bologna, Viale Berti Pichat 5, Bologna, Italy

**Lennon, S.**
Department of Occupational and Physiotherapy, University of Ulster at Jordanstown, Newtownabbey, Co. Antrim, BT37 0QB, Northern Ireland

**Menghini, G.**
Centro Ricerche, Clinica S. Lucia, Roma, Italy

**Miozzo, M.**
Dipartimento di Psicologia Generale, Università di Padova, Piazza Capitaniato 3, 35139 Padova, Italy

**Mitchum, C.C.**
Department of Neurology, University of Maryland School of Medicine, 22 S. Greene Street, Box 175, Baltimore, Maryland 21201-1595, USA

**Patterson, K.**
MRC Applied Psychology Unit, 15, Chaucer Road, Cambridge CB2 2EF, UK

**Pickering, A.D.**
Department of Psychology, St. George's Hospital Medical School, London SW17 0RE, UK

**Pilgrim, E.**
Physiotherapy Department, Radcliffe Infirmary, Oxford OX2 6HE, UK

**Riddoch, M.J.**
Cognitive Science Research Centre, School of Psychology, University of Birmingham, Edgbaston, Birmingham B15 2TT, UK

**Robertson, I.**
MRC Applied Psychology Unit, 15, Chaucer Road, Cambridge CB2 2EF, UK

**Sartori, G.**
Dipartimento di Psicologia Generale, Università di Padova, Piazza Capitaniato 3, 35139 Padova, Italy

**Schacter, D.**
Department of Psychology, University of Havard, Cambridge, MA 02138, USA

**Seymour, P.H.K.**
Department of Psychology, The University of Dundee, Dundee DD1 4HN, UK

**Siegel, L.S.**
Ontario Institute for Studies in Education, 252 Bloor St. West, Toronto, Ontario, Canada M5S 1V6, Canada

**Umiltà, C.**
Dipartimento di Psicologia Generale, Università di Padova, Piazza Capitaniato 3, 35139 Padova, Italy

# Preface

This book has its origins in a conference on Cognitive Neuropsychology and Cognitive Rehabilitation held at the University of Birmingham in 1990. That conference brought together researchers in cognitive neuropsychology and rehabilitationists in order to evaluate the relations between the two areas. It also provided a forum for the presentation of new empirical studies of cognitive neuropsychological approaches to rehabilitation. The conference used a format in which keynote addresses, dealing with recent developments in theory, generated a framework for subsequent empirical papers, and this has been retained in the book, with overview chapters adopting the role of the keynote talks. The book differs from previous works in the field containing this mixture of theoretical and empirical research. Cognitive neuropsychological rehabilitation (if that is indeed the correct term) is in its infancy, and perhaps more than anything else, there is simply a need for a larger data base of relevant studies. This book helps provide some of this data base. The book also arrives at a time when the first rush of cognitive neuropsychological studies of rehabilitation has finished, and researchers are beginning to evaluate the success (or otherwise) of the approach. We believe this evaluation is a necessary and positive step and it will be needed to advance the field. Many of the opening chapters to each section are concerned with this evaluation, and with seeking ways in which cognitive neuropsychology can be made yet more applicable to rehabiliation practice. We hope that many of the arguments are taken on board, and will influence future work.

As with any book, there are many people to thank. In this case we thank the editorial and production teams of Lawrence Erlbaum UK, and especially Michael Forster for bearing with us as we struggled to bring things to fruition despite many other competing demands.

M. Jane Riddoch
Glyn W. Humphreys

# PART ONE

## Overview

CHAPTER ONE

# Cognitive Neuropsychology and Cognitive Rehabilitation: A Marriage of Equal Partners?

M. J. Riddoch and G. W. Humphreys
*Cognitive Science Research Centre, School of Psychology, University of Birmingham, UK*

## INTRODUCTION

Over the past 15 years, there have been significant advances in the cognitive analyses of many neuropsychological syndromes, including neuropsychological disorders of reading (e.g. Coltheart, 1985; Coltheart, Patterson, & Marshall, 1980), spoken language (e.g. Coltheart, Sartori, & Job, 1987), visual object recognition (Humphreys & Riddoch, 1987a; Humphreys & Riddoch, 1987b), memory (Parkin, 1987; Mayes, 1988) and attention (Jeannerod, 1987; Robertson & Marshall, in press). In such analyses, investigators aim to understand cognitive deficits in patients in terms of impairments to particular processes within a model of normal cognitive function. In addition, evidence from cognitively impaired patients can be used to constrain the functional models of normal cognitive performance. For example, some of the clearest evidence for a so-called "direct" route for naming words (going direct from a lexical representation of the word's spelling to a lexical representation of its name) comes from neuropsychology (e.g. the finding that patients may retain the ability to read irregular words requiring lexical mediation, while concurrently showing poor word comprehension; Schwartz, Marin, & Saffran, 1979; Funnell, 1983).

Thus there is a two-way relationship between neuropsychological data and cognitive theory; the discipline of cognitive neuropsychology is based upon this two-way relationship (see Coltheart, 1984). However, until relatively recently, cognitive neuropsychological analyses have had little impact on the practice of clinical rehabilitation. The reasons for this have been considered in some detail in a number of recent publications (e.g. Wilson & Patterson, 1990), and are outlined in several chapters in the present volume (see the chapters by Patterson and by Hillis & Caramazza). Some accounts stress sociological factors for the lack of close links. (Those undertaking cognitive neuropsychological research have typically been academics, interested in finding out why a patient has a particular deficit rather than in trying to remedy it. In contrast, clinicians undertaking clinical rehabilitation may either be unaware of current theoretical accounts of a given neuropsychological disorder or they may fail to see the relevance of these accounts to the day-to-day treatment being carried out.) Others point to matters of substance that separate the diagnosis-based research typical of cognitive neuropsychology from issues that are at the heart of therapy research, such as how to choose the appropriate therapy for a particular patient. More recently, definite attempts have been made to relate cognitive neuropsychology to cognitive rehabilitation (Seron & Deloche, 1989). This book continues this trend.

## CHARACTERISTICS OF COGNITIVE NEUROPSYCHOLOGY

### 1. Cognitive Theory and Cognitive Neuropsychology

For many areas of study, cognitive neuropsychological research is carried out against the backdrop of existing information processing theories of task performance. For instance, studies of acquired dyslexia have undoubtedly been influenced by theories of word reading that distinguish lexical from (rule-based) non-lexical procedures for translating between spelling and sound. Tests can be designed which selectively tap the different parts of the information processing model (contrasting the reading aloud of irregular words with that of regular words and nonwords), and the performance of a given patient can then be interpreted according to the pattern of performance across the different tests and according to the underlying processing model. Models of this sort have also directed cognitive rehabilitation strategies. For instance, de Partz (1986) retrained word naming in a deep dyslexic patient (described later) by re-establishing a non-lexical procedure for translating graphemes into phonemes. It can be argued that this procedure was directly influenced by the cognitive model stressing dual lexical and non-lexical routes to word naming as training of the non-lexical process was conducted using nonwords in order to prevent the lexical route being used (see Seron, van der Linden, & de Partz, 1992).

As we have already noted, studies of patients with selective cognitive deficits hold additional promise in that they can facilitate the development of information processing models, by demonstrating selective patterns of breakdown within a given task. Patients can be shown to have selective problems with one task but not with another, though previously both might have been thought to be subsumed by a single (undifferentiated) processing system. Take again the example of patients able to read aloud irregular words without comprehending their meaning. Early models of reading made no distinction between lexical processes for direct translation from spelling to sound and those involved in extracting meaning from words (Coltheart, 1978). Dissociations showing good naming of irregular words without comprehension show that such an account must be incorrect; procedures exist for lexical reading without comprehension. Inferences of separable processing modules within a cognitive system are made even more secure by the existence of patients showing the opposite profile, so that the two patients doubly dissociate from one another (Shallice, 1988). In the case of reading, some patients can show access to the meaning of words without demonstrating direct access to phonology (i.e. "deep dyslexic" patients who make semantic rather than phonologically based errors in reading aloud; Coltheart, et al., 1980), and so doubly dissociate from patients who cannot extract meaning from print but can read irregular words aloud.

Using evidence from double dissociations, cognitive neuropsychologists can identify the separable processing modules comprising a given cognitive system. They can then proceed to outline a "functional architecture" for a given task, typically in the form of a "boxes and arrows" diagram, where the separable modules may conform to different "routes" between the boxes and arrows (see Coltheart, 1985, for this argument as applied to word reading; Humphreys & Riddoch, 1987c, for a similar argument concerning object recognition).

## 2. Cognitive Neuropsychology as a Method of Analysis

Much cognitive neuropsychological research has taken the form described, and it has concentrated on specifying the "routes" through the cognitive system mediating a given task. Researchers have been less specific about the nature of the representations "within the boxes" (Seidenberg, 1988; see also the chapters by Berndt & Mitchum and by Hillis & Caramazza in this volume). This may be a fault as far as cognitive rehabilitation is concerned. Keeping our examples from the field of word recognition, attempts to restore impaired lexical knowledge in a patient may differ according to whether the lexicon is thought to contain representations of whole words or of parts of words (e.g. separating word onsets from the body or rhyming section). If the lexicon contains segmented representations of words, then training using a whole-word "look and say" method may fail to restore lexical knowledge, and instead it may lead to a set of item-specific procedures being established that may fail to generalise when applied to new stimuli (see Humphreys & Riddoch, this volume, for evidence on item-specific learning in studies attempting to retrain patients with impaired visual object recognition). In many areas, theories have tended to be agnostic on issues concerning the nature of the representations mediating cognitive performance.

Berndt and Mitchum (this volume) also point out that theorists have tended to be somewhat cavalier in their labelling of the "boxes and arrows" of information processing models. Very often no distinction is made between stored representations and the processes operating on those representations, though again the outcome of therapy might differ according to whether a general process is treated (perhaps leading to generalization to new stimuli) or whether specific representations are restored (when perhaps little generalization might occur). At present we simply do not know whether therapy might be differentially successful if targeted at processes rather than representations (or vice versa).

However, in criticising cognitive neuropsychology thus, we need to ensure that we do not throw away the baby with the bathwater. To begin with, the criticisms apply only to some examples of cognitive neuropsychological theories; in other cases, theorists have gone into considerable detail in their attempts to separate representations and processes, and to specify the contents of the "boxes" within a model (e.g. Caramazza & Hillis, 1990). Further, the question should not be whether cognitive neuropsychology, as an approach, has delivered all it promised, but whether the approach can lead to useful developments in cognitive rehabilitation *in principle*. As we discuss below, an analysis of cognitive neuropsychologically oriented therapy does indicate that it can contribute to neuropsychological remediation over and above approaches that do not utilize a cognitive theory to direct therapy. This is a point made in a number of the chapters in this volume (Coltheart, Bates, & Castles; Ellis, Franklin, & Crerar). If this analysis is valid, then the "in principle" argument is won.

A somewhat different, and all too often ignored point, concerns the fact that cognitive neuropsychology is an *approach* to understanding cognitive dysfunction; it is not simply a recipe book with set procedures for assessing and rehabilitating neuropsychological patients. There are important implications here for therapy research. These can be illustrated first by considering the question of diagnosis. Cognitive neuropsychology has been useful for diagnosis of the functional locus of cognitive deficits in patients, but we should not think that diagnosis simply involves taking a given theory and applying it to a patient. More often, the diagnosis involves working through a series of tests that are set up in order to establish the functional deficit in a given patient, with the experimenters thinking on their feet as the tests are designed and carried out. In such instances, the tests with the patient contribute directly towards the theoretical framework for understanding the deficit.

In many areas cognitive neuropsychological analyses take this form because theories are underspecified. Our own work on ideomotor apraxia can be used as an example here. We (Riddoch, Humphreys, & Price, 1989) noted a patient C.D., who, following a left-parietal lesion, was unable to gesture with his right hand to seen objects. C.D. showed good recognition of the objects, so the problem in gesturing was not due to impaired recognition; he was also able to make right-hand gestures when given the names of objects. The problem with right-hand actions to seen objects was overcome to some degree when bimanual actions were performed to visual stimuli. Using such results, we suggested that there exist direct routes to action from vision, unmediated by the semantic system. C.D. had an intact route from the semantic system to the system controlling right-hand actions, hence the good performance when gesturing to names. His problem lay within the direct route from vision to action. We proposed that, for C.D., there was increased noise within this route, leading to interference when visual objects "afforded" several competing actions (cf. Gibson, 1979). The competition between competing actions could be reduced in bimanual tasks where the left-hand actions constrained those made by the right hand. Tests with C.D. led to the proposed theoretical framework. The framework is by no means complete, and many questions concerning, for example, the nature of the actions systems governing each hand, remain unanswered.

Nevertheless, this approach of designing tests according to a theoretical model derived as a patient is evaluated, can be useful for therapy research. In their chapter in the current volume, Pilgrim and Humphreys report a patient with a problem similar to C.D.'s; he also found it particularly difficult to make gestures towards visually presented objects. Pilgrim and Humphreys used a modified form of conductive education training, emphasising verbal mediation of action, with the aim of producing verbal constraints on the actions afforded by the direct visual route. The therapy was shown to have a successful effect with trained objects. Such cases illustrate that complete theories do not need to be realized before cognitive neuropsychology, as an approach, can contribute towards cognitive rehabilitation. What is crucial is that diagnosis and therapy are carried out in the light of some form of theoretical framework that specifies the underlying processing mechanisms (in this case, that there exist at least two routes from vision to action, one direct and the other indirect, involving semantic mediation, so that one route can be used to constrain interference within the other). The approach can be valid even if the framework is generated only with respect to the patient being treated.

## 3. Modularity

The main contributions from cognitive neuropsychology to the development of cognitive theory have come through the study of dissociations between patients (Shallice, 1988). Dissociations, by their very nature, lead to an emphasis on the modular structure of the information processing systems underlying particular tasks. This may be adequate as far as theory-building is concerned, but it is less satisfactory for clinical rehabilitation. In the clinic the rehabilitationist will typically be faced with patients with multiple deficits, where the damage has not respected the strict boundaries between functionally independent processing modules. It may be clinically relevant to understand how much one deficit impinges on another, or even more particularly, whether an associated deficit constrains rehabilitation of a given ability. This topic is discussed in some detail by Berndt and Mitchum, this volume, who discuss the constraints imposed by impaired phonological processing and by impaired verbal short-term memory on the rehabilitation of reading.

There may well be a useful distinction that can be drawn here between modular representations and processes, and non-modular factors. Modular processes operate on their own inputs and generate their own outputs without affecting processing within other parts of the cognitive system. Non-modular factors operate to modulate processing within the stimulus- and task-specific modular processing systems. Examples of non-modular factors might be the rate of learning or consolidation, or the level of arousal. Impairments to these non-modular factors might influence many modular sub-systems, and also impinge directly on rehabilitation. For instance, Sartori, Miozzo, and Job, this volume, discuss the influence of anterograde amnesia on their attempts to rehabilitate category-specific recognition problems in an agnosic patient. Rehabilitationists clearly need to be interested in issues concerning the non-modularity of information processing, as well as the nature of modular subsystems. So far, cognitive neuropsychology has tended to down-play such issues.

Once the role of non-modular factors becomes recognised, theories can be developed that specify the relations between non-modular factors and modular processes. Rehabilitation can then be directed at the non-modular factors in a theoretically-informed way. One area where progress is beginning to be made in this respect is in the study of attention. The relations between arousal and attentional modulation of sensory and response processes were the subject of considerable study in the early 1960s and 1970s (Broadbent, 1971; Posner, 1978). More recently, attempts have been made to map both sensory- and response-oriented attentional systems and arousal systems onto specific brain sites (Posner & Rothbart, 1992). These studies provide a means of relating theoretical accounts of the connection between attention and arousal to patients with selective brain lesions. Some aspects of unilateral visual neglect, for example, can be related to deficits within right-hemisphere systems dominant in the control and maintenance of arousal levels, while specific disruption of processing operations concerned with engaging, disengaging and moving attention may also be apparent (see Riddoch & Humphreys; Robertson, this volume). At least some of the effects of rehabilitation may be related to altering levels of arousal in patients; systematic studies are now underway to tease apart effects on arousal from effects on specific attentional operations (Robertson, this volume).

A moral from this work on attention is that cognitive neuropsychology can be sensitive to relations between modular and non-modular processes, but that more detailed theories of these relations are needed to understand how complex behaviour can emerge from interactions within processing networks. The potential importance of such interactions has not been stressed in cognitive neuropsychology due to the emphasis on dissociations between patients. Interactions between processing modules may govern the operation of the processing system, even though the modules may be functionally isolatable following brain damage. For rehabilitation, such interactions may be crucial.

## 4. Connectionist Modelling

Although we have discussed cognitive neuropsychological theories in terms of "box and arrows" models, a more recent trend has been towards the development of connectionist models of human cognition. In these models, performance emerges from interactions between large numbers of processing units, each of which performs a computationally simple task. Connectionist models have been applied to all the topic areas covered in this book (Visual object recognition, Visual attention, Motor performance, Spoken language, Written language and Memory), and they may provide an alternative to "box and arrows" accounts of behaviour. In particular, some connectionist models blur the distinction between the different processing routes apparent in "box and arrows" models, because the patterns of performance attributed to the different routes can be captured within a single network capable of representing several different associations simultaneously. Despite the use of only a single network, simulated lesioning can lead to processing disorders similar to those of some neuropsychological patients (Hinton & Shallice, 1991; Humphreys, Müller, & Freeman, in press; Mozer, 1991; Mozer & Behrmann, 1990; Patterson, Seidenberg, & McClelland, 1989).

Connectionist models may provide us with one way of understanding the relations between modular and non-modular processes in cognition as the effects of particular non-modular processes can be simulated to observe their general effects on the system and also on particular modules. From such simulations predictions can also be made concerning which modular processes might benefit most from gains in the non-modular factor. Cognitive neuropsychological rehabilitation may be modelled.

Connectionist models also take a step towards linking functional analyses of performance to the neurophysiology of brain functions. In crude terms, these models respect the general idea that neural processing is based on complex interactions between very many computationally simple processing units. And even though the activation functions and learning rules of many of the models are currently a long way from those used in the brain, general analyses of factors such as the size and nature of the lesion can begin (e.g. contrasting the effects of adding noise to a processing system relative to the effects due to "silencing" processing units, see Humphreys et al., in press).

In the future, we expect cognitive neuropsychological theories to go beyond verbal "box and arrow" formulations, and to take the form of fully articulated working computational models. We may hope that such models begin to remedy some of the characteristics of cognitive neuropsychology that are unsatisfactory for cognitive rehabilitation. Included among these, as we have noted, are a failure to specify the representations at different processing levels of a system; the failure to distinguish representations and processes; the failure to account for non-modular as well as modular processes.

## COGNITIVE NEUROPSYCHOLOGY AND COGNITIVE REHABILITATION

Hillis and Caramazza (this volume) propose that cognitive neuropsychology is *necessary* for cognitive rehabilitation, but it is not *sufficient*. That is, cognitive neuropsychology is necessary in order to provide accurate diagnoses of the functional loci of any impairments in patients. It is not sufficient, however, because the design and application of therapy would still need to be accomplished.

Some of the characteristics of the cognitive neuropsychological approach, outlined in the first section, lend themselves to cognitive rehabilitation more than others. For example, the emphasis on designing tests to help guide the interpretation of the deficits in a given patient, and on the use of an adaptive framework that can be updated as the research progresses, is directly relevant to therapy studies. Also, as clearer models of the interactions between modular and non-modular processes should emerge, so cognitive neuropsychological models should provide a useful framework for understanding general therapy effects that do not operate on specific modules. Connectionist models may prove particularly useful for this.

However, it might be argued cognitive neuropsychology provides little guidance as far as designing therapy is concerned; as Wilson and Patterson (1990) note, the therapy chosen following a cognitive neuropsychological diagnosis may differ hardly at all from more traditional therapies, designed without a specific process-model of task performance in mind. If this is so, what benefit is there from taking a cognitive neuropsychological approach? Specific issues here concern: designing therapy and understanding how learning might take place.

### 1. Designing Therapy

Designing the most appropriate therapy for a given patient is often thought to be more of an art than a science, and the most appropriate therapy probably depends upon many factors that will always be difficult to legislate for. These include: the interests and motivation of the patient, pre- and post-insult; the age of the patient; and the nature of the support systems provided. As noted earlier, the therapy actually done following a cognitive neuropsychological analysis may not differ greatly from what might have been done traditionally (see Wilson & Patterson, 1990). This would not necessarily be a problem, except that cognitive neuropsychological analyses are notoriously time consuming.

Is this criticism valid? We suggest that it is not. The example of de Partz's (1986) treatment of a deep dyslexic patient that we referred to illustrates this. De Partz set out to re-establish a non-lexical procedure for translating print to sound, consistent with the cognitive neuropsychological diagnosis that non-lexical reading procedures are impaired in deep dyslexia. Her treatment focused on the use of nonwords, because, in a patient with at least partial access to lexical knowledge (as occurs in deep dyslexia), lexical reading processes would probably dominate any attempt to re-establish a non-lexical procedure using words. As Seron et al. (1992) discuss, this choice of material may well not have been made without the framework of an explicit theory that distinguished lexical from non-lexical processes. At least in principle, cognitive neuropsychology can be of direct relevance to cognitive rehabilitation.

In other cases, cognitive models play a more abstract role in guiding therapy; for example, they can provide guidance for choosing a therapy to remediate a particular processing route, rather than dictating the nature of the therapy or the material to use. Thus Pilgrim and Humphreys (this volume) chose a therapy that aimed to utilize a semantic route to action, to help constrain a problem diagnosed as residing within a separate visual route to action. The cognitive model of visually directed actions was not specified in sufficient detail to determine the optimum material or remediation strategy (amongst a range that tap a semantic route to action), but it still served to indicate the general kind of approach needed.

Against this positive linkage of cognitive neuropsychology to rehabilitation, it could be argued (for example) that the therapy chosen by Pilgrim and Humphreys—conductive education—is one with a long history in the treatment of motor disorders, and one that might have been chosen by therapists not using a cognitive neuropsychological approach. The latter may well be true, but we suggest it is irrelevant to the argument of whether cognitive neuropsychology remains useful in such instances. Therapists may happen upon a good choice of therapy for a variety of reasons, many of them (we would argue) to do with the therapist's implicit model of the disorder in question. The cognitive neuropsychological approach attempts to replace such implicit models with an explicit account of the cognitive ability; it does not deny that implicit theories can be useful too. What is more relevant is that the cognitive neuropsychological model—even when not fully formulated in terms of the nature of the representations within the different processing routes—provides a framework for understanding why therapy is effective. This may only be the beginning of a proper analysis of the rehabilitation process. For instance, if the model of visually directed actions used by Pilgrim and Humphreys is correct, other procedures which utilize the semantic route to action should be useful for similar patients, and success should not be tied to the use of conductive education.

Thus cognitive neuropsychological analyses encourage evaluations of the nature of therapy to understand why any success occurs. In the case of conductive education, the effects of using a verbalised strategy may be separated from the effects of breaking complex actions down into components which are then chunked together into larger segments. The general point here is that cognitive models can provide a means of understanding why two apparently different therapies can work for patients with the same functional processing disorder. The models may predict success in both cases, providing the specific processes thought to be affected are treated. Note that the practicalities of carrying out cognitive neuropsychological analyses, typically using single patients who are studied in depth, lend themselves to therapy studies where the therapist adapts the nature of the therapy in the light of properly analyzed outcome evaluations (see Berndt & Mitchum, Mitchum & Berndt, this volume; Seron et al., 1992). Hence we argue that cognitive neuropsychology has been useful for therapy, both when models are used at the macro-scopic and at the micro-scopic levels (respectively in Pilgrim & Humphreys, this volume; and in de Partz, 1986).

Indeed, even the problem of time consuming testing is not necessarily critical. Many of the best cases of cognitive neuropsychological rehabilitation have been conducted on patients with long-standing clinical problems, perhaps many years after their lesion occurred. Accurate diagnosis and targeting of treatment would save time in the long run for such patients. Also, as models and tests become more sophisticated, so *guided* evaluations should emerge. Patients need not be subjected to all cognitive neuropsychological tests of a given ability, rather tests are needed that focus on a problem in a more detailed way only once the problem is exposed. Such guided assessment should be less time consuming.

## 2. Learning

Cognitive models have not traditionally been models of learning. Hence they provide little guidance as to why one patient can learn using a strategy to remediate a particular process, whilst another, with the same apparent functional problem, fails to learn (cf. de Partz, 1986, with Berndt & Mitchum, this volume). In part, this is because the present models provide no analysis of motivational or other apparently ancillary factors. Also, because the models are functional descriptions, they are not tied to neurophysiological analyses of the nature and size of the lesion. We believe this is unfortunate, because neurophysiological data are likely to be relevant for understanding recovery after brain insult. This point is explored more thoroughly in the chapter concerned with the rehabilitation of visual recognition disorders (Humphreys & Riddoch, this volume).

One way that cognitive models may become more closely allied with neurophysiology is through the development of connectionist simulations. Although, as we have already noted, such simulations often do not incorporate the same activation or learning routines as the brain, they nevertheless enable some issues to be explored: for instance, the effects of the size of the lesion on re-learning, the effects of lesions at different loci in the model etc. (see Humphreys & Riddoch, this volume). We look forward to thorough analyses along these lines.

In addition to providing a closer link to neurophysiology, connectionist models also speak to the issue of development—a much remarked-on fault of more traditional cognitive models (Patterson & Morton, 1985). Models can explore whether particular tasks can be learned in an unsupervised way; whether training with one task ought to generalise to another (given that assumptions made in the model, concerning the nature of the representations, are correct; see Plaut, 1992) and so forth. The models also emphasise that learning can continue throughout life, and is not confined to a "plastic" period during early development. Whilst this may be questioned, recent analyses in the field of vision (an area where the argument has been made previously) indeed suggest that learning continues to take place into adulthood (see Humphreys & Riddoch, this volume). By addressing developmental aspects of performance, connectionist models do not just deal with the effects of damage on the adult system; they can also be useful for analysing developmental disorders (e.g. by examining how learning varies as a function of the number of processing units at different levels of the system; see Seidenberg & McClelland, 1989). Developmental disorders of cognition have often not been dealt with in great detail within cognitive neuropsychology, at least in part because models were oriented towards the adult system. Connectionist models may help herald a change. Certainly there is considerable interest in developmental disorders, reflected by several chapters in the present volume (de Haan & Campbell; Johnston, Anderson, & Duncan; Seymour & Bruce; Siegal).

In sum, cognitive models have often had little to say about learning. This is not to argue that they should be aloof from the topic; on the contrary, we propose that models need to tackle the topic head-on. One way in which this is taking place is through the development of connectionist models of cognition.

### 3. From Cognitive Rehabilitation to Cognitive Models

Several authors have recently pointed out that the relationship between cognitive rehabilitation and cognitive modelling should not be one-way (Patterson, this volume; Seron et al., 1992; Wilson & Patterson, 1990). In addition to models being used to direct therapy, the results of therapy studies should also be used to influence theory-development. Indeed, rehabilitation studies can play a special role here because they provide examples of direct attempts to manipulate particular factors within a model. The theorist is no longer left simply as an explorer of nature's whims, able only to examine the ways in which particular lesions affect performance.

Already pieces of evidence are beginning to emerge indicating the utility of therapy studies. We pick out one example from the present volume. Hillis and Caramazza report a rehabilitation study on a patient with a semantic disorder affecting picture naming. Training via one modality (treating picture naming by giving sentence completion and phonemic cues) resulted in generalised improvement not only to stimuli presented within the trained modality, but also to stimuli presented in an untrained modality (naming written words rather than pictures; see also Riddoch, Humphreys, Coltheart, & Funnell, 1988, for a similar example). Generalisation might be expected if the semantic system mediating performance were amodal, and so used both for picture and for word naming.

It is in this last respect that cognitive neuropsychology and cognitive rehabilitation may be thought to be equal partners in their marriage. Rehabilitation studies should be of the same relevance to theorists as theories are to rehabilitationists.

## THE BOOK

The book contains 24 chapters concerned with the relations between cognitive neuropsychology and cognitive rehabilitation. It is divided into topic areas: Visual object recognition, Visual attention, Motor performance, Spoken language, Written language, and Memory. Within each area there is an overview chapter, and this is followed by a series of empirical chapters. The overview chapters aim to highlight theoretical developments within the given areas, and so should provide a framework for the following empirical chapters. There is also a general overview chapter by Coltheart et al., that attempts to speak to issues spanning a number of areas. By bringing together theoretical and empirical chapters in this way, we hope to highlight the importance of theory for the empirical studies of rehabilitation, and the importance of the studies for the theories. It is on this reciprocal relationship that we believe the future of cognitive neuropsychological approaches to rehabilitation depends.

## REFERENCES

Broadbent, D. E. (1971). *Decision and stress*. London: Academic Press.

Caramazza, A., & Hillis, A. E. (1990). Levels of representation, co-ordinate frames, and unilateral neglect. *Cognitive Neuropsychology, 7,* 391-445.

Coltheart, M. (1978). Lexical access in simple reading tasks. In G. Underwood (Ed.), *Strategies of information processing*. London: Academic Press.

Coltheart, M. (1984). Editorial. *Cognitive Neuropsychology, 1,* 1-8.

Coltheart, M. (1985). Cognitive neuropsychology and the study of reading. In M. I. Posner & O. S. M. Marin (Eds.), *Attention and performance*. Hillsdale, N.J.: Lawrence Erlbaum Associates Inc.

Coltheart, M., Patterson, K., & Marshall, J. C. (Eds.) (1980). *Deep dyslexia*. London: Routledge & Kegan Paul.

Coltheart, M., Sartori, G., & Job, R. (1987). *The cognitive neuropsychology of language*. Hillsdale: N.J.: Lawrence Erlbaum Associates Inc.

De Partz, M.-P. (1986). Re-education of a deep dyslexic patient: Rationale of the method and results. *Cognitive Neuropsychology, 3,* 149-177.

Funnell, E. (1983). Phonological processes in reading:New evidence from acquired dyslexia. *British Journal of Psychology, 74,* 159-180.

Gibson, J. J. (1979). *The ecological approach to visual perception*. Boston: Houghton Mifflin.

Hinton, G. E., & Shallice, T. (1991). Lesioning an attractor network: Investigations of acquired dyslexia. *Psychological Review, 98,* 74-95.

Humphreys, G. W., Müller, H., & Freeman, T. (in press). Lesioning a connectionist model of visual search: Selective effects on distractor grouping. *Canadian Journal of Psychology* .

Humphreys, G. W., & Riddoch, M. J. (1987a). *To see but not to see: A case of visual agnosia*. London: Lawrence Erlbaum Associates Ltd.

Humphreys, G. W., & Riddoch, M. J. (1987b). *Visual object processing: A cognitive neuropsychological approach*. London: Lawrence Erlbaum Associates Ltd.

Humphreys, G. W., & Riddoch, M. J. (1987c). The fractionation of visual agnosia. In G. W. Humphreys & M. J. Riddoch (Eds.), *Visual object processing: A cognitive neuropsychological approach*. London: Lawrence Erlbaum Associates Ltd.

Jeannerod, M. (Ed.). (1987). *Neurophysiological and neuropsychological aspects of spatial neglect*. Amsterdam: North Holland.

Mayes, A. R. (1988). *Human organic memory disorders*. Cambridge: Cambridge University Press.

Mozer, M. C. (1991). *The perception of multiple objects: A connectionist approach*. Cambridge, MA: MIT Press.

Mozer, M. C., & Behrmann, M. (1990). On the interaction of selective attention and lexical knowledge: A connectionist account of neglect dyslexia. *Journal of Cognitive Neuroscience, 2,* 96–123.

Parkin, A. J. (1987). *Memory and amnesia.* Oxford: Blackwell.

Patterson, K. E., & Morton, J. (1985). From orthography to phonology: An attempt at an old interpretation. In K. E. Patterson, J. C. Marshall, & M. Coltheart (Eds.), *Surface dyslexia.* London: Lawrence Erlbaum Associates Ltd.

Patterson, K. E., Seidenberg, M. S., & McClelland, J. L. (1989). Connections and disconnections: Acquired dyslexia in a computational model of reading processes. In R. G. M. Morris (Ed.), *Parallel distributed processing: Implications for psychology and neurobiology.* New York: Oxford University Press.

Plaut, D. C. (1992). Relearning after damage in connectionist networks: Implications for patient rehabilitation. Paper presented to the *Cognitive Science Society,* May.

Posner, M. I. (1978). *Chronometric explorations of mind.* Hillsdale, N.J.: Lawrence Erlbaum Associates Inc.

Posner, M. I., & Rothbart, M. K. (1992). Attentional mechanisms and conscious experience. In A. D. Milner & M. D. Rugg (Eds.), *The neuropsychology of consciousness.* London: Academic Press.

Riddoch, M. J., Humphreys, G. W., Coltheart, M., & Funnell, E. (1988). Semantic systems or system? Neuropsychological evidence re-examined. *Cognitive Neuropsychology, 5,* 3-25.

Riddoch, M. J., Humphreys, G. W., & Price, C. J. (1989). Routes to action: Evidence from apraxia. *Cognitive Neuropsychology, 6,* 437-454.

Robertson, L., & Marshall, J. C. (Eds.). (in press). *Unilateral neglect.* Hove: Lawrence Erlbaum Associates Ltd.

Schwartz, M. F., Marin, O. S. M., & Saffran, E. M. (1979). Dissociations of language function in dementia: A case study. *Brain, 7,* 277-306.

Seidenberg, M. (1988). Cognitive neuropsychology and language: The state of the art. *Cognitive Neuropsychology, 5*, 403-426.

Seidenberg M. S., & McClelland, J. L. (1989). A distributed, developmental model of word recognition and naming. *Psychological Review, 96,* 523-568.

Seron, X., & Deloche, G. (Eds.) (1989). *Cognitive approaches in neuropsychological rehabilitation.* Hillsdale, N.J.: Lawrence Erlbaum Associates Inc.

Seron, X., van der Linden, M., & de Partz, M.-P. (1992). In defence of cognitive approaches in neuropsychological therapy. *Neuropsychological Rehabilitation, 1,* 303-318.

Shallice, T. (1988). *From neuropsychology to mental structure.* Cambridge: Cambridge University Press.

Wilson, B. A., & Patterson, K. E. (1990). Rehabilitation and cognitive neuropsychology. *Applied Cognitive Psychology, 4,* 247-260.

CHAPTER TWO

# Cognitive Neuropsychology and Rehabilitation

Max Coltheart, Andree Bates, and Anne Castles
*School of Behavioural Sciences, Macquarie University, Sydney, Australia*

## INTRODUCTION

Since our intention here is to make some remarks about relationships between cognitive neuropsychology and rehabilitation, a description of cognitive neuropsychology makes a convenient starting point. Cognitive neuropsychologists appear to agree that their discipline, the intersection of cognitive psychology and neuropsychology, has two essential features:

1. The use of models of normal cognitive processing to interpret impairments of cognition caused by damage to the brain.
2. The use of data collected in experimental studies of people with such impairments as evidence for adjudicating between, testing, or developing models of normal cognitive processing.

Many cognitive neuropsychologists have over the past decade also come to be interested in the application of cognitive neuropsychology to the rehabilitation of people who have suffered some form of cognitive impairment after brain damage The general idea here has been that in order to treat such an impairment one must first *understand it;* and understanding it means being able to describe which components of the relevant cognitive processing system are still relatively intact and which have been affected by the neurological damage. Those who have adopted this approach generally also argue that directing treatment towards components of the processing system that are relatively intact is unlikely to help. Hence treatment should be preceded by theoretical analysis; and this analysis cannot be carried out without a model, simply because the model specifies what the relevant set of processing components are.

At least in Britain, ideas like this were developing just as views concerning the lack of efficacy of speech therapy were in circulation because of studies such as that by Lincoln et al. (1984). These studies of aphasia therapy made no attempt at analysing language disorders in relation to models of normal language processing, and hence invited criticism of the following kind: If the normal language-processing system has many separate processing subcomponents, there will be a very large number of different ways in which damage to that system will produce a person with an acquired impairment of language. Hence in any group of aphasics there are likely to be many different patterns of impairments and preservations of the set of processing subcomponents. If so, applying the same treatment to all of these different disorders is unlikely to be effective. Each different pattern of impairment will require a different pattern of treatment. Therefore, it was argued, it would not be surprising if group studies of the efficacy of aphasia therapy did not yield positive results.

It is because of this line of reasoning that those interested in the application of cognitive neuropsychology to rehabilitation came to the view that only the single-case approach was appropriate for research on the efficacy of treatment methods. What is more, it was also argued that this emphasis on the single-case approach was just as important in clinical practice as in rehabilitation research; any attempt at treatment of an acquired impairment of cognitive processing should be preceded by an assessment of that impairment based upon a model of the relevant cognitive processing system. So, for example, object naming depends upon a processing system involving at least half a dozen different processing components, and hence there are at least half a dozen different forms of anomia, which will require different kinds of treatment. Worries that the use of single-case studies would raise insuperable statistical or methodological problems led to statistical methods and experimental designs appropriate for single-case study research being drawn to the attention of those interested in this approach by, for example, Coltheart (1983) and Pring (1986).

This approach to the rehabilitation of acquired cognitive impairments has gained widespread acceptance. It is common now to come across such views as these:

> "The starting point for neuropsychological rehabilitation should be a secure model of the cognitive function to be restored." (Lesser, 1989);

> "It would be difficult to expose the logic of memory therapies without first making explicit the way in which mnemonic activities are conceived in normal subjects nowadays." (van der Linden & van der Kaa, 1989);

> "Any theoretical interpretation of any disorder of cognitive processing ... aims at identifying which aspects of cognitive processing are impaired and which remain intact. If such identification is successful, then a focus for treatment is provided. Without the prior theoretical analysis, treatment can only be unfocused." (Coltheart & Byng, 1989).

What has developed, then, is an approach to rehabilitation possessing these features:

1. Rehabilitation research, and the practice of treatment, must be organised in a single-case study mode;
2. The first step in treatment is an analysis of the patient's impairments in relation to some model of normal processing, identifying which components of that model are relatively spared and which are impaired;
3. Treatment studies must be designed in such a way that any improvement at post-test that is due to the specific treatment adopted can be distinguished from improvements due to spontaneous recovery, practice effects, or general effects of treatment.

One might offer this list of features as a characterisation of the cognitive neuropsychological approach to rehabilitation; and in the second half of the 1980s numerous studies using this approach were carried out (e.g. Bachy-Langedoch & de Partz, 1989; Behrmann, 1987; Byng, 1988; Coltheart & Byng, 1989; de Partz, 1986; Jones, 1986; Scott & Byng, 1988). This body of literature documents positive effects of cognitive neuropsychological treatment of numerous different forms of language impairment: surface dyslexia, deep dyslexia, surface dysgraphia, deep dysgraphia, "agrammatic" sentence comprehension, and "agrammatic" sentence production.

However, very recently, cognitive neuropsychologists have begun to scrutinise this work, interested in characterising more precisely what cognitive neuropsychology's contribution has actually been. A warning note was sounded by Howard and Patterson (1989):

> "There is a widespread (though, one could argue, unsubstantiated) belief that the development of treatment methods depends on, or at least will be facilitated by, analysis of underlying impairments. The claim is made (often, as Saffran (1986) noted, in the last line of applications for research grants) that better understanding of both the surface and deep structure of neuropsychological deficits will enable design of more rational and coherent treatment techniques. Is the claim true?"

And now doubts as to just how important the contributions of cognitive neuropsychology to rehabilitation really have been are explicitly expressed:

> "I find that the promise of cognitive neuropsychology as a guide for the choice of intervention strategies is still largely unfulfilled." (Caramazza, 1989);

> "Our assessment suggests that at present theories from cognitive psychology have little impact on the majority of treatment programmes." (Wilson & Patterson, 1990).

Thus it is clear that there is considerable controversy here. We believe that good progress in resolving these controversies may be made if we analyse in a little more detail what has been meant by the term "cognitive neuropsychological rehabilitation".

By definition, this term refers to the use of models of normal processing as an aid to rehabilitation. When one looks closely at discussions of the nature of cognitive neuropsychological rehabilitation, it becomes clear that there are three quite different kinds of contribution that people have thought models might make. These are:

*As a basis for rational assessment techniques.* Typically, a cognitive model tells you that the cognitive process that you wish to assess depends upon a particular set of processing subcomponents. These models are generally sufficiently explicit so that it is not difficult to deduce from the model what would be an appropriate assessment technique for each of these different subcomponents. Hence the model helps in the creation of a battery of subtests which represents a system for detailed assessment of the broad cognitive ability under investigation.

*As a way of defining what the focus of treatment should be.* If, within the set of processing components that make up the whole system, the assessment methods provided by the model identify which subcomponent is specifically impaired, this allows the treatment to be specific rather than general. In cases where an attempt will be at *restoring* function (rather than reconstitution—see Howard & Patterson, 1989), it would seem essential for treatment to be focused in this way.

*As a source of ideas about treatment methods.* If assessment has identified a specific subcomponent of processing that is the source of the patient's difficulties, and if treatment is to be focused on this specific subcomponent, we still need to decide *how* this subcomponent is to be treated. Knowing exactly how this subcomponent actually carries out its job in the intact system might help here.

What one needs to do, if considering the contributions of models to rehabilitation, is to discuss these three types of possible contribution separately. In order to illustrate the general points we would like to make, we will use an actual example from cognitive neuropsychological rehabilitation, namely, the work on treatment of acquired dyslexia by Coltheart and Byng (1989).

## ASSESSMENT

In our view, there can be no question about the major contributions that models have made to neuropsychological assessment techniques in the past decade. As models of language-processing are more advanced and more detailed than models of other forms of cognitive activity, contributions of models to assessment are most obvious in the domain of language, but are by no means confined to this domain. Models suggest distinctions, suggest contrasting classes of stimuli which highlight selective impairments that might otherwise have gone unnoticed. This is easily seen when one contrasts assessment procedures which are not model-based with those which are, contrasting, for example, the non-model-based Boston Diagnostic Aphasia Examination (Goodglass & Kaplan, 1972), Western Aphasia Battery (Kertesz, 1979) or Schuell examination (Schuell, 1965) with the model-based PALPA (Kay, Lesser, & Coltheart, 1992). Distinctions such as word vs. nonword, irregular word vs. regular word, abstract word vs. concrete word, content word vs. function word, morphologically complex vs. morphologically simple word, are examples of model-based distinctions which generate contrasting stimulus sets which can bring out in sharp relief selective impairments of language processing. Dual-route models of reading prescribe that the distinction between regular and irregular words, and the distinction between words and nonwords, are significant. For example, it is possible that the representations used in the orthographic input lexicon are morphemes rather than words (Murrell & Morton, 1974), so one ought to assess the processing of single-morpheme vs. multi-morpheme words, and so on. Assessment procedures which are not model-based simply lack materials of this kind. As a result, such procedures cannot yield detailed profiles of impairments and preservations of specific aspects of language-processing.

This is easily demonstrated using the Coltheart and Byng (1989) example. Their patient E.E. suffered from acquired dyslexia, acquired dysgraphia, and anomia, after a head injury caused by a fall. Treatment was for the reading difficulty. As this was cognitive-neuropsychological treatment, it began by using a model of normal reading as a basis for assessing E.E.'s acquired dyslexia. This was a dual-route model of reading (see e.g. Coltheart, 1985; Ellis & Young, 1988; Patterson & Shewell, 1987); Fig. 2.1 provides a simplified description of such a model. Hence an assessment of the integrity of each of these two reading routes was carried out. The straightforward way of doing this includes comparing the reading of irregular words to the reading of regular words, as one of the two routes, the lexical route, must be intact if irregular words are read well. In E.E.'s case, irregular words were read much less well than regular words, implying that the lexical route of E.E.'s reading system was selectively impaired. A consequence of any such impairment would be that sometimes when trying to read an irregular word, E.E. would have to use the nonlexical route, and the reading of irregular words by the nonlexical route will yield incorrect responses. What is more, these should be "regularisation errors"—reading an irregular word as if it were regular. The diagnosis that E.E. had a selective impairment of the lexical route for reading was confirmed by the fact that he made many regularisation errors when reading irregular words aloud.

This assessment was however not sufficiently detailed for treatment purposes. Reflection upon the model given in Fig. 2.1 reveals that someone who reads *yacht* as "/jætʃt/" might do so for either of two very different reasons:

1. the word has not been recognised by the visual word recognition system, and so is treated as a completely novel letter-string that is read aloud using the grapheme-phoneme correspondence rules of the nonlexical reading route;
2. the word is successfully recognised by the visual word recognition system but attempts to retrieve its pronunciation from the spoken-word pronunciation system fail; the only way to produce a spoken response to the letter-string is to generate this from use of the nonlexical reading route.

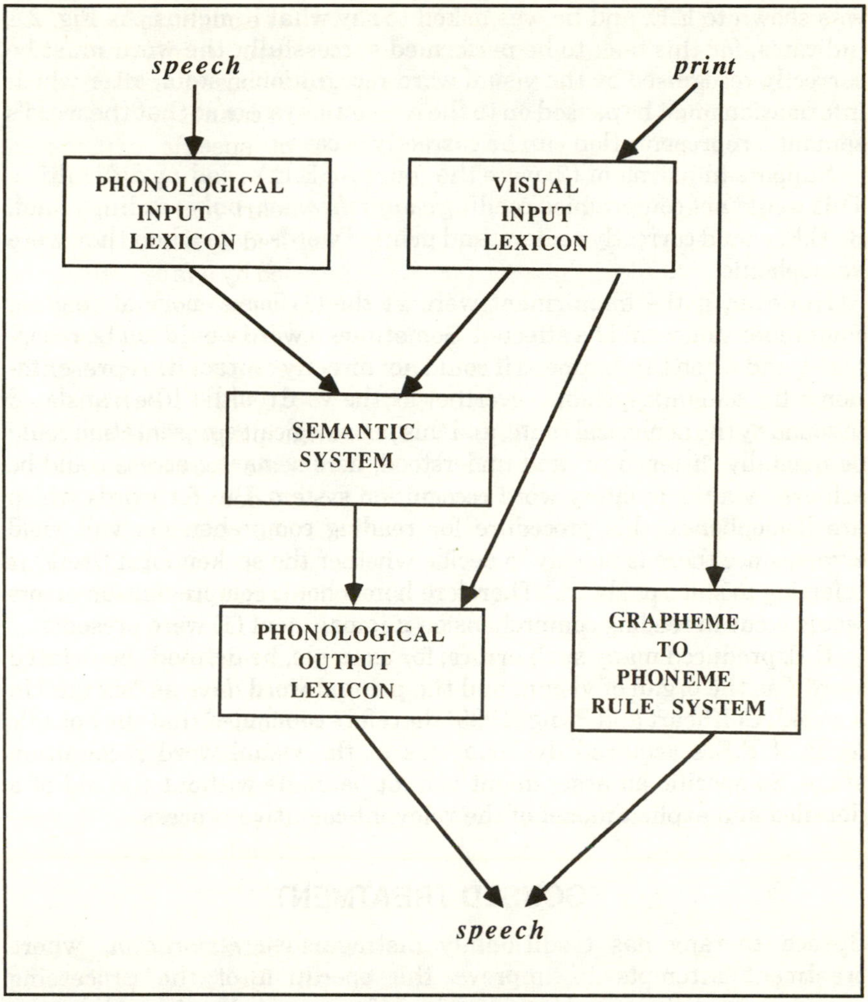


FIG. 2.1. A model of some of the language-processing system.

Clearly, these two different kinds of impairment, one a visual deficit and the other an anomia, would require different kinds of treatment. Consequently, treatment could not be planned until it was established which kind of impairment E.E. had actually suffered.

How can this differential diagnosis be made? Here again the model aids assessment, since reflecting on it leads to the realisation that testing the ability to comprehend printed homophones allows one to decide which impairment is present. Suppose the homophonic word *sale* was shown to E.E. and he was asked to say what it means. As Fig. 2.1 indicates, for this task to be performed successfully, the word must be correctly recognised by the visual word recognition system, after which information must be passed on to the semantic system so that the word's semantic representation can be correctly accessed.

Suppose impairment (2) were the source of E.E.'s reading difficulties. This would not compromise reading *comprehension,* only reading aloud. So E.E. would correctly understand printed words even when they were homophonic.

However, if the impairment were at the (1) locus, normal reading comprehension would be affected. Sometimes a word would not be recognised, and when this happens it could not directly contact its representation in the semantic system. Nevertheless, the word could still be translated to sound by the nonlexical route, and this phonological representation could be mentally "listened to" and understood; here semantic access could be achieved via the auditory word recognition system. But for words which are homophones, this procedure for reading comprehension will yield errors, since there is no way to decide whether the spoken form "/seɪl/" is referring to ships or shops.[1] Therefore homophonic comprehension errors would occur in reading comprehension if impairment (1) were present.

E.E. produced many such errors; for example, he defined the printed word *I* as the organ of vision, and the printed word *daze* as "six (sic) in a week". Coltheart and Byng (1989) therefore concluded that the specific locus of E.E.'s acquired dyslexia was at the visual word recognition stage. So specific an assessment cannot be made without the aid of a detailed and explicit model of the relevant cognitive process.

## FOCUSED TREATMENT

Speech therapy has traditionally distinguished *restoration,* where treatment attempts to improve the operation of the processing subcomponent that has been impaired, from *reconstitution,* where the aim is "to use the patient's remaining processing abilities to achieve the same functional result in another (abnormal/unusual) way" (Howard & Patterson, 1989, p.50). Clearly, restoration is desirable; but in sufficiently severe cases only reconstitution may be possible. We listed earlier seven case studies of cognitive neuropsychological rehabilitation. All aimed at restoration. The study of treatment of deep dysgraphia by Bachy-Langedoch and de Partz (1989) contrasts with the study of treatment of deep dysgraphia by Hatfield (1982, 1983): Hatfield's work was not model-based, and it was reconstitutive in character, whilst Bachy-Langedoch and de Partz's work was model-based and took a restorative approach.

Why this emphasis on the restorative approach within the cognitive neuropsychological camp? One reason is that, if a model allows one to identify in detail precisely what part of the system is specifically impaired, this permits treatment to be focused on this specific cognitive sub-ability, whereas an assessment method which is not model-based might make it difficult to design appropriate restorative treatments, because what needs to be restored has not been identified.

A second reason is that models allow identification of circumstances in which reconstitutive treatments could not be fully successful. For example, if a patient can still use letter-sound rules to read aloud, but has a specific impairment of visual word recognition, using the patient's remaining reading abilities *cannot* achieve the functional result of making reading as good as it was premorbidly, because no amount of virtuosity with rule-based reading procedures will permit correct processing of highly irregular words. In such circumstances, the choice appears to be between adopting a restorative approach or acknowledging that the ability in question can never be returned to premorbid levels.

Comparable points can be made in relation to other cognitive domains. Imagine a prosopagnosic who can no longer recognise his wife's face. Instead of using some model of face-recognition to identify the specific source of this impairment and then attempting to direct treatment at the specific processing subcomponent responsible for the prosopagnosia, a therapist could propose that the wife could begin to wear a distinctive pair of glasses, offering the patient a visual cue to identification. This is reconstitutive in the sense that some visual ability other than the impaired one (face-recognition) is used to achieve the function that is lacking. But of course this will not assist in the recognition by sight of other family members. Similarly, using mnemonic techniques to teach an amnesic patient to remember details about their immediate neighbours may succeed in avoiding some embarrassing moments in the street, but will not provide any general help with memory difficulties.

We do not for a moment wish to deny that there may be many cases in which restorative treatments may simply not be effective whilst reconstitutive treatments can nevertheless achieve their specific aims. Our point is only to emphasise the distinction between the two treatment approaches, and to note that the studies of cognitive neuropsychological rehabilitation published so far have been largely of the restorative kind. This, however, is not necessarily characteristic of all cognitive neuropsychological rehabilitation; one can imagine the decision being taken that a component of the processing system that has been identified as impaired is not going to respond to treatment, and then working out how the remaining, intact, components of the system might be able to accomplish a task in which the patient is currently experiencing difficulties.

Returning to E.E.: As the model-based assessment had identified an impairment of the visual word recognition system as the source of E.E.'s reading difficulties, the treatment chosen was one which focused on attempts to restore the functioning of this particular processing subcomponent. That is, the aim of the treatment was to improve E.E's ability to recognise previously familiar words which he once was able to recognise but which were now unfamiliar to him.

## DEVISING TREATMENT METHODS

Suppose it were agreed that cognitive neuropsychology has made valuable contributions to the development of assessment methods, and that the focused treatment approach, restorative in nature, and characteristic of model-based rehabilitation, has also achieved valuable results. After the assessment, and the subsequent identification of a specific sub-ability that is to be treated, a method for treatment will have to be worked out before treatment can begin. Have models helped here?

It seems to us that the answer is no, but that the reason for this is *not* because models cannot help. It is because current models are not sufficiently specific to provide this kind of help. Consider semantic processing. Many models (e.g. Riddoch, Humphreys, Coltheart, & Funnell, 1988) suggest that there is a single semantic system that is accessible from spoken words, printed words, pictures, and objects, by whatever perceptual modality these are presented. It follows that picture-word matching is an appropriate way of assessing semantic processing, and this and other such assessment tasks can help to identify selective impairments of semantic processing. In order to try to treat such an impairment, more needs to be known about semantic processing. The difficulty might be in the process of access to semantics, or it might be that semantic representations themselves are damaged or erased. To devise a treatment method for the former, the models need to describe how the semantic system is accessed. To devise a treatment method for the latter, the models need to explain what semantic representations are actually like. No extant model of language-processing has anything useful to say here.

This is a rather general point that has already been made by Seidenberg (1988). What cognitive neuropsychology has succeeded in doing is relating patterns of cognitive impairment to the architectures of processing models of cognition. For a particular architecture, many patients' impairments can be interpreted as consequent upon one or other pattern of disruptions to individual processing subcomponents or pathways of communication between processing subcomponents. What cognitive neuropsychology has *not* succeeded in doing is relating patterns of cognitive impairment to theoretical ideas about how individual processing subcomponents actually work.

This is partly because the models of normal processing often do not include proposals about how such subcomponents actually work, but this is by no means the whole story. There are theories about how processing components actually work—the cohort model of auditory word recognition (e.g. Marslen-Wilson, 1987), the spreading-activation model of spoken word production (Dell, 1986), and search models of visual word recognition (Forster, 1979) are examples—and such theories have been used disappointingly rarely in cognitive neuropsychological research. If it is shown that a patient has a specific impairment of spoken word production, it should be possible to use data from such a patient to learn more about how this particular process actually works, or to adjudicate between competing theories about this. Seidenberg (1988) points out that this kind of work is not common in cognitive neuropsychology. It would seem important for the future progress of the subject that this omission be remedied.

A possible consequence, if cognitive neuropsychology did move in this direction, is that models might begin to say something useful about treatment methods. Wilson and Patterson (1990) give an example. They consider a specific theory about how visual word recognition is achieved, the parallel-distributed processing model of Seidenberg and McClelland (1989), and point out that this model predicts that, if a patient with impaired visual word recognition is successfully treated with a fixed set of words, there should be considerable generalisation to the recognition of untreated words. Alternative theories of visual word recognition which do not postulate distributed representations do not make this prediction. Coltheart and Byng (1989) did observe a generalisation effect of this kind.[2]

There seems to be some ground for optimism about future contributions from models *vis-à-vis* treatment methods, but so far such contributions have been minimal. After the specific sub-ability to be treated has been specified, it has usually been up to the therapist's ingenuity to work out methods by which performance of this impaired sub-ability might be improved.

What of E.E.? The model allowed Coltheart and Byng (1989) to pinpoint E.E.'s processing impairment, and his treatment was targeted at this impairment. But the treatment method used was not suggested by the model. No attempt was made to deduce, from anything known about how the visual word recognition system actually works, what methods might be efficacious in getting the system to work again. The mnemonic technique used for treatment was a product of the ingenuity of the therapist, not of insights provided by the model.

## ANOTHER ILLUSTRATIVE CASE STUDY BRIEFLY DESCRIBED

Q.N., a 57-year-old university lecturer in a literary subject, poet, and broadcaster, suffered a CVA which produced a large left temporal/parietal lesion. This resulted in a variety of cognitive impairments including a Gerstmann syndrome, mild impairments of spoken language including mild anomia, a complete inability to produce written language, and very impaired reading. Given that reading was essential for his occupation and was one of his main interests in life, it was the function which we (Coltheart, Castles, Bates, & Reid, submitted) sought to treat.

The most prominent form of error he made was to omit, add or alter the endings of suffixed words, making errors such as *creation* → "create", *dancer* → "dancing", and *speak* → "speaking". As he also made visual errors involving ends of words which were not suffixes, it was possible that these apparently morphological errors were really visual (Funnell, 1987), and this needed investigation if the treatment were to be chosen rationally. This was done using material devised by Funnell in which pseudosuffixed words such as *quarter* are closely matched to genuinely suffixed words such as *speaker*. Q.N. correctly read 29/32 pseudosuffixed words and only 10/32 genuinely suffixed words. So his reading problem is genuinely morphological.

But is it genuinely a reading problem? Here we need to make the model of reading shown in Fig. 2.1 more detailed—in particular, we must add some form of central knowledge of morphological structure to the model. We presume that this system of knowledge is independent of the semantic system in Fig. 2.1 (although, if it were not, the arguments given here would still hold); and by the term "central" we mean that this body of morphological knowledge is used for both input and output of both written and spoken language. The model we use to analyses Q.N.'s deficit further is given in Fig. 2.2.

This model makes it clear that there are three different processing loci at which a morphological impairment might arise and cause morphological errors in reading—within the visual input lexicon, within the system of central morphological knowledge, or within the phonological output lexicon.[3] Quite different treatments would be appropriate for these quite different impairments. So Q.N.'s disorder must be localised to one or other of these processing stages before one can begin to think about devising treatment methods.

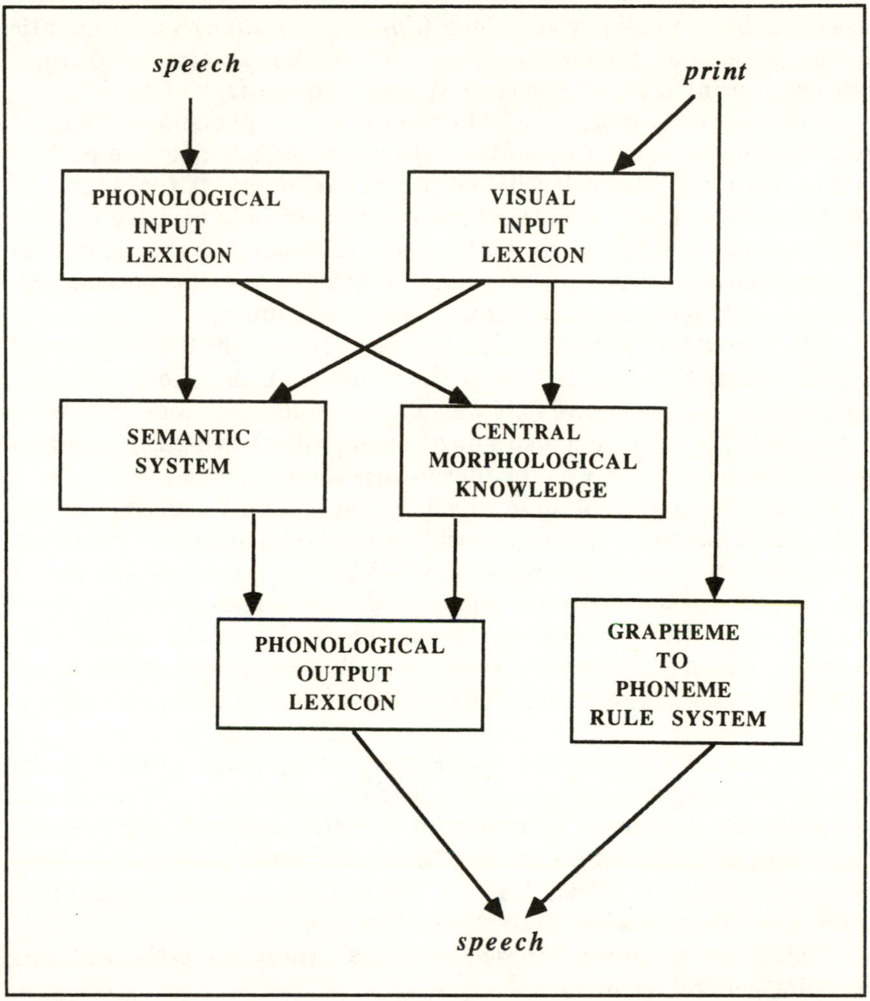


FIG. 2.2. A model of some of the language-processing system including morphological knowledge.

The model tells us how to do this (Coltheart, 1985). The task needed is "morphological comprehension"—a task which requires accessing the meanings of suffixes for successful performance. The subject is asked whether single words refer to people or not; the target words are affixed (e.g. *dancer, musician*) and there are "morphological foils" consisting of the same roots but different suffixes (e.g. *dancing, musical*). In order to classify the targets as referring to people and the morphological foils as not, all the suffixes must be correctly understood. Visual errors are assessed by including visual foils (*danger, munition*) and semantic errors by semantic foils (*ballet, piano*). The task is administered twice, once with printed words and once with spoken words.

If the source of morphological errors is in the phonological output lexicon, comprehension of suffixes will not be affected, so the patient will succeed in this task with both types of input. If the source of morphological errors is in the central morphological knowledge system, the patient will fail with both types of input. If the source of morphological errors is in the visual input lexicon, the patient will succeed with auditory input but fail with visual input.

Q.N. scored 98/100 with auditory input but only 69/100 with visual input. Visual or semantic errors were rare; but the choice between targets and morphological foils was not much above chance. Hence we know that Q.N.'s problem is specifically to do with the visual recognition of suffixes. This, then, was the therapeutic target.

Here we have a situation in which the use of a model has allowed an exact identification of a highly specific selective impairment of reading, in a highly motivated subject who, what is more, has a sophisticated knowledge of the relevant linguistic domain; conversations about morphology with him were entirely possible, and he could explain such matters as the distinction between inflectional and derivational morphology, or the differences between prefixes, infixes and suffixes, perfectly well.

We chose five singular nouns and their five regular plural forms, the initial aim being for Q.N. to learn to read all ten correctly. When shown a picture of a tree, or the written word *tree*, and asked to say the plural, he had no difficulty in responding "tree", so we were optimistic about the treatment, and indeed designed the study so that we could obtain answers to the following interesting questions:

If Q.N. learns to read these five plural words correctly, will this learning generalise to:

(a) the plural forms of untrained nouns?
(b) the suffix -*s* when it is not a plural (*likes, John's*)?
(c) other inflectional suffixes?
(d) all suffixes?

Answers to these questions would obviously provide valuable constraints upon models of the morphological processing system—a clear illustration of the way in which rehabilitation studies have a valuable potential role for developing testing models of normal processing.

However, despite the apparently highly favourable circumstances, we were unable to make any improvements at all in Q.N.'s ability to read even just these five plural nouns correctly, although a number of different treatment methods were tried. He remained unable even to judge consistently that the two printed words

*tree* *trees*

were different (these words being presented simultaneously and side-by-side), whilst being confident that

*see* *seed*

were different.

The model-based interpretation of Q.N.'s acquired dyslexia was particularly precise. The treatment was particularly unsuccessful (we have been unable to decide why this was so). His case highlights the gulf which can exist between theoretical interpretation and choice of efficacious treatment method. No model exists which explains exactly how visual word recognition deals with suffixed words. If we knew in detail how this happens in the intact system, would such knowledge tell us what treatment methods to use?

## DEVELOPMENTAL COGNITIVE NEUROPSYCHOLOGY

Cognitive neuropsychology offers a perspective not only upon acquired disorders of cognition but also upon developmental disorders. If one has a model of the processing system used for the skilled performance of some cognitive process, one can think of the child's gradual acquisition of this skill as a journey towards acquisition of a fully functioning model. Assessment of children then takes the form of deciding whether the particular child has acquired as much of the processing system as would be normal for the child's age. It is therefore worth studying whether the selective losses of specific subcomponents of a processing system that one sees after brain damage in adults have a developmental analogue in selective failures to acquire normally specific subcomponents of the processing system.

The acquisition of reading and of spelling has been investigated in this way (Marshall, 1984; Seymour, 1986). The most obvious first step here has been to adopt a dual-route model of reading and to investigate whether in cases of developmental dyslexia it is ever the case that there is selective poverty of acquisition of one route or the other. Such selectivity has been reported: The lexical route may lag behind ("developmental surface dyslexia" — Coltheart, Masterson, Byng, Prior,

& Riddoch, 1983; Holmes, 1973) or the nonlexical route may be less developed ("developmental phonological dyslexia"—Snowling & Hulme, 1989; Temple & Marshall, 1983). Other cases of these two contrasting patterns have been described, using slightly different terminology, by Seymour (1986).

These case studies suggest that, at least for reading, the cognitive neuropsychological approach could be as fruitful for developmental disorders as it has been for acquired disorders. It is possible, however, that the clear developmental dissociations shown in the case studies are a rare phenomenon, and that the bulk of dyslexic children do not show such clear patterns. If so, the approach would not be very useful in clinical settings, for assessment and treatment.

This question was pursued by Castles and Coltheart (1993). They administered a battery of irregular words, nonwords and regular words to a group of 56 developmentally dyslexic boys. This group yielded 10 very clear examples of developmental surface dyslexia—10 children whose reading of exception words was far worse than that achieved by a normal control group but whose nonword reading was within the normal range. There were also eight very clear examples of developmental phonological dyslexia—8 children whose reading of nonwords was far worse than that achieved by the normal control group, but whose exception-word reading was within the normal range. Thus about one-third of the sample of dyslexic children showed a marked dissociation, in one direction or the other, between how well the lexical route for reading was being acquired and how well the non-lexical route was being acquired.

Whether it is correct to use the term "dyslexic" of these children is arguable, but irrelevant here; the point being made is that, when one studies the acquisition of the two routes of the dual-route model, one finds a number of children who are acquiring the lexical route much more successfully than the nonlexical route, and a number of children for whom the opposite is the case. In assessing learning to read, then, it would seem that the model is going to be valuable; its components are independently acquirable, and so should be independently assessed.

## DEVELOPMENTAL READING REHABILITATION

The model can help with rehabilitation too. Model-based material administered to J.F., a 24-year-old woman who complained of reading difficulties (ongoing work in collaboration with S. Benson) revealed that her reading of irregular words (80% correct) was much better than her reading of pronounceable monosyllabic nonwords (32% correct). In terms of the model in Fig. 2.1, this implies a specific difficulty in learning the grapheme-phoneme rule system; if an important aid in building up the visual input lexicon as a child learns to read is "decoding" (see e.g. Harris & Coltheart, 1986, for a review of evidence for this), then one would expect her to have had some difficulty in acquiring the lexical route too, and hence some difficulty in reading irregular words. Her occupation sometimes required the ability to read novel letter-strings, so this nonlexical deficiency was particularly troublesome: hence it was the focus of treatment.

A model of the processing subcomponents comprising the nonlexical reading route that is part of the Fig. 2.1 model was sketched by Coltheart (1985) and is further discussed by Berndt and Mitchum (this volume). According to this model, nonlexical translation of print to speech requires three stages:

(1) Graphemic parsing—here "grapheme" means the written representation of a phoneme, and graphemic parsing is the translation of a letter-string into a string of graphemes, such as *thatch* →<th> <a> <tch>.
(2) Phoneme assignment—every grapheme has a corresponding phoneme, and at this stage the grapheme string is translated into a phoneme string.
(3) Blending—at this stage the string of phonemes is blended into a single syllable or single polysyllabic representation.

Defective operation of the nonlexical route can arise at any or all of these three stages. The case reported by Berndt and Mitchum had a particular problem at the third stage. Such considerations are important for the planning of treatment, as different loci of breakdown of the nonlexical route would suggest different types of treatment. Hence we needed to analyse J.F.'s nonword reading deficit further.

With nonwords which did not require graphemic parsing because they have a one-to-one mapping between letters and phonemes—nonwords such as *gop* or *lif* —J.F.'s nonword reading was 100% correct. For nonwords containing multiletter graphemes (i.e. where a phoneme was represented by two letters rather than one), such as the vowel grapheme in *hoil* or the initial consonant grapheme in *chut*, reading was poor (30% correct). This indicates that J.F. had some knowledge of phoneme assignment, but very poor ability at graphemic parsing.

A structured phonics treatment programme (Hornsby & Shear, 1976) was adopted, as the treatment was directed at the nonlexical rather than the lexical reading route; and the phonics treatment focused specifically upon material that required graphemic parsing—teaching JF that sometimes during reading two or more letters must be taken as a group and assigned an individual phoneme, and that this is true for both vowels and consonants. Progress has been slow, but it has been steady; J.F.'s ability to read nonwords has improved significantly (from 8/25 correct to 15/25 correct) and her error pattern has changed from consisting mostly of refusals to respond at all to consisting mostly of responses containing only minor inaccuracies in the application of letter-sound rules (refusals to respond have decreased from 15 to nil).

## CONCLUSIONS

At least as far as language is concerned, it has become clear, we believe, that cognitive neuropsychological rehabilitation is here to stay. Its contributions to the devising of treatment methods have as yet been, at best, minimal; perhaps explicit recognition of this point will encourage efforts in this direction in the future. On the other hand, the contributions of cognitive neuropsychology to assessment, and the success of rehabilitation studies which have focused in a cognitive neuropsychological way upon attempts at restoring impaired processing subcomponents, are indisputable. What is more, we have offered some reasons to believe that developmental language disorders are as amenable to the cognitive neuropsychological approach as acquired language disorders, in the sense that one can use models of normal language development as tools for identifying the specific way in which language is impaired in specific developmental cases.

As cognitive neuropsychology expands, models of normal processing are being applied to acquired disorders of various forms of cognitive processing other than language — see, for example, the sections in this book on attention, vision, motor skills and memory. We may expect these endeavours to yield rational assessment methods for these various cognitive domains. If they do, we may then expect to see targeted treatment studies in these domains too.

## NOTES

1. Since in at least some cases of surface dyslexia (e. g., Bub, Cancelliere and Kertesz, 1985), high-frequency words are recognised much better than low-frequency words one might expect that homophone confusions would occur more often with low-frequency than with high-frequency words.
2. Matters are actually somewhat more complicated than this paragraph suggests. Firstly, the generalisation effect of therapy in a PDP network was actually demonstrated by Hinton, McClelland, and Rumelhart (1986) with a rather different kind of network; we do not see why the specific network

architecture of the Seidenberg and McClelland model should yield such an effect. Secondly, the generalisation effect can occur even in a model which uses local representations in a word recognition system: If the patient's problem is not damage to these representations, but impairment of the procedure which accesses these representations, a treatment which improved this access would generalise to untreated words. Nevertheless, the general point—that as models become more specific, they begin to have something to say about what treatment effects one might expect to see—remains correct.

3. These three processing stages are all components of the lexical route for reading aloud. Of course, morphologically complex words could also be read aloud correctly by the non-lexical (GPC) route, when they are regular in spelling-to-sound correspondence. Hence a morphological impairment of one of the three lexical processing stages would only show up as a serious impairment of reading if the patient had an additional deficit, an impairment of the GPC reading route. This was true of Q.N.: he was very poor at reading nonwords aloud.

## REFERENCES


Bachy-Langedoch, N. & de Partz, M.-P. (1989). Coordination of two reorganisation therapies in a deep dyslexic patient with oral naming disorders. In X. Seron, & G. Deloche (Eds.), *Cognitive approaches in neuropsychological rehabilitation* (pp. 211-248). Hillsdale, N.J.: Lawrence Erlbaum Associates Inc.

Behrmann, M. (1987). The rites of righting writing: Homophone remediation in acquired dysgraphia. *Cognitive Neuropsychology, 4,* 365-384.

Bub, D., Cancelliere, A., & Kertesz, A. (1985). Whole-word and analytic translation of spelling to sound in a non-semantic reader. In K. Patterson, J.C. Marshall, & M. Coltheart (Eds.), *Surface dyslexia: Cognitive & neuropsychological studies of phonological reading* (pp.15-34). London: Lawrence Erlbaum Associates Ltd.

Byng, S. (1988). Sentence processing deficits: Theory and therapy. *Cognitive Neuropsychology, 5,* 629-676.

Caramazza, A. (1989). Cognitive neuropsychology and rehabilitation: An unfulfilled promise? In X. Seron & G. Deloche (Eds.), *Cognitive approaches in neuropsychological rehabilitation* (pp. 383-398). Hillsdale, N.J.: Lawrence Erlbaum Associates Inc.

Castles, A. & Coltheart, M. (1993). Varieties of developmental dyslexia. *Cognition, 47,* 149–180.

Coltheart, M. (1983). Aphasia therapy: A single-case-study approach. In C. Code & D. Müller (Eds.), *Aphasia therapy.* London: Edward Arnold.

Coltheart, M. (1985). Cognitive neuropsychology and the study of reading. In M. I. Posner & O. S. M. Marin (Eds.), *Attention and performance XI.* Hillsdale. N.J.: Lawrence Erlbaum Associates Inc.

Coltheart, M. & Byng, S. (1989). A treatment for surface dyslexia. In X. Seron & G. Deloche (Eds.), *Cognitive approaches in neuropsychological rehabilitation.* (pp.159-174). Hillsdale, N.J.: Lawrence Erlbaum Associates Inc.

Coltheart, M., Castles, A., Bates, A., & Reid, L. (submitted). *Morphological processing and visual word recognition: Evidence from acquired dyslexia.*

Coltheart, M., Masterson, J., Byng, S., Prior, M., & Riddoch, M. J. (1983). Surface dyslexia. *Quarterly Journal of Experimental Psychology, 35A,* 469-495.

de Partz. M. P. (1986). Re-education of a deep dyslexic patient: Rationale of the method and results. *Cognitive Neuropsychology, 3,* 149-177.

Dell, G. (1986). A spreading-activation theory of retrieval in sentence production. *Psychological Review, 93,* 283-321.

Ellis, A. W. & Young, A. W. (1988). *Human cognitive neuropsychology.* London: Lawrence Erlbaum Associates Ltd.

Forster, K. I. (1979). Levels of processing and the structure of the language processor. In R. J. Wales & E. C.Walker (Eds.), *New approaches to language mechanisms.* Hillsdale, N.J.: Lawrence Erlbaum Associates Inc.

Funnell, E. (1987). Morphological errors in acquired dyslexia: A case of mistaken identity. *Quarterly Journal of Experimental Psychology, 39A,* 497-538.

Goodglass, H. & Kaplan, E. (1972). *The assessment of aphasia & related disorders.* Philadelphia: Lea & Ferbiger.

Harris, M. & Coltheart, M. (1986). *Language processing in children and adults.* London: Routledge & Kegan Paul.

Hatfield, F. M. (1982). Diverses formes de désintégration du langage écrit et implications pour la rééducation. In X. Seron & C. Laterre (Eds.), *Rééduquer le cerveau: logopédie, psychologie, neurologie.* Brussels: Pierre Mardaga.

Hatfield, F. M. (1983). Aspects of acquired dysgraphia and implications for re-education. In C. Code, & D. Müller (Eds.), *Aphasia therapy.* London: Edward Arnold.

Hinton, G. E., McClelland, J. L., & Rumelhart, D. E. (1986). Distributed representations. In D. E. Rumelhart & J. L. McClelland (Eds.), *Parallel distributed processing Vol.1* (pp.71-109). Boston: Bradford Books.

Holmes, J. M. (1973). *Dyslexia: A neurolinguistic study of traumatic and developmental disorders of reading.* Unpublished PhD. thesis, University of Edinburgh.

Hornsby, B. & Shear, F. (1976). *Alpha to Omega.* London: Heinemann Educational Books.

Howard, D. & Patterson, K. (1989). Models for therapy. In X. Seron, & G. Deloche (Eds.), *Cognitive approaches in neuropsychological rehabilitation* (pp. 39-64). Hillsdale, N.J.: Lawrence Erlbaum Associates Inc.

Jones, E. (1986). Building the foundations for sentence production in a non-fluent patient. *British Journal of Disorders of Communication, 21,* 63-82.

Kay, J. M., Lesser, R., & Coltheart, M. (1992). *PALPA: Psycholinguistic assessments of language processing in aphasia.* Hove: Lawrence Erlbaum Associates Ltd.

Kertesz, A. (1979). *Aphasia and associated disorders of language.* New York: Grune & Stratton.

Lesser, R. (1989). Some issues in the neuropsychological rehabilitation of anomia. In X. Seron, & G. Deloche (Eds.), *Cognitive approaches in neuropsychological rehabilitation* (pp. 65-104). Hillsdale, N.J.: Lawrence Erlbaum Associates Inc.

Lincoln, N. R., McGuirk. E., Mulley, G. P.. Lendrem, W., Jones, E., & Mitchell, J. R. A. (1984). Effectiveness of speech therapy for aphasic stroke patients: A randomised controlled trial. *Lancet, 1,* 1197-1200.

Marshall, J. C. (1984). Toward a rational taxonomy of the developmental dyslexias. In R. N. Malatesha & H. A. Whitaker (Eds.), *Dyslexia. A global issue* The Hague: Martinus Nijhoff.

Marslen-Wilson, W. D. (1987). Functional parallelism in spoken word recognition. *Cognition, 25,* 71-102.

Murrell, G. A. & Morton, J. (1974). Word recognition and morphemic structure. *Journal of Experimental Psychology, 102,* 963-968.

Patterson, K. & Shewell, C. (1987). Speak and spell: Dissociations and word-class effects. In M. Coltheart, G. Sartori, & R. Job (Eds.), *The cognitive neuropsychology of language.* (pp.273-292). London: Lawrence Erlbaum Associates Ltd.

Pring, T. R. (1986). Evaluating the effects of speech therapy for aphasics and volunteers: Developing the single case methodology. *British Journal of Communication Disorders, 13,* 65-73.

Riddoch, M.J., Humphreys, G.W., Coltheart, M., & Funnell, E. (1988). Semantic systems or system? Neuropsychological evidence re-examined. *Cognitive Neuropsychology, 5,* 3-25.

Schuell, H.M. (1965). *Differential diagnosis of aphasia with the Minnesota Test.* Minneapolis: University of Minnesota Press.

Scott, C. & Byng, S. (1988). Computer assisted remediation of a homophone comprehension disorder in surface dyslexia. *Aphasiology, 3,* 301-320.

Seidenberg, M.S. (1988). Cognitive neuropsychology and language: The state of the art. *Cognitive Neuropsychology, 5,* 403-426.

Seidenberg, M.S. & Mclelland, J.L. (1989). A distributed, developmental model of word recognition and naming. *Psychological Review, 96,* 523-568.

Seymour, P.H.K. (1986). *Cognitive analysis of dyslexia.* London: Routledge & Kegan Paul.

Snowling, M. & Hulme, C. (1989). A longitudinal case study of developmental phonological dyslexia. *Cognitive Neuropsychology, 6,* 357-378.

Temple, C.M. & Marshall, D.C. (1983). A case study of developmental phonological dyslexia. *British Journal of Psychology, 74,* 517-534.

van der Linden, M. & van der Kaa, M.-A. (1989). Reorganization therapy for memory impairments. In X. Seron & G. Deloche (Eds.), *Cognitive approaches in neuropsychological rehabilitation.* (pp.39-64). Hillsdale, N.J.: Lawrence Erlbaum Associates Inc.

Wilson, B. & Patterson, K. (1990). Rehabilitation and cognitive neuropsychology—does cognitive psychology apply? *Applied Cognitive Psychology, 4,* 247-260.

# PART TWO

## Visual Object Recognition

CHAPTER THREE

# Visual Object Processing in Normality and Pathology: Implications for Rehabilitation

G. W. Humphreys and M. J. Riddoch
*Cognitive Science Research Centre, School of Psychology, University of Birmingham, UK*

## ABSTRACT

In this Chapter we discuss some of the general implications for understanding visual object processing that emerge from recent cognitive neuroscientific studies of vision in both humans and non-human primates. This work stresses the modular organisation of visual processing and the role of learning upon particular visual processing modules. We go on to outline some of the implications of this work for attempts to remediate visual processing in brain damaged patients, and we evaluate previous rehabilitation studies within the light of the work on both the functional components and the physiological organisation of vision. We propose that any full theory of rehabilitation should be underpinned by a physiological account of the changes that occur after brain damage and during learning. Because of the inter-linking of cognitive and physiological research in vision, vision is one area of research where there are signs of such theory emerging.

## INTRODUCTION

At a conservative estimate, around 60% of the monkey cortex is devoted to vision (e.g. see Desimone & Ungerleider, 1989). This estimate includes the striate cortex, the area receiving the main cortical projections from the retina, and areas of pre-striate cortex extending anteriorly into both the temporal and parietal lobes; all these areas contain cells specialised for processing visual signals. Given the extent of cortex concerned with visual processing, neurological disturbances of vision are frequently encountered following damage to posterior regions of the brain. Disturbances in visual perception, diagnosed even through relatively non-analytic clinical tests such as copying and line cancellation, have also been related to the recovery of cognitive and motor function after brain damage (Andrews et al., 1982; Denes et al., 1982). Thus it is important to try to understand the nature of neurological disturbances of vision, and to try to design appropriate rehabilitation strategies to improve visual function wherever possible.

As a first step in this process, we believe it is necessary to specify the processes normally subserving visual perception, because it is only by generating such a normal framework that we can understand how vision can break down. We may then go on to use the framework to help the design and evaluation of rehabilitation programs for vision.

In writing this Chapter we have several aims. First, we will sketch a framework for normal visual processing. This framework will concentrate almost exclusively on the processes leading up to the recognition of visually presented, static objects. To cover the whole of vision, including topics such as motion, colour and depth perception, is beyond the scope of the Chapter, and mention of these topics will be made only when they impinge on static visual object recognition. Somewhat unusually, and at slight variance with the other chapters in this book, we will also try to construct a framework from physiological as well as from cognitive studies of normal human performance. We discuss our reasons for this in the following section. Second, we aim to review (albeit briefly and selectively) attempts to rehabilitate visual processing impairments. Third, we will raise several issues concerning earlier work in the field, in the hope of establishing pointers for future research.

## 1. NORMAL VISUAL OBJECT PROCESSING

### A Physiological Perspective

Cognitive neuropsychology is concerned with the relations between neuropsychological disturbances of cognitive function and normal cognitive performance (e.g. Coltheart, 1984; Riddoch & Humphreys, Chapter 1, this volume). By and large, workers trying to specify this relationship have stressed functional disturbances of human performance, rather than the physiological underpinnings of the behaviour (e.g. Mehler, Morton, & Jusczyk, 1984). One reason for this is that, for many topics such as language, problem solving and reasoning, physiological accounts of human performance lag behind functional models. Hence physiological and functional models cannot be easily related to one another (see Humphreys & Riddoch, 1987a). However, this situation is not universal, and it does not hold as far as vision is concerned. Indeed, it can be argued that current physiological studies are a major driving force in vision research, providing an essential converging line of evidence linked to computational, experimental and neuropsychological studies (e.g. Humphreys & Quinlan, 1987; Kosslyn & Koenig, 1992). Physiological studies may be particularly important as far as understanding how learning takes place, and we shall go on to argue that a physiological theory of brain damage and learning should be a necessary part of any complete theory of rehabilitation.

We thus begin with a short tour of physiological studies of visual object processing, which will then attempt to link to a functional model. We subsequently return to the physiological data when we review the success of attempts to rehabilitate object processing deficits in brain-damaged humans.

## Multiple Visual Areas and Functional Specialisation

One of the most important insights provided by physiological studies of vision is that there is a good deal of functional specialisation of visual processing in the brain. Recent reviews of physiological work with monkeys suggest that there are at least 20 separate cortical areas concerned with visual functions, and there are unlikely to be fewer such cases in humans (e.g. see Van Essen, 1985). These areas differ in several ways including: histology, connectivity with other areas and functional specialisation.

Cells in the "early" parts of the visual cortex, such as the primary visual striate cortex or area V1, tend to respond to simple image characteristics such as the presence of an edge of a particular width (or spatial frequency) of a particular orientation (e.g. Hubel & Wiesel, 1959). Many of these cells are also selectively specialised for processing colour, luminance or motion (e.g. Livingstone & Hubel, 1988; Thorell, de Valois, & Albrecht, 1984), suggesting some degree of functional specialisation even at this stage. V1 cells are also topographically mapped, so that they only respond when their preferred stimulus is placed within their receptive field, and local relations in the visual field are maintained by 1 to 1 mapping between field position and the receptive field tuning of neighbouring cells. Thus the outputs of these cells do not generalise across retinal positions. Position-coding within area V1 is non-linear, however. The few degrees of space surrounding the fovea of the retina are allocated vastly more cells than areas of space going out from the fovea to the retinal periphery; this is the cortical magnification factor (see Cowey, 1979). Hence we can expect lesions of a given size in area V1 in humans to produce differentially large field defects, according to whether the lesion affects cells turned to foveal or peripheral retinal regions. This is indeed the case. Small lesions to cells encoding peripheral retinal regions produce much larger field defects than lesions of the same physical size but affecting cells turned to the fovea (Holmes, 1918).

In more anterior visual areas, cells can respond to different image characteristics than those to which their connected Vl cells are sensitive, suggesting that these cells in higher-level visual areas compute new properties from the outputs of two or more earlier cells. An example of this is the report by Von der Heydt and Peterhans (Peterhans & Von der Heydt, 1989; Von der Heydt & Peterhans, 1989) that cells in area V2 can respond to the presence of an "illusory contour", present between the ends of co-linear edges (see Fig. 3.1). The illusory contour is not present in the image itself, and cells in VI tuned to its orientation and position are not activated. The cells in V2 that are activated seem to be computing collinearity between edge-coding cells in V1 tuned to the bordering spatial positions. Such "filling-in" processes are likely to be fundamentally important in the grouping of local elements into organised perceptual structures, and hence likely perform a critical role in object recognition. They may also play a role in the perceptual filling-in reported by many patients with small field defects (e.g. Gerrits & Timmerman, 1969), and by us all for the blind spot (e.g. Grossberg & Mingolla, 1985; O'Regan, 1992).

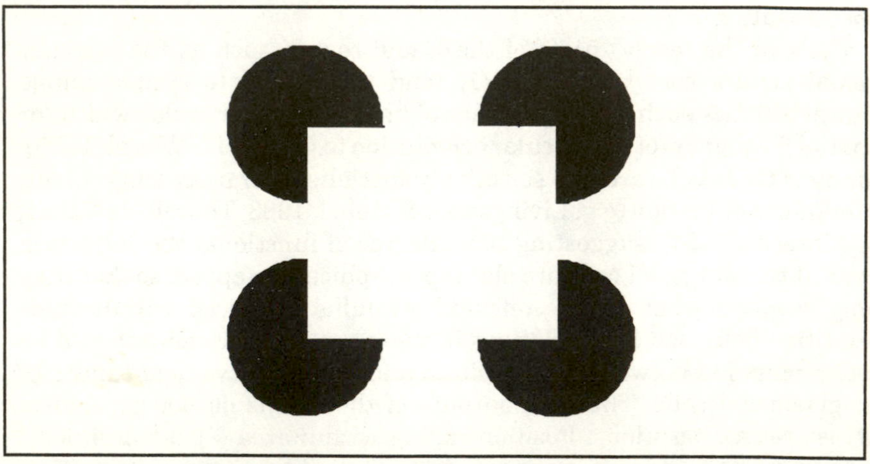

FIG. 3.1. Example of a figure with illusory contours.

One general distinction that has greatly influenced physiological thinking about vision over the past ten years is that between the so-called dorsal "where" and the ventral "what" system. This distinction follows the divergence between the visual pathways projecting from the occipital lobe to the parietal (dorsal) and temporal (ventral) lobes. Cells in specialised regions of the parietal lobe (area 7a) respond according to the conjunction of the presence of stimuli in particular retinal positions and to the position of the eye, suggesting they encode visual stimuli in a head-centred co-ordinate system (e.g. Andersen, 1988). Lesions of parietal regions in both humans and monkeys tend to produce impaired spatial processing, leading to problems such as mislocalisation (e.g. Ratcliff & Davies-Jones, 1972) and poor memory for location (Ungerleider & Mishkin, 1982). In contrast to cells in area V1, a majority of cells in some parietal regions can be tuned to peripheral parts of the retina and not the fovea (e.g. Colby et al., 1983; Van Essen, 1985). Clearly such cells play a different computational role in vision than do cells tuned to the retina; for instance, they may be involved in computing the location of future eye movements.

Whilst cells within different regions of the *occipital-parietal* pathway remain tuned to spatial positions (albeit if this coding is based on a different co-ordinate system or focused on different retinal regions to cells in V1), one general trend that characterises cells within the visual areas extending anteriorly along the *occipital-temporal* pathway is decreasing sensitivity to retinal position. Within the infero-temporal lobe, for example, many cells have extremely large receptive fields encompassing nearly all the retina, with these receptive fields centred on the fovea (e.g. Gross, Rocha-Miranda, & Bender, 1972). Such cells respond irrespective of the position of their preferred stimulus on the retina, and so manifest position-invariance. Cells at this highest end of the "what" system can show selectively tuned responses to complex visual stimuli such as faces (Perrett et al., 1984, 1985) and hands (Gross et al., 1972). They also show orientation-tuning, responding most when the preferred stimulus is presented at a particular orientation. Many also respond selectively to moderately complex parts of an image, including the presence of particular combinations of features (e.g. combinations of shape, colour and texture; Tanaka, Saito, Fukada, & Moriya, 1991). These results suggest that images of objects are encoded in terms of combinations of such cells, each of which represent the presence of partial features or feature combinations. Recognition, taking place at the highest levels of the system, may be orientation- but not position-specific.

Cells within earlier parts of the "what" system, mediating the passage of activity from the occipital to the temporal lobe, also seem to play specific roles in object processing. For instance, Zeki (1977; 1980) first documented an area termed V4 where many of the cells respond selectively to particular colours and some appear also to exhibit colour constancy (i.e. to respond to the same colour even when the wavelength changes with variations in lighting). This is also probably the last area prior to the temporal lobe in which cells preserve a topographic map of the retina. He suggested that such cells play a crucial role in colour perception. More recent work, however, suggests that cells in this area do more than register the presence of particular visual properties in images. Moran and Desimone (1985) reported that the receptive-field tuning of these cells could be altered dynamically by having a monkey attend to a spatial position where a target was presented. This allowed the monkey to "gate out" distractor stimuli represented within what was formerly the receptive field of the cell, mapped when a distractor was not present. Schiller and Lee (1991) also report that lesions of V4 produce problems for monkeys in tasks requiring the discriminatation of low saliency stimuli presented against high saliency backgrounds; this problem did not occur when the low saliency stimuli were presented in isolation. Further, Schiller and Lee attempted to retrain the V4 lesioned monkeys to discriminate the low saliency targets amongst high saliency backgrounds. They found that the monkeys were able to improve with practice, but this failed to generalise both when a new task was introduced, and when the trained patterns were shifted on the retina. These results indicate that V4 is not simply a transit-station for visual processing along the occipital-temporal pathway. Rather it forms a crucial role in selecting less salient stimuli against a background and in generalising learning across visual tasks and retinal ocations.

Previous work on the effects of learning on visual processing suggested that the tuning of cells to particular visual inputs (e.g. edges of a given orientation) could be altered during a period of plasticity in young animals, but that retuning did not occur thereafter (e.g. Blakemore & Cooper, 1970; LeVay, Wiesel & Hubel, 1980). This might be taken to indicate that there can be little modification of visual encoding in adults. However, recent work indicates that cells in the visual cortex can undergo modification even in adulthood. For instance, Gilbert and Wiesel (1992) lesioned the retinae of cats and monkeys. They found that, over time, cortical cells with receptive fields covering the lesioned retinal regions recovered visual activity, and responded to regions bordering the lesioned area. This occurred only for cells within the cortex. Cells in the lateral geniculate nucleus (LGN), which provides the visual input to the cortex, failed to recover activity. Such results suggest that there remains considerable scope for visual cortical reorganisation in adult as well as in immature visual systems (see also

Heinen & Skavenski, 1991). Such reorganisation seems to be mediated by synaptic changes within the cortex, and does not operate in more primitive visual areas, such as the LGN. We should note two things. One is that there is modification of position coding here (i.e. the remapping of receptive field positions), rather than modification of tuning to stimulus properties (e.g. retuning responses to line orientations or combinations of orientations). The other is that any reorganisation that occurs may be constrained by the properties of the visual system where damage has taken place. Thus there may be little generalisation of learning across position if the cells that mediate position-generalisation are damaged (cf. the effects of V4 lesions on discrimination learning).

### Summary and Implications

Some of the broad implications that arise from physiological evidence on visual processing are the following:

1. The visual system divides up many of the different tasks of object processing, such as grouping parts into wholes, colour perception, the coding of the object relative to the body, viewpoint-independence and so forth; separate tasks are allocated to different cortical regions. That is, there is some degree of both functional and anatomical modularity.
2. Hard computational problems, such as generalisation across location, seem to be handled in a relatively simple way, via summation across units tuned to increasingly more coarsely tuned spatial areas.
3. Visual processing is subject to learning in brain damaged adult animals, and to modulation via attention.

These points will be returned to when we discuss attempts to rehabilitate visual processing in neuropsychological patients. First, though, we discuss cognitive neuropsychological work on both models of object recognition and on object recognition disorders.

## 2. A COGNITIVE NEUROPSYCHOLOGICAL PERSPECTIVE

### Cognitive Models

Cognitive models of visual object recognition, like the physiological data discussed above, suggest the existence of several separate stages of processing. One of the most well-known accounts of object recognition is that proposed by Marr (1982). Marr argued that object recognition can be broken down into at least three broad stages, each characterised by the generation of a new form of representation of the image. Marr termed these representations as follows:

1. The Primal Sketch: A retinally-specific representation of raw edge-based primitives derived from intensity changes in the image.
2. The 2½D Sketch: Another viewpoint-dependent representation of the image, but this time incorporating information about surface orientation and depth (with the surface information being derived from stereopsis, texture analysis etc.).
3. The 3D Model Representation: A view-independent representation of the major parts of an object, coded with respect to a salient geometric property of the whole object, such as its principal axis.

Marr emphasised that the problem of viewpoint-invariant object recognition could be solved by constructing an object-centred representation, such as the 3D Model Representation, and matching that to a single stored representation of the object in memory. It was also proposed that the above three representations were encoded sequentially and hierarchically. Consequently, impairments to a higher-order representation, such as a 3D Model Representation, ought not to affect earlier processes. This proposal was itself partly based on evidence from studies of patients with object recognition impairments (visual agnosia), who performed well on tests of early visual processing (e.g. Warrington & Taylor, 1973, 1978).

One criticism of Marr's approach has concerned its emphasis on recognition requiring the construction of a surface-based representation (the 2½ D Sketch) as one necessary part of a sequential hierarchy of processing stages. This does not fit with several pieces of evidence on human object recognition suggesting that adding surface details (colour, texture) has relatively little effect on recognition, at least when objects are presented briefly (e.g. Biederman & Ju, 1988; Davidoff & Ostergaard, 1988; though see Price & Humphreys, 1989). A contrasting account, put forward by Biederman (1987), emphasises that recognition can be based directly on edge-based descriptions of objects, without surface-based descriptions necessarily being involved. Biederman also emphasises that recognition is mediated by the decomposition of objects into their basic volumetric parts—their "geons". He suggests that very many objects can be constructed simply by varying the relations between a simple set of component geons, such as cylinders, spheres and bricks, and variations of these basic components created by altering their cross-sectional dimensions and degree of symmetry. Recognition requires that these components first be encoded, followed by an encoding of the relations between the geons, and a matching of this representation to memory (see Hummel & Biederman, 1992).

According to Biederman, geons are encoded by detecting the presence of certain non-accidental properties in an image. For instance, a brick can be detected from the presence of three parallel edges, an inner Y vertex, and three outer arrow vertices (see Fig. 3.2). These properties are nonaccidental, in the sense that they are unlikely to be created simply by noise in an image. By registering the presence of such properties in the appropriate spatial positions in an image, the presence of particular geons can be encoded, and recognition proceeds by matching this geon-based representation to memory.

Within this scheme, recognition is relatively robust to changes in viewpoint, providing sufficient geons remain visible to support matching to memory.

Biederman's account can be criticised because the representation of objects in terms of a primitive set of geons is probably insufficient to make finer-grained identifications within classes of objects with visually-similar examples (such as many biological categories). For this, specific attributes may also need to be added, both to the object representation encoded from the image and to memory. Indeed, this may

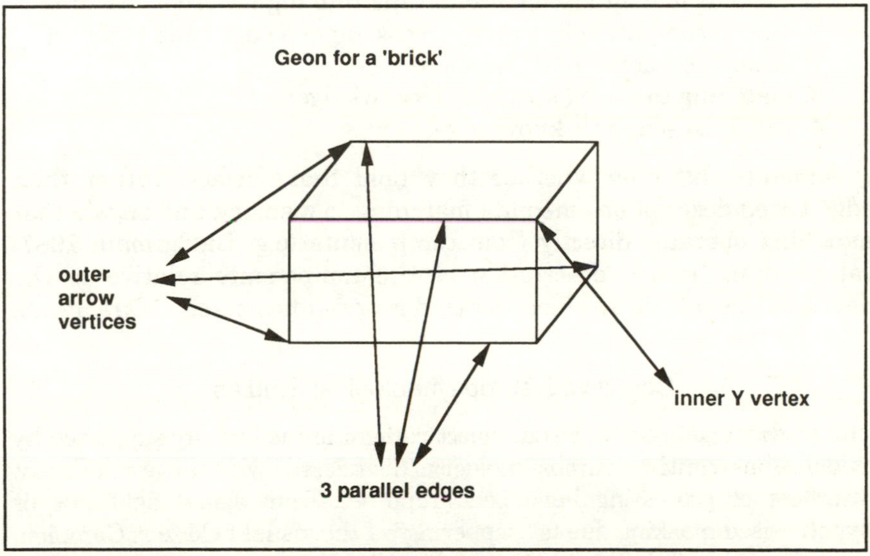


FIG. 3.2. Example of the non-accidental properties of a 'brick' geon.

be at least one role of the "complex feature detectors" in the inferotemporal lobe, as reported by Tanaka et al. (1991).

Both Biederman's and Marr's accounts discuss object recognition up to the process of matching input representations to memory. The nature of the memory representations was not considered in detail. Nevertheless, one common view of the memory representations mediating object recognition is that distinctions can be drawn between representations of the structure of objects ("structural descriptions", following Riddoch & Humphreys, 1987a,b) and semantic representations specifying the object's function and prior associations (e.g. see Seymour, 1979). Such a distinction is implicated by evidence showing that patients can have poor semantic knowledge, even when they appear able to access structural knowledge about objects (e.g. being able to judge whether objects are familiar or not; see Riddoch & Humphreys, 1987a; Sheridan & Humphreys, in press; see also Schacter, 1990, who provides supporting evidence for the distinction with normal subjects).

## Summary

In sum, models of object recognition emphasise a series of modular processes, and a common theme is that there is:

1. an initial coding of edges;
2. some form of grouping or encoding into higher-order features (e.g. to compute collinearity across aligned edges and to detect other "non-accidental" relations);
3. matching to stored structural knowledge;
4. access to semantic knowledge.

Accounts differ on whether they hold that surface- rather than edge-based descriptions mediate matching to memory, and on whether matching operates directly from components (e.g. Biederman, 1987) rather than from a description of the components relative to the perceptual whole, in an object-centred representation (e.g. Marr, 1982).

## Cognitive Neuropsychological Studies

The modular analysis of visual object recognition is broadly supported by evidence on cognitive neuropsychological disorders. A wide range of different disorders of processing have been reported, from visual field loss or hypothesised masking due to "peppering" of the visual field (e.g. Campion, 1987; Campion & Latto, 1985), to failure to derive semantic information about objects although access to structural knowledge seems intact (Riddoch & Humphreys, 1987a; Sheridan & Humphreys, in press; see earlier).

Recent attempts to classify patients with visual object processing disorders into discrete groups, reflecting damage to a series of hierarchically organised processes, have been made by Warrington (1982, 1985; Kartsounis & Warrington, 1991) and Humphreys and Riddoch (1987b; Humphreys et al., in press a). Warrington has argued that disorders of object processing can lead to:

1. problems in coding simple properties of shapes,
2. impaired figure-ground segmentation,
3. impaired perceptual classification (judging that two objects are the same across changes in view), and
4. impaired semantic classification (judging that two physically different objects are functionally related).

Humphreys and Riddoch have proposed separate deficits to:

1. the coding of primitive features at particular spatial scales,
2. the grouping and integration of these features,
3. the processes mapping these features to stored knowledge, from different viewpoints,
4. access to stored structural knowledge, and
5. access to semantic knowledge.

Whilst these proposed disorders do not map exactly onto the stages of object recognition proposed by Marr, Biederman and others (see earlier), some are nevertheless clearly related. For instance, most cognitive models would predict that stages concerned with feature coding, grouping, access to structural knowledge and access to stored semantic knowledge, could be selectively disrupted. Hence, such models can be used initially to provide a framework for diagnosing visual object processing problems in patients, and subsequently, helping target rehabilitation at the impaired components. In cases where current theories do not accurately account for particular patients, the theories may be in need of modification, with the aim being that, once modified, they can be used as an even more accurate framework for future studies (see Riddoch & Humphreys, Chapter 1, this volume).

## CONSTRAINTS FROM A MODULAR APPROACH

We also suggest that, in addition to using specific theories as a framework for rehabilitation, some general constraints can be derived from the cognitive neuropsychological approach to vision. Such constraints can be useful even in the absence of proper theory for a given case.

Two such constraints concern the modular approach to vision. One is that, within a modular system, there will be a tendency to develop task and stimulus-specific organisation in order to optimise performance. For instance, as we have already intimated, differentiation within classes of objects with visually similar examples may be difficult to achieve, and the system may need to develop complex feature representations to individuate particular items. Such developments may be optimised by storing such representations together, minimising long connections (cf. Cowey, 1985), and enabling rapid collateral inhibition between competing representations. A consequence of this will be the development of anatomically-organised modules for specific stimulus classes (e.g. for faces as opposed to other classes of object). Cognitive neuropsychological evidence indeed points to stimulus and task-specific modularity (e.g. de Renzi, 1986; McCarthy & Warrington, 1986): We simply suggest that this may be characteristic of the whole system.

A second and related constraint is that, within a modular system, it is possible that direct (task-based) connections exist between input and output modules without mediation by some central set of representations. Recent evidence on visual processing disorders is consistent with this. Milner et al. (1991) documented a patient who, following carbon monoxide poisoning, was markedly impaired at object recognition, which itself could be attributed to her poor orientation discrimination on standard matching and same-different judgement tasks. Yet, despite the poor performance on these tasks, the patient was able to reach accurately to post a letter through a letter box! Milner et al. suggest that there may be a direct mapping of orientation information to an action system concerned with locomotion and reaching responses, and that this is independent of the mapping of orientation to an object recognition system.

In a rather different case, Riddoch and Humphreys (1987a) documented a patient, J.B., able to perform accurate gestures to visually presented objects, but who was markedly impaired at matching associatively related objects. This was not due to impaired semantic knowledge *per se*; J.B. could perform associative matching when given the names of the objects. J.B. also seemed to have intact structural knowledge; for example, he was able to discriminate familiar from unfamiliar (meaningless) objects in (relatively difficult) object decision tasks. The problem seemed to be in mapping visually accessed structural knowledge onto semantic knowledge (e.g. to allow him to carry out visual associative matching). In this context. J.B.'s impressive gestures to visual objects suggest that there may be direct connections between stored structural knowledge and learned actions to objects, by-passing semantic knowledge.

The relevance of this to visual rehabilitation is that, due to the existence of such direct (input and output) connections, patients may show discriminations using some output systems whilst failing to show any discrimination using others. It may then be possible to utilise intact input-output systems to provide feedback for the retraining of the impaired system. We return to this point when we discuss studies of "covert" visual processing.

## 3. VISUAL REHABILITATION

Given an accurate cognitive neuropsychological classification of a patient, it may be possible to design a therapy targeted at the impaired stage(s) of processing. In fact, there have been remarkably few cognitive neuropsychological studies of visual rehabilitation, and those that have been carried out have, to date, shown little success.

### Cognitive Neuropsychological Studies

By cognitive neuropsychological studies of rehabilitation, we refer to a particular class of studies characterised by:

1. an attempt to diagnose a visual processing disorder in terms of a model of normal visual processing, and
2. an attempt to design and evaluate a therapy in terms of its effect on the impaired component(s).

### Restoring Visual Memories

*Case I* One study that can be viewed as an attempt to restore impaired visual memory in a patient was presented by Wilson and Ratcliff (1982). They reported the case of a 22 year-old head injured patient, H.S., who, despite apparently (and interestingly) good recognition of faces and good reading, was poor at visual object identification. H.S. was worse at identifying line drawings than real objects, she made visual misidentification errors, and she made errors by pointing to visually related distractors in picture-word matching. She also made some errors on matching objects photographed from different views ("unusual-view matching").

Unusual-view matching is often assumed to tap pre-semantic visual processing as patients may perform such matching perfectly and yet show poor object recognition, due perhaps to impaired semantic knowledge (Warrington & Taylor, 1978). The assessment points to H.S. having a visual processing deficit prior to accessing semantic knowledge about objects, perhaps in perceptual coding or in stored structural knowledge. H.S. was given various retraining tasks, including being told the right name for a pictured object when she failed to name it, being given the correct name for the object along with pictures of different examples of the object, and being told the correct name for the target object along with being shown examples of the object she'd previously labelled as the target. These tasks may be viewed as attempts to restore stored visual knowledge about the impaired items, and/or to restore visual knowledge about items that were competitors during the identification of a given target. Relative to a baseline where objects were re-tested without training, H.S. improved at object naming having learned to re-associate the name with the object. However, training with other examples of the target object led to less facilitation, and training with examples of competitor objects led to no facilitation. Re-training the name for the object also produced no generalisation when different pictures of the same object were used (see also Sergent & Signoret, 1992, for a similar result when retraining face identification in prosopagnosic patients).

In this case, the patient, H.S., was able to learn new visual-verbal associations. However, the lack of generalisation suggests that this was being done in a rote fashion, perhaps without re-representing the object in the stored visual recognition system. According to at least some models of object recognition (e.g. Marr, 1982), stored structural descriptions, being object-centred, should lead to generalisation across views. Indeed, in a further test, Wilson and Ratcliff found that H.S. was as able to learn incorrect as correct associations, indicating that there was no general improvement to her accessing previously stored object knowledge.

*Case 2* A second case with a diagnosed deficit in stored visual knowledge for objects is that of patient D.W. (see Riddoch & Humphreys, 1992, for a preliminary report). D.W. suffered a head injury producing right frontal and bilateral occipital lobe damage, in addition to having had long-standing temporal lobe epilepsy. He had marked problems in visually recognising visually presented animate objects, along with rather milder problems in recognising inanimate objects (see also Sartori, Miozzo, & Job, this volume). His problems were not confined to visual recognition. For instance, D.W. was unable to draw inanimate objects from memory, he was unable to give verbal definitions of their visual characteristics, and he was poor at answering definitions stressing the visual characteristics of objects (e.g. questions of the form: what wild and ferocious animal is like a large cat with orange and black stripes?). In contrast to this, he had good verbal knowledge and could answer correctly definitions stressing the verbal and functional properties of objects (e.g. what wild and ferocious animal was hunted in the jungles of India in the days of the Raj?). D.W.'s perceptual-matching performance also seemed relatively intact; he was able to copy accurately and could perform unusual-view matches (see earlier). This pattern of good perceptual performance, along with poor knowledge of the visual properties of objects, suggests an impairment of stored visual knowledge.

We attempted to use D.W.'s good verbal knowledge to help restore his impaired stored visual knowledge about objects. To do this, we gave him a set of definitions to learn, which stressed both visual and verbal/functional characteristics about objects. For instance, he was asked to learn the name "lion" to the definition: "a large cat-like animal, with a long tail with a hairy tuft at the end; the male has a large furry mane around his head; it is the king of the beasts". He was able to learn a set of 12 such definitions over a two-week period. For the next week he was given reduced versions of the definitions, only stressing visual properties of the items. He continued to perform well at answering these definitions, and showed improvement relative to his previous ability to answer visual definitions concerning the same set of items, and his ability to answer visual definitions concerning a matched, untreated set of items (see Table 3.1). This suggests that his learning of the definitions was not simply based on the verbal functional characteristics they originally contained. However, of more importance is whether learning these visual definitions had any carry-over effects to his ability to identify objects from vision.

At the time of the initial test of D.W.'s ability to name visually based definitions, he was also tested at naming pictures of the items for whom definitions had been constructed. The same items were then re-tested after his learning of visual definitions. Unfortunately, there were few signs of an improvement in naming the pictures at post-relative to pre-test. This also held for tests of picture-word matching, where target pictures were placed amongst visually and semantically similar items (e.g. lion, leopard, tiger, panther; see Table 3.1).

The data suggest that, although D.W. was able to learn visually based definitions, this learning did not involve the re-laying down of stored visual representations, which might aid subsequent visual object recognition. Rather, he seemed to learn such visually based definitions as just another form of *verbal* knowledge. For subseqent on-line object recognition, this served little purpose. We propose that, because of D.W.'s degenerate visual knowledge, the representations of many objects became activated during on-line object recognition, leading to the misidentification of a target object in terms of a visually similar (often highly familiar) competitor. This continued to take place even when D.W. possessed verbal knowledge about visual features of objects that could

TABLE 3.1
D.W.'s Ability to Answer Visual Definitions, to Name Pictures and to Perform Picture-word Matching when Tested Pre- and Post-training on a Set of Visual+Verbal, then Purely Visual, Definitions

| | *Treated items* | *Untreated items* |
|---|---|---|
| *Naming visual definitions* | | |
| Pre-test | 0/12 | 13/26 |
| Post-test | 11/12 | 12/26 |
| *Picture naming* | | |
| Pre-test | 0/12 | 4/26 |
| Post-test | 1/12 | 3/26 |
| *Picture-word matching* | | |
| Pre-test | 4/12 | 10/26 |
| Post-test | 5/12 | 11/26 |

have helped him to identify objects. In part this may be because visual activation of stored knowledge about objects is difficult to prevent (Boucart & Humphreys, 1992), even when the stored knowledge is degenerate and automatic access to the knowledge representations leads to misidentifications.

These two cases indicate that, whilst patients with impaired visual object recognition can re-learn certain types of knowledge about objects, it does not necessarily lead to improvements that generalise beyond the stimuli given.

## Retraining a Patient with Impaired Local Grouping

H.S. and D.W. can both be viewed as having poor stored visual knowledge about objects. We (Humphreys & Riddoch, 1987a; Humphreys et al., in press b; Riddoch & Humphreys, 1987c) have documented the case of a rather different patient, H.J.A., with marked problems in visual object recognition but with good stored visual knowledge. H.J.A. had poor visual object recognition, being impaired at deciding whether he was presented with real or meaningless objects (in object decision tasks), as well as being poor at semantic categorisation and naming objects. Despite this, he was able to draw objects from memory and he could give accurate verbal descriptions concerning many visual attributes of objects.

We have argued that his deficit occurs in stages of visual processing preceding access to stored knowledge, and that it reflects poor grouping and segmentation of visual forms. Consistent with this proposal, the deficit is most obviously manifest in circumstances where H.J.A. needs to segment a stimulus from a complex background. For instance, in visual search tasks, H.J.A. is particularly poor at detecting the presence of simple form conjunction targets (e.g. ⊥) embedded amongst multiple, identical nontargets sharing some of the same visual features as the target (e.g. T's or ⊣ ). He is not impaired at detecting the same form conjunction targets presented in isolation in the field (Humphreys et al., in press b). Normally, the detection of such targets is strongly determined by the degree of grouping between nontargets and between nontargets and targets. With identical (i.e. homogeneous) nontargets, search is efficient because the nontargets group together and can be segmented easily from targets. With heterogeneous nontargets, search can be inefficient because nontargets do not group together and can even group with the target, making target detection difficult (see Duncan & Humphreys, 1989, 1992; Humphreys & Müller, 1993). A patient may show selectively poor detection of form conjunction targets amongst multiple homogeneous nontargets because of poor grouping between the local forms. Grouping background elements together may also play a crucial role in selecting the less salient stimuli in a complex visual field (cf. Schiller & Lee, 1991).

Humphreys, Freeman and Müller (in press) were able to simulate the pattern of search deficits shown by H.J.A. in a connectionist model of visual search. The selective pattern of deficits occurred when lesions affected the representations mediating grouping between the visual forms, or when increased levels of noise operated in the encoding of local form information, which in turn disrupted grouping. This provides converging evidence for the argument that, in H.J.A.'s case, there is disruption of early grouping processes involved in the organisation of local parts into perceptual wholes.

We have investigated the object processing deficits in H.J.A. for over ten years. During this time, his performance has remained essentially stable, with his identif1cation of line drawings being little better than when it was first studied some two months after his lesion. We have observed some improvement in his ability to identify real common objects (see Humphreys & Riddoch, 1987c), and this we attribute to an improved ability to utilise non-form information (such as surface texture, brightness gradients, stereo-depth and motion parallax) to faciliate his grouping and segmentation of the parts of objects.

## Training on Grouping Tasks

In an attempt to remedy H.J.A.'s deficit in visual grouping, we have given him extensive practice on visual search tasks sensitive to grouping between background stimuli. For instance, in one retraining exercise,

H.J.A. was given over 3000 trials of practice, with feedback, on a task requiring him to detect the presence of an inverted T target amongst homogeneous T nontargets. The data from this are presented in Fig. 3.3. As can be seen in Fig. 3.3, H.J.A. was initially considerably slower than both the young and the age-matched control subjects. This is not simply because he is generally slow at search tasks: H.J.A. can perform well on search tasks that are difficult for normal subjects, where grouping between targets and nontargets disrupts performance (e.g. with form conjunction targets and heterogeneous nontargets).

Giving him 3000 trials of practice on the task with homogeneous nontargets led to some reaction time (RT) decreases, but it failed to eliminate the effects of the number of nontargets on search and H.J.A. continued to make numerous errors. H.J.A. also remained severely agnosic in everyday life. Unfortunately, giving him extensive practice and feedback on a task sensitive to grouping and image segmentation led neither to the resolution of his major deficit in everyday life, nor even to normal performance on the grouping and segmentation task he was trained on.

## Training Object Identification

We have also examined the effects of retraining object identification directly with H.J.A. Within separate test sessions H.J.A. was trained to identify six line drawings of common objects and six photographs of faces of famous people. The retraining was then repeated in a subsequent session one month later. One further week later he was retested with either (a) the stimuli he had been trained on, (b) pictures of the same items but taken from a different viewpoint (view changes were relatively small, typically involving a rotation of around 45 degrees in depth), or (c) new (untrained) items. For the line drawings of objects, he was also tested on other drawings of items from the same basic category as the items he had been trained on (e.g. a picture of a different dog from the dog he had been trained to identify). H.J.A. showed good item-specific learning; he learned the stimuli within one session and retained that learning on both the subsequent retraining and test sessions, scoring 6/6 on each occasion. For the line drawings of objects there was some apparent generalisation to the same items depicted in a changed view: he scored 4/6 relative to an unchanging baseline of 1/18 on a set of matched, untrained items. There was no generalisation to objects from the same basic level category (0/6). For the photographs of faces there was no generalisation even to the new viewpoints (0/6; baseline items: 0/12). We do not think that any differences in generalisation across viewpoints for objects and faces reflect any intrinsic differences between

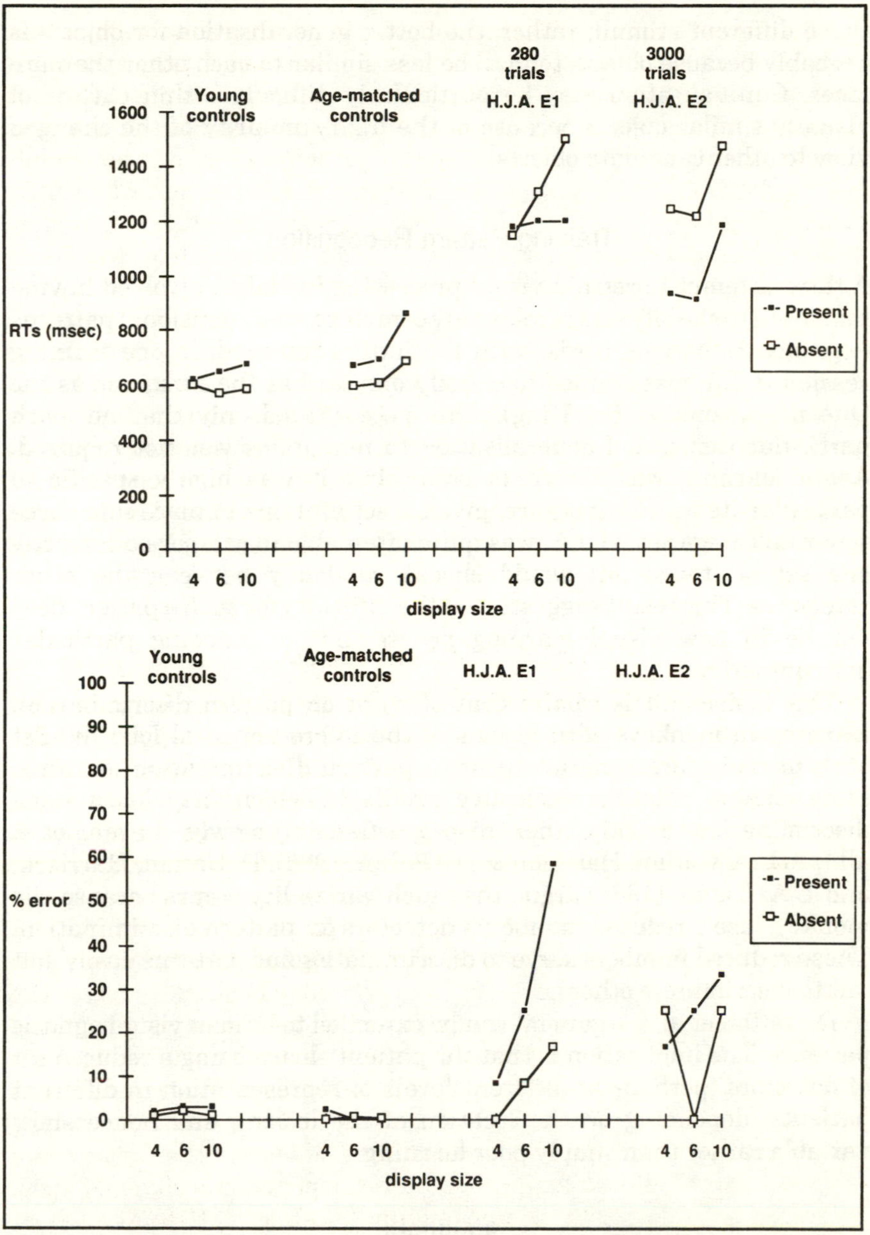


FIG. 3.3. Reaction time and error search functions for the agnosic patient H.J.A. and for both young control subjects and control subjects age-matched fo H.J.A. The task required the detection of an inverted T target against varying numbers of T distractors.

these different stimuli; rather, the better generalisation for objects is probably because objects tend to be less similar to each other than are faces. Generalisation may be particularly difficult within classes of visually similar objects because of the high similarity of the changed view to other candidate objects.

## Training Pattern Recognition

A third attempt to retrain visual processing in H.J.A. involved having him learn to classify sets of relatively complex two-dimensional patterns (e.g. picture playing cards, with the letters removed; in one training session H.J.A. was trained to classify one card as the Jack, one as the Queen and one as the King). This necessitated only that he learn particular items, and generalisation to new items was not required. Again learning was shown to occur, but it was highly specific to particular items. For instance, given a set of items to place into three separate categories, H.J.A. was quite often able to categorise correctly one set of items, but would choose randomly between the other categories. This result suggests that the difficulty for such a patient does not lie in new visual learning *per se*, but in learning particular discriminations.

This last result is reminiscent of work on pattern discrimination learning in monkeys with lesions of the infero-temporal lobe. Whilst such monkeys are generally poor at pattern discrimination learning, some show a relatively selective profile in which they learn some discriminations quickly, others disproportionately slowly, or even not at all (see E.A. Gaffan, Harrison & D. Gaffan, 1986). D. Gaffan, Harrison, and E.A. Gaffan (1986) argue that such variability occurs because the monkeys use a reduced number of detectors for pattern discrimination. These reduced numbers serve to discriminate some patterns easily, but fail to discriminate others.

D. Gaffan et al.'s argument can be extended to human visual agnosic patients. The implication is that the patients learn using a reduced set of detectors (perhaps at different levels of representation in different patients, depending on the location of the lesion), and hence show variable rather than simply poor learning.

## Summary

These training examples, with patients H.S., D.W. and H.J.A., have been relatively unsuccessful. One particular difficulty has been in showing any generalisation from a training set to a new set of items. In order to make practical advances in retraining object recognition, we need to understand why generalisation did not occur in these cases, and how it might best be fostered. Accordingly, it is useful to consider studies of learning in normal visual perception, and studies that attempt to relate visual learning to the physiological mechanisms in vision. In the fourth section of the Chapter, we review some of the implications of work on normal visual learning for the cognitive neuropsychlogical rehabilitation of vision. We argue that, at least as far as visual re-learning is concerned, a thorough grounding in physiological theory is a reasonable place to start.

## 4. NORMAL VISUAL LEARNING

### The Discrimination of Primitive Visual Properties

It is a commonly held view that the first stages of object processing involve coding the stimulus in terms of a set of primitive visual properties—its colour, orientation, size (or spatial frequency) etc. Can learning influence even these early stages of object processing? Using experimental procedures that eliminate response biases, research shows that practice can improve the discrimination of basic attributes of visual stimuli, such as the detection of particular spatial frequencies (Fiorentini & Berardi, 1981) and judgements of the direction of motion (Ball & Sekuler, 1987). However, the mechanisms of learning in such instances remain unclear. Studies have now begun to illustrate the nature of training effects on the discrimination of primitive visual properties, the most relevant being those showing that such training effects can be position-specific.

### Position-specific Visual Learning

As we have noted earlier, many visual areas in the cortex contain cells which maintain a topographic map of the retina. We might expect, therefore, that visual learning mediated through such cells would be specific to the stimuli being presented on the same place on the retina. That is, we need not expect visual pattern learning to be invariant to position.

Two recent studies have shown that it is indeed possible to demonstrate position-specific visual learning. For instance, Nazir and O'Regan (1990) had subjects learn to discriminate between a previously unknown target and two nontargets, visually similar to the target. The stimuli were presented at a fixed retinal position during training, and subjects were prevented from making eye movements. Nazir and O'Regan found that, although subjects could learn the discrimination, there was little transfer of learning when the stimuli were presented at a new location (equally far from fixation as the training location). that is, learning with these unfamiliar patterns was specific to the retinal location of the training.

Karni and Sagi (1992) trained subjects to discriminate a simple difference in the orientation of a target line relative to a background of lines at a constant orientation. The background lines were presented across the field, but the target was always presented within the same quadrant on the screen during training. Brief stimulus exposures were used, minimising eye movements. Several interesting results emerged.

1. Subjects improved at the discrimination task, but there was no transfer of training when the target was presented in an "untrained" quadrant.
2. There was no transfer of training across eyes when subjects were trained using one eye and tested using the other.
3. There was little training within an experimental session, but substantial training across sessions.
4. Performance was drastically affected by changing the orientation of the background stimuli after training, but not by changing the orientation of the target and keeping that of the background constant.
5. Despite substantial training, subjects remained unable to identify the orientation of target and background stimuli.

These results suggest the following. First, as in the Nazir and O'Regan study, training was position-specific. Second, it occurred at a level at which visual coding is still monocular. Third, training led to a long-term improvement in sensitivity. Fourth, the fact that training was dependent on the orientation of the background rather than the target elements, while also depending on the location where the target appeared, suggests that subjects were sensitised to the presence of orientation differences relative to a given background, at particular retinal locations. This last point is reinforced by the finding that subjects found it difficult to identify the particular orientations involved even after training. Van Essen et al. (1989) found cells in area V1 that responded to orientation differences in textures, but not to uniform textures themselves; also orientation-selective monocular cells are found only in V1. Thus we can suggest that training affected the sensitivity of cells in area V1, and that there remains a degree of plasticity in the primary visual cortex of adults.

The last conclusion is of course good news as far as the perceptual retraining of adults who have suffered neurological damage is concerned. However, two further points should be emphasised. One is that training at this level of the visual system does not generalise across retinal position. Thus there are limitations on the gains involved. Second, training improved the sensitivity in detecting orientation differences, but not the ability of subjects to identify the orientations themselves. Karni and Sagi discuss the training effects in terms of improving the sensitivity of detecting *where* differences in orientation-textures appear in the field, without there being any necessary improvement in the discrimination of *what* differences are present. In terms of visual neurophysiology, the training seems to lead to better discrimination within the dorsal "where" systems, but not within the ventral "what" system (cf. Ungerleider & Mishkin, 1982). Again there would appear to be limitations here for training patients with visual recognition impairments, reflecting impairments within the "what" pattern recognition system. For instance, patients may learn to make correct localisation judgements, but this need not improve pattern recognition.

## On the Learning of New Perceptual Attributes

Learning to discriminate primitive visual properties, such as orientation differences, could involve amplification of the responses in cells already tuned to a particular image property, or it could be based on a reduction in the variance of neural responses to the signal. Such work does not speak to the issue of whether sensitivity to *new* properties can be established, yet it is just such sensitivity that we may wish to increase by re-training patients who have lost selective perceptual abilities. Relevant to this last issue are studies on perceptual expertise in object classification and identification tasks. We consider three apparently diverse examples of normal visual learning: (1) perceptual expertise in chicken sexers, (2) learning to detect targets defined by conjunctions of features in visual search tasks ("developing blue T detectors"), and (3) perceptual expertise in face recognition. These examples allow us to make a distinction between the computation of "first-order" non-accidental features in images and the computation of "second-order" spatial relations between such features, that may help to separate different types of perceptual learning.

### *Perceptual Expertise in Chicken Sexers*

For the uninitiated, it is extremely difficult to decide the sex of young chickens from visual inspection. This apparently esoteric ability can be learned, however, and professional chicken sexers can reach classification rates of over 1000 per hour with an accuracy level of around 98%. Indeed, the success of the modern hatchery industry is dependent on the ability of such sexers to establish rapid and accurate visual classification procedures. On what is this perceptual expertise based?

Biederman and Shiffrar (1987) examined this. They interviewed and observed an expert "chicken sexer" at work. They noted that he used a particular visual attribute of the chickens to make his decision: Namely, whether the sexual eminence (the "bead") is convex or concave in contour. Such a visual attribute is of interest for psychologists working on visual object recognition because it is relatively invariant to transformations of viewpoint. Biederman (1987) and Lowe (1987) have argued that attributes such as the direction of surface curvature (convex or concave) are useful in object recognition because they are non-accidental (see Section 2 on cognitive models of object recognition). Non-accidental higher-order features may form the building blocks from which descriptions of the component parts of objects (the geons, in Biederman's terms) are encoded. In this sense, we may term them "first-order" features.

Biederman and Shiffrar went on to test their idea that the non-accidental property of convexity/concavity was crucial for discriminating the sex of chickens. They instructed a set of undergraduates to attend to this critical feature and showed that they were able to achieve 84% correct discriminations. This compares with 60% correct discriminations achieved by the same subjects before they were given the specific instructions and with 70% correct discriminations achieved by a group of professional chicken sexers on the same set of chickens.

The point about this example is that perceptual expertise in chicken sexing can be gained by instructing subjects to use a higher-order, non-accidental attribute that is probably an inherent part of the normal perceptual processing armoury: a "first-order" feature. Training improves the expert's ability to utilise this attribute, but in this case there is no evidence to suggest that expertise involves the computation of new first-order features from the image. A similar lesson can also be drawn from studies of the effects of perceptual training on visual search in normal observers.

### *Detecting "blue T's"*

In studies of visual search, subjects are asked to detect the presence of a pre-defined target relative to varying numbers of background items. When the target and background items differ on the basis of some salient visual property—such as their colour or orientation—search is easy and little affected by the number of background items (e.g. the search functions of reaction time against the display size are flat; Treisman & Gelade, 1980). There are grounds for suggesting that search in these cases can involve the detection of activity within early parts of the visual system where cells are tuned to simple image properties like colour and orientation (e.g. see Treisman & Gormican, 1988). In contrast to this, search is difficult when the target is defined by certain conjunctions of simple properties, when each of the relevant properties also occurs in different nontarget stimuli. For instance, search is normally slowed by between 20–30 msec by each additional nontarget for a target such as a blue T presented amongst red T and blue O nontargets. This is so even when search for the same target against each type of nontarget alone is unaffected by the number of nontargets present.

Treisman and her colleagues suggest that colour-form conjunctions, such as blue T's, are difficult to detect because neurons are not specifically tuned to encode arbitrary conjunctions. If visual neurons were tuned to such conjunctions, then conjunction targets may be detected by the activation of the particular neuron(s), and the number of nontargets present may have little effect. Given such a hypothesis, it is of some interest to examine the effects of learning on search for conjunctions of this type. Can cells become selectively tuned to arbitrary colour-form conjunctions, giving rise to flat search functions?

This issue was examined by Treisman and Gelade (1980). They gave a small group of subjects extended practice on a colour-form conjunction search task (as above). With practice, the slopes of the RT-display size search functions decreased. However, they did not become flat. Also, even after extended practice, the slopes for present to absent responses retained a ratio of around 1:2. This last result is consistent with subjects continuing to conduct a serial and self-terminating search of the displays. The slopes for present responses are about half those for absent responses because, on average, subjects search half the items in the display on present trials.

Treisman and Gelade's results provide no evidence for subjects being able to develop representations of arbitrary conjunctions of simple visual features that enable such conjunctions to pop out against backgrounds containing similar features. This may in turn suggest that it is (at the very least) difficult for visual neurons to become tuned to higher-order conjunctive features. This was the account put forward by Treisman and Gelade. It again follows that there are constraints on normal visual learning.

There are caveats to this conclusion, though. One is that Treisman and Gelade examined conjunctions defined across dimensions that may be processed independently of one another in the brain (cf. Livingstone & Hubel, 1988). It is possible that neurons are tuned to conjunctions defined within a single dimension (such as two lines of different orientations). It may also be crucial that these higher-order attributes fall within a relatively confined spatial area (perhaps scaled by the size of the stimulus), so that the attributes can be computed by the summation of local retinally-coded features. Indeed, the evidence that we have already noted, that normal subjects can detect form conjunctions amongst homogeneous nontargets on the basis of a spatially parallel search (e.g. Duncan & Humphreys, 1989; Humphreys & Müller, 1993), is consistent with the existence of detectors tuned to higher-order conjunctive features within the form domain. Such effects are also highly sensitive to the distances between the stimuli (scaled by stimulus size; Humphreys, Quinlan & Riddoch, 1989). The development of higher-order detection units in the form domain also presumably plays a major role in learning to read, since in reading there is good evidence for parallel processing beyond the simple feature level (e.g. involving letters and even words as perceptual units; see Humphreys & Bruce, 1989, for a review).

The second caveat is that visual search tasks may not provide a transparent window onto the tuning of visual neurons. Search tasks may be influenced by similarity relations between nontargets and targets such that, even if neurons are selectively tuned to a particular target (and even one defined by local, complex combinations of image features), that target may remain difficult to detect because the neurons are partially activated by the nontargets present (e.g. see Duncan & Humphreys, 1989). Given this second caveat, it is possible to derive a rather different conclusion from the Treisman and Gelade study to the one they themselves offered: Namely, that it is difficult for us to learn to prevent partial activation of higher-order detectors, rather than it being difficult to develop such detectors in the first place. In effect the net result may be the same: Practice alone may fail to help resolve a problem arising from either the loss of higher-order detectors for complex visual features or noise in their operation (cf. the study of the agnosic patients D.W. and H.J.A., discussed in Section 3).

### *Second-order Features: Expertise in Face Recognition*

There is one class of visual stimulus for which nearly all normal human observers can be said to be expert at identifying: namely faces. As a general class, faces are visually very similar to one another, yet normal subjects are able to identify many hundreds of different faces. If this ability were found with other visual stimuli, it would undoubtedly be broadly recognised as a perceptual expertise.

Studies of face recognition suggest that it is crucially dependent on the perception of subtle relations between what would commonly be taken as internal facial features, such as the eyes, nose and mouth. For instance, in simple matching tasks requiring the matching of a full face to a part (just the internal features or the external, outline features), familiar faces are matched faster to their internal features than they are to their external features (Young et al., 1985). This is not because internal features are necessarily easier to match than external features. With unfamiliar faces there are no differences in matching time, and the times to match the external features of familiar and unfamiliar faces do not differ. It appears rather that internal features play a special role in the recognition of familiar faces. This advantage for matching the internal over the external features of familiar faces is lost, however, when the faces are inverted (Young, Hellawell & Hay, 1987). Inversion seems to make it more difficult to perceive the relations between the internal features of faces (see also Yin, 1969). Interestingly, this appears to hold not only for faces, but it also occurs with observers expert in the identification of other animate objects, when those objects are inverted (e.g. Diamond & Carey, 1986).

One reason why inversion may render face recognition particularly difficult is that face recognition depends on the computation of metric relations between first-order features (e.g. for faces, the spacing between the nose and mouth). Such metric relations may require the coding of angles and distances relative to a standard perceptual reference frame (such as the centre of gravity of the face), and may thus be sensitive to changes in the orientation of that frame. This suggestion also allows us to distinguish two types of perceptual expertise, characterised by the differences between chicken sexing and face recognition. Expertise in chicken sexing seems dependent on the presence of a contrastive first-order, non-accidental feature—the direction of surface curvature of the sexual eminence in chickens. Expertise in face recognition depends on the presence of second-order metric relations between separate contrastive first-order features. Whilst there is evidence that second-order metric relations can be learned (e.g. when we learn to identify new faces), there is little evidence for the learning of first-order non-accidental features.

## Some Conclusions from Normal Visual Learning

The work on normal visual learning provides a mixed prognosis for the retraining of visual recognition disorders. The work suggests that visual cells in the cortex remain modifiable by experience for adult subjects, and that this may be true even of cells in the primary visual cortex, area V1 (Karni & Sagi, 1992). However, training effects on cells within early parts of the visual cortex do not necessarily generalise across retinal location.

There may also be separable training effects on detection responses, mediated by the dorsal "where" visual system, and on pattern recognition responses, mediated by the ventral "what" system. Perceptual expertise in some complex real-life pattern recognition tasks (such as chicken sexing) seem to involve subjects making better use of first-order perceptual features normally computed from the image, rather than the development of new higher-order feature detectors (Biederman & Shiffrar, 1987). Indeed it appears difficult either to develop such higher-order feature detectors or, where they exist, to learn to prevent their partial activation by visually similar stimuli (Treisman & Gelade, 1980). In contrast, studies of face recognition suggest that it is possible to learn new metric relations between separate first-order features (e.g. Diamond & Carey, 1986). If this argument holds, one general implication for neuropsychological rehabilitation is that we may expect differential success for attempts to remediate impairments in the operation of first-order feature detectors, and for attempts to retrain the perception of second-order relations between perceptual features. The learning of second-order relations between perceptual features may be the more tractable.

A further point here is that, in the work on position-specific learning (Karni & Sagi, 1992; Nazir & O'Regan, 1990), subjects were prevented from moving their eyes. It is possible that eye movements play a crucial role in our being able to generalise newly learned shapes across retinal locations so that position-specific learning is shown only under conditions where eye movements are prevented. For instance, knowledge that an eye movement has been made within an objects may enable the visual system to associate the features encoded at one retinal location, within one fixation, with features encoded at a different retinal location on a different fixation. The utility of training a scanning path across objects for patients with impaired visual object recognition has been been little explored.

## 5. VISUAL REHABILITATION REVISITED

Although work on the rehabilitation of visual recognition disorders has so far failed to produce positive evidence of generalised success, this is not true for all areas of visual rehabilitation. In particular, work by Zihl and his collaborators suggests that perceptual training can help reduce visual field defects in neurological patients. This work can be understood in terms of the effects of the training on cells in early visual cortex. It serves as a model of how we can approach the remediation of higher-level recognition disorders.

## Zihl's Studies

When visual field defects occur after a stroke, there seems to be little spontaneous recovery (e.g. Wilbrand & Saenger, 1917), at least after the initial 48 hours (Haerer, 1973).[1] Nevertheless, Zihl (1981; Zihl & Von Cramon, 1979, 1985), working with groups of stroke patients, found that having them take part in simple perceptual detection tasks had specific effects on reducing the area of their blind field. In these tasks the patients had to detect low contrast lights presented in both their good and their impaired field. No feedback was given concerning whether their detection responses were correct or not. Even so, the patients were observed subsequently to perform better in light detection tasks within their affected visual fields. The improvement was not due to spontaneous recovery as performance was shown to improve only within a training session and then to be constant, across time, between training sessions.

These effects of training on the recovery of field defects can be linked to the properties of cells in the early parts of the visual cortex. For instance, the spatial area over which recovery could be observed was scaled according to the retinal location where training took place: training at a more peripheral retinal location led to a recovery over a broader spatial area than training nearer the fovea. This is consistent with cells tuned to more peripheral retinal regions having larger receptive fields. Also, training with just one eye led to recovery of the visual field when the patient was tested with the other eye. This suggests that recovery took place within cells tuned to binocular input. Zihl and his colleagues further found that the training effects were modulated by attention. Performance was better when subjects were instructed to attend to the region of stimulation than when training stimuli were presented randomly across retinal positions. These findings are consistent with there being recovery within binocular cells that maintain a topographic mapping to the retina, and that are modulated by attention. The training effects are also reported as having some generalised benefits on the patients' visual performance, including leading to some improvements in colour perception and to the patients making more accurate eye movements into their affected field.

Zihl and Von Cramon's work is very clear in suggesting a close link between perceptual training effects and underlying physiological mechanisms, though it should be noted that not all researchers have found the same benefits when using quite similar training regimes (Balliet, Blood & Bach-Y-Rita, 1985; Blythe, Kennard & Ruddock, 1987). One moral of the work may be that, in carrying out perceptual retraining, we should aim to capitalise on known properties of cells in different areas of the visual cortex. We list one example. Work on the retraining of object recognition in patients has shown that there may often be little generalisation to new objects. While any of several reasons could cause this, one possibility is that patients learn using cells within those early parts of the visual cortex that remain intact after the lesion. Such cells compute simple visual properties and maintain a topographic mapping to the retina making generalisation difficult. Training regimes may thus need to prevent learning at such early levels of the cortex and force learning at higher cortical levels. For example: By presenting stimuli at different retinal locations across trials, or by having patients follow eye movement scan paths across objects.

## The Degree of Deficit and Separate Processing Routes

One other result that emerged from Zihl and Von Cramon's studies is that, for an individual patient, recovery was greatest within areas of visual field where the defect was less severe. This suggests that attempts to restore visual functions may have the greatest chance of success when there is partial rather than complete damage to a given region. Again, this possibility has been little explored as far as rehabilitating visual recognition is concerned, but, if valid, it would have important implications.

One implication is that training ought to extend to patients with less severe recognition problems as well as to those with obvious clinical deficits. We note here that clinically-apparent deficits in visual object recognition are typically associated with bilateral lesions, presumably because many visual functions are bilaterally represented. Nevertheless, subtle problems may be encountered after unilateral lesions, and testing needs to be sensitive to this.

Linked to the last point is that rehabilitationists need to have assessment tools that are sensitive to gradations of deficit. Ideally, such tools should also to be easy to use, not time-consuming, and not require specialist equipment. It is here that recent work on so-called "covert" recognition may be relevant. There is now relatively strong evidence that, in patients with marked impairments in the "overt" recognition of particular objects (e.g. when asked to judge whether the object is familiar), recognition may take place "covertly". For instance, some prosopagnosic patients, unable to demonstrate overt recognition even on forced-choice familiarity decisions with faces, nevertheless match familiar faces more rapidly and accurately than unfamiliar faces (e.g. de Haan, Young & Newcombe, 1987). Such covert recognition can be manifested on tasks where the patients do not need to have conscious knowledge that recognition is taking place. In addition to matching tasks, this can include simple learning tasks such as where patients have to learn either correct face-name or incorrect face-name pairings. Covert recognition can be shown by prosopagnosic patients learning correct face-name pairings more rapidly than incorrect face-name pairings (e.g. de Haan et al., 1987; Young & de Haan, 1988). Face-name learning tasks can easily be incorporated into clinical testing procedures, and can rapidly show whether patients show signs of covert recognition.

It may be of clinical interest to assess whether a given patient exhibits covert recognition, if covert recognition is apparent in patients with less severe recognition problems (though see McNeil & Warrington, 1991). Patients who manifest covert recognition may be those most likely to benefit from treatment. Sergent and Poncet (1990) reported the case of a prosopagnosic patient who showed covert recognition in a face-name learning task. In one investigation, the patient was presented with sets of faces of people from the same profession. She was initially unable to identify the individual faces. However, when presented with the faces together simultaneously, and told that they belonged to the same profession, she was able to identify the profession and then proceeded to identify the faces. This benefit in face identification occurred only if the patient was able to identify the profession of the people herself. This result has been replicated by Young and de Haan (1992). One way of accounting for the finding is that, by presenting faces from the same occupation together, the level of semantic activation created by the faces can be sufficient to activate individual stored face representations above their thresholds. The patient is then able to identify the faces. Whatever the cause of the phenomenon, it suggests a promising avenue to explore for rehabilitating face recognition, and one that can easily be incorporated into clinical settings.

There is also a second way to consider covert recognition, in addition to it possibly reflecting a milder perceptual deficit. This is that it may reflect the preservation of a direct (input-output) processing channel, which continues to operate even though overt recognition is impaired. A suggestion along these lines concerning covert face recognition in prosopagnosia was made by Bauer (1984). Bauer (see also Tranel & Damasio, 1985) noted that some patients with impaired overt recognition of faces could nevertheless show evidence of covert recognition via autonomic responses (such as changes in galvanic skin responses when presented with familiar relative to unfamiliar faces). He suggested that this reflected the operation of a direct route between face inputs and emotional responses, unmediated by access to detailed semantic knowledge about the person. It may be possible to capitalise on such direct responses to facilitate learning—for instance, by giving patients feedback from their autonomic responses.

## SOME CONCLUSIONS

We have discussed studies examining the effects of perceptual retraining on patients with severe problems in visual object recognition. To date, retraining studies have met with limited success. In part this may well be because few studies have diagnosed the deficit relative to an accurate model of normal visual object recognition, and hence they may not have targeted rehabilitation at the appropriate component within the model. This is an argument that echoes throughout this book. We also propose that, within the area of visual object recognition, we have the opportunity to link studies not only to cognitive models of performance, but also to physiological research on the underlying neural mechanisms. In doing this we can gain further insight into the nature of the functional disrurbance, as we have tried to show in our example linking learning in agnosia to studies of learning in infero-temporal lesioned monkeys (D. Gaffan et al., 1986). By linking remediation studies with patients to neurophysiological research, we can also acquire increased knowledge about whether retraining influences particular neuronal populations, how effects vary as a function of the size and location of the lesion (and the degree of deficit), and how particular neuronal populations can be targeted by tasks. And, in a very direct manner, neurophysiological studies can indicate whether damaged cell populations can be influenced by training regimes. This foundation work ought to be coupled to human studies that provide sensitive measures that are clinically relevant to rehabilitation (e.g. being sensitive to the functional locus and degree of deficit). In sum, within this field, we can begin to build bridges between neuropsychological, cognitive and neurophysiological work, that we believe will have important pay-offs for neuropsychological rehabilitation.

## ACKNOWLEDGEMENTS

This work was supported by grants from the Human Science Frontier and from the Medicial Research Council of Great Britain.

## NOTES

1. The same may not hold true for other types of brain damage, such as head injury (Poppelreuter, 1917; Teuber et al., 1960).

## REFERENCES


Andersen, R.A. (1988). Visual and visual-motor functions of the posterior parietal cortex. In P. Rakic & W. Singer (Eds.), *Neurobiology of neocortex.* London: Wiley & Sons.

Andrews, K., Brocklehurst, J.C., Richards, B., & Laycock, P.J. (1982). *Recovery of severely disabled stroke patients.* Paper presented to the 9th scientific meeting of the Society for Research in Rehabilitation, Bristol.

Ball, K & Sekular, R. (1987). Direction-specific improvement in motion discrimination. *Vision Research, 27.* 953-965.

Balliet, R., Blood, K.M.T., & Bach-Y-Rita, P. (1985). Visual field rehabilitation in the cortically blind? *Journal of Neurology. Neurosurgery and Psychiatry, 48,* 1113-1124.

Bauer, R.M. (1984). Recognition of names and faces in prosopagnosia: A neuropsychological application of the guilty knowledge test. *Neuropsychologia, 22,* 457-469.

Biederman, I. (1987). Recognition-by-components: A theory of human image understanding. *Psychological Review 94,* 115-147.

Biederman, I. & Ju, G. (1988). Surface versus edge-based determinants of visual recognition. *Cognitive Psychology, 20,* 38-64.

Biederman, I. & Shiffrar, M.M. (1987). Sexing day-old chicks: A case study and expert systems analysis of a difficult perceptual-learning task. *Journal of Experimental Psychology: Human Perception and Performance, 13,* 640-645.

Blakemore, C. & Cooper, G.F. (1970). Development of the brain depends on the visual environment. *Nature, 228,* 477-478.

Blythe, I.M., Kennard, C., & Ruddock, K.H. (1987). Residual vision in patients with retrogeniculate lesions of the visual pathways. *Brain, 110,* 887-905.

Boucart, M. & Humphreys, G.W. (1992). Global shape cannot be attended without object identification. *Journal of Experimental Psychology: Human Perception and Performance,*

Campion, J. (1987). Apperceptive agnosia: The specification and description of concepts. In G.W. Humphreys & M.J. Riddoch (Eds.), *Visual object processing: A cognitive neuropsychological approach.* London: Lawrence Erlbaum Associates Ltd.

Campion, J. & Latto, R. (1985). Apperceptive agnosia due to carbon monoxide poisoning. An interpretation based on critical band masking from disseminated lesions. *Behavioural Brain Research, 15,* 227-240.

Colby, C.L., Gattass, R., Olson, C.R., & Gross, C.G. (1983). Cortical afferents to visual area PO in the macaque. *Society for Neuroscience Abstracts, 9,* 152.

Coltheart, M. (1984). Editorial. *Cognitive Neuropsychology, 1,* 1-8.

Cowey, A. (1979). Cortical maps and visual perception. The Grindley Memorial lecture. *Quarterly Journal of Experimental Psychology, 31,* 1-17.

Cowey, A. (1985). Aspects of cortical organisation related to selective attention and selective impairments of visual perception: A tutorial review. In M.I. Posner & O.S.M. Marin (Eds.), *Attention & performance XI.* Hillsdale, N.J.: Lawrence Erlbaum Associates Inc.

Davidoff, J.B. & Ostergaard, A.L. (1988). The role of colour in categorical judgements. *Quarterly Journal of Experimental Psychology, 40A,* 533-544.

de Haan, E.H.F., Young, A.W., & Newcombe, F. (1987). Face recognition without awareness. *Cognitive Neuropsychology, 4,* 385-415.

Denes, C., Semenza, C., Stoppa, E., & Lis, A. (1982). Unilateral spatial neglect and recovery from hemiplegia. *Brain, 105,* 543-552.

de Renzi, E. (1986). Current issues in prosopagnosia. In H.D. Ellis, M.A. Jeeves, F. Newcombe, & A.W. Young (Eds.), *Aspects of face processing.* Dordrecht: Martinus Nijhoff.

Desimone, R. & Ungerleider, L.G. (1989). Neural mechanisms of visual procesing in monkeys. In F. Boller & J. Grafman (Eds.), *Handbook of neuropsychology, Vol. 2,* Amsterdam: Elsevier Science.

Diamond, R. & Carey, S. (1986). Why faces are and are not special: An effects of expertise. *Journal of Experimental Psychology: General, 115,* 107-117.

Duncan, J. & Humphreys, G.W. (1989) Visual search and stimulus similarity. *Psychological Review, 96,* 433-458.

Duncan, J., & Humphreys, G.W. (1992). Beyond the search surface: Visual search and attentional engagement. *Journal of Experimental Psychology: Human Perception and Performance, 18.*

Fiorentini, A. & Berardi, N. (1981). Learning in grating waveform discrimination: Specificity for orientation and spatial frequency. *Vision Research, 21,* 1149-1158.

Gaffan, D., Harrison, S., & Gaffan, E.A. (1986). Visual identification following inferotemporal ablation in the monkey. *Quarterly Journal of Experimental Psychology, 38B*, 5-30.

Gaffan, E.A., Harrison, S., & Gaffan, D. (1986). Single and concurrent discrimination learning by monkeys after lesions of inferotemporal cortex. *Quarterly Journal of Experimental Psychology, 38B,* 31-52.

Gerrits, H.J. & Timmerman, G.J. (1969). The filling-in process in patients with retinal scoomata. *Vision Research, 9,* 439-442.

Gilbert, C.D. & Wiesel, T.N. (1992). Receptive field dynamics in adult primary cortex. *Nature, 356,* 150-152.

Gross, C., Rocha-Miranda, C.E., & Bender, D.B. (1972) Visual properties of cells in inferotemporal cortex of the macaque. *Journal of Neurophysiology, 35,* 96-111.

Grossberg, S. & Mingolla, E. (1985). Natural dynamics of perceptual grouping: Textures, boundaries and emergent segmentations. *Perception & Psychophysics, 38,* 141-161.

Haerer, A F. (1973). Visual field defects and the prognosis of stroke. *Stroke, 4,* 163-168.

Heinen, S.J. & Skavenski, A.A. (1991). Recovery of visual responses in foveal V1 neurons following bilateral foveal lesions in adult monkey. *Experimental Brain Research, 83,* 670-674.

Holmes, G. (1918). Disturbances of vision by cerebral lesions. *British Journal of Ophthalmology, 2,* 12-25.

Hubel, D.H. & Wiesel, T.N. (1959). Receptive fields of single neurons in the cat's striate cortex. *Journal of Physiology, 148,* 574-591.

Hummel, J. & Biederman, I. (1992). Dynamic binding in a neural network for shape recognition. *Psychological Review.*

Humphreys, G.W. & Bruce, V. (1989). *Visual cognition: Computational, experimental and neuropsychological perspectives.* London: Lawrence Erlbaum Associates Ltd.

Humphreys, G.W., Freeman, T.C.A., & Müller, H.M. (1992). Lesioning a connectionist model of visual search: Selective effects on distractor grouping. *Canadian Journal of Psychology.*

Humphreys, G.W. & Müller, H.M. (1993) Search via Recursive Rejection (SERR): A connectionist model of visual search. *Cognitive Psychology.*

Humphreys, G.W. & Quinlan, P.T. (1987). Normal and pathological processes in visual object constancy. In G.W. Humphreys & M.J. Riddoch (Eds.), *Visual object processing: A neuropsychological approach.* London: Lawrence Erlbaum Associates Ltd.

Humphreys, G.W., Quinlan, P.T., & Riddoch, M.J. (1989). Grouping effects in visual search: Effects with single- and combined-feature targets. *Journal of Experimental Psychology: General, 118,* 258-279.

Humphreys, G.W. & Riddoch, M.J. (1987a) Cognitive neuropsychology and visual object processing. In G.W. Humphreys & M.J. Riddoch (Eds.), *Visual object processing: A cognitive neuropsychological approach.* London: Lawrence Erlbaum Associates Ltd.

Humphreys, G.W. & Riddoch, M.J. (1987b). The fractionation of visual agnosia. In G.W. Humphreys & M.J. Riddoch (Eds.), *Visual object processing: A cognitive neuropsychological approach.* London: Lawrence Erlbaum Associates Ltd.

Humphreys, G.W. & Riddoch, M.J. (1987c) *To see but not to see: A case study of visual agnosia.* London: Lawrence Erlbaum Associates Ltd.

Humphreys, G.W., Riddoch, M.J., Donnelly, N., Freeman, T.C.A., Boucart, M., & Müller, H.M. (in press a). Intermediate visual processing and visual agnosia. In M. Farah & G. Ratcliff (Eds.), *Neural bases of high-level vision.* Hillsdale, N.J.: Lawrence Erlbaum Associates Inc.

Humphreys, G.W., Riddoch, M.J., Quinlan, P.T., Donnelly, N., & Price, C.J. (in press b). Parallel pattern processing and visual agnosia. *Canadian Journal of Psychology.*

Karni, A. & Sagi, D. (1992). Where practice makes perfect in texture discrimination—evidence for primary visual cortex plasticity. *Spatial Vision, 5,* 1-20

Kartsounis, L.D. & Warrington, E.K. (1991). Failure of object recognition due to a breakdown of figure-ground discrimination in a patient with normal acuity. *Neuropsychologia, 29,* 969-980.

Kosslyn, S.M. & Koenig, O. (1992). *Wet mind: The new cognitive neuroscience.* New York: Free Press.

LeVay, S., Wiesel, T.N., & Hubel, D.H. (1980). The development of ocular dominance columns in normal and visually deprived monkeys. *Journal of Comparative Neurology, 191,* 1-51.

Livingstone, M.S. & Hubel, D.H. (1988). Segregation of form, color, movement and depth: Anatomy, physiology and perception. *Science, 240,* 68-75.

Lowe, D.G. (1987). Three-dimensional object recognition from single two-dimensional images. *Artificial Intelligence, 31,* 355-395.

Marr, D. (1982). *Vision.* San Fransisco: W.H. Freeman.

McCarthy, R.A. & Warrington, E.K. (1986). Visual associative agnosia: A clinico-atomical study of a single case. *Journal of Neurology, Neurosurgery and Psychiatry, 49,* 1233-1240.

McNeil, J.E. & Warrington, E.K. (1991). Prosopagnosia—a reclassification. *Quarterly Journal of Experimental Psychology, 43A,* 267-287.

Mehler, J., Morton, J., & Jusczyk, P.W. (1984). On reducing language to biology. *Cognitive Neuropsychology, 1,* 83-116.

Milner, A.D., Perrett, D.I., Johnston, R.S., Benson, P.J., Jordan, T.R., Heeley, D.W., Bettuci, D., Mortara, F., Mutani, R., Terazzi, E., & Davidson, D.L.W. (1991). Perception and action in visual form agnosia. *Brain, 114,* 405-428.

Moran, J. & Desimone, R. (1985). Selective attention gates visual processing in the extrastriate cortex. *Science, 229,* 782-784.

Nazir, T.A. & O'Regan, J.K. (1990). Some results on translation invariance in the human visual system. *Spatial Vision, 5.*

O'Regan, K. (1992). Solving the real myteries of visual perception. *Canadian Journal of Psychology, 46,* 461-488.

Perrett, D.I., Smith, P.A.J., Potter, D.D., Mistlin, A.J., Head, A.S., Milner, A.D., & Jeeves, M.A. (1984). Neurones responsive to faces in the temporal cortex: Studies of functional organisation, sensitivity to identity and relation to perception. *Human Neurobiology, 3,* 197-208.

Perrett, D.I., Smith, P.A.J., Potter, D.D., Mistlin, A.J., Head, A.S., Milner, A.D., & Jeeves, M.A. (1985). Visual cells in the temporal cortex sensitive to face view and gaze direction. *Proceedings of the Royal Society, London, B223,* 293-317.

Peterhans, E. & Von der Heydt, R. (1989). Mechanisms of contour perception in monkey visual cortex. 2: Contours bridging gaps. *Journal of Neuroscience, 9,* 1749-1763.

Poppelreuter, W. (1917). *Die Psychischen Schadigungen durch Kopfschuss im Kriege 1914/16. Band I: Die Storungen der Niederen und Hoheren Sehleistungen durch Verletzungen des Opzipalhirns.* Leipzig: L. Voss.

Price, C.J. & Humphreys, G.W. (1989). The effects of surface detail on object categorisation and naming. *Quarterly Journal of Experimental Psychology, 41A,* 797-828.

Ratcliff, G. & Davies-Jones, G.A.G. (1972). Defective visual localisation in focal brain wounds. *Brain, 95,* 49-60.

Riddoch, M.J. & Humphreys, G.W. (1987a). Visual object processing in optic aphasia: A case of semantic agnosia. *Cognitive Neuropsychology, 4,* 131-185.

Riddoch, M.J. & Humphreys, G.W. (1987b). Picture naming. In G.W. Humphreys & M.J. Riddoch (Eds.), *Visual object processing: A cognitive neuropsychological approach.* London: Lawrence Erlbaum Associates Ltd.

Riddoch, M.J. & Humphreys, G.W. (1987c). A case of integrative visual agnosia. *Brain, 110,* 1431-1461 .

Riddoch, M.J. & Humphreys, G.W. (1992). The smiling giraffe: An illustration of a visual memory disorder. In R. Campbell (Ed.), *Mental lives: Case studies in cognition.* Oxford: Blackwells.

Schacter, D.L. (1990). Perceptual representation systems and implicit memory: Toward a resolution of the multiple memory systems debate. *Annals of the New York Academy of Sciences, 608,* 543-571.

Schiller, P.H. & Lee, K. (1991). The role of the primate extrastriate area V4 in vision. *Science, 251,* 1251-1253.

Sergent, J. & Poncet, M. (1990). From covert to overt recognition of faces in a prosopagnosic patient. *Brain, 113,* 989-1004.

Sergent, J. & Signoret, J.L. (1992). Functional and anatomical decomposition of face processing: Evidence from prosopagnosia and PET study of normal subjects. *Philosophical Transactions of the Royal Society, London, B.*

Seymour, P.H.K. (1979). Human visual cognition. London: Collier MacMillan.
Sheridan, J. & Humphreys, G.W. (in press). A verbal-semantic category-specific recognition impairment. *Cognitive Neuropsychology.*
Tanaka, K., Saito, H.A., Fukada, Y., & Moriya, M. (1991). Coding visual images of objects in the infero-temporal cortex of the macaque monkey. *Journal of Neurophysiology, 66,* 170-189.
Teuber, H-L., Battersby, W.S., & Bender, M.B. (1960). *Visual field defects after penetrating missile wounds of the brain.* Cambridge, Mass.: Harvard University Press.
Thorell, L.G., De Valois, R.L., & Albrecht, D.G. (1984). Spatial mapping of monkey V1 cells with pure color and luminance stimuli. *Vision Research, 24,* 751-769.
Tranel, D. & Damasio, A.R. (1985). Knowledge without awareness: An autonomic index of facial recognition by prosopagnosics. *Science, 228,* 1543-1554.
Treisman, A. & Gelade, G. (1980). A feature-integration theory of attention. *Cognitive Psychology, 12,* 97-136.
Treisman, A. & Gormican, S. (1988). Feature analysis in early vision: Evidence from search asymmetries. *Psychological Review, 95,* 15-48.
Ungerleider, L.G. & Mishkin, M. (1982). Two cortical visual systems. In D.J. Ingle, M.A. Goodale & R.J.W. Mansfield (Eds.), *Analysis of visual behavior.* Cambridge, Mass.: MIT Press.
Van Essen, D.C. (1985). Functional organisation of primate visual cortex. In A. Peters & E.G. Jones (Eds.), *Cerebral cortex, Vol. 3: Visual cortex.* New York: Plenum Press.
Van Essen, D.C., de Yoe, E.A., Olavarria, J.F., Knierim, J.J., Fox, J.M., Sagi, D., & Julesz, B. (1989). Neural responses to static and moving texture patterns in visual cortex of the macaque monkey. In D.M.K. Lam & C. Gilbert (Eds.), *Neural mechanisms of visual perception.* Texas: Portfolio Publishing.
Von der Heydt, R. & Peterhans, E. (1989). Mechanisms of contour perception in the monkey visual cortex. 1: Lines of pattern discontinuities. *Journal of Neuroscience, 9,* 1731-1748.
Warrington, E.K. (1982). Neuropsychological studies of object recognition. *Philosophical Transactions of the Royal Society, London, B298,* 15-33.
Warrington, E.K. (1985). Agnosia: The impairment of object recognition. In J.A.M. Frederiks (Ed.), *Handbook of Clinical Neurology, Vol.1: Clinical Neuropsychology.* Amsterdam: Elsevier Science.
Warrington, E.K. & Taylor, A.M. (1973). The contribution of the right parietal lobe to object recognition. *Cortex, 9,* 152-164.
Warrington, E.K. & Taylor, A.M. (1978). Two categorical stages of object recognition. *Perception, 7,* 695-705.
Wilbrand, H. & Saenger, A. (1917). *Die Homonyme nebst ihren Beziehungen zu den Anderen Cerebralen Herderscheinungen.* Wiesbaden: J.F. Bergmann.
Wilson, B. & Ratcliff, G. (1982). *Learning of object names in a case of visual agnosia without amnesia.* Paper presented to the International Neuropsychology Society.
Yin, R.K. (1969). Looking at upside-down faces. *Journal of Experimental Psychology, 81,* 141-145.
Young, A.W. & de Haan, E.H.F. (1988). Boundaries of covert recognition in prosopagnosia. *Cognitive Neuropsychology, 5,* 317-336.

Young, A.W. & de Haan, E.H.F. (1992). Face recognition and awareness after brain injury. In A.D. Milner & M.D. Rugg (Eds.), *The neuropsychology of consciousness*. London: Academic Press.

Young, A.W., Hay, D.C., McWeeny, K.H., Flude, B.M., & Ellis, A.W. (1985). Matching familiar and unfamiliar faces on internal and external features. *Perception, 14,* 737-746.

Young, A.W., Hellawell, D., & Hay, D.C. (1987). Configurational information in face perception. *Perception, 16,* 747-759.

Zeki, S. (1977). Colour coding in the superior temporal sulcus of rhesus monkey cortex. *Proceedings of the Royal Society, London, B197,* 195-223.

Zeki, S. (1980). The representation of colours in the cerebral cortex. *Nature, 284,* 412-418.

Zihl, J. (1981). Recovery of visual functions in patients with cerebral blindness: Effect of specific practice with saccadic localisation. *Experimental Brain Research, 44,* 159-169.

Zihl, J. & Von Cramon, D. (1979). Restitution of visual function in patients with cerebral blindness. *Journal of Neurology, Neurosurgery and Psychiatry, 42,* 312-322.

Zihl, J. & Von Cramon, D. (1985). Visual field recovery from scotoma in patients with postgeniculate damage: A review of 55 cases. *Brain, 108,* 335-365.

CHAPTER FOUR

# Developmental Prosopagnosia: A Functional Analysis and Implications for Remediation

Ruth Campbell
*Department of Psychology, Goldsmiths College, University of London, UK*

Edward De Haan
*Russell-Cairns Head Injury Unit, Radcliffe Infirmary, Oxford, UK; Cognitive Neuropsychology Division, Department of Psychonomics, Utrecht University, The Netherlands*

## ABSTRACT

A single case of prosopagnosia is described, which is a follow-up to an earlier report (McConachie, 1976). The case, A.B., had a developmental aetiology that seems to have been unique at the time of the first report. Visuo-sensory function was essentially intact. Face recognition was very severely compromised in contrast to her other recognition skills. There was evidence of mild impairment in the precise identification of other visually presented objects. Detailed exploration of her face-processing deficit showed (a) that although A.B. could make face vs. non-face judgements, her ability to make other decisions about faces, including those based on expression, gender, age and direction of gaze, was compromised; (b) that she showed reasonable (borderline) performance on Benton and Van Allen's face-matching task, but had very impaired immediate memory for unknown faces; and (c) that she showed no covert recognition ability for faces, despite good knowledge of those individuals from names. In terms of a cognitive model of face recognition (Bruce & Young, 1986), we argue that A.B. has underspecified *structural encoding* of faces. We speculate on this deficit in A.B. in terms of her other perceptual disorders as well as her close similarity to a case of childhood prosopagnosia: discussed in K.F. Young and Ellis (1989) and her differences from a new case of developmental prosopagnosia. We offer some suggestions for remediation in this and similar cases, based on a review of the small extant literature.

## INTRODUCTION

In this chapter we describe a young woman, A.B., who is unable to recognise familiar people by looking at the face. She can identify people quite well by voice, gait and other cues. She has no obvious problems in tasks of auditory or visual language processing. Her memory is excellent. She has learned several foreign languages and had no difficulty in learning to read or write (even in non-roman scripts). She is not autistic, and maintains social relationships, although face-to-face meetings may seem to lack adequate nonverbal communication. She leads an independent and fulfilling life as a university researcher and teacher. Interestingly, she appears always to have had these problems; they do not seem to be due to complications during birth, or brain damage following injury or neurological disease later life. A.B. is *developmentally prosopagnosic*. Her mother reports having similar problems, too, but we have not yet investigated this.

We will attempt here to fill out this sketch of A.B. in order to pinpoint exactly which processes are intact and which impaired. A.B. is clearly very unusual and we offer some speculations on the rarity of this problem. A number of people have now been described who lose their ability to recognise faces following brain injury. We will try to put A.B.'s problems in the context of those acquired impairments in order better to assess whether, and to what extent, any program for improving her skills in this area is indicated. This study, which we believe to be the first to look in systematic detail at such a developmental problem, will be *diagnostic* in nature. Only then will we have a basis for discussing remediation.

### Background

A.B. was born at 37 weeks gestation, and is an only child. She reports that she was never able to recognise people, apart from the most familiar ones, by their face. She came to the attention of medical experts and neuropsychological researchers in 1974 when she was twelve years old. Her parents were concerned that her school progress was impeded by 'clumsy writing' but were primarily seeking general medical advice on a longstanding medical complaint that had kept A.B. off school for long periods during childhood. Much later the medical problems were diagnosed and treated successfully.

Neurological examination at that time showed no sign of clinical impairment, and she had no visual field defects. A C.T. scan taken in 1980 revealed no radiological abnormalities with contrast injection. Neuropsychological investigation at that time, and again when she was 20 years old, indicated very superior verbal skills but poor nonverbal performance scores on standardised intelligence tests. For example, on WISC testing the discrepancy between verbal and nonverbal scores was statistically significant (140/100). However, not all nonverbal tasks were poorly performed. For example, Block Design matching (Koh's task) was performed quickly and accurately. She was noted to be clumsy in writing and in her actions generally.

At the time of testing when she was 12 years old, A.B. fell uneasily between adult and child test procedures that may have given a clearer picture of the extent and nature of her abnormalities. Therefore, McConachie (1976) described her tentatively as a *possible* case of developmental prosopagnosia. That report was unique in drawing attention to this. Only in the last few years have other reports of developmental prosopagnosia surfaced, and A.B. is still the only well documented, reported case. But in follow-up testing of A.B. at age 20, the diagnosis of a *specific* face processing deficit was questioned by Dr M. Wyke (personal communication).

## Recent Developments

We have been fortunate to be able to investigate A.B. more fully since 1986. In the 15 years since her first investigation, the topic of face recognition and its disorders has become the focus of much research resulting in the formulation of theoretical models within the framework of cognitive neuropsychology. These models attempt a functional description of cognitive deficits in terms of discrete and separable stages in information processing. Descriptions have been accumulating of *acquired* prosopagnosia; that is, of people who, following brain injury, lose a previously good ability to recognise faces (see de Renzi, 1986 and also Damasio, Damasio & van Hoesen, 1982). Locating such deficits in particular brain systems is a secondary part of this enterprise, which aims to describe and explain how normal face processing works (Ellis & Young, 1988).

Other advances have also occurred in the last 15 years. One major advance has been in the development of machine theories of vision that now guide anatomical and theoretical approaches (Humphreys & Bruce, 1989). Also, certain aspects of visual function are now examined more closely than before. In particular, contrast sensitivity at different spatial frequencies (see Fig. 4.1) is now a mandatory part of the assessment of visuosensory functions.

Our objective was to re-investigate A.B. with three questions in mind:

1. What, if anything, is amiss in her visuo-sensory functioning?
2. Which precise processes are compromised in her recognition of faces?
3. To what extent is her problem restricted to recognising faces, or does she show a more general identification impairment? Only when this has been accomplished will we be able to suggest remedial possibilities.

## VISUO-SPATIAL PROCESSING: PERCEPTION AND MEMORY

If A.B. had some problem in the elementary processing of visual information (e.g. colour, CSF, acuity) then this could, perhaps, explain her problems in face identification. Earlier tests had established full field vision in A.B. In contrast to acquired prosopagnosia which is typically (but not always) accompanied by a left upper quadrantanopia (Meadows, 1974).

### *Colour vision tests*

Simple tests of colour matching were well performed. Using a full Farnsworth-Munsell test battery under appropriate lighting conditions, A.B. showed normal performance and worked quickly. However, in arranging tokens in order of increasing and decreasing 'whiteness or blackness' (i.e. in grey-sensitivity) she consistently made small errors and was prone to hesitations. These were not sufficient to classify her as 'abnormal' in the clinical sense, but they were anomalous.

### *Contrast sensitivity at different spatial frequencies*

We tested A.B.'s contrast sensitivity (Fig. 4.1) with gratings of different spatial frequencies (Wilkins & Robson, 1986). In this task, the subject has to say whether they see a grid pattern or just a grey field as the contrast between the bars and the background is systematically changed. A.B. showed normal sensitivity for the spatial frequencies tested. Sergent (1989) has suggested that a loss of contrast sensitivity in the low spatial frequency range causes face recognition problems. However, Newcombe, De Haan, Ross, and Young (1989) found no consistent relationship between contrast sensitivity function and face recognition proficiency in neurological patients.

So it seems that apart from A.B.'s slight problem with greyness sensitivity, we can detect no purely perceptual problem that would contribute to her face-recognition difficulties to any marked extent.

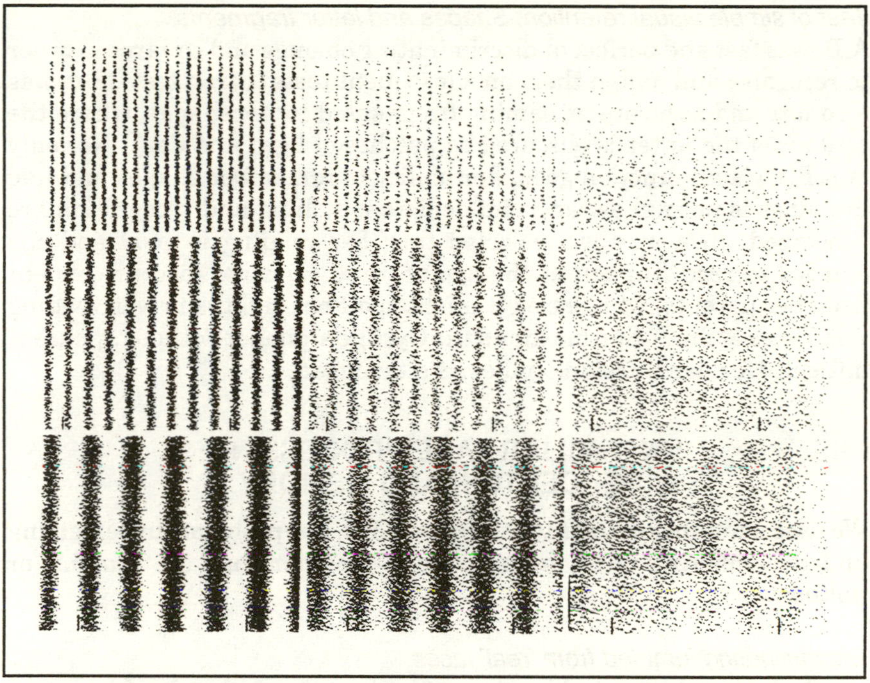

FIG. 4.1. Examples of three different levels of contrast (changing from high to low contrast; right → left), for three different spatial frequencies (ranging from high to low; top → bottom).

Perhaps she cannot *retain* visual information? We looked next at tasks of simple visual matching and recognition.

*Matching of line orientation*

This requires the subject to match two lines, each 2cm. long and of a given orientation, to an array of lines of different orientations. The test line and the match set are on different pages of a test booklet, requiring eye-movements to make the match (Benton, Varney, & Hamsher, 1978). A.B. made no errors and was very fast at this task.

*Retention of simple line drawings*

On this test (Benton & Van Allen, 1973a) a line drawing of three geometrical figures is presented for three seconds. Subsequently, the subject is required to select the correct line drawing from a set with three visually similar decoys, seen immediately afterwards. A.B.'s score of 28/32 is well within normal range.

### *Test of simple visual retention: Shapes and letter fragments*

A.B. was fast and perfect at discriminating oblongs and squares in order to recognise and match them on subsequent tests (Efron test). She was also fast and accurate at naming fragmented letter shapes, where the contour of the letter is obscured by patches of light and dark. Not only is A.B.'s visual function good, her ability to remember shapes and line drawings is normal as far as immediate matching and recognition are concerned. In a way we expected this; her reading is good and she learned to read English at the age of three. (Despite discouragement from her parents, who feared it might spoil her sight, she was reading *The Times* at four). She mastered the Cyrillic alphabet without apparent difficulty for her Russian studies as a teenager.

## UNFAMILIAR FACE PROCESSING: PERCEPTION AND MEMORY

We used a number of tests to establish if A.B. has problems in perceiving and remembering faces, irrespective of whether they are familiar or unknown.

### *Discriminating jumbled from 'real' faces*

If A.B. had problems in knowing a face 'as a face', she should be slow and inaccurate when asked to make face judgements on displays of scrambled face features compared with real face pictures (see Fig. 4.2). A.B. was shown slides of faces comprising scrambled features within a face frame intermixed with properly positioned features for the decision: is it a face or not? Compared to four control subjects, matched to A.B. for age and educational level, she was entirely normal, both for response speed and accuracy (A.B.: mean RT=713m.sec; 0 errors: Controls; mean RT=696m.sec (S.D.=113); 2.1 errors (S.D.=2.1).

### *Unfamiliar face matching*

The Benton and Van Allen test (1973b) comprises a series of sheets containing a single photographed target face to be matched to a set of six face photographs. In the first five trials, an identical face has to be selected from among five decoys. In the remaining 17 trials, three different views (changed in orientation or lighting conditions compared to the target photograph) have to be discriminated from three incorrect alternatives. The faces are physically similar, without spectacles or facial hair, and wear caps to eliminate hairline cues. A.B.'s score of 39 was on the borderline between normal performance and that of right hemisphere-lesioned patients who do not have prosopagnosia but do have more generalised visual/perceptual problems. It has come to be a

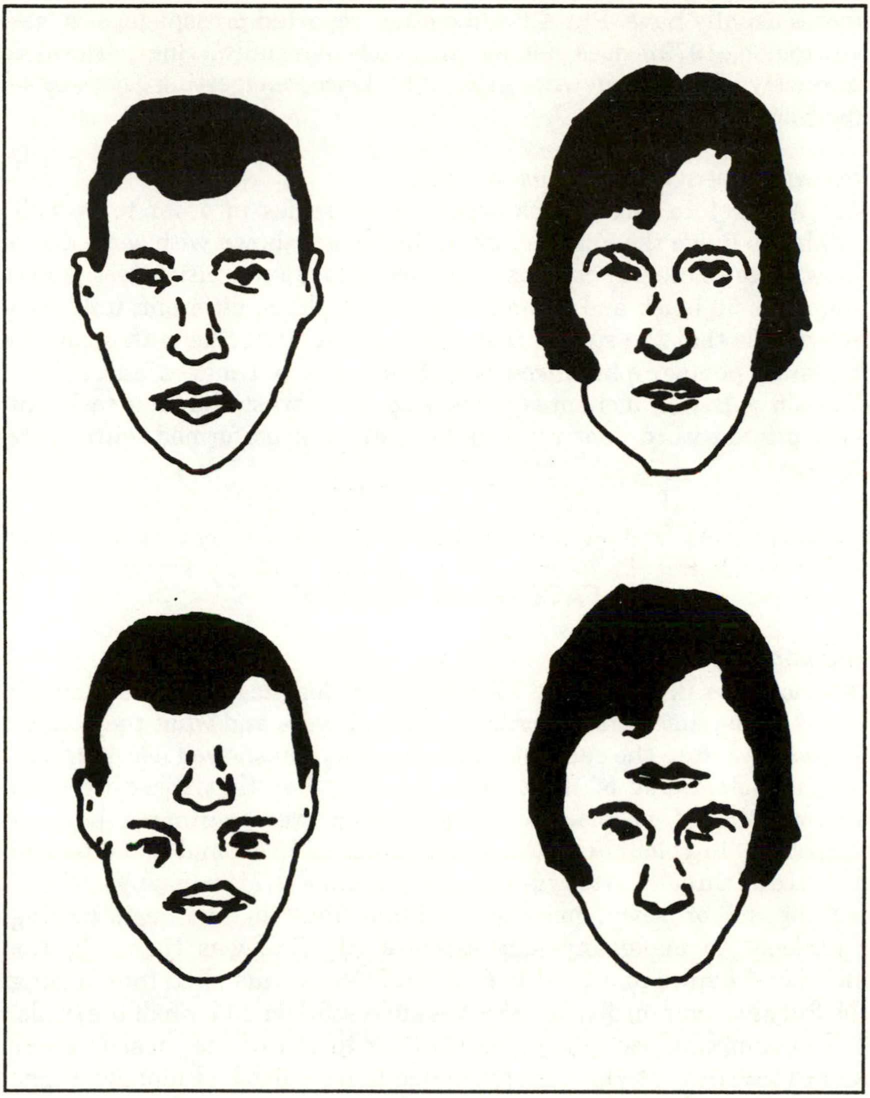

FIG. 4.2. Examples of stimuli used in the "face-nonface" decision task.

defining symptom of prosopagnosia that patients can do quite well on this test despite their everyday face recognition failure. That is, prosopagnosia can be distinguished, using this test, from 'purely perceptual' problems which may affect any sort of visual stimulus with the physical characteristics (contrast, line detail, colour) that faces in photos usually have. But A.B., like other reported prosopagnosics (see Newcombe, 1979), does not do this task 'normally'. She performed extremely slowly and with little confidence, suggesting the use of idiosyncratic strategies.

*Immediate memory for unfamiliar faces*

Can A.B. retain face photos presented in series in order to be able reliably to judge them as 'old' when they are reshown with some decoy ('new') face photographs? The Warrington face recognition test (1984) comprises 50 black and white face photographs of different, unknown individuals that the subject inspects one at a time. She is then shown the same photographs mixed with new ones and makes an old-new decision. A.B. was at chance on this task. In contrast, the same task, but with printed words not faces as stimuli, was performed with 100% accuracy.

## FACE IDENTIFICATION

*Familiar people*

We showed A.B. a series of 40 names of colleagues. She was familiar with all the names and described who they were and what they did as well as how often she encountered them. We then showed her 40 recent colour photographs of these people, telling her that these were all photographs of people she knew. These were ordinary portrait snapshots, in colour and in monochrome, of head and shoulders in full-face or three-quarter view. She was unable to identify any of them; making six or seven misidentifications and, for the rest, lacking confidence to make any judgement at all. She was then told the individual names and tried to find the face that matched from among the forty pictures on display. She was successful on under half the trials.

Ten snapshot portraits corresponding to ten of the most familiar names among the forty, were presented to her mixed with photographs of ten people whose names she did not know, and whom we thought she was unlikely to have met (these were mainly ex-employees from the same place of work). She was at chance in judging these faces as familiar or unfamiliar and expressed little confidence in her choice. She used both categories of decision equally often. Among the familiar faces were those of people who had taught her for several years as well as those of close colleagues. These included people who worked in the same office as she did—she saw all of these people regularly, some of them every day.

*Famous faces*

The only face that A.B. ever named in photographs or in line drawings (caricature) was that of Mrs. Thatcher, but even then she was hesitant and did not always name her correctly. Although she has a postcard of the wedding of Prince Charles and Princess Diana above her desk she was unable reliably to name these or other members of the British Royal Family in other photographs. Other popular icons (Marilyn Monroe, Winston Churchill, Che Guevara, Elvis Presley, James Dean, John F. Kennedy, Mikhail Gorbachev) were not named reliably. On a test of familiarity of famous faces (Newcombe et al., 1989), where she was shown a series of individually presented famous and unknown faces for familiar versus unfamiliar decision, she performed at chance level. However, when a forced choice paradigm was introduced (De Haan & Campbell, 1991; Young & De Haan, 1988) A.B. was slightly better than chance. That is, when pairs of faces were presented, one of which was famous, she chose the familiar one in 75/128 trials, which is statistically above chance though very impaired. On the other hand she always knows who these people are when given information other than faces; she correctly distinguished famous names (Elvis Presley) from non-famous names (Winston Dean) and knew why they were famous.

In summary, A.B. knows that a (photofit-style) face is a face and is able, painstakingly, to match photographs of faces across different views and lighting conditions (a *hard* visual matching task). But she cannot judge whether she has just seen face photographs of unfamiliar people that were identical from test to retest (an *easy* test of visual recognition). Neither personally familiar nor famous faces are familiar to her, though she has no problem with the identities of these people when tested by their names. She knows who these people are, though not by face.

A.B., we safely conclude, cannot recognise faces with anything like normal proficiency, though many of the visual skills that might be thought necessary to support face recognition do not appear to be badly compromised.

## OTHER FACE PROCESSING SKILLS

To what extent are A.B.'s face-problems confined to face *identification*? If we find that other aspects of face processing are compromised, then a theoretical account of her difficulties that focuses on the identification of distinctive individuals within a given category (within-category discrimination) may not be well directed.

Apart from being the major source of identification of others, faces tell us many things. We know the sex, age, race of the other person from their face. We can tell if they are angry or happy, sad or surprised

(Darwin, 1872). We make all sorts of judgements of the face—attractiveness, trustworthiness, criminality. These may be inaccurate because they are stereotypical, but they are nevertheless systematic. We rely on faces in communicating with other people. We know if someone is ready to engage in conversation by the way they orient their face and eyes to us. Direction of eye-gaze tells us where someone is looking and, often, where we should look. Most of us are extremely sensitive to direction of gaze and use it to modulate conversation and interaction with others. Even autistic children, who cannot understand beliefs and desires of other people (i.e. they cannot take the mental perspective of another person) can nevertheless reliably indicate 'where someone else is looking' (Baron-Cohen, 1992). Moreover, all of us can lipread—insofar as we can tell whether someone is speaking by noticing if their mouth moves (Campbell, 1989). These are everyday skills, not dependent on special expertise other than exposure to people and their faces.

We have tested A.B. on several of these face processing tasks. She is slow and inaccurate at judging age or expression from face photographs, being significantly worse than (unselected) normal controls. Her ability to judge expression and sex of speaker from voice is normal. Her mistakes in judging seem to be visual and/or semantic. For example, she misidentified a face showing disgust as one of surprise—they are visually and also semantically close. She relied on hairstyle in making gender judgements: long haired men without beards were misidentified as women.

A.B. was unable to discriminate eye-gaze direction in a simple task where one selects which of two coloured face photographs is 'looking straight at you'. In these pictures a head could be facing left or right while the eyes look at the camera; that is, head orientation and eye-gaze direction were independently varied (see Fig. 4.3). Her performance was entirely predicted by the direction of the *head,* not of the eyes in the head (Campbell et al., 1990b).

She was able to lipread in that she could identify a lip-spoken digit (i.e. we mouthed numbers at her, silently) and she could classify pictures of faces as speaking or pulling faces. However, when she was shown a speaking face saying 'ga' while a dubbed synchronous sound track said 'ba' she reported the heard 'ba', and not a combination of the heard and the seen sound. Normal subjects cannot separate the two sources of information (Campbell et al., 1990a).

So A.B.'s face-processing problems are not confined to identification. Faces are more difficult in all respects. She cannot reliably do with faces what most of us can do; she fails even at expression and gaze judgement—tasks which are extremely salient for the control of person

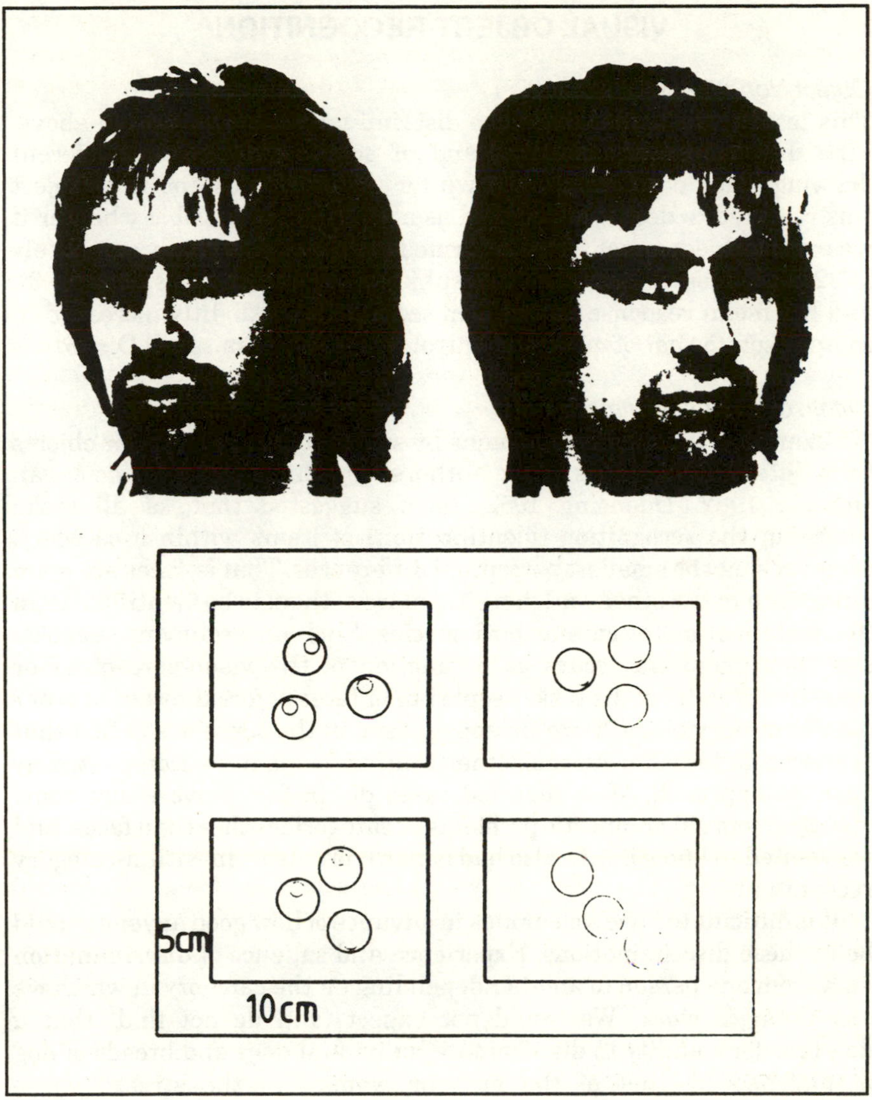


FIG. 4.3. Direction of eye gaze. A.B. could not say which of the two face photographs was "looking at her", but could discriminate the "odd-one-out" in the concentric circles task.

to person interaction. It is often unclear whether A.B. knows who is speaking and where they are, and her own responses, particularly at the start of a conversation often reflect this; speaking with her can be like talking to someone on the telephone.

## VISUAL OBJECT RECOGNITION

*Object/Non-object discrimination*

This test corresponds to the face discrimination test described above. Line drawings of real objects and of scrambled parts of different drawings (non-objects) were shown for three seconds and the subject was required to decide as fast and as accurately as possible whether it was a real object or not. A.B. performed this task reasonably accurately (3/32 errors; four matched control subjects mean=0.8 errors, S.D.=1 .3), and her mean response time (982m.sec) was only slightly increased in comparison to that of matched control subjects (858m.sec; S.D.=65).

*Within category discriminations*

We examined A.B.'s ability to name by sight pictures of familiar objects from different categories. Some authors (e.g. Damasio, Damasio & van Hoesen, 1982; Duensing 1952) have suggested that, of all tasks requiring the recognition (identification) of items within a category, faces present the smallest perceptual differences. That is, faces are more alike, each to the other, and there are more of them to be identified, than (for instance) motor cars or bird species. Such an argument suggests that prosopagnosia occurs as a function of the visuo-perceptual or mnestic difficulty of the task. People fail at faces before they fail at other discriminatory tasks. 'Pure' prosopagnosia, in the sense of a deficit that is special to faces for reasons other than these, is not encompassed by such an approach. Most reported cases do, in fact, have either some visuo/perceptual or mnestic problems in categories other than faces, and we wanted to know if A.B. also had general problems in within-category recognition.

It is difficult to have a clear idea in advance of how good anyone should be at these discriminations. Experience and salience of discrimination vary from one person to another depending on the category in which we ask them to work. We would not expect (and do not find) that a dog-breeder's ability to discriminate individual dogs and breeds of dog is matched by that of the man or woman in the street (whose discriminations may be more concerned with the dog's behaviour than its appearance). However, although we do not have norms for all these tests—such norms may be meaningless in the face of such wide variation—we can still gain some impression of ease or difficulty.

*Food:* Food is a salient discrimination for everyone. Does A.B. have difficulty in recognising pictures of different foodstuffs? Using photographs (coloured and monochrome) and line drawings, we found that she named most fruit and vegetables quite accurately and was similarly quite good at identifying cooked food. Nevertheless her abilities were not very impressive: She could not distinguish between cooked lamb chops and cooked beefsteak seen in full colour photographs and mistook a colour photograph of a parsnip for a carrot.

*Flowers:* A.B. made many mistakes in naming line drawings and colour photographs of flowers (19/26 errors; four matched controls made a mean 9.5 errors, S.D.=0.5). She was much more accurate at matching full colour photographs of flowers to their spoken names in a forced choice task where just two flower names were spoken for each flower picture seen (5/26 choices were wrong; controls made a mean 1.2 errors, S.D.=1.3). A.B. has a garden which she tends herself.

*Cars:* Makes of automobile were not identified by A.B. and it is unclear that she knows anything about the different makes of car. A.B. does not drive and is not interested in cars.

*Other categories:* Other identifications were tested with line drawings. These were obtained from the Oxford Illustrated Dictionary and were enlarged to triple-page size. A.B. was shown a page and asked to name every drawn item. She was good at naming household utensils (vacuum cleaner, bucket, etc). She made some errors in naming animals.

A.B. mis-named items that had visual and/or semantic properties in common with the target. Thus a beaver would be misidentified as a rabbit, both are smallish furry quadruped mammals; a lupin as a delphinium, both are tall, blue-coloured border perennials.

*Tests of pictured objects shown in unusual views*

Warrington (see Warrington, 1984; Warrington & James, 1991) has developed a number of tests of visual object recognition which specifically examine changes in viewpoint. These are tests of *object invariance.* This term refers to the fact that despite the changes afforded by change of viewpoint or illumination of the two-dimensional representation of the object (as in a photograph of an object rotated through different orientations, for example) objects are readily recognised for what they are. Nevertheless, most objects that we see have a preferred orientation. We recognise faces best when they are the right way up and full to three-quarter face view. Cups, teapots, cars, lions, rabbits, all have *canonical* viewpoints from which their salient distinctive features are most apparent, and they, too, have a right (and a wrong) way up. On Warrington's 'unusual views' test, which presents photographs of real objects from non-canonical viewpoints, A.B. scored at below the fifth percentile compared with elderly controls. That is, she was worse than 95% of tested controls at this task. This test, however, was developed 25 years ago and includes objects which are not particularly familiar to young people (e.g. a hand-held mechanical egg-whisk) and norms are no longer available for people of A.B.'s age. Norms are available, however, for a test of *silhouette* recognition, where silhouette pictures of objects are presented at unfamiliar angles. These are of objects (cat, elephant, basket) which A.B. was able to name correctly and easily as line drawings in the usual orientation. She scored at below the fifth percentile for her age group in naming silhouettes from unusual views. In another silhouette test an outline of an object (a revolver or a trumpet) is seen from a very unfamiliar view and in subsequent pictures it is gradually rotated towards the canonical orientation. The test score reflects the view at which the subject correctly names the object. A.B. was again below the 5% level for age-norms on this task.

*Object naming*

On the Oldfield-Wingfield naming task (Newcombe, Oldfield, Ratcliff, & Wingfield, 1971), the subject is presented with 26 line drawings of objects varying in familiarity (e.g. a tap and a gyroscope) and asked to name the object as quickly as possible. A.B. made two naming errors (i.e. 'distance, goggles, sort of thing' for binoculars), but more importantly, made seven recognition errors (such as saying 'violin' for guitar) which is clearly outside the normal range. Thus, there is evidence for a (mild) degree of object agnosia on a standard clinical object recognition task.

Overall the evidence strongly suggests that A.B.'s visual recognition problems are not restricted to faces. But her recognition deficit for these other types of stimuli is clearly less marked than her face-processing deficit and is not apparent, for instance, in meeting her and interacting with her. She would never mistake a hat stand for a woman (as did a prosopagnosic patient described by Sacks (Sacks, 1986) and even quite detailed discriminations (e.g. knives, forks, spoons) do not appear to cause her problems. De Renzi (1986) reports a case of 'pure' prosopagnosia where the patient identified all his clothes and personal belongings correctly by sight when these were mixed up with those of others. Only faces caused him problems. A.B., too, never seems to make mistakes in finding her coat or bag when they are mixed up with those of others. Indeed she claims that she identifies people in part by their typical clothing, hairstyle and so forth. Only on careful testing with many types of pictured object were *some* problems apparent.

In object identification her mistakes are 'plausible' on visual/semantic grounds; they are the types of error we might expect of someone who has had little experience with these pictures or the objects to which they correspond. So, too, for her problems with unusual views: Experience with objects should allow skill to develop at interpreting odd orientations or lighting of familiar objects. For some reason visual experience has failed to improve A.B.'s discrimination abilities when it comes to these tasks.

## THEORETICAL AND REMEDIAL CONSIDERATIONS

Here we will try to interpret A.B.'s problems so that they cast light on theories concerning normal face perception and recognition and on ideas about the neurological basis for face-processing skill.

### Face Recognition: A Cognitive Neuropsychological Perspective

Bruce and Young (1986) have proposed a multi-stage model of the processes needed to recognise faces. This is reproduced in Fig. 4.4.

Each of the stages is taken to be a necessary functional component for normal face recognition. This model has guided research in normal populations (Bruce, 1988) and in people with face-processing deficits (see De Haan, 1989). Can we locate A.B.'s problems in this model, or will developmental prosopagnosia in general, and A.B. in particular, demand a different sort of model? A.B. can discriminate photofit-style faces from non-faces; her problem is not at the level of achieving a structural representation of the face in terms of which features should go where. Also, A.B. can (slowly) match unfamiliar faces across different views and lighting conditions; this simultaneous-matching process is not badly compromised. However, such matching need not always require that the face be recognised as a face; we will return to this point later.

A.B. is poor at judging age, expression and some aspects of speech from the face. She cannot discriminate eye-gaze. All these tasks (on the model) require good structural encoding of the face. However, her difficulties with faces are not so profound that faces are meaningless; her judgements of facial expression and of gender were not completely wrong, but *underinformed.* Some information about faces is achieved, but it is insufficient to support reliable representations in various face judgements. Thus, in this framework, A.B.'s problems are within the box labelled 'structural encoding'; they may be described as due to *underspecified structural encoding.*

In the terminology of clinical neuropsychology, A.B.'s problems with faces are *perceptual* rather than *amnesic* (memory based). Perceptual

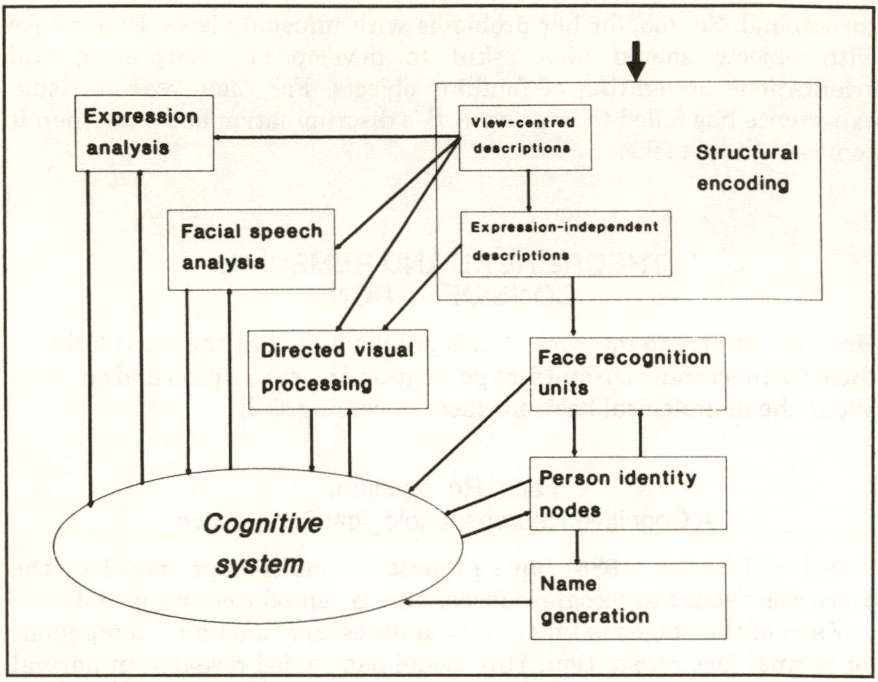


FIG. 4.4. An information processing model of the stages in face recognition. Adapted from Bruce and Young (1986).

refers here to those 'higher-order' processes required to develop coherent representations or specifications on which further cognitive processes can be based. Her deficits do not seem to be primarily amnesic, since she is unimpaired in recognising and remembering people by description, name or voice, and her recognition problem affects all visual information processing of physiognomy.

Inspection of the model in Fig. 4.4 shows that there is an alternative functional explanation. It could be argued that despite impoverished structural encoding processes, Face Recognition Units have been created but their outputs fail to reach subsequent stages because of faulty connection. This possibility is suggested by recent studies with acquired prosopagnosic patients who show clear evidence of *covert* processing of face familiarity (Bauer, 1984; De Haan, Young, & Newcombe, 1987). That is, indirect measures which do not require the patient to make an overt identification response (e.g. skin conductance responses, or interference from unrelated familiar faces on the classification of names) can show preserved face recognition effects, while the patient has no conscious access to this information.

The possibility of covert face recognition in A.B. is not indicated by what we know of her condition. Her problem affects many aspects of the way she deals with faces. Her verbal descriptions of faces are very sparing of visual detail—so while she may say (of a photograph) that the person portrayed has blue eyes she would not say that these were large, or dark or far apart; even when the face is being described as it is being viewed. Her descriptions of famous people from memory emphasise their non-visual aspects; she finds it difficult to provide more than a very sparse answer in response to questions such as 'What does Marilyn Monroe look like?' If one assumes that face imagery depends on intact FRUs, then her problems in this respect suggest absent FRUs, rather than FRUs disconnected from perceptual input processes (they could still be due to an impaired ability to access FRUs for description).

We directly investigated the possibility of covert face recognition in A.B. with the 'Associative Priming' paradigm (Young, Hellawell & De Haan, 1988). This reaction-time experiment involves the presentation of printed names of famous and unknown people for a familiarity decision. Response speed decreases significantly in normal subjects when prior to the name (e.g. Princess Diana), a related face (e.g. Prince Charles) has been shown compared to the conditions where the 'prime' face was of an unfamiliar person or an unrelated famous person (e.g. Mick Jagger). The results on this task established the absence of covert recognition in A.B. (De Haan & Campbell, in press). This suggests that A.B. has problems in setting up and maintaining useful representations of other people's faces sufficient to support any further processing. Internal representations of faces are poorly established, hindering all further information processing, including the build up of Face Recognition Units.

The absence of an intact FRU system has important repercussions for the selection and development of possible remedial programmes. If her problems had been restricted to overt face processing tasks we could, in principle, attempt to improve access to such representations by training. This general point is well illustrated by the work of Schacter who demonstrated dramatic improvements in amnesic patients with a rehabilitation programme that takes advantage of preserved covert processes (Glisky, Schacter, & Butters, this volume). More specifically, Sergent and Poncet (1990) have shown that in certain cases of acquired prosopagnosia with covert face recognition, *overt* face recognition can be achieved under very specific conditions. They presented their patient with a large number of photographs of faces of media celebrities drawn from a number of categories (singers, politicians, comedians, etc.). When these faces were presented in isolation the patient, as expected, recognised none of them. However, when all the faces belonging to one category were presented simultaneously (e.g. the faces of eight comedians), she could spontaneously recognise some of the *categories* and was subsequently able to recognise some of the individual faces within that category. However, if she failed to identify the category, she was then not helped in identifying the faces when the experimenter gave her the category-name. It seems that spontaneous overt recognition of the individual faces was only possible if cumulative activation from the different faces surpassed a certain threshold, and this could only occur when all the faces had some semantic (category) information in common. Unfortunately, there was very little generalisation, for the patient again failed to recognise individual face photographs when they were presented at a later stage. Studies in our laboratory (De Haan, Young, & Newcombe, 1991) have recently replicated this finding. The prosopagnosic patient P.H. (De Haan, Young, & Newcombe 1987), who has good covert recognition and no overt face recognition, shows similar effects to those described by Sergent and Poncet, although to a less marked degree. In P.H., however, overt recognition following such procedures was somewhat longer lasting than in Sergent and Poncet's patient. Although we still know very little about this phenomenon, it clearly holds promise for remediation.

## A WIDER PERSPECTIVE

Although the Bruce and Young face processing model allows us to make a reasonable attempt at functional localisation of A.B.'s face processing deficit, it cannot tell us how we may link these problems to her other visual apperceptive problems. Are her problems unitary and associated (all objects including faces) or separable and dissociated (objects—slight, faces—severe)?

While A.B. is not perfect at within-category discrimination, her impairments are not as striking as her face impairments. For example, outside the realm of personal interactions, her everyday behaviour shows little sign of the sort of mistakes or uncertainties we might expect of someone who could not, for instance, distinguish a knife from a spoon by sight. By contrast, her encounters with other people can exhibit a tentative quality. For example, she often appears nervous and will say 'hello' in an uncommitted way which invites the other person to speak. This may then enable her to identify who is speaking.

Could a deficit in higher visual function—one that is signalled by her problems in recognising familiar objects from an unfamiliar viewpoint—be *sufficient* to cause her severe visual face processing problems and (somewhat less marked) object processing impairments? Arguably, face processing makes higher demands on visual processing than does the recognition of other objects or relevant aspects of them, but we cannot find any evidence that poor acuity, poor colour vision, or reduced contrast sensitivity at particular spatial frequencies are responsible for A.B.'s problems. If 'vision' is compromised, it must be at a particularly central and general level to account for the specificity of A.B.'s problems. At what level could this be? What aspect of the full structural code for faces is so hard for A.B. to achieve?

In A.B., performance on the silhouette task (poor) and line-drawing object decision task (relatively good), suggests that she has more of a problem with the global and spatial aspects than the local (lines and edges) aspects of object recognition. Furthermore, her errors of misidentification, although often respecting local salient information (flower colour, number of florets in flower naming) seem to be most pronounced where spatial properties might have helped make the correct decision. One example might be the ability to distinguish relative length and shape of different parts (she could not distinguish a parsnip from a carrot). A.B.'s quick and unimpaired ability to read and remember forms such as line-drawn shapes, letters, or numbers further supports the possibility that local information, particularly when it can be interpreted in terms of 'flat', two-dimensional attributes, is intact and effectively processed. Another distinction in A.B.'s abilities may also indicate this: A.B. was unable to discriminate with any certainty eye-gaze in photographs. Yet when she was asked to indicate the odd one out of three sets of concentric circles in which one set had an inner circle in a different orientation than the others, she was accurate and fast (see Fig. 4.3). She can distinguish the local (relative orientation) visual features that are required to perform the gaze task when these are presented as two-dimensional line drawings, out of a face context, but appears to be unable to incorporate them into a judgement on the face as a whole, three-dimensional pattern.

It appears that A.B. may have particular problems in establishing a *spatial framework* into which salient feature information might fit. Her problems with facial expressions also fit this account. For example, in identifying surprise on a face, it is the *distance* between the eyes and eyebrows—as much as the shape of the features themselves—that signals the expression. And the difference between a surprised face and a disgusted or a happy one is not signalled by any one feature but rather by the attributes of a spatially defined *set* of features.

As A.B. has such dense problems, we could infer that such a spatial framework is needed for all good face processing to develop. Without such an underpinning it may be difficult to integrate the specific values of features in order to identify an individual, their facial expression, or even gender. To test the strength of this assertion, try to make any sort of judgement about a face when you inspect it upside-down or in photographic negative. Faces, much more than other sorts of visual stimulus, are particularly affected by manipulations that impair the construction of a spatial representation that is independent of viewpoint and lighting (see Galper, 1970; Phillips, 1972; Yin, 1969).

We have arrived at the possibility that while A.B.'s deficit in face processing is indeed severe compared with her deficit in object recognition, this severity could be explained in terms of a disruption of some general perceptual processes, rather than a deficit in a specific face processing module. But these general perceptual processes are at a high level and may concern the ways in which two- and three-dimensional knowledge of objects in the world is integrated and represented in the brain. A.B. is impaired at tasks that require spatial rather than purely visual analysis: Face processing may be particularly demanding of both, so that a weakness in the former, or in linking the two (hypothesised) processes, will be particularly debilitating in trying to identify people and making sense, generally, of their appearance.

This story does not, however, seem to take account of two face tasks that A.B. could do. She matched face photographs reasonably well in the Benton and Van Allen task and she made correct face/nonface decisions. How is this possible if she lacks a spatial frame for faces? We would like to argue that some of the Benton pictures can be matched by looking for an *unchanging face feature* (such as a hairline feature) across the array of photographs. One would not need a spatial framework to match the faces on such a local basis. She was very slow indeed at this task, which suggests idiosyncratic strategies. And, after all, she was not as accurate as a normal control subject would be at this task.

The face/non-face decision can be made by checking the order of identified features ("two eyes above a nose above a mouth"), and we assume that face features are not too much of a problem for A.B., particularly when they are presented in a fairly schematic form, as in the photofit style pictures used in this test. In addition, the ability to detect face-like configurations (even three blobs arranged in the positions of the eyes and mouth in an upright face frame) can be based on a separate process than that used for identifying faces. For instance, such schematic faces are extremely powerful in attracting babies' attention. Some research in infant perception and behaviour suggests that this may reflect a basic, innate and *independent* system for responding to members of our own species (de Schonen & Mathivet, 1989; Johnson, 1988).

## COMPARISON WITH OTHER PATIENTS

Developmental prosopagnosia is a rare condition and although A.B. was unique as a reported case when we started our investigation, another case has come to our attention recently. It is possible that the reported incidence of prosopagnosia will increase as clinicians and researchers become aware of its existence. We will now compare A.B. with one other case of developmental prosopagnosia (Temple, 1992) and one case of acquired childhood prosopagnosia following meningitis at fourteen months (Young & Ellis, 1989).

Temple (1992) describes a woman, now middle-aged, who, like A.B. reports that she always had difficulty with faces. On formal testing, she displays a severe impairment in famous face recognition. In this case, however, the pattern of disorder is very different. Temple's case can recognise unfamiliar faces (i.e. in Warrington's old-new faces task she performs normally), and can analyse facial expressions. Her problem is in linking the achieved representation of a seen face to the semantic information specific to that individual. In terms of the model, her deficit can be conceptualised as a defect in the FRUs or a disconnection between the FRUs and the subsequent processes (see Fig. 4.2). Detailed investigation of covert face recognition might distinguish between these alternative explanations. If covert face recognition were to be found, suggesting intact FRUs, it might be possible to provoke overt recognition capitalising on this preserved, currently covert abilities (Sergent & Poncet, 1990). Therefore, remedial programmes for this patient and A.B. should focus on different types of training.

The patient K.D. (Young & Ellis, 1989) contracted meningococcal meningitis at the age of fourteen months. There followed almost two years of medical complications including a period of cortical blindness. After a partial recovery, she was left with poor vision and prosopagnosia. The authors argue convincingly that, although her visuo-sensory problems are severe, they cannot explain the face recognition deficit, as other children with equally poor vision are not prosopagnosic. Detailed investigations revealed a similar pattern of performance as those described for A.B.: Some degree of impaired object recognition (especially when presented in unusual views); impaired performance on tasks for expression analysis, gender discrimination, and unfamiliar face matching (although she was by no means completely unable to do these tests), and a complete inability to recognise familiar faces. In addition, K.D. failed to show covert recognition effects on implicit tasks. By contrast she had achieved a reading level which was near normal for her age. An attempt to remediate K.D., using a paired-associate learning approach for combining information (occupations, names, etc.) to faces with the aid of a portable computer, produced very disappointing results (Ellis & Young, 1988).

## CONCLUSIONS

We have argued that a congenital inability to recognise familiar faces can be caused by inadequate development of a perceptual stage of face processing which in turn has led to a failure of development in the mechanisms that, in normal children, operate on the output of this particular process. In terms of the Bruce and Young (1986) model the functional locus of deficit is in structural encoding. The mechanism here is essentially combinatorial and is used to construct a coherent, abstract representation of a person's face from diverse features, viewpoints, expressions. We would claim that normal face identification processes are not learnable by A.B.; as they did not develop at the right time they will not develop at all. This very negative conclusion seems to be at odds with the more common-sense view that because most of us continue to learn new faces through our adult life, there is no need to posit age-specific face-recognition maturation. Against this, we would argue that we also continue to learn new words into adult life; learning new vocabulary items may indeed implicate, indirectly, those processes that were used to achieve mastery of the language system as a whole and which were probably laid down early in life. Adult face and word learning, however, does suggest one way in which A.B. may be helped in recognising faces. The analogy here is with learning words in a foreign language: While it is hard to acquire a vocabulary in, say, Chinese, after infancy, it is possible. Such second language learning may be idiosyncratic. Similarly, it is possible that A.B. could learn some more faces idiosyncratically, for instance, by relying on specific features that are always reliably associated with that face, and that do not require spatial processing. Unfortunately, such features tend not to be permanent; hairstyle, spectacles, facial hair can be altered readily. However there are some features that are less likely to change and could form the basis for identification; skin-tone, texture and (within limits) colour (eye colour) are examples that come to mind. And, if idiosyncratic strategies fail for *face* recognition, *person* recognition might be improved by learning to concentrate on (relatively) unique features of the body, and the way it moves. In this context, 'experienced' acquired prosopagnosic patients could, themselves, teach us which characteristics are most promising. This requires the assessment of the efficiency of the different alternative ways of identification which they might have developed spontaneously.

An important difference in these cues might be those that the patient may control (e.g. "I'll recognise father as long as he always wears a green tie"), which will allow easy recognition of a limited number of significant people, and those that promote more generalisation. The latter are likely to involve combinations of relatively constant features; face shape, eye colour, size of eyebrows, etc.

The main implication of our studies with A.B. is that careful diagnosis, preferably in the context of a functional model, is crucial for directing rehabilitation programmes. Although covert face recognition has, as yet, not been demonstrated in developmental prosopagnosia, it is clear that knowledge about what the patient still can do and cannot do with visual face information is pertinent for the design of remedial programmes.

## ACKNOWLEDGEMENTS

We are grateful to Dr E. Warrington and to Dr M. Wyke for making tests and results available to us and to J. Garwood for running some of these tests. Charles Heywood was instrumental in testing visual function. We are particularly grateful to him, as we are to A.B. for her patience and insights during these investigations. This work was supported by the Medical Research Council of Great Britain through project grant no. G8811259N to R.Campbell and G890469N to E.H.F. De Haan and A.W Young. An Oxford University Pump-priming grant to R.C. also supported some early stages of this work.

## REFERENCES

Baron-Cohen., S. (1992). The girl who laughed in church. In R.Campbell (Ed.), *Mental lives. Case studies in cognition*. Oxford: Blackwell

Bauer, R.M. (1984). Autonomic recognition of names and faces in prosopagnosia: A neuropsychological application of the guilty knowledge test. *Neuropsychologia, 22,* 457-469.

Benton, A.L. & van Allen, M.W. (1973a). *Tests of Visual Function.* Iowa, U.S.A.

Benton, A.L. & van Allen, M.W. (1973b). *Test of face recognition manual,* Neurosensory Center Publication number 287, Iowa, U.S.A: Department of Neurology

Benton, A.L., Varney, N.R., & Hamsher, K. DeS. (1978). Visuo-spatial judgement: A clinical test. *Archives of Neurology, 35,* 364-367.

Bruce,V. (1988). *Recognising faces.* Hove: Lawrence Erlbaum Associates Ltd.

Bruce, V. & Young, A.W. (1986). Understanding face recognition *British Journal of Psychology, 77,* 305-327.

Campbell, R. (1989). Lipreading. In A.W. Young & H.D. Ellis (Eds.), *Handbook of research on face processing.* (187-234). Amsterdam: Elsevier.

Campbell, R., Garwood, J., Franklin, S., Howard, D., Landis, T., & Regard, M. (1990a). Neuropsychological studies of the auditory-visual fusion illusion. *Neuropsychologia. 28,* 787-802

Campbell, R., Heywood, C., Cowey, A., Regard, M., & Landis, T. (1990b). The detection of eye-gaze direction in macaque and prosopagnosic subjects. *Neuropsychologia, 28,* 1123-1142.

Damasio, A.R., Damasio, H., & van Hoesen, G.W. (1982). Prosopagnosia: Anatomic basis and behavioral mechanisms. *Neurology, 32,* 331-334.

Darwin, C. (1872, reprinted 1965) *The expression of the emotions in man and animals.* Chicago: University of Chicago Press.

De Haan, E.H.F. (1989). The case for case studies and functional models. In A.W. Young & H.D. Ellis (Eds.), *The handbook of face processing,* Amsterdam: North Holland.

De Haan, E.H.F. & Campbell, R. (1991). A fifteen year follow-up of a case of developmental prosopagnosia *Cortex, 27,* 489-509.

De Haan, E.H.F., Young, A.W., & Newcombe, F. (1987). Face recognition without awareness. *Cognitive Neuropsychology, 4,* 385-415.

De Haan, E.H.F., Young, A.W., & Newcombe, F. (1991). Covert and overt face recognition in prosopagnosia. *Brain, 14,* 2575-2591.

De Renzi, E. (1986). Current issues in prosopagnosia. In H.D. Ellis, M.A. Jeeves, F. Newcombe, & A. Young (Eds.), *Aspects of face processing: A NATO Symposium* (pp. 279-290). Dordrecht: M.Nijhoff.

de Schonen, S. & Mathivet, E. (1989). First come, first served; a scenario about the development of hemispheric specialization in face recognition during infancy. *Cahiers de Psychologie Cognitive, 9,* 3-46.

Duensing, F. (1952). Beitrag zur Frage der optischen Agnosie. *Archiv für Psychiatrie und Nervenkrankheiten, 188,* 131-161.

Ellis, A.W. & Young, A.W. (1989). *Cognitive Neuropsychology.* Hove: Lawrence Erlbaum Associates Ltd.

Ellis, H.D. & Young, A.W. (1988). Training in face processing skills for a child with acquired prosopagnosia. *Developmental Neuropsychology, 4,* 283-294.

Galper, R.E. (1970). Recognition of faces in photographic negative. *Psychonomic Science, 19,* 207-208.

Humphreys, G.W. & Bruce, V. (1989). *Visual cognition.* Hove: Lawrence Erlbaum Associates Ltd.

Johnson, M. (1988). Memories of mother. *New Scientist, 2,* 18th February, 60-62.

McConachie, H.R. (1976). Developmental prosopagnosia. A single case report. *Cortex, 12,* 76-82.

Newcombe, F. (1979). The processing of visual information in prosopagnosia and acquired dyslexia. In D.J. Osborne, M.M. Gruneberg, & J.R. Eiser (Eds.), *Research in Psychology and Medicine, 1* (pp. 315-322). London: Academic Press.

Newcombe, F., De Haan, E.H.F., Ross, J., & Young, A.W. (1989). Face processing, laterality and contrast sensitivity. *Neuropsychologia, 27,* 523-538.

Newcombe, F., Oldfield, R.C., Ratcliff, G.G., & Wingfield, A. (1971). Recognition and naming of object-drawings by men with focal brain wounds. *Journal of Neurology, Neurosurgery and Psychiatry, 34,* 329-340.

Phillips, R. (1972). Why are faces hard to recognise in photographic negative? *Perception and Psychophysics, 12,* 425-426.

Sacks, O. (1986). *The man who mistook his wife for a hat.* London: Duckworth.

Sergent, J. (1989). Structural processing of faces. In A.W. Young & H.D. Ellis (Eds.), *Handbook of face processing* (pp. 57-93). Amsterdam: North Holland.

Sergent, J. & Poncet, M. (1990). From covert to overt recognition of faces in a prosopagnosic patient. *Brain*, *113*, 989-1004

Temple, C.R.M. (1992). A case of developmental prosopagnosia. In R.Campbell (Ed.), *Mental lives: Case studies in cognition* (pp. 201-215). Oxford: Blackwell.

Warrington, E. (1984). *Recognition memory test*. U.K.: NFER-Nelson.

Warrington, E. & James, M. (1991). *The VSOR test of visual function*. Berkshire: NFER.

Wilkins, A.J. & Robson, J.G. (1986). *The Cambridge Low Contrast Gratings*. U.K.: Clement Clerk International.

Yin, R. (1969). Looking at upside-down faces. *Journal of Experimental Psychology, 81,* 141 -145.

Young, A.W. & de Haan, E.H.F. (1988). Boundaries of covert recognition in prosopagnosia. *Cognitive Neuropsychology, 5,* 317-336

Young, A.W. & Ellis, H.D. (1989). Childhood prosopagnosia. *Brain and Cognition, 9,* 16-47.

Young, A.W., Hellawell, D., & De Haan, E.H.F. (1988). Cross-domain semantic priming in normal subjects and a prosopagnosic patient. *Quarterly Journal of Experimental Psychology, 40A*, 561-580.

CHAPTER FIVE

# Rehabilitation of Semantic Memory Impairments

Giuseppe Sartori, Michele Miozzo, and Remo Job
*Università di Padova, Dipartimento di Psicologia Generale, Padova, Italy*

## ABSTRACT

The semantic memory rehabilitation programme of two post-encephalitic patients (Michelangelo and Giulietta) is presented. The programme was tailored on the previous neuropsychological evaluation, which showed that the symptoms requiring treatment were a category specific deficit restricted to living things and anterograde amnesia. As for the former, as both patients had problems in processing information about the structural properties of living things, the tasks developed for rehabilitation concerned visual attributes of items. Neither patient benefitted from cognitive therapy, as a similar representation deficit was detected in pre- and post-therapy test sessions. We interpret this lack of benefit as being due to the concurrence of semantic disturbance with anterograde amnesia that made impossible the restoring of the lost information.

## INTRODUCTION

According to recent cognitive models, memory is viewed as a multiple system that is divisible into several sub-systems differing in the nature of information stored, and in the way they represent and process this information. Probably these functional distinctions reflect the organisation of the memory in the brain, so that each subcomponent is allocated different neurological structures. One of the most important approaches to partitioning memory is that proposed by Tulving (1983; 1984), who differentiated between what he called semantic memory and episodic memory. Semantic memory encompasses the encyclopedic knowledge of the world and the meaning of words and concepts. In contrast, episodic memory is an autobiographical record of personally experienced, unique events encoded in relation to a spatial-temporal context. Referring to this distinction from a neuropsychological perspective, we could expect to find patients showing a dissociation where semantic memory is damaged and episodic memory is spared. The opposite dissociation (i.e. episodic memory impaired while semantic memory is spared) is a typical observation in anterograde amnesic patients (for a review see Shallice, 1988).

In these last years, neuroscientists have presented experimental evidence for a particular kind of impairment of semantic memory, producing the so-called category specific disorders. The distinctive feature of this semantic disturbance is an impairment of specific domains of knowledge; that is, the selective impairment of the ability to process exemplars of some semantic categories and the selective preservation of the ability to process exemplars from other semantic categories. The first detailed investigation of category specific disorders was performed by Warrington and Shallice (1984), who reported four patients performing very poorly in identifying elements of particular categories such as living things and foods whereas non-living things were relatively spared. All four of these patients had recovered from herpes simplex virus encephalitis (HSVE), and all had sustained bilateral temporal lobe damage. Generally, herpes simplex viral infection causes acute necrosis, oedema and haemorrhage commonly involving bilaterally or unilaterally the temporal portion of the brain and extending into orbitofrontal regions, while neurological sequelae can range from severe dementia to mild anomic and amnesic disorders.

These original observations were replicated in several recent accounts of neuropsychological studies of HSVE patients such as those reported by Pietrini et al. (1988), Sartori and Job (1988), Sartori, Zago, and Miozzo (1990), Silveri and Gainotti (1988), Stewart, Parkin, and Hunkin (1992). In the study of De Renzi, Liotti, and Nichelli, 1987 and in that of Ratcliff and Newcombe, 1982, cases of presumptive diagnosis of HSVE are presented.

Nevertheless, category-related defects can be caused by other pathologies. For instance, Hart, Berndt, and Caramazza's (1985) patient developed category specific impairment for living items following cerebral infarction (other examples include Basso, Capitani, & Laiacona, 1988; Farah, Hammond, Mehta, & Ratcliff, 1989; Hillis & Caramazza 1990; Yamadori & Albert, 1973). It is important to note that all these cases had unilateral or bilateral involvement of inferior temporal lobes, thus mimicking lesions induced by herpes simplex virus.

The opposite category deficit, namely damaged knowledge of non-living elements with relatively preserved knowledge of living elements, have also been described, thus suggesting the possibility of a double dissociation (see Hillis & Caramazza, 1991; Warrington & McCarthy, 1987). Further, apart from the main distinction between living and non-living things, finer-grained disruption of specific domains of knowledge have been discovered. For instance Yamadori and Albert (1973) presented a patient who appeared to have more difficulty comprehending the names of indoor objects than the names of outdoor objects.

Category impairments are commonly associated with other neuropsychological deficits that seemed to vary according to the pathologies determining the semantic impairment. Whereas, for example, all HSVE patients exhibiting category specific damage are amnesic (usually severe anterograde amnesia accompanied by mild retrograde amnesia) and disoriented to time and place, there are patients with categorical impairments who did not show any amnesic disturbances (see Yamadori & Albert's, 1973, case).

Interpreting various cases of category specific impairments, Humphreys, Riddoch, and Quinlan (1988) proposed that such disturbances could arise from single or multiple selective damage on at least three different levels: the structural description, the semantic memory or the phonological output. This explanation is in accordance with recent cognitive models proposing that at least three different stored mental representations have to be accessed for correctly identifying and naming an object. According to these models, after preliminary processing of low-level visual information, the structural description containing information about the objects' visual features and their spatial relations is accessed. Then, we encounter a semantic representation that encompasses functional, perceptual and associative information about objects. Finally a phonological representation that makes available the name of the object for articulation is accessed.

In the light of such multi-component models, it is important to diagnose the stage of the processing at which category specific disorders occur. In addition, it is important to establish whether the disorder is due to impaired access to intact knowledge representations, or due to impairment to the knowledge representations themselves. In the first case the representation is intact but at present is inaccessible. In the latter case, either the visual perceptual, the semantic, or the phonological representations (or part of them) may be lost (see Shallice, 1988). A representational impairment may be discriminated from an access or retrieval impairment because of inter-trial consistency (i.e. whether the patient misidentifies the same items performing the same tasks at different times) and inter-task consistency (i.e. the patient misidentifies the same items in different tasks).

Category specific disorders could then be categorised according to at least the following criteria:

1. the kind(s) of category damaged, that is the type of dissociations among impaired and spared categories;
2. the locus of the impairment, that is the cognitive structure selectively affected by the semantic damage;
3. the distinction among access and representation deficits;
4. the pathology that caused the semantic deficit;
5. the cognitive impairments associated with semantic damage.

In our opinion, these criteria are important not only for the interpretation of category specific impairment but also for planning cognitive rehabilitation. In these last years, increasing attention has been paid to the application of cognitive neuropsychological theories to cognitive rehabilitation (Byng & Coltheart, 1986; Howard & Hatfield, 1987). For example Byng and Coltheart (1986) have shown promising results from the application of cognitive models to the development of rehabilitation programmes for agrammatism, traditionally a field in which rehabilitation has not given significant results. By analogy with other fields of cognitive neuropsychology, we presume that cognitive therapy for patients with impairments within the semantic domain should be adapted to the specific functional deficit inferred. Furthermore, disorders of access should require a different treatment programme from disorders of semantic knowledge *per se*.

Previous research in this field is minimal. Behrmann and Lieberthal (1989) planned a cognitive remediation programme with a global aphasic patient showing a category specific impairment restricted to some categories of objects (e.g. furniture and transport). For improving the semantic knowledge of single items, a category specific treatment programme including the re-acquisition of generic and specific details about items, was adopted. Post-therapy evaluation revealed a significant improvement on treated and some untreated items of treated categories, but limited generalisation to items of untreated categories. However, the evidence in support of the statement that their patient has category deficits seems quite weak as it is based only on a categorisation task.

In our study we will present two rehabilitation case reports on patients who have been interpreted as having a representational deficit, confined to the categories of living things. We will show that a cognitive rehabilitation programme focused on the treatment of the semantic memory disorder was not effective on those tasks requiring the retrieval of specific semantic information about living things. Given that both patients suffered from a severe memory amnesia, which was also treated but did not recover, it is probably the case that the absence of anterograde amnesia is the logical requirement for the success of the cognitive rehabilitation programmme. Our two patients seem to have some features in common with Behrmann and Lieberthal's (1989) case C.H., because they all showed a category specific impairment due to a loss of semantic information. The main difference among the three cases seems to be the absence of anterograde amnesia that patient C.H. did not seem to exhibit. In the present study we will argue that the absence of this memory impairment is crucial for the success of the therapy.

## CASE REPORTS

The two patients reported in this paper underwent cognitive rehabilitation before a full and exhaustive evaluation was performed. This means that we are not able to provide data collected exactly on the same tasks before and after therapy. However, pre-therapy results were sufficient to establish the existence of a specific memory disorder. Post-therapy experiments also confirm this hypothesis.

Immediately below we will present pre-therapy data collected on two patients affected by HSVE. Then, we will describe the therapy programmme in detail and, finally, we will show the data collected after the treatment.

## PRE-THERAPY NEUROPSYCHOLOGICAL EVALUATION

### Patient 1

Michelangelo was a 38 year old man was working as clerk at the Health Services and was an active member of the World Wildlife Fund (for a more detailed description of this case see Sartori & Job, 1988, and for additional experimental data see Sartori, Job, & Coltheart, in press). As such, according to his wife and colleagues he was able to identify huge numbers of animals, fish and birds premorbidly. In May 1984 he suddenly developed temporo-spatial disorientation and a severe amnesia. A few days post-onset he was admitted to the Neurological Department of Treviso. E.E.G. was normal but C.T. scan showed two areas of hypodensity in right and left anterior temporal lobes. Increase of intratecal herpes antibodies was found by serially analysing the liquor and serum. He was immediately treated with Acyclovir. At an initial neuropsychological examination conducted at the bedside, the patient was found to be severely anomic with comprehension disorders, anterograde amnesia and anosognosia. Twenty days post-onset, WAIS verbal I.Q. was 82, performance I.Q. was 76 and overall I.Q. 78. On the Wechsler Memory Scale he scored 57. Auditory comprehension, as tested with the Token test, was fairly good (33/36) showing that the initial auditory comprehension disorder disappeared very quickly. Performance in a retrograde memory test was clearly related to the temporal distance from onset. Tested on four alternative forced choice questions about events that happened in 1978-1979 he scored 12.5% correct (mean of controls=79%) whereas for 1966-1967 accuracy was 50% (mean=73.3). In a recognition memory test he scored 26/50 (z=-2.23; chance=25/50) for faces and 38/50 (z=-1.3) for words. He was able to recall only 1/10 of a list of words presented to him. No apraxic nor ideomotor disorders were recorded. Presented with the pictures from Snodgrass and Vanderwart's (1980) set, Michelangelo was able to correctly name only 31%, 35% and 75% of animals, vegetables and objects, respectively. In a second naming session it was observed that the non-identified pictures were mostly the same as in the first session. Copying tasks were performed well, but he showed a category-specific disturbance in drawing from memory. Although his drawings of objects were well portrayed with no important details omitted, he drew animals in such a way that an observer was unable to recognise what he had portrayed. Commonly, Michelangelo drew animals with additional parts that were well portrayed but wrong. Clinical observation points out that it was impossible for the patient to learn new faces; for example, he still has great problems in recognising the authors after having seen them for years. On the contrary he apparently has no problems in recognising his relatives and other familiar persons known before onset. Michelangelo was 100% correct in naming overlapping figures or degraded pictures, provided that they did not represent living things, and he was able to identify objects seen from an unusual view. These data rule out the presence of a low-level visual processing deficit. He was able to sort ferocious from non-ferocious animals, judge if a given animal sound corresponded to a given animal's name, and match a verbally presented environment (e.g. desert) to the verbally presented name of a given animal (e.g. camel), thus showing that non-perceptual knowledge about animals was much better preserved than his visual knowledge.

## Patient 2

Giulietta, a 55-year-old right-handed housewife, with five years of schooling, was hospitalised on 20.7.1988 at the Department of Neurology, at the Ospedale Civile of Treviso, for confusion, malaise and fever. Initial neurological evaluation revealed a severe amnesia and an impairment in understanding complex orders, but no motor deficit. C.T. scan (performed at the time of admission) revealed no signs of abnormality while E.E.G. showed periodic lateralised epileptiform discharges (P.L.E.D.s), predominantly in the left hemisphere. The clinical diagnosis of H.S.V.E. was confirmed by viral antibodies studies. A second C.T. scan (carried out a few days after the first one), like N.M.R., revealed bilateral, temporal and hippocampal lesions. An acyclovir (Zovirax) treatment (5mg/kg every 8 hours) was started. In the following days the patient showed a recovery of consciousness and a rather complete normalisation of E.E.G.

Giulietta was referred to the Neuropsychological Laboratory on 12.08.88 for a detailed assessment of her residual cognitive disorders. On the WAIS the patient obtained the following scores: Verbal I.Q.=85, Performance I.Q.=93 and full Scale I.Q.=87. On the Buscke-Fuld Memory Test she scored 3 standard deviations below normals and 2.5 standard deviations below the other cognitive functions as estimated with the WAIS. The patient showed no apraxic deficits and she was able to copy drawings. No abnormalities were evident in her spontaneous speech or in verbal comprehension (Token Test 33/36). Moreover, Giulietta was perfectly able to repeat words or sentences verbally presented. Reading, writing, and calculating were normal. When given 233 pictures taken from the Snodgrass and Vanderwart (1980) set, she was able to name correctly only 109/233 pictures (46.47%) (mean control subjects=211/233, s.d.=3.98, z=25.58). Giulietta's naming performance was worse with pictures representing living things such as animals (percentage correct naming with Animals: 29.09%; with Objects: 52.24%). Giulietta's scores in this latter test reveal a disorder in naming pictures, particularly pictures of living things. On a replicated presentation of the Snodgrass and Vanderwart picture set, Giulietta tended to name incorrectly the same items as she had done first time. She had no problems in recognising people known before onset by their faces, but she had great problems with people known only post-onset. Even if the patient copied pictures correctly, she commonly failed to draw animals from memory. On tasks tapping low level visual processing (such as figure/ground discrimination, line detection, usual/unusual view matching, etc.) her performance was normal. Giulietta was also unimpaired in an "Object decision test" in which she had to sort real from non-existing animals that, in some cases, were perceptually similar to existing animals (see task number 6). However, she did sometimes fail to give a correct definition of living things; in particular she found difficulty in retrieving information about the physical appearance of living elements.

Category specific naming deficit and amnesia (both retrograde and anterograde) are the major features of both patients' deficits. As referred to earlier, these cognitive deficits are possible sequelae of H.S.V.E. (e.g. Warrington & Shallice, 1984).

## COGNITIVE REHABILITATION PROCEDURE

The patients underwent cognitive rehabilitation two times a week for 12 months in the case of Michelangelo and for 8 months in the case of Giulietta. The treatment was carried out by a speech-therapist.

The aims of the rehabilitation programme were, first, to restore the patients' perceptual knowledge of living things in order to enable them to process correctly this kind of information and, second, to improve their episodic memory capabilities. According to the double aims of the remediation programme, we designed different tasks for improving semantic and episodic memory.

In the tasks planned for the recovery of the category specific deficit, we always used stimuli belonging both to impaired and preserved categories. Even with the impaired categories of living things, we always gave a mixture of items that, on previous assessments, were either damaged or preserved. The list of the tasks subject to the rehabilitation procedure is presented below.

*Categorisation tasks* In several sessions the subjects were required to sort pictures, and spoken and printed words into various broad categories (animals, fruits, vegetables and objects). The therapist said the name of the category (e.g. "Animals") and the patients had to choose, among a set of about 20 pictures or words, those belonging to the category. In a second version of the test, the patients had to sort elements of broad categories into subcategories. Presented with a set of 20 animals, the patients had to divide them into mammals, birds, fish and insects. In the same way with objects, the patients classified vehicles, weapons, food, furniture, kitchen utensils, clothing and musical instruments. Reinforcement was given immediately after the patient's response.

*Verbal description of concepts* The patients were asked to define verbally a concept provided (orally) by the therapist. In this task the patients were encouraged to retrieve all semantic and perceptual knowledge of an animal or an object they knew. The therapist always pointed out errors to the patients, providing the correct attribute of the item.

*Description of perceptual attributes* The patients were specifically asked to describe verbally the visual appearance of animals and objects. As an aid, the subject was instructed to construct a mental image of the item to be decribed. After the description, a picture of the target item was shown and the patients were asked to verify their responses.

*Naming with verbal definitions* A list of 50 verbal definitions of animals, vegetables and objects was read to the patients. The definitions were taken from Italian dictionaries. In each definition, both perceptual and functional information about the item were included. This task was first administered to normal subjects who easily named the items correctly. When the patients did not name the item, or when they gave a wrong response, the therapist repeated the definition. After two consequent wrong responses or omission, the therapist gave the correct name of the item.

*Word-picture matching* The patients had to point to a target picture named by the therapist from among about 10-20 pictures laid on a table. For every trial, roughly half the pictures were of living things. In another version of this test the patients had to match pictures with printed words. The therapist always reinforced the patients' correct responses.

*Drawing tasks* In an initial session, the patients were asked to copy some pictures of living and non-living things (stimuli were taken from Snodgrass and Vanderwart, 1980). Then, in the following session, the patients had to draw from memory the same pictures previously copied. When drawing from memory was completed, a picture of the item was shown to the patients, asking them to detect the parts wrongly depicted or omitted in their drawings.

Antrograde amnesia was treated by teaching the patients to utilise mnemonics in learning a list of unrelated words. Two techniques requiring mental-imagery were adopted for improving episodic memory: the Link-method and the Loci-method. With the first technique, the patient was instructed to encode aurally presented items by creating a linked image. For instance, given the words *cat* and *table*, the patient was invited to visualise the cat and the table, and then create a unique image depicting "a cat on the table". In the Loci-method an image-link is created among a sequence of spatially ordered loci and the items of the list to be remembered.

## POST-THERAPY NEUROPSYCHOLOGICAL EVALUATION

The tests used in the post-therapy evaluation were administered on different occasions over a period of about two months. This evaluation started a month after completion of the therapy programme. For each task the patients' performances were evaluated with respect to their respective control group. Each group was composed of ten non-hospitalised normal subjects, matched for age and school level.

### *Task 1: Picture naming*

Snodgrass and Vanderwart's (1980) study on picture naming in normal subjects reveals that naming accuracy and speed are affected by factors such as picture familiarity, picture complexity, word frequency and semantic membership. It could be that our patients' category specific effect, shown in picture naming, is confounded by a significant effect from the other factors implicated in this task. The following naming task was designed in order to document this effect. Sixty-four pictures, some taken from Snodgrass and Vanderwart's (1980) list, were selected. For all items, ratings for picture familiarity and complexity had been collected from 20 university-aged students using a seven-point scale. Half the pictures were of living things and the remainder were of inanimate objects. The factors taken into account were varied orthogonally. Michelangelo and Giulietta, and their respective control groups, were given these 64 pictures to name (see Table 5.1). The performance of each patient was evaluated by calculating the z-score of the patient's performance in relation to their own control group.

TABLE 5.1
Percentage of Correct Responses in Naming Pictures Task

| | *STRUCTURALLY** | | | |
|---|---|---|---|---|
| | *SIMILAR (Animals+Fruits)* | | *DISSIMILAR (Objects)* | |
| | *Frequency* | | *Frequency* | |
| | *High* | *Low* | *High* | *Low* |
| Complexity | | | | |
| – High | | | | |
| Michelangelo | 2/6 | 2/6 | 6/6 | 6/6 |
| Giulietta | 3/6 | 5/6 | 6/6 | 5/6 |
| – Low | | | | |
| Michelangelo | 5/6 | 4/6 | 5/6 | 6/6 |
| Giulietta | 3/6 | 5/6 | 4/6 | 6/6 |

*The structurally similar and dissimilar items have a mean rate of familiarity of 3.49 and 3.20, respectively (Mann Whitney U = 328.5, $P > 0.05$).

The patients' naming performance showed a naming deficit limited primarily to pictures of living things (Michelangelo: living things z=-14.7; non living things z=0.27; Giulietta: living things z=-13.9; non living things z=-1.08). Their performance was not affected by other variables such as name frequency, picture familiarity and complexity. This result rules out the possibility that category damage is arising solely as a side effect of visual complexity (cf. Stewart, Parkin, & Hunkin, 1992), visual familiarity and word frequency. A qualitative analysis of the errors in the naming task showed that the patients were able to access general information about living things. Even when the patients were unable to name correctly the picture of an animal, they recognised the depicted object as an animal. There were, however, a high proportion of semantically related errors (e.g. deer → goat), suggesting that they were unable to access more specific perceptual or semantic information about animals.

*Task 2: Naming with phonemic cues*

If the patients' impairment is due to an inability to select the correct phonological form from among the set of activated forms in the (output) phonological system, then providing phonological information should reduce the probability of selecting an incorrect alternative (see Caramazza & Hillis, 1991; but see Kay & Ellis, 1987, for a contrasting case). To assess this, Michelangelo and Giulietta were presented with the same set of 64 pictures used in the naming test (see task 1). When the patients were unable to name a picture, giving no responses or an incorrect one, the experimenter said the initial sound of the appropriate word. The patients' performances in this task do not differ substantially from their performances in picture naming (see Table 5.2); there was a minor improvement, but still a substantial category specific deficit. This evidence demonstrates that supplying a phonemic cue is not an effective tool for improving naming performance in patients with disturbances at the level of the semantic representation.

*Task 3 Consistency of naming responses*

According to Shallice, (1987; 1988), representational deficits are characterised by consistency in the item correctly identified and

TABLE 5.2
Percentage of Correct Responses in Naming Pictures
(with Phonological Cues)

| | *Michelangelo* | *Giulietta* |
|---|---|---|
| Living Things | 53% | 66% |
| Inanimate Things | 94% | 91% |

misidentified (but see Caramazza et al., 1990). If semantic information is degraded or lost, leading to a naming deficit, a similar problem is expected in a second presentation of the same task. Access and retrieval deficits cause, on the contrary, "noisy", and hence inconsistent, responses.

The two patients were given the same list of pictures ten days after the first presentation. On 90% of the trials Giulietta gave correct and incorrect responses to the same pictures of living things and consistent responses to the same pictures of non-living things in 83% of the trials. Michelangelo gave the same response in 90% of the trials with living things, and 84% with non-living things. Thus the patients were highly consistent with pictures they could name and those that they could not. We interpreted the evidence of high consistency as reflecting knowledge loss affecting particular classes of categories.

*Task 4: Part-whole matching*

This task (see Riddoch & Humphreys, 1987) was devised for investigating the information concerning the perceptual features of the parts of a given concept and the spatial relations among parts—information that we assume is contained in the structural description (see Introduction). In this experiment, a set of 16 animals and 50 objects was selected. For each animal, the body with a part missing was presented to the patient, along with four instances of the missing parts (one target and three distractors). The patient was asked to match the body with, respectively, the correct head, paws, tail, horn and beak. The same procedure was used for objects, but only two alternatives were presented due to the difficulty in finding different

FIG. 5.1. Examples of stimuli presented to the patient in the part-whole matching test.

instances of a given feature. The isolated parts were also magnified (x4) in relation to the body to avoid perceptual cues. The position of the target was varied over the stimulus set. Neither with animals nor with objects were targets presented more than once.

Data reported in Table 5.3 clearly show that Giulietta was unable to match correctly a part with the whole in both sets. It should be noted that the patient's performance with objects was similar to that with animals (percentage correct responses with animals: 56.25%; with objects: 66.0%). Michelangelo, on the contrary, although being able to complete correctly the task with objects, shows a dramatic impairment with animals (more than six standard deviations below what would be expected from his performance with objects).

*Task 5: Object decision task*

An object decision task (e.g. Kroll & Potter, 1984; Riddoch & Humphreys, 1987) consists in asking the subject to decide if a given picture is of a real object or a non-existing one. Such a task, especially in the variation proposed by Riddoch and Humphreys (1987) where non-existing things are derived by real ones by interchanging some parts, is designed to use the perceptual knowledge about the stimulus.

The test that we devised consisted of 48 pictures, 24 were of real things. Examples of the pictures used in this task are presented in Fig. 5.2. The controlled variable for real items was the category: animal and object. For unreal items, the combination of parts (e.g. animals+animals, objects+objects and animals+objects) and the general overall shape (whether maintained with respect to a target picture or not) was controlled. Patients' results on this task are summarised in Table 5.3.

TABLE 5.3
Michelangelo and Giulietta's Correct Responses in the Part-Whole Matching Test

| | *ANIMALS* *n = 16* *(chance = 4/16)* | *OBJECTS* *n = 50* *(chance = 25/50)* |
|---|---|---|
| Michelangelo | 5 (31%) | 41.0 (82%) |
| Controls (mean) | 14.7 (92%) | 44.0 (88%) |
| (s.d.) | 1.2 | 2.1 |
| | (z = −8.16) | (z = −2.06) |
| Giulietta | 9 (56%) | 33 (66%) |
| Controls (mean) | 14.2 (88%) | 42.0 (84%) |
| (s.d.) | 0.8 | 2.0 |
| | (z = −6.37) | (z = −4.47) |

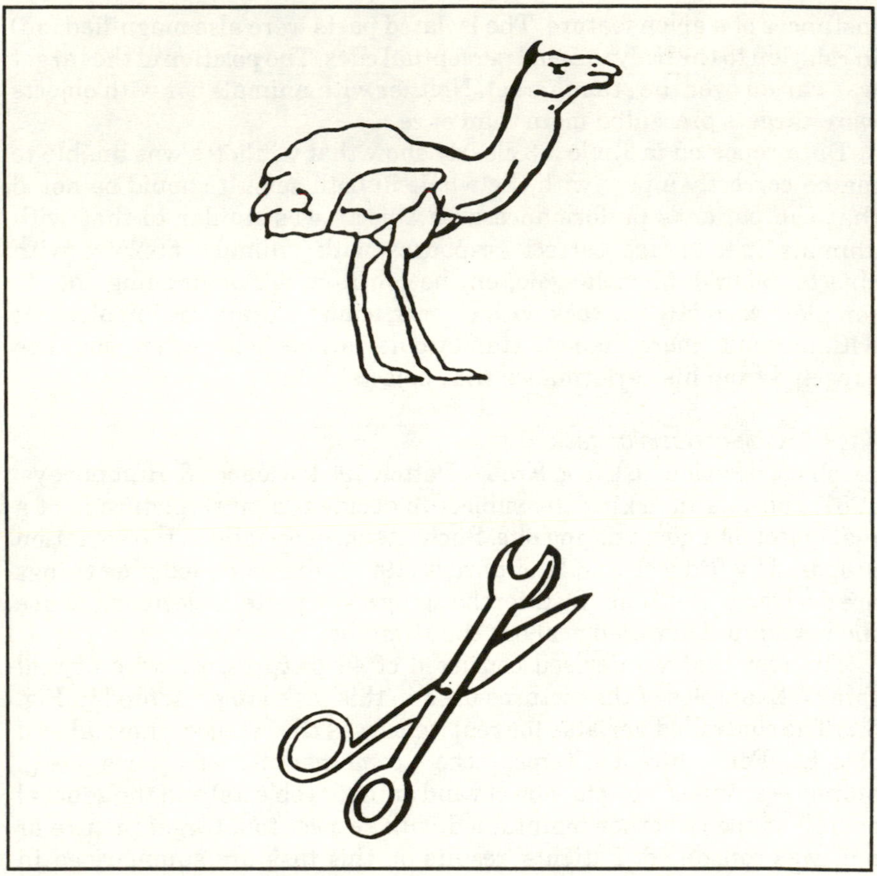

FIG. 5.2. Meaningless stimuli for the reality decision task.

Both patients performed correctly with objects. With animals, Giulietta correctly judged all the real elements but rejected non-existing ones at about chance level. Her performance may thus reflect the tendency of accepting as real any item presenting some recognisable features. Such a tendency was even more strongly adopted by Michelangelo, who was severely impaired in recognising as unreal the non-existing animals.

*Task 6: Perceptual properties decision task*

To verify whether the deficit in processing information about visual elements of objects also occurred in the verbal domain, the patient was asked to judge the relationship between a given perceptual attribute

TABLE 5.4
The Number of Correct Responses in the Object Decision Task

| | *ANIMALS* | | *OBJECTS* | |
|---|---|---|---|---|
| | *Real* *n = 16* | *Unreal* *n = 16* | *Real* *n = 8* | *Unreal* *n = 8* |
| Michelangelo | 16 | 4 | 8 | 7 |
| Controls (mean | 14.4 | 14.1 | 7.4 | 7.2 |
| (s.d.) | 0.8 | 1.5 | 1.7 | 1.3 |
| | (z = +2.05) | (z = –6.5) | (z = +0.35) | (z = –0.15) |
| Giulietta | 16 | 9 | 6 | 8 |
| Controls (mean) | 13.7 | 13.3 | 6.8 | 6.7 |
| (s.d.) | 1.7 | 2.1 | 2.0 | 2.2 |
| | (z = +1.32) | (z = –2.02) | (z = –0.40) | (z = +0.57) |

and a given concept. For each concept, eight perceptual attributes (half belonging and half not) were selected. A set of ten animals and ten objects were used for a total of 80 attributes per category. The performance of the patients and controls is summarised in Table 5.5. It is important to note that the performance of both patients in this test is similar to tasks in which pictures were presented: This could be considered evidence favouring the account that these tasks draw upon a single body of visual information about objects.

*Task 7: Drawing from memory*
In this task, the experimenter spoke the name of an object or an animal, and the patient was asked to draw it from memory. Some examples of their drawings are in Fig. 5.3. Patients' drawings show the same kinds of errors that the patients made when processing pictures or giving answers to questions about the visual properties of objects.

TABLE 5.5
The Number of Correct Responses in the Perceptual Properties Decision Task

| | *ANIMALS* *n = 80* | *OBJECTS* *n = 80* |
|---|---|---|
| Michelangelo | 48 (60%) | 71 (89%) |
| Controls (mean | 69.5 (87%) | 72.6 (87%) |
| (s.d.) | 4.1 | 2.9 |
| | (z = –5.24) | (z = –0.18) |
| Giulietta | 50 (62%) | 72 (90%) |
| Controls (mean) | 69.3 (91%) | 69.7 (87%) |
| (s.d.) | 4.5 | 5.3 |
| | (z = –4.28) | (z = –0.43) |

Michelangelo portrayed an oyster with legs, an eel with ears and legs, a squid with quills, and so on. Similarly, as can be seen in Giulietta's drawing of a turtle, her errors consisted in omitting some specific features of the animal or in attaching well portrayed, but wrong parts, in the "correct" position. Both patients have effortlessly drawn objects, omitting no important components.

*Mental imagery tasks*

There is the possibility that Michelangelo and Giulietta's problem is mental imagery rather than perceptual knowledge. They may have intact knowledge but fail to generate properly a visual image, possibly

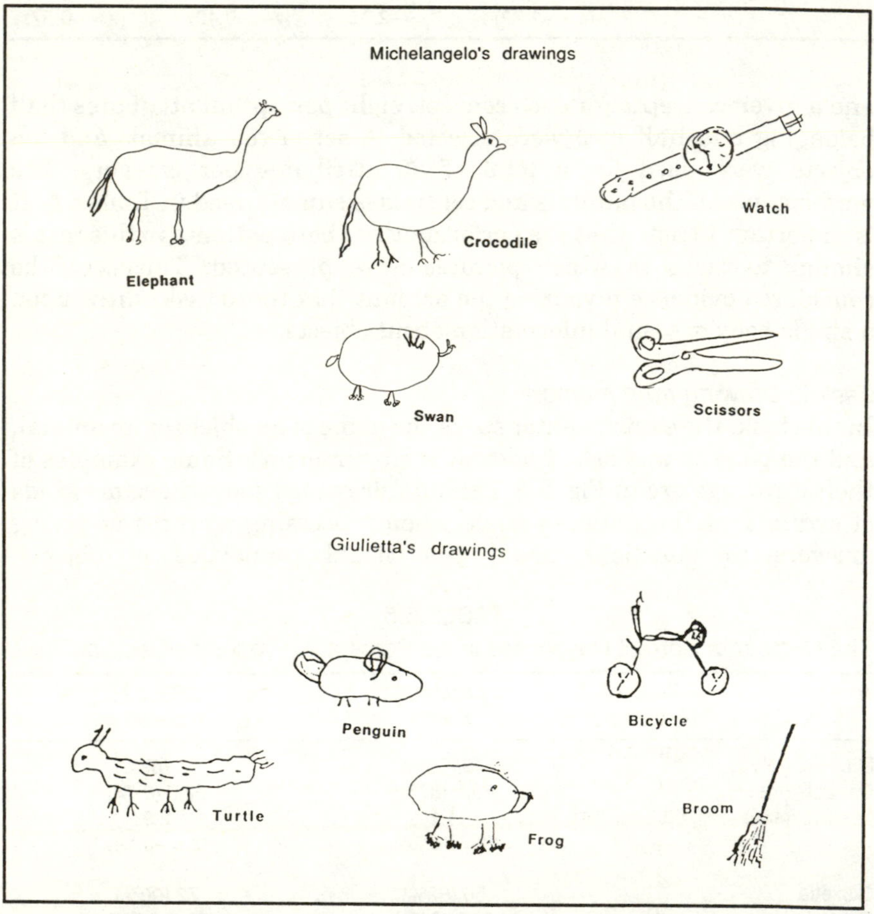


FIG. 5.3. Examples of patients' drawings of animals and objects.

due to a problem in a visual buffer required to hold images, (cf. Farah, 1984), then we would expect them to fail in most of the tasks. An imagery impairment could also be related to the effects of the therapy. In fact, we could suppose that imaging an object could be a useful means of retrieving some perceptual features of that object.

The tasks we used for analysing this possibility were taken from Kosslyn, Holtzman, Farah, and Gazzaniga (1985), and have been used by them to study mental imagery in split-brain patients, after being validated in normal subjects. The first task, a "straight-curved judgment test" (Coltheart, Hull, & Slater, 1975), consists in asking if an uppercase letter has a straight line or not. This task is supposed to require the generation of a visual image of a letter. The ability to generate a skeletal image was tested asking the subject to image a given animal (e.g. a goat), and deciding if a number of other animals were bigger or not. The capacity to generate specific parts of animals and to add them to the skeletal image in the visual buffer was tested by asking whether a given animal had floppy ears or not ("detail analysis" task). The results are reported in Table 5.6.

The patients were able to perform every task except when they were required to image parts of animals; here their performance was at chance (Michelangelo) or close to chance (Giulietta). This pattern of performance is consistent with the interpretation that the patients can generate images and manipulate them by analysing their parts, providing their long term visual memory contains that information (as in the case of objects). Parts of animals are not properly represented and therefore their performance on tasks such as requiring them to judge animals' ears, is extremely poor. These data therefore rule out a deficit of imaging as the cause of Michelangelo and Giulietta's symptoms.

## GENERAL DISCUSSION

Michelangelo and Giulietta exhibited category specific impairment restricted to living things followed H.S.V.E. infection. The cognitive rehabilitation programme was guided by previous neuropsychological evaluations, in which we concluded that the core symptoms that required treatment were semantic disturbance and anterograde amnesia. Despite the strict relationship between the theoretical framework and the tasks devised for the rehabilitation programme, patients' performance on the post-treatment tests revealed no significant benefit from the therapy. In the post-therapy test sessions it was clear that the category specific impairment was still present and could not be a side effect of some factors known to affect picture naming, such as name frequency, picture complexity or familiarity.

TABLE 5.6
Percentage Correct Responses in Mental Imagery Tasks

| | | |
|---|---|---|
| | *Straight/curved judgement task (n = 40)* | |
| | (Es. "Has the uppercase letter "A" only straight lines?") | |
| Michelangelo | 98% | |
| Control Subjects | 91% | |
| Giulietta | 100% | |
| Control Subjects | 97% | |
| | *Large/small judgement task* | |
| | Animals (n = 20) (Es. "Is a fox larger than a goat?") | Objects (n = 20) (Es. "Is a car longer than higher?") |
| Michelangelo | 100% | 94% |
| Control subjects | 95% | 95% |
| Giulietta | 90% | 95% |
| Control Subjects | 95% | 92% |
| | *Detail analysis* | |
| | *Animals (n = 18)* (Es. "Has a rabbit floppy ears?") | |
| Michelangelo | 50%* | |
| Control Subjects | 90% | |
| Giulietta | 67%** | |
| Control Subjects | 85% | |

*z = −6.00
**z = −2.51

Given that Giulietta and Michelangelo misnamed the same pictures in two separate naming sessions, we argue that they have lost some information regarding living things. More specifically, their semantic knowledge of living things seemed better preserved than the knowledge of perceptual appearance of the same elements. In fact, although Michelangelo was able, for instance to recognise from a picture if an animal is ferocious or not, he was at about chance in the object decision task, in which he had to sort real from unreal pictures of animals. And Giulietta, as mentioned in the Case Report, when asked to define names verbally found it more difficult to retrieve perceptual than semantic attributes of animals. Our patients' category specific damage also occurred irrespective of the modality of presentation. Michelangelo was unable to judge correctly the reality of pictures of animals, and to decide correctly if a given part, verbally named by the experimenter, belonged to a certain animal. On the other hand, in the part-whole matching task Giulietta could not attach the correct feature to a picture of an animal in which that feature was missing, and her performance in the perceptual properties decision task resembled Michelangelo's. Our patients' performance was similarly impaired in all the tasks requiring the processing of information about the physical properties of animals. This evidence supported the conclusion that the information stored in the structural description is lost. This hypothesis could account for our patients' deficit in tasks such as picture naming, object decision task, perceptual properties decision task, part-whole matching, and drawing from memory.

Despite the fact that we did not give the patients exactly the same tasks before and after the remediation programme, the qualitative conclusion at which we arrived seems to be defendable.

Neither patient benefitted from cognitive therapy because a similar perceptual representation deficit was detected in pre- and post-therapy tests. A first explanation of this fact is that our treatment was not properly designed. However, an alternative account could be advanced based on the observation that our patients, as most patients with category specific disorders, are affected by anterograde amnesia. According to this explanation, the concurrence of semantic disturbance with anterograde amnesia does not permit the re-learning of the lost information. In other words, if the patient does not recall that, for instance, an elephant has a proboscis, that information cannot be retained after being presented in a therapy session because the fixation in long-term semantic memory is limited by anterograde amnesia (though see Humphreys & Riddoch, this volume).

An analogous conclusion was advanced interpreting data on impairments in learning semantic knowledge in amnesic patients. For instance Gabrieli, Cohen, and Corkin (1988) tested semantic knowledge in H.M. (see Scoville & Milner, 1957) a case whose anterograde amnesia followed bilateral resection of medial temporal-lobe structures, including the amygdala and hippocampus. These authors showed that while semantic knowledge acquired before the onset of H.M.'s amnesia was intact, the patient was unable to learn the meaning of new words that appeared in the English language after the brain-damage. So, the patient failed to learn new semantic information irrespective of the way in which it was presented (by means of definitions, synonyms, and semantic context). In a lexical decision test he treated new words as unreal ones. In contrast Berhmann and Liebarthal (1989) were successful in their rehabilitation programme of category specific impairment perhaps because of the absence in their patient of anterograde amnesic deficits.

In order to circumvent the patients' anterograde amnesic problems, we devised a series of tasks tapping implicit memory. It has been shown (for a review see Schacter, 1985; see also Glisky, Schachter, & Butters, this volume) that amnesic patients can learn new associations between words when the stimuli presented require an "indirect" memory task, such as the completion of word fragments, rather than conscious recall. We have constructed word-pairs in which the first word was the name of an animal (e.g. deer) and the second was the name of a specific feature of that animal (e.g. horns). After studying these pairs, patients are required to complete two- and three-letter fragments of targets. Some of the targets are presented in the same context as the completion test and others are presented in a different context.

It is premature to draw any conclusion based on implicit memory from the rehabilitation programme while it is still in progress. However, we suspect that a good performance in an implicit memory task does not necessarily mean that new information will be fixed in semantic memory.

In conclusion, the ability to retain episodic information seems essential for building a permanent store of new information. Consequently, treatment of specific semantic memory loss should be considered impossible if accompanied by a severe anterograde amnesia. If amnesia is absent, some rehabilitation techniques seem to show some efficacy (see Berhmann & Lieberthal, 1989).

## ACKNOWLEDGEMENTS

Thanks are given to the patients Michelangelo and Giulietta for their participation to the experimental post-therapy sessions. The collaboration of S. Zago in collecting data is gratefully acknowledged. We wish to thank Glyn Humphreys and Jane Riddoch for their comments on an early draft of the manuscript.

## REFERENCES

Basso, A., Capitani, E., & Laiacona, M. (1988). Progressive language impairment without dementia: A case with isolated category specific semantic defect. *Journal of Neurology, Neurosurgery, and Psychiatry, 51,* 1201-1207.

Behrmann, M. & Lieberthal, T. (1989). Category-specific treatment of a lexical-semantic deficit: A single case study of global aphasia. *British Journal of Disorders of Communication, 24,* 281-299.

Byng, S. & Coltheart, M. (1986). Aphasia therapy research: Methodological requirements and illustrative results. In L.G. Nillsen & E. Hjelmquist (Eds.), *Communication and Handicap: Aspects of psychological compensation and technical aids.* Amsterdam: North Holland.

Caramazza, A. & Hillis, A.E. (1990). Where do semantic errors come from? *Cortex, 26,* 95-122.

Caramazza, A., Hillis, A.E., Rapp, B.C., & Romani, C. (1990). The multiple semantic hypothesis: Multiple confusions? *Cognitive Neuropsychology, 7,* 161-189.

Coltheart, M., Hull, E., & Slater, D. (1975). Sex differences in imagery and reading. *Nature, 253,* 438-440.

De Renzi, E., Liotti, M., & Nichelli, P. (1987). Semantic amnesia with preservation of autobiographic memory. A case report. *Cortex, 23,* 575-579.

Farah, M.J. (1984). The neurological basis of mental imagery: a componential analysis. *Cognition, 18,* 245-272.

Farah, M.J., Hammond, K.M., Mehta, Z., & Ratcliff, G. (1989). Category-specificity and modality-specificity in semantic memory. *Neuropsychologia, 27,* 193-200.

Gabrieli, J.D.E., Cohen, N.J., & Corkin, S. (1988). The impaired learning of semantic knowledge following bilateral medial temporal-lobe resection. *Brain and Cognition, 7,* 157-177.

Hart, J., Berndt, R.S., & Caramazza, A. (1985). Category-specific naming deficit following cerebral infarction. *Nature, 316,* 439-440.

Hillis, A.E. & Caramazza, A. (1991). Category specific naming and comprehension impairment: A double dissociation. *Brain, 114,* 2087-2094.

Howard, D. & Hatfield, F.M. (1987). *Aphasia therapy: Historical and contemporary issues.* London: Lawrence Erlbaum Associates Ltd.

Humphreys, G.W., Riddoch, M.J., & Quinlan, P. T. (1988). Cascade processes in picture identification. *Cognitive Neuropsychology, 5,* 143-150.

Kay, J. & Ellis, A.W. (1987). A cognitive neuropsychological case study of anomia. Implications for psychological models of word retrieval. *Brain, 110,* 613-629.

Kosslyn, S., Holtzman, J., Farah, M.J., & Gazzaniga, M.S. (1985). A computational analysis of mental image generation: Evidence from functional dissociations in split-brain patients. *Journal of Experimental Psychology: General, 114,* 311-341.

Kroll, J.F. & Potter, M.C. (1984). Recognising words, pictures, and concepts: a comparison of lexical, object, and reality decision. *Journal of Verbal Learning and Verbal Behaviour, 23,* 39-66.

Pietrini, V., Nertempi, P., Vaglia, A., Revello, M.G., Pinna, V., & Ferro Milone, F. (1988). Recovery from herpes simplex encephalitis: Selective impairment of specific semantic categories with neuroradiological correlation. *Journal of Neurology, Neurosurgery and Psychiatry, 51,* 1284-1293.

Ratcliff, G. & Newcombe, F. (1982). Object recognition: Some deduction from the clinical evidence. In A.W. Ellis (Ed.), *Normality and pathology in cognitive functions.* New York/London: Academic Press.

Riddoch, M.J. & Humphreys, G.W. (1987). Visual object processing in optic aphasia: A case of semantic access agnosia. *Cognitive Neuropsychology, 4,* 131-185.

Sartori, G. & Job, R. (1988). The oyster with four legs: A neuropsychological study on the interaction of visual and semantic information. *Cognitive Neuropsychology, 5,* 105-132.

Sartori, G., Job, R., & Coltheart, M. (in press). The neuropsychology of visual semantics. In D.E. Meyer & S. Stamblum (Eds.), *Attention & Performance. XV.* London: Lawrence Erlbaum Associates.

Sartori, G., Zago, S., & Miozzo, M. (1990, May). *Selective impairment of perceptual knowledge: Further investigation.* Work presented at the European Brain and Behaviour Society. Workshop on Cognitive Neuroscience, Padova.

Schacter, D.L. (1985). Multiple forms of memory in humans and animals. In N. Weinberger, J. McGaugh, & G. Lynch (Eds.), *Memory systems of the brain*. New York: Guilford.

Scoville, W.B. & Milner, B. (1957). Loss of recent memory after bilateral hippocampal lesions. *Journal of Neurology, Neurosurgery and Psychiatry, 20*, 11-21.

Shallice, T. (1987). Impairment of semantic processing: Multiple dissociations. In M. Coltheart, G. Sartori & R. Job (Eds.), *The cognitive neuropsychology of language*. London: Lawrence Erlbaum Associates Ltd.

Shallice, T. (1988). *From Neuropsychology to mental structure*. Cambridge: Cambridge University Press.

Silveri, M.C. & Gainotti, G. (1988). Interaction between vision and language in category specific semantic impairment. *Cognitive Neuropsychology, 3*, 677-709.

Snodgrass, J.G. & Vanderwart, M. (1980). A standardised set of 260 pictures: Norms for name agreement, image agreement, familiarity, and visual complexity. *Journal of Experimental Psychology: Human Learning and Memory, 6*, 174-215.

Stewart, F., Parkin, A.J., & Hunkin. H.N. (1992). Naming impairments following recovery from herpes simplex encephalitis. *Quarterly Journal of Experimental Psychology, 44A*, 261-284.

Tulving, E. (1983). *Elements of episodic memory*. Oxford: Clarendon Press.

Tulving, E. (1984). Precis of elements of episodic memory. *The Behavioral and Brain Sciences, 7*, 223-268.

Warrington, E.K., & McCarthy, R.A. (1987). Categories of knowledge: Further fractionations and an attempted integration. *Brain, 110*, 1273-1296.

Warrington, E.K. & Shallice, T. (1984). Category specific semantic impairments. *Brain, 107*, 829-853.

Yamadori, A. & Albert, M.L. (1973). Word category aphasia. *Cortex, 9*, 112-125.

# PART THREE

## Visual Attention

CHAPTER SIX

# Towards an Understanding of Neglect

M. J. Riddoch and G. W. Humphreys
*Cognitive Science Research Centre, School of Psychology, University of Birmingham, UK*

## TOWARDS AN UNDERSTANDING OF UNILATERAL NEGLECT

A common neurological syndrome that may occur as a result of brain damage is that of unilateral neglect. Neglect is commonly associated with right hemisphere strokes, although it may also result from cerebral tumour or head injury. Using a simple form of assessment requiring the crossing through of a number of randomly scattered lines (Albert, 1973), neglect has been reported present in 49% of patients with right hemisphere lesions and 25% of those with left hemisphere lesions (Fullerton, McSherry, & Stout, 1986). Neglect resulting from left hemisphere lesions, although not so frequent as that resulting from right hemisphere lesions, also tends to be less severe (Caramazza & Hillis, 1990; Friedrich, Walker, & Posner, 1985; Ogden, 1985; Warrington, 1991). The characteristic features of the syndrome are a failure either to perceive or respond to stimuli presented on the side of space contralateral to the cerebral lesion; a failure to initiate movements in the side of space contralateral to the lesion; and extinction (i.e. when both contralateral and ipsilateral stimuli are presented simultaneously, only the ipsilateral stimulus will be reported).

## THE HETEROGENEOUS NATURE OF THE ANATOMY OF NEGLECT

Neglect phenomena in humans have been reported following lesions to many distinct anatomical areas of the brain. This can hardly be surprising because many different brain structures and systems are likely to be involved in normal attentional processes (Colby, 1991). Most frequently, neglect is reported following posterior parietal lesions of the right hemisphere (Bisiach, Capitani, Luzzatti, & Perani, 1981; Critchley, 1953; Hecaen & Angelergues, 1963). Additionally, there have been reports of neglect following right-hemispheric frontal lesions and lesions of the cingulate gyrus (Coslett, Bowers, Fitzpatrick, Haws, & Heilman, 1990; Damasio, Damasio, & Chang Chui, 1980; Gloning, 1965; Heilman & Valenstein, 1972). Other reports have implicated the thalamus and basal ganglia (Damasio et al., 1980; Watson & Heilman, 1979).

The precise nature of the neglect symptoms shown by a given patient may vary according to the anatomical locus of lesion. Coslett et al. (1990) have argued that the inferior and posterior parietal cortex may be critical for monitoring and directing attention within the *visual environment*. More anterior lesions may result in difficulties in initiating or executing *movements* in or towards the side of space contralateral to the lesion. Consistent with this distinction, some patients only show neglect in tasks requiring movement of the contralesional limb or movements within the contralesional hemispace (Coslett et al., 1990; Laplane & Degos, 1983; Tegner & Levander, 1991). Others show neglect only when stimuli are presented in the contralesional visual field (Coslett et al., 1990).

Evidence from the animal literature indicates that there are also quantitative differences in the neglect resulting from different frontal lesions. For instance, Rizzolatti and his colleagues have shown that lesions of the frontal eye fields (area 8) result in a marked decrease of spontaneous and saccadic eye-movements towards the side contralateral to the lesion, the animals show extinction to double simultaneous stimulation, and the impairment is more apparent with stimuli further away from the animal's body than those close to it ("extrapersonal neglect"). A rather different disorder is shown as a result of lesions to area 6 of the frontal lobes of monkeys. Such monkeys show a reluctance to use the contralateral arm spontaneously or in response to sensory stimuli (this occurs in the absence of any paralysis). They do not show extrapersonal neglect. The disorder is more apparent in the monkey's immediate environment ("peri-personal neglect") and in relation to the monkey's body ("personal neglect"). Peri-personal neglect is also shown in monkeys with unilateral lesions of the rostal part of the inferior parietal lobule (area 7b)(Rizzolatti et al., 1985). Attempts to relate

Rizzolatti's distinctions to neglect in humans have been made by Halligan and Marshall (1991). They report a patient who showed neglect in a paper and pencil line bisection task (a test of personal or peri-personal neglect), but not in playing darts (apparently no extra-personal neglect).

Different forms of neglect may also result from lesions to different areas of the parietal lobes. Areas within the parietal lobes may be distinguished not only by morphology but also by connectivity. For instance, Goldman-Rakic (1988) discusses a number of the feed-forward pathways from the parietal to the frontal lobes in the monkey brain. Area 7a (situated caudally and medially on the lateral surface of the parietal lobe) maps onto the frontal eye fields while area 7b (situated more rostally in the lateral part of the posterior parietal cortex) maps onto area 6. Of these two parietal areas, area 7a receives visual input from the occipital lobes. Area 7b, on the other hand, receives input from the somatosensory cortex. We might therefore expect the nature of the neglect deficit to differ in patients with parietal lesions implicating area 7a as opposed to those patients whose lesion may implicate area 7b.

Thus, any discussion of neglect simply in anterior/posterior (motor/sensory) terms will very much understate the complex nature of the syndrome. Mesulam (1981) was one of the first to propose that these different brain areas may be linked to form an attentional circuit. Lesions to different parts of the circuit may result in quantitatively different forms of neglect[1]. Mesulam's account too, is probably an over-simplification. The interactions between the many brain structures involved in attentional control are complex. The brain must achieve a balance between reflexive (data-driven) and goal-oriented (knowledge-driven) behaviour (Colby, 1991). Different neuronal mechanisms come into play depending on whether the source of information selected for attentional processing is external (a current sensory stimulus) or internal (a representation of a previous stimulus)(Colby, 1991). The implication is that, in any one patient, not only may the nature of the neglect vary according to the locus of lesion but also as a function of the task, or as a function of the required modality of response. We will return to this issue in the section entitled "Functional fractionations of neglect".

## THE ASYMMETRICAL NATURE OF NEGLECT DEFICITS

During the acute phase of the illness, neglect seems to appear with equal frequency in both left and right hemisphere brain damaged groups (Albert, 1973; Ogden, 1985; Sieroff, Pollatsek, & Posner, 1988). However, as previously noted, neglect appears to be more severe and long lasting following right cerebral lesions (Ogden, 1987)(although see the section on Rehabilitation at the end of this chapter).

The asymmetry of the incidence of neglect following right or left hemisphere lesions has been accounted for in several different ways. For instance, Heilman and his co-workers have proposed that the attentional neurones of the right hemisphere may have bilateral receptive fields whereas the homologous cells of the left parietal cortex have only contralateral receptive fields (Heilman, Bowers, Valenstein, & Watson, 1987; Heilman & Van den Abel, 1980). Thus, the effect of lesioning attentional neurones in the left hemisphere may be compensated for by the neurones in the right hemisphere, which allow attentional orienting to both sides of space. There is no corresponding compensation for lesioning the attentional neurones in the right hemisphere, because the left hemisphere allows orienting only to the right. A similar view is expressed by Mesulam (1981), although Mesulam argues that the predominant tendency of the right hemisphere is to attend to the contralateral hemispace (despite bilateral receptive fields), and that more synaptic space is devoted to attentional functions in the right hemisphere than the left, so that most attentional tasks involving either hemispace generate greater activity in the right hemisphere.

A more analytic view of the nature of the attentional properties of the right hemisphere has been taken by Posner and his colleagues. For instance, they have argued that although both hemispheres may be involved in the orienting of attention to the contralesional side of space (an ability that may be impaired equally by lesions of the left or right parietal lobes), one crucial function of the right hemisphere is the maintenance of the alert state. Posner and Peterson (1990) cite studies showing that: (i) lesions of the right hemisphere cause difficulty in alerting (as measured by galvanic skin responses (Heilman, Watson & Valenstein, 1985), or heart rate responses (Yokoyama, Jennings, Ackles, Hood, & Boller, 1987) and (ii) in vigilance tasks, where cerebral blood flow and metabolism have been measured, the right cerebral hemisphere is shown to be strongly, and selectively, activated (Deutsch, Papanicolaou, Bourbon, & Eisenberg, 1988). Such results may be due to the asymmetric organisation of the norepinethrine transmitter system in the brain; thus lesions of the right, but not of the left hemisphere of the rat can deplete norepinethrine input to the cortex (Posner & Rothbart, 1992).

What may be the implications of the proposed asymmetric distribution of attentional resources? Patients suffering a right hemisphere lesion may show decreased arousal (see Posner & Peterson, 1990), and a decreased ability to direct attention to the left. However, it is unlikely that the entire attentional potential of the right hemisphere will be lost as a result of the lesion given the distributed nature of attentional resources at both cortical and subcortical level (Colby, 1991). Tasks that make demands on right hemisphere resources (e.g. spatial tasks; left limb tasks) may have the effect of boosting the depleted attentional resources of the right hemisphere causing increased arousal and decreased left-side neglect. Similarly, in patients with left hemisphere lesions, tasks that make demands on left hemisphere resources (e.g. verbal tasks; right limb tasks) may have the effect of decreasing right-side neglect. We will return to this issue in the section entitled "Rehabilitation of neglect" (p. 141).

## EYE MOVEMENTS AND NEGLECT

There is a clear relationship between eye movements and shifts in attentional focus; gaze direction and focus of attention normally coincide although it has been shown that attention can be moved across space independently of eye movements (Posner, Snyder & Davidson, 1980; Posner & Cohen, 1984). Patients with neglect may show restricted eye movements. For instance, in patients with right parietal lesions (and no clinical manifestations of neglect), leftward eye movements have been found to be significantly slower to initiate, and to have a longer movement time than rightward eye movements (Girotti, Casazza, Musicco, & Avanzini, 1983; Heilman & Van den Abel, 1980; Johnston, 1988). Patients with right sided brain lesions and unilateral neglect are more likely to make multiple saccades than patients with either right or left sided lesions who show no neglect in tasks requiring detection of visual targets situated to the right or left of fixation (Girotti et al., 1983). Rightward saccades also do not appear normal in cases of patients with right sided lesions and unilateral neglect. For instance, control subjects were able to locate a right-side target with only one saccade on 60% of trials and with two saccades on 40% of trials. Patients with right sided lesions and unilateral neglect were able to locate a right-side target with only one saccade on approximately 40% of trials, with two saccades on 40% of trials and on about 20% of trials, three saccades were necessary (Girotti et al., 1983).

The eye movement studies performed by Girotti et al. (1983) have shown that the eye movement system in patients with unilateral neglect can be impaired when patients are required to detect peripherally presented targets, whether the movement is in a left or a rightward direction; clearly impaired eye movements may contribute to many impaired functional manifestations seen in patients with unilateral neglect. It remains unclear whether such impairments are always linked to attentional deficits in neglect or whether eye movement and attentional deficits are separable. Nevertheless, an obvious implication is that rehabilitation programmes should incorporate some aspect of eye movement training.

## FUNCTIONAL FRACTIONATIONS OF NEGLECT

Given the heterogeneity across patients of the lesion site within each hemisphere, it seems likely that the neglect syndrome will fractionate in a number of different ways. Indeed, recent studies have shown that neglect may fractionate into several discrete syndromes, each of which may occur in isolation in a single patient. We have already suggested that the nature of neglect may vary according to the anatomical locus of lesion. For instance, anterior (frontal) lesions may result in motor neglect and posterior (parietal) lesions resulting in sensory neglect (Coslett et al., 1990). Even more specific fractionations have also been reported. For instance, neglect in reading has been described in isolation from generalised neglect (i.e. neglect on other visual tasks) (Baxter & Warrington, 1983; Patterson & Wilson, 1990; Riddoch, Humphreys, Cleton, & Fery, 1990; Warrington, 1991). However, reading may be considered a particularly visually demanding task. It therefore remains possible that in all these cases, general neglect may have been elicited if performance had been assessed under more stringent conditions than those generally available clinically. For instance, M.O. (Riddoch et al., 1990) showed no neglect in everyday life nor in typical clinical tests (such as the Rivermead Star Cancellation Test). He also showed no clinical neglect in reading words or complex passages of text. However, under reduced exposure conditions (words being presented for a limited period) he showed the typical symptoms of a right hemisphere lesioned neglect dyslexic: that is, the initial part of the word was misread.

Clearly more stringent tests of general neglect should be devised and applied before claims of a selective deficit (e.g. in reading) may be upheld. None the less, it appears that with even a specific task, such as reading, several different forms of neglect may be shown. In some patients, single word reading may be selectively impaired although the reading of text may be intact (Costello & Warrington, 1987; Patterson & Wilson, 1990; Riddoch et al., 1990). The alternative impairment, that of intact reading of single words but impaired text reading, has been reported by Kartsounis and Warrington (1989). Thus, there is a double dissociation between the neglect in reading text and the neglect with single words. Double dissociations such as this are typically taken to indicate the involvement of separate processes in tasks, in this case involving words and text. Only the processes involved in text reading are impaired in some patients, whilst others only have impaired word processing.

Dissociations in neglect may not only occur over different patients or groups of patients, but may even be shown in an individual patient (Costello & Warrington, 1987; Cubelli, Nichelli, Bonito, De Tanti, & Inzaghi, 1991; Kashiwagi, Kashiwagi, Nishikawa, Tanabe, & Okuda, 1990; Humphreys & Riddoch,[2]; Riddoch, Humphreys, Luckhurst, & Burroughs[3]). Although some of these cases are reported to have bilateral lesions on C.T. scan (e.g. Costello & Warrington, 1987; Humphreys & Riddoch,[2]) others do not (e.g. Cubelli et al., 1991; Kashiwagi et al., 1990; Riddoch et al.[3]). These cases are significant in showing that the neglect phenomenon cannot simply be explained in terms of a single underlying mechanism. Neuronal activity may be determined by the nature of the task to be performed, or by the motor system used to undertake that task.

### *I. Neglect as a Function of Task*

Several cases have been reported recently where the side of space neglected varies according to the task performed by the patient. For instance, Costello and Warrington (1987) reported the case of a right handed man who suffered a left-sided lesion as a result of a parieto-occipital tumour. The tumour extended across the corpus callosum into the right hemisphere. In visuo-spatial tasks (such as line bisection and copying), J.O.H. demonstrated a *right side* neglect. When asked to read single words, however, *left side* neglect was shown. In this instance, Costello and Warrington have argued that visuo-spatial tasks result in right hemisphere activation and left-side orienting of attention, resulting in right side neglect. Reading tasks produce strong left hemisphere activation and right-side orienting of attention, causing left side neglect.

A similar hemisphere-activation account can be applied to the patient described by Kashiwagi and his associates (Kashiwagi, et al., 1990). Y.Y., a right-handed government official, suffered multiple lesions as a result of a cerebral thrombosis. M.R.I. scans showed lesions in the posterior half of the genu and the whole trunk of the corpus callosum, the postero-superior portion of the left medial frontal lobe and the left medial temporo-occipital lobes. Y.Y. showed left-side neglect on visuo-spatial tasks such as copying and line bisection tasks. Neglect was only shown when the tasks were performed with the right hand. When the left hand was used, no neglect was shown. Left-side neglect was also apparent in tasks such as the identification of chimeric figures, and in reading aloud multiple digit numbers. Interestingly, when asked to copy multiple digit numbers, *left-side* neglect was shown when the digits were copied with the right hand, but *right-side* neglect was shown when the digits were copied with the left hand. Kashiwagi et al. (1990) base their interpretation of Y.Y.'s deficits on the assumption that an asymmetry exists in the cerebral representation of directed attention and that hemispheric activation is dependent on task demands. For instance, left hemisphere activation will result when verbal or right manual performance is required; right hemisphere activation will result when visuo-spatial or left manual performance is required. Activation of either hemisphere results in attention being directed towards the contralateral hemispace, and activation of the right hemisphere will also allow attention to be directed ipsilaterally. Y.Y., having a callosal lesion, is unable to benefit from information transmitted between the hemispheres. The reading of multiple digit strings aloud, or the identification of chimeric figures will theoretically result in left hemisphere activation (as will the use of the right hand); attention will then be directed to the right, and left neglect will result. In theory, no neglect should occur when the left hand is used because the activated right hemisphere is able to direct attention both to the left and to the right hemispace. However, neglect was also shown when the patient had to copy digit strings with his left hand. The point is not really addressed by Kashiwagi et al., (1990) who note that while the "bilateral attention of the right hemisphere is activated", without any input from the left hemisphere, "the total amount of right-sided attention may be decreased to some extent".

A further case showing different patterns of dissociation in unilateral spatial neglect is reported by Cubelli et al. (1991). A.R. suffered a left parieto-occipital lesion resulting in a mild dysphasia, severe right hemiparesis and a dense right homonymous hemianopia. A.R. neglected the right side of space in visuo-spatial tasks (e.g. copying, line cancellation, figure search and word finding tasks), but the left side of space in reading single words. Cubelli et al. (1991) conclude that "the left-neglect in reading, suffered by A.R., was an independent deficit to the right-neglect apparent in spatial tasks".

The above cases show different patterns of neglect within a single patient according to whether the task can be described as verbal (e.g. reading) or visuo-spatial (line bisection, copying etc.). A further case of our own provides an even finer-grained distinction. This patient, J.R., tended to make errors identifying single objects by omitting or misidentifying parts on the left-side of the objects (see Fig. 6.1). Similarly, when asked to bisect individually presented lines, bisections tended to be towards the right of centre, again indicating left-side neglect. However, when presented with multiple objects, omissions would occur on the right. For instance, J.R. was asked to cross through a number of lines randomly ordered across a page; or he was asked to identify words or pictures that were scattered at random across a sheet of A4 paper. In these circumstances, J.R. tended to omit items on the right of the page, though concurrently misidentifying the left parts of individual stimuli (see Fig. 6.1). Neglect for the left side of single objects or the right side of multiple objects could not be accounted for in terms of the differential visual angle being subtended by the different items. When presented with individual words that were enlarged to fit on a single page, J.R. continued to misidentify left-side letters, and there were no omissions of right-side letters (though the same letters were missed when in the same location but scattered as individual letters). Humphreys and Riddoch argue that the pattern of performance shown by this case suggests that the visual system may represent the visual world in different ways according to whether visual elements combine to form a single coherent object or whether elements form discrete objects in their own right. Different forms of neglect can emerge depending on which form of representation is affected. Thus, the neglect shown with single objects may reflect a difficulty in engaging attention on the contralesional side of any single stimulus. The neglect shown with multiple objects may reflect a difficulty in orienting contralesionally, an ability which may be particularly affected by the number of items in the field (Kaplan, Verfaellie, Meadows, Caplan, Pessin, & DeWitt, 1991; Riddoch & Humphreys, 1987). J.R. had suffered bilateral damage as a result of his stroke (C.T. scan showed right cerebellar and fronto-parietal lesions and a left occipital lesion), and the two forms of neglect shown are likely to be the result of the different cerebral lesions. In his case, a problem in orienting may be linked to his left occipital lesion, with the orienting system subsequently being less activated than normal. The problem in engaging attention in the appropriate location within an object may be linked to the right fronto-parietal lesion.

### *2. Neglect as a Function of Hand Use*

The degree of neglect shown in a task may be significantly influenced by the hand used to perform the task. For instance, significant attenuation of left neglect has been shown in some patients when the left hand as opposed to the right hand is used in pointing (Joanette, Brouchon, Gauthier, & Sampson, 1986) or line bisection tasks ( Halligan & Marshall, 1989; Halligan, Manning, & Marshall, 1991). Halligan and Marshall (1989) argued that this effect may also be due to hemisphere-specific arousal (see earlier). When the patient employs the right hand, the (undamaged) left hemisphere will be activated causing a rightwards orienting of attention and left-side neglect. When the patient uses the left hand, the (damaged) right hemisphere will be

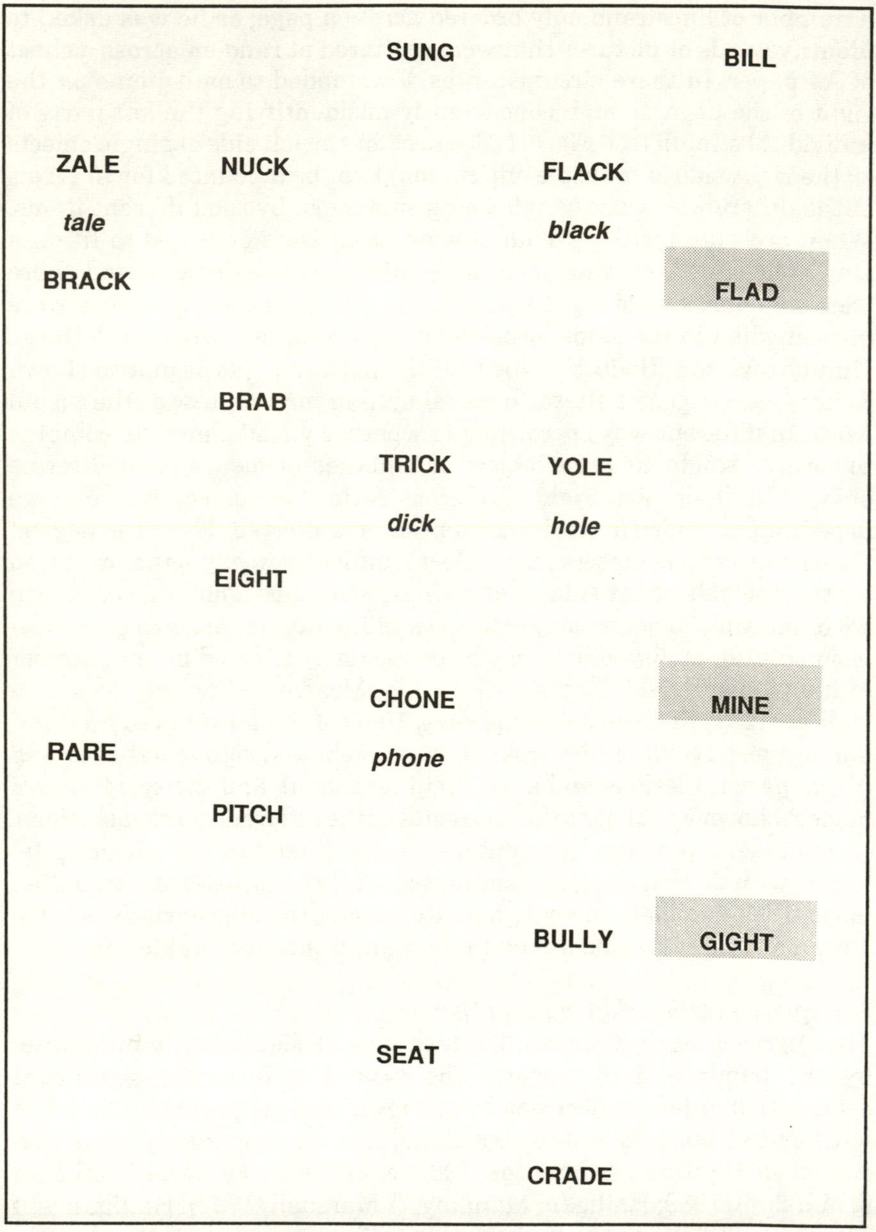


FIG.6.1. Example stimuli and responses from the study of patient J.R. Words and nonwords were placed randomly in the field (in capitals). Strings shown with a grey background were omitted by J.R. Lower-case items are J.R.'s "neglect" errors to the corresponding upper-case string. All other strings were identified correctly.

activated resulting in a leftwards orienting of attention and an attenuation of neglect.

An alternative account proposed by Halligan et al. (1991) is that hand position may act as a spatial cue, attracting the patient's attention to the left. This possibility was explored with patients using either the right or left hand in a line bisection paradigm; in addition, the bisecting hand was placed at either the right or the left side of the line. In two patients with right parietal lesions, attenuation of neglect was most marked when the bisecting hand (either the right or the left hand) was initially positioned in the left side of space. This effect cannot easily be explained in terms of differential hemisphere activation, because there should not be differential right hemisphere activation from the right hand. Halligan et al. (1991) therefore propose that positioning either hand to the left of the line has a cueing effect (cf. Riddoch & Humphreys, 1983).

In summary, recent data show that the locus of neglect deficit may vary:

1. As a function of task: Verbal tasks result in left hemisphere activation. This may cause right side orienting and left neglect. Spatial tasks result in right hemisphere activation. If it is assumed that there is little ipsilateral allocation of attention as a result of right hemisphere activation, right-side neglect may be shown in spatial tasks.

2. As a function of hand use: Use of the left hand results in right hemisphere activation, and leftward orienting of attention; use of the right hand results in left hemisphere activation and rightward orienting of attention. We might also speculate that hand use effects contribute to the asymmetric manifestation of neglect following right and left hemisphere lesions. Patients with right hemisphere lesions will be able to continue to use the dominant right hand in activities of daily living (as any paralysis will be on the left); this may have the effect of increasing left hemisphere activation and rightward orienting of attention. The reverse effect in patients with left hemisphere lesions may not occur since use of the nondominant left hand is often very difficult (if the contralesional side is paralysed). Hand effects may also interact with the effects of task.

3. According to the nature of the material: Internal representations of single complex objects may differ from those of multiple objects. Either these representations may be selectively damaged or attentional processes operating on them may be selectively impaired (e.g. attentional engagement processes may be important for identifying single objects, whereas attentional orienting processes may be important for shifting attention between separate objects, see Humphreys & Riddoch, 1993).

## NATURE OF THE IMPAIRED MECHANISM(S)

The emphasis of the chapter so far has been on neglect as an attentional deficit. For instance, it has been argued that patients fail to attend appropriately to the contralesional side of stimulus items (Humphreys & Riddoch, 1992; Riddoch, et al., 1990), and so are unable to derive appropriate information for object or word recognition; or patients fail to attend to the contralesional side of space (Riddoch & Humphreys, 1983; Heilman, 1979) so that contralesional stimuli are processed more poorly than ipsilesional stimuli. However, it is also possible to consider neglect (at least *visual* neglect) in terms of degradation to some form of internal representation (or representations). Any from a number of different representations could be affected. The impairment may be in an early sensory representation (due to some form of visual field deficit) or in a higher level abstract representation, specific to particular cognitive ability such as reading or visual object recognition (Bisiach & Luzzati, 1978; Driver & Halligan, 1991).

### Attentional Accounts

Attentional accounts of neglect have typically been considered because: (1) neglect can be improved by cueing patients to attend to the neglected side (Posner, Cohen, & Rafal, 1982; Riddoch & Humphreys, 1983), and (2) neglect can be exacerbated by presenting stimuli on the non-neglected side simultaneously with stimuli on the neglected side (the phenomenon of extinction). Thus processes sensitive to voluntary (attentional) control, and to competition for selection between simultaneous events (e.g. for identification responses) seem to play a part in the syndrome.

Given the wide distribution of attentional processes in the brain, attention cannot be conceived as a unitary process. Posner and his colleagues have distinguished at least three attentional deficits that may result from lesions to different areas of the brain: Impaired attentional engagement on a stimulus may result from thalamic lesions (Rafal & Posner, 1987); impaired movement of attention may result from mid-brain lesions (Posner, Rafal, Choate, & Vaughan, 1985) and impaired ability to disengage attention may result from parietal lesions (Posner, Walker, Friedrich & Rafal, 1984). How the thalamic effects observed by Rafal and Posner relate to the problems in engaging attention in a case like J.R. (Humphreys & Riddoch[2] discussed earlier), which we link to a fronto-parietal lesion, are not fully understood.

A more functional approach has been adopted by Humphreys and Riddoch (1992). They have argued that different attentional states (such as engage, disengage and move) arise from interactions between components of an attentional network. Evidence from normal and brain damaged subjects has been used to specify these component attentional mechanisms and the ways in which they interact. Humphreys and Riddoch (1992) argue for the existence of at least three component attentional mechanisms in the attentional network: One concerned with maintaining attention at its current focus; another concerned with orienting attention in response to appropriate data-driven signals; and a third concerned with voluntary orienting of attention to new locations. These components interact in a mutually antagonistic way, so that activation of one component leads to inhibition of the others (see Fig. 6.2). By relating different attentional components in this way it becomes apparent that an attentional impairment (e.g. a problem with disengaging from ipsilateral stimuli) may arise from either of two causes: From a unilateral deficit in an orienting mechanism such that contralateral stimuli no longer *attract* attention normally; or from abnormal inhibition of the orienting system(s) by the maintenance

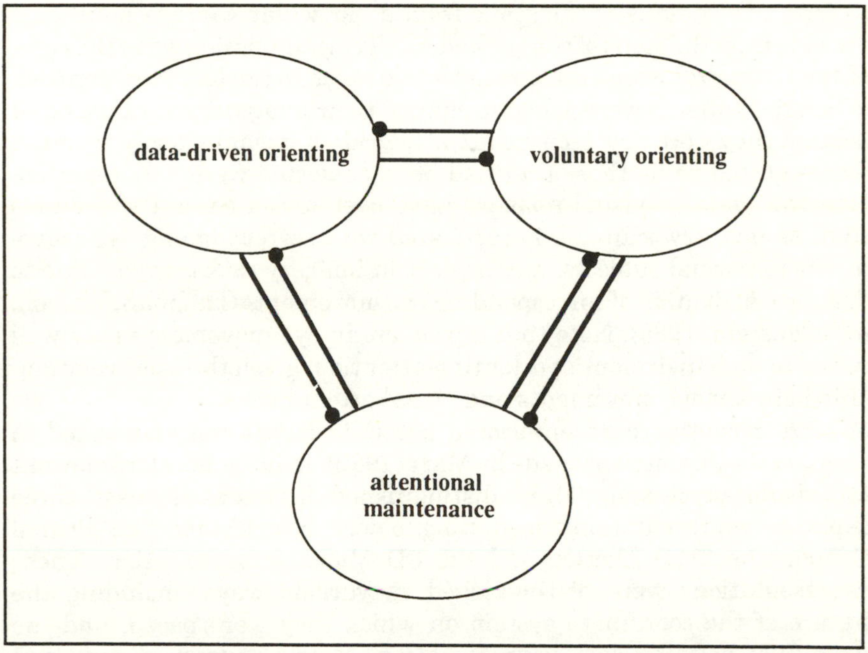


FIG. 6.2.

system. Similarly, problems in engaging attention could arise because either ipsilatral stimuli produce stronger orienting signals, pulling attention to the non-affected side, or there is unilateral damage to the system that maintains attention on the affected side of an object.

An attentional framework of this sort allows some insight into instances where the neglected side may vary as a function of the task performed by the patient (see Humphreys & Riddoch[2]). As we noted earlier, J.R. tended to neglect the left side of individual objects but tended to omit right-side items from multi-item displays. In his case, neglect of the left side of individual objects may reflect inappropriate engaging of attention on their right sides. Omissions of right-side objects may reflect a difficulty in orienting attention to right-side stimuli.

## Representational Accounts

Two representational accounts can be distinguished. The first holds that neglect is due to an impaired internal representation of space. This has been shown in a series of intriguing imagery experiments by Bisiach and colleagues (see Bisiach & Luzzati, 1978). Here, patients were asked to image a familiar scene (the Piazza del Duomo in Milan). They were to report the details of the scene from a particular vantage point (e.g. viewing from the steps of the Cathedral). Typically, buildings to the right of the Cathedral were enumerated while those to the left were omitted. When the patients were asked to change their imaginary vantage point (so that they were now facing the Cathedral), items previously reported were omitted while those that had been neglected were now reported. However, data on visual imagery have been criticised on the grounds that, as imagery scanning is correlated with corresponding eye movements in normal subjects, any neglect in imagery tasks may be due to defective activation of corresponding eye movements (Heilman, Watson, & Valenstein, 1985). Note that a problem in eye movements may well relate to an impairment in orienting attention, given the close relationship between eye movements and visual attention.

More recently, representational accounts have been elaborated in terms of the distinctions made by Marr (1982). In his general framework for visual processing, Marr distinguished between at least three separate representations mediating object recognition: The Primal Sketch, the 2½D Sketch, and the 3D Model representation. These representations were distinguished in various ways, including the nature of the coordinate system on which they were based, and the primitives defining each representation. Marr's suggestion was that multiple descriptions of objects are elaborated during object processing, and that this is necessarily the case as these descriptions serve different computational purposes in making different kinds of information explicit. Different representational levels may be selectively affected in unilateral neglect.

Caramazza and Hillis (1990; see also Monk, 1985) have applied Marr's notion of different levels of representation to models of reading (cf. Marr, 1982). Initial word processing occurs at a retinotopic level of representation. Later processing occurs at a "string-level" representation. This representation is viewpoint dependent but not retinotopic; it is centred on the string as a single object, so that impairments at this level of processing will affect the contralesional portion of the string wherever it falls within the visual field. The neglected part of the word will depend on the orientation of the string. The final level of representation is termed the "word-level". This representation is based on the word itself; in particular, the relative locations of individual letters within that word. Impairments at this level affect the contralesional side of the word whatever its orientation. Patients with impairments at one or more of the different representational levels should generate different behaviours, reflecting the nature of the underlying representation that is impaired. For instance, retinal level deficits can be claimed if the position of the stimulus in the visual field affects performance. Impairments of the string-level representation should result in deficits in object or word identification wherever items are presented in the visual field. Performance should improve with vertical presentation of words since the string is no longer coded in terms of left and right but in terms of top and bottom (and indeed, reading is improved in some cases of neglect dyslexia with vertical presentation of words; Behrmann, Moscovitch, Black, & Mozer, 1990; Young, Newcombe, & Ellis, 1991). Word-level deficits should be characterised by impairments in reading that are independent both of the field and the orientation of the stimulus; for instance, neglect of one part of a word should occur despite the topographic orientation of the stimulus, because the position of the letter in the word-level representation remains the same.

With regard to object recognition, the performance of some patients in copying tasks suggests that neglect may operate in object-centred coordinates. Thus, if a patient is asked to copy a scene, the contralesional side of *each* object in the scene may be neglected (Gainotti, D'Erme, Monteleone, & Silveri, 1986; Ogden, 1987). Driver and Halligan (1991) argue, however, that copying tasks are very unconstrained, and that the effects described above may simply be due to a realignment of a retinal reference frame to each item in the array. To disconfound these two possibilities, Driver and Halligan required patients to perform same/different judgements on two simultaneously presented objects arranged one above the other. Differences between the objects could arise in the arrangement of their parts aligned along a main axis of elongation. The two objects were either aligned with the environmental vertical (which corresponded to retinal vertical when as the patient sat with her head in the upright position), or were rotated (the principal axis of both objects was rotated 45° clockwise or anti-clockwise, and the patient's head was in the upright position). In this latter condition, a "different" part in the two objects could fall into the patient's right visual field, while remaining on the left side of the object's main axis (i.e. on the left-side of an object-centred representation). A single patient with a right temporo-parietal lesion took part in the study. Driver and Halligan found that, over stimuli, the patient was worse at detecting differences in parts on the left versus parts on the right of the object's principal axis, even when the differences were in the patient's right visual field.

While neglect may be described in terms of damage to one or more internal representations, some form of attentional involvement cannot be ruled out. For instance, the ability of neglect patients to describe an imaged scene is improved if they are specifically cued to report items on the contralesional side (Bisiach & Luzzati, 1978). Similarly, reading performance can be improved if cues are placed on the contralesional side (Riddoch et al., 1990; Riddoch et al.[3]).

Thus, whatever theoretical stance is taken with regard to the mechanisms of neglect, our suggestion is that the implications for rehabilitation are the same. Attempts should be made to improve attentional processes. There are several reasons for arguing this. One is that attempts to reconstruct degenerate internal representations—and especially those involved in vision—that are generated rapidly on-line and with often little conscious mediation—may be fundamentally limited. How can a patient be helped to reconstruct a Primal Sketch or a retinotopic representation of a word? Mere practice at object recognition or at reading tasks does not suffice, because patients may have chronic neglect despite everyday stimulation in object recognition tasks. A second reason for arguing this is that, where studies of rehabilitation and/or training of visual processes have had some success, this success seems related to training subjects to attend better to the output of processes that seem otherwise unaffected (see Humphreys & Riddoch, Chapter 3, this volume). Thus attentional training is both more tractable and *a priori*, more likely to prove successful.

## REHABILITATION OF NEGLECT

### Spontaneous Recovery

Several questions must be addressed before considering approaches to the rehabilitation of neglect: In particular, is rehabilitation necessary? For instance, it has been claimed that neglect is only apparent in the early stages post insult, and frequently it disappears completely (Gainotti, 1968). However, the issue of spontaneous recovery needs to be considered with caution. There have been few systematic investigations, and there is no consensus as to the most effective way of assessing neglect (it may be that neglect persists, but simply less floridly in the later stages following the initial brain damage; Seron, Deloche, & Coyette, 1989). Neglect symptoms may be reinstated in "recovered" patients under short exposure conditions or conditions of double simultaneous stimulation (Riddoch et al., 1990). Hence subtle problems may well remain.

### Assessment

Another pertinent issue is the assessment of neglect. Before considering rehabilitation, accurate assessment of the deficit is necessary. Standard clinical assessment tools tend to lack sophistication (e.g. copying or drawing from memory tasks are difficult to quantify), and they also may not be sensitive to distinctions between different forms of neglect. As a result, patients with different underlying problems may be categorised and treated in similar ways. Detailed clinical assessments of neglect should examine several different behaviour domains (including both visual and motor domains). We have indicated earlier that eye movements may be impaired in patients with unilateral neglect. Detailed testing of eye movements is frequently impractical in the clinical situation; however it is possible to perform some elementary testing. For instance, the ability to scan smoothly may be assessed by asking the patient to follow the point of a pencil as it is moved smoothly by the examiner into both left and right sides of space. Orienting ability may be assessed by visual monitoring of eye movements when the patient is asked to scan and report the contents of a scene.

Other neglect deficits may include impaired engagement and disengagement of visual attention. Attentional engagement may be assessed by identification tasks. Stimuli should consist of both pictures and words, as there may be differences in performance with these two sorts of stimulus item. Misidentification errors (such as reading LAND as SAND) may imply that attention has been engaged at an inappropriate location (e.g. too far to the right in a word). A disengagement problem may not be implicated in the circumstance because attentional disengagement may not usually be required when reading short words (e.g. LaBerge, 1983).

Attentional disengagement may be assessed in tests of visual extinction. Patients may engage attention correctly on single objects but fail to detect items on the affected side under bilateral presentation conditions once attention is engaged by ipsilesional stimuli. This pattern of performance suggests some form of disengagement problem. Although, ideally, these hypotheses concerning the deficits should be explored in a more rigorous experimental fashion, the demonstrations may serve as a starting point for rehabilitation.

A number of simple clinical tests of neglect incorporate both visual and motor elements. They include: Cancellation tasks; copying tasks; and drawing from memory. Tests specifically examining for the presence of motor neglect are not so easy to devise because some form of input is typically required; hence neglect related to the input may be implicated. One procedure may be to contrast tasks which require a hand response with one that has minimal motor demand—for instance, copying letters placed randomly across a page as opposed to naming the same letters. Here the stimulus is kept constant but the nature of the motor response is varied. Patients whose problem is due to under-use of the affected limb should be impaired particularly in the copying task.

Different patients may exhibit different performance profiles on tests such as those outlined above. Any such difference would suggest the presence of different underlying attentional deficits; rehabilitation should be directed towards the specific area of impairment to achieve maximum effect. Given the heterogeneity of the neglect syndrome, it is hardly surprising that group studies of the effects of rehabilitation on neglect have mixed results (see Robertson, 1990; Webster et al., 1984; Weinberg et al., 1979). For example, the training of orienting via visual detection tasks may help behaviour on tasks that require detection of items that appear on the periphery of the subject (e.g. allowing the patient to detect people who approach from the neglected side) but is unlikely to help the patient who has difficulty due to "overmaintenance" of attention particularly when there are many objects present or an object is very complex. Rehabilitation studies tend not only to have equivocal success but there may often be problems in generalising the improvement over tasks (see Robertson, this volume, for a review).

## General Attentional Training and Rehabilitation

Robertson (this volume) makes a first attempt to distinguish between different training strategies. General attentional training is contrasted with the rehabilitation of unilateral neglect. Using Robertson's terms, attentional training usually comprises visual search or reaction time tasks, and is aimed at supramodal aspects of attention, such as increasing arousal levels. Unilateral neglect rehabilitation focuses on the use of cues[4] to draw attention to the affected side. The results of such studies using both approaches tend to be mixed, but Robertson argues that attentional training may be more effective than attempts to rehabilitate unilateral neglect where training effects have not been shown to generalise to different tasks or to generalise over time. Note though that a failure to generalise should not be taken as a failure to rehabilitate. In practical terms, effective training on just one task may be useful if that task is functional in everyday life (see Lennon, this volume).

## Specific Attentional Training and Rehabilitation

We propose that, to be maximally effective, rehabilitation should be directed towards the specific area of impairment. For instance, it is important to determine whether the impairment may be characterised mainly in visual or mainly in motor terms. If the impairment is largely in the visual domain, we need to ask: What form does the deficit take (e.g. an impairment in engaging or in disengaging attention from the stimulus, and in each case, is this due to poor orienting, over-maintenance, or unilateral problems in attentional maintenance?) Once the deficit has been defined, specific rehabilitation strategies should be applied. Thus, if the particular difficulty shown by the patient is in orienting attention to the contralesional side of space, tasks requiring orienting (such as cancellation or visual detection tasks) which gradually increase in difficulty, may be used.

Different forms of orienting should also be examined—for instance, contrasting voluntary orienting (to internally driven signals) to more automatic or "reflexive" orienting (cf. Müller & Rabbitt, 1989) to appropriate data-driven signals (see Humphreys & Riddoch, 1993). It is possible that patients are impaired in one rather than the other process, and therefore treatment might only be directed at the affected process. For instance, it is commonly noted that patients may voluntarily orient to cues but may fail to orient their attention contralesionally more automatically (e.g. Riddoch & Humphreys, 1983). Attempts to ensure ways of more automatic orienting may therefore be worthwhile exploring. Seron, Deloche, and Coyette (1989) first attempted to rehabilitate neglect in a patient by training scanning patterns, using both visual scanning tasks and verbal instruction (cf. Diller & Weinberg, 1977). While performance was good during therapy sessions, it failed to generalise outside. In contrast to this, some success outside the therapy session was achieved when the patient was fitted with a "warning signal" device placed in his left shirt pocket. This device sounded a high pitched sound at random intervals of 5 to 20 seconds. The authors argue that the warning signal device may have helped to orient attention automatically to the affected side, and allowed performance to generalise. The training of scanning, on the other hand, emphasised voluntary orienting of attention. This may fail to generalise to broader contexts as the patient's attention may then be engaged elsewhere.

Seron et al.'s (1989) report is interesting and attempts to pick up on the distinction between automatic and voluntary orienting processes. However, it is very much a first step in the area, and we are some way from tying down exactly why performance may have improved more generally with the auditory warning signal. For instance, such a signal may not only lead to automatic orienting of attention, it might also lead to generalised increases in arousal. Improving arousal levels may in itself improve orienting. Controlled studies are needed to tease apart general arousal effects in therapy from specific effects upon visual orienting.

Seron et al.'s warning signal might also have been effective because it increased the overall sensory input on the affected side. The relations between overall sensory input and attentional orienting remain little understood, though there are some suggestions that increasing the sensory input on the affected side can decrease neglect. For instance, vestibular stimulation (in the form of irrigation of the contralesional ear with ice cold water for one minute) has been shown to have a significant effect (albeit temporary) on the reduction of neglect and hemianesthesia (Vallar, Sterzi, Bottini, Cappa, & Rusconi, 1990). Again these effects may, at least in part, be due to generalised increases in arousal.

One final point is that, for both automatic and voluntary orienting processes, cueing effects may be modality specific, and their utility will depend on whether neglect is of a sensory (e.g. visual) or motor variety. Consider the case reported by Riddoch et al.[3]). As a result of a left-side lesion, the patient, E.L. showed *left* neglect in reading single words but *right* neglect in cancellation tasks or in copying words. Performance in reading improved if E.L. was asked to report the colour of a left-side cue prior to reading the word; neglect in copying was improved if E.L. placed a finger on the neglected (right-side). *No* improvement in performance was observed, however, if a finger was placed on the left-side of the word in reading tasks or if a right-side colour cue was reported prior to copying words. The visual task (reading) appeared to benefit from a visual but not a motor cue, the reverse was apparent for the motor task, where benefit was obtained from a motor but not a visual cue. For E.L., the effectiveness of rehabilitation was dependent on congruity between the mode of cueing and a given task.

Overall, our theoretical analysis of unilateral neglect has stressed the heterogeneity of the syndrome, both anatomically and functionally. This heterogeneity indicates that blanket treatments of the neglect syndrome are unlikely to prove successful, and that therapy needs to be directed at the specific deficit in a given patient, indeed even in a given task. As a richer and more elaborate theoretical picture becomes clearer, we look forward to more controlled studies assessing the utility of theory-driven therapies. More optimistically, we also look forward to the promise of such therapies being verified.

## ACKNOWLEDGEMENTS

This work was supported by grants from the Human Science Frontier and the Medical Research Council of Great Britain.

## NOTES

1. For instance, according to Mesulam, reticular lesions will result in decreased arousal, cingulate lesions in decreased motivation, frontal lesions in motor neglect and parietal lesions in sensory neglect (Mesulam, 1981).
2. Humphreys, G.W. & Riddoch, M.J. *Within-object and between-object spatial coding and visual neglect.*
3. Riddoch, M.J., Humphreys G.W., Luckhurst, L., & Burroughs, E. *Modality specific cueing effects in neglect.*
4. Cues may either be visual such as red anchor lines on the neglected side of text; or motor, where the patient may be asked to position their affected limb prior to performing any functional activity.

## REFERENCES


Albert, M.L. (1973). A simple test of visual neglect. *Neurology, 23,* 658-664.

Baxter, D.M. & Warrington, E.K. (1983). Neglect dysgraphia. *Journal of Neurology, Neurosurgery and Psychiatry, 46,* 1073-1078.

Behrmann, M., Moscovitch, M., Black, S.E., & Mozer, M. (1990). Perceptual and conceptual mechanisms in neglect dyslexia: Two contrasting case studies. *Brain, 113,* 1163-1183.

Bisiach, E., Capitani, E., Luzzati, C., & Perani, D. (1981). Brain and conscious representation of outside reality. *Neuropsychologia, 19,* 543-551.

Bisiach, E. & Luzzati, C. (1978). Unilateral neglect of representational space. *Cortex, 14,* 129-133.

Caramazza, A. & Hillis, A.E. (1990) Levels of representation, co-ordinate frames, and unilateral neglect. *Cognitive Neuropsychology, 7,* 391-445.

Colby, C.L. (1991). The neuroanatomy and neurophysiology of attention. *Journal of Child Neurology, 6,* S90-S118.

Coslett, H.B., Bowers, D., Fitzpatrick, E., Haws, B., & Heilman, K.M. (1990). Directional hypokinesia and hemispatial inattention in neglect. *Brain, 113,* 475-486.

Costello, A. de L. & Warrington, E. (1987). Word comprehension and word retrieval in patients with localised cerebral lesions. *Brain, 101,* 163-185.

Critchley, M. (1953). *The parietal lobes.* London: Hafner Press.

Cubelli, R., Nichelli, P., Bonito, V., De Tanti, A., & Inzaghi, M.G. (1991). Different patterns of dissociation in unilateral neglect. *Brain and Cognition, 15,* 139-159.

Damasio, A.R., Damasio, H., & Chang Chui, H. (1980). Neglect following damage to frontal lobe and basal ganglia. *Neuropsychologia, 18,* 123-132.

Deutsch, G., Papanicolaou, A.C., Bourbon, T., & Eisenberg, H.M. (1988). Cerebral blood flow evidence of right cerebral activation in attention demanding tasks. *International Journal of Neuroscience, 36,* 23-28.

Diller, L. & Weinberg, J. (1977). Hemi-inattention in rehabilitation: The evolution of a rationale treatment program. In E.A. Weinstein & R.P. Friedland (Eds.), *Advances in neurology,* Volume 18, New York: Raven Press.

Driver, J. & Halligan, P. W. (1991). Can visual neglect operate in object-centred coordinates? An affirmative single-case study. *Cognitive Neuropsychology, 8,* 475-496.

Friedrich, F.J., Walker, J.A., & Posner, M.I. (1985). Effects of parietal lesions on visual matching: Implications for reading errors. *Cognitive Neuropsychology, 2,* 253-264.

Fullerton, K.J., McSherry, D., & Stout, R.W. (1986). Albert's Test: A neglected test of visual neglect. *The Lancet, 334,* 430-432.

Gainotti, G. (1968). Les manifestations de negligence et d'inattention pour l'hemispace. *Cortex, 4,* 64-91.

Gainotti, G., D'Erme, P., Monteleone, D., & Silveri, M.C. (1986). Mechanisms of unilateral spatial neglect in relation to laterality of cerebral lesion. *Brain, 109,* 599-612.

Girotti, F., Casazza, M., Musicco, M., & Avanzini, G. (1983). Occulomotor disorders in cortical lesions in man: The role of unilateral neglect. *Neuropsychologia, 21,* 543-553.

Gloning, K. (1965). *Die cerebral bedingten storungen des raumlichen sehen und des raumerlebens.* Wien: Maudrig.

Goldman-Rakic P.S. (1988). Changing concepts of cortical connectivity: Parallel distributed cortical networks. In P. Rakic & W. Singer (Eds.), *Neurobiology of neocortex.* Chichester: John Wiley and Sons.

Halligan, P. W. & Marshall, J.C. (1989). Perceptual cueing and perceptuo-motor compatibility in visuo-spatial neglect: A single case study. *Neuropsychologia, 27,* 423-435.

Halligan, P.W. & Marshall, J.C. (1991). Left neglect for near but not far space in man. *Nature, 350,* 498-500.

Halligan, P. W., Manning, L., & Marshall, J.C. (1991). Hemispheric activation vs spatio-motor cueing in visual neglect: A case study. *Neuropsychologia, 29,* 165-176.

Hecaen, H. & Angelergues, R. (1963). *La cecité psychique.* Paris: Masson.

Heilman, K.M. (1979). Neglect and related disorders. In K.M. Heilman & E. Valenstein (Eds.), *Clinical neuropsychology.* New York: Oxford University Press.

Heilman, K.M., Bowers, D., Valenstein, E., & Watson, R.T. (1987). Hemispace and hemispatial neglect. In M. Jeannerod (Ed.), *Neurophysiological and neuropsychological aspects of spatial neglect.* North Holland: Elsevier Science Publishers.

Heilman, K.M. & Valenstein, E. (1972). Frontal lobe neglect in man. *Neurology, 22,* 660-664.

Heilman, K.M. & Van den Abel, T. (1980). Right hemisphere dominance for attention. The mechanism underlying hemispheric asymmetries of attention (neglect). *Neurology, 30,* 327-330.

Heilman, K.M.,Watson, R.T., & Valenstein, E. (1985). Neglect and related disorders. In K.M. Heilman & E. Valenstein (Eds.), *Clinical neuropsychology.* New York: Oxford University Press.

Humphreys, G.W. & Riddoch, M.J. (1992). Interactions between object and space systems revealed through neuropsychology. In D.E. Meyer & S. Kornblum (Eds.), *Attention and performance XIV.* Hillsdale, N.J.: Lawrence Erlbaum Associates Inc.

Humphreys, G.W. & Riddoch, M.J. (1993). Interactive attentional systems and unilateral visual neglect. In I. Robertson & J.C. Marshall (Eds.), *Unilateral neglect: Clinical and experimental studies.* Hove: Lawrence Erlbaum Associates Ltd.

Joanette, Y., Brouchon, M., Gauthier, L., & Sampson, M. (1986). Pointing with left vs right hand in left visual field neglect. *Neuropsychologia, 24,* 391-396.

Johnston, C.W. (1988). Eye movements in visual hemi-neglect. In C.W. Johnston & F.J. Pirozzolo (Eds.), *Neuropsychology of eye movements.* Hillsdale, N.J.: Lawrence Erlbaum Associates Inc.

Kaplan, R.F., Verfaellie, M., Meadows, M.E., Caplan, L.R., Pessin, M.S., & De Witt, D. (1991). Changing attentional demands in left hemispatial neglect. *Archives of Neurology, 48,* 1263-1266.

Kartsounis, L.D. & Warrington, E.K. (1989). Unilateral neglect overcome by cues implicit in stimulus displays. *Journal of Neurology, Neurosurgery and Psychiatry, 52,* 1253-1259.

Kashiwagi, A., Kashiwagi, T., Nishikawa, T., Tanabe, H., & Okuda, J. (1990). Hemispatial neglect in a patient with callosal infarction. *Brain, 113,* 1005-1023.

LaBerge, D. (1983). The spatial extent of attention to letters and words. *Journal of Experimental Psychology: Human Perception and Performance, 9,* 371-379.

Laplane, D. & Degos, J.D. (1983). Motor neglect. *Journal of Neurology, Neurosurgery and Psychiatry, 46,* 152-158.

Marr, D. (1982). *Vision.* New York: W. H. Freeman & Co.

Mesulam, M.M. (1981). A cortical network for directed attention and unilateral neglect. *Annals of Neurology, 10,* 309-325.

Monk, A.F. (1985). Co-ordinate systems in visual word recognition. *Quarterly Journal of Experimental Psychology, 37(A),* 613-625.

Müller, H. J. & Rabbitt, P.M.A. (1989). Reflexive and voluntary orienting of visual attention: Time course of activation and resistance to interruption. *Journal of Experimental Psychology: Human Perception and Performance, 15,* 315-330.

Ogden, J.A. (1985). Contralesional neglect of constructed images in right and left brain damaged patients. *Neuropsychologia, 23,* 273-277.

Ogden, J.A. (1987). The "neglected" left hemisphere. In M. Jeannerod (Ed.), *Neurophysiological and neuropsychological aspects of spatial neglect.* North Holland: Elsevier Science Publishers.

Patterson, K.E. & Wilson, B. (1990). A ROSE is a ROSE or a NOSE: A deficit in initial letter identification. *Cognitive Neuropsychology, 7,* 447-477.

Posner, M.I. & Cohen, Y. (1984). Components of visual orienting. In H. Bouma & D.G. Bowhuis (Eds.), *Attention and performance X,* 531-556. Hillsdale, N.J.: Lawrence Erlbaum Associates Inc.

Posner, M.I., Cohen, Y., & Rafal, R.D. (1982). Neural systems of spatial orienting. *Philosophical Transactions of the Royal Society of London, B298,* 187-198.

Posner, M.I. & Peterson, S.E. (1990). The attention system of the human brain. *Annual Review of the Neurosciences, 13,* 25-42.

Posner, M.I., Rafal, R.D., Choate, L.S., & Vaughan, J. (1985). Inhibition of return: Neural basis and function. *Cognitive Neuropsychology, 2,* 211-228.

Posner, M.I. & Rothbart, M. (1992). Attentional mechanisms and conscious experience. In A.D. Miller & M. Rugg (Eds.), *The neuropsychology of consciousness.* London: Academic Press.

Posner, M.I., Snyder, C.R., & Davidson, B.J. (1980). Attention and the detection of signals. *Journal of Experimental Psychology: General, 109,* 160-174.

Posner, M.I., Walker, J.A., Friedrich, F.J., & Rafal, R.D. (1984). Effects of parietal injury on the covert orienting of attention. *Journal of Neuroscience, 4,* 1863-1874.

Rafal, R.D. & Posner, M.I. (1987). Deficits in human visual spatial attention following thalamic lesions. *Proceedings of the National Academy of Science, 84,* 7349-7353.

Riddoch, M.J. & Humphreys, G.W. (1983). The effect of cueing on unilateral neglect. *Neuropsychologia, 21,* 589-599

Riddoch, M.J. & Humphreys, G.W. (1987). Perceptual and action systems in unilateral visual neglect. In M. Jeannerod (Ed.), *Neurophysiological and neuropsychological aspects of spatial neglect.* Amsterdam: Elsevier.

Riddoch, M.J., Humphreys, G.W., Cleton, P., & Fery, P. (1990). Interaction of attentional and lexical processes in neglect dyslexia. *Cognitive Neuropsychology, 7,* 479-517.

Rizzolatti, G. & Carnarda, R. (1987). Neural circuits for spatial attention and unilateral neglect. In M. Jeanerrod (Ed.), *Neurophysiological and neuropsychological aspects of visual neglect.* North Holland: Elsevier Science Publishers.

Rizzolatti, G., Gentilucci, M., & Matelli, M. (1985). Selective spatial attention: One centre, one circuit or many circuits? In M.I. Posner & O. Marin (Eds.), *Attention and performance XI.* Hillsdale, N.J.: Lawrence Erlbaum Associates Inc.

Robertson, I. (1990). Does computerised cognitive rehabilitation work? A review. *Aphasiology, 4,* 381-405.

Seron, X., Deloche, G., & Coyette, F. (1989). A retrospective analysis of a single case neglect therapy: A point of theory. In X. Seron & G. Deloche (Eds.), *Cognitive approaches in neuropsychological rehabilitation.* Hillsdale N.J.: Lawrence Erlbaum Associates Inc.

Sieroff, E., Pollatsek, A., & Posner, M.I. (1988). Recognition of visual letter strings following injury to the posterior visual spatial attention system. *Cognitive Neuropsychology, 5,* 427-449.

Tegner, R. & Levander, M. (1991). Through a looking glass: A new technique to demonstrate directional hypokinesia in neglect. *Brain, 114,* 1943-1951.

Vallar, G., Sterzi, R., Bottini, G., Cappa, S., & Rusconi, M.L. (1990). Temporary remission of left hemianaesthesia after vestibular stimulation. A sensory neglect phenomenon. *Cortex, 26,* 123-131.

Warrington, E.K. (1991). Right neglect dyslexia: A single case study. *Cognitive Neuropsychology, 8,* 193-212.

Watson, R.T. & Heilman, K.M. (1979). Thalamic neglect. *Neurology, 29,* 690-694.

Webster, J., Jones, S., & Blanton, P. (1984). Visual scanning training with stroke patients. *Behavioural Therapy, 15,* 129-143.

Weinberg, M., Diller, L., Gorden, W., Gerstman, L.J., Lieberman, A., Lakin, P., Hodges, G., & Ezrachi, O. (1979). Training sensory awareness and spatial organisation in people with brain damage. *Archives of Physical Medicine and Rehabilitalion, 60,* 491-496.

Yokoyama, K., Jennings, R., Ackles, P., Hood, P., & Boller, F. (1987). Lack of heart rate changes during an attention-demanding task after right hemisphere lesions. *Neurology, 37,* 624-630.

Young, A.W., Newcombe, F., & Ellis, A.W. (1991). Different impairments contribute to neglect dyslexia. *Cognitive Neuropsychology, 8,* 177-191.

CHAPTER SEVEN

# On the Rehabilitation of Hemispatial Neglect

Elisabetta Làdavas
*Dipartimento di Psicologia, Università di Bologna, Bologna, Italy*

Giacomo Menghini
*Centro Ricerche, Clinica S. Lucia, Roma, Italy*

Carlo Umiltà
*Dipartimento di Psicologia Generale, Università di Padova, Padova, Italy*

## ABSTRACT

This paper aims to show that hemispatial neglect can be rehabilitated by a treatment that manipulates spatial attention, and elucidates some issues relevant either to theories of hemispatial neglect or to theories of normal spatial attention.

The first section deals with theories of neglect. In particular, the representational, arousal and attentional hypotheses are discussed. The attentional hypothesis is considered to be the one that accommodates all the features that characterise the deficit. The second section is devoted to discussing attentional-orienting in normals. The problems addressed are the distinction between covert and overt orienting, the distinction between voluntary and automatic orienting, the relation between attention orienting and eye movements, and whether there is a single mechanism or several modular mechanisms capable of orienting attention.

The final section outlines the rationale and the results of our research on the rehabilitation of neglect. In this study spatial neglect was manipulated by the use of either overt or covert orienting but only voluntary attention was trained. Although the treatment was limited to the visual modality, extinction and neglect were tested in both visual and tactile modalities, before and after the treatment.

The results showed a clear-cut improvement of visual neglect. Considering that the treatment was based exclusively on manipulating attention, this constitutes strong evidence in favour of the attentional hypothesis. Overt

… orienting were equally effective in improving visual extinction …ct. This result supports those hypotheses that assume a close relationship between eye movements and attention shifts. No improvement was observed for those tests that involved the tactile modality. This result shows that the mechanisms for shifting of attention in the visual and tactile modalities are largely independent. Therefore the modularity view of attention mechanisms was supported.

## INTRODUCTION

### Hemispatial Neglect as an Attentional Deficit

Hemispatial neglect (neglect, for brevity) occurs when patients do not report, respond, or orient to stimuli presented contralaterally to the lesioned hemisphere, provided the deficit cannot be attributed to sensory or motor impairments (see e.g. Jeannerod, 1987). Because neglect is more commonly observed after right, rather than left, parietal lesions (Vallar & Perani, 1987), in what follows we will consider only neglect for the left side of space.

In the literature, one can find the distinction between motor neglect and hypokinesia on one side and sensory neglect on the other. Motor neglect refers to patients who have difficulty moving the contralateral limbs (Heilman et al., 1987). Sensory neglect manifests itself when patients fail to report stimuli shown in the left hemispace even when the task does not require overt movements in that direction. However, as noted by Bisiach and Vallar (1988), whereas cases showing only motor neglect have been described (Laplane & Degos, 1983), the opposite dissociation (i.e. sensory neglect without motor neglect) has not been reported so far. In this paper we will confine ourselves to discussing left sensory neglect.

A different taxonomy was proposed by Bisiach and Vallar (1988), who distinguished neglect for extrapersonal space, neglect for one half of the patient's body, and motor neglect. Extrapersonal neglect affects stimuli coming from the environment and extends also to internally generated visuo-spatial representations. When neglect affects one half of the body, the patient may comb, shave, wash and dress only the non-neglected side. Motor neglect can be seen as a poverty, or total lack, of movements within the affected hemispace during spontaneous actions. Accepting this taxonomy, it can be said that the present paper is concerned with extrapersonal neglect.

There are three main hypotheses attempting to explain neglect: The representational hypothesis, the arousal hypothesis and the selective attention hypothesis. The best known instance of a representational hypothesis is the one advocated by Bisiach (Bisiach & Berti, 1987;

Bisiach & Vallar, 1988) according to which neglect is caused by a deficit in the ability to form a whole representation of space. Patients do not react to information originating from the affected spatial region simply because that region is impoverished in the internal representation.

The arousal hypothesis proposed by Heilman (Heilman et al., 1985; Heilman et al., 1987) maintains that each side of the brain contains its own activation system. When one system is lesioned, the corresponding hemisphere cannot process sensory information and organise motor responses due to the arousal deficit. As a consequence, there would be a selective loss of the orienting response to the space contralateral to the lesion.

The attentional hypothesis was proposed by Kinsbourne (1977, 1987; see also De Renzi et al., 1989; Làdavas, 1987; Làdavas et al., 1990) and maintains that each hemisphere is responsible for shifting attention in the contraversive direction either in the ipsilateral or contralateral hemispace. Damage to one hemisphere causes an imbalance in the attentional system in favour of shifts contraversive to the intact side.

The three hypotheses face the problem of explaining why neglect occurs much more frequently, if not exclusively, after right rather than left parietal lesions. Bisiach and Vallar (1988) suggest a skewed representation of space. In other words, the ipsi-contralateral gradient characterising space representation is assumed to be steeper in the left than in the right hemisphere. Heilman and Van den Abel (1980) suggest instead that the left hemisphere controls orienting to the right side of space only, whereas the right hemisphere controls orienting towards both sides. Kinsbourne (1987) assumes that the leftward bias caused by the right hemisphere is weaker than the rightward bias caused by the left hemisphere. Hence neglect is more pronounced after right hemisphere lesions.

In the present paper we will accept the attentional hypothesis essentially for two reasons. First, by assuming that each hemisphere controls attention shifts in both halves of space, it can easily explain why neglect patients show a reduced responsivity to the leftmost stimuli also in the intact right visual field, that is, in the field ipsilateral to the lesion (De Renzi et al., 1989; Làdavas, 1987; Làdavas et al., 1989, 1990). Second, the attentional hypothesis is the only one that can accommodate some recent results showing neglect patients to outperform controls in detecting stimuli in the intact visual hemifield. This finding is easily interpreted if one assumes that focal attention is "captured" by the most ipsilesional location. By contrast, it is difficult to conceive of a lesion that produces a better representation, or a higher level of activation, in any portion of space (Làdavas et al., 1990). This interpretation was corroborated by another study of Làdavas (1990) showing that in patients with visual extinction, the accuracy and speed of responses to the most ipsilesional position did not change when the task required focusing attention or distributing it along the horizontal dimension.

It must be considered, however, that the attentional bias towards the right side cannot be the sole explanation of the neglect phenomenon. Normal observers do not neglect stimuli in one hemifield when attention is narrowly focused on a location in the other hemifield. Under these conditions, responses are slower when stimuli appear in the hemifield opposite to the one where attention is directed, but omissions are exceedingly rare. In the case of neglect patients, an additional deficit is likely to play a role. Perhaps, not only is attention captured by the rightmost location but in addition contralesional stimuli cannot activate the right hemisphere, as suggested by Heilman (e.g. Heilman et al., 1987). However, it should be noted that there is evidence in the literature that contradicts Heilman's hypothesis, indicating that contralateral stimuli cannot activate the contralateral hemisphere (Riddoch & Humphreys, 1983).

## ORIENTING OF ATTENTION AND REHABILITATION OF NEGLECT

Since we consider neglect to be an attentional deficit, it is necessary to take into consideration some aspects of the orienting of attention in normals before discussing how neglect can be rehabilitated.

An important distinction is that between overt orienting, which is accompanied by head and eye movements, and purely covert orienting, which can be achieved in the absence of body movements (see e.g. Posner, 1978; 1980).

As pointed out by Shepherd, Findlay, and Hockey (1986; also see Umiltà, 1988) the relationship between eye movements and spatial attention can logically manifest itself in three forms. According to the identity hypothesis, the mechanisms involved in the generation of eye movements are identical to those that produce attention shifts. The independence hypothesis maintains that there are two mechanisms, one for eye movements and one for attention shifts, which are not functionally related. A third view, the interdependency hypothesis, is that the two mechanisms are neither identical nor completely independent, so that the functioning of one can be facilitated or inhibited by the other.

The identity hypothesis has been disproved by a number of experiments clearly demonstrating that attention can be directed to different points in space, regardless of eye position (see, e.g. Jonides, 1983; Posner, 1978, 1980; Umiltà, 1988). The evidence concerning the independence hypothesis and the interdependence hypothesis is less decisive, even though several attempts have been made to compare them (Klein, 1980; Posner, 1980; Remington, 1980; Rizzolatti, Riggio, Dascola, & Umiltà, 1987; Shepherd et al., 1986; Shepherd & Müller, 1989).

When all is considered, it seems to us that the evidence available to date favours the interdependence hypothesis. A strong version of this is the premotor hypothesis (Rizzolatti et al., 1987; Tassinari, Alioti, Chelazzi, Marzi & Berlucchi, 1987), which postulates a strict link between covert orienting of attention and the programming of ocular movements. The basic idea is that overt orienting and covert orienting are both controlled by the neural mechanisms that are also in charge of saccade programming. Upon presentation of a directional cue, a motor program for the saccade is prepared, which specifies the direction and the amplitude of the eye movement. This would occur regardless of whether the saccade is actually executed (i.e. overt orienting) or is not executed (i.e. covert orienting).

The issue of the type of link between orienting of attention and eye movements is no doubt relevant to the rehabilitation of neglect. The acceptance of the independence view should logically lead to the use of two procedures, one aimed at rehabilitating overt orienting and the other aimed at rehabilitating covert orienting. This is because, by rehabilitating, for example, the mechanism of overt orienting, one cannot affect the mechanism for covert orienting or vice-versa.

It is worth noting that the outcome of the rehabilitation procedure can help to distinguish between the two hypotheses. The interdependence hypothesis would be supported if rehabilitation of one type of orienting also had a beneficial effect on the other. The independence hypothesis would instead be supported if the recovery were to be confined to the type of orienting directly employed in the rehabilitation procedure.

A second important distinction that emerges from the study of normal subjects is that between voluntary and automatic orienting (Müller & Findlay, 1988; Müller & Rabbitt, 1989; Spencer, Lambert, & Hockey, 1988; Yantis & Jonides, 1984).

It is known that attention can be directed to the position of an impending target by the use of centrally located cues or of peripherally located cues. In the first case, a cognitive cue shown at or around fixation indicates the position to which attention must be directed. In the second case, a peripheral marker, in the form of a salient discontinuity in a non-foveal area is shown near the location to which attention must be directed. Based on criteria such as capacity demands, resistance to suppression, and sensitivity to expectancy, peripheral cues are shown to cause automatic shifts of attention, whereas central cues cause voluntary shifts. This has led to the notion that automatic and voluntary orienting can be achieved by two separate mechanisms (Müller & Findlay, 1987; Müller & Rabbitt, 1989). Posner (1980) and Jonides (1981) have, instead, assumed that there was one mechanism only, which could be triggered automatically by peripheral cues or initiated voluntarily by central cues. In their view, the two modes of orienting were thought to differ only in the ways attention shifts were initiated, rather than in the mechanisms that guided them.

The distinction between automatic and voluntary shifts of attention is also relevant here. First, it is important when choosing the rehabilitation procedure. The acceptance of the two-mechanism view leads to the use of two rehabilitation procedures, one for automatic and the other for voluntary orienting. The acceptance of the single-mechanism view leads to the use of only one procedure, based on either automatic or voluntary orienting. Second, again the outcome of the treatment can help to distinguish between the two hypotheses. The single-mechanism hypothesis would be supported if recovery caused by automatic orienting were to extend also to voluntary orienting or vice-versa. The dual-mechanism hypothesis would instead gain support if the effect of treatment remained confined to the mode of attention shift, automatic or voluntary, employed in the rehabilitation procedure.

Another issue that must be taken into consideration is the existence in the brain of a single central mechanism, or several modular mechanisms, capable of controlling attention. If there were a "general" attentional centre, possibly located in the parietal lobe, then one should expect that neglect manifests itself across sensory modalities. That is to say, a lesion to the right parietal lobe should produce neglect for any stimulus that occupies a left position in space, regardless of the sensory modality under investigation (i.e. visual, auditory or tactile). It is worth stressing that the notion of a unified central mechanism for orienting in space also predicts that motor neglect and hypokinesia (see definition given earlier) should not be observed in isolation, but should always coexist with perceptual neglect in all sensory modalities.

The attentional hypothesis, however, is not necessarily dependent on the notion of a single mechanism for attention. As suggested by Mesulam (1981; also see Rizzolatti & Gallese, 1988), attentional mechanisms can be present in various cerebral areas intermixed with neurons having sensory or motor functions. These attentional mechanisms may be connected and thus form an attentional circuit. Lesions of the cerebral areas endowed with attentional mechanisms will produce modality specific forms of neglect, along with different sensory and motor deficits. This view, of course, predicts that neglect can manifest itself in one sensory modality (e.g. vision) without affecting other sensory modalities (e.g. audition and touch).

The available evidence is in favour of the modular view because neglect has been shown to be confined often to one or two modalities (Halsband, Gruhn, & Ettlinger, 1985; however, see Farah, Wong, Monheit, & Morrow, 1989). In addition, there are well documented cases of dissociations between motor neglect and directional hypokinesia on one side and sensory neglect on the other (Laplane & Degos, 1983). More generally, it can be said that sensory components of neglect predominate after parietal lobe lesions, whereas motor components predominate after frontal lobe lesions (Laplane & Degos, 1983).

Evidence from rehabilitation studies can be important for clarifying the relationship among the various attentional mechanisms that together form the overall "attentional circuit". If attentional mechanisms located in different brain areas are independent and separately disrupted, one should expect that a rehabilitation procedure involving a specific domain does not extend its effects to other domains. Instead, if there is a single attentional mechanism, then recovery achieved in one domain might well extend to other domains. Of course, the observation of intermodality rehabilitation effects would also be in accordance with the view of a single attentional mechanism.

## SOME GENERAL ISSUES ON THE REHABILITATION OF NEGLECT

In this section we will briefly discuss some issues that should be considered before starting a rehabilitation study of neglect.

It is well known that many neglect patients show spontaneous recovery (Gainotti, 1968). The deficit is evident immediately after the stroke and then performance improves over a period of several months. In some cases the recovery is complete, but more often it reaches a stage where only extinction can be observed. In some other cases, the deficit stabilises in the form of chronic neglect. In order to test properly the effects of a treatment, one has to select patients who have already reached the chronic stage of the deficit. Based on the available literature (Colombo, De Renzi, & Gentilini, 1982; Gainotti, 1968) it can be estimated that a period of six months after the onset of the cerebral accident is enough. However, it is advisable to collect direct evidence by submitting the patient to tests for the assessment of neglect on at least two separate occasions separated by a month. If no improvement is observed, one can be reasonably sure that the phase of spontaneous recovery has ended.

Neglect is very often accompanied by visual field defects, such as a left hemianopia. If the extent of visual field defects is not properly determined, artificial negative results can occur because stimuli may not be detected due to their falling in the blind field. Also artificial positive results might be obtained. This is because the treatment can lessen the effect of anosognosia, which often accompanies neglect, inducing compensatory head and eye movements.

Because, as we have already seen, different types of neglect may occur after purely posterior lesions or antero-posterior lesions, the investigator should make sure that an equal number of patients with posterior and antero-posterior lesions are included in the two groups. Better still, one should have four groups, that is, an experimental and a control group with posterior lesions, and an experimental and a control group with antero-posterior lesions.

## RATIONALE FOR THE REHABILITATION PROCEDURE

In this section we will outline those points that were taken into consideration in choosing the rehabilitation procedure adopted in our study.

The choice of the rehabilitation procedure must be guided by an explanatory hypothesis of neglect. As stated, we are convinced that the most important feature of neglect is an imbalance in spatial attention, which is compulsively captured by the most ipsilesional stimuli. Therefore, we devised a rehabilitation procedure aimed at correcting this rightward bias. The procedure was in part borrowed from a study by Posner, Walker, Friedrich, and Rafal (1987), who showed that in patients with visual extinction, the attentional imbalance could be compensated for by directing attention towards the affected hemispace through the use of visual cues.

Our procedure involved a contrast between overt and covert orienting. That is to say, one group of patients was induced to turn the eyes to the left hemispace, whereas another group was induced to orient attention to the left hemispace while maintaining the eyes at fixation. This experimental manipulation was introduced to test the relationship between eye movements and attention shifts. It was reasoned that if the independence hypothesis holds true, the effect of training covert orienting should not extend to overt orienting and vice-versa. In contrast, the interdependence hypothesis, and, more specifically, the premotor hypothesis of spatial attention (Rizzolatti et al., 1987; Tassinari et al., 1987), predicts that by improving one type of orienting one should bring about beneficial effects also for the other type.

In our study we trained the voluntary orienting of attention. This prevented us from testing the single- or dual-mechanism distinction of attention orienting. As might be remembered, the single-mechanism hypothesis maintains that automatic orienting, caused by peripheral cues, and voluntary orienting, caused by central cues, are both subserved by the same mechanism. Instead, the dual-mechanism hypothesis maintains that automatic and voluntary orienting are subserved by separate mechanisms. By using both peripheral and central cues we could have gathered evidence for discriminating between the two hypotheses. However, we decided to use only central cues for the following reasons.

First, Posner et al. (1987) had already shown that, at least for extinction, central cues bring about a clear-cut improvement. Second, it seemed very unlikely that peripheral cues could produce an improvement. As said before, neglect patients may fail to report stimuli shown in the left hemispace, not only because attention is permanently directed to the right, but also due to a deficit in arousal in the right hemisphere. This being the case, it is difficult to imagine how a stimulus shown to the left could cause a reorienting of attention to that side by automatically capturing attention. In this connection, it is important to report that some preliminary trials had confirmed that patients were completely unable to direct attention to the left in response to peripheral cues (Làdavas, in preparation).

Although our rehabilitation procedure was limited to the orienting of attention in the visual modality, the battery for the assessment of extinction and neglect before and after the treatment also included tests for the assessment of extinction and neglect in the tactile modality. These tests were aimed at testing the so-called modularity hypothesis of attention. As stated earlier, this view holds that there is no unitary centre for spatial attention, but orienting attention in space depends on a multitude of mechanisms. This hypothesis clearly predicts that the recovery brought about by the treatment should be limited to the modality in which the rehabilitation took place. In contrast, if it were shown that practising orienting of attention in the visual modality also improves orienting of attention in the tactile modality, then the modularity view would be rendered much less tenable.

However, it must be stressed that the observation of inter-modality effects caused by the treatment would not necessarily imply that there is a unitary centre for spatial attention. It might well be that there are several intimately interrelated mechanisms and that recovery of one of them causes an improvement that extends its effects to the entire system.

## A REHABILITATION STUDY

In what follows, we will describe a rehabilitation study and report a brief summary of the results (for more details see Làdavas, Menghini, & Umiltà, 1993).

*Subjects*

A total of 12 patients with CT-confirmed unilateral lesions involving the right parietal lobe participated in the study (see Table 7.1). There were four patients in each of the three groups (covert-orienting group, overt-orienting group, and control group). All patients showed visual and tactile neglect, visual and tactile extinction, as well as hemiplegia or hemiparesis (contralateral to the lesion). Neglect was stable as proved by the second assessment carried out one month after the first. Only those patients who showed the same degree of neglect in the two assessments were included in the study.

*Assessment of Neglect Before and After the Treatment*

Visual field defects were determined by standard campimetry. The presence/absence of visual neglect was assessed by a number of tests. In the present paper we will take into consideration only those that lend themselves to a quantitative analysis.

The patients were asked: 1. to cross out "Hs" in a structured array of letters (Diller et al., 1977); 2. to cross out variously oriented lines displayed on a sheet of paper (Albert, 1973); 3. to cross out bells displayed among others objects in a sheet of paper (Gauthier, Dehaut, & Joanett, 1989); and 4. to pick up ten objects spread on a table. In addition they were given a test introduced by Làdavas (1987) that allows assessment of both visual extinction (double presentation) and visual neglect (single presentation). In this test, the computer-controlled visual display consisted of four squares forming the four corners of an imaginary square around a central fixation point. A trial began with a continuously displayed central fixation stimulus following by a target

TABLE 7.1

| *Case* | *Age* | *Onset of Illness* | *Visual field* | *CT scan* |
|---|---|---|---|---|
| O1 | 65 | 6 mth | Normal | R fronto-parietal |
| O2 | 83 | 5 yr | L inf. deficit | R fronto-temp.-parietal |
| O3 | 77 | 9 mth | Normal | R fronto-temp.-parietal |
| O4 | 69 | 6 mth | L inf. deficit | R parieto-occipital |
| C1 | 67 | 11 yr | L sup. deficit | R parieto-occipital |
| C2 | 60 | 6 mth | L inf. deficit | R parieto-temporo-occipital |
| C3 | 74 | 6 mth | L inf. deficit | R fronto-temporo-parietal |
| C4 | 64 | 4 yr | L inf. deficit | R temporo-parietal |
| CG1 | 67 | 6 mth | L sup. deficit | R parieto-temporo-occipital |
| CG2 | 67 | 29 mth | L inf. deficit | |
| CG3 | 43 | 6 mth | L inf. deficit | R fronto-temporo-parietal |
| CG4 | 68 | 13 mth | Normal | R temporo-parietal |

("x"). There were three possible stimulus conditions: either two x's were briefly displayed centred in two of the squares, equally distributed across each of the six possible between and within-field combinations (double presentation), or one x was displayed (single presentation), or no x's were displayed (catch trials). The patients were required to indicate, by pointing with the index finger of the hand ipsilateral to the lesion, which of the squares had contained an "x".

The presence/absence of tactile neglect was assessed by alternately touching with a finger the dorsal part of the left or right hand. The patient had to report the stimulus and to indicate which hand was stimulated. The presence/absence of tactile extinction was assessed by simultaneously touching the left and right hand. Double presentations were alternated with single presentations, and the patient had to report the number of stimuli perceived and the hand(s) touched.

The patients performed all these tests three times. On the first occasion, the tests were aimed at showing the presence of neglect. On the second occasion, one month later, they were performed to assess the stability of the deficit. If the patient did not show any kind of spontaneous recovery, they were included in the rehabilitation group and performed all the tests for the third time after completing the rehabilitation procedure. Patients in the control group also performed the tests three times but they did not undergo any kind of rehabilitation procedure specific to neglect between the second and the third assessment. They were, however, subjected to a sensory-motor rehabilitation treatment between the two assessments.

### *Apparatus and Procedure*

The performance of the three groups was compared using the battery of tests described, before and after the treatment.

The patient sat in front of a video screen driven by an Apple IIe microcomputer. The head was positioned on an adjustable head and chin rest, so that the distance between the eyes and the screen was approximately 50cm.

The visual display comprised one central fixation mark and four boxes for stimulus presentation. Two boxes were arranged vertically in the upper and lower quadrants of the left hemifield and the other two in the upper and lower quadrants of the right hemifield. The inner vertex of each box was located at 7° above or below the horizontal meridian and at 11° to the right or left of the vertical meridian.

In every condition, the cue used for directing attention was an arrow presented at the fixation. The stimulus was an "x" that appeared in one of the boxes. The response was signalled by pressing the spacebar of the computer keyboard using the index finger of the right hand.

On each trial, the sequence of events was as follows: First, the fixation point was presented along with the four boxes. After a 500msec interval, a symbol appeared at fixation indicating either that the stimulus would subsequently be shown with high probability within the corresponding box (an arrow) or that all four boxes were equiprobable (a cross). In the covert attention condition, the patient's task was to fixate the central point while directing attention to the cued box or, if the boxes were equiprobable, to pay attention to all boxes. In the overt attention condition, the patient had to look directly at the cued box or, if the boxes were equiprobable, to fixate the central point. Following a further interval, varying randomly from 800–1500msec, the stimulus was shown for 75msec and the subject had to respond to it as fast as possible, regardless of its position. The response ended the trial and was followed for one second by feedback about speed and accuracy. The display was on until a response was made or a three second interval had elapsed.

In each session the patient was cued to direct attention to one of the boxes on 80% of the trials, and to pay attention to all of them on 20% of the trials. When a specific box was cued, 70% of the times the stimulus would appear in it and 30% of the times the stimulus would appear in one of the non-cued boxes (10% each). The experimental group attended 30 sessions of about 50–60 minutes on different days for a total of six weeks.

### *Results*

The results discussed here concern the second and the third assessment of neglect and extinction, before and after the treatment. One analysis of variance was performed on data collected with the neglect tests in the visual modality. It is worth noting that there was a considerable difference, regardless of the group, in the patient's performance on the different tests. We do not think that different tasks measure different aspects of visual neglect, but rather that these differences merely reflected different degrees of difficulty of the task.

The analysis showed that the two experimental groups improved significantly in all tests after the treatment. By contrast, the control group did not show any significant differences between the second and the third assessment (Fig. 7.1). Improvement after the treatment did not differ for the two experimental groups (Figs. 7.2 and 7.3). Note that the performance of the three groups was not significantly different with regard to the results obtained at the second assessment, the one that preceded the treatment.

A second analysis of variance was conducted on the data collected with the Làdavas test and the tactile test. This analysis had three main

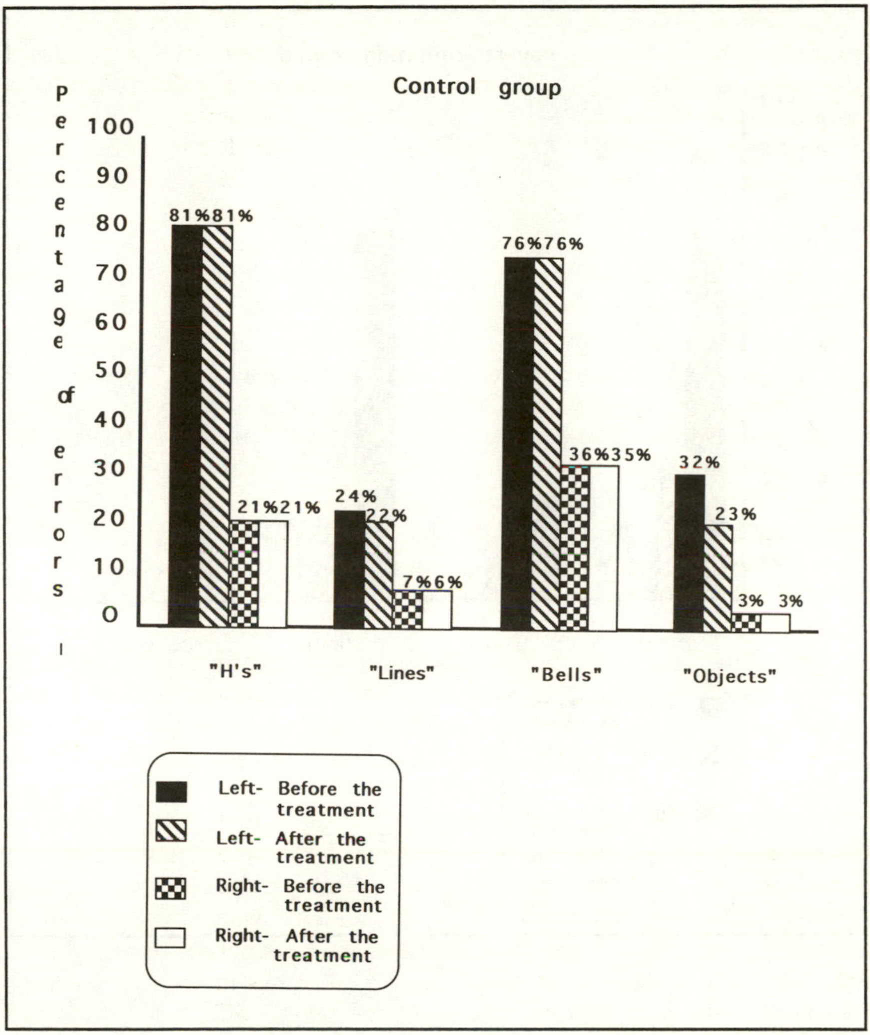


FIG. 7.1

purposes: 1. to assess the effect of the treatment on neglect; 2. to assess the effect of treatment on extinction; and 3. to compare the effect of treatment in the visual and tactile modalities.

This analysis showed a significant improvement for both neglect and extinction in the visual modality for the two experimental groups. There was no difference in the amount of improvement between the group that performed covert orienting (Fig. 7.4) and the group that performed overt

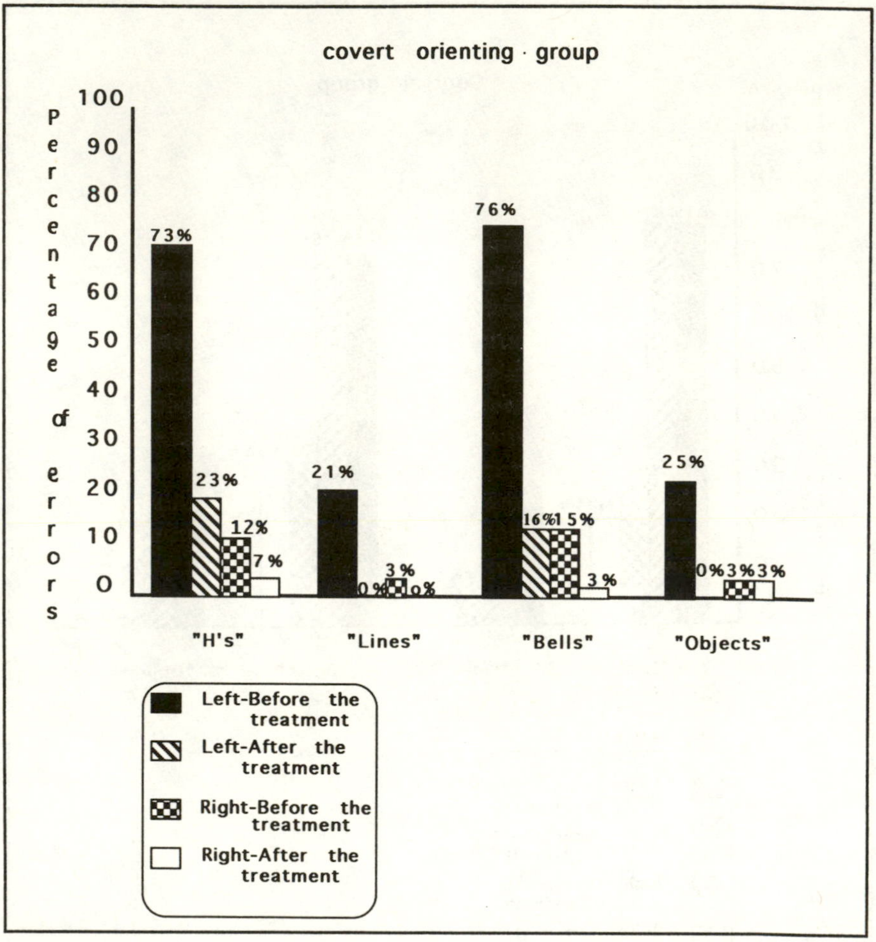


FIG. 7.2.

orienting (Fig. 7.5). The control group did not improve from the second to the third assessment (Fig. 7.6).

In the tactile modality, the results were strikingly different from those obtained in the visual modality because none of the three groups showed an improvement in either neglect or extinction from the second to the third assessment. The small differences observed did not even approach statistical significance.

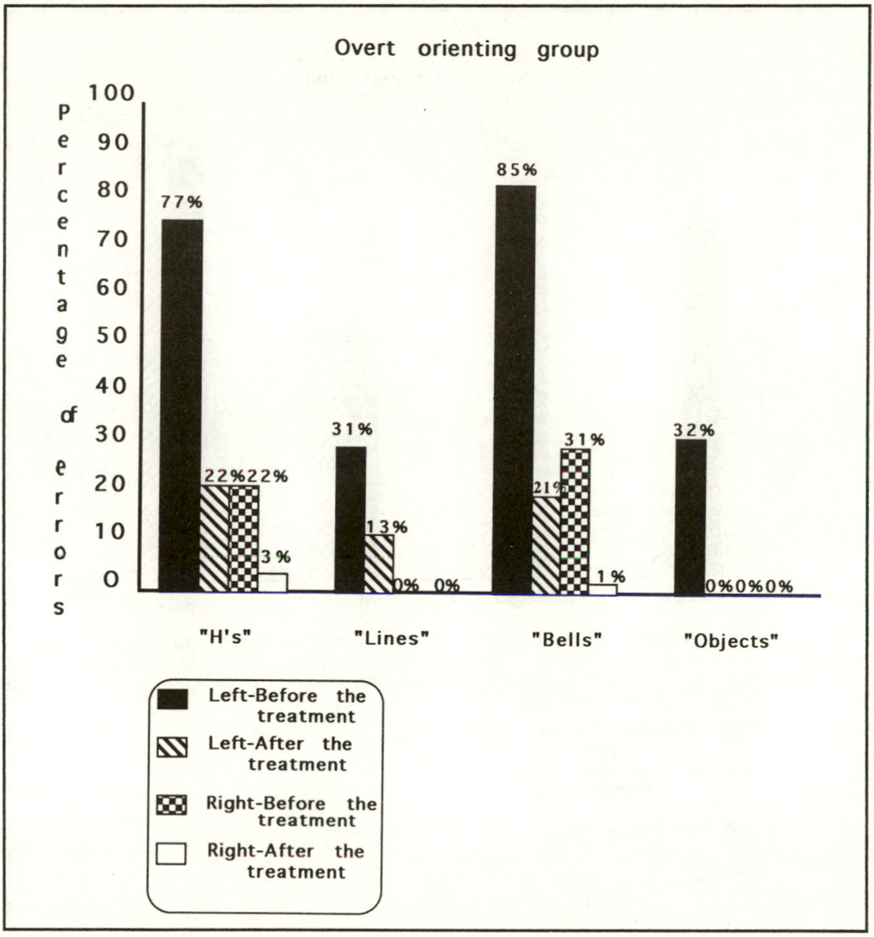


FIG. 7.3.

## DISCUSSION

The results of this rehabilitation study will be discussed with reference to some of the points raised in the previous sections.

The treatment brought about a clear-cut improvement of visual neglect. This outcome, besides its obvious practical implications, also constitutes strong evidence in favour of the attentional hypothesis, according to which the main cause of neglect is a bias of spatial attention, which is captured by the stimuli in the right visual field.

The rehabilitation procedure adopted in our study was aimed at training the patients to overcome the rightward bias by also voluntarily

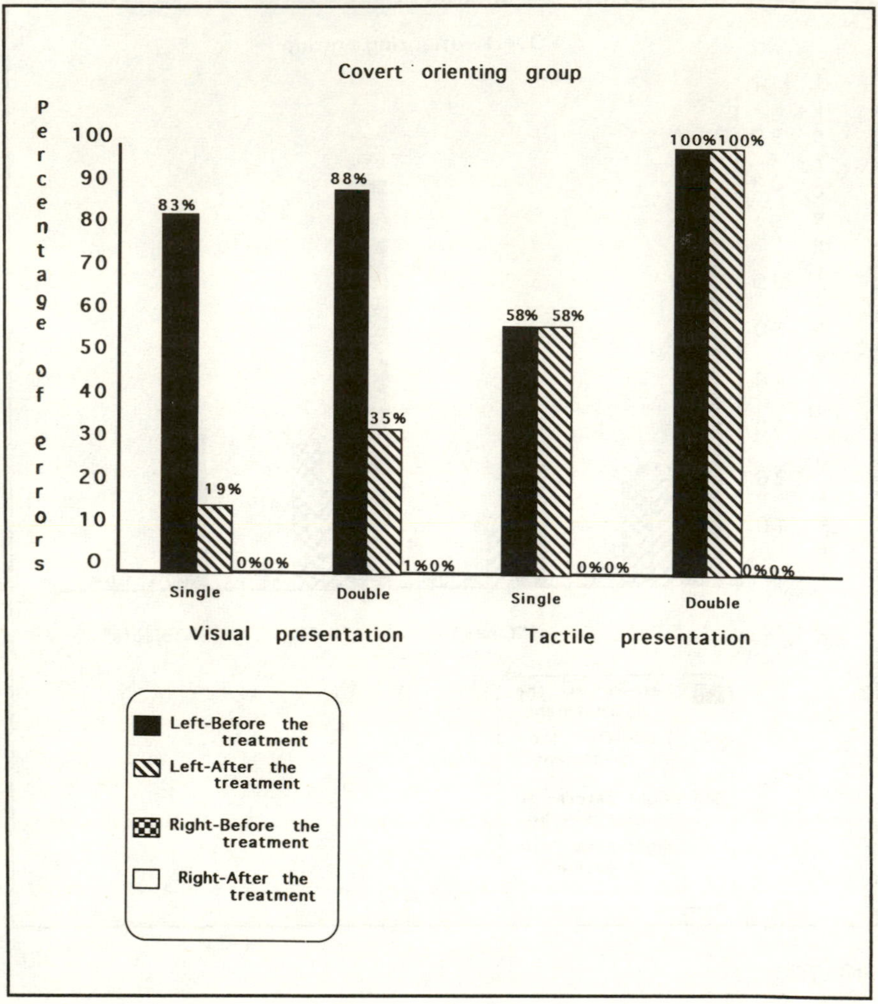


FIG. 7.4.

directing attention to stimuli shown in the neglected left visual field. Apparently, only mechanisms specific for the orienting of attention were involved in the treatment. In particular, no attempt was made at enhancing arousal in the right hemisphere or at manipulating the internal representation of the left side of space. Thus, the favourable outcome of the treatment provides evidence that right parietal lesions cause neglect by damaging the mechanisms that normally allow attention to be oriented leftwards.

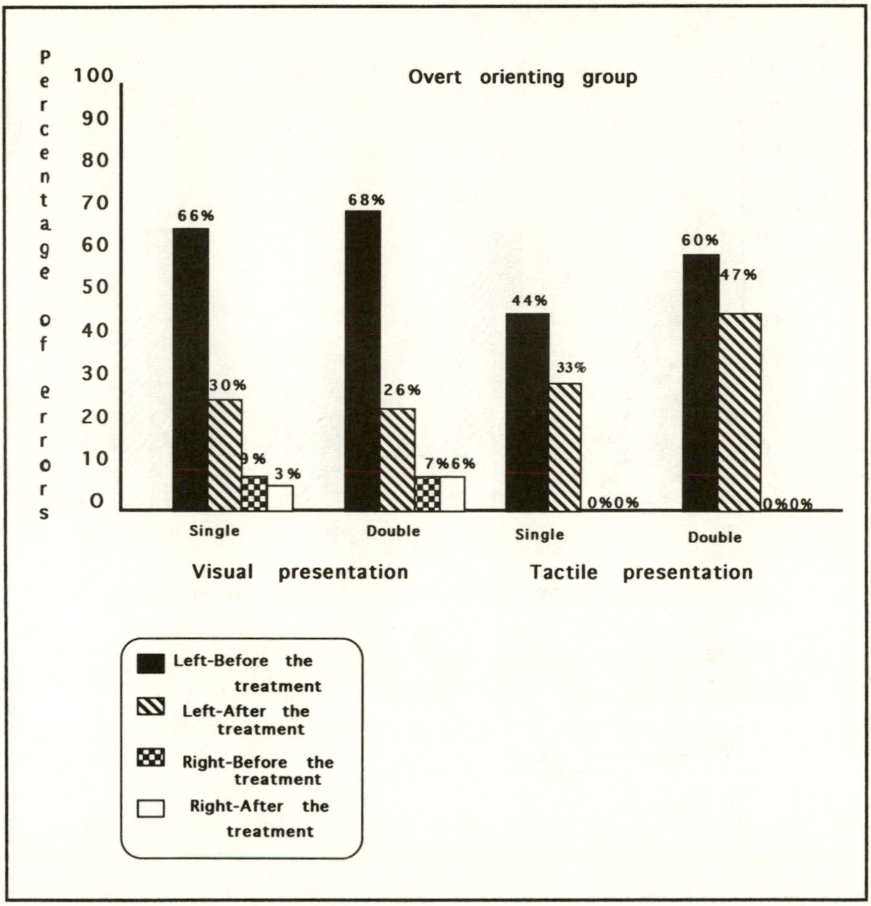


FIG. 7.5

The same reasoning also applies to visual extinction, which also improved after the treatment. A prevalent view is that extinction is a mild attentional deficit that manifests itself only when attention is biased ipsilesionally by a concurrent stimulation. However, extinction may also be considered to be a mild sensory impairment that emerges only in the presence of competing stimuli in the visual field ipsilateral to the lesion (De Renzi, 1982). If extinction were sensory in origin, it would be rather difficult to explain the beneficial effects yielded by a treatment that manipulated exclusively spatial attention. It would seem, therefore, that the mere fact that our treatment was successful again supports an attentional account.

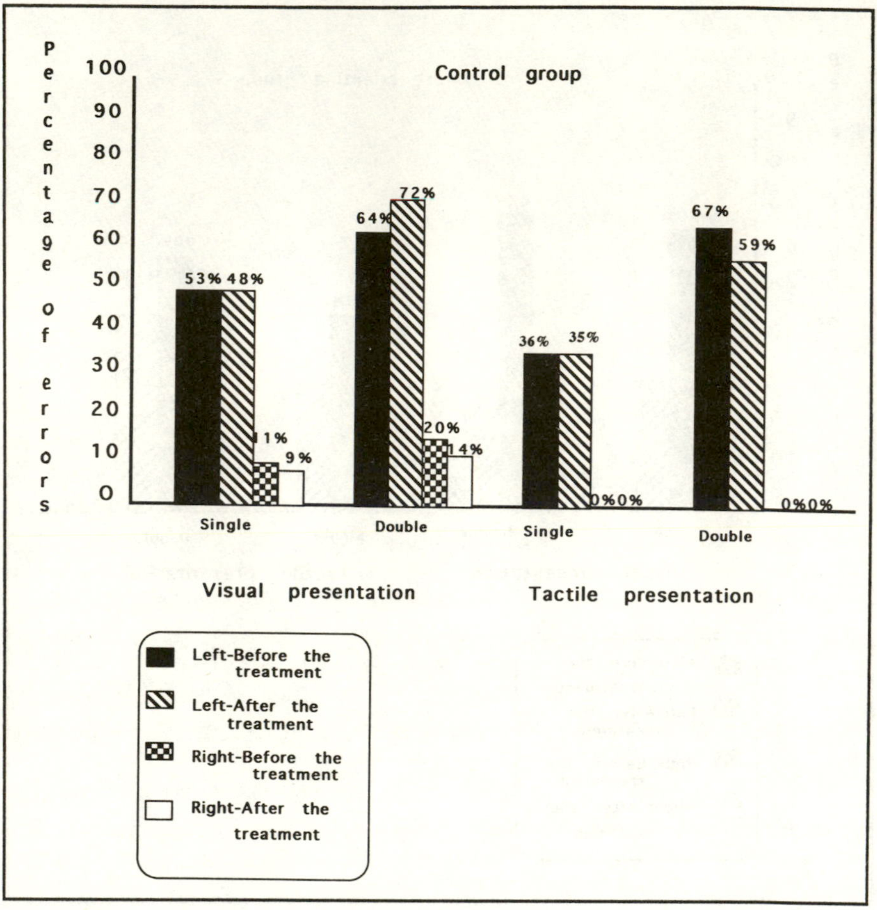


FIG. 7.6.

It was found that overt orienting and covert orienting were equally effective in improving visual extinction and visual neglect. This result, which must be viewed with caution because of the risks inherent in the acceptance of the null hypothesis, especially when few subjects are tested, seems to be in favour of those hypotheses that assume a close relationship between eye movements and attention shifts.

In the literature there are some other studies that support this wiew. Chedru, Leblanc, and Lhermitte (1973) found that marked left unilateral neglect was associated with increased time for leftward eye movements, and the degree of asymmetry in eye movement exploration was positively correlated with the degree of unilateral inattention.

Another study by Girotti, Casazza, Musicco, and Avanzini (1983) presented evidence supporting a unidirectional intentional gaze defect in patients with neglect without gaze paresis. However, in order to draw valid conclusions about the relationship between mechanisms for performing movements of the eyes and those for performing shifts of attention, eye movements should be recorded before and after the treatment. If the two mechanisms were strictly linked, a rehabilitation procedure that exploits only covert orienting should also have effects on tasks that require movements of the eyes.

Our rehabilitation procedure was confined to the visual modality. When the tests administered before and after treatment were in this modality, a clear-cut improvement was observed. By contrast, no improvement was observed for those tests that were given in the tactile modality. Although this was also a negative result, the lack of intermodality effects can be taken as preliminary evidence in favour of the modularity view of spatial attention. In fact, if there were a unique "central" mechanism for orienting attention, one would expect that rehabilitating orienting in one modality should also affect orienting in other modalities. Instead, it seems that the mechanism for shifting attention in the tactile modality is largely independent from the mechanism for shifting attention in the visual modality.

As for the dissociation between motor neglect and directional hypokinesia on one side and sensory neglect on the other (Laplane & Degos, 1983), the results of the present study do not provide relevant information, because the patients were not tested for motor neglect and directional hypokinesia. Note that the condition in which patients were required to pick up objects is not informative for this purpose because the deficit could be due to either hypokinesia or a perceptual deficit. It would be interesting to verify whether a rehabilitation procedure for sensory neglect also extends its effects to motor neglect and directional hypokinesia. As stated earlier, the observation of any rehabilitation effects in domains different from that specifically rehabilitated would be in accordance with the view of a single attentional mechanism.

At this stage we have not yet formally tested our patients for the automatic orienting of attention. Therefore, we cannot be sure that a procedure that involves exclusively voluntary orienting produces an improvement in automatic orienting. However, based on the observation of the behaviour of patients and reports from their relatives, it would seem that the improvement also extends to everyday life, where automatic orienting no doubt plays an important role. Admittedly, it is very difficult to draw sound conclusions on the basis of these observations because in everyday life a voluntary scan of the environment may also play a crucial role. If such anecdotal observations were confirmed by standard tests (see, e.g. Tassinari et al., 1987), that would be evidence in favour of the single-mechanism view. In fact, if there were two mechanisms, one for voluntary orienting and the other for automatic orienting, a rehabilitation procedure that depended exclusively on the former should not yield an improvement for the latter. At any rate, the question of whether a procedure based on voluntary orienting can produce an improvement in automatic orienting will receive a clear answer only through tests that employ peripheral cues, which are known to cause an automatic orienting of spatial attention (see e.g. Müller & Rabbitt, 1989).

We would like to conclude by stressing that rehabilitation studies, like the one reported in this paper, are important not only from a practical point of view, but can also shed light on the causes of neglect and on the basic mechanisms subserving spatial attention in normals.

## REFERENCES

Albert, M.L. (1973). A simple test of visual neglect. *Neurology, 23,* 658-664.

Bisiach, E. & Berti, A. (1987). Dyschiria: An attempt at its systemic explanation. In M. Jeannerod (Ed.), *Neurophysiological and neuropsychological aspects of spatial neglect* (pp.183-201). Amsterdam: North-Holland.

Bisiach, E. & Vallar, G. (1988). Hemineglect in humans. In F. Boller & J. Grafman (Eds.), *Handbook of neuropsychology* (pp.195-222). Amsterdam: Elsevier.

Chedru, F., Leblanc, M., & Lhermitte, F. (1973). Visual searching in normal and brain-damaged subjects: Contribution to the study of unilateral inattention. *Cortex, 9,* 94-111.

Colombo, A., De Renzi, E., & Gentilini, M. (1982). The time course of visual hemi-inattention. *Archives für Psychiatrie und Nervenkrankheiten, 29,* 644-653.

De Renzi, E. (1982). *Disorders of space exploration and cognition*. London: Wiley.

De Renzi, E., Gentilini, M., Faglioni, P., & Barbieri, C. (1989). Attentional shift towards the rightmost stimuli in patients with left visual neglect. *Cortex, 25,* 231-237.

Diller, L. & Weinberg, J. (1977). Hemi-inattention in rehabilitation: The evolution of a rational remediation program. In Weinstein E.A. & Friedland R.P. (Eds), *Hemi-inattention and hemispheric specialisation advances in neurology, Vol. 18* (pp.63-82). New York: Raven Press.

Farah, M.J., Wong, A.B., Monheit, M.A., & Morrow, L.A. (1989). Parietal lobe mechanisms of spatial attention: Modality-specific or supramodal? *Neuropsychologia, 27,* 461-470.

Girotti, F., Casazza, M., Musicco, M., & Avanzini, G. (1983). Oculomotor disorders in cortical lesions in man: The role of unilateral neglect. *Neuropsychologia, 21,* 543-553.

Gainotti G. (1968). Les manifestations de negligence et d'inattention par l'hemispace. *Cortex, 4,* 64-91.

Gauthier, L., Dehaut, F., & Joanett, J. (1989). The bells test: A quantitative and qualitative test for visual neglect. *International Journal of Clinical Neuropsychology, 11,* 49-54.

Halsband, V., Gruhn, S., & Ettlinger, G. (1985). Unilateral spatial neglect and defective performance in one half of space. *International Journal of Neuroscience, 28,* 173-195.

Heilman, K.M., Bowers, D., Coslett, H.B., Whelan, H., & Watson, R.T. (1985). Directional hypokinesia. *Neurology, 35,* 855-859.

Heilman, K.M., Bowers, D., Valenstein, E., & Watson, R.T. (1987). Hemispace and hemispatial neglect. In M. Jeannerod (Ed.), *Neurophysiological and neuropsychological aspects of spatial neglect* (pp.115-150). Amsterdam: North-Holland .

Heilman, K.M. & Van den Abel, T. (1980). The right hemisphere dominance for attention: The mechanism underlying hemispheric asymmetries of inattention (neglect). *Neurology, 30,* 327-330.

Jeannerod, M. (1987). *Neurophysiological and neuropsychological aspects of spatial neglect.* Amsterdam: North-Holland.

Jonides J. (1983). Further toward a model of the mind's eye's movement. *Bulletin of Psychomomic Society, 21,* 247-250.

Kinsbourne, M. (1977). Hemineglect and hemisphere rivalry. In E.A. Weinstein, & R.P. Friedland (Eds.), *Hemi-inattention and hemisphere specialisation* (pp.69-86). New York: Raven Press.

Kinsbourne, M., (1987). Mechanisms of unilateral neglect. In M. Jeannerod (Ed.), *Neurophysiological and neuropsychological aspects of spatial neglect.* Amsterdam: North-Holland.

Klein, R., (1980). Does oculomotor readiness mediate cognitive control of visual attention? In R. S. Nickerson (Ed.), *Attention and performance, VIII* (pp.259-276). Hillsdale, NJ: Lawrence Erlbaum Associates Inc.

Làdavas, E. (1987). Is the hemispatial deficit produced by right parietal lobe damage associated with retinal or gravitational coordinates? *Brain, 110,* 167-180.

Làdavas, E. (1990). Selective spatial attention in patients with visual extinction. *Brain, 113,* 1527-1538.

Làdavas, E., Del Pesce M., & Provinciali, L. (1989). Unilateral attention deficits and hemispheric asymmetries in the control of visual attention. *Neuropsychologia, 27,* 353-366.

Làdavas, E., Petronio, A., & Umiltà, C. (1990). The deployment of visual attention in the intact field of hemineglect patients. *Cortex, 26,* 307-317.

Làdavas, E., Menghini, G., & Umlità, C. (in press). A rehabilitation study of hemispatial neglect. *Cognitive Neuropsychology.*

Làdavas, E. (in preparation). A dissociation between automatic and voluntary orienting mechanisms in patients with visual neglect.

Laplane D. & Degos J.D. (1983). Motor neglect. *Journal of Neurology, Neurosurgery and Psychiatry, 46,* 152-158.

Müller H.J. & Findlay J.M. (1987). Sensitivity and criterion effects in the spatial cueing of visual attention. *Perception and Psychophysics, 42,* 383-399.

Müller H.J. & Findlay J.M. (1988). The effect of visual attention on peripheral discrimination threshold in single and multiple element displays. *Acta Psychologica, 69,* 129-155.

Müller H.J. & Rabbitt P.M. (1989). Reflexive and voluntary orienting of visual attention: Time course of activation and resistance to interruption. *Journal of Experimental Psychology: Human Perception and Performance, 15,* 315-330.

Posner, M.I. (1978). *Chronometric exploration of mind.* Hillsdale, N.J.: Lawrence Erlbaum Associates Inc.

Posner, M.I. (1980). Orienting of attention. *Quarterly Journal of Experimental Psychology, 32,* 3-25.

Posner, M.I., Walker, J.A., Friedrich, F.A., & Rafal, R.D. (1987). How do the parietal lobes direct covert attention? *Neuropsychologia, 25,* 135-145.

Remington, R.W. (1980). Attention and saccadic eye movements. *Journal of Experimental Psychology: Human Perception and Performance, 6,* 726-744.

Riddoch, M.J. & Humphreys, G.W. (1983). The effect of cueing on unilateral neglect. *Neuropsychologia, 21,* 589-599.

Rizzolatti, G. & Gallese, V. (1988). Mechanisms and theories of spatial neglect. In F. Boller and J. Grafman (Eds.), *Handbook of neuropsychology* (pp.223-246). Amsterdam: Elsevier.

Rizzolatti, G., Riggio, L., Dascola, I., & Umiltà, C. (1987). Reorienting attention across the horizontal and vertical meridians: Evidence in favour of a premotor theory of attention. *Neuropsychologia, 25,* 31-40.

Shepherd, M. & Müller, H.J. (1989) Movement versus focusing of attention. *Perception and Psychophysics, 46,* 146-154.

Shepherd, M., Findlay J.M., & Hockey R.J. (1986) The relationship between eye movements and spatial attention. *Quarterly Journal of Experimental Psychology, 38A,* 475-491.

Spencer, M.B.H., Lambert, A.J., & Hockey, R. (1988). The inhibitory component of orienting, alertness and sustained attention. *Acta Psychologica, 69,* 165-184.

Tassinari, G., Alioti, S., Chelazzi, L., Marzi, C., & Berlucchi, G. (1987) Distribution in the visual field of the costs of voluntary allocated attention and of the inhibitory after-effects of covert orienting. *Neuropsychologia, 25,* 55-71.

Umiltà, C. (1988) Orienting of attention.In F. Boller and J. Grafman (Eds.), *Handbook of neuropsychology, Vol. 1* (pp.175-193). Amsterdam: Elsevier.

Vallar, G. & Perani, D., (1987) The anatomy of spatial neglect in humans. In M. Jeannerod (Ed.), *Neurophysiological and neuropychological aspects of spatial neglect,* 235-258, Amsterdam: North-Holland.

Yantis S. & Jonides, J. (1984) Abrupt visual onsets and selective attention: Evidence from visual search. *Journal of Experimental Psychology, 10,* 601-620.

CHAPTER EIGHT

# The Rehabilitation of Attentional and Hemi-inattentional Disorders

Ian H. Robertson
*MRC Applied Psychology Unit, Cambridge, UK*

## ABSTRACT

There is much evidence to suggest a close link between attentional and hemi-inattentional disorders. It is proposed in this chapter that the results of neglect rehabilitation are actually less encouraging than has previously been assumed. Many apparently positive results, it is argued, are actually attributable to similarities between training and test materials. Attempted replications of some of the New York training procedures have frequently found generalisation only to tests similar to the training procedures. One reason proposed for this is that visual neglect is associated with more general attentional problems that may impede recovery.

The evidence for the effectiveness of rehabilitation of attentional disorders is more positive than it is for visual neglect, though there are also negative findings here. The possibility of training neglect by attempting to modify nonlateralised attentional difficulties is discussed.

Furthermore, the author describes some preliminary studies on the rehabilitation of visual neglect which attempt to bypass the presumed limited attentional resources of neglect patients. One method evaluated in this way involved teaching patients to use their partially hemiplegic left arms as "perceptual anchors" to which leftward scanning responses were conditioned. A related method involved an avoidance conditioning paradigm where left arm responses (if necessary aided by the right arm) were made on the neglected side. The positive results of these studies suggest that neglect rehabilitation may in the future produce more positive results.

## INTRODUCTION

In this paper, it is argued that hemi-inattentional disorders are closely associated with non-lateralised attentional deficits, and that this fact has important implications for cognitive rehabilitation. Given the close links between attentional and hemi-inattentional disorders, it makes sense also to review the evidence for the effectiveness of attentional rehabilitation in the same chapter.

The paper is divided into four sections. First, evidence for a close link between attentional and hemi-inattentional disorders is provided. Secondly, evidence for the effectiveness of rehabilitation of hemi-inattention is reviewed. Thirdly, evidence for the effectiveness of attentional rehabilitation is reviewed, with the prospects for effective rehabilitation of hemi-inattentional disorders being tackled in the final section.

## EVIDENCE OF A LINK BETWEEN ATTENTIONAL AND HEMI-INATTENTIONAL DEFICITS

Robertson (1989), among others, has proposed the existence of a non-lateralised attentional deficit associated with unilateral left visual neglect, and predicted that one result of this would be a significant increase in right sided omissions as compared with controls when left neglect patients were cued to the left during the presentation of rapid single or double stimuli. Subjects had to report what they saw on a computer screen—for example a square on the right and a cross on the left. In the normal condition they would tend to make errors to the left, and not report the cross. When their attention was focused on the left by means of reading a word written under the left stimulus, subjects showed one of two patterns. Approximately half would make most of their omissions on the right in the cueing condition, while the others would correctly read the word on the left, but neglect the stimulus immediately above it. For the group as a whole, the effect of the cueing was to equalise the left and right omissions.

Robertson (1990a) found that the degree of neglect was highly correlated with the discrepancy between forward and backward digit span. Forward digit span tends to be relatively preserved following brain damage (Benton et al., 1983). Backward digit span, on the other hand is more demanding of attentional resources, requiring as it does rehearsal of the forward string while simultaneously repeating it backwards. Hence digit discrepancy can be regarded as a measure of some aspect of attentional functioning.

Other indices of possible mental deterioration such as verbal memory or perseveration were uncorrelated with degree of neglect, and the digit span-neglect relationship remained even when the effects of visuo-spatial efficiency were partialled out. This latter finding argues against the view that poor ability to represent spatially the digits in backward span underlies both the span performance and the neglect.

In another paper, Robertson and Frasca (1991) had ten subjects, suffering from left unilateral neglect, carry out a letter cancellation task under normal conditions, while counting forward, and when generating random numbers, respectively. The index of neglect was significantly greater for the random number generation condition than for the standard cancellation condition; the forward counting had an intermediate position.

In a second study in the same paper, Robertson and Frasca studied four left unilateral neglect subjects and four right brain damaged controls who carried out a simple reaction time task. Stimuli appeared randomly to the left and right, with and without the simultaneous performance of a secondary task (counting backward in threes from 100). The discrepancy between left versus right latencies increased significantly (three way analysis of variance) in the secondary task condition for two patients in the neglect group but not for the other two. None of the control group showed this effect.

Rapcsak, Verfaellie, Fleet, and Heilman (1989) examined the degree of left hemi-inattention shown by a group of patients in a simple cancellation task under three conditions. The first required the patient to cancel all of a group of simple stimuli. The second required cancellation of only those of a group of similar stimuli which differed from the other stimuli by one simple feature—a "dot" in the top right hand corner. In the third condition, the stimulus to be cancelled had a dot in the top right hand corner but, in addition to the foils used in the first condition, there were additional foils that had a dot in the bottom right hand corner that were also not to be cancelled.

The last condition differed only from the other two in that it required more selective attention from the subject; i.e. the subjects had to select stimuli from among a greater variety of competing stimuli. The authors found that the degree of neglect in the latter condition was significantly greater than in the other two, suggesting a deterioration in hemi-inattention under greater non-lateralised attentional load.

Lecours et al. (1987) studied brain damaged illiterates and found that left brain damaged patients who explored both sides of space when tested with simple linguistic stimuli tended to restrict visual search to the left side of space when syntactically more complex sentences were used. Right brain damaged patients were unaffected by sentence complexity in their visual search.

Weintraub and Mesulam (1987) analysed cancellation scores and found that neglect patients not only made more left sided omissions than controls and left brain damaged patients, but also made more right sided omissions than either of these groups. They interpreted this as providing further evidence for the proposition that while the left hemisphere controls attention only to the right side of space, the right hemisphere controls attention in both hemifields. Hence right brain damage should result, as they found, in both lateralised and bilateral attentional difficulties.

Pillon (1981) has also shown with left neglect subjects how decreasing the complexity of the Rey complex figure reduces the amount of neglect shown for the left half of the figure, even though the retinal size of the total shape to be copied remained the same.

The theoretical explanations for these diverse findings vary widely; what is in common to them all is the notion that it cannot simply be the ability to attend to one side of space which is impaired in neglect. One view is to explain this in terms of Weintraub and Mesulam (1987): i.e. that the right hemisphere has bilateral attentional responsibilities, resulting in bilateral deficits.

However, several studies have failed to establish in normals that left and right hemispheres differ in their attentional responsibilities in the way that Weintraub and Mesulam describe (e.g. Roy et al., 1987).

## EFFECTIVENESS OF REHABILITATION

One of the earliest studies of attempts to remediate visual neglect was by Lawson (1962) in Aberdeen. He treated two cases of neglect by frequently reminding the patients to "look to the left", and also to use their fingers to guide their vision while reading. They were also encouraged to find the centre of a book or food-tray by using touch and then to use their finger position as a reference point from which to explore systematically the page or the tray. It is interesting to note that Lawson reported that generalisation to untrained tasks was poor.

### The New York Studies

Weinberg et al., (1977) carried out a controlled study of 20 hours of training with 25 right C.V.A. patients suffering from left hemi-inattention, defined by a range of cancellation, reading and other tests. These were compared with a randomly selected group of 32 patients satisfying similar criteria. The mean time post-stroke was ten weeks, though the range was considerable. Control subjects received the same normal occupational therapy programme as the experimental subjects, and no attempt was made to control for the non-specific effects of being in a novel treatment programme.

The experimental treatment consisted of a number of tasks designed to "compensate for faulty scanning habits" (p. 481). These included use of a "scanning machine", reading and cancellation tasks where the subjects were provided with a thick red vertical line down the left side of the page, and which the patients are taught to use as an anchor by always bringing it (the line) into vision before beginning the task in hand and a number of other strategies which have been well described elsewhere. Performance on a wide range of reading, cancellation and other tests showed significant benefit to the treated group relative to the controls, particularly for the group showing severe neglect.

In a partial replication study using identical selection criteria, Weinberg et al. (1979) carried out a further randomised trial, in this case with the control group being given an extra hour of occupational therapy each day to match the extra treatment time given to the treatment group.

The procedures were similar to the previous study, with the addition of two extra training tasks relating to tactile location training and length estimation training. The treated group did better than the controls on a number of neuropsychological tests, and again this was particularly prominent among the severe group.

A further partial replication of this type of training procedure was carried out by Young, Collins, and Hren (1983) who also found results suggesting a significant treatment effect.

Gordon et al., (1985) attempted a further replication of the training procedures developed by Weinberg et al., though this time not using a randomised design. Instead, one institution supplied the control group for one period, and another institution supplied the experimental group. This was then reversed on an unspecified number of occasions.

The experimental (n=48) and control (n=29) subjects were well matched on all neurological and neuropsychological measures. Eighty five hours of training showed the experimental group performing significantly better than the control group on cancellation, arithmetic, reading comprehension, line bisection, and on a search task. By four months however, there were no significant differences between the two groups except that the control group showed significantly less lateral bias on Ravens Coloured Progressive Matrices, and the treatment group reported significantly less anxiety and hostility.

## Poor Generalisation in Attempted Replications of the New York Studies

In yet another attempted replication of the Weinberg et al. methods, (Webster et al., 1984) used a multiple-baseline by subject single case design with three males showing left neglect; i.e. treatment onset was staggered for the three subjects in order to determine whether improvements in neglect corresponded with the onset of treatment. Performance was measured by having the subjects navigate an obstacle course in wheelchairs and counting the number of times they collided with markers on the course (see also Lennon, this volume).

The training relied on the scanning machine used by Weinberg et al., and scanning was trained while moving in the wheelchair. Significant improvements in wheelchair navigation appeared in each case, though only for frontal collisions with the obstacles, but not with collisions with the rear of the wheelchair.

In replication of the previous study, Gouvier et al., (1984) found similar results, though it was interesting to note that improvement on wheelchair and scanning board performance did not generalise to letter cancellation performance.

Another study by this group (Gouvier et al., 1987) tended to support the view that the effects of training were much more consistently observed in tasks similar to the training procedure. For instance training using a light-board (detecting lights on a two metre wide board) produced improvements on this measure, but not on cancellation, while training in cancellation resulted in improvements in cancellation tests but not on light-board performance.

## Failure of Computerised Versions of the New York Methods

Finally, Robertson et al. (1990) carried out a randomised controlled trial of computerised training with 36 patients suffering unilateral neglect. One group of 20 subjects received a mean of 15.5 (sd 1.8) hours of computerised scanning and attentional training which drew on many of the methods of the New York group (e.g. perceptual anchoring), while a second group of 16 subjects received a mean of 11.4 (sd 5.2) hours of recreational computing selected in order to minimise scanning and timed attentional tasks.

Training consisted of computerised procedures such as matching to sample tasks, where the computer would not accept a response before the subject pressed an "anchor bar" on the left of the touch-sensitive screen. Blind follow-up at the end of training and six months follow-up revealed no statistically or clinically significant results between groups (which were extremely well matched prior to training) on a wide range of relevant tests. This was not because of large improvements on the part of the control group, as neither group showed dramatic improvements in neglect over six months.

### Conclusions

The rehabilitation of hemi-inattentional disorders is probably the most researched area of neuropsychological rehabilitation outside of the language disorder area. Results have tended to be positive, but closer inspection of the data suggests the following:

1. Training effects tend to be restricted to measures that show stimulus characteristics of the training materials. For instance, the Weinberg procedures lean heavily on reading and cancellation training. Testing tends to rely on measures with similar stimulus characteristics, and hence generalisation to different tasks has not been demonstrated clearly.
2. Training effects have not been shown clearly to generalise over time.

In short, the promise shown by training in this area may not be quite so clear as might first appear. One hypothesis to explain this may be that a major problem in neglect—non-lateralised attentional loss—may not have been properly addressed in most training programmes to date. The next section considers the effectiveness of training of such attentional loss.

## EFFECTIVENESS OF REHABILITATION OF ATTENTIONAL DISORDERS

Much of the early work on non-lateralised attentional training was carried out by Ben-Yishay and colleagues at the New York University Medical Center (e.g. Ben-Yishay et al., 1979; 1980). Subjects were trained in such skills as time estimation and reaction time tasks, among others. Unfortunately, no randomised controlled trials or controlled single-case studies have been carried out, and simple A-B designs have been used, with all the methodological problems involved (e.g. Robertson, 1990b).

This holds also for the work of Prigatano et al. (1984) who reported the results of a comprehensive head-injury rehabilitation programme including attentional training. The study by Scherzer (1986) also deals with a comprehensive rehabilitation programme where the effects of attentional training cannot be partialled out.

## Negative Findings

Malec et al. (1984) compared performance of ten head-injured patients, having a mean of 80 days post-injury, using a randomised double-crossover study, i.e. one group was treated while the other acted as control, and then the experimental conditions were reversed. While large improvements in attentional tests were found over four weeks of training, there was no significant difference after training versus non-training weeks, leading to the conclusion that the observed improvements had nothing to do with the training given. This study illustrates well the pitfalls of relying on simple before-after data as illustrated in several of the studies already reviewed.

In a preliminary report of a study published (Fasotti, 1988), Fasotti describes a randomised trial where 17 head-injured patients received 30 half-hour sessions of reaction time training to a variety of dual tasks, combining auditory and visual stimuli. A control group of ten matched patients received no training. No significant differences between groups on various standardised tests of cognitive function, including the block design subtest of the WAIS, were found.

Ponsford and Kinsella (1988) trained ten severely head-injured patients using a multiple-baseline-by-subjects design. The first procedure was a no-training condition, the second a computerised attentional training condition, the third a condition of the latter plus therapist feedback and reinforcement and the final one a return to baseline condition. The baseline lengths were three and six weeks respectively. Training included simple reaction time training, a visual search/matching task, choice/go-no go reaction time, vigilance ("spot the (target) letter" of a series of random letters appearing on the screen) and a number detection task ("spot the numbers that are either even or a multiple of five"). Performance was assessed by neuropsychological tests and a rating scale of attentional behaviour by occupational therapists of the patient's behaviour in day-to-day activities. In addition, a video of performance on a clerical task was taken, which was assessed at the beginning and end of each phase.

Though there were steady improvements over time on these measures for the ten subjects, this improvement bore no significant relationship to the training offered. In conclusion, this study found no training effects of computerised attentional training.

## Positive Findings

Sohlberg and Mateer (1987) carried out four single-case studies of attentional training, using computer-based procedures including simple reaction time, choice reaction time, alternating attention tasks that included arithmetical exercises, and divided attention tasks. The trainees received seven to nine sessions of attentional training per week for between four to eight weeks and repeated measures of one attentional task, PASAT (Paced Auditory Serial Addition Test), were given, as well as control measures of non-attentionally relevant tasks. PASAT is a test of serial arithmetic that requires fairly complex mental manipulations in a correct sequence under time pressure.

In one case, a dramatic improvement in PASAT followed the instigation of training, and this was too great to be attributed to a practice effect, and less dramatic effects were also observed in the other cases. There were no measures of wider generalisation other than to the PASAT test.

Sturm et al. (1983) matched two groups, each of 15 mixed head-injured and stroke patients, testing them on a comprehensive neuropsychological battery of 16 tests at intake, four weeks, and then at eight weeks. The battery included German standardised tests of attention, memory, reasoning and visuo-perceptual functioning. The first group received 14 training sessions of mean length 15 minutes for the first four weeks, and nothing for the second four weeks. The reverse was true for the second group. Test scores were compared in this crossover design at both four and eight weeks.

Training took place on the Vienna Test System, consisting of a range of attention and perceptual speed tasks, including simple and choice reaction time to visual and acoustic stimuli and reaction to target pictorial stimuli embedded within several similar stimuli. The difficulty of these tasks was steadily increased, for instance, requiring different reactions to different and complex combinations of stimuli in various modalities.

The results were impressive. Significant improvements in test scores were observed following training but not following the non-training period in both groups. These improvements were particularly evident on tests that were similar in form to the training tests (e.g. reaction-time and perceptual discrimination tasks), but they were also apparent on a wide range of less closely related tests of psychomotor function, logical thinking, word fluency and spatial reasoning. These effects were stable for at least four weeks following cessation of training, and no comparable effects were obtained for the control groups.

Though the study was not without methodological flaws (e.g. lack of blind assessment, matching of subjects rather than randomisation), and though no generalisation to everyday life was sought or demonstrated, this study does represent a high-quality and important contribution to the literature, indicating that computerised attentional training may produce relatively enduring changes in neuropsychological tests dissimilar to the tasks used for training.

Gray and Robertson (1989) carried out three single-case studies that also suggested promising effects of attentional training. This led to a randomised controlled trial of attentional training between an attentionally-trained group of 17 brain-damaged subjects and a control group of 14 randomly allocated control subjects with similar problems in attention (17 subjects had closed head injury; 14 had other types of injury). Training consisted of a mean of 15.3 hours of computerised training on reaction-time tasks, rapid number comparison, digit symbol transfer, as well as a number of arcade-type divided reaction time tasks, some of which had been specially written for brain-injured patients.

The control group received a mean of 12.7 hours of recreational computing, consisting of computer quizzes and games that the authors judged made few attentional demands on the patients.

On six month blind follow-up, clear improvements for the experimental group were found on PASAT and WAIS-R Arithmetic, after covariance of relevant pretreatment variables (Gray et al., 1992).

## Conclusions

A number of studies of attentional training suggest that some types of training may produce changes in cognitive functioning that cannot be explained by stimulus-specific learning effects, and which therefore may reflect some improvement on certain related cognitive functions. None of these studies demonstrates, however, that such effects generalise to the everyday functioning of the treated patients.

Of the positive studies, three showed immediate effects of training, and only one of these (Sturm et al., 1983) demonstrates any maintenance of improved performance over time (only four weeks, in this case). Gray, Robertson et al. (1988), on the other hand, find a delayed effect of training that is difficult to square with the findings of these other studies.

In short, the current state of the literature suggests that attentional training shows more promise than training of most other cognitive functions apart from certain types of language problems (see Robertson, 1990b).

## PROSPECTS FOR REHABILITATION OF HEMI-INATTENTION

The first section of this chapter suggested that the presence of hemi-inattention may be associated with the presence of non-lateralised attentional disorders. The second section suggested that training strategies for hemi-inattention may be more task-specific than had previously been suggested, for instance by Weinberg and his colleagues in the New York group. What implications does this have for the rehabilitation of hemi-inattentional disorders in the future?

The first implication is that training should be tied to specific cues that are likely to be present in the everyday life of the person. Robertson, North, and Geggie (1992) taught a person with unilateral left neglect to place his hemiplegic arm as a perceptual anchor immediately to the left of any area in which he was working. So, for instance, while reading, he was taught to lay his left arm along the left margin of the book. When eating, he was taught to hold (with the little residual power he had in the limb) the arm to the left of the plate. While playing games or working in occupational therapy, he similarly was taught the overlearned response of laying his left arm along the margins of the working area. Using a multiple-baseline design, clear improvements in a number of tests, including dialling a telephone, reading and letter cancellation were observed.

In two further single-case studies in the same paper, Robertson et al. (1991) used an avoidance conditioning paradigm to train two patients to press a switch on their left side in order to prevent an unpleasant buzzing sound occurring. The time before the buzzer would go off varied randomly and could not be predicted by the subjects. Significant improvements in tests of neglect were observed, as well as improvements in blind ratings of everyday problems such as collisions with doorways.

In another study, neglect of the left leg, leading to walking problems due to a raised heel habit, was treated by means of a simple heel buzzer feedback system (Robertson & Cashman, 1991). Lennon (this volume) gives a further example of treament tied to functionally important tasks.

If future studies can demonstrate that the types of nonlateralised attentional disorders shown by people with unilateral neglect can be rehabilitated in ways similar to those outlined in the previous section on attentional rehabilitation, then the prospects for the rehabilitation of unilateral neglect may be enhanced.

The common feature of these approaches is that they may rely on learning mechanisms (such as avoidance conditioning) that are less dependent on conscious attention than many types of teaching/learning procedures. Their apparent effectiveness may relate partly to the fact that responses are being taught that will tend not to be affected by attention being occupied by other tasks or by fluctuations in arousal.

Posner and Peterson (1990) propose a three factor account of attention: Selection, vigilance and orientation. They suggest that neglect may be associated with difficulties in disengaging attention (one of the sub-mechanisms of the orientation system) from stimuli on the ipsilesional side. They also suggest, however, that there is a right-hemisphere based vigilance control system. It is possible, therefore, that the association between neglect and non-lateralised attentional disorders noted earlier in this chapter may be related to damage to the vigilance system in the right hemisphere. Such an account would also explain the preponderance of left over right neglect. In other words, the severity of, and recovery from, visual neglect may be substantially increased by non-lateralised vigilance difficulties, though the relative contribution of the orientation and vigilance problems respectively cannot yet be quantified.

If this is the case, then the importance of learning strategies which endure even when arousal and vigilance are low is obvious. Whether strategies to modify arousal can be developed that affect degree of neglect remains to be seen. One study by Fleet and Heilman (1986) suggests some promise in this area. They compared the performance of neglect patients on repeated letter cancellation administrations under two conditions—one with feedback of results, one with no feedback. With serial administrations in a short time period, neglect increased in the latter condition, but decreased in the former condition. The authors interpret this as being due to improved arousal as a result of feedback of results causing a reduction in neglect. This result, along with the rest of the evidence reviewed in this chapter, suggests promising future developments in the rehabilitation of unilateral neglect.

## REFERENCES

Benton, A., Hamsher, K., Varney, N., & Spreen, O. (1983). *Contributions to neuropsychological assessment.* Oxford: Oxford University Press.

Ben-Yishay, Y., Rattock, J., & Diller, L. (1979). A clinical strategy for the systematic amelioration of attentional disturbances in severe head trauma patients. In *Working approaches to remediation of cognitive deficits in brain damaged patients.* Rehabilitation Monograph No. 60. New York: New York University Medical Center.

Ben-Yishay, Y., Rattock, J., Ross, B., Lakin, P. , Cohen, T., & Diller, L. (1980). A remediation "module" for the systematic amelioration of attentional disturbances in severe head trauma patients. In *Approaches to remediation of cognitive deficits in brain damaged persons.* Rehabilitation Monograph No. 61. New York: New York University Medical Center.

Fasotti, L. (1988). *Computerised training of attentional deficits after closed head injury.* Unpublished manuscript, University of Hunsbruck, The Netherlands.

Fleet, W.S. & Heilman, K.M. (1986). The fatigue effect in unilateral neglect. *Neurology, 36* (Supplement 1), 258.

Gordon, W., Hibbard, M.R., Egelko, S., Diller, L., Shaver, P., Lieberman, A. and Ragnarson, L. (1985). Perceptual remediation in patients with right brain damage: a comprehensive program. *Archives of Physical Medicine and Rehabilitation, 66,* 353-359.

Gouvier, W., Bua, B., Blanton, P., & Urey, J. (1987). Behavioural changes following visual scanning training: observation of five cases. *International Journal of Clinical Neuropsychology, 9,* 74-80.

Gray, J. & Robertson, I. (1988). Microcomputer-based attentional retraining after brain injury: A randomised group-controlled trial. *Journal of Clinical and Experimental Neuropsychology, 10,* 332. (Abstract).

Gray, J. & Robertson, I. (1989). Remediation of attentional difficulties following brain-injury: Three experimental single case studies. *Brain Injury 3,* 163- 170.

Gray, J., Robertson, I., Pentland, B., & Smith, S. (1992). Microcomputer based attentional training after brain damage: A randomised group controlled trial. *Neuropsychological Rehabilitation, 2,* 97-115.

Lawson, I.R. (1962). Visual-spatial neglect in lesions of the right cerebral hemisphere. *Neurology, 12,* 23-33.

Lecours, A.R., Mehler, F., Parente, M.A. et al. (1987). Illiteracy and brain damage: II. Manifestations of unilateral neglect in testing "auditory comprehension" with iconographic materials. *Brain and Cognition, 6,* 243-265.

Malec, J., Jones, R., Rao, N., & Stubbs, K. (1984). Video-game practise effect on sustained attention in patients with craniocerebral trauma. *Cognitive Rehabilitation 2,* 18-23.

Pillon, B. (1981). Negligence de l'hemi-espace gauche dans des spreuves visuo-constructives. *Neuropsycholgia, 19,* 317-320.

Ponsford, J. & Kinsella, G. (1988). Evaluation of a remedial programme for attentional deficits following closed head-injury. *Journal of Clinical and Experimental Neuropsychology 10,* 693-708.

Posner, M.I. & Peterson, S.E. (1990). The attention system of the human brain. *Annual Review of Neuroscience 13,* 25-42.

Prigatano, P. , Fordyce, D., Zeiner, H., Roueche, J., Pepping, M., & Wood, B. (1984). Neuropsychological rehabilitation after closed head injury in young adults. *Journal of Neurology, Neurosurgery and Psychiatry, 47,* 505-513.

Rapcsak, S.Z., Verfaellie, M., Fleet, S., & Heilman, K.M. (1989). Selective attention in hemispatial neglect. *Arch. Neurol. 46,* 172-178 .

Robertson, I. (1989). Anomalies in the lateralisation omissions in unilateral left neglect: Implications for an attentional theory of neglect. *Neuropsychologia, 27,* 157-165.

Robertson, I. (1990a). Digit span and visual neglect: A puzzling relationship. *Neuropsychologia, 28,* 217-222.

Robertson, I. (1990b). Does computerised cognitive rehabilitation work? A review. *Aphasiology, 4,* 381-405.

Robertson, I. & Cashman, E. (1991). Auditory Feedback for Walking Difficulties in a Case of Unilateral Neglect. *Neuropsychological Rehabilitation, 1,* 175-183.

Robertson, I. & Frasca, R. (1991). Attentional load and visual neglect. *International Journal of Neuroscience, 62*, 45-56.

Robertson, I., Gray, J., Pentland, B., & Waite, L. (1990). Microcomputer-based rehabilitation of unilateral left visual neglect: a randomised controlled trial. *Archives of Physical Medicine and Rehabilitation, 71,* 663-668.

Robertson I., Gray J., & McKenzie, S. (1988). Microcomputer-based cognitive rehabilitation of visual neglect: Three multiple baseline single-case studies. *Brain Injury, 2,* 151-163.

Robertson, I., Gray, J., Pentland, B., & Waite, L. (1990). A randomised controlled trial of computer-based cognitive rehabiliation for unilateral left visual neglect. *Archives of Physical Medicine and Rehabilitation, 71,* 663-668.

Robertson, I., North, N., & Geggie, C. (1992). Spatio-motor cueing in unilateral neglect: three single case studies of its therapeutic effectiveness. *Journal of Neurology, Neurosurgery and Psychiatry, 55,* 799-805.

Roy, E., Reuter-Lorenz, P. , Roy, L., Copland, S., & Moscovitch, M. (1987). Unilateral attention deficits and hemispheric assymetries in the control of attention. In M. Jeannerod (Ed.), *Neurophysiological and Neuropsychological Aspects of Neglect.* North Holland, Elsevier.

Scherzer, B. (1986). Rehabilitation following severe head trauma: Results of a three-year program. *Archives of Physical Medicine and Rehabilitation, 67,* 366-374.

Sohlberg, M. & Mateer, A. (1987). Effectiveness of an attention-training programme. *Journal of Clinical and Experimental Neuropsychology, 9,* 117-130.

Sturm, W., Dahmen, W., Hartje, W., & Willmes, K. (1983). Ergebnisse eines Trainingsprogramms zur Verbesserung der visuellen Auffassungsshnelligkeit und Konzentrationsfahigkeit bei Hirngeschaditgten. *Archive für Psychiatrie und Nervenkrankenheiten 233,* 9-22.

Webster, J., Jones, S., Blanton, P. , Gross, R., Beissel, G., & Wofford, J. (1984). Visual scanning training with stroke patients. *Behaviour Therapy, 15,* 129-143.

Weinberg, J., Diller, L., Gordon, W., Gerstman, L., Lieberman, A., Lakin, P., Hodges, G., & Ezrachi, O. (1977). Visual scanning training effect on reading-related tasks in acquired right brain damage. *Archives of Physical Medicine and Rehabilitation, 58,* 479-486.

Weinberg, M., Diller, L., Gordon, W., Gerstman, L., Lieberman, A., Lakin, P. , Hodges, G., & Ezrachi, O. (1979). Training sensory awareness and spatial organisation in people with right brain damage. *Archives of Physical Medicine and Rehabilitation, 60,* 491-496.

Weintraub, S. & Mesulam, M. (1987). Right cerebral dominance in spatial attention. Further evidence based on ipsilateral neglect. *Arch. Neurol. 44,* 621-625.

Young, G., Collins, D., & Hren, M. (1983). Effect of pairing scanning training with block design training in the remediation of perceptual problems in left hemiplegics. *Journal of Clinical Neuropsychology, 5,* 201-212.

CHAPTER NINE

# Task Specific Effects in the Rehabilitation of Unilateral Neglect

Sheila Lennon
*Department of Occupational and Physiotherapy, University of Ulster at Jordanstown, Newtownabbey, Northern Ireland*

## ABSTRACT

A therapy programme was designed to measure unilateral neglect and to assess the effects of both a visual and a tactile cueing strategy on a variety of functional tasks. The patient's scanning, assessed in reading and cancellation tasks, improved spontaneously. Unilateral neglect was reduced in negotiating an obstacle course using a colour cueing strategy. Standard physiotherapy practice in the form of increased afferent input with repetitive motor practice (the tactile cueing strategy) did not improve the patient's spatial awareness or motor neglect. The implications for the understanding and the rehabilitation of unilateral neglect are discussed.

## INTRODUCTION

Unilateral neglect can be defined as the failure of brain damaged individuals to report, respond or orient to stimuli to the side of space contralateral to the lesion (Heilman & Valenstein, 1979). Neglect is more common and more severe following right brain damage (Albert, 1973; Kinsella & Ford, 1985; see D'Erme et al., this volume) and it may be observed in as many as 40% of all patients with right brain damage (Wade, Wood, & Langton Hewer, 1988).

The importance of perceptual dysfunctions such as neglect in rehabilitation is well documented. Studies have shown that despite severe handicap due to language dysfunction, left hemisphere lesioned patients without neglect make a better functional recovery than right hemisphere lesioned patients with neglect (Feigenson et al., 1977; Kinsella & Ford, 1980).

From a theoretical perspective, it is now generally accepted that neglect is not a sensory disorder, but rather a reflection of a higher level processing deficit. Posner, Walker, Friedrich, and Rafal (1984) proposed that neglect is due to a disorder of attention; this claim is based on the effects of cueing on neglect. They showed that patients with neglect could shift their attention to both the neglected and the unaffected side, providing they were cued to the same side as the target. If they were cued to attend to a location contralateral to their lesion, their ability to re-orient attention to a target on the opposite side declined dramatically. Riddoch and Humphreys (1983) further hypothesised that neglect was a deficit of automatic orienting; again their patients showed a marked decrease in neglect on line bisection tasks when cued to shift their attention voluntarily into their neglected field. Robertson (1989) supports this view; he suggests that visual neglect is closely associated with a non-lateralised general attentional deficit. In his study, there was a significant increase in right sided omissions when patients with neglect were cued to the left compared to controls. It would seem that neglect is not simply the omission of one side of space that is impaired in neglect. The above work suggests that theoretically motivated rehabilitation of neglect should include the use of cueing to direct the patient's attention to the affected side.

## EVALUATION OF NEGLECT

Traditionally, four specific types of task have been used to evaluate neglect: Copying and drawing tasks; line bisection; cancellation and visual search tasks. Although all these tasks measure the amount of information omitted from the neglected side, they vary in their ability to provide a detailed account of omissions on the neglected side. Furthermore, neglect does not appear to be a unitary phenomenon, but may have multiple components. Some studies have shown clear dissociations of neglect on different types of task; neglect on reading, but not on drawing (Lawson, 1962); motor neglect (an under-utilisation of the neglected arm) with normal performance on copying and drawing tasks (Laplane & Degos, 1983). A recent case report even documents a patient with right neglect on drawing tasks and left neglect when reading (Costello & Warrington, 1987). Are these diverse assessment procedures measuring the same underlying deficit? For the clinician, it is difficult to gauge the relevance of these pen and paper tasks to everyday skills. Often the real life difficulties experienced by patients with neglect remain, even though neglect on specific tasks such as cancellation appears resolved. A recent measurement tool, the Behavioral Inattention Test (BIT) designed by Wilson, Cockburn, and Halligan (1987), unlike the other tests used to measure neglect, relies on a range of measures closely related to everyday function, and may prove to be more clinically relevant.

## EFFECTIVENESS OF REHABILITATION IN NEGLECT

Four group studies have showed a consistent and positive training effect in patients with neglect. Weinberg et al. (1977) improved scanning skills in a series of reading-related tasks, which included the use of a scanning machine and a coloured anchor line as a cueing strategy. Weinberg et al. (1979) added a sensory awareness (non-visual) task and size estimation training as a spatial organisation task to their training regime, and again reported significant effects. Young et al. (1983) also reported benefits from this type of training, in addition they incorporated block design training as a non-visual task. Gordon et al. (1985) also found significant training effects using the procedures developed by Weinberg et al., however, these results were not maintained on follow-up four months later.

Although the results of these studies have tended to be positive, training effects have been measured on pen and paper tasks, not the patient's real life difficulties. Webster et al. (1984) in a multiple baseline single case design with three neglect patients measured the patients'' performance on a wheelchair obstacle course, based on the number of collisions with markers on the course. Training using the scanning machine developed by Weinberg et al. (1977) significantly reduced the patients' number of frontal, but not rear collisions on the wheelchair obstacle course. Gouvier et al. (1987) in a similar study on five patients, improved the patients' performance in wheelchair navigation and with the scanning machine, but not on a letter cancellation task. In summary there is evidence that neglect can be re-educated, however, training effects only tend to generalise to tasks that are similar to the training tasks. Even though patients may improve on the pen and paper tasks with training, neglect remains unchanged in their everyday function. There is good evidence that visual scanning is amenable to treatment, some treatment effects have also been obtained in more complex spatial tasks. It would seem that training strategies for neglect may be both cue and task dependent. Any therapy programme designed to rehabilitate neglect would need to consider these factors. It should incorporate training strategies that are specific and relevant to the tasks and cues that patients are likely to encounter in everyday life.

This single case study attempts to assess and remediate unilateral neglect in a series of tasks designed to simulate the functional difficulties experienced in everyday life by a right hemisphere lesioned patient.

## Method

The patient, J.D., was a 74 year old male who suffered a right cerebrovascular accident on 23 August 1988. J.D. presented with a dense left hemiplegia. There was no hemianopia, as tested by a visual field confrontation test. His range of eye movements and gaze appeared normal. Intensive physiotherapy commenced twice daily in September 1988.

At the time of this study, in November 1988, J.D. was emotionally labile with occasional periods of confusion, thought to be due to a recurrent urinary tract infection. Despite a moderate degree of motor recovery with minimal sensory deficit, J.D. did not attempt to use his left arm. He walked independently using a stick in his right hand, but was constantly bumping into obstacles on his left side; consequently J.D. experienced frequent falls. Functionally J.D. remained dependent, scoring 8/20 on the Barthel activities of daily living index (Mahoney & Barthel, 1965). This index scores individuals on ten everyday activities according to whether or not they are dependent, require assistance or are independent. J.D. scored zero points on the following activities: grooming; toilet use; dressing and bathing.

Clinically J.D. showed signs of unilateral neglect during grooming, dressing, changing his position and walking. The therapy team felt that unilateral neglect was impeding J.D.'s return to functional independence, even though his sensorimotor abilities continued to improve steadily.

Preliminary investigations revealed that J.D. did not have any gross intellectual impairment. His language function was intact. J.D.'s short term memory was mildly impaired; both his auditory and visual digit spans were five. His general knowledge, and recall of autobiographical and recent events was intact. Functionally he could not remember his telephone number or his daily treatment timetable. He did however remember the exercises taught in therapy from one session to the next.

Perceptually, J.D. was neither agnosic nor dyspraxic, though he did present with neglect and dressing apraxia. Neglect was evaluated by copying and drawing, cancellation, reading tasks and informal clinical observation. J.D. showed no evidence of neglect on copying shapes, drawing a man, a house or a clock. He did show neglect on three cancellation tasks: line bisection (Albert, 1973); letter cancellation

(Diller & Weinberg, 1977) and star cancellation (Bhavnani et al., 1983). Interestingly enough, J.D. only showed neglect consistently on the star cancellation task. He did not neglect the left side of space when reading, though he did make substitution errors (e.g. “rockstar” instead of “megastar”) and jumped from one line to another when scanning connected text. Clinically, J.D. showed signs of unilateral neglect. He did not shave the left side of his face; he did not use his left arm; he bumped into obstacles on his left side experiencing frequent falls and he reported that he was unable to read.

This study took place from November 1988 to March 1989, when further intervention was halted to J.D.’s increasing confusion resulting in an inability to comply with testing. Throughout this study, J.D. continued his normal physiotherapy programme consisting of twice daily sessions as an inpatient. He was discharged home in December 1988 and attended as an outpatient twice a week. Treatment focused on integrating his left side into the following activities: rolling; lying to sitting; sitting to standing and facilitating the return of normal movement in his left arm. In April 1989, J.D. was hospitalised on a psychogeriatric ward for investigation of confusion, aggression and incontinence. A diagnosis of multi-infarct dementia was made. However these symptoms were later attributed to the presence of a large bladder stone, which was surgically removed on 8 June 1989. His symptoms resolved, J.D. was discharged home in July 1989.

## Procedure

A multiple baseline procedure was used to monitor five tasks, designed to measure different aspects of J.D.’s neglect over a four month period. Four of these tasks were invented by the therapist to relate to three specific functional difficulties identified by the patient; these were: Problems in reading text, bumping into obstacles, and failure by J.D. to use his left arm spontaneously.

Task one was star cancellation. This was chosen as J.D. consistently showed neglect on this task during the assessment period. While seated in front of a large table (90cm x 122cm), J.D. was instructed to place a line through all the small stars printed on a sheet of paper placed centrally (Bhavnani et al., 1983). The therapist noted the number of stars omitted on either side of the page.

In task two, the therapist compiled 20 versions of a tabloid newspaper with an equal number of headlines on the left and right pages. J.D. was instructed to read aloud all the headlines in bold type that he could see on the page in front of him. The newspaper was placed centrally on the table. The therapist then noted the number of headlines read aloud correctly on either side of the page. It proved impossible to obtain 20 versions with exactly the same number of headlines.The numbers were therefore transformed into percentages so that comparisons could be made between the twenty versions.

Task three required that J.D. negotiate a pre-arranged circuit of the gym (Fig. 9.1). The circuit was designed so that ten obstacles were situated on either side for a total of twenty obstacles. The obstacles were placed at the same level approximately two feet apart. J.D. had one trial run through the circuit by following the therapist. He was then requested to follow the circuit on his own. The therapist then noted the number of obstacles that he bumped into on either side.

For task four, the therapist attempted to assess J.D.'s awareness of the position of his left arm in space. The therapist placed J.D.'s left arm randomly in ten previously determined set positions (Table 9.1). While blindfolded, J.D. was asked to "mirror" the position of the arm as moved by the examiner, with his right arm. For each position, J.D. was given a score of zero if no movement occurred; a score of one if part of the position was correctly assumed, and a score of two if the position was correct. For each trial, J.D. could obtain a maximum score of twenty points for each arm.

In task five, the therapist measured J.D.'s ability to use his left arm spontaneously in a bimanual task. The therapist placed twenty matchboxes, randomly spaced in equal numbers on either side of the large table. J.D. was instructed to place all the matchboxes in a shallow red box placed in the centre of the table under two conditions: Condition A—his choice (anyway he wished to do so); condition B—bilaterally (using the left hand on the left and the right hand on the right). The therapist noted the number of boxes collected by either hand and the time it took to finish the task. For each of the tasks, the therapist demonstrated the task then asked J.D. to explain in his own words what was required to ensure that he understood the task.

TABLE 9.1
Testing Positions for Spatial Awareness (Task Four)

| | | |
|---|---|---|
| 1. | Shoulder flexion | – 60 degrees |
| 2. | Shoulder abduction | – 60 degrees |
| 3. | Shoulder extension | – 30 degrees |
| 4. | Shoulder – neutral | – NO MOVEMENT |
| 5. | Elbow flexion with supination | – 120 degrees |
| 6. | Elbow extension | – 30 degrees |
| 7. | Elbow supination | – 3/4 R.O.M. |
| 8. | Full wrist extension with finger flexion | – 1/2 R.O.M. |
| 9. | Full wrist and finger extension | |
| 10. | Thumb opposition to the third digit | |

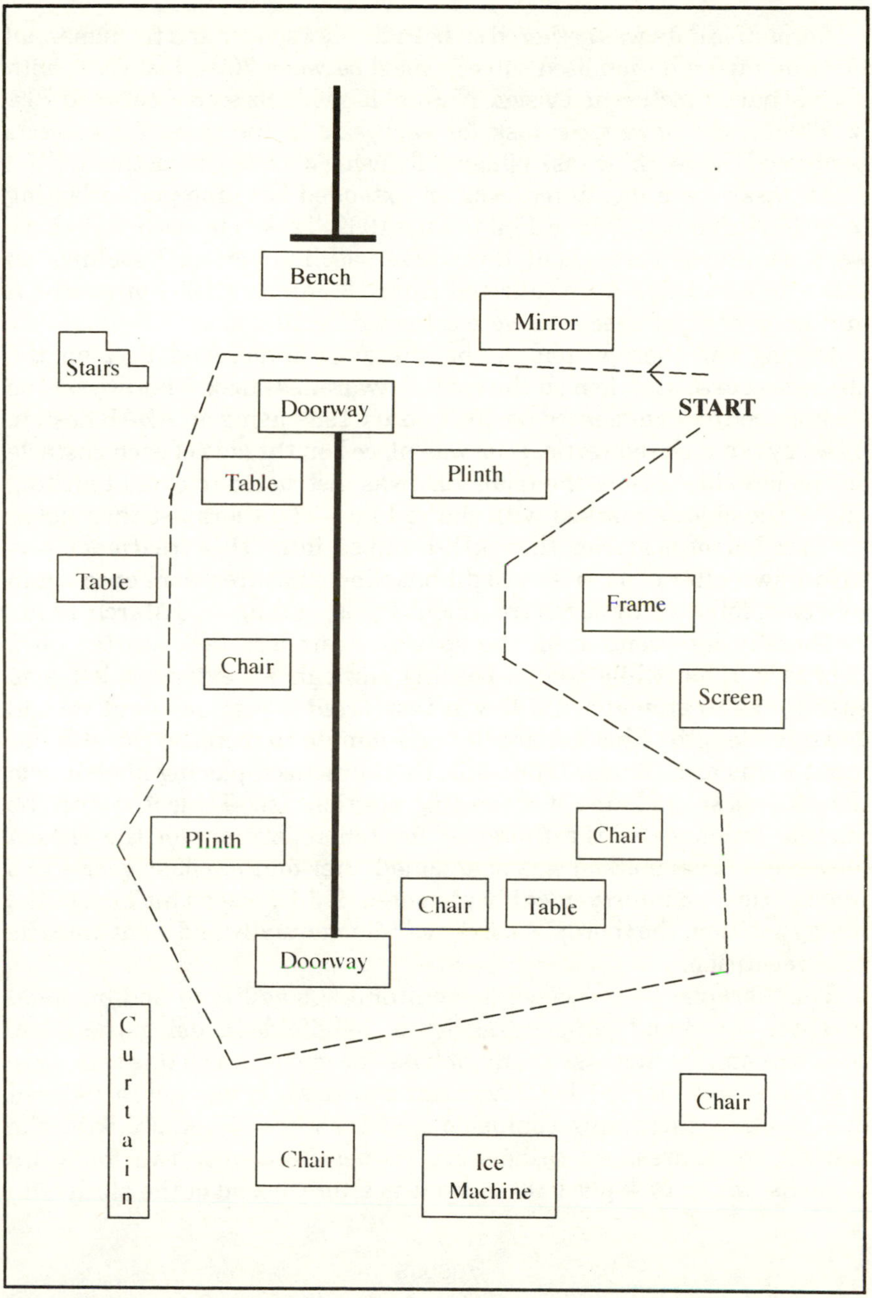


FIG. 9.1. Task 3: Obstacle Course.

Normative data was gathered on both the newspaper and the bimanual tasks on fifteen hospitalised subjects aged between 70 and 90 years with normal hand function and vision. Normal individuals scored between 70% to 90% on the newspaper task for each side of the page. All subjects performed the reaching task bimanually using a variety of methods.

All tasks were monitored over an extended baseline period lasting from 16 November 1988 to 17 January 1989. Tasks one, two, and three were monitored throughout the whole baseline period. Baselines on tasks four and five were collected from 13 January 1989 onwards. A minimum of eight baselines were collected on all tasks.

During the therapy phase, the therapist intervened first on the obstacle course and then on the spatial awareness task. Therapy on the obstacle course commenced on 20 January 1989 using an ABAB design. A two by ten inch red vertical cue was placed on the side of each obstacle on the left side. Before the trial, J.D. was instructed to avoid touching any of the objects marked with the red line. The therapist then noted the number of obstacles that J.D. bumped into. This treatment was withdrawn after eight trials. Eight baseline measures were once again collected, followed by seven treatment trials, ending on 8 March 1989.

Therapy intervention on the spatial awareness task started on 8 February 1989; while weight-bearing through an extended left arm sitting on a treatment bed, J.D. was instructed to vigorously rub up and down the length of his left arm for one minute to increase the afferent input to his arm (Musa, 1986). J.D. then practised placing his left arm in positions six and nine of the testing positions (see Table 9.1) with the manual guidance of the therapist for ten repetitions of the chosen movement. This method was abandoned after four sessions over a two week period, no improvement being noted. If J.D. placed his arm in the wrong position, the therapist corrected him manually and went onto the next repetition.

The therapist then decided to monitor J.D.'s ability to find his hand in space (i.e. hand pin-pointing while blindfolded), using the same positions and scoring system. Eight baseline measures on this task were completed on 8 March 1989. The treatment strategy was not introduced due to J.D.'s increasing confusion and inability to comply with the testing procedures. All tasks were re-measured over two follow-up sessions, which took place three months after the end of the study.

## Results

At the end of the first baseline period, only the baselines for tasks three, four, and five remained stable. Baseline readings for star cancellation (task one) were within normal limits. Linear regression analysis for left sided stimuli showed a gradual improvement in J.D.'s performance level from 19 December 1987 onwards (r=-0.77). His performance on right sided stimuli remained consistent throughout the testing period (r=-0.23). There was a significant difference between J.D.'s performance on this task pre and post discharge (Mann Whitney test, $P < 0.005$). From 5 March 1989, J.D. once again shows evidence of neglect corresponding to a deterioration in J.D.'s mental status (see Fig. 9.2).

Baselines for reading the headlines (task two) were also approaching normal limits ranging from 67% to 71% (normal range: 70% to 90% ; see Fig. 9.3). J.D. improved spontaneously in his ability to read headlines. Although there was a significant difference in his performance during the baseline period (Wilcoxen test, $P < 0.005$); from 13 January 1989, the difference between left and right stimuli was no longer significant.

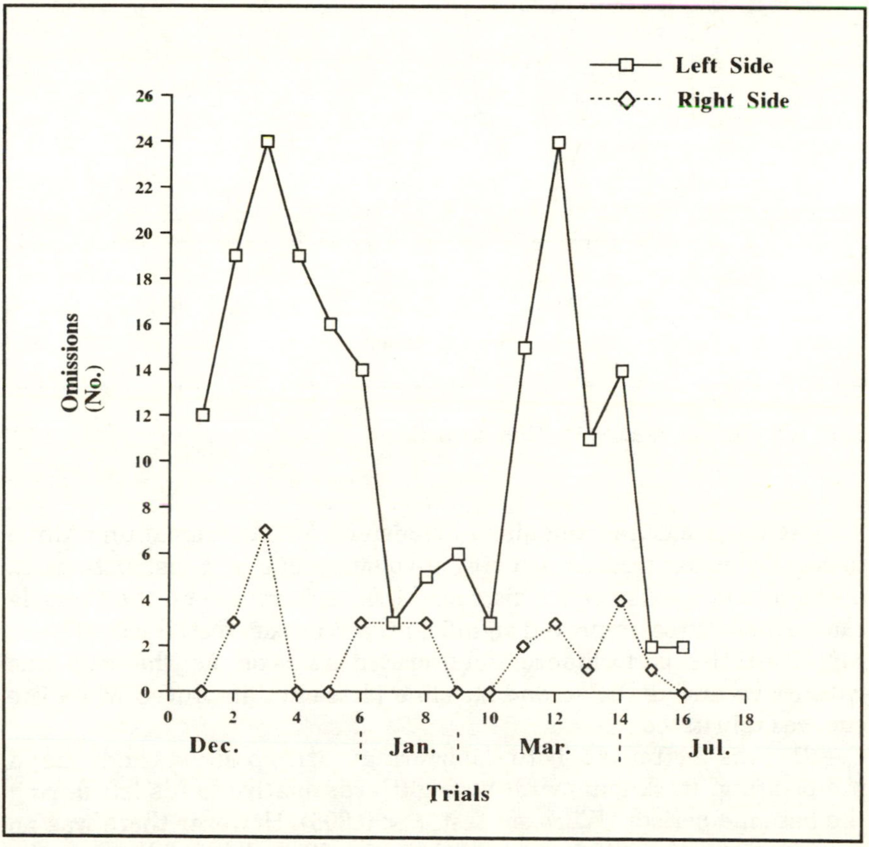


FIG. 9.2. Task 1: Star Cancellation.

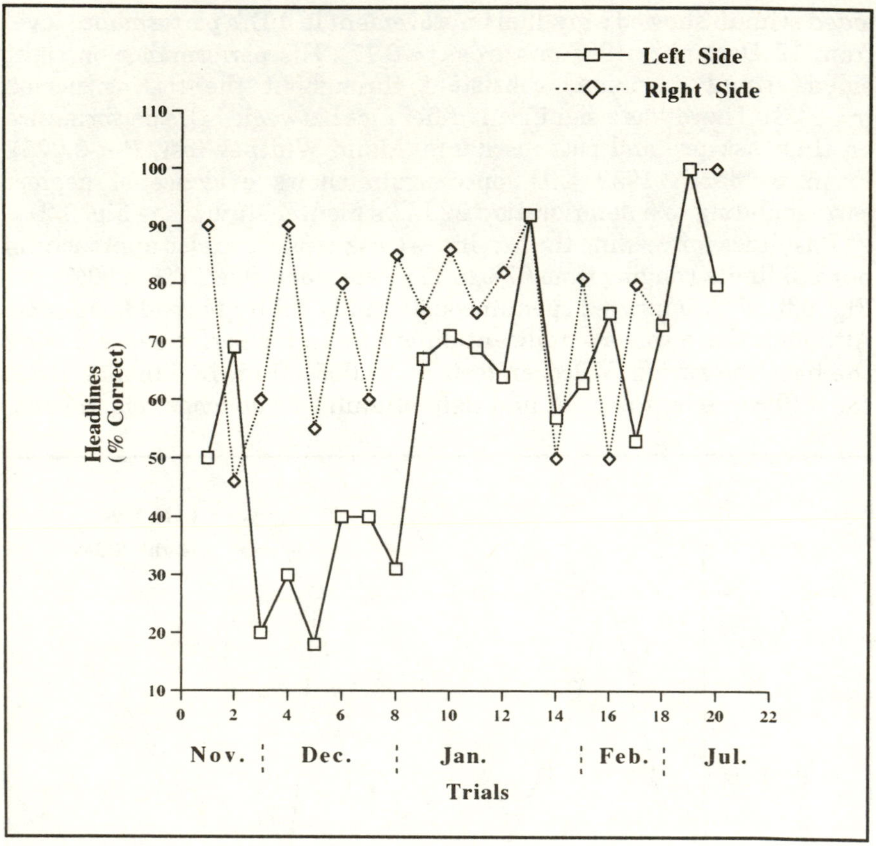


FIG. 9.3. Task 2: Reading the "Newspaper".

Baseline measures remained consistent for the remaining three tasks. Following treatment using a coloured cue and instructions to avoid objects marked with this cue, J.D.'s performance on the obstacle course (task three) improved significantly (Wilcoxen test, $P < 0.005$; see Fig. 9.4). His performance deteriorated as soon as the cue was withdrawn during the second baseline phase and improved when the cue was reinstated.

J.D. was better at both "mirroring" arm position and "hand pin-pointing" (task four) with his right arm relative to his left during the baseline periods (Wilcoxen test, $P < 0.005$). However there was no difference on the "mirroring" task with either hand following the implementation of the treatment strategy (Chi square test: last four baselines vs four treatment trials, $\chi^2$=0.29 (L); $\chi^2$=0.31 (R), $P$=NS ).

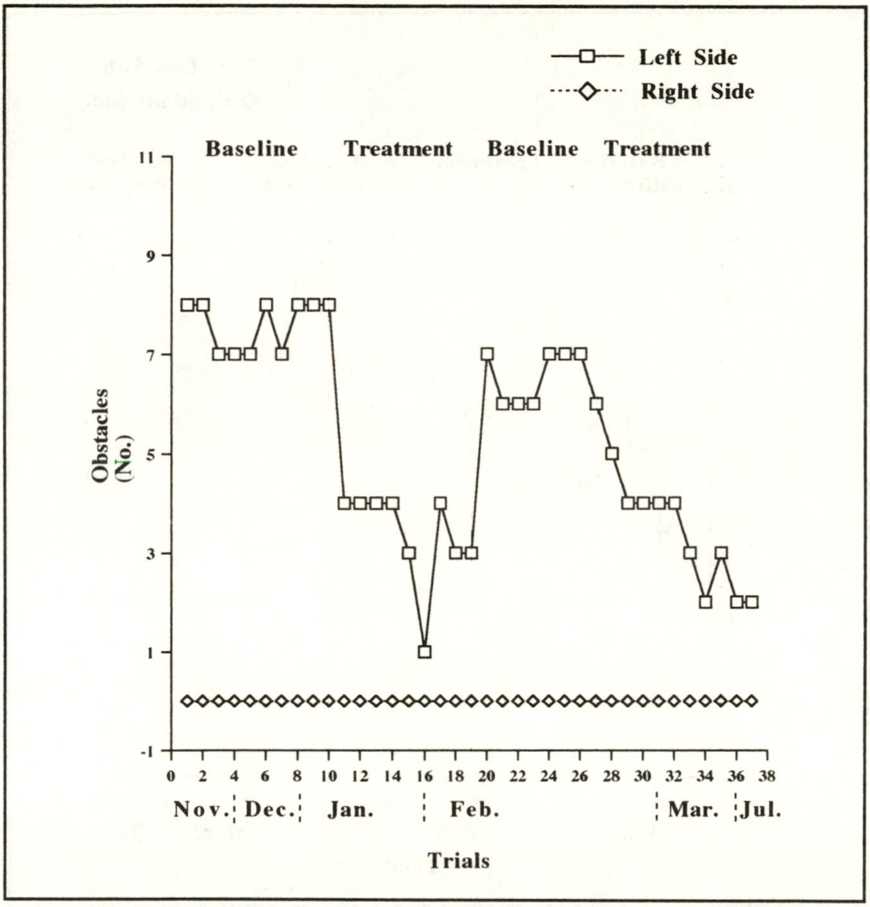


FIG. 9.4. Task 3: Obstacle Course.

Performance of the left arm relative to the right arm differed significantly on the reaching task (task five), as illustrated in Fig. 9.6 (Wilcoxen test, $P < 0.005$). There was a trend for J.D.'s left hand performance to improve (Linear regression analysis, r=-0.78), whilst his right hand performance, if anything, worsened (Linear regression analysis, r=0.60). Given the choice condition, J.D. always performed the task with his right hand except on three occasions. His average time for collecting ten boxes with his right hand was 32 seconds as compared to 3 minutes and 35 seconds with his left hand (see Fig. 9.6).

All measurements and tasks were retested three months later in July 1989. When reading connected text, J.D. was much faster and made

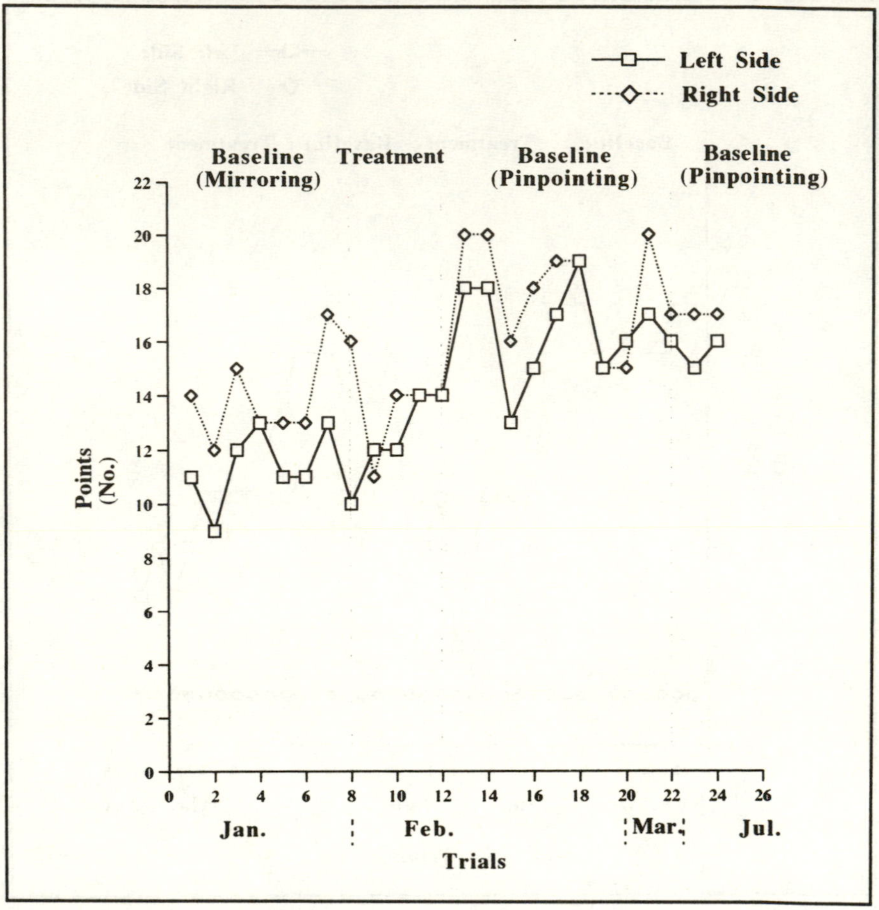


FIG. 9.5. Task 4: "Spatial Awareness".

fewer substitution and scanning errors (November 1988: 2 minutes and 50 seconds, 4 omissions; July 1989: 1 minute and 20 seconds, 2 omissions). He was now able to read the newspaper every day. His performance on copying, drawing, and cancellation tasks remained unchanged. From a sensorimotor viewpoint, he scored 16/20 on the Barthel Index as compared to 15/20 in February 1989; he continued to have difficulty in the following areas: Bladder control, feeding, dressing and washing. Clinically observed neglect was less obvious, but still present. He occasionally used his left arm to push himself into standing or to get in and out of bed. He did not use his left arm in manual tasks, but was often seen exercising his left arm spontaneously. The star

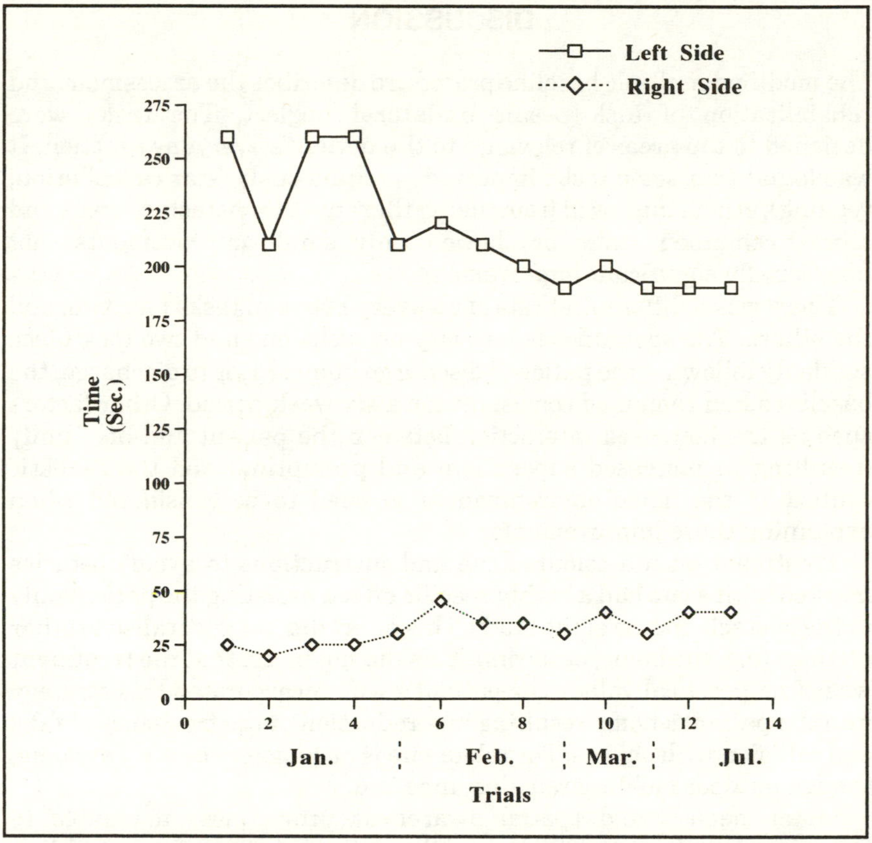


FIG. 9.6. Task 5: "Reaching".

cancellation and the reading tasks remained within normal limits (see Figs. 9.2 and 9.3). He maintained his performance on the obstacle course without cueing, only bumping into two out of ten obstacles (see Fig. 9.4). There was no change on the hand pin-pointing or reaching tasks (see Figs. 9.5 and 9.6).

In summary, spontaneous recovery occurred in the star cancellation and the reading tasks. There was a task-specific treatment effect on the obstacle course, which had no effect on the spatial awareness or reaching task. The second treatment strategy, a form of tactile cueing, did not decrease the patient's neglect on the spatial awareness, it also had no effect on the other tasks.

## DISCUSSION

The modified multiple baseline procedure describes the assessment and rehabilitation of task-specific unilateral neglect. The tasks were designed to tap areas of relevance to the patient's everyday function. It was found that some tasks improved spontaneously (star cancellation, reading), others improved from cueing therapy (the obstacle course), and others remained static or showed only small improvements (not functionally significant improvement).

There was a differential rate of recovery between tasks one, two, and the others. The spontaneous recovery on tasks one and two took place suddenly following the patient's discharge home. Prior to discharge, the baselines had remained consistent for a six week period. Other factors such as the increased interaction between the patient and his family (resulting in increased supervision and prompting) and the realistic context of the home environment also need to be considered when explaining these improvements.

Treatment with a coloured cue and instructions to avoid obstacles marked with a cue had a highly specific effect, assisting the patient only in the obstacle course of the study. This effect did not generalise to other settings (e.g. the home, outdoors). This did not mean that the treatment was of no practical value. The patient's wife incorporated this strategy into the patient's home resulting in a reduction of the frequency of falls and collision with objects. The colour cue is no longer necessary at home, though outdoor mobility remains impaired.

Motor neglect and spatial awareness proved less amenable to treatment in this study. The tactile cueing strategy (i.e. stroking) combined with weight bearing and repetitive motor practice did not produce any significant improvement. Perhaps the task chosen to assess spatial awareness is simply a reflection of the patient's joint proprioception sense and does not measure awareness in any broader sense. Effectively there appeared to be a dissociation between J.D.'s ability to mirror the position of his right arm with his left arm and his ability to find his right arm in space with the left. It would have been interesting to try a different form of afferent input (e.g. vibration) to measure its effect on both types of spatial awareness task. The lack of an effect on mirroring contradicts the assumption made by physiotherapists, that increasing afferent input and repetitive motor practice, as part of a therapy programme designed to encourage the patient to integrate his affected side into everyday activities, will decrease unilateral neglect. In addition to the trial of a specific tactile cueing strategy, J.D. had undergone 12 weeks of twice-daily physiotherapy sessions using the standard physiotherapy approach

(Davies, 1985). This approach, which encourages all individuals to direct the patient's attention to his affected side, did not seem to have any effect on the patient's unilateral neglect. Neither of the cueing strategies (i.e. visual or tactile) influenced J.D.'s ability to use his left arm spontaneously in the bimanual task. It would appear that colour cueing is only effective in reducing visual neglect. However, it is difficult with functional tasks to determine which aspects are visual, spatial or motor. Certainly the obstacle course would appear to have both visual and spatial components.

The data from this study supports the hypothesis that at least some aspects of the neglect syndrome reflect a disorder of attention, in accordance with the view of Riddoch and Humphreys (1983), that patients with neglect fail to allocate their attention automatically to the affected side. J.D. was able to process stimuli on his affected side when explicitly requested to do so, assisted by additional cueing strategies.

The differential rates of recovery in the different tasks, and the lack of carry-over of training across tasks, suggest a further and interesting possibility that neglect is not a unitary phenomenon (Costello & Warrington, 1987; Laplane & Degos, 1983). Laplane and Degos (1983) suggest that motor neglect is a result of a defect of movement reprogramming and organisation. If this were the case, it is unlikely that remediation aimed at improving scanning ability or reducing the number of bumping errors on an obstacle course will influence tasks relating to spatial awareness or the spontaneous use of the neglected arm. The type of cue required to redirect the patient's attention to his neglected side will differ depending on either the form of neglect or the task involved. Lack of generalisation across tasks and indeed to untrained tasks has been highlighted in several studies (Lawson, 1962; Webster et al., 1984; Weinberg et al., 1979). In the context of the present study, non-generalisation does not necessarily reflect a failure of the rehabilitation task *per se*, but could be due to the underlying nature of the disorder, which has multiple components.

Against this view of separate components in neglect, there is the possibility that the differential recovery and lack of training generalisation simply reflect the difficulty of the individual tasks. Harder tasks may take longer to recover than easy tasks; hence a homogeneous recovery pattern should not be expected. Though this task difficulty account cannot be overruled from the present data, it seems unlikely to be true. Most of the tasks are trivially easy for normal subjects, and there seems no reason *a priori* to think that reaching to pick up objects is more difficult than searching through a complex visual display. The task difficulty account may be discounted if, in further studies, other cases are found that show a different pattern of recovery.

This highlights the importance of replication and of case series in this field. In sum, this paper makes a first attempt at identifying different components of neglect in complex functional tasks with a view to their remediation. This single case study design shows that a therapy programme can be tailor-made to suit an individual's specific problems. Repeated baseline measuring enabled the therapist to document a differential rate of recovery in different tasks relating to unilateral neglect. The therapist was able to devise her own testing methods to assess neglect and evaluate the outcome of her treatment. These tasks remain relevant for the assessment of unilateral neglect and can easily be replicated in other single case studies of patients with unilateral neglect. This type of study can easily be incorporated into normal clinical practice as a useful tool for evaluation of outcome.

## REFERENCES

Albert, M.C. (1973). A simple test of visual neglect. *Neurology, 23,* 658-644.

Bhavnani, G., Cockburn, J., Whiting, S. & Lincoln, N. (1983). The reliability of the Rivermead Perceptual Assessment and implications for some commonly used assessments of perception. *British Journal of Occupational Therapy, 46,* 17-19.

Davies, P.M. (1985). *Steps to follow,* Heidelberg: Springer Verlag.

Costello, A. & Warrington, E.K. (1987). The dissociation of visuospatial neglect and neglect dyslexia. *Journal of Neurology, Neurosurgery and Psychiatry, 50,* 1110-1116.

Diller, L. & Weinberg, J.V. (1977). Hemi-inattention in rehabilitation: The evolution of a rational remediation programme in Weinstein, E.A. and Friedland, R.P. (Eds.), *Advances in Neurology, Vol. 18,* Raven Press.

Feigenson, J.S., McDowell, F.H., Meese, P., McCarthy, M.L., & Greenberg, S.D. (1977). Factors influencing outcome and length of stay in a stroke rehabilitation unit. Part I. *Stroke, 8,* 651-662

Gordon, W.A., Ruckdescel-Hibbard, M., Egelko, S., Diller, L., Scotzin-Shaver, M., Lieberman, A., & Ragnarsson, K. (1985). Perceptual remediation in patients with right brain damage. A comprehensive programme. *Archives of Physical Medicine and Rehabilitation, 66,* 353-359.

Gouvier, W., Bua, B., Blanton, P., & Urey, J. (1987). Behavioural changes following visual scanning training: observation of five cases. *International Journal of Clinical Neuropsychology, 9,* 74-80.

Heilman, K.M. & Valenstein, E. (1979). Mechanisms underlying hemispatial neglect. *Annals of Neurology, 5,* 166-170.

Kinsella, G. & Ford, B. (1985). Hemi-inattention and the recovery patterns of stroke patients. *International Journal of Rehabilitation Medicine, 7,* 102-106.

Laplane, D. & Degos, J. (1983). Motor neglect. *Journal of Neurology, Neurosurgery and Psychiatry, 46,* 152-158.

Lawson, I.R. (1962). Visual-spatial neglect in lesions of the right hemisphere. *Neurology, 12,* 23-33.

Mahoney, F.I. & Barthel, D. (1965). Functional evaluation: The Barthel Index. *Maryland State Medical Journal, 14,* 61-65.

Musa, I. (1986). The role of afferent input in the re-education of spasticity: An hypothesis. *Physiotherapy, 72,* 179-182.

Posner, M.I., Walker, J.A., Friedrich, F.J., & Rafal, R.D. (1984). Effects of parietal injury on covert orienting of visual attention. *Journal of Neuroscience, 4,* 1863-1874.

Riddoch, M.J. & Humphreys, G.W. (1983). The effect of cueing on unilateral visual neglect. *Neuropsychologica, 21,* 589-598.

Robertson, I. (1989). Anomalies in the lateralisation omissions in unilateral left neglect: Implications for an attentional theory of neglect. *Neuropsychologia, 27,* 217-222.

Wade, D.T., Wood, V.A., & Langton Hewer, R. (1988). Recovery of cognitive function soon after stroke: a study of visual neglect, attention span and verbal recall. *Journal of Neurology, Neurosurgery and Psychiatry, 51,* 10-13.

Webster, J., Jones, S., Blanton, P., Gross, R., Beissel, G., & Wofford, J. (1984). Visual scanning training with stroke patients. *Behaviour Therapy, 15,* 129-143.

Weinberg, J., Diller, L., Gordon, W.A., Gerstman, L.J., Lieberman, A., Lakin, P., Hodges, G., & Ezrachi, O. (1977). Visual scanning training effect on reading related tasks in acquired right brain damage. *Archives of Physical Medicine and Rehabilitation, 58,* 479-482.

Weinberg, J., Diller, L., Gordon W.A., Gerstman, L.J., Lieberman, A., Lakin, P., Hodges, G., & Ezrachi, O. (1979). Training sensory awareness and spatial organisation in people with right brain damage. *Archives of Physical Medicine and Rehabilitation, 60,* 491-494.

Wilson, B., Cockburn, J., & Halligan, P. (1987). Development of a behavioural test of visuospatial neglect. *Archives of Physical Medicine and Rehabilitation, 68,* 98-102.

Young, G.C., Collins, D., & Hren, M. (1983). Effect of pairing scanning training with block design training in the remediation of perceptual problems in left hemiplegics. *Journal of Clinical Psychology, 5,* 201-212.

CHAPTER TEN

# Early Ipsilateral Orienting of Attention in Patients with Contralateral Neglect

Patrizia D'Erme, Guido Gainotti, and Paolo Bartolomeo
*Institute of Neurology of the Catholic University, Rome, Italy*

Ian Robertson
*MRC Applied Psychology Unit, Cambridge, UK*

## ABSTRACT

Three experiments were carried out to investigate whether early orienting of attention to the side of space ipsilateral to the lesion could mediate unilateral spatial neglect.

The first was designed to evaluate forms of lateral orienting of attention so severe as to provoke an overt gaze deviation; this was achieved by assessing systematically the phenomenon of "magnetic gaze attraction".

The second investigation evaluated milder forms of automatic orienting of attention by analysing the temporal sequence followed by patients in identifying the pictures of an overlapping figures task: A tendency to initiate the scanning of the pattern from the half space ipsilateral to the lesion was predicted in neglect patients.

The third investigation tested whether the ipsilateral orienting of attention would be observed also in conditions requiring central eye fixation. Simple reaction times were recorded in contrasting conditions with and without positional expectancy square "boxes": The ipsilesional box was predicted to attract the patients' attention, increasing reaction times to contralesional targets.

The results showed that: 1. right brain-damaged patients tend automatically to orient attention toward the ipsilesional half space more than left brain-damaged patients; 2. this tendency is tightly linked to the presence of behavioural manifestations of neglect; 3. the early rightwards orienting of attention can be observed both in tasks requiring central eye fixation and in tasks where no such constraint is given, provided that stimuli (not necessarily targets) coexist on both sides of space.

Our data are consistent with the hypothesis viewing unilateral spatial neglect as a multi-component syndrome with one characteristic being early orienting of attention toward the half space ipsilateral to the lesion.

## INTRODUCTION

The neuropsychological literature on unilateral spatial neglect has recently emphasised the pre-eminent role of the attentional mechanisms in the syndrome. For example, Posner (1980) and Posner et al., (1982) analysed the process of moving attention and distinguished three different mental operations involved in covert orienting of attention: 1. disengaging from the current focus; 2. moving toward the target and 3. engaging the novel target (Posner et al., 1984).

These authors also suggested that parietal lobe injuries specifically affect the ability to disengage attention automatically from its previous focus, resulting in the phenomenon of visual extinction (i.e. failure to report a previously perceived stimulus when another stimulus is simultaneously applied elsewhere in the visual field).

Clinical observations and neuropsychological data (De Renzi et al., 1989; Karnath, 1988; Mark et al., 1988; Marshall & Halligan, 1989) suggest, however, that the difficulty in disengaging attention from its previous focus could be but one aspect of a more complex disturbance characterised by an early automatic orienting of attention toward the half of space ipsilateral to the lesion.

To verify this hypothesis we designed three neuropsychological investigations, aiming to take into account both severe and subtle forms of automatic orienting of attention to the ipsilesional side in patients with and without unilateral spatial neglect.

A clinical phenomenon which seems to express a severe form of automatic sidewards orienting of attention is that of "magnetic gaze attraction" described by Cohn (1972) in patients with homonymous hemianopia, and considered as an "oculomotor analog of extinction" (Friedland & Weinstein, 1977). This phenomenon, which is usually observed while assessing the visual field of a patient with the confrontation technique, involves a tendency to spontaneously orient the gaze toward the side ipsilateral to the brain lesion as soon as the examiner stretches out her/his arms and prior to the actual administration of the stimuli.

In order to study the relationship between magnetic gaze attraction and unilateral spatial neglect, we assessed systematically, in our first investigation, the incidence of this phenomenon in unselected groups of right and left brain-damaged patients with and without evidence of neglect (Gainotti et al., 1991).

A second clinical phenomenon possibly indicative of milder forms of early ipsilateral orienting is the scanning pattern shown by brain-damaged patients while identifying pictures represented in an overlapping figures test. If patients tend to orient first toward stimuli lying in one half of space, they should identify first pictures placed in that part of the composite diagram and afterwards pictures on the opposite side of the display. An analysis of the temporal sequence followed by right and left brain-damaged patients while identifying the items of an overlapping figures test was therefore performed in our second investigation (Gainotti et al., 1991).

As the previous two investigations analysed situations likely involving eye movements, we aimed to check if the phenomenon of ipsilateral orienting could also be observed in right and left brain-damaged patients in conditions requiring only covert orienting of attention. For this purpose we examined reaction time performance to lateralised visual stimuli under different conditions—with and without square boxes on both sides of a computer screen. We assumed that the ipsilesional box would automatically attract the patient's attention, thus increasing the reaction times to contralateral stimuli and decreasing those to ipsilateral stimuli.

The general hypothesis was: If automatic orienting of attention toward the ipsilateral half of space is an important component of unilateral spatial neglect, then a strong relationship should exist between presence and severity of the lateral orienting bias and presence and severity of unilateral spatial neglect (D'Erme et al., 1992).

## EXPERIMENT 1

This investigation was designed to analyse the relationship between magnetic gaze attraction and unilateral spatial neglect, particularly taking into account two problems: 1. the relationship between magnetic gaze attraction and laterality of lesion, to see whether magnetic gaze attraction prevails in right brain-damaged patients, as unilateral spatial neglect usually does (Brain, 1941; Gainotti et al., 1972; Heilman et al., 1985); 2. the relation between magnetic gaze attraction, homonymous hemianopia, visual extinction and unilateral spatial neglect.

Our prediction was that if the magnetic gaze attraction is part of the unilateral spatial neglect syndrome, then it should clearly prevail in right brain-damaged patients with severe manifestations of hemi-neglect.

## Method

### *Subjects*

Fifty-three right brain-damaged and thirty-three left brain-damaged patients participated. There was no significant difference between the groups as regards age and mean educational level. The groups were also well matched with respect to aetiology and intra-hemispheric locus of lesion.

### *Testing procedures*

Four aspects of the patients' behaviour were considered:

1. the presence of a visual field defect, assessed by means of a perimetric examination;
2. the presence and severity of unilateral spatial neglect, assessed by means of a standard battery comprising tests of line cancellation (Albert, 1973), line bisection (D'Erme et al., 1987), copying drawings (Gainotti et al., 1989), identification of overlapping figures and searching for animals on a large board (Gainotti et al., 1986).
3. the incidence and severity of visual extinction;
4. the presence of a magnetic gaze attraction.

For each test, normative data obtained with control subjects allowed us to distinguish normal from pathological performance. Within the latter, arbitrary cut-off points were drawn in order to distinguish, respectively, a "severe" and a "mild to moderate" form of unilateral spatial neglect (Gainotti et al., 1991).

To detect the presence of visual extinction and magnetic gaze attraction toward the unaffected field, patients were submitted to a visual field assessment with the confrontation technique. Patients were seated at a distance of about one metre from the confronting examiner who, after having stretched out her/his arms, moved her/his fingers either in one hemifield or in both hemifields simultaneously, according to a previously randomised pattern. The sequence consisted of 36 stimuli distributed as follows: 9 right and 9 left single stimuli, 18 double simultaneous stimulations, administered in the upper or lower quadrant of each hemifield and on the horizontal midline.

Patients were defined as affected by a severe form of visual extinction when more than 60% of left sided stimuli were omitted on double simultaneous stimulation. Rates of extinction ranging from 16% to 60% were considered as mild. Extinction was obviously also found in patients with a visual field defect (quadrantanopia or hemianopia), together with a higher number of omissions of single stimuli applied to the affected field.

Patients were considered as presenting with magnetic gaze attraction when the examiner detected the consistent occurrence of spontaneous, automatic shifts of the patient's eyes toward the side ipsilateral to the lesion, triggered by the stretching of the examiner's hands (prior to the administration of the stimulus).

## Results

The phenomenon of magnetic gaze attraction was observed in 12 right brain-damaged patients out of 53 (23%) but only in one left brain-damaged patient out of 33 (3%). This difference was highly significant ($\chi^2$=6.09; $P < 0.02$). Magnetic gaze attraction was brief and reversible in most patients (10 right and 1 left), but strong and persistent in 2 right brain-damaged patients, preventing them from correctly performing the confrontation test and the perimetric assessment of the visual field. Therefore these two patients were not considered in the statistical analysis concerning visual field defect and visual extinction.

The incidence of visual field defect was very similar in right brain-damaged patients (17 out of 51) and in left brain-damaged patients (11 out of 33).

In contrast, we observed a significantly higher incidence of unilateral spatial neglect in right brain-damaged than in left brain-damaged patients: 40 right brain-damaged patients out of 53 (75%), as opposed to 6 left brain-damaged patients out of 33 (18%), showed evidence of contralateral neglect ($\chi^2$=26.83; $P < 0.001$).

Finally, the phenomenon of visual extinction was observed significantly more often in right brain-damaged than left brain-damaged patients ($\chi^2$=8.39; $P < 0.004$) and this difference persisted even when patients with visual field defect were excluded from the analysis ($\chi^2$=13.1; $P < 0.001$).

In order to analyse the relationships between magnetic gaze attraction, unilateral spatial neglect and visual extinction, we distinguished two levels of severity of neglect (i.e. mild to moderate vs. severe) and two levels of visual extinction, according to the criteria mentioned in the Method. We observed that magnetic gaze attraction is almost always found in patients with severe unilateral spatial neglect and consistent visual extinction. Less striking is the link between magnetic gaze attraction and visual field defect because 7 out of 10 right brain-damaged patients with magnetic gaze attraction showed no evidence of homonymous hemianopia or quadrantanopia.

Taken together, these results suggest that magnetic gaze attraction and unilateral spatial neglect are highly interconnected. Both are, indeed, significantly more frequent in right than in left brain-damaged patients and magnetic gaze attraction is only observed in patients with severe neglect for the contralateral half of space.

## EXPERIMENT 2

Our second investigation assessed whether milder forms of lateral orienting of attention could be detected in patients with less striking manifestations of neglect, by analysing their scanning pattern when required to identify overlapping figures (Gainotti et al., 1986).

We hypothesised that automatic ipsilateral orienting should occur in neglect patients when presented with the bilaterally placed figures in the test. Consequently, right brain-damaged patients, who show a higher incidence of neglect, should be more likely than left brain-damaged patients to identify first figures lying on the half of space ipsilateral to their lesion. This phenomenon should be most apparent in patients with severe unilateral spatial neglect, but it should also be associated with milder forms of neglect.

### Method

#### *Subjects*

Thirty-five non brain-damaged control subjects, 88 right and 64 left brain-damaged patients were examined. There was no difference between the three groups with regards to age and educational level; aetiology and site of lesion were also well matched in the two patient groups.

#### *Testing procedures*

In the overlapping figures test, subjects were requested to recognise the overlapping figures of four common objects (two on the right and two on the left), drawn on a card (14cms x 21cms) and overlapping a fifth centrally located figure (see Fig. 10.1). Subjects were presented with a total of five cards (plus a practice one) one at a time and were instructed to recognise the figures by pointing to identical figures interspersed with distractors vertically aligned on a multiple choice card placed below the stimulus pattern.

We analysed three aspects of the subjects' behaviour:

1. The tendency to initiate the scanning of the overlapping figures from the ipsilesional side was evaluated by counting the number of first recognitions made on the right side in each of the five cards.

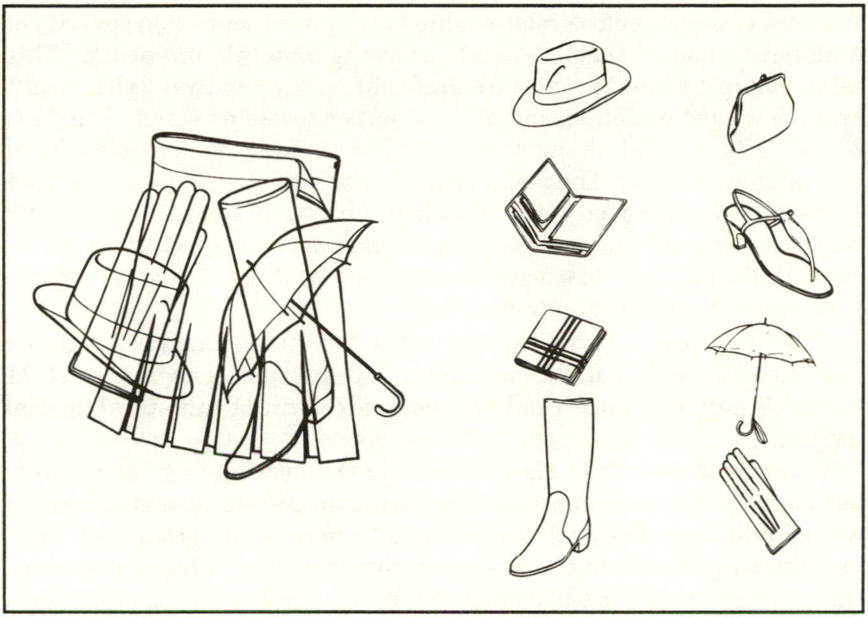

FIG. 10.1. An item from the "Overlapping Figures" test. In testing sessions the eight alternatives were vertically aligned just below the stimulus pattern.

2. Unilateral spatial neglect was recorded either when one or more figures were omitted on the side contralateral to the lesion (in the absence of ipsilateral omissions), or when at least double the figures were omitted on the contralateral than on the ipsilateral side (Gainotti et al., 1986).

3. Severe unilateral spatial neglect, exhibited by patients who were unable to identify contralesional figures in at least three out of five cards, was distinguished from mild to moderate unilateral spatial neglect, shown by patients who identified the majority of figures on both sides of space.

## Results

Right brain-damaged patients consistently analysed the stimulus pattern by identifying first figures lying on the right side of space, their mean score being 3.4. This behaviour significantly differs from that observed in control subjects and in left brain-damaged patients; both groups showed, in fact, a marked tendency to make their first choice on the left side of space and did not differ significantly from each other, their respective mean scores being 1.4 and 1.01.

There was also a close relationship between presence and severity of unilateral spatial neglect and early ipsilateral orienting. This relationship however was significant only within the right brain-damaged patients, where 51 subjects showed no signs of neglect, 26 subjects a mild to moderate neglect and 11 a severe form of contralateral neglect. The mean value for the first choice scores was 2.64 for right brain-damaged patients without unilateral spatial neglect, 3.92 for those with mild to moderate unilateral spatial neglect and 4.72 for right brain-damaged patients with severe unilateral spatial neglect (One-way ANOVA: $F=31.06$; $P < 0.001$).

The corresponding values within the left brain-damaged patients were 1.05 for the 57 patients without unilateral spatial neglect and 0.71 for the 7 patients with a mild to moderate form of unilateral spatial neglect.

In terms of their first choice scores in the overlapping figures test, left brain-damaged patients with and without unilateral spatial neglect were undistinguishable from controls, whereas all groups of right brain-damaged patients made more right-half first choice responses than the controls (post-hoc statistics by non-orthogonal comparisons, respectively: $F_1=21.00$, $F_2=61.78$, $F_3=60.29$; $P < 0.01$).

## Discussion

The first two experiments strongly suggest that a bias in early ipsilateral orienting contributes to both dramatic and less severe forms of unilateral spatial neglect.

In Experiment 1 the phenomenon of magnetic gaze attraction toward the unaffected field occurred far more frequently in right than in left brain-damaged patients, and was more strongly associated with severe hemi-neglect than with homonymous hemianopia. Furthermore, the occurrence of magnetic gaze attraction before the actual presentation of a stimulus shows that hemi-neglect cannot be reduced to a difficulty in disengaging attention from its previous target.

Experiment 2 used a subtler index of the ipsilateral orienting bias, but again suggested that the bias is shared by right brain-damaged patients with severe and milder forms of unilateral spatial neglect. These patients tend to identify first figures lying on the right side of the pattern, whereas the opposite trend is shown by left brain-damaged patients and control subjects. A rightwards orienting tendency was also found in right brain-damaged patients without clinical signs of unilateral spatial neglect, who were able to explore thoroughly both sides of the pattern. This finding confirms that the observed pattern of scanning is not an artifact due to the inability to analyse the contralesional side of the composite diagram and it might thus represent a subtle index of subclinical forms of unilateral spatial neglect.

## EXPERIMENT 3

Experiment 3 examined simple reaction times to peripheral targets under conditions where lateralised position expectancy boxes either were or were not present. This test aimed to be more sensitive to covert attentional processes than the previous tests. In one experimental condition, prior to the occurrence of each target, patients were given a cue indicating the likely location of the target. We expected reaction times of neglect patients to contralesional stimuli to be slowed by cueing attention to the side ipsilateral to the lesion (cf. Posner et al., 1984). According to our prediction, this effect should also be elicited by the peripheral boxes in conditions without lateralised cueing. In patients with left-sided neglect, the right-sided of the two simultaneously appearing boxes is expected to summon attention, thus mimicking the effect of an invalid cue on reaction times to left targets. In addition, if the ipsilateral box captures the patient's attention, a facilitatory effect may be expected for targets appearing on that side.

### Method

#### *Subjects*

Five right brain-damaged patients with moderate to severe unilateral spatial neglect, five right brain-damaged patients with mild neglect and five left brain-damaged patients without signs of neglect participated. The three groups of patients did not differ with regards to age, educational level and severity of lesion. The groups were also well matched on aetiology and intrahemispheric site of lesion. Either confrontation or perimetric visual field assessment was carried out for all patients.

The presence and severity of unilateral spatial neglect was assessed by means of a battery of tests including: Letter cancellation, line cancellation (Albert, 1973), and a test of copying a drawing consisting of many horizontally arrayed elements (Gainotti et al., 1989). The occurrence of visual extinction to double simultaneous stimulation was also taken into account in the final evaluation. In order to distinguish mild from moderate to severe forms of unilateral spatial neglect, we adopted as a cut-off score a frequency of left-sided omissions of 20% of the overall items of each test (the cut-off was raised to 50% as regards visual extinctions). No left brain-damaged patient showed signs of unilateral spatial neglect.

All patients used their preferred hand to respond, with the exception of three left brain-damaged patients who used their left hand, due to right-sided motor impairment.

*Procedure*

Subjects were seated in a dimly illuminated room, facing a computer screen. They were asked to fix their gaze on a black dot drawn on the centre of the screen throughout the block of trials. Eye fixation was monitored by an experimenter standing behind the computer, and trials in which an eye deviation was observed were not considered in the successive analysis.

Subjects were asked to press the spacebar of the keyboard as soon as they detected the target, which consisted of a black asterisk (see Fig. 10.2) subtending 1.29 x 0.96 degrees of visual angle, appearing 7.86 degrees to the left or right of the fixation point.

In two of the experimental conditions the target was preceded by a cue consisting of a black ellipse of 0.65 x 0.80 degrees of visual angle. In two further conditions, the target (or cue and target) appeared within one of two empty boxes (one right and one left) subtending 1.92 x 1.30 degrees of visual angle. In addition, a number of catch trials were given, where a small dot appeared at the usual location of the target.

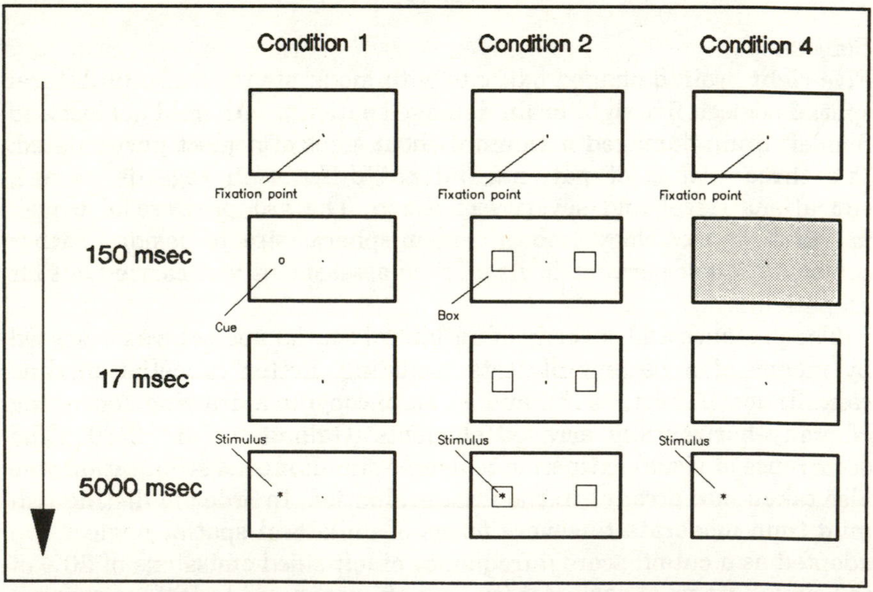


FIG. 10.2. Scheme of the conditions of Experiment 3 (see text for details).

Prior to each experiment subjects were given a minimum of ten practice trials.

*Experimental Conditions (see Fig. 10.2)*

*Condition 1. Cues but no boxes.* In this condition cues and targets appeared unbounded by boxes. A cue appeared for 150msec (left or right), followed by an interval of 17msec after which the target appeared either in the same or in the contralateral location (on valid and invalid trials). The target remained either until the subject pressed the spacebar, or for a maximum of 5000msec, if no response was made. Response latencies were recorded by the computer. There were a total of 80 trials, the target being 40 on the left and 40 on the right (32 valid, 8 invalid trials).

Trials were presented in four blocks of twenty-four each, with a brief rest for subjects between each block. The order of presentation of trials was randomised by the computer prior to each block in all conditions.

*Condition 2. Boxes but no cue.* In this condition, only the target appeared, bounded within either of the two boxes, 167msec after their appearance. As in the first condition, the boxes remained on the screen as long as the target also remained there. Twenty trials (ten left, ten right), were given (plus four catch trials).

*Condition 3.* This was a combination of the previous two. However, results obtained in this condition will not be taken into account here. (see D'Erme et al., 1992).

*Condition 4. No boxes, no lateralised cue.* Here, the trial began with the darkening of the white area of the screen for 150msec, followed by a gap of 17msec and then by the appearance of the target. The number and distribution of trials were the same as in condition 2.

## Results

Median reaction times (in msec) were calculated for each subject in each condition. All responses with reaction times either less than 100msec or more than 4500msec were excluded from the analysis. All the patients who entered the study performed the catch trials correctly and did not exceed the established limit of 10% errors. The means of median reaction times for each patient group in each condition are reported in Table 10.1.

It must be noted that the different experimental conditions do not appear intrinsically to affect performances of each group of patients in responding to ipsilesional targets, thus showing the substantial similarity of the task demands.

TABLE 10.1
Mean Values of Median Reaction Times of Right Brain-damaged Patients with Severe (RSN) and Mild Neglect (RMN) and of Left Brain-damaged Patients (LBD) in Each Experimental Condition
(ipsi = ipsilesional, cont = contralesional target)

| | *Condition 1* (*no boxes*) | | | | *Condition 2* (*boxes, no cue*) | | *Condition 4* (*no boxes, no cue*) | |
|---|---|---|---|---|---|---|---|---|
| | *valid cue* | | *invalid cue* | | | | | |
| | *ipsi* | *cont* | *ipsi* | *cont* | *ipsi* | *cont* | *ipsi* | *cont* |
| RSN | 555.4 | 850.2 | 638.2 | 1415.6 | 583.8 | 2007.2 | 621.4 | 1433.8 |
| | (261.9) | (440.2) | (242.7) | (804.8) | (176.1) | (757.3) | (142.4) | (897.1) |
| RMN | 531.4 | 656.4 | 625.0 | 759.2 | 525.0 | 593.8 | 601.2 | 670.2 |
| | (179.7) | (208.9) | (188.6) | (312.9) | (116.9) | (161.9) | (116.3) | (141.9) |
| LBD | 402.6 | 398.8 | 405.4 | 411.4 | 428.6 | 436.2 | 422.8 | 447.2 |
| | (102.6) | (91.5) | (121.2) | (125.4) | (126.1) | (131.9) | (101.9) | (113.2) |

To verify whether in right brain-damaged patients with neglect, the simultaneous appearance of two boxes would produce a slowing of reaction times to left targets analogous to that produced by a right-sided (invalid) cue, we compared results of condition 1 (lateralised cue, no boxes) and condition 2 (boxes, no cue).

An analysis of variance was carried out contrasting data on the invalid cue trials of condition 1 and on condition 2. The results are reported in Table 10.2 and were subjected to *post hoc* comparisons by means of Duncan's Multiple-Range Test. The right-sided severe neglect group differs significantly both from right-sided mild neglect and left brain-damaged groups ($P < 0.01$). This effect is not due to responses to ipsilesional targets, which do not differ significantly in the three groups; on the contrary, when contralesional targets are considered, right-sided

TABLE 10.2
Statistical Analysis on Median Reaction Times of Left Brain-damaged (LBD) and Right Brain-damaged Patients with Moderate-severe (RSN) and Mild (RMN) Neglect, in Condition 1 (Invalid Cue) and Condition 2

| *ANOVA* | F | (df) | *P* |
|---|---|---|---|
| GROUP (RSN, RMN, LBD) | 11.413 | (2) | .002 |
| EXPERIMENT (1 invalid/2) | .464 | (1) | n.s. |
| Group – Experiment | 2.228 | (2) | .149 (n.s.) |
| TARGET SIDE (Left/Right) | 23.269 | (1) | < .001 |
| Group – Target side | 17.542 | (2) | < .001 |
| Experiment – Target side | 2.232 | (1) | .158 (n.s.) |
| Group – Experiment – Target side | 3.048 | (2) | .084 |

severe neglect patients show slower reaction times than right-sided mild neglect and left brain-damaged patients ($P < 0.01$). Right-sided severe neglect patients exhibit "costs" in responding to contralesional as compared to ipsilesional targets in both experimental conditions.

Although the magnitude of the slowing of reaction times to left targets is greater in the presence of the boxes than after the appearance of a right-sided cue, the difference between the two conditions is not statistically significant.

The slowing of reaction times to contralesional, as compared to ipsilesional targets observed in right-sided severe neglect patients in the valid cue trials of condition 1, was not significant at the statistical control (ANOVA performed on results of the four conditions, *post hoc* analysis by means of Duncan's Multiple-Range test). Our results thus suggest that the phenomenon described by Posner et al. (1984) as an "extinction-like" reaction time pattern (i.e. the effect of ipsilateral cues in slowing responses to contralateral targets) can be elicited either by a transient invalid cue or by two permanent boxes of which no processing is explicitly requested in order to perform the task correctly.

To test the prediction of an advantage for responses to ipsilateral targets bounded in boxes as compared to targets appearing on the blank hemispace, the results of condition 2 and 4 were contrasted. Although the reaction times of right-sided severe neglect patients tended to be faster when right-sided targets appeared within boxes than when they appeared on the blank screen (condition 4), this difference was not statistically significant. Right-sided mild neglect and left brain-damaged patients did not show similar trends.

We might therefore assume that early ipsilateral orienting of attention dramatically hampers the reorienting of attention toward the opposite side. Responses to ipsilateral targets show a less pronounced benefit from attention being already engaged on that side.

## Discussion

The results of Experiment 3 show that, in simple reaction time tasks to lateralised visual stimuli, the simultaneous presence of boxes on each side of the computer screen induces early rightwards orienting in right brain-damaged patients with severe unilateral spatial neglect. However, right-sided mild neglect patients unexpectedly did not share this behaviour with right-sided severe neglect patients, their performance being substantially similar to that of the left brain-damaged patients.

This discrepancy between the results of Experiment 2 and Experiment 3 as regards right-sided mild neglect patients could be due to the different kinds of attentional orienting elicited by the two experimental situations. In Experiment 2 no constraints were put on the patient's spatial exploration, so that the natural tendencies to orient automatically first to the right side of the figures could fully be appreciated. In Experiment 3, only part of these tendencies could be evaluated, as patients were requested to maintain central eye fixation. It is therefore likely that, in this condition, the effect of the boxes could be fully appreciated only in patients with marked orienting tendencies and severe contralateral neglect. The possibility of a major salience of the left side targets of Experiment 3 as compared to those of Experiment 2 should also be taken into account to explain the observed discrepancy.

Our results also bear methodological implications for the construction of reaction time tests in neglect patients. Far from being facilitated, right brain-damaged patients with severe neglect are likely to be further hampered in responding to left-sided targets by the presence of positional expectancy boxes.

## GENERAL DISCUSSION

The results of our investigations show that one of the major aspects that characterises the behaviour of patients with unilateral spatial neglect is an early orientation of attention toward the side of space ipsilateral to the brain lesion. This attentional bias significantly hinders the apprehension of information from the contralesional hemispace, both in tasks requiring central eye fixation (Experiment 3) and in tasks where overt orienting of attention is allowed (Experiment 2).

Furthermore, the data show that early ipsilateral orienting is much more frequent and severe in right than in left brain-damaged patients, thus raising the problem of the mechanism underlying this asymmetry in orienting tendencies.

The claim that an ipsilateral orienting bias may contribute to unilateral spatial neglect in right brain-damaged patients is supported by data obtained with different methodologies in different laboratories. Mark et al. (1988) recently tested right brain-damaged neglect patients in an ingenious variation of a line cancellation task. In one version the lines were to be erased, in the other version cancelled by pencil strokes. The authors concluded that neglect was increased in the second version by stimuli remaining in the non-neglected half of space that attracted the patient's attention.

Similarly, De Renzi et al. (1989) observed a gaze displacement toward the rightmost of four stimuli in neglect patients in a search task confined to the right hemispace. They viewed this finding as manifesting an imbalance of lateral orienting tendencies.

Taken together, these findings support the suggestion, advanced by Karnath (1988), that unilateral spatial neglect might be considered as a multi-component syndrome, with one component consisting of spontaneous ipsilateral orienting of attention.

Three different interpretations have been advanced to explain the prevalence of unilateral spatial neglect in right brain-damaged patients:

The first is based on the hypothesis developed by Heilman et al. (1985; 1987). These authors suggested that neglect is induced by an "attentional-arousal disorder". Hemispheric asymmetries result from the unequal distribution within the two cerebral hemispheres of neurons with bilateral receptive fields. Heilman et al. suggested that left "attentional neurons" have mainly contralateral receptive fields, whereas right attentional neurons are more likely to have bilateral receptive fields. As a consequence of this asymmetry, the right hemisphere can attend to novel or significant stimuli on both sides of space, whereas the left hemisphere only attends to contralateral stimuli. Right hemisphere lesions would thus cause unilateral spatial neglect more often than left-sided lesions.

This hypothesis, although explaining the prevalence of unilateral spatial neglect in right brain-damaged patients, suggests a spatial distribution of attentional disorders inconsistent with the result of the present research and of other recent studies. Heilman's model predicts, indeed, that right brain-damaged patients should present, in addition to a strong contralateral neglect, a mild ipsilateral inattention. This prediction has been partly supported by previous investigations (Heilman & Van den Abel,1980; Weintraub & Mesulam, 1987), but has been recently refuted by data obtained in our laboratory (Gainotti et al., 1990). Results from that study showed that ipsilateral attentional disorders are not more frequent in right than in left brain-damaged patients if we exclude attentional defects extending across the midline as a consequence of severe contralateral neglect. Furthermore, the same feature of Heilman's model is inconsistent with our present data, suggesting the existence of an automatic orienting of attention toward the ipsilesional side, and even more with the above mentioned findings of De Renzi et al. (1989), which suggest a kind of over-attention for the right side rather than a mild inattention for this side, as predicted by the model.

The second interpretation, by Kinsbourne (1975; 1987), claims that the left hemisphere is endowed with a stronger orienting response to the contralateral side, compared with the right hemisphere. A lateralised cerebral lesion produces an activation imbalance, which is more likely to cause neglect if the damage is confined to the right rather than to the left hemisphere because it would enhance the spontaneous rightwards orienting bias. At first sight it might seem that Kinsbourne's model fits our data. However, according to Kinsbourne's theory, in Experiment 2 here, normal subjects should show a mild tendency to first orient their attention to the right side items in the overlapping figures task (due to more powerful rightwards orienting tendencies). This prediction was not confirmed because the opposite trend was observed.

Moreover, in the fourth condition of Experiment 3, ipsilesional reaction times obtained from right brain-damaged patients should be faster than ipsilesional reaction times of left brain-damaged patients due to the stronger rightwards orienting tendencies of the intact left hemisphere. The opposite result was in fact obtained (see Table 10.1).

We should like to emphasise that the ipsilateral bias is highly stimulus-dependent. Our simple reaction time experiment (Experiment 3) shows that in right-sided severe neglect patients the presence of bilateral boxes induced a statistically significant slowing of reaction times to stimuli on the left side, compared with stimuli on the right side of the screen. On the other hand, in the blank screen condition, such slowing, although detectable, was not statistically significant. This finding might therefore suggest that the rightwards orienting bias is most likely a compulsory phenomenon elicited by the simultaneous presence of stimuli on both sides of space, rather than a spontaneous tendency to orient preferentially to the right hemispace, resulting from a right cerebral lesion. It is therefore unlikely that the striking prevalence in right brain-damaged patients of the phenomena associated with ipsilateral orienting of attention simply reflects the magnification of normal physiological asymmetries in lateral orienting tendencies.

The third interpretation is that the major interhemispheric differences may reflect the selective disruption in right brain-damaged patients of a mechanism linked to the normal automatic orienting reaction. On the other hand, voluntary orienting mechanisms may be equally affected by lesions in either the right or left hemispheres. If this interpretation holds, then two outcomes could be predicted:

The first is that a severe imbalance in automatic orienting of attention should result from large right hemisphere lesions. When stimuli appear in the right hemifield or in both visual hemifields, attention is readily captured by the right-sided stimulus and automatically oriented toward that side of space. This rightwards orienting occurs at the expenses of the left hemifield; thus left-sided stimuli are obscured or alternatively, can be attended to with a delay that reflects the time-consuming process of reorienting attention from the right to the left side of space. This delay is clearly demonstrated in our Experiment 3 by the extinction-like reaction time pattern exhibited by right-sided severe neglect patients in condition 2. Furthermore, the rightward orienting behaviour might be enhanced by non-lateralised stimuli or by conditions that act phasically by increasing the level of arousal.

This hypothesis is in agreement with the observation reported by Marshall and Halligan (1989), who suggest that an "ipsilateral capture" of attention rather than a contralateral neglect, might underlie the neglect syndrome. Similarly, Riddoch and Humphreys (1987) pointed out that ipsilateral stimuli might effect a stronger hold on attention in neglect patients than in normal subjects, or alternatively, that contralateral stimuli might fail to capture attention in patients with unilateral spatial neglect. Riddoch and Humphreys hypothesised that unilateral spatial neglect is due to some breakdown in the attentional capture mechanisms.

The second predicted outcome is that neglect in right brain-damaged patients should prevail in tasks requiring a partly automatic orienting of attention, relative to those involving a more intentional activity of visual searching. This assumption is supported by the finding of a striking prevalence of neglect in right brain-damaged (compared with left brain-damaged) patients on a task of identification of overlapping figures, whereas an approximately equal incidence of neglect was observed in right brain-damaged and left brain-damaged patients on a task of searching for animals on a large board (Gainotti et al., 1986; 1989).

This second point, concerning a possible dissociation between lost automatic orienting tendencies and preserved voluntary orienting of attention, could have important implications for rehabilitation. The behavioural difficulties resulting from an impaired tendency automatically to orient attention toward novel or significant stimuli arising on the neglected half of space, could indeed be overcome by teaching the patient to pay deliberate, continuous attention to that part of space. Although this rehabilitative strategy has been explicitly mentioned by only a few authors (Seron et al., 1989), some techniques used empirically in rehabilitation programs probably act through this mechanism.

Finally, the notion of attention being captured by ipsilateral stimuli should suggest a careful monitoring of the effect of ipsilateral distractors on rehabilitative tasks. The presence of stimuli attracting the patient's attention further away from the neglected side should be avoided in the earlier stages of rehabilitation of severe neglect patients. Ipsilesional distractors could be introduced in a subsequent stage, and their number and/or salience gradually enhanced. The patient could be instructed to overcome the impasse due to lingering on the right side of the structured space by shortly interrupting the ongoing task to look in a different direction; we observed that this procedure, either suggested by the examiner or casually adopted by the patient, often allows fixation to be restored to the left of the previous focus, so that a partial or complete scanning of the neglected field can be achieved.

## REFERENCES

Albert, M.L. (1973). A simple test of visual neglect. *Neurology, 23,* 658–64.

Brain, W.R. (1941). Visual disorientation with special reference to lesions of the right cerebral hemisphere. *Brain, 64,* 244–272.

Cohn, R. (1972). Eyeball movements in homonymous hemianopia following simultaneous bitemporal object presentation. *Neurology, 22,* 12–14.

D'Erme, P., De Bonis, C., & Gainotti, G. (1987). Influenza dell'emi-inattenzione e dell'emianopsia sui compiti di bisezione di linee nei pazienti cerebrolesi. *Archivio di Psicologia, Neurologia e Psichiatria, 48(2),* 193–207.

D'Erme, P., Robertson, I., Bartolomeo, P., Daniele, A., & Gainotti, G. (1992). Early rightwards orienting of attention on simple reaction times performance in patients with left-side neglect. *Neuropsychologia, 30(11),* 989-1000.

De Renzi, E., Gentilini, M., Faglioni, P., & Barbieri, C. (1989). Attentional shifts towards the rightmost stimuli in patients with left visual neglect. *Cortex, 25,* 231–237.

Friedland, R.P., & Weinstein, E.A. (1977). Hemi-inattention and hemisphere specialisation: Introduction and historical review. In: E.A. Weinstein & R.P Friedland (Eds.), *Advances in Neurology, 18.* New York: Raven Press.

Gainotti, G., D'Erme, P., & Bartolomeo, P. (1991). Early orientation of attention toward the half space ipsilateral to the lesion in patients with unilateral brain damage. *J Neurol Neurosurg Psych, 54,* 1082–1089.

Gainotti, G., D'Erme, P., & De Bonis, C. (1989). Aspects cliniques et mecanismes de la negligence visuo-spatiale. *Rev Neurol (Paris), 145,* 8–9:626–634.

Gainotti, G., D'Erme, P., Monteleone, D., & Silveri, M.C. (1986). Mechanisms of unilateral spatial neglect in relation to laterality of cerebral lesion. *Brain, 109,* 599–612.

Gainotti, G., Giustolisi, L., & Nocentini, U. (1990). Contralateral and ipsilateral disorders of visual attention in patients with unilateral brain damage. *J Neurol Neurosurg Psych, 53,* 422–426.

Gainotti, G., Messerli, P., & Tissot, R. (1972). Qualitative analysis of unilateral spatial neglect in relation to laterality of cerebral lesion. *J Neurol Neurosurg Psych, 35* , 545–550.

Heilman, K.M., Bowers, D., Valenstein, E., & Watson, R.T. (1987). Hemispace and hemispatial neglect. In: M. Jeannerod (Ed.), *Neurophysiological and neuropsychological aspects of spatial neglect* (pp. 115-150). Amsterdam: Elsevier Science Publishers B.V. (North-Holland).

Heilman, K.M., Valenstein, E., & Watson, R.T. (1985). The neglect syndrome. In: P.J. Vinken & G.J. Bruyn (Eds.), *Handbook of Clinical Neurology, 1* (pp.153-183). Amsterdam: North Holland Publishing Company.

Heilman, K.M., & Van Den Abel, T. ( 1980). Right hemispheric dominance for attention: The mechanism underlying hemispheric asymmetries of inattention (neglect). *Neurology, 30,* 327–30.

Karnath, H.O. (1988). Deficits of attention in acute and recovered visual hemi-neglect. *Neuropsychologia, 20,* 27-45.

Kinsbourne, M. (1975). The mechanisms of hemispheric control of the lateral gradient of attention. In: P.M.A. Rabbitt & S. Dornic (Eds.), *Attention and performance.* London: Academic Press.

Kinsbourne, M. (1987). Mechanisms of unilateral neglect. In: M. Jeannerod, (Ed.), *Neurophysiological and neuropsychological aspects of spatial neglect* (pp. 69-86). Amsterdam: Elsevier Science Publishers B.V. (North Holland).

Mark, V.W., Kooistra, C.A., & Heilman, K.M. (1988). Hemispatial neglect affected by non-neglected stimuli. *Neurology, 38,* 1207-1211.

Marshall, J.C. & Halligan, P.W. (1989). Does the midsagittal plane play any privileged role in "left" neglect? *Cognitive Neuropsychology, 6(4),* 403–422.

Posner, M.I. (1980). Orienting of attention. The VIIth Sir Frederic Bartlett Lecture. *Quarterly Journal of Experimental Psychology, 32,* 3-25.

Posner, M.I., Cohen, Y., & Rafal, R.D. (1982). Neural system control of spatial orienting. *Philosophical Transactions of the Royal Society, London, 298,* 187–198.

Posner, M.I., Walker, J.A., Friedrich, F.A., & Rafal, R.D. (1984). Effects of parietal injury on covert orienting of attention. *Journal of Neuroscience, 4(7),* 1863–1874.

Riddoch, M.J. & Humphreys, G.W. (1987). Perceptual and action systems in unilateral visual neglect. In: M. Jeannerod (Ed.), *Neurophysiological and Neuropsychological Aspects of Spatial Neglect* (pp. 151-181). Amsterdam: Elsevier Science Publishers B.V. (North-Holland).

Seron, X., Deloche, G., & Coyette, F. (1989). A retrospective analysis of a single case neglect therapy: A point of theory. In: X. Seron & G. Deloche (Eds.), *Cognitive approach to neuropsychological rehabilitation.* Hillsdale, N.J: Lawrence Erlbaum Associates Inc.

Weintraub, S. & Mesulam, M.M. (1987). Right cerebral dominance in spatial attention: Further evidence based on ipsilateral neglect. *Archives of Neurology, 44,* 621–625.

# PART FOUR

## Motor Performance

CHAPTER ELEVEN

# From Motor Images to Motor Programs

M. Jeannerod and J. Decety
*Vision et Motricité, Bron, France*

## ABSTRACT

This chapter reviews findings from different experiments that were designed to explore the nature of mentally represented actions. Insight into motor images was obtained using several methods. Chronometric analysis revealed a striking similarity between the duration of actually executed actions and their represented counterparts. A significant vegetative activation (as tested by studying cardiorespiratory changes) was found during represented actions. This activation was proportional to the degree of imagined effort. These results suggest that motor images share the same neural mechanisms as those that are responsible for programming and preparing real movements. Information provided by regional cerebral blood flow mapping, showing that the same brain areas are involved in the two conditions, tends to confirm this hypothesis. On the basis of these results it is concluded that mental rehearsal techniques, using controlled motor imagery in patients with motor disorders of central origin, should become a valuable technique for rehabilitation.

## INTRODUCTION

The debate on the nature of mental images is still very open. It has long been assumed that mental images were abstract propositional entities, neutral with respect to stimulus modality and response systems. This theory, which is congruent with the classical computational approach to cognition, implies that there should be no difference in how perceptually-based and verbally-based information is represented and, therefore, that mental images would be best described as "sentence-like" expressions (e.g. Pylyshyn, 1981). However, the arguments put forward by the tenants of the computational approach—for instance, the fact that images can be generated by verbal description or can be described verbally by the subject who experiences them—are not sufficient to demonstrate that these images are built in the same way as language propositions.

An alternative view on the nature of mental images is based on the empiricist assumption that representations derive from interaction with the external world and are built from perceptual-motor experience. This implies that the information represented in mental images should be modality-specific, rather than being amodal as assumed by the computational theory. Mental images could therefore be conceived as analogue (as opposed to digital) representations, isomorphic with perceptual information (see Paivio, 1986). This distinction between the two theories, however, may be too simplistic. It could be, for example, that the way the images are induced (e.g. by verbal instructions, or by showing pictures) determine the mode of processing of the represented information (Riddoch, Humphreys, Coltheart, & Funnell, 1988)

The theory of a modality-specific representation has generated a large body of experimental work. These experiments have provided evidence that the information stored in visual images of objects preserve the metric spatial properties of the represented objects. Shepard and Metzler (1971) first showed that represented three-dimensional shapes are mentally manipulated in the same way as if they were real 3-D objects; the time taken by the subjects mentally to rotate such shapes increases linearly with the angle of rotation. In a more recent experiment Georgopoulos and Massey (1987) requested subjects to perform reaching movements at various angles from a stimulus direction and found that duration of reaction times of these movements was proportional to the size of the angle. They proposed that the increase in reaction time was related to rotating mentally the movement vector until the angle of rotation corresponded to the size required. This relationship, which is reminiscent of the classical relation between movement time and task difficulty observed during execution of real movements (Fitts, 1954), suggested to Georgopoulos and Massey that both real and imagined motions might be governed by the same principles.

Further interest in the mental manipulation paradigm arose from an experiment by Kosslyn, Ball, and Reiser (1978). These authors asked subjects first to memorise complex visual stimuli (e.g. a map of an island) and then to generate a mental image of these stimuli. They found that the time needed to travel from one point of the image to another (as inferred from the time taken by the subjects to arrive at the prescribed point) increased linearly with the distance to be scanned. This result, as well as those of the mental rotation experiments, suggests that processes underlying mental movements within visually represented space might be similar to those underlying actual movements within physical space. Indeed, in a replication of the Kosslyn et al. experiment, Denis and Cocude (1989) found that the time taken to travel mentally between points on the memorised map was closely similar to the time actually taken to scan between the same points on the real map. Decety and Michel (1989) also reached the same conclusion in comparing actual and mental movement times in a graphic task. The time taken by right-handed subjects to write their signature or a piece of text was the same whether the task was executed actually or mentally. This temporal invariance was maintained, though at different rates, with the right and the left hand.

These experiments suggest that mental imagery is not a genuine phenomenon but, rather, that it pertains to the same class of mechanisms as those which are involved in processing incoming or outgoing information. In the visual domain, for example, a large number of experimental studies in normal subjects (using evoked potentials or mapping of brain metabolic activity), as well as in brain-damaged patients, have shown quite convincingly that the distribution of brain activation during visual imagery is the same as during visual perception (for a review, see Farah, 1989). Our aim in this chapter was to extend the same reasoning to motor imagery, by assuming that motor images share the same neural mechanisms as those that are also responsible for preparation and programming of actual movements. This assumption seems to receive support from the effects produced by the use of mental imagery during motor training. It has been convincingly shown that this technique (the so-called "mental rehearsal" or "mental practice", now an accepted procedure in the preparation of athletes; e.g. Richardson, 1967; Suinn, 1984) improves motor performance during execution of the previously represented action. Particularly clear data were obtained by Mendoza and Wichman (1978) for the improvement of dart-throwing performance. A recent meta-analysis of the effects of mental practice, performed by several groups (Decety & Ingvar, 1990; Feltz & Landers, 1983; Swets & Bjork,1990) have validated this technique. Decety and Ingvar ended their review, which included not only behavioural data but also neurophysiological correlates, by suggesting mental practice to involve the primary stages of motor programming.

This hypothesis implies several specific predictions. First, in accordance with some of the foregoing results, the time to travel mentally to places in memorised space and the time to travel physically to the homologous places in actual space should be similar. This prediction was tested in the first experiment, in which we undertook a direct comparison of the duration of movements actually performed with that of movements mentally represented by the same subjects. A simple walking task was used, where blindfolded subjects were requested either to walk, or to imagine themselves walking, towards previously inspected targets. The second prediction was that one should be able, by indirect measurements, to identify within motor images, parameters that are normally encoded within motor programs. In order to test this prediction, a second experiment using the same walking task was performed. In this case, however, an extrinsic constraint was imposed on execution of the task. Subjects carried a heavy load while they walked, both actually and mentally, such that they had to produce a greater amount of force to perform the task. The effects of this constraint were observed on motor timing. Finally, the third prediction was that the degree of activation of brain mechanisms by imagined action should be reflected in some way at the level of peripheral effectors. This prediction was tested in a third experiment where cardiorespiratory changes were monitored and compared during actual and mental effort.

## EXPERIMENT 1

### Method

The subjects were ten university students studying physical education selected for their imaging ability. Prior to the experimental sessions, three different tests were applied to subjects to evaluate their imagery ability, the Sheehan (1967) Mental Imagery Questionnaire, the Hall, Pongrac and Buckholz (1985) Movement Imagery Questionnaire, and the Gordon Test of Visual Imagery Control (Gordon, 1949; Richardson, 1969). All subjects scored as good imagers. Finally, another questionnaire (Denis & Carfantan, 1985) was administered after termination of the experiment in order to check subjects tacit knowledge about mental imagery. In response to the relevant questions in this questionnaire, all subjects rejected the idea that visual imagery might produce effects on motor learning.

The experiment was conducted on a running track of an outdoor stadium. Three white marks (30cm x 20cm) were traced on the ground with white chalk and used as targets. The targets were located 5 metres apart from each other. The subject's starting position on the track was such that their distance from the targets could be either 5, 10 or 15 metres. Starting position was varied from trial to trial.

At the beginning of each trial subjects were placed on the track. They were then allowed to look for 5sec at one of the targets. After being blindfolded they were instructed to construct a mental representation of the track and the target. Finally, after another 5sec delay, they were requested either to walk at a normal pace to the target and to stop when they thought they had reached its location (actual walking condition), or to imagine themselves walking to and stopping at, the target (mental walking condition). Ten trials were performed in each of the two conditions and for each of the three target distances (60 trials per subject). Conditions and target distances were randomly distributed in order to avoid block effects.

Walking times were measured in both the actual and the mental walking conditions. Subjects held an electronic stopwatch in their right hand. They switched the stopwatch on when they started to walk (actually or mentally) and off when they stopped. Walking time was read directly by the experimenter on the stopwatch. This experiment also involved measurements of errors made by the subjects in reaching the targets. This aspect of the results is not reported here (see Decety, Jeannerod, & Prablanc, 1989). Subjects were given no information on their spatial or temporal errors.

### Results

In the actual walking condition, walking time varied across subjects (between 3.8sec and 7.2sec for targets at 5m, between 6.9sec and 12.9sec for targets at 10m, and between 10.8sec and 19.3sec for targets at 15m). In each individual subject, walking time was found to increase with the distance covered (Fig. 11.1, upper).

In the mental walking condition, walking times were found to be very close to those measured in the actual walking condition for the same subjects and for the corresponding distances. The similarity of the two distributions of walking times was confirmed statistically. An intrasubject paired t test showed no significant differences between the means of the two distributions. T(19) ranged between 0.2 and 1.1 for 5m; 0.2 and 1.3 for 10m; 0.3 and 1.7 for 15m, $P > 0.5$. In addition, the mean values of travel time for the actual and the mental walking conditions were plotted against each other for each target. Intrasubject linear correlation coefficients ranged between r=0.89 and r=0.99. Figure 11.1 (lower) shows the highly linear aspect of the distribution.

A two-way intersubject analysis of variance was conducted on walking times x distance (5, 10, 15m) x modality (actual, mental). No difference was found between actual and mental walking times, $F(1,54)=0.02$, $P > 0.5$; there was a significant difference between the three distances, $F(2,54)=131.7$, $P < 0.001$. No interaction was significant, $F(2,54)=0.2$, $P > 0.5$.

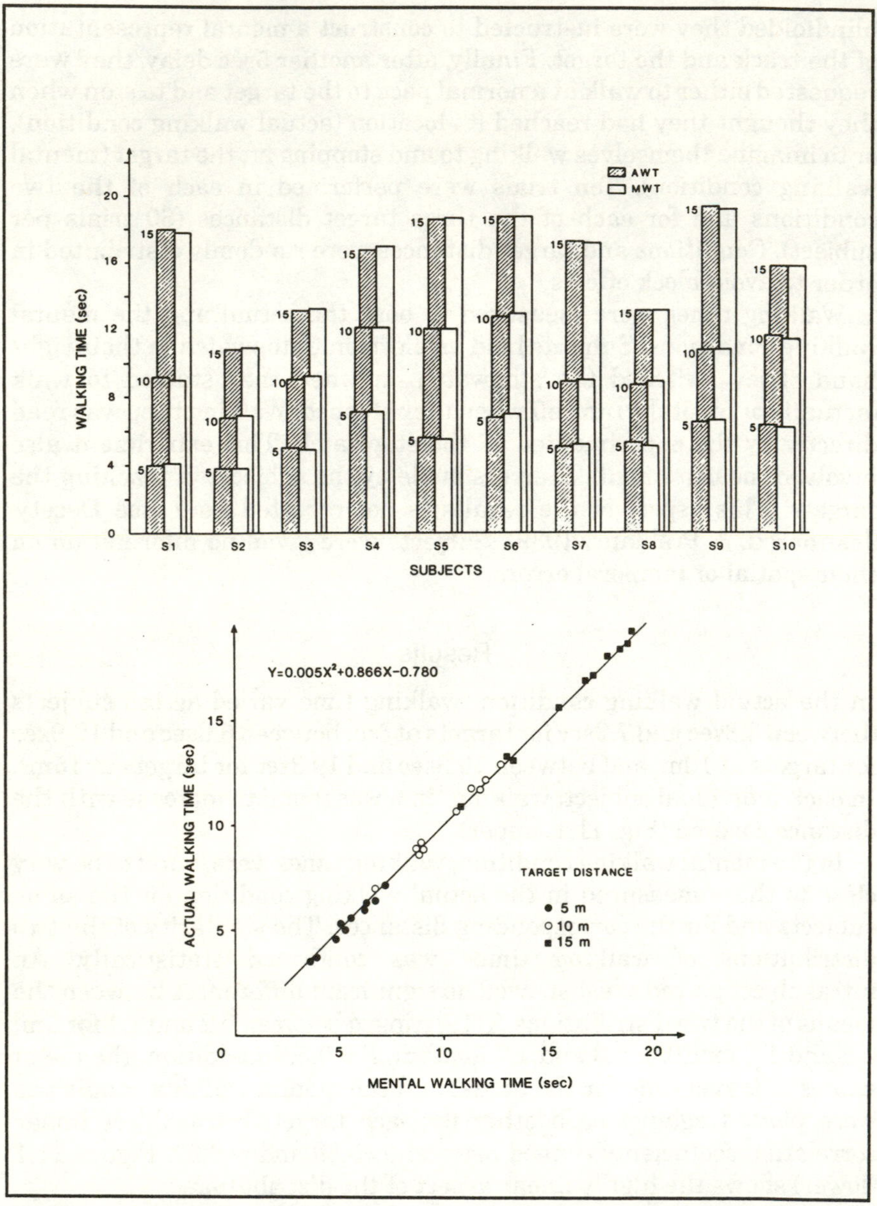


FIG. 11.1. Upper: Mean walking time (in seconds) for the 10 subjects (S1–S10) of Experiment 1. AWT: Actual Walking Time; MWT: Mental Walking Time. Values at top of histograms: distance of targets (5, 10, 15m) Lower: Intrasubject distribution of mean Mental Walking Times plotted against mean Actual Walking times in the 10 subjects of Experiment 1. From Decety et al., 1989.

### Discussion

Our first prediction, namely that actual and walking times should be within the same range, was fulfilled by the results of Experiment 1. First, walking times increased with target distance, in both the actual and the mental walking conditions, a finding that replicates and extends that of Kosslyn et al. (1978) and Denis and Cocude (1989) in their visual scanning experiments. In addition, and most importantly, walking times were invariant *across* actual and mental conditions.

The second finding raises an important question. It might be, as has been suggested by several authors, that our subjects had tacit knowledge of what should happen when they had to walk longer distances, namely, that duration of the action should increase. If this were the case, the observed temporal invariance could be simply due to a strategy of the subjects of replicating in the mental condition the temporal sequence registered in the actual condition. (Pylyshyn, 1981; see also Mitchell & Richman, 1980; Richman, Mitchell, & Reznick, 1979).

One possible way to answer this question is to introduce an external constraint on the motor task, such that the subjects would have to produce a greater effort to execute the same task. It was conjectured that, if time was the variable represented in the motor image, this external constraint should not affect the duration of the imagined action. If, on the other hand, other variables, such as muscular force, were represented, then the durations of the imagined and the actually executed movements should differ because the constraint would exert its effect only in the actual condition and not in the mental condition.

A second experiment was thus performed in the same subjects as in Experiment 1 by using a condition involving an external constraint on movement execution. The constraint was a heavy load carried by the subjects while they actually walked or imagined themselves walking towards the targets. The purpose of this experiment was therefore twofold: Refuting the tacit knowledge objection; and getting insight into the contents of motor images.

## EXPERIMENT 2

### Method

The same ten subjects as in Experiment 1 were used in this experiment, which was carried out several weeks after completion of Experiment 1. The same running track with the three targets was used.

A 25kg. weight was placed on subjects' shoulders in a rucksack. Subjects were placed on the track and were instructed to look at one of the targets for 5sec. Then they were blindfolded and were requested either to walk and reach the target location (actual walking condition) or to imagine themselves walking to it (mental walking condition). Each subject received ten trials for each of the three target distances in each of the two conditions (60 trials per subject). Trials were randomly alternated in order to avoid block effects. Walking time was measured as in Experiment 1.

## Results

Walking times in the actual walking condition with the 25kg. load were in the same range as those measured in the same subjects in Experiment 1 (actual walking condition) (paired t test, $P > 0.5$). By contrast, travel times in the mental walking condition with the load were significantly increased in all subjects and for all target distances (paired t test, T (9) ranging between 6.9 and 7.2 for 5m; 8.3 and 9.6 for 10m; 6.5 and 6.9 for 15m, $P < 0.001$ (Fig. 11.2, upper). This increase was not linear across distances. The distribution of actual walking times vs. mental walking times for the three target distances fitted a polynomial equation (Fig. 11.2, lower). This distribution was clearly different from that observed in Experiment 1.

The intrasubject variability was relatively small in both the actual and the mental conditions. In the actual condition, coefficients of variation ranged between 1.4% and 6.3% for 5m targets, 3.4% and 9.2% for 10m targets, 2.8% and 4.4% for 15m targets. In the mental condition, coefficients of variation ranged between 2.8% and 10% for 5m targets, 2.6% and 6% for 10m targets, 1.2% and 11% for 15m targets.

A two-way intersubject analysis of variance was conducted by using walking time data in the mental conditions from Experiments 1 and 2, on load conditions (with or without 25kg. load) x target distances (5, 10, 15m). There was a significant difference between the two load conditions, $F(1,54)=23.4$, $P < 0.001$. In addition significant differences were found between distances, $F(2,54)=104.7$, $P < 0.001$. No interaction was found between those two factors, $P > 0.5$.

It is interesting to note that in the mental walking condition subjects spontaneously reported a strong sensation of effort that they felt to increase with the distance of targets.

## Discussion

As predicted, the results from Experiment 2 showed a clear dissociation between actual and mental walking times. It took about 30% longer to the subjects carrying a 25kg. load to walk mentally towards the targets than actually to perform the task. Because actual walking times with

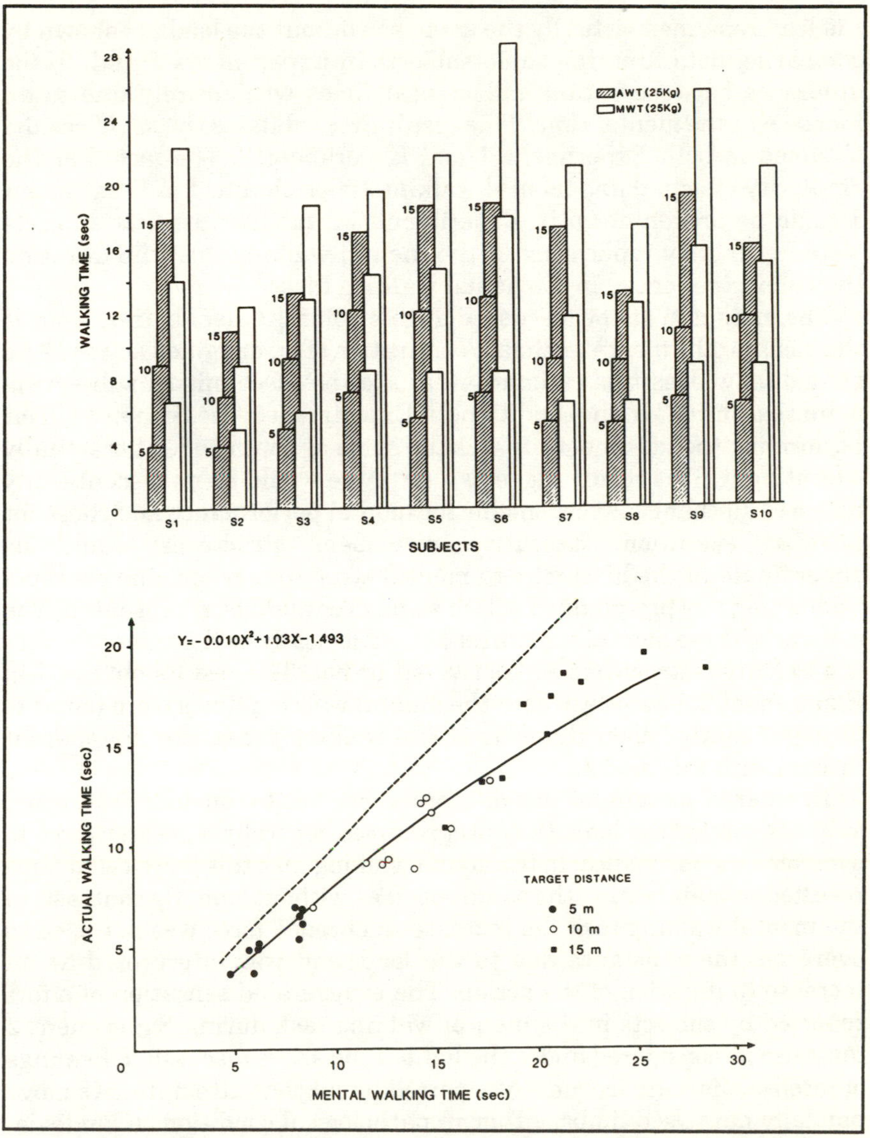


FIG. 11.2. Upper: Mean walking time (in seconds) for the 10 subjects (S1–S10) of Experiment 2. Subjects carried a 25kg. load on their shoulders. AWT: Actual Walking Time; MWT: Mental Walking Time. Values at top of histograms: distance of targets (5, 10, 15m). Lower: Intrasubject distribution of mean Mental Walking Times plotted against mean Actual Walking Times in the 10 subjects of Experiment 2. The solid line represents the fitting curve for this distribution. The dashed line reproduces the regression line calculated for the same subjects in Experiment 1 (see Fig. 11.1). From Decety et al., 1989.

the load remained virtually the same as without the load (as shown by comparing data from the same subjects in Experiments 1 and 2), the difference between actual and mental times was entirely due to an increase in the mental time. This result first validates the set of results obtained in both Experiment 1 and Experiment 2. The fact that the similarity of actual and mental walking times obtained in Experiment 1 could be broken down in Experiment 2 demonstrates that subjects were not merely replicating in the mental walking task the duration they had experienced in the actual walking task.

The main issue to be discussed at this point is twofold: first, what is the basis for the mental estimate of duration of an imagined action? And second, how does this estimate relate to the mechanisms subserving actual execution? In the conditions of Experiment 1, the time needed for performing the task mentally was the same as that needed for actually executing it. This result suggests that there would be no discontinuity between mechanisms responsible for mental performance and those for physical execution. Executive movement structures would be subordinate in the hierarchy to mental structures where the concepts underlying any pre-planned action sequence would be represented. The content of these mental structures should logically be the same whether the executive structures are activated or not. The results obtained in Experiment 2, however, where the mental walking times were found to be significantly longer than the actual walking times, are in apparent discord with this model.

In order to account for this difference, one has to consider that, when subjects carried the load, they programmed centrally a greater force to overcome the resistance. In the actual walking task this increase in force resulted in maintaining the same speed as without load. By contrast, in the mental walking task the increase in encoded force was not used to overcome the resistance due to the load, and was interpreted as an increase in duration of the action. The exaggerated sensation of effort reported by subjects in the mental walking task during Experiment 2 may also be considered under the light of the above discussion. Feelings of intense effort are frequently reported by subjects attempting to move partially paralysed limbs, either in pathological conditions (Gandevia, 1982) or following local curarisation. Gandevia and McCloskey (1977), in an attempt to objectify these sensations, used the curarisation technique for measuring the quantity of effort that subjects have to exercise to achieve a given task with partially paralysed limbs. They asked subjects to press a lever with one thumb in order to produce a reference tension, displayed visually on an oscilloscope screen. With the other thumb, the subjects had to press another lever so as to match the muscular effort produced by the reference thumb. During partial curarisation on the side of the reference thumb the subjects indicated with their other (nonparalysed) thumb, a much larger muscular effort than normally required to produce the same tension. The exaggerated sensation of effort reported by our subjects in the present experiment may thus also be interpreted as a subjective correlate of the increased effort specified by the program in order to overcome the weight.

These results stress the fact that not only time is a represented variable in motor imagery, but that other parameters related to the effort needed to execute the action, also seem to be represented. This point was tested in the third experiment.

## EXPERIMENT 3

### Method

A different group of eleven young subjects was used (for a full account of this experiment, see Decety, Jeannerod, Germain, & Pastene, 1991). They scored at an average of 3.2 (sd, 0.4) for visual imagery and 3.3 (sd, 0.5) for kinaesthetic imagery (highest score on the scale, 4.0) with the Sheehan's questionnaire. Each subject came for two sessions separated by a one week interval. During the first session, subjects were placed on a treadmill. Following a three minutes rest period, the treadmill was started and the subjects locomoted for three minutes at $5km.h^{-1}$, then for three minutes at $8km.h^{-1}$ and finally for three minutes at $12km.h^{-1}$ (actual locomotion session). During the second session subjects were placed again on the treadmill. They were blindfolded and wore earphones connected to a portable tape recorder. Following a three minutes rest period, subjects heard through the earphones a record of the noise of the treadmill running at $5km.h^{-1}$ This record lasted for three minutes. Immediately prior to the treadmill noise, they received taped verbal instructions to "imagine themselves locomoting at the speed corresponding to the heard noise". The same was repeated for $8km.h^{-1}$ and for $12km.h^{-1}$ (mental locomotion session). The presentation of the treadmill noise was intended to help the subjects to carry on the mental imagery task, and to ensure that each condition had the same duration.

During the mental locomotion session, one control subject, after the three minutes rest period, received the treadmill noise through the earphones without instructions to imagine walking.

During both the actual and the mental locomotion sessions, electrodes were placed on the subject's chest for recording heart rate using a digital electrocardiograph. In addition, a respiratory mask was placed on the subject's face during the last 30sec of each condition (e.g. resting, $5km.h^{-1}$, etc) for measuring respiratory parameters. These measurements, which were made using a spirometer and Beckman gas analysers, included: Pulmonary ventilation (VE) in litres.min$^{-1}$; Oxygen consumption ($VO_2$) in litres.min$^{-1}$. An index for oxygen uptake (true $O_2$) and $CO_2$ elimination (in % by litre of expired air) were also computed.

## Results

The main finding in this experiment was that both heart rate and pulmonary ventilation increased during the mental imagery of locomotion, proportional to the imagined walking speed. Concerning heart rate, a monotonic increase was observed, which correlated positively with the speed of imagined walking ($r=0.39$, $P < 0.009$). The mean heart rate was 84.8.min (sd, 14.0) in the resting condition and was raised to 101.3.min (sd, 17.0) during the 12 km.h$^{-1}$ condition.

The rate of increase of the frequency of heart beats during the mental locomotion session was about 1.4 beat.min$^{-1}$ per km.h$^{-1}$, as compared with the rate of increase of 7.5 beats.min$^{-1}$ per km.h$^{-1}$ observed during the actual locomotion session (Fig. 11.3A). This effect of imagined speed on heart rate was present in the 10 subjects who passed the mental locomotion session (Fig. 11.3B). In the control subject, no increase in heart rate was observed; on the contrary, the heart rate tended to be lower during exposure to the treadmill noise than at rest (Fig. 11.3B).

The analysis of changes in respiratory parameters during the mental locomotion session first revealed an increase in VE. As shown by Fig. 11.4, the mean VE increased from 9.5 (sd, 2.9) l.min$^{-1}$ in the resting condition, to 19.5 (sd, 10.2) l.min-1 in the 12km.h$^{-1}$ condition. A highly significant correlation was found between VE and imagined speed ($r=0.47, P<0.001$). This increase in VE corresponded to a rate of increase of 0.83 l.min$^{-1}$ per km.h$^{-1}$, as compared to the value of 5.1 l.min$^{-1}$ per km.h$^{-1}$ observed during actual locomotion.

The increase of VE during mental locomotion was accompanied by a small but consistent increase in oxygen consumption ($VO_2$), which also correlated positively with walking speed ($r=0.44$, $P < 0.005$). It was observed that $VO_2$ increased from 0.26 (sd, 0.05) l.min$^{-1}$ at rest, up to 0.36 (sd, 0.07) l.min$^{-1}$ at 12 km.h$^{-1}$. By comparison, during actual locomotion, $VO_2$ increased from 0.33 (sd, 0.10) l.min$^{-1}$ to 2.83 (sd, 0.43) l.min$^{-1}$ (Fig. 11.5).

As a consequence of the disparity between the increase in VE and the less important increase in $VO_2$ in the mental condition, the oxygen uptake (true $O_2$) decreased as a function of imagined locomoting speed, such that the estimated proportion of oxygen per litre of expired air during the resting condition (3.70%), dropped to 2.66% during the 12km.h$^{-1}$ condition ($P < 0.009$). By contrast, during actual locomotion,

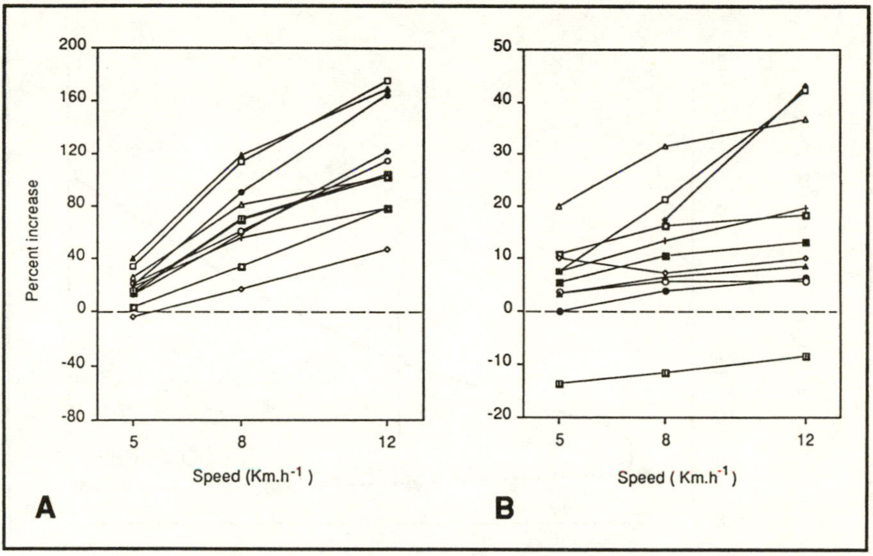


FIG. 11.3. Increase in heart rate during actual (A) and mental (B) effort, as a function of speed, in the 11 subjects of Experiment 3. Values are expressed in percent of resting value. The control subject (below the zero line in B) had a decrease in heart rate during the mental locomotion session. From Decety et al., 1991.

the oxygen uptake was increased from 3.32% at rest up to 4.74% at 12km.h$^{-1}$ ($P < 0.0001$) (Fig. 11.6). The same effect was observed with $CO_2$, which showed a decrease in expired air as a function of imagined speed during the mental session (from 3.3% per litre at rest, down to 2.3 % at 12km.h$^{-1}$ ), although it increased during the actual session (from 2.7% at rest, up to 4.6% at 12km.h$^{-1}$).

Finally, in the control subject, VE (Fig. 11.5), as well as oxygen uptake and $CO_2$ elimination remained unchanged during the control mental session.

## Discussion

A number of points must be discussed before the observed changes in vegetative functions during motor imagery can be considered as a specific effect. Similar changes, including increase in heart rate and respiration, have often been reported during situations of mental imagery where psychogenic and emotional factors are manipulated. In such situations the conceptual content processed during imagery (e.g. fear) and the vividness of the image determine the amplitude and pattern of this coincident efferent activity (Lang, Kozak, Miller, Levin,

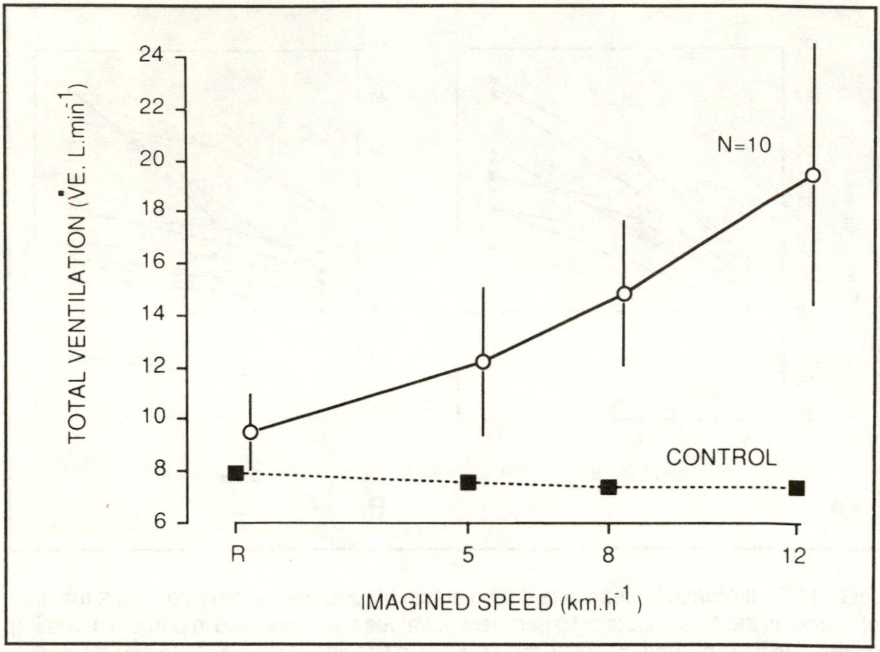


FIG. 11.4. Mean increase in total ventilation (VE, in litres per minute), as a function of imagined locomotory speed in the 11 subjects of Experiment 3. Open circles, mean value of VE for each condition. R, resting condition. Vertical bars represent one standard deviation. Black squares, values of VE in one control subject who was exposed to the noise of the treadmill running at different speeds without being given any instruction for mental imagery of locomotion. From Decety et al., 1991.

& McLean, 1980; Morgan, 1985). It has been proposed that cognitive or affective arousal could involve a global increase in muscle tone, hence producing an increase in metabolic demands.

It could be that, in the present experiment, the subjects who imagined running at increasing speeds, produced a proportional increase in muscular activity by co-contracting antagonist muscle groups. This explanation, based on the observation that mental images imply arousal and increase in muscular tension, would account for the increase in oxygen consumption in the mental condition. This assumption has recently been ruled out by Decety et al. (1993) in a study during motor imagery in which cardiorespiratory parameters were recorded simultaneously to measurements of muscular metabolism using 31P nuclear magnetic resonance (NMR) spectroscopy. During motor imagery, NMR spectra remained unchanged with respect to the testing values. Although this cannot be ruled out without a direct measurement

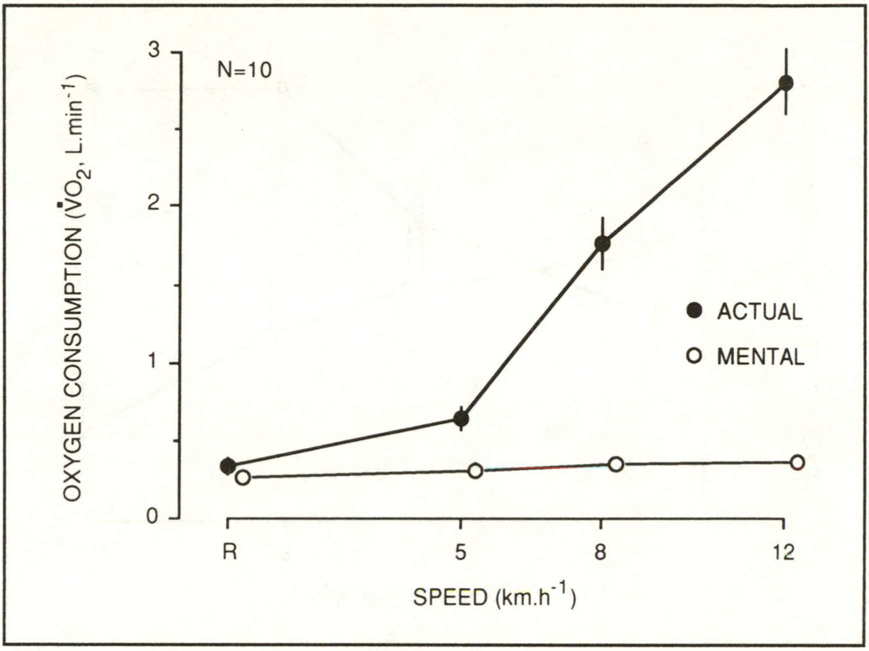


FIG. 11.5. Comparison of oxygen consumption ($VO_2$, in litres per minute) during actual and mental locomotion. Filled circles, mean values of $VO_2$ for the 11 subjects of Experiment 3 during the resting condition (R) and locomotion at 5, 8 and 12 km.h$^{-1}$. Open circles, values of $VO_2$ for the same 11 subjects during the resting condition and mentally simulated locomotion at 5, 8 and 12 km.h$^{-1}$. Vertical bars represent one standard deviation. Note lack of change in oxygen consumption during the mental conditions. From Decety et al., 1991.

of muscular activity, a closer inspection of the present results reveals a discrepancy between the degree of vegetative activation and the change in oxygen consumption. Indeed, if the increase in oxygen consumption corresponded solely to an increase in peripheral metabolic demands due to muscular contraction, the oxygen uptake should also increase, as it is the case during actual physical effort. Our results clearly show instead that oxygen uptake decreased during mental effort.

This finding demonstrates that the vegetative activation during motor imagery is greater than required by the increase in metabolic demands and, therefore, that a significant fraction of this vegetative activation has to be of a central origin. The fact that vegetative activity during mental effort increases beyond the level of metabolic demands supports our initial hypothesis of a commonality of mechanisms between actual and imagined action. This effect can be considered as a

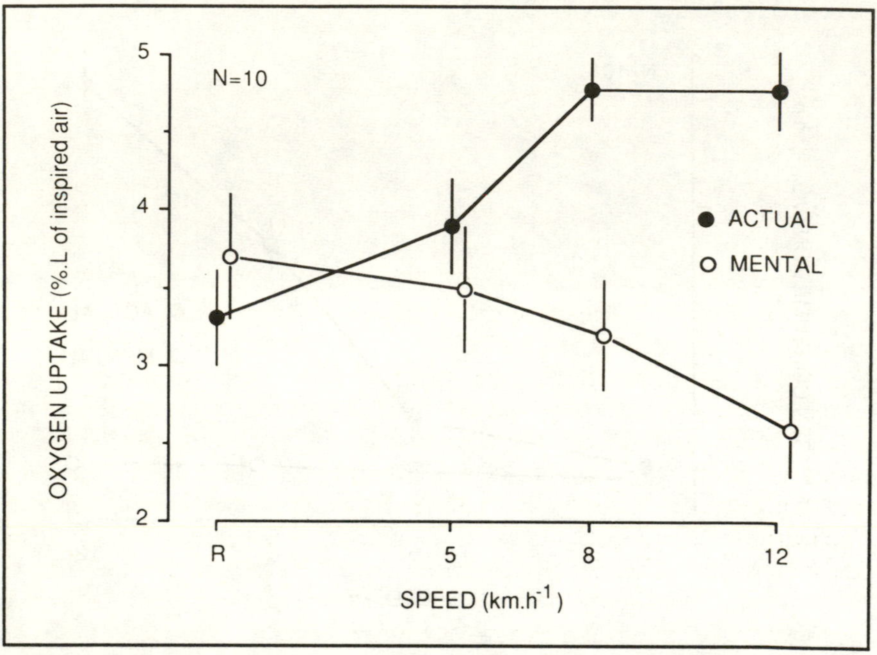


FIG. 11.6. Comparison of changes in oxygen uptake during actual and mental locomotion in the 11 subjects of Experiment 3. Filled circles, values of parameter true $O_2$ (in percent by litre of inspired air) during actual locomotion, as a function of locomotory speed (R, resting condition). Open circles, values of parameter true $O_2$ during mental simulation of locomotion, as a function of imagined speed. Vertical bars represent one standard deviation. Note decrease in oxygen uptake in the mental condition, due to increase in total ventilation and correlative stability of oxygen consumption. From Decety et al., 1991.

vegetative response pertaining to the normal pattern of activation that occurs during motor programming. In this way, the central programming structures would anticipate the need for energetic mobilisation required by the planned movement, to the same extent as they anticipate the amount of activity needed in the motor pathways for producing the movement.

## CONCLUSION

Our initial hypothesis that motor images share the same neural mechanisms as those that are also responsible for preparation and programming of actual movements was therefore supported by the present results. Other confirmatory arguments can be drawn from experiments using functional mapping of the regional cerebral blood flow. Cortical motor areas have been shown by this technique to be activated during a mentally imagined sequence of movements. The pattern of cortical activation, which includes the premotor areas and the supplementary motor area, is strikingly similar to that observed during actual execution of the same sequence of movement. The only marked difference between the two situations is that the primary motor cortex is activated only if movements are actually executed (Roland, Skinhoj, Lassen, & Larsen, 1980). Moreover, in a recent experiment, Decety, Sjoholm, Ryding, Sternberg, and Ingvar (1990) demonstrated that, in addition to cortical areas, the cerebellar metabolism also increased by about 19% during motor imagery and by 10% in the basal ganglia. These results suggest that the neural structures involved in planning and programming motor output could be preactivated or "primed" during motor imagery. They can be interpreted as a direct support to mental practice that has been used empirically for more than 10 years, particularly in the sport context. A similar experimental design, adapted to brain-damaged patients, should logically contribute to improving recovery from motor deficits of central origin, by helping the patients to use alternative motor strategies and by improving efficiency of spared performance. The question of whether mental practice has any relevance to physiotherapy has not, to our present knowledge, been addressed experimentally. This might be due to the difficulty of evaluating the effectiveness of mental practice in groups of patients. Measurement of brain metabolism (e.g. using positron emission tomography) could be of interest for selecting those patients who show increased activity in the relevant brain areas.

## REFERENCES

Decety, J. & Michel, F. (1989). Comparative analysis of actual and mental movement times in two graphic tasks. *Brain & Cognition, 11,* 87-97 .

Decety, J. & Ingvar, D.H. (1990). Brain structures participating in mental simulation of motor behavior: a neuropsychological interpretation. *Acta Psychologica, 73,* 13-34.

Decety, J., Jeannerod, M., Durozard, D, & Baverel, G. (1993). Central activation of autonomic effectors during mental representation of motor actions in man. *Journal of Physiology, London, 461,* 549-563.

Decety, J., Jeannerod, M., & Prablanc, C. (1989). The timing of mentally represented actions. *Behavioural Brain Research, 34,* 35-42.

Decety, J., Jeannerod, M., Germain, & Pastene, J. (1991). Vegetative response during imagined movement is proportional to mental effort. *Behavioural Brain Research, 42,* 1-5.

Decety, J., Sjoholm, H., Ryding, E., Stenberg, G., & Ingvar, D. (1990). The cerebellum participates in mental activity: Tomographic measurements of regional cerebral blood flow. *Brain Research, 535,* 313-317.

Denis, M. & Carfantan, M. (1985). People knowledge about images. *Cognition, 20,* 49-60.

Denis, M. & Cocude, M. (1989). Scanning visual images generated from verbal descriptions. *European Journal of Cognitive Psychology, 1,* 293-307.

Farah, M.J. (1989). The neural basis of mental imagery. *Trends in Neurosciences, 12,* 395-399.

Feltz, D.L. & Landers, D.M. (1983). The effects of mental practice on motor skill learning and performance: A meta analysis. *Journal of Sport Psychology, 5,* 25-57.

Fitts, P.M. (1954). The information capacity of the human motor system in controlling the amplitude of movement. *Journal of Experimental Psychology, 47,* 381-391.

Gandevia, S.G. (1982). The perception of motor commands or effort during muscular paralysis. *Brain, 105,* 151-159.

Gandevia, S.G. & McCloskey, D.I. (1977). Changes in motor commands, as shown by changes in perceived heaviness, during partial curarisation and peripheral anaesthesia in man. *Journal of Physiology, 272,* 673-689.

Georgopoulos, A.P. & Massey, J.T. (1987). Cognitive spatial-motor processes. *Experimental Brain Research, 65,* 361-370.

Gordon, R.A. (1949). An investigation into some of the factors that favour the formation of stereotyped images. *British Journal of Psychology, 39,* 156-157.

Hall, C., Pongrac, J., & Buckholz, E. (1985). The measurement of imagery ability. *Human Movement Science, 4,* 107-118.

Johnson, P. (1982). The functional equivalence of imagery and movement. *Quarterly Journal of Experimental Psychology, 34A,* 349-365.

Kosslyn, S.M., Ball, T.M., & Reiser, B.J. (1978). Visual images preserve metric spatial information. Evidence from studies of image scanning. *Journal of Experimental Psychology: Human Perception and Performance, 4,* 47-60.

Lang, P.J., Kozak, M.J., Miller, G.A., Levin, D.N., & McLean, A. (1980). Emotional imagery: Conceptual structure and pattern of somato-visceral response. *Psychophysiology, 17,* 179-192.

Mendoza, D.W. & Wichman, H. (1978). "Inner" darts: Effects of mental practice on performance of dart throwing. *Perceptual and Motor Skills, 47,* 1195-1199.

Mitchell, D.B. & Richman, C.L. (1980). Confirmed reservation: Mental travel. *Journal of Experimental Psychology: Human Perception Performance, 6,* 58-66.

Morgan, W.P. (1985). Psychogenic factors and exercise metabolism. A review. *Medicine and Science in Sports and Exercise, 17,* 309-316.

Paivio, A. (1986). *Mental representations: A dual coding approach.* New York: Oxford University Press.

Pylyshyn, Z.W. (1981). The imagery debate: Analogue media versus tacit knowledge. *Psychological Review, 88,* 16-45.

Richardson A. (1967). Mental practice: A review and discussion. *Research Quarterly, 38,* 95-107.

Richardson, A. (1969). *Mental imagery.* New York: Springer.

Richman, C.L., Mitchell, D.B., & Reznick, J.S. (1979). Mental travel: Some reservations. *Journal of Experimental Psychology: Human Perception and Performance, 5,* 1, 13-18.

Riddoch, M.J., Humphreys, G.W., Coltheart, M., & Funnell, E. (1988). Semantic systems or system? Neuropsychological evidence re-examined. *Cognitive Neuropsychology, 5,* 3-25.

Roland, P.E., Skinhoj, E., Lassen, N.A., & Larsen, B. (1980). Different cortical areas in man in organisation of voluntary movements in extrapersonal space. *Journal of Neurophysiology, 43,* 137-150.

Sheehan, R.N. (1967). A shortened form of Betts' questionnaire upon mental imagery. *Journal of Clinical Psycholology, 23,* 386-389.

Shepard, R.N. & Metzler, J. (1971) Mental rotation of three-dimensional objects, *Science, 171,* 701-703.

Suinn, R.M. (1983). Imagery and sports. In: A.A Sheikk (Ed.), *Imagery, current theory, research and application.* John Wiley and Sons.

Suinn, R.M. (1984). Imagery and sports. In: W.F. Straub & J.M. Williams (Eds.), *Cognitive sport psychology.* Lansing, New York: Sport Science Associates.

Swets, J.A. & Bjork, R.A. (1990). Enhancing human performance: An evaluation of "new age" techniques considered by the U.S. army. *Psychological Science, 1,* 85-95.

CHAPTER TWELVE

# Prevention of Early Immobility in Patients with Parkinson's Disease: A Cognitive Strategy Training for Turning in Bed and Rising from a Chair

Y.P.T. Kamsma, W.H. Brouwer, and J.P.W.F. Lakke
*Traffic Research Centre and Department of Neurology of the University Hospital, University of Groningen, The Netherlands*

## ABSTRACT

In this study it was attempted to develop a method of intervention with regard to specific motor impairments in Parkinson's disease (PD) that do not respond well to pharmacological treatment and may lead to early invalidity: execution of global postural changes such as turning in bed and rising from a chair.

In a first experiment, turning in bed and rising from a chair, were kinesiologically assessed in ten healthy young subjects (20-30 yrs), ten healthy elderly (60-70 yrs) and ten PD patients. In healthy subjects, turning can be characterised as a complex motor task, in which the components need delicate tuning in terms of sequential and simultaneous execution. Essential is the formation of an "arch", formed by one leg and one shoulder, which enables a person to lift the body from the mattress and rotate the body along this arch. This results in a stable position of lying on the side without lateral displacement. PD patients show difficulties in the tuning and execution of the components. Formation of an arch is problematical and this affects the quality of turning to a great extent. Also, they tend to execute the components in a fragmented and ineffective manner and frequently components are not executed at all. In rising from a chair, similar problems in the execution of the components of this global postural change were

observed. In healthy controls, rising from a chair occurs fluently with initial displacement of legs and arms, eventually shifting to a support function, and acceleration of the trunk leading to horizontal and vertical displacement of the body's centre of gravity.
In a second experiment, alternative movement strategies for turning and rising from a chair were taught to ten, not demented, PD patients: three mildly affected, three moderately affected and four strongly affected. These strategies had to meet demands imposed on them on neuropsychological and kinesiological grounds: the large complex movement was divided into simple partial movements, each leading to a stable in-between-position and with a logical and strict sequence. An individual training of six sessions of one hour duration was set up to teach these new movement strategies. After the training, patients of mild and moderate severity showed good results: they hardly made any errors in the execution of the learned strategies that lead to better movement results. The strongly affected patients performed less successfully. Improvement was present but not sufficient.

## GENERAL INTRODUCTION

In Parkinson's disease, a deficient neurotransmitter system, most prominent in the dopaminergic nigrostriatal pathways of the basal ganglia, leads to certain pathological motor symptoms that progressively debilitate freedom of movement. Major motor symptoms are a resting tremor (4-6Hz), muscle rigidity, and akinesia. Tremor and rigidity are thought to be produced secondarily by the action of intact brain mechanisms that have been released from the influence of the impaired dopaminergic neurotransmission in the basal ganglia (positive symptoms). Akinesia, a negative symptom, is regarded as the principal motor symptom (Hallett & Khoshbin, 1980; Lakke, Van Den Burg & Wiegman, 1982; Marsden, 1982), likely to be due directly to the loss of function of the deficient neurotransmitter system. Akinesia is a collective noun for the following symptomatology:

1. An inability or delay in initiating and continuing movement.
2. Hypokinesia: Poverty of movement. Examples are reduced or absent armswing during walking and lack of facial expression.
3. Bradykinesia: Slowness of movement. (Marsden, 1989).

These symptoms strongly influence motor functioning in general. Drug therapy is rather effective in diminishing tremor and rigidity. It may also induce a remarkable effect regarding akinesia in distal movements (e.g. movements of the limbs). However, more basic movements that are related to the axis of the body remain disturbed, and when PD progresses, initiation and execution of these movements become more and more problematic (Lakke et al., 1982; Lakke & Kamsma, 1992).

The different effects of medication on distal and more proximal movements support a division of motor functioning in two major groups. The first major group may be called axial motor functions because they are directly related to the axis of the body. Axial motor functions are important for human posture, postural adaptation and locomotion. A subdivision can be made into posture, an active process involving the maintenance of a certain position, and axially related movements required to shift from one position to the other: global postural changes. Examples of these global postural changes are: turning in bed, rising from a chair, and also walking and crawling.

The second major group of motor functions may be called distal motor functions. These distal motor functions are motor behaviour performed with the limbs as in perceptual-motor skills. Axial motor functioning forms a basis for distal motor functioning: it creates and maintains positions from where distal movements can be optimally performed.

The effects of drugs such as L-dopa are basically to reduce tremor, rigidity and akinesia with regard to distal motor functions. Difficulties in the execution of global postural changes remain, even with optimal drug prescription. An illustration of this fact is that, according to Lakke et al. (1980), 80% of 103 patients, investigated by questionnaire, reported persistent problems in turning in bed, and 75% of this group found no improvement in this symptom from medication.

The axial akinesia seems to result in a situation that can be described as apraxic in the literal sense of the word: the patient does not succeed in executing the intended action. This kind of apraxia has been called "axial apraxia" (Lakke, 1985). Contrary to classical apraxia, which by definition is a result of lesions of the cortex and affects voluntary movement, axial apraxia is caused by a degenerative process in the subcortical regions and involves automatically executed movements. Figure 12.1 provides a framework illustrating the relations between the three main symptoms of PD and possible underlying divisions of motor function.

Problems with global postural changes can influence the life of the PD patient even from a relatively early stage of the disease. A recent assessment (of physical independency, social involvement and subjective wellbeing) at our department (Lakke, Brouwer, & Broersma, 1988) illustrates the disabling character of impaired global postural changes. Patients who were not able to turn in bed at night, to get up from a chair or couch, or who did not succeed in covering a certain distance on foot, were early invalids with the quality of their life strongly affected. This stresses the importance for the PD patient to remain physically independent for as long as possible. When drugs can only relieve the motor impairment to a limited extent, it becomes especially

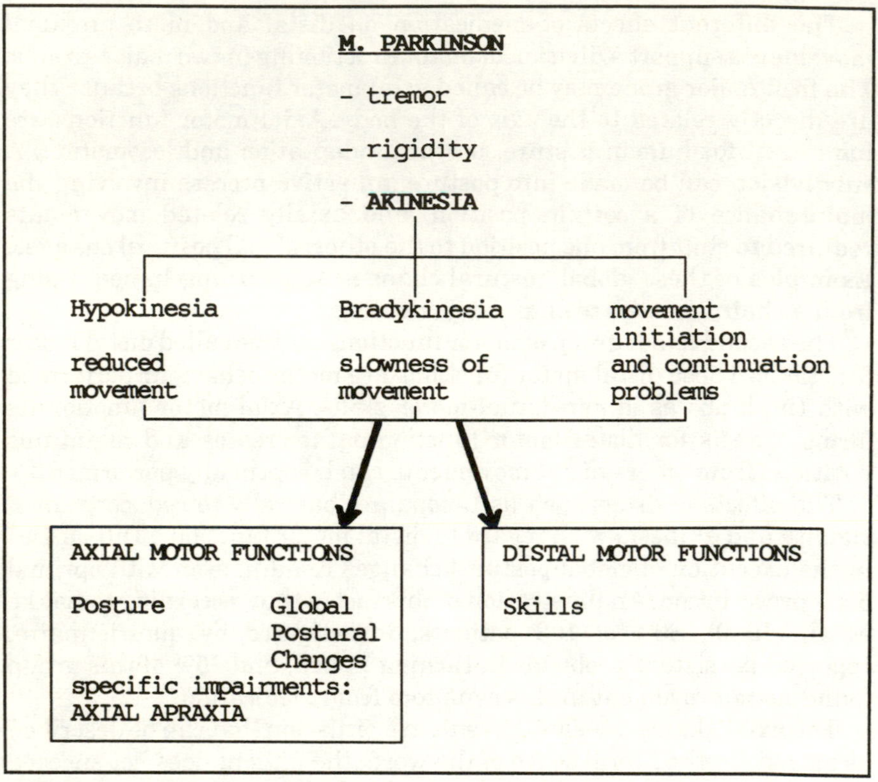


FIG. 12.1. Impairments of movement in Parkinson's disease.

worthwhile to develop a concept in which additional forms of therapy might be successful (Weiner & Singer, 1989).

Reports of attempts to assess different forms of movement therapy (Rose & Capildeo, 1981) contain disappointing results (Franklyn et al., 1981; Gibberd et al., 1981). In the traditional movement therapies described, the focus had been on the training of the impaired functions with the aim of strengthening these. An alternative method of training that has not yet been systematically investigated, is a form of strategy training in which an activity is reorganised in such a way that the demands on the impaired function are minimised. In movement therapy of PD, this goes back to Luria's old principle of "inter-systematic reorganisation" (1963). In individual cases of PD he reported remarkable improvements in finger tapping and walking when higher order cortical systems were used to control or initiate the movement. It is the object of our research to study the possibilities of strategies for the control of global postural changes that can be executed under conscious cortical control.

Two global postural changes, essential to everyday life, were studied. These were turning in bed and rising from a chair. In a first experiment, a kinesiological analysis was conducted in order to understand how these are executed in healthy subjects and PD patients, and to find out which aspects of the global postural changes generate problems. In a second experiment, kinesiological and neuropsychological knowledge were put together. New motor strategies were designed, trained and evaluated in PD patients.

## EXPERIMENT 1: KINESIOLOGY OF TURNING IN BED AND RISING FROM A CHAIR

### Methods

#### *Subjects*

The group of normal subjects consisted of ten university students (age 20-30yrs, five males, five females) and ten healthy elderly (age 60-70yrs, five males and five females). The PD group consisted of ten outpatients (age 50-70yrs, six males and four females, attending the Department of Neurology of the University Hospital of Groningen for routine investigation. Two patients were rated as belonging to stage II, six to stage III and two to stage IV on the Hoehn and Yahr five-point rating-scale that measures overall disability. None of the patients was clinically demented and they all received medication for treatment of PD.

#### *Materials*

*Chairs.* The chairs were identical and of a standard type with two arms and four legs. The chair had the following dimensions: seating area: 51cm x 46cm (width x depth), height of the seating area 43cm at the front and 40cm at the rear. The angle between the seat and the back: 110deg. Height of back: starting at 63cm and ending at 82cm. Height of the arm rests: 68.5cm, length: 46cm, horizontally placed and made of plastic. Seats and backs were covered with imitation leather.

*Bed.* A standard hospital bed. Dimensions: height 0.80m, with a wooden bed-base. The size of the mattress: 1.90m x 0.80m x 0.10m, covered with a cotton sheet. A cushion provided support for the head.

*Video.* Recordings were taken with a VHS-camcorder from a fixed point in the room (distance 1.80m, viewing the bed in length and facing the right corner of the foot of the bed, and 4m from the chairs, height

2m), over a fixed angle and with a fixed focus. With the help of an additional character generator, a date and stopwatch facility was brought into the video picture. Observation and scoring was done with a VHS-video recorder with remote control, the facilities for slow motion, still, and frame by frame operation, and a full colour monitor.

*Procedure*

*Turning in bed.* The subjects were asked to lie down on their backs on the bed. Immediately after a visual sign (lightflash) was given, they had to turn to one side. They had to stay in this position for five seconds after which they were allowed to turn on their back again. This procedure was repeated six times. Turning was alternately conducted to the right and to the left side.

*Rising from a chair.* This was assessed in the same group of normals and PD patients. Two chairs were placed facing each other three metres apart. Subjects were asked to rise directly after the visual sign (lightflash), walk to the opposite chair and sit down on it. This procedure was also repeated six times.

*Observation and scoring*

Analysis of the performances was conducted by observation in the form of time-sampling of the video recordings of turning and rising by normals and PD patients. An observation scheme involved separate scoring for the limbs, head, shoulders, trunk, and pelvis. For each of these categories, several movements were qualitatively distinguished. The stopwatch in the video picture made it possible to score temporal aspects of the actions that took place. In this way, quantitative, qualitative, and temporal aspects of rising from a chair and turning in bed could be analysed.

In order to test the reliability of the observation method and inter-observer agreement, three observers were trained in the use of the observation schema. After this, each scored 11 videotaped performances of normals and PD patients turning in bed and rising from a chair. These were chosen at random in advance. Inter-observer reliability was assessed by the determination of Cohen's Kappa (k), which measures the proportion of agreement (Pa) between the observers and corrects for the proportion of chance (Pc) inherent to the method of timesampling.

$$k = (Pa - Pc)/(1 - Pc).$$

For turning in bed the mean Cohen's Kappa was 0.72; for rising from a chair it was 0.84. A Cohen's Kappa of 0.60 is regarded as sufficient.

TABLE 12.1
Observation Schema for the Analysis of Turning in Bed

| Category | | Subcategory | Time samples | | | |
|---|---|---|---|---|---|---|
| Head | | displacement | | | | |
| | | support | | | | |
| | | roll | | | | |
| | | turn | | | | |
| Arms | homolat. | displacement | | | | |
| | | support | | | | |
| | heterolat. | displacement | | | | |
| | | support | | | | |
| Shoulders | homolat. | displacement | | | | |
| | | support | | | | |
| | heterolat. | displacement | | | | |
| | | support | | | | |
| | hom + het | roll | | | | |
| | | turn | | | | |
| Legs | homolat. | displacement | | | | |
| | | support | | | | |
| | heterolat. | displacement | | | | |
| | | support | | | | |
| Pelvis | | displacement | | | | |
| | | support | | | | |
| | | roll | | | | |
| | | turn | | | | |

## Results and Discussion

### *Turning in bed*

This showed characteristic movement patterns in normal subjects. Figure 12.2a illustrates what was frequently seen. Between points of support, the heterolateral leg and homolateral shoulder, an arch is formed, and the body can be lifted from the mattress. An axial rotation along the arch can be executed. This results in a stable position of lying on one side of the body, while a lateral displacement in bed is prevented.

In healthy controls there was little variation in the choice of points of support and the time necessary to perform the action of turning in bed. In young adults the mean turning time was 2.62sec. (sd=0.60sec.) and in healthy elderly it was 3.64sec. (sd=0.47sec.). The combinations of letters on the basis of the diagrams correspond with the different body parts shown in Fig. 12.2a, used to form an arch. Figures 12.2b and 12.2c illustrate that more arches arose between the homolateral shoulder (B) and the heterolateral leg (G) than between any other possible parts of the body.

The prevention of lateral displacement is an essential quality of turning. It constitutes the difference between merely rolling over to the side and turning to the side. When a person rolls instead of turns, a lateral displacement to, or over, the edge of the bed is inevitable, resulting in an uncomfortable position.

Turning in bed in PD patients is clearly different from normal turning. This may be seen in Fig. 12.2d. PD patients use a great variety of points of support and frequently recapture these positions in order successfully to turn in bed. In a large proportion of turnings, there is no

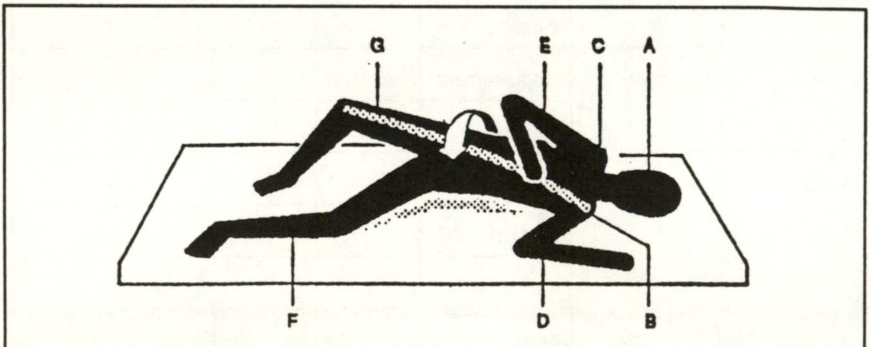


FIG. 12.2a. Turning, as was generally seen in normal subjects. Between the heterolateral leg (G) and the homolateral shoulder (B) an arch is formed: the body can be lifted and rotated without lateral displacement.

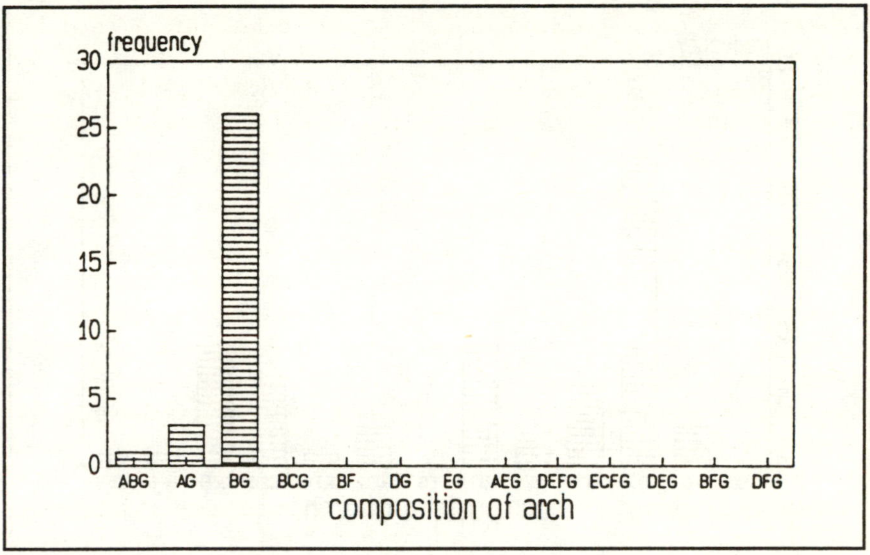


FIG. 12.2b. The frequency and composition of arches during turning, scored by three observers in ten healthy young adults. Each subject turned once. The letter combinations refer to Fig. 12.2a. They represent the body parts that are used in the formation of an arch.

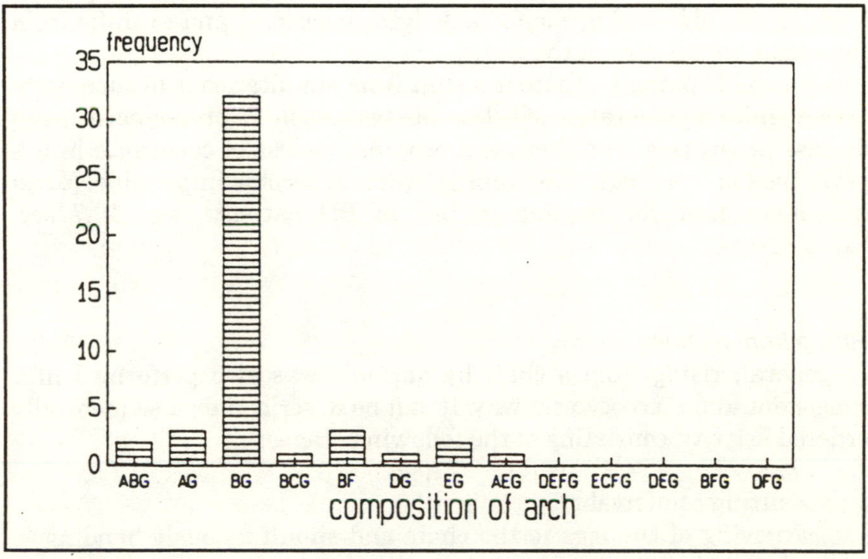


FIG. 12.2c. The formation of arches during one turning in healthy elderly (N=10, 3 observers).

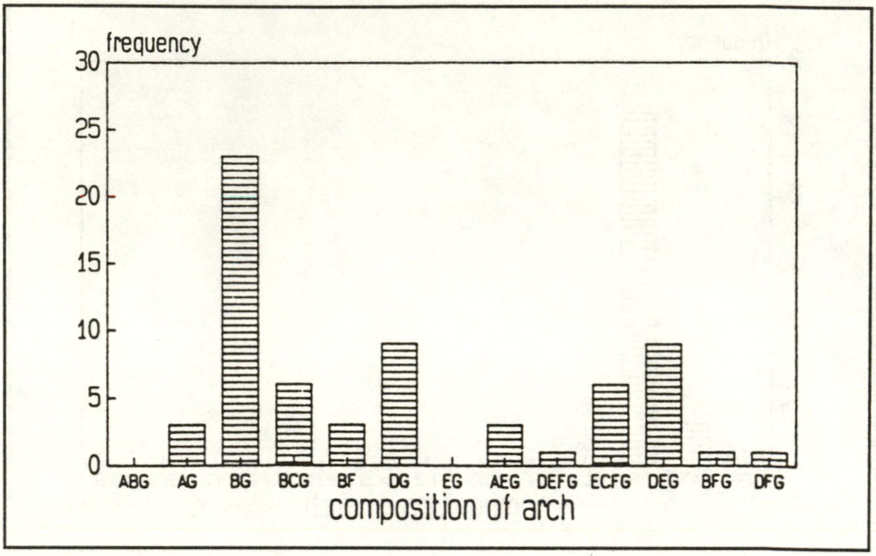


FIG. 12.2d. The formation of arches (or attempts) during one turning in PD patients (N=10, 3 observers).

actual formation of an arch, and turning evolves into rolling over to the side. In the latter case the points of support are used for pushing. This leads to unstable and uncomfortable lying positions, and to shifts from the centre to the edge of the bed.

Also, in PD patients, there is a shift from simultaneous to successive action. This fragmentation of action can become more pronounced as the disease progresses, and there is a progressive loss of coherence in the performed movements. Even rolling over can become impossible. Mean movement time for turning in bed in PD patients was 10.71sec. (sd=3.82sec).

*Rising from a chair*

In general, rising from a chair by normals was also performed in a consistent and stereotypical way. It can be described as a sequentially ordered activity, consisting of the following stages:

- sitting comfortably in chair,
- moving of the legs to the chair and simultaneously bending forward of the trunk,
- taking support on legs, frequently on arms also, and rising from the chair.

The initial horizontal displacement of the trunk fluently shifts into a vertical direction. The only inter-subject variation that could be detected was the difference in the use of the arms. When they were used for support, they were either placed on the armrests of the chair, the seat or the subject's own legs. Frequently they were not used for support at all. It was in the use of the arms that some slight disagreement in scoring by the observers was present. Mean rise times were as follows: young adults 1.89sec. (sd=0.40sec.); healthy elderly 1.97sec. (sd=0.25sec.).

In PD patients, rising from a chair was not conducted in the same consistent way. They showed the following anomalies:

- an uncomfortable flexed position in the chair,
- inadequate or absent displacement of the legs and arms,
- a tendency to avoid simultaneous movement of legs, arms and other parts of the body,
- a tendency to more pronounced arm activity and premature knee extension,
- absent or slowly performed bending forward of the trunk,
- a fragmented, interrupted execution of the action as a whole,
- extended rise time (mean 2.50sec.; sd=0.85sec.).

Typically, the action was not fluent and required more effort than for normal controls.

## EXPERIMENT 2: THE RESEARCH ON TRAINING PD PATIENTS

### Introduction

When we attempt to describe the execution of turning in bed and rising from a chair, it becomes clear that these actions have certain specific properties in common:

- they may be performed automatically, without the need of conscious control and without interference with mental activities. In this regard the total action may be seen as "open loop", i.e. preprogrammed and unfolding automatically.
- they may be considered as complex motor tasks for which complex motor plans are required that lead to rapid sequences of movements and to simultaneous movement elements.

To our knowledge, no systematic neuropsychological research regarding motor behaviour involved in turning in bed and rising from a chair has ever been conducted. A considerable amount of research has been conducted however, on akinetic symptoms in voluntarily induced distal movements both in non-medicated and medicated PD patients. Although there can be considerable improvement in execution of this type of movement when L-dopa therapy is applied, more or less subtle impairments remain detectable.

As the pattern of results with regard to akinesia in distal movements may also be relevant to global postural changes and the reorganised strategies, a short review of the relevant findings will be attempted:

1. Ballistic movement over large trajectories are particularly impaired. In ballistic movement, the initial impulsive activity of the agonist is inadequate (reduced EMG-burst: Berardelli et al, 1986; Hallett & Khoshbin, 1980; Stelmach & Worringham, 1988), which leads to impairment of high velocity movements: patients tend to shift from open loop to visually controlled closed loop action (Flowers, 1978).
2. Concurrent movements are particularly impaired. Benecke et al. (1986) found that simultaneous execution of two distal movements (flexion of the elbow and squeezing of the hand) leads to a greater slowness than would be expected from the motor time of the movements when executed in isolation. They concluded that simultaneous execution of two motor programmes in PD is disturbed.
3. Rapid switching between motor programmes is problematic. Sequential execution of the same two distal movements showed an additional slowness of the separate single movements and a comparatively long delay between the two movements when compared with healthy control subjects (Benecke et al., 1987); sequential execution of different motor programs is also disturbed in PD.

One might think that these aspects provide an explanation for the difficulties the PD patient encounters in the execution of the global postural changes (because of their open loop character and the concurrent and sequential movements required). But then one must also wonder why patients do benefit from L-dopa on a great variety of skills that have these same properties in common. Clinical reports of PD patients who can play the piano again, who can knit again, who can dress themselves again and who can drive cars without any problem when on L-dopa, are numerous. So the aforementioned aspects that can be detected in clinical tests, even when the patient is on L-dopa, are not sufficient to understand problems in global postural changes. When the sequential, simultaneous and open loop aspects would be the only factors, improvement induced by pharmacological therapy would be evident, though not necessarily perfect. As this is not the case there might be another explanation: There is an additional non-dopaminergic transmitter system affected in PD that regulates axial motor functioning (Teelken et al., 1989).

Another aspect related to global postural changes is the fact that people do not "know" at a conscious level how to perform them. They are by definition pre-programmed, automatically executed, open loop and complex. One actually doesn't know how one does it. The fact that a kinesiological analysis was necessary to understand the structure of turning and rising, illustrates this. The PD patient has no clue whatsoever to know where he or she is going wrong.

Considering this, it can be understood that a movement therapy designed to restore or retrain the original global postural change will not be successful. For one thing it is (was) not clear how these actions are performed. And when it is, it cannot be expected that the dynamic and automatic execution can be relearned.

It is not likely that the PD patient will benefit from mere rolling instead of turning. As pointed out in Experiment 1, rolling leads to considerable lateral displacement in bed. One can also expect difficulties in the execution of the fast movements that are required to rapidly accelerate the pelvis and the trunk to overcome gravity before the point of equilibrium is reached and rolling can be completed. Conceivably, in many PD patients, this momentum cannot be made in time because it requires a ballistic movement over a wide angle, and this is impaired. Therefore global postural changes must be reorganised, new movement strategies must be developed. Optimal use of distal motor functioning can compensate for impaired axial motor functioning. The phenomena observed in voluntarily induced distal movements in PD patients, should be well regarded in the design of new motor strategies and general knowledge about skill learning should be taken into account (Welford, 1982).

In the learning of motor skills three levels of skill may be distinguished (Cranenburgh & Mulder, 1986; Fitts & Posner, 1967): the learning develops from an initial cognitive stage via an associative stage to an automatic stage.

1. The cognitive stage is viewed as a period of introduction. It has also been termed verbal motor stage indicating the importance of language in the initial stages of skill learning. On the basis of external and internal feedback (verbal, visual and kinaesthetic), internalisation of the skill (memory and

perception track) develops. Execution of the skill will depend on conscious attentional control and therefore be slow and sequential. Parallel execution of other consciously controlled actions is impaired.
2. In the associative stage, external feedback becomes less prominent. Components of the skill that must be learned are associated and become chunks, invoked as single actions.
3. The automatic stage: In this phase execution of the skill requires no conscious control and the isolated actions are hardly accessible.

If we compare global postural changes with motor skills, an important difference appears to be that the former have developed in a prelingual period of life, so without a verbal stage. This might explain part of the problems in spontaneous discovery of alternative strategies: There is no verbal cognitive schema to recall and modify. The likely lack of such a schema is another motivation to develop alternatively structured motor strategies that do have a schema that remains accessible.

In the planned training it is not necessary to pass through all three stages of motor learning as it is a method that is specifically linked to the cognitive stage. As PD patients have particular difficulty in the performance of automatic motor actions, automatisation of the alternative strategies cannot happen because it implies lack of conscious control. Some chunking may be allowed but only when the separate actions are directly related to each other and when operation of the combined-action chunk can be controlled. In training, it is essential that the PD patient develops a precise mental perception of how the strategy is to be executed. Emphasis must be put on the execution of the separate parts of the strategy. Training can thus be regarded as execution oriented (cognitively directed) instead of goal oriented (automatically produced) (Cranenburgh & Mulder, 1986).

Based on the above considerations, new motor strategies for turning in bed and rising from a chair were designed. These strategies had the following features:

- the complex movement was divided into small steps, which comprise singular simple movements that are distally initiated,
- these separate steps were arranged sequentially, avoiding the need for simultaneous action,
- the separate steps could be executed under conscious control, if possible, visually or tactually guided,

- between the separate steps, a pause was inserted to detach the following phase from the previous one, avoiding interference and giving time to return to the verbal representation of the strategy,
- every separate step led to a stable in-between position from where a new phase could be initiated, until the whole sequence of phases has been passed through,
- axial components were limited to a minimum and, when they could not be prevented, they had to be as simple as possible and executed with a maximum of conscious control.

Also, it was decided to make use of the technique of mental practice in the learning process (see Jeannerod & Decety, this volume). It may be defined as a frequent imaging and a cognitive analysis of the execution of movement(s) without actual performance of this (these) movement(s) and can be considered as a form of self-instruction. Mental practice can be useful in many ways. For one thing, it can help the patient to concentrate on the training. Another positive aspect is the fact that an easily fatigued PD patient can practice without physical performance. And, as pointed out, when the patient is performing the strategy, it helps to regenerate the mental perception of the execution. This indicates the importance of sufficient time intervals between the parts of the strategy: It facilitates consciously controlled execution and reduces the chance of chunking and automatisation.

The possible value of strategies for turning in bed and rising from a chair, designed as described, was assessed in a group of ten PD patients. A research protocol was designed, a training programme set up and an evaluation of results executed. The investigation was whether PD patients can learn the new movement strategies, and whether these strategies, at least in the experimental context, can provide better movement results.

## Methods

### *Subjects*

A group of patients with PD, who visit the department of Neurology of the University Hospital of Groningen on a regular basis, was approached. From this group, ten patients were selected. Criteria for selection were absence of clear cognitive deterioration or dementia, and clinically established existence of problems in axial motor functioning. Details of the ten patients are shown in Table 12.2. All patients received L-dopa medication.

TABLE 12.2
Patient Characteristics

| *Subject* | *Sex* | *Age (yrs)* | *Duration of the illness (yrs)* | *Hoehn and Yahr rating* |
|---|---|---|---|---|
| 1 | F | 64 | 14 | III |
| 2 | F | 57 | 16 | III |
| 3 | M | 57 | 17 | IV |
| 4 | F | 57 | 10 | II |
| 5 | M | 63 | 6 | III |
| 6 | M | 82 | 6 | II |
| 7 | F | 59 | 10 | II |
| 8 | M | 65 | 23 | IV |
| 9 | F | 65 | 8 | IV |
| 10 | M | 68 | 10 | IV |

*Materials*
For the training and evaluation, the same materials as mentioned in Experiment 1 were used. During measurements, the same positions and conditions for the video equipment were established.

*Strategies*
In this study, alternative strategies for turning in bed and rising from a chair were the following:

*Turning in bed.* The initial position is lying in the centre of the bed.

1. Move the arms to the sides and put the hands on the edge of the mattress.
2. Pull the legs up one after the other until the knees are flexed at right angles.
3. Lift the pelvis from the mattress and move it, in small steps, as far as possible in the direction, opposite to the intended turning direction. Reposition the feet in the same direction after every displacement of the pelvis.
4. Lower the legs sideways to the mattress in the intended turning direction.
5. Bring the outer arm to the other side of the bed.
6. Make the rest of the body roll over immediately after moving the outer arm, until there is a stable and comfortable position, lying on the side.

*Rising from a chair.* Starting point is an erect and comfortable position, the spine touching the back of the chair.

1. Take hold of the arms of the chair, or, when absent, the sides of the seat.
2. Move the legs to the chair, heels just in front of its legs.
3. Bend forward and come to sit on the edge of the seat.
4. Put full weight on the legs and rise from the chair. When necessary, use the arms as support.

*Training Procedures*

The training programme consisted of six sessions. The first two were exclusively used for learning the strategy of turning in bed. During the next four sessions rising from a chair was also learned and practiced.

Every session took one hour and had the following structure:

- At the beginning of each session, an initial measurement was conducted in the form of a video recording of turning in bed and rising from a chair (in the last four sessions). No feedback from the trainer was given yet.
- After this, training started with turning in bed. Instructions were given and errors were discussed. An instructive video tape of the right execution served as a reference.
- In the next part of the session the actual training took place, starting with physical practice, followed by mental practice and ending with a last physical performance of the strategy.
- A video recording of turning in bed, without any feedback from the trainer, formed a final measurement.
- The training of turning was followed by the training of rising from a chair. It was conducted in exactly the same way and also ended with a final measurement without any feedback from the trainer.

In the course of the training the physical and mental practice gradually changed from trainer-instructed to self-instructed. The patient had to verbalise the phases of the strategies that were physically or mentally executed. During mental practice this also served as a check for the trainer. The sessions were planned with a progressive time interval, increasing from three days between the first and the second session to two weeks between the fifth and sixth.

*Observation and Scoring*

Raw data were the video recordings of two sets of two performances of each strategy, taken at the beginning (initial recording) and at the end (after the training) of each training session. From the recordings, qualitative and quantitative data, that were directly related to the execution of the strategies, could be scored. As the strategies could be regarded as blueprints for performance, clearly divided into discrete steps, it was possible to analyse whether the right movements were made and whether they were performed in the right way and in the right order. Three types of errors were distinguished: executional, sequential, and intentional errors. An executional error was scored when a step of the strategy was not performed perfectly (incomplete, not executed in full, e.g. no maximum displacement of the pelvis to the edge of the mattress in turning). When the steps were performed in the wrong order, (e.g. pulling the legs up and moving the pelvis while the arms have not yet been moved to the side) this was scored as a sequential error. Occasionally patients tended to make movements that were not part of the strategies. These movements were scored as intentional errors (e.g. stretching of legs during the turning strategy).

Maximum error rate per strategy was the number of steps of which the strategy consists, multiplied by three (the number of error types). For rising, this resulted in a maximum of 4 x 3 = 12 errors; for turning this was 6 x 3 = 18 errors. The video tapes were systematically observed and scored. Two observers were trained, the inter-observer agreement for turning was 82.22 %, for rising 98.8% (for the scoring of five turnings and five risings).

For each strategy, a three point rating scale was constructed that could indicate the quality of the initial position before execution of the strategy and the quality of the final position after the execution. Within these scales a rating of 1 represents a poor position, a rating of 2 represents a moderate position and 3 a good position. All position ratings were exactly defined. Again two observers were trained and five turnings and five risings were scored. For turning there was a disagreement of one rating out of ten, which means that inter-observer agreement was 90%. For rising this was 100%.

## Results and Discussion

As we intended to assess which patients would learn the strategies best, a subdivision of the PD patients group was made on the basis of severity of motor impairment, rated with the Hoehn-and-Yahr-scales (H+Y). Three groups were formed (H+Y II, H+Y III and H+Y IV), and differences between them became apparent. By plotting the error scores of the performances it is possible to show the rate of improvement in the execution of the strategies in the course of the training sessions. The mean percentage of errors, made by the three groups of patients during each execution, could be calculated.

Figures 12.3a and 12.3b illustrate that in all three groups less errors were made in the course of the training. For the patients in groups H+Y II and III, the number of sessions was sufficient to arrive at perfect results. Group IV might have benefited from a larger number of sessions, though diminishing effect of training in the form of a less steep slope can be detected.

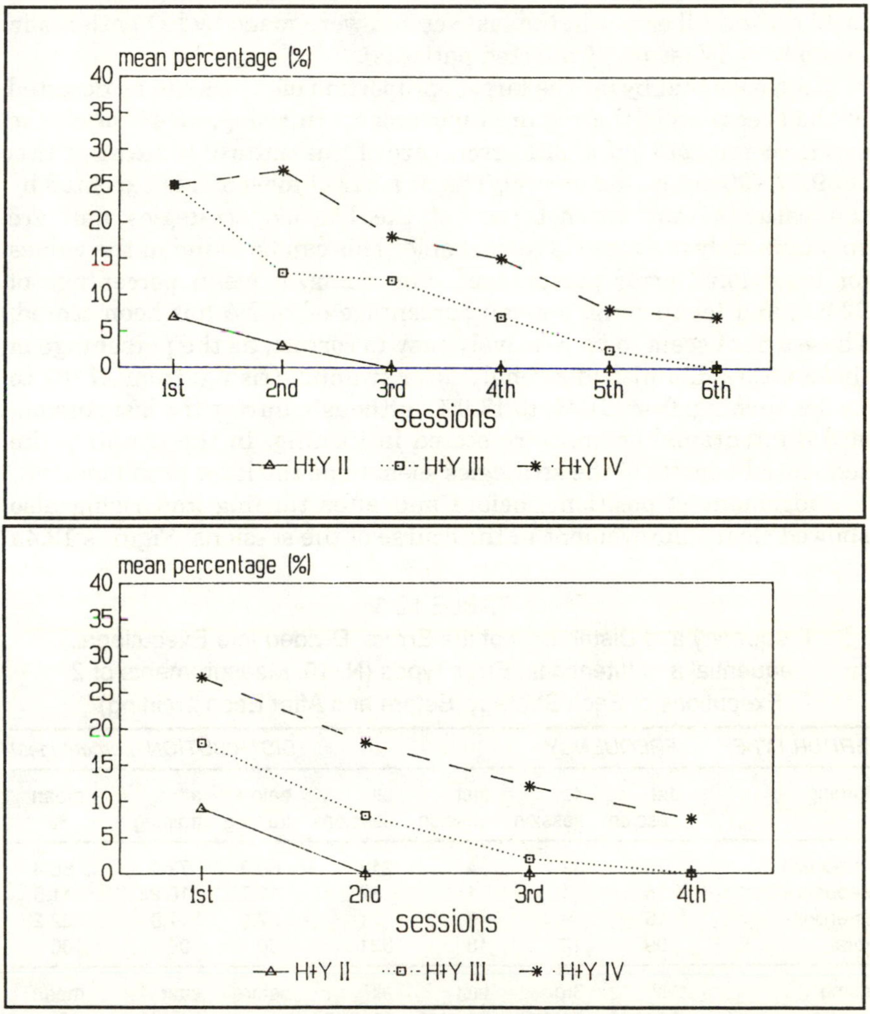


FIGS.12.3a & b. Mean percentages of scored errors made in the course of the training found in three groups of PD patients: H+Y II (mildly affected), H+Y III (moderately affected), H+Y IV (strongly affected.).
a. Error percentages in turning. b. Error percentages in rising.

The types of errors that were scored during the initial measurement before and the final measurement after training were also studied. As mentioned, three types of errors were discriminated: executional, sequential, and intentional errors. In Table 12.3 the composition of the total number of errors is shown. When the first session is compared with the last, the decrease in the number of errors is substantial. In turning, the number dropped from 109 to 13 errors; in rising, it dropped from 86 to 12 errors. All errors in the last session were made by PD patients in group H+Y IV (strongly affected patients).

It appears that by far the largest proportion of errors can be detected in the execution of the required movement. In rising, 66.4% of all the errors scored (213 out of 321 errors) are of this nature. In turning, this is 59.5% (96 out of 162 errors). The number of movements executed by the patients that are not part of the learned strategies and are spontaneously produced is remarkable. This can be found in the values for intentional error percentages. For rising, a mean percentage of 22.2%, and for turning, a mean percentage of 24.2% has been scored. These errors seem to be relatively easy to correct, as the percentage of these errors diminished strongly after training (rising: from 27.0% to 17.3%, turning: from 31.4% to 17.0%), although, during the last session, still 8 intentional errors were scored in turning. In the training, the sequential aspects of the strategies seem to be the least problematical.

Judgement of positions, before and after turning and rising also showed clear improvement in the course of the sessions. Figures 12.4a

TABLE 12.3
Frequency and Distribution of the Errors, Divided Into Executional, Sequential and Intentional Error Types (N=10, Measurements of 2 Executions of Each Strategy, Before and After Each Training)

| *ERROR TYPE* | *FREQUENCY* | | | | *DISTRIBUTION (percentages)* | | |
|---|---|---|---|---|---|---|---|
| turning | 1st session | 4th session | last session | all sessions | before training | after training | mean % |
| execution | 76 | 32 | 4 | 213 | 60.3 | 72.4 | 66.4 |
| sequence | 15 | 1 | 1 | 37 | 12.7 | 10.2 | 11.5 |
| intention | 18 | 9 | 8 | 71 | 27.0 | 17.3 | 22.2 |
| total | 109 | 42 | 13 | 321 | 100 | 100 | 100 |
| rising | 1st session | 3rd session | last session | all sessions | before training | after training | mean % |
| execution | 43 | 15 | 6 | 96 | 52.9 | 66.0 | 59.5 |
| sequence | 15 | 1 | 3 | 27 | 15.7 | 17.0 | 16.4 |
| intention | 28 | 6 | 3 | 39 | 31.4 | 17.0 | 24.2 |
| total | 86 | 22 | 12 | 162 | 100 | 100 | 100 |

and 12.4b show that positions in bed before and after applying the turning strategy showed clear improvement in all groups of patients. But only groups II and III managed to produce perfect or near perfect results. Learning the strategy for rising from a chair gave very little trouble to patients in groups II and III. Figure 12.4c shows that from the first session onwards they were capable of taking perfect or near perfect positions before rising. The execution itself resulted in perfect positions after rising (Fig. 12.4d). Group IV, however, did not score so well. This can partly be due to the fact that subject No.8 had extreme problems in getting out of the chair. Throughout the four sessions, when recordings were made, she did not succeed once. This also explains the difference between the higher rated initial position before rising when compared to the ratings after rising. Improvement of the position of the patient after rising or turning may have been a direct result of the execution of the strategies. It may also in part have been due to the better positions learned at the outset of the strategies. These two factors cannot easily be separated, but a fact is that a poor position at the outset

FIGURE 12.4 (a, b, c & d)
Mean rating scores for positions in three groups of patients (H+Y II, III & IV). Each patient performed both strategies twice

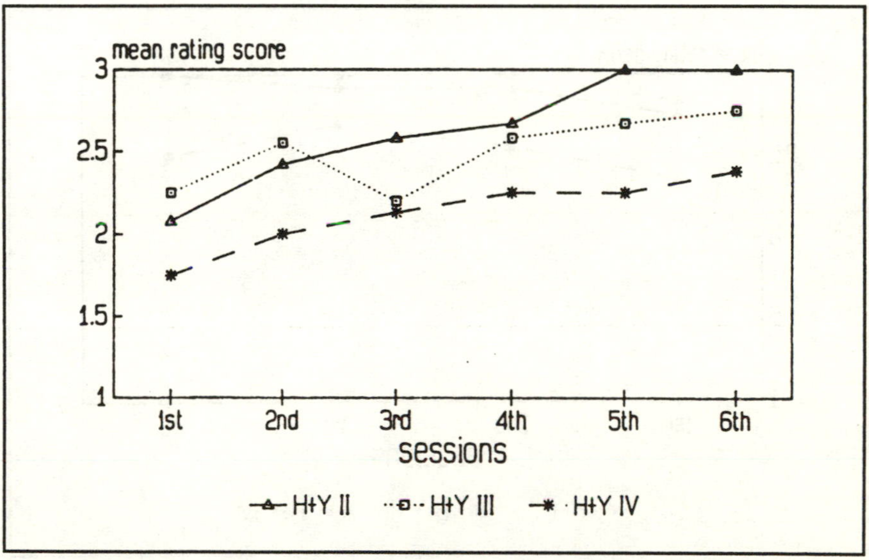


FIG. 12.4a. Mean rating of position before turning.

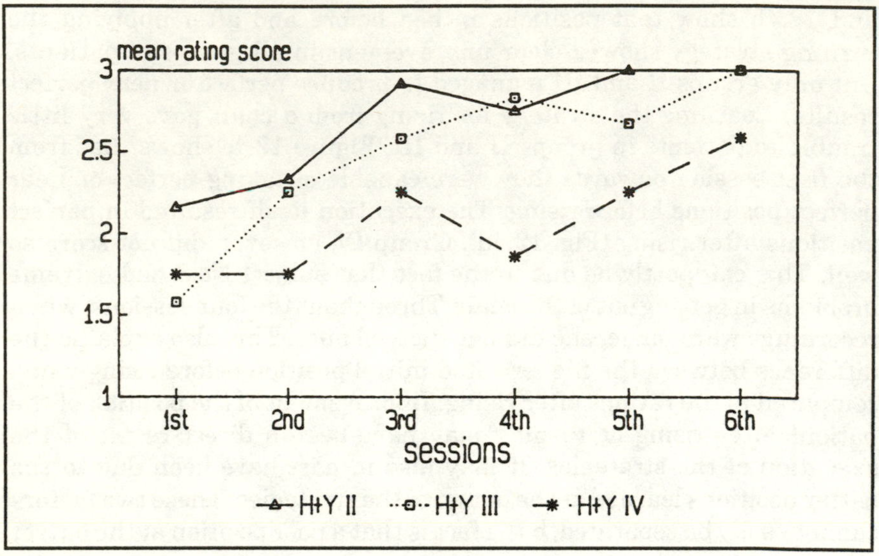


FIG. 12.4b. Mean rating of position after turning.

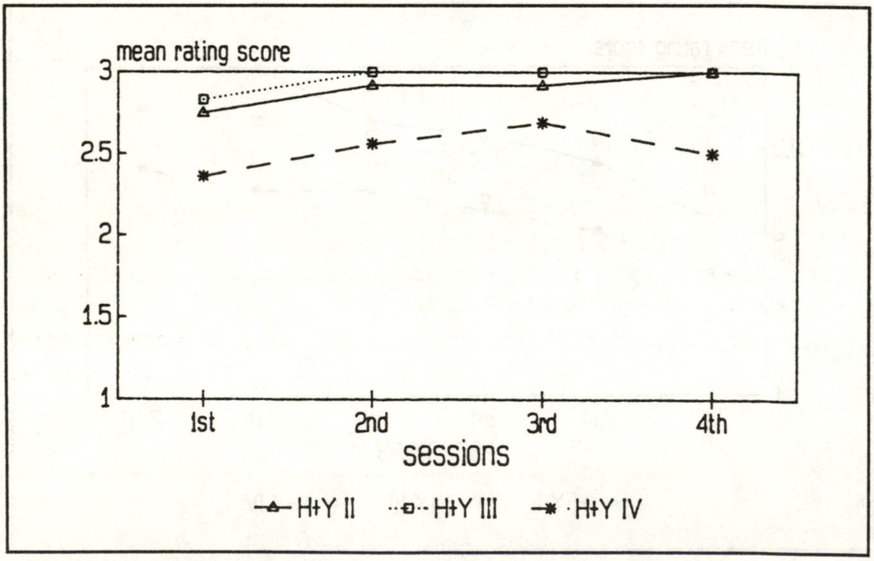


FIG. 12.4c. Mean rating of position before rising.

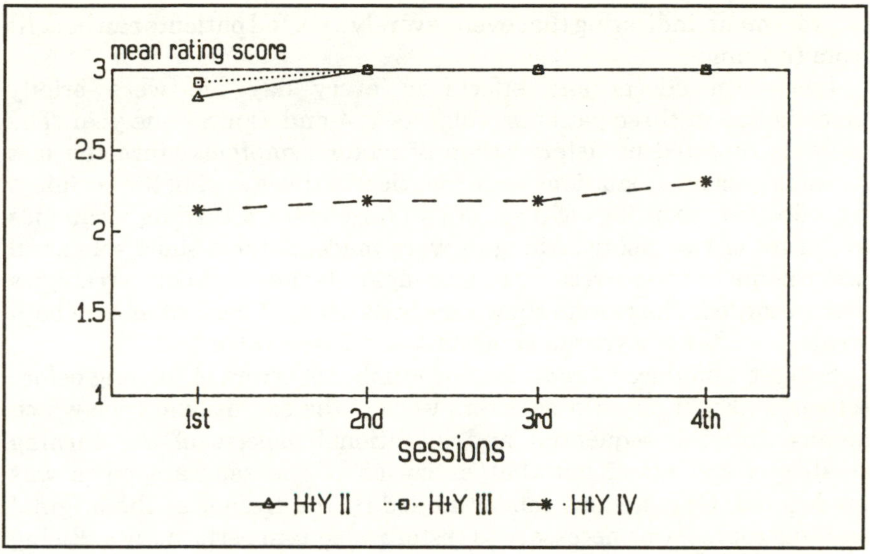


FIG. 12.4d. Mean rating of position after rising.

of the turning strategy changed in many cases into moderate or even good positions after the execution of the strategy. This implies that the strategies can lead to positive results even when initial positions are not perfect.

## GENERAL DISCUSSION

The results indicate that the new strategies improved performance in patients in the experimental situation. Thus the method of instruction works, at least at the short term and in the training situation. In addition, alternative strategies can be learned and lead to better movement results when compared to the original execution of global postural changes in patients with PD.

As a possible movement therapy is intended to prevent early problems in the execution of global postural changes, patients in stadium II and III on the Hoehn-and-Yahr-scales are perhaps the best people to be trained. When the disease progresses and the specific motor impairment regarding global postural changes becomes manifest, such patients might be able to apply the learned strategies and overcome problematic movement situations. A further positive aspect of the procedure is the relatively small number of sessions necessary to give maximal results in patients of group II and III. In these groups major improvement was noticed. Indeed even group IV patients showed some improvement, indicating that even severely affected patients can benefit from training.

Long-term effects and effects in every day life were briefly investigated in three patients (subjects 1, 4 and 7) after one year. The patients reported no deterioration of motor symptoms since the last training session. Conditions were identical to those during the training. Initial video recordings of a set of two unrehearsed turning strategies and a set of two rising strategies were made. After a short rehearsal programme of the correct strategies, again two sets of both strategies were recorded. The results show very little decay of performance of both strategies after one year in subjects 4 and 7 (see Table 12.4.).

Subject 1 produced a considerable number of errors in turning before rehearsal. Eight out of nine errors were of the executional type which means that the sequential and intentional aspects of the turning strategy were intact, but that execution of the separate parts was inadequate. Only a short rehearsal, led by the trainer of the original training course, was necessary to restore adequate performance. Rising delivered no problems. Subject 4 produced two errors of the sequential type: She moved the feet first, then the arms. This is of no importance to the actual result of the strategy. Again a short rehearsal was sufficient for good results.

The scored errors in execution of the turning strategy before rehearsal affected the position after turning for all subjects. Subject 1 scored a rating of 1, subject 4 a rating of 2.5, subject 7 a rating of 2. After rehearsal, the positions were respectively rated at 2.5 for subject 1, and 3 for subjects 4 and 7. Ratings for the positions before and after rising, were perfect in all three subjects.

Some remarks about the use in daily life and transition of strategies to other situations and other forms of global postural changes can be made: All three previously mentioned patients reported the use of at least parts of the strategies. For example, in repositioning in a chair or in bed, and in getting out of bed or difficult chairs. Subject 7 reported that the strategy for rising enabled her to rise from a chair in company in such a way that people wouldn't notice her disease.

TABLE 12.4

Results in Three PD Patients (Subjects 1, 4 and 7), 1 Year After Training

| | *turning* | | *rising* | |
|---|---|---|---|---|
| errors<br>subject | before | after | before | after |
| 1 | 9 (25%) | 1 (2.8%) | 2 (8.3%) | 1 (4.2%) |
| 4 | 2 (5.6%) | 0 | 2 (8.3%) | 0 |
| 7 | 4 (11.5%) | 1 (2.8%) | 3 (12.5%) | 0 |

At present, we are in the early stage of a larger scale study in which the effectiveness of the training, with regard to short- and long-term effects on the trained activities, activities of daily life and subjective well-being in an experimental group of PD patients, will be evaluated in comparison with a control group that is treated in a conventional manner. Besides turning in bed and rising from a chair, akinetic problems with regard to walking will be the subject of study. Again cognitively directed strategies will be designed and tested. A consciously controlled emphatically executed heel-strike, foot-roll and toe-off will be essential.

## ACKNOWLEDGEMENTS

This study was supported by the Praeventiefonds (Dutch Prevention Fund) grant 28-1572 to W.H. Brouwer and J.P.W.F. Lakke. We would like to thank M.J. Driesens-Start, R. Elting, E. Holtjer, B. Rubingh, H.K. Slager, F. Vos and W. Zijlstra for their creative support.

## REFERENCES

Arling, G. (1987). Strain, social support, and distress in old age. *Journal of Gerontology, 42,* 107-113.

Benecke, R., Rothwell, J.C., Dick, J.P.R., Day, B.L., & Marsden, C.D. (1986). Performance of simultaneous movements in patients with Parkinson's disease. *Brain, 109,* 739-757.

Benecke, R., Rothwell, J.C., Dick, J.P.R., Day, B.L., & Marsden, C.D. (1987). Disturbance of sequential movements in patients with Parkinson's disease. *Brain, 110,* 361-379.

Berardelli, A., Dick, J.P.R., Rothwell, J.C., Day, B.L., & Marsden, C.D. (1986). Scaling of the size of the first agonist EMG-burst during rapid wrist movements in patients with Parkinson's disease. *Journal of Neurology, Neurosurgery and Psychiatry, 49,* 1273-1279.

Cranenburgh, B. van & Mulder, Th. (1986). *Van contractie naar actie.* Utrecht: Bohn, Scheltema en Holkema.

Cratty, B.C. (1973). *Movement behavior and motor learning,* 3rd edition. Philadelphia: Lea and Febiger.

Fitts, P.M. & Posner, M.I. (1967). *Human performance.* Belmont, CA: Brooks Cole Publishing Co.

Flowers, K. (1978). Some frequency response characteristics of Parkinsonism on pursuit tracking. *Brain, 101,* 19-34.

Franklyn, S., Kohout, L.J., Stern, G.M., & Dunning, M. (1981). Physiotherapy in Parkinson's Disease. In F.C. Rose & R. Capildeo (Eds.), *Research progress in Parkinson's disease.* London: Pitman Books Ltd.

Gibberd, F.B., Page, N.G.R., Spencer, K.M., Kinnear, E., & Hawksworth, J.B. (1981). A controlled trial of physiotherapy for Parkinson's disease. In F.C. Rose & R. Capildeo (Eds.), *Research progress in Parkinson's disease.* London: Pitman Books Ltd.

Hallett, J. & Khoshbin, S. (1980). A physiological mechanism of bradykinesia. *Brain, 103,* 301-314.
Hoehn, M.M. & Yahr, M.D. (1967). Parkinsonism: Onset, progression and mortality. *Neurology, 17,* 427-442.
Lakke, J.P.W.F. (1985). Axial Apraxia in Parkinson's Disease. *Journal of the Neurological Sciences, 69,* 37-46.
Lakke, J.P.W.F., Brouwer, W.H., & Broersma, T.T.W. (1988). Measuring the quality of life in neurological degenerative diseases. *TGO Tijdschrift voor Therapie, Geneesmiddel en Onderzoek, 13,* 176-180.
Lakke, J.P.W.F., Jong, P.J. de, Koppejan, E.H., & Weerden, T.W. (1980). Observations on postural behavior: axial rotation in the recumbent position in Parkinson patients after L-dopa treatment. In: U.K. Rinne, M. Klinger, & G. Stamm (Eds.), *Parkinson's Disease current progress, problems and management.* Amsterdam: Elsevier/NorthHolland Biomedical Press.
Lakke, J.P.W.F. & Kamsma, Y.P.T. (1992). Parkinson's disease and the axial component of motor behaviour. *Focus on Parkinson's Disease, 4(1),* 9-13.
Lakke, J.P.W.F., Van Den Burg, W., & Wiegman, J. (1982). Abnormalities in postural reflexes and voluntarily induced automatic movements in Parkinsonian patients. *Clinical Neurology and Neurosurgery, 84,* 227-235.
Luria, A.R. (1963). *Restoration of Function after Brain Injury.* London: Pergamon Press.
Marsden, C.D. (1982). The mysterious motor function of the basal ganglia. *Neurology, 32,* S14-539.
Marsden, C.D. (1989). Slowness of movement in Parkinson's disease. *Movement Disorders, Supplement 4,* S26-S37.
Rose, F.C. & Capildeo, R. (Eds.) (1981). *Research progress in Parkinson's disease.* London: Pitman Books Ltd.
Stelmach, G.E. & Worringham, C.J. (1988). The preparation and production of isometric force in Parkinson's disease. *Neuropsychologia, 1,* 93-103.
Teelken, A.W., Berg, G.A. van den, Muskiet, F.A.J., StaalSchreinemachers, A.L., Wolthers, B.G., & Lakke, J.P.W.F. (1989). Catecholamine metabolism during additional administration of DL-threo-3,4-dihydroxyphenylserine to patients with Parkinson's disease. *Journal of Neural Transmission, 1,* 177-188.
Weiner, W.J. & Singer, C. (1989). Parkinson's disease and nonpharmacologic treatment programs. *Journal of the American Geriatrics Society, 4,* 359-363.
Welford, A.T. (1982). Motor skills and aging. In J.A. Mortimer, F.J.Pirozzolo, & G.J. Maletta (Eds.), *The aging motor system.* New York: Praeger.

CHAPTER THIRTEEN

# Rehabilitation of a Case of Ideomotor Apraxia

Emerita Pilgrim
*Department of Physiotherapy, Radcliffe Infirmary NHS Trust, Oxford, UK*

G. W. Humphreys
*Cognitive Science Research Centre, School of Psychology, University of Birmingham, UK*

## ABSTRACT

The case of a left-handed head injured patient (G.F.), with ideomotor apraxia of his left upper limb, is presented. The purpose of the study was to present an analysis of the nature of the apraxia and the results of a rehabilitation strategy (modified 'Conductive Education') used to change G.F.'s left hand performance. The results showed a positive effect of therapy, but little carry-over to everyday life. The implications of the study for understanding the nature of apraxia, and for its rehabilitation are discussed.

## INTRODUCTION

The term "apraxia" is widely applied to deficits affecting the purposeful organisation of voluntary actions, not caused by weakness, akinesia, abnormal tone or posture, intellectual deterioration, poor comprehension or unco-operativeness (Heilman, 1979). Often such patients demonstrate normal unhesitating use of the affected limb in everyday tasks such as reaching out to shake hands or to open a door, and even tying shoe laces. However, when asked to demonstrate how to use an object or how to carry out an action involving a single or a series of components of movements, then the patient's performance is distorted and not smoothly executed; it lacks correct spatial and temporal order and is sometimes incomplete.

A number of different theories have been generated to account for the different dyspraxic subtypes. For instance, one traditional proposal maintains that certain centres within the cortex are the locus of 'motor programmes' for skilled movements (Faglioni & Basso, 1985; Heilman, 1979; Liepmann, 1900). It is thought that the supramarginal gyrus of the left parietal lobe plays a pivotal role in movement control and indeed, may be the site of the motor programme. Information is thought to be transmitted from the left supramarginal gyrus by two direct routes: One to the right premotor area via the corpus callosum (which in turn would control the left hand via the right motor area), and the other to the left premotor area then to the motor area for the control of the right hand (Faglioni & Basso, 1985). Apraxia will result from damage to the parietal site of the motor programme.

In contrast, apraxia could result from damage to the pathways transmitting information from the primary auditory and visual areas to the motor area in the brain (a disconnection account). This account does not imply that any specific area is responsible for generating action. In the case of pantomiming to the names of objects, auditory stimuli travel to the primary auditory cortex (Heschl's gyrus) and the auditory association area (in the left hemisphere, Wernicke's area, important in language comprehension), then to the motor association area (Area 6) and the primary motor area (Area 4); apraxia occurs when the damage interrupts the transmission of the sensory information to the motor areas (Geschwind & Kaplan, 1962).

Evidence from patients suggests that actions may be triggered in different ways according to the input modality of the stimulus. For instance, as a result of their systematic investigation of left brain-damaged patients on the use of ten objects in three modalities (auditory, visual and tactile presentation of an object), de Renzi, Faglioni and Sorgato (1982) proposed that the same type of gesture can be differentially impaired according to the modality of input. Thus, 90% of patients were found to be worse given verbal as opposed to visual input, 5% of patients were found to be worse given visual as opposed to verbal input and 9% of patients worse given visual as opposed to tactile input, suggesting modality-specific impairments and at least three "routes to action".

The possibility that there may exist relatively direct links between visual descriptions of objects and learned actions has been little discussed in neuropsychological theory. As an example of this, the ability of a patient to make an appropriate gesture to a visually presented object is often taken to indicate normal access to semantic information about the object's function, even in the absence of any ability to retrieve phonological information concerning the object's name (e.g. L'hermitte

& Beauvois, 1973). Such an assumption holds only if there is a single route from vision to action, mediated by access to semantic knowledge.

At least two pieces of evidence contradict this assumption. Riddoch and Humphreys (1987) reported the case of a patient (J.B.) who was impaired both at naming and at matching functionally associated objects, from vision. In contrast, when given the names of the objects J.B. performed at ceiling level. Despite his apparent problems in visual access to semantic or functional knowledge, J.B. was generally good at making correct gestures to objects he failed to identify. This relatively preserved ability to gesture to visually presented objects thus appears to reflect a non-semantic route between vision and action. This route could involve direct associations between stored item-specific "structural knowledge" (learned information about the structure of individual objects), or directly-computed visual information not contingent on item-specific knowledge (e.g. a container may be associated with a pouring or drinking action, a spiralled shaft might be associated with a screwing action and so forth). In J.B.'s case, it seems likely that gestures were based on stored item-specific knowledge because: (1) he was able to distinguish between known objects and novel nonobjects constructed by inter-changing the parts of known objects; and (2) his gestures could be very specific (e.g. he made a right-hand cutting gesture to a knife, and a left hand "prodding and lifting" gesture to a fork).

Riddoch, Humphreys, and Price (1989) reported a contrasting case, of an apraxic patient who was impaired at making gestures, but only to visually presented objects. This patient, C.D., was typically unable to initiate the appropriate right-hand action when confronted with a visually presented object. Nevertheless, he could gesture to the same objects with his left hand, and he could gesture with his right hand when the objects were removed and he was given only their names. C.D. also identified and retrieved appropriate semantic knowledge about all the objects concerned, indicating intact visual access to semantic knowledge (contrary to J.B. earlier). Also, the route from semantics to action seemed intact, given his ability to make right-hand gestures to object names. The problem related to the coupling of vision to the system governing right-hand actions. To account for the pattern of results, Riddoch et al. proposed that visually presented objects activate a set of competing actions from vision-action associations that are not contingent on item-specific knowledge. Expressed in terms of direct perception (Gibson, 1979), we might say that visually presented objects afford various actions. Appropriate gestures to visually presented objects require that there is selection between competing affordances. For C.D., visual input seemed to inhibit the action system controlling his right hand, so that he was impaired at initiating right hand actions.

When visual input was removed and C.D. was given only the object's name, the right-hand action system seemed to be accessed appropriately via the semantic system. Riddoch et al. conclude that C.D.'s impairment was linked to abnormal inhibition in a route linking visual input descriptions of objects to action.

The present paper reports an apraxic patient, G.F., who complements the case of C.D. (Riddoch et al., 1989). G.F. presented with a unimanual left-handed apraxia following multiple lesions of the right temporal and frontal lobes. He was particularly impaired at making learned left-handed gestures to visual stimuli, and he was rather better at left-handed gestures when given joint visual and tactile input and when asked to gesture to the name of the object. G.F. was relatively good at making right hand gestures to objects irrespective of the modality of presentation. We first outline a set of tests that aimed to identify the locus of G .F.'s impairment in terms of a model of how known actions might be retrieved and carried out (see Pilgrim & Humphreys, 1991, for further details); we then outline a rehabilitation study aimed at remediating his specific deficit.

## CASE HISTORY

G.F. suffered a head injury at age 29 in January 1987 when he was knocked down by a car. C.T. scan showed extensive brain injury and multiple lesions in the right temporal and frontal region.

Pre-morbidly G.F. was left-handed. He had seven years of secondary school education, and was working in a shoe factory at the time of the accident.

G.F. entered a rehabilitation centre two months after his accident. Though initially mute, he gradually became able to speak fluently but with some perseverative features. He had a left upper quadrantinopia, intact sensation but some neglect of his left limbs (e.g. he tended not to use his left limbs despite their having intact strength). He also showed extinction to bilateral simultaneous tactile stimulation. However, there was no sign of unilateral visual neglect in drawing and cancellation tasks. This pattern of underuse of the affected side, along with a lack of visual neglect, is consistent with a form of motor neglect (see LaPlane & Degos, 1983).

A WAIS-R test, given nine months after admission, showed a verbal I.Q. score of 91 and a performance I.Q. score of 57. G.F. had particular problems with visual memory and construction tasks.

The tests reported in this study were carried out over a three month period (commencing twenty three months post injury), during which time G.F.'s condition remained stable.

## ASSESSMENT 1: PROPRIOCEPTIVE AND/OR KINAESTHETIC KNOWLEDGE

To test G.F.'s stored knowledge about the correct action for the use of objects he was evaluated on whether he could judge whether an action passively performed with his left hand was correct or not using only proprioceptive and/or kinaesthetic feedback.

### *Materials*

G.F.'s performance was assessed on the use of twenty common objects (see Table 13.1) and recorded on videotape.

### *Method*

G.F. was blindfolded and each of the twenty objects was placed consecutively in his left hand. This was done twice; once for when the correct action was performed for each object, and once for when the incorrect action was performed. On each trial, G.F. was told what the object was (e.g. a hammer), and then one of the experimenters moved his hand passively in either the correct gesture for the object (moving his hand in short firm repetitive downward motions and up) or in a gesture appropriate for one of the other objects in the set (e.g. turning his hand in a spiral motion, then pulling his clenched hand in a short firm movement upwards). G.F. was asked to say yes or no according to whether the correct gesture was performed.

### *Results and Discussion*

G.F. scored 40/40; his decisions were made rapidly and there were no problems in discriminating the correct from the incorrect gestures. This indicates that G.F. has intact stored proprioceptive and/or kinaesthetic knowledge about the correct actions for objects.

TABLE 13.1
Twenty Common Objects Used to Test Gesturing Use of Objects Under Different Modalities

| | |
|---|---|
| Beaker | Pencil |
| Hammer | Toothbrush |
| Teapot | Fork |
| Corkscrew | Key |
| Milk bottle | Saw |
| Razor | Teacup |
| Milk jug | Whistle |
| Tin opener | Paintbrush |
| Clothes brush | Trowel |
| Scissors | Nailbrush |

## ASSESSMENT 2: G.F.'s PERFORMANCE GESTURING THE USE OF OBJECTS

This assessment was carried out to quantify G.F.'s ability to gesture to common objects with his right and left hands.

### *Method*

The 20 objects were equally divided into 5 sets of 4, and the sets of items were rotated across conditions using a Latin Square design. There were two presentation conditions: Vision-only and vision-and-touch. In the vision-only condition, G.F. was asked "Show me how you would use this object", and in the vision-and-touch condition he was allowed to hold the object. His performance was videotaped and the tapes were subsequently scored by five independent assessors. The assessors were asked to rate G.F.'s gestures on a 7-point scale: 1 being poor (incomplete, exaggerated, distorted or inappropriate), 7 being good (unhesitating, smoothly executed, fluent sequencing, correct spatial arrangement).

### *Results*

G.F.'s gestures were analysed by taking the means of the assessors' ratings for each gesture and by conducting within-items ANOVAs. The mean ratings on the gestures are given in Table 13.2.

There were reliable effects of presentation condition (vision-only vs vision-and-touch) ($F(1,19)=33.09$, $P<0.01$) and of hand ($F(1,19)=235.13$, $P<0.001$). His performance was better under the vision-and-touch condition than the vision-only condition, and it was better with the right hand than the left hand.

There was also an interaction between the presentation condition and the hand of response ($F(1,19)=38.58$, $P<0.01$). With visual stimuli, G.F.'s performance with his left hand was worse than his right hand performance with both vision and vision and touch ($P<0.05$, Newman-Keuls test, for both comparisons).

### *Discussion*

Assessment 2 demonstrates that G.F. has a unimanual apraxia, in that his gestures are worse with his left, relative to his right, hand. Interestingly, G.F. was formerly left-hand dominant. Unimanual

TABLE 13.2
Mean Ratings of G.F.'s Gestures in Assessment 2
(1 = Poor Performance, 7 = Good Performance)

| | Vision only | Vision and touch |
|---|---|---|
| Left hand | 1.83 | 4.28 |
| Right hand | 5.96 | 5.93 |

apraxias are commonly found for the non-dominant rather than the dominant limb (Faglioni & Basso, 1985). Non-dominant limb apraxia can be linked to the existence of a single bimanual action system controlling responses for both hands, with this action system being sited in the dominant hemisphere. Unimanual apraxia of the nondominant hand can then be attributed to disconnection of the non-dominant hand from the controlling action system (Faglioni & Basso, 1985).

G.F.'s problem with his formerly dominant hand can be interpreted in at least two ways. On one account, there is a disconnection within G.F.'s right hemisphere of left-hand responses from a bi-manual action system (see Fig. 13.1). Alternatively, there may exist separate action systems for each hand, in which case, G.F's problem may be attributed to an impairment of the left-hand action system (see Fig. 13.2). In other studies, we showed that G.F. was relatively good at making bimanual actions, using his apraxic left hand (Pilgrim & Humphreys, 1991). Good bimanual actions can be attributed to facilitatory cross talk from an intact (right hand) action system for the impaired (left hand) system, in line with the idea of action systems being hand-specific (Fig. 13.2). It is less easy for the proposal of a single, bimanual action system, to account for the result.

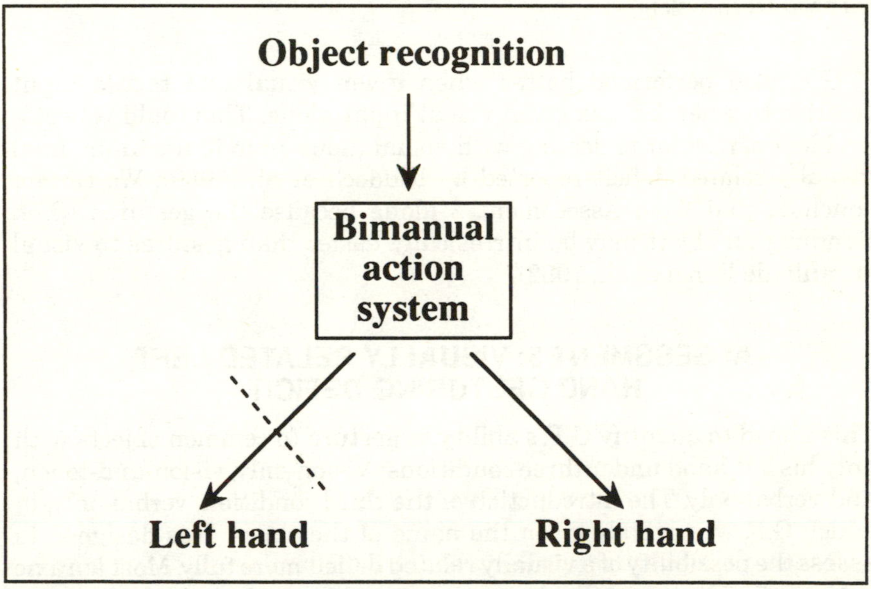


FIG. 13.1. Hypothesised model for making learned gestures to seen objects (G.F.'s lesion disconnects the left hand motor responses from the controlling bimanual action system).

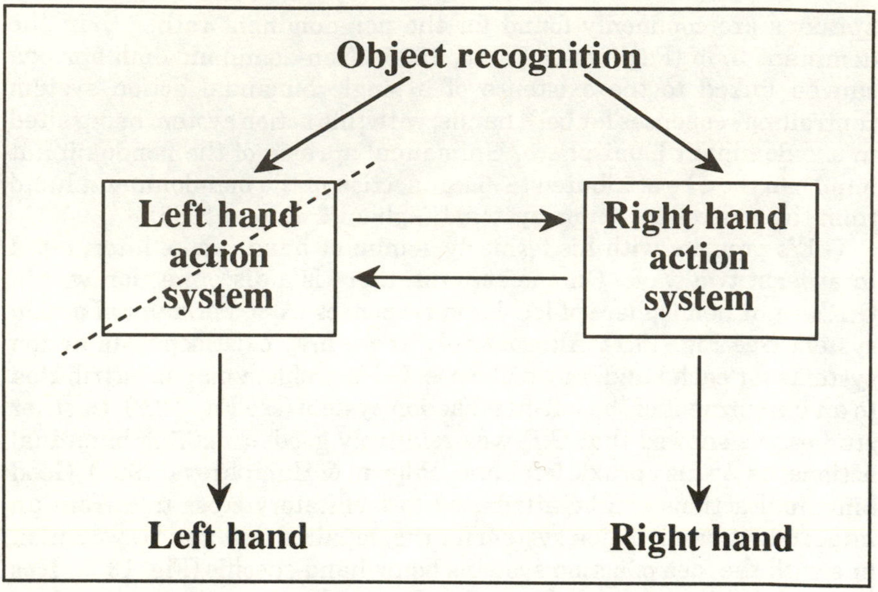


FIG. 13.2. Hypothesised model for making learned gestures to seen objects, with separate action systems specified for each hand (G.F.'s lesion selectively disrupts the left hand action system).

G.F. also performed better when given visual and tactile input relative to when he was given visual input alone. This could reflect a problem particular to dealing with visual input, akin to the unimanual visually related deficit reported by Riddoch et al. (1989). We cannot conclude that from Assessment 2 alone because the gestures when handling an object may be intrinsically easier than gestures to visual stimuli (de Renzi et al., 1982).

## ASSESSMENT 3: VISUALLY RELATED LEFT HAND GESTURING DEFICIT

This aimed to quantify G.F.'s ability to gesture to common objects with only his left hand under three conditions: Vision-only, vision-and-touch, and verbal-only. The introduction of the third condition, verbal-only, in which G.F. was merely given the name of the object, was designed to assess the possibility of a visually related deficit more fully. Most apraxic patients find it more difficult to gesture to object names than to gesture to the same objects presented visually (Rothi & Heilman, 1985), so it cannot be argued that gesturing to object names is intrinsically easier than gesturing to visually presented objects.

*Method*

The same 20 objects were used as in Assessments 1 and 2. Each of the objects was presented in each of the three conditions with the order of the stimuli being randomly determined. The data were scored and analysed as for Assessment 2.

*Results*

The mean ratings given to gestures are shown in Table 13.3. There was a main effect of condition ($F(1,19)=31.33$, $P<0.01$). G.F.'s performance in the vision-and-touch condition was better than in the verbal-only condition ($P<0.01$, Newman Keuls test), and his performance in the verbal-only condition was better than in the vision-only condition ($P<0.05$, Newman-Keuls test).

*Discussion*

Assessment 3 confirms that G.F.'s problem with left-hand gestures is especially marked with visually presented stimuli because performance in the visual condition was worse even than performance when he was given the names of the object alone. Indeed, as his performance improves when he is given the name alone, it would appear that the visual object interferes with his gesturing ability. Visual interference in gesturing may be attributable to the multiple action sets afforded by visually presented objects. When multiple actions are activated within an action system, G.F. may find it particularly difficult to select the appropriate action: We can think here that G.F.'s left-hand actions are normally made on the basis of a "noisy" left-hand action system. Performance is worst when that level of noise is maximised—when input occurs via a visual route that normally raises "noise" in the system. Note also that G.F. is far from perfect at making left-hand gestures when given object names or visual-plus-tactile input. This fits with the idea that visual input acts to exacerbate the operation of an already impaired action system.

G.F. had shown that he had knowledge of the correct action to particular objects by making rapid and correct judgements when having to discriminate between correct and incorrect actions (Assessment 1); also he was able to carry out gestures with his right hand. In devising a rehabilitation strategy, we therefore attempted to capitalise upon his

TABLE 13.3
Mean Ratings of G.F.'s Left Hand Gestures in Assessment 3
(1 = Poor Performance, 7 = Good Performance)

| Vision only | Vision and touch | Name only |
|---|---|---|
| 1.80 | 4.33 | 2.60 |

intact verbal knowledge. This was done by devising a goal-directed verbal strategy, in which G.F. articulated the serial order of the component parts of each action, whilst performing the actions with his left hand.

*Treatment*

Conductive education (CE) is an educational approach for the attainment of functional motor goals in the rehabilitation of brain-damaged children and adults. The process is a structured one through the subject's active participation in goal-directed actions that are broken down into component parts, performed serially and rhythmically verbalised simultaneously. A "conductor" provides the goal-directed instructions (Cotton & Sutton, 1986).

A modified form of CE was used to re-educate G.F.'s left hand movements. This consisted of a task-analysis of the movements involved in using common objects, and verbalised articulation of the goal-directed task.

*Training*

G.F. received training daily in the use of objects with his left hand over three weeks, using the modified version of CE Practice involved the use of the objects with *goal-directed verbalisation*. The first session consisted of physical assistance plus verbal instructions based on the task analysis (e.g. for the object: beaker)

"*Reach* the beaker,
*clasp* the beaker,
*carry to my lips*,
*drink*,
*Stop*"

Once a set of actions becomes learned, the number of verbal directions can be reduced, until performance attains a criterion level in the absence of verbalisation. At such a stage, it is possible that the task has become automatised, and no longer dependent on the same supporting structures (e.g. Logan, 1985).

Two training sessions were observed by G.F.'s wife and she was given written instructions (as described earlier) for the practice to continue daily for 15 minutes under her supervision and feedback. The experimenter (E.P.) directed a session once a week after the initial two training sessions.

## ASSESSMENT 4: EFFECT OF TREATMENT

### *Method*

A multiple-baseline procedure was used with G.F. being given a set of "trained" objects and a set of "control" objects, for which no training was given.

Five objects were used in the training group (see Table 13.4 - Group A), and five in the control group (Table 13.4 - Group B). These ten objects had been rated with the lowest scores by the independent assessors and so they were considered as being sensitive to change. Pre-therapy results were based on G.F.'s performance on Assessment 3, and involved three testing conditions for each object: Vision-only, vision-and-touch, verbal-only. At the end of three weeks training, G.F. was re-assessed for each object under each test condition.

### *Results*

The data from the five objects in Group A and the five objects in Group B, scored prior to training, and after training, were analysed by conducting a mixed design ANOVA, with one between-items factor (Trained vs. Control Objects) and two repeated measures factor (presentation condition and time of testing; see Table 13.5).

There was no main effect of whether items were trained or control ($F<1.0$). There was a main effect of the presentation condition ($F(2,16)=51.79$, $P=<0.001$); G.F.'s performance was better in the vision-and-touch condition and vision-only was better than verbal-only. G.F.'s initial assessment was minimally better in the verbal presentation than in the visual presentation condition, but after treatment, performance in the visual presentation condition was minimally better than in the verbal presentation condition.

TABLE 13.4
Two Groups of Objects Exposed to Different Input

| |
|---|
| Group A: Training group with modified "Conductive Education" (with verbal feedback) |
| Fork |
| Trowel |
| Corkscrew |
| Beaker |
| Teapot |
| Group B: Control group "experience" (handling only, without verbal feedback) |
| Hammer |
| Scissors |
| Key |
| Toothbrush |
| Nailbrush |

TABLE 13.5
Mean Ratings of G.F.'s Left Hand Performance Under Three Modalities: Pre- and Post-training

| | Verbal only | | Vision only | | Vision & touch | |
|---|---|---|---|---|---|---|
| | Pre- training | Post- training | Pre- training | Post- training | Pre- training | Post- training |
| Group A: (training) | 1.64 | 2.72 | 1.16 | 3.08 | 3.72 | 5.4 |
| Group B: (control) | 2.32 | 2.16 | 1.6 | 2.52 | 3.68 | 4.24 |

There was also a significant main effect of time of testing ($F(1,8)=15.59$, $P=<0.01$); performance was better on the second (post-treatment) relative to the first (pre-treatment) test.

The only interaction that approached significance was between the treatment group and the item group ($F(1,8)=4.89$, $P=<0.058$). Pre-treatment performance on treated and control items did not differ; after treatment, performance on treated items was significantly better than pre-treatment performance with both treated and control items ($P<0.01$ and $P<0.05$, Newman-Keuls). There was no pre- vs. post-treatment difference for control items.

These findings suggest that a modified form of Conductive Education treatment had an effect on G.F.'s performance, and that there was no general improvement over time on untreated objects.

### *Discussion*

G.F.'s performance under visual presentation of objects in Assessment 3 was shown to be worse relative his performance when given object names (the verbal-only condition). There was a minimal improvement in G.F.'s performance on control items under visual presentation after treatment. In addition, there was a more substantial improvement in his performance with the objects treated, relative to his performance with the same objects tested prior to treatment. There are various ways in which this treatment effect could occur. For instance if one assumes that verbal inputs activate semantic knowledge directly (as proposed by Riddoch et al., 1989), then verbalisation may be seen as augmenting G.F.'s semantic knowledge, and perhaps inhibiting inappropriate actions that are afforded from visually presented objects. One might also speculate that the minimal improvement in his performance under visual presentation conditions for all (untreated as well as treated) objects could be due to his developing a strategy of trying to inhibit activation within a left-hand action system.

Alternatively, as G.F. has the knowledge that his left-hand performance is inappropriate and inaccurate (Assessment 1), verbalisation could help specifically in generating a correct action sequence. For instance, verbalisation of the first part of the action could raise activation for that component of the action, allowing it to be selected successfully. Note that this idea is not incompatible with the proposal that verbalisation works via inhibiting inappropriate actions with an action system. One effect of verbalising the first component of an action may be also to inhibit inappropriate activation. Whichever account holds true, the lack of a generalised effect on control items also indicates some degree of item-specificity in the activation and/or inhibition passed from the semantic system to the action system.

## GENERAL DISCUSSION

G.F. is an apraxic patient who was initially particularly poor at making gestures to seen objects with his previously dominant (left) hand (Assessments 2 and 3). That this problem was initially worse for visually presented objects, relative to when objects were presented visually and tactilely, or relative to when object names were given, is of some interest for theories of action. In particular, this pattern of performance dissociates from the usual pattern of poor gesturing to object names (Rothi & Heilman, 1985), and so supports the existence of separate routes to action (see also Riddoch et al., 1989). In G.F.'s case we propose that the problem resides within the action system controlling his left hand (see Pilgrim & Humphreys, 1991). Performance is worse when objects are presented visually because visual objects normally activate a set of actions, and so raise the background noise in what we take is an already noisy action system (in G.F.'s case).

After training, testing showed that a modified form of CE had an effect on G.F. 's apraxic use of objects with his left hand. The basic principle of CE is the restoration of performance through a restructuring of the functional system by incorporating the role of speech in the regulation of motor acts. We have suggested that it may affect performance both by activating the appropriate initial components of an action sequence, and also by inhibiting inappropriate actions afforded by vision-action associations.

The use of goal-directed verbalisation may also be of general use in apraxia, and need not be confined to gesturing to objects. For instance, G.F. also demonstrated apraxic agraphia (Ellis, Young, & Flude, 1987). Pilgrim (1989) carried out an evaluation of G.F.'s apraxic agraphia and was able to show that he had good knowledge of the letter form and that there were beneficial effects on his writing of single letters when G.F. verbalised each letter form into its component parts and reconstructed the letter in serial order.

Although the role of speech in a modified form of CE was shown to have an effect on G.F.'s use of objects and writing ability, it should also be noted that G.F. needed considerable prompting to use a verbalisation strategy, and he failed to use it spontaneously after the training period. This could be accounted for as part of the heterogeneity of behaviour after frontal lobe damage. It has been reported that although patients with frontal lobe damage can learn, they continue to make perseverative errors and also fail to improve their performance due to an inability to use that knowledge spontaneously (Milner, 1963, 1965). Goldberg (1985) proposed that goal-setting is carried out by the pre-frontal cortex. Frontal lesions may impair the setting up of goals, and hence self-adoption of rehabilitation strategies. This can be related to the distinction drawn by Ellis et al. (1987) between availability and utilisation of feedback. They demonstrated in their patient V.B., and in normals, that the ability to fully utilise feedback in writing was dependent on the degree of attention applied.

A goal for future research could be to separate potential ways in which CE might help in rehabilitation. Two potential effects of CE might be: (1) augmenting semantic knowledge and reducing the options afforded from pure visual structural information—through inhibiting inappropriate actions; and (2) reducing a defect with motor programming—by guiding the serial ordering of motor components of goal-directed actions. Work is needed to separate these different potential effects of CE. Such research is necessary to gain knowledge of the most suitable areas in rehabilitation in which CE might be used appropriately and effectively. Finally, we need to consider whether the effect of CE, for example, on gesturing to objects and writing, has the potential to generalise to other tasks, and whether skills need to be practised repeatedly until they become automatic.

## REFERENCES

Cotton, E. & Sutton, A. (Eds.) (1986). *Conductive education: A system of overcoming motor disorder.* Beckenham: Croom Helm

de Renzi, E. (1985). Methods of limb apraxia examination and their bearing on the interpretation of the disorder. In E.A. Roy (Ed.), *Neuropsychological studies of apraxia and related disorders*. Amsterdam: Elsevier Science Publishers BV, North Holland.

de Renzi, E., Faglioni, P., & Sorgato, P. (1982). Modality-specific and supramodal mechanisms of apraxia. *Brain, 105;* 301-312.

Ellis, A.W., Young, A.W., & Flude, B.M. (1987). "Afferent dysgraphia" in a patient and in normal subjects. *Cognitive Neuropsychology, 4*, 465-486.

Faglioni, P. & Basso, A. (1985). Historical perspectives on neuroanatomical correlates of limb apraxia. In E.A. Roy (Ed.), *Neuropsychological studies of apraxia and related disorders*. Amsterdam: Elsevier Science Publishers BV, North Holland.

Geschwind, N. & Kaplan, E. (1962). A human cerebral deconnection syndrome. A preliminary report. *Neurology. Minneapolis, 12*, 675-685.

Gibson, J.J. (1979). *The ecological approach to visual perception*. Boston: Houghton-Mifflin.

Goldberg, G. (1985). Response and projection: A reinterpretation of the premotor concept. In E.A. Roy (Ed.), *Neuropsychological studies of apraxia and related disorders*. Amsterdam: Elsevier Science Publishers BV, North Holland.

Heilman, K.M. (1979). Apraxia. In K.M. Heilman & E. Valenstein (Eds.), *Clinical Neuropsychology. V.1*. Oxford University Press, New York.

Laplane, D. & Degos, J.D. (1983). Motor neglect. *Journal of Neurology. Neurosurery and Psychiatry, 46*, 152-158.

L'hermitte, F. & Beauvois, M.F. (1973). A visual-speech disconnexion syndrome. Report of a case with optic aphasia, agnosic alexia and colour agnosia. *Brain. 96*, 695-714.

Liepmann, H. (1900). The syndrome of apraxia (motor asymboly) based on a case of unilateral apraxia. (Translation). In D.A. Rottenberg & F.H. Hochberg (Eds.), *Neurological classics in modern translation*.

Logan, G.D. (1985). Skill and automaticity: Relations, implications and future directions. *Canadian Journal of Psychology, 39*, 367-386.

Milner, B. (1963). Effects of different brain lesions on card sorting. *Archives of Neurology, 2*, 90-100.

Milner, B. (1965). Visually guided maze-learning in man: Effects of bilateral hippocampal, bilateral frontal and unilateral cerebral lesions. *Neuropsychologia, 3*, 317-338.

Pilgrim, E.J. (1989). *A single case report of unimanual apraxia and agraphia in a lefthanded head injured patient*. (MSc. thesis, London University).

Pilgrim, E.J. & Humphreys, G.W. (1991). Impairment of action to visual objects in a case of ideomotor apraxia. *Cognitive Neuropsychology, 8*, 459-473.

Riddoch, M.J. & Humphreys, G.W. (1987). Visual object processing in a case of optic aphasia: A case of semantic access agnosia. *Cognitive Neuropsychology, 4*, 131-185.

Riddoch, M.J., Humphreys, G.W., & Price, C.J. (1989). Routes to action: Evidence from apraxia. *Cognitive Neuropsychology, 6*, 437-454.

Rothi, L.J.G. & Heilman, K.M. (1985). Ideomotor apraxia: Gesture discrimination, comprehension and memory. In E.A. Roy (Ed.), *Neuropsychological studies of apraxia and related disorders*. Amsterdam: Elsevier Science Publishers BV, North Holland.

# PART FIVE

## Spoken Language and Phonological Skills

CHAPTER FOURTEEN

# Cognitive Neuropsychology and the Remediation of Disorders of Spoken Language

Andrew W. Ellis and Sue Franklin
*Department of Psychology, University of York, UK*

Alison Crerar
*Department of Computer Studies, Napier University and Department of Speech Pathology and Therapy, Queen Margaret Polytechnic, Edinburgh, UK*

## INTRODUCTION

The growth of cognitive neuropsychology in the 1970s was stimulated in large measure by the incursion into the field of experimental cognitive psychologists who brought with them their armoury of cognitive theories, experimental methods and statistical techniques (Shallice, 1988a). These psychologists were typically concerned to understand the nature and organisation of cognitive processes in the neurologically intact individual. They saw neuropsychological patients as a source of insights into normal cognitive processes that could complement and extend the insights gained from experiments in the laboratory. In the words of Wilson and Patterson (1990), "As practiced by the majority of cognitive neuropsychologists, ... this approach to research is indeed just a variant of cognitive psychology. The source of evidence may be different ... but the techniques tend to be similar and, more importantly, the goals are the same."

The early development of the field was inevitably influenced by the nature of the pre-existing interests of these cognitive psychologists. It happened, for example, that reading and memory were skills of great interest at the time, and so the study of acquired dyslexia and forms of short- and long-term memory disorder rather dominated cognitive neuropsychology in the early years. This emphasis was not entirely unreasonable: cognitive neuropsychology is based on the application to neuropsychology of theories or models of normal cognitive processing, and at the time when this seminal work was being done, theories of reading and memory were much better developed than, say, theories of object recognition or spoken word comprehension.

As cognitive neuropsychology has matured, it has also diversified into other areas of cognition (Ellis & Young, 1988). Part of this expansion has been a growth in research on disorders of spoken language processing. In keeping with the major concerns of cognitive neuropsychology, this work has largely (though, as we shall see, not exclusively) focused on what can be learned from the study of patients with spoken language deficits about the organisation of language processes in the normal (neurologically intact) mind and brain. It has, however, also refined our ability to pinpoint the impairments underlying dysphasic symptoms. In the early part of this paper we shall review a small number of studies which concentrate in particular on research into disorders of auditory word comprehension and naming. We will then briefly discuss the contribution of model-based assessments in the accurate diagnosis of aphasia. In the third section of the paper we will consider the importance of accurate diagnoses in the general management of the dysphasic person's difficulties. Finally, we will assess the contribution of the cognitive neuropsychological approach to direct therapeutic intervention.

## UNDERSTANDING SPOKEN WORDS

Problems understanding heard words are common in aphasia. Too often in the past, however, aphasiologists have been content to apply a label such as 'fluent aphasia' or 'Wernicke's aphasia', distinguishing at best between comprehension impairment with or without intact repetition, and have not enquired further as to the underlying causes of the problem. In contrast, cognitive neuropsychologists have begun to delineate several different patterns of disorder and to devise tests that will allow the level(s) of breakdown to be identified in a particular patient.

Consider three patients (E.S., A.H., and C.J.) selected from the set of nine reported by Franklin (1989). Each patient was given a set of tests designed to identify different patterns of auditory word comprehension deficit. The tests included:

1. *lexical decision*—discriminating between heard words and invented nonwords,
2. *phoneme discrimination*—same-different judgements on pairs of syllables, and
3. *semantic processing*—deciding whether pairs of words had similar or dissimilar meanings.

The results are summarised in Table 14.1. The three patients in question showed three quite different patterns of auditory word comprehension deficit. In fact, when examined closely, all nine patients reported by Franklin (1989) showed qualitatively different patterns of impaired and intact performance across the different tests of auditory word and nonword perception, and comprehension.

Patient E.S. was poor at all these three tasks (though good at others). His pattern is indicative of a relatively peripheral impairment of phoneme discrimination known as *word-sound deafness* (or *pure word deafness* where there are no additional impairments). Because he was poor at perceiving and discriminating speech sounds, E.S. was also poor at repeating both words and nonwords, telling words from nonwords, and comprehending heard words. The literature contains a number of case studies of patients with what would appear to be the same deficit (e.g., Auerbach et al. 1982; Saffran, Marin, & Yeni-Komshian, 1976). It should be noted that E.S.'s impairment was *not* a pure one; he also had a semantic deficit, indicated by the fact that he was far from perfect at comprehending written words.

Patient A.H. was good at phoneme discrimination but poor at lexical decision and semantic processing. This pattern was shared by two other patients in the Franklin (1989) study and may be termed *word-form deafness*.

Patient C.J. was good at both phoneme discrimination and auditory lexical decision but was poor at semantic processing. He had comparable

TABLE 14.1
Patterns of Performance on Phoneme Discrimination, Auditory Lexical Decision, and Semantic Processing (Synonym Judgements) in Three Patients with Auditory Word Comprehension Deficits (from Franklin, 1989)

| | *PATIENT* | | |
|---|---|---|---|
| | *ES* | *AH* | *CJ* |
| Phoneme discrimination | Severely impaired | Good | Good |
| Lexical decision (auditory) | Severely impaired | Severely impaired | Good |
| Semantic processing | Severely impaired | Severely impaired | Severely impaired |

problems comprehending written words, and the deficit affected the comprehension of both concrete and abstract words. Thus, C.J. may be considered to suffer from a *general semantic deficit*.

Two other patients in Franklin's study showed good phoneme discrimination and auditory lexical decision performance in the context of poor comprehension of heard words. One patient, D.I., had comprehension problems for both heard and written words, again suggesting a central semantic impairment, but the problem only affected the comprehension of abstract words. Comprehension of concrete, imageable words was good. This *abstract semantic deficit* would nowadays be counted as an example of *category-specificity*, and might be used as the basis of claims about the possible internal structure of the semantic system (e.g. Riddoch, Humphreys, Coltheart, & Funnell, 1988; Shallice, 1988b). We would prefer not to become embroiled in the debate currently surrounding the interpretation of category-specific impairments, and will content ourselves with pointing out that comprehension problems are capable of differentially affecting one type of word more than another, and that diagnostic procedures need to be alert to this possibility.

Another patient in the Franklin (1989) study, D.R.B., was poor at comprehending heard words (despite good phoneme discrimination and auditory lexical decision performance), but had no comparable problems comprehending written words. With written words he was good at synonym judgements and other tasks requiring comprehension of word meanings. This remarkable pattern has been called *word-meaning deafness*. It was the object of a classic, if somewhat anecdotal, case study by Bramwell (1897), and a more recent investigation by Kohn and Friedman (1986). Patients with word-meaning deafness can *hear* words clearly and can show good repetition, yet they fail to understand many of the words they hear. The deficit is specific to heard words. In some cases, the patient may be able to write down a heard word and then understand it by reading what he or she has just written!

We have described five of the nine patients from the Franklin (1989) study in some detail, but have already said that although there were similarities between some of them, there were aspects of each patient's performance that made that patient different from the others in the study. A cognitive neuropsychological analysis was able to reveal those differences in a way that should have practical as well as theoretical implications. We have given names to some of the patterns, but we should not confuse naming with understanding. Cognitive neuropsychology is about more than just labelling disorders; it is about understanding them; that is, being able to specify precisely which aspects of normal cognitive processing are impaired in a given patient, generating a particular pattern of performance. The labels we use ('word sound deafness', 'word meaning deafness' etc) refer to *symptoms* not syndromes: As such, they can occur in combination with a wide range of other symptoms, so that two patients who both show, for example, word sound deafness could differ greatly in terms of their other linguistic deficits or other neuropsychological impairments generally.

## MODELLING AUDITORY WORD COMPREHENSION AND ITS DISORDERS

The different patterns of auditory word comprehension deficit observed by Franklin (1989) can be captured to some degree by a model like that shown in Fig. 14.1. This is meant to illustrate some of the processes involved in *normal* auditory word comprehension, but will also provide a framework for analysing the various disorders of spoken word recognition that we have just described. The model (which can at best only be a simplified first approximation to a final acceptable account) identifies three distinct components responsible for three different aspects of word recognition and comprehension.

The job of the *auditory analysis system* is to identify speech sounds (possibly, but not necessarily phonemes) in the speech wave. The results of that analysis are passed to the *auditory input lexicon*. Its role is to identify strings of speech sounds as familiar words. In order to do that it must contain stored descriptions (or 'representations') of the spoken forms of words known to the listener. If the input received from auditory analysis matches one of the stored descriptions in the auditory input lexicon, then a portion of the speech wave will be known to be familiar.

At the stage of the auditory input lexicon the listener does not yet know the meaning of the word. For comprehension to be complete, the representation of a word's meaning must be activated within the *semantic system*. Psychologists know very little about how word meanings are represented (see Garnham, 1985), but representations of some sort there must be.

The various tasks employed in the Franklin study were designed to tap separately each of the components of Fig. 14.1. If the auditory analysis system is intact, the listener will be able to do phoneme discrimination. They will also be able to say whether two words or nonwords sound the same or different, even though they may not know which are words and which nonwords, or what the words mean. Word-sound deafness in which the patient has impaired phoneme discrimination is assumed to be the result of damage to the auditory analysis system.

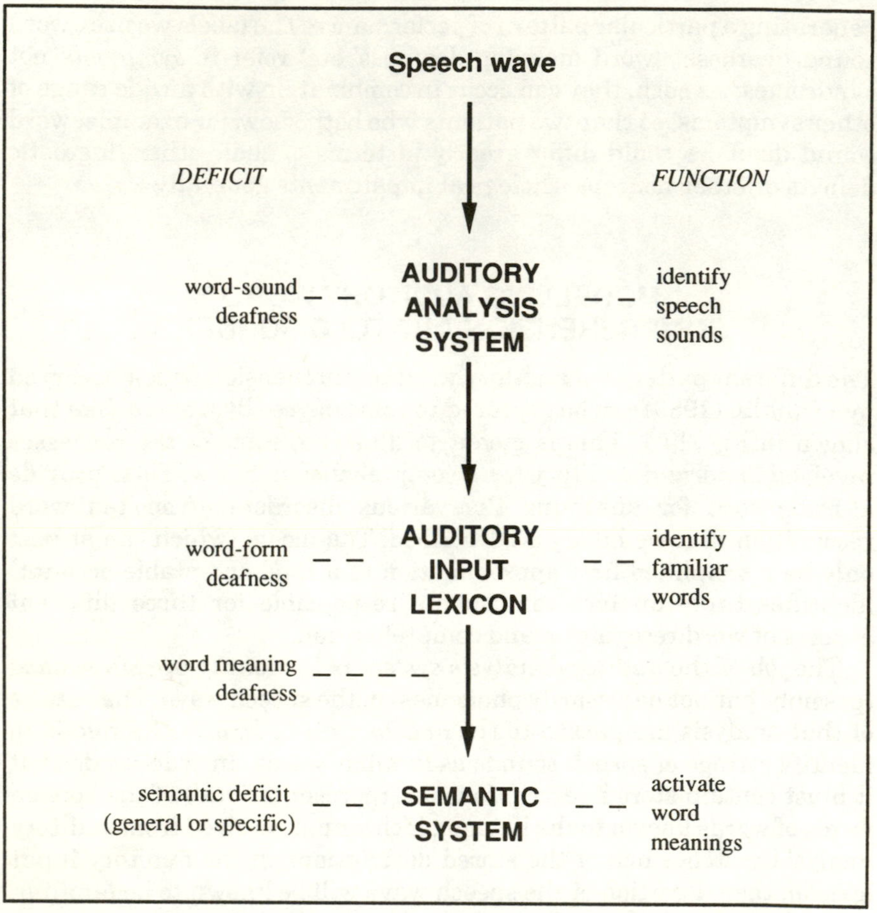


FIG. 14.1. A simple functional model for auditory word comprehension, showing the disorders associated with impairment at each stage.

If both the auditory analysis system and the auditory input lexicon are intact, then the listener will be able to do both phoneme discrimination and auditory lexical decision. If the auditory analysis system is intact but the auditory input lexicon is damaged, then the patient will be good at phoneme discrimination but poor at auditory lexical decision. This is the pattern that Franklin (1989) called *word-form deafness*. Prior to the work of Kohn and Friedman (1986) and Franklin (1989) this form of auditory word comprehension deficit had not been distinguished from word-sound deafness and word-meaning deafness. Yet with a cognitive model and a set of well-chosen tasks it is possible to make a clear distinction between these different patterns.

All three components and their interconnections must be intact if phoneme discrimination, auditory lexical decision and synonym judgements are all to be performed accurately. In word-meaning deafness, phoneme discrimination and auditory lexical decision are still performed accurately, but the patient fails on tasks like synonym judgements that require a precise understanding of the meanings of heard words. The patient with word-meaning deafness can, however, understand written words. If we assume that the same semantic system is involved in representing the meanings of words that are either heard or read, then we must conclude that the semantic system is intact. The only remaining option would be to explain word-meaning deafness in terms of a *disconnection* (complete or partial) between the auditory input lexicon and the semantic system (Ellis, 1984). The representations of spoken word-forms in the auditory input lexicon can be activated (hence the preserved ability to make lexical decisions), but those representations can no longer make contact with the corresponding representations of word meanings in the semantic system.

Patients with either general or category-specific semantic deficits can again perform phoneme discrimination and auditory lexical decision tasks accurately, but not synonym judgements or other tasks that require access to word meanings. Unlike patients with word-meaning deafness, these patients have equal difficulty understanding written words. The assumption, therefore, is that such patients have impairments internal to the semantic system itself—widespread in the case of generalised semantic impairment; more restricted in the case of category-specific semantic impairment.

The right-hand side of Fig. 14.1 shows the localisation of these different patterns of auditory word comprehension deficit within the model. One point to note is that damage to an early stage in a sequence will have knock-on effects for processes downstream of the damaged component because those later stages, though they may themselves be intact, will be receiving defective input. Hence, patients with word-sound deafness are poor at auditory lexical decision and comprehension of heard words, even though the auditory input lexicon and the semantic system may be intact. Similarly, although phoneme discrimination remains possible for the patient with word-form deafness, damage to the auditory input lexicon means that the semantic system, though it may be intact, is receiving inadequate input, so the patient is poor at understanding heard words.

## MODELLING NAMING AND ITS DISORDERS

We have endeavoured to explain disorders of auditory word comprehension in terms of a sequence of processing operations which can be damaged at a number of different levels (and perhaps in a number of different ways). It is possible to offer a similar analysis of the production of single spoken words as in naming (by which we will mean the retrieval and production of single words, typically object names). We will make the common assumption that word retrieval is initiated by the same semantic representations whose activation marks the successful completion of the comprehension process. When word retrieval is being tested, semantic representations may be activated by definitions, sentences cues or pictures, though in normal speech production word retrieval is often under less direct stimulus control, being driven, for example, by the flow of meanings in a conversation.

Figure 14.2 shows a simple model for naming. The first stage in that model is the semantic system. At that stage, words are represented as meanings only. Spoken word forms are retrieved from the next component in the sequence—the *speech output lexicon*. In fact, there is debate as to whether we should talk in terms of separate input and output lexicons for speech and writing (Coltheart & Funnell, 1987; Monsell, 1987), and it may be that what we have called the auditory input lexicon and the speech output lexicon are in truth the same phonological wordstore operating in two different modes for comprehension and production. For the present paper, however, we will assume that two different lexical stores mediate the recognition of heard words and the retrieval of word forms in speaking.

The third component in Fig. 14.2 is the *phoneme level*. There is evidence to suggest that in normal speech production, word retrieval can run some way ahead of articulation, so that a speaker may have selected all the words of a phrase or clause before beginning to articulate the first one (Garrett, 1982). If that is so, then there must exist a stage in the production process at which words can be stored prior to articulation. That, we believe, is at least part of the purpose of the phoneme level.

Hence, the phoneme level holds words in the interval between their being selected from the speech output lexicon and their being prepared for overt production. The phoneme level cannot be the last stage in spoken naming: various co-articulatory and other processes must intervene in order to translate phoneme strings into speech movements. Disorders of those processes presumably result in so-called *dyspraxia of speech*. In this paper, however, we will confine ourselves to the earlier stages of word production shown in Fig. 14.2.

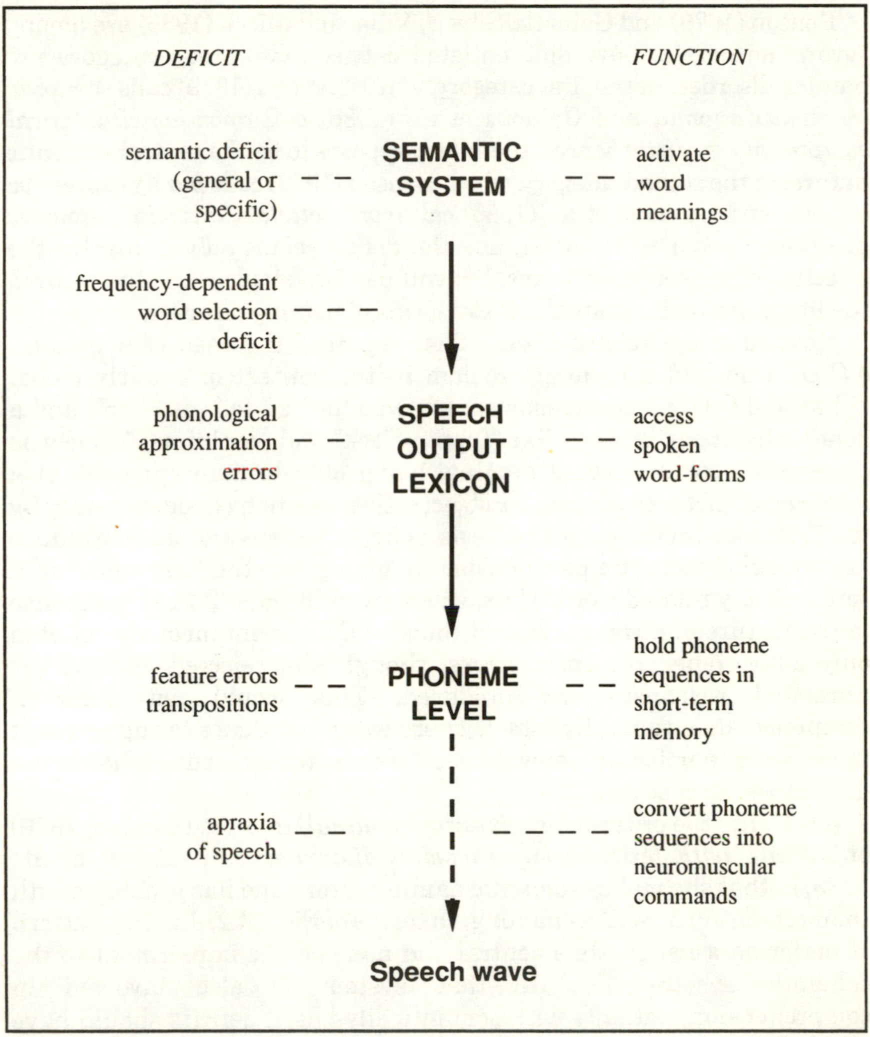


FIG. 14.2. A simple functional model for naming (word finding), showing the disorders associated with impairment at each stage.

It is sometimes claimed that speech production is more difficult to investigate experimentally than speech comprehension and that it is harder to devise tasks to tap each stage separately. Nevertheless, we shall argue that it is possible using cognitive neuropsychological methods to establish the likely locus of the breakdown in patients showing qualitatively different patterns of naming disorder (see Ellis, Kay & Franklin, 1992, for a fuller discussion).

Benson (1979) and Gainotti, Silveri, Villa, and Miceli (1986) are among several authors to have differentiated between two broad categories of naming disorder. In the first category, which Benson (1979) calls *semantic (nominal) anomia* and Gainotti et al. (1986) call *anomia with lexical comprehension disturbances*, the deficit appears to be of a central semantic nature. In the second category, which Benson (1979) calls *purely expressive anomia* and Gainotti et al. (1986) call *word selection anomia*, semantic processes appear to be intact, and the deficit seems only to involve the selection of spoken word forms. We will use two single case studies from the literature to illustrate these two forms of naming disorder.

Howard and Orchard-Lisle (1984) reported the case of a patient, J.C.U., who had a naming problem in the context of a fairly global aphasia. J.C.U.'s spontaneous speech was limited to "yes", "no", and a small selection of phrases like "flipping 'eck" and "cor blimey". She was extremely poor at picture naming, being able to name just 3% of a selection of pictures of familiar objects. She was helped significantly by the first sound of the target name as a cue, but it was also easy to induce her to make semantic paraphasias by giving her the first sound of a semantically related word. Thus, when given the cue "l" (/l/) in response to the picture of a tiger, she said "lion". J.C.U. spontaneously rejected only 24% of her semantic errors, though she rejected 86% of the unrelated responses she produced. This would not occur if comprehension were fully intact. There was no evidence to suggest that there were particular categories of words which caused her more difficulties than others.

J.C.U. fits the criteria for *semantic (nominal) anomia* (Benson, 1979) or *anomia with lexical comprehension disturbances* (Gainotti et al., 1986) in that she makes semantic naming errors and has problems with comprehension as well as naming. In terms of Fig. 14.2, J.C.U.'s pattern of performance suggests a central and non-specific impairment to the semantic system. Because that system is also involved in comprehension, patients with semantically-based deficits should have problems understanding the same words that they have difficulty accessing in speech. That was the case with J.C.U.

Purely expressive anomia (Benson, 1979) or word selection anomia (Gainotti et al.,1986) can be illustrated with reference to patient E.S.T. of Kay and Ellis (1987). E.S.T. was successfully operated upon to remove a large but benign tumour from his left hemisphere. Though he made a good recovery, he was left with considerable word-finding difficulties. He became quite accomplished at masking these in spontaneous speech by the strategy of replacing words he found difficult with easier ones. His problems became more apparent in object naming tasks when he could no longer employ that strategy.

E.S.T.'s capacity to produce an object name could be shown to depend on the name's frequency of use. He was much more likely to be able to retrieve commonly used names correctly than less commonly used names. The effect seemed to be tied to how often the object name was used in speech, rather than how often an object might be seen because he had difficulty naming objects, like a brick or a cloud, that are seen all the time but whose names are not used particularly often in speaking.

E.S.T.' s attempts at word retrieval were sometimes helped by the provision of a phonemic cue, though he often knew with what sound a target word began, even when he was unable to recall the word in full. Unlike J.C.U., he could not be induced to make semantic errors by misleading phonemic cues. Shown a picture of a baseball bat and told, "it's r" (for racquet) he replied, "Doesn't begin with that though, does it? It's a b"!

Quite often E.S.T. made what might be termed *phonological approximation errors* in which he produced an attempt at the target word that contained some of the right phonemes without being wholly correct. For example, asked to name a picture of a stool he said, "Stop, step ... seat, small seat, round seat, sit on the ... sit on the stuh, steep, stone ... it's stole, stay, street". He similarly named a strawberry as a "sumberry", and a balloon as a "ballow".

Table 14.2 shows the results of asking E.S.T. to name a set of 260 line drawings of objects published by Snodgrass and Vanderwart (1980). The table shows the mean frequencies for object names eliciting different types of response from E.S.T. where frequency is measured in terms of the number of times a given word occurs per million words of (written) English. As can be seen, the mean frequency of words named correctly and without delay was substantially higher than the mean frequency of words named correctly after a delay or with the aid of an initial sound cue. Target words to which E.S.T. could only produce an approximation, an entirely incorrect word, or no response at all, had the lowest mean frequencies.

TABLE 14.2
EST's Responses to a Set of 260 Object Pictures Published by Snodgrass and Vanderwart (1980). Data from Kay and Ellis (1987)

| *RESPONSE TYPE* | *Mean frequency per million words of English* |
|---|---|
| Immediately correct (N = 97) | 82.5 |
| Correct after delay of 5 secs or more (N = 27) | 38.0 |
| Correct after an initial sound cue (N = 27) | 27.8 |
| Phonological approximation (N = 22) | 13.6 |
| Phonological approximation after initial sound cue (N = 37) | 7.9 |
| Incorrect/omission (N = 50) | 16.3 |

Kay and Ellis (1987) tried to explain both the frequency effect and the phonological approximation errors in terms of damage to the connection between the semantic system and the speech output lexicon. More recent work has shown that a marked frequency effect may be observed in patients who do not make phonological approximation errors (Hirsh, Ellis, & McCloskey, 1990; Miceli, Giustolisi, & Caramazza 1991; Zingeser & Berndt, 1988). This suggests that the two phenomena arise at different loci. One possibility suggested by Ellis, Kay and Franklin (1991) is that the frequency effect arises in the connection between the semantic system and the speech output lexicon while phonological approximation errors which do not involve the substitution or reversal of similar phonemes (Miller & Ellis, 1987) are a consequence of damage internal to the lexicon. Further detailed single case studies of anomic patients are required to resolve this issue.

If a patient has an impairment at the level of lexical output, that patient should show preserved comprehension of words that they have that difficulty in producing. E.S.T. showed good comprehension of object names that he was unable to retrieve in naming. This was demonstrated on a range of tasks and again differentiates E.S.T. from J.C.U. and similar patients with central semantically-based naming problems.

## THE ROLE OF MODELS

Though models like Figs. 14.1 and 14.2 may be simple, they are demonstrably useful when it comes to helping us distinguish between, and understand, different forms of auditory word comprehension and naming deficit. Models of this sort are commonplace within cognitive neuropsychology but may still appear somewhat off-putting to practitioners. We would like to make a few more general points about the role and value of models, not only to the development of cognitive neuropsychological theories, but also to the practical application of the discipline.

When most people hear the word *model* they probably think of a scaled-down replica of a physical object like a model car or plane. Models can, however, take many different forms. The static two-dimensional representation on paper of a geographical area is a model—we usually call it a map. For an economist, a model may be a complex series of equations that express hypothetical relationships between key factors in an economic subsystem. A particularly powerful way of using models is to use a model developed to account for one set of findings to predict findings in another area of research. Cognitive neuropsychology has, with some success, used models developed to explain the way that normal subjects process language to predict characteristics of dysphasic language. Models are now being implemented on computers, to simulate various aspects of cognition. By comparing the performance of the simulation with the performance of the real-world system it is modelling, its shortcomings can be identified and it can possibly be modified to give a better account.

Considerable progress is possible using such models provided that certain assumptions are made. These assumptions have been articulated by Caramazza (1984; 1986), Saffran (1982) and Shallice (1988a) among others. The very existence of models like Figs. 14.1 and 14.2 assumes that it is reasonable and profitable to think of the mind as being composed of many discrete and separable functional components, each responsible for a different aspect of mental processing (see Patterson, this volume). It must be possible to interrogate the functioning of selected components using well chosen tasks, and it must be possible to infer which components are damaged and which are intact from the pattern of performance shown by individual patients. The performance of a patient should be interpretable as arising from the workings of the intact cognitive system minus those components that have been damaged.

Without assumptions of this sort, the kind of interpretations we have just given to different patterns of auditory word comprehension and naming deficit would not be possible. Such interpretations will be much easier if another commonly made assumption is correct, namely the assumption that the mature brain does not develop entirely new functional components following brain injury. It is reasonable to expect that new strategies may be devised which allow tasks to be performed in new ways using old components, but cognitive neuropsychology is going to be much harder (though not impossible) if it ever transpires that the adult brain can develop, say, a new auditory input lexicon following destruction of the old one. At present there is no firm evidence to suggest that such things can happen.

It is possible, therefore, for progress to be made in cognitive neuropsychology if certain assumptions are made. A model like Fig. 14.1 can account for patterns of auditory word comprehension deficit if the components are assumed to be separate and distinct, and if symptoms can be assumed to arise either from damage to the components themselves (as in word-sound deafness, word-form deafness and central semantic impairments) or from damage to the connection between two components (as in word-meaning deafness).

We argued earlier that Franklin's (1989) patient E.S. had a combination of word-sound deafness and a semantic impairment. Such an argument is neither surprising nor problematic. Although it may be that the relatively pure cases are the ones that tend to be picked up for scientific investigation and reported in the literature, the typical patient is more likely to be someone whose brain injury has resulted in a cluster of deficits. These should be interpretable as combinations of deficits that may be seen in isolation in rare patients with relatively pure impairments of single processing stages.

Even a very simple model predicts the existence of several pure deficits, plus many more combinatory patterns. There is no good reason to suppose that all these different profiles will be capable of being subsumed under a small number of headings such as have been used previously in aphasiology. This does not mean that comparisons between patients will be impossible: two patients will, for example, share certain features in common if both have suffered damage to the auditory input lexicon, even if their impairments are such that they differ greatly in other respects.

There is nothing in a diagrammatic model that could not be expressed in verbal form, but just as it is easier to find one's way around a town using a map than using a verbal account of the layout of the streets, so it is easier to follow an hypothesised account of the layout of the cognitive system when that account is represented diagrammatically . As with a map, it is far simpler, using a diagram, to envisage certain pathways being blocked while others remain open, allowing point A to be reached from point B, even if by an unusual route.

Models are of immense value for cognitive neuropsychologists struggling to get to grips with the bewildering range of ways in which even apparently simple functions like single word comprehension can break down. We would argue, though, that cognitive neuropsychological models can be equally useful to speech therapists and other professionals who work with brain injured patients on a day-to-day basis.

The value of models in providing a standardised conceptual framework and accompanying terminology is enormous yet easily overlooked. Models provide standardised forms of representation, giving tangible expression to theories and providing a communicative device through which the state of knowledge can be expressed, disseminated and systematically explored. We would suggest that cognitive neuropsychological modelling offers a conceptual framework and vocabulary that are well suited to meet the needs of speech therapists who, with practice and experience, can use the theory to discuss patients, therapeutic possibilities, and outcomes with one another. With suitable modification, the approach can also help the therapist to inform patients and relatives about the nature of a language disorder. In what follows, we will discuss the contribution that cognitive neuropsychology can make to the diagnosis of aphasia, to the patient's own understanding of his or her condition to the day-to-day management of patients, and to devising and evaluating therapies.

## CLINICAL APPLICATIONS

### Diagnosis

Cognitive neuropsychology, suitably applied, equips the therapist with a far better diagnosis and understanding of the nature of a patient's language disorder than has been provided by traditional aphasiology and traditional aphasia tests. The latter have been overly concerned with assigning patients to one of an unreasonably small set of syndrome categories, whereas any cognitive model worth its salt will inevitably represent a large number of components and interconnections, all capable of being impaired separately or in different combinations. There is little to be gained from attempting to reduce this complexity to a few categories like *non-fluent aphasia* or *Wernicke's aphasia*. Besides, as we have noted, there is more to diagnosis than mere labelling. We believe that cognitive neuropsychology also represents an advance over previous approaches in the degree to which it enables the practitioner to *understand* what has gone wrong for a given aphasic patient.

Cognitive neuropsychologists have sometimes been tempted to replace old syndrome categories such as *fluent* and *nonfluent aphasia* with new categories such as *deep* and *surface dyslexia*. Such terms should be treated with care. The main objection is that the new categories are scarcely more homogeneous than their predecessors. No sooner are they postulated than new evidence requires that they be break up (fractionate) into subtypes which in turn break up, and so on. What then of terms like word-sound deafness and central semantic deficit that we have been using freely in this chapter? As noted earlier, the crucial difference is our view that these terms refer to collections of *symptoms* that arise from damage to a single functional component or connection. Word-sound deafness is a collection of symptoms that arises as a consequence of damage to the auditory analysis system. It may very occasionally be seen in isolation, but will be more likely to co-exist with a range of other deficits in an aphasic patient. From our point of view there is nothing problematic about asserting that a patient has word-sound deafness combined with central semantic impairment: indeed, we have argued that Franklin's (1989) patient E.S. displayed precisely that combination. All attempts to force patients into mutually exclusive syndrome categories are a waste of time.

Present cognitive neuropsychological categories should not be expected to last for ever. Auditory analysis probably involves many cognitive processes, each of which may be capable of separate impairment. Models will need to evolve to take account of advances in our understanding of cognition, and new terms will be needed as shorthand labels for symptoms that arise from damage to different components within the models. Theoretical debate should concentrate on relating patients to models, rather than relating categories like word-sound deafness to models (Ellis, 1987). The good speech therapist must keep in touch with the evolution of our understanding of language disorders and consequent changes in terminology, just as the good doctor must keep in touch with developments in medical science.

Cognitive neuropsychological assessment involves giving the patient tests designed to determine the intactness or otherwise of each hypothesised processing component. We have tried to show for the cases of auditory word comprehension and naming how that might be done. It is common, though, for an aphasic patient to be able to produce and/or comprehend some words but not others. The therapist will therefore want to discover what the relevant dimensions of difficulty are for each patient. Candidate factors that have been shown to be influential for at least some patients include part of speech, imageability (abstractness), frequency of use, age of acquisition, morphological complexity, phonological complexity, and length (measured in phonemes or syllables). Where repetition is concerned, lexicality (whether an item is a word or nonword) can be a very important determiner of success or failure.

Until recently, therapists have been frustrated by the lack of test materials that would allow them to assess the influence of these sorts of factors. Traditional aphasia tests are not ideal for doing cognitive neuropsychology for a number of reasons, including the fact that they do not allow the therapist to assess the contribution of factors like morphological complexity or imageability to a patient's performance (Byng, Kay, Edmundson, & Scott, 1990). Fortunately, that need should be met in large measure by publication of the Psycholinguistic Assessment of Language Performance in Aphasia (PALPA) Battery (Kay, Lesser, & Coltheart, 1992). The PALPA Battery contains materials in the form of word lists and picture sets, carefully selected to manipulate one factor at a time while keeping constant as many other factors as possible. It makes use of procedures such as lexical decision, repetition and picture naming to assess word- and sentence-level processing of spoken and written language. Tests are explicitly related to a cognitive model of normal language processing.

A commitment to cognitive neuropsychology undoubtedly implies a commitment to a degree of methodological rigour in everyday practice. Arguably, good clinical practice demands a shade more rigour than may have been commonplace in the past. We would reject any suggestion, though, that cognitive neuropsychology is excessively time consuming. Apart from querying whether a therapist can afford to do a worthwhile assessment, we would note that with experience it is possible to home in rapidly on a patient's main areas of deficit and to select just those tests that will be maximally informative regarding the aspects of language functioning that are of most concern.

## Feedback to Patients

Traditional assessment procedures allow a speech pathologist to inform a patient that they have a certain aphasic syndrome, and that as a result they are likely to have difficulty with A, B and C. It may help the patient, and their relatives, to be able to put a label on their condition, but leaving aside the theoretical arguments about syndrome categories, all speech pathologists know that many patients do not fit neatly into the standard categories, and that there can be considerable variability even among those that do. We would argue that a cognitive neuropsychological assessment provides a far more useful profile of a patient's pattern of cognitive and linguistic strengths and weaknesses, and that armed with better functional diagnosis, the speech pathologist is also in a better position to explain to the patient and their relatives what has gone wrong.

Very often one of the most difficult things for a patient to cope with is the apparent unpredictability of aphasic performance. Take the case of word-finding problems. Patients can be puzzled, frustrated and frightened by their ability to recall one word but not another. A cognitive neuropsychological assessment that has sought to tease apart the different aspects of complexity and difficulty, may reveal that the patient has particular difficulty with, say, low frequency and abstract words. Very few patients will be capable of working this out for themselves, but simply to *understand* why one word can be recalled with ease though another remains elusive can help to reduce the sense of chaos and the feeling of being out of control that can easily afflict a patient. It can also help the relatives to see the order behind the apparent chaos, and as a consequence to be more sympathetic and understanding.

In allowing the therapist to convey better feedback to patients and relatives, cognitive neuropsychology is helping with the important social aspects of a therapist's work. In some cases the reason why a given patient is not responding to therapy will be a cognitive reason to do with the nature of the underlying deficits, but in other cases the reason may be social or motivational. Counselling and family therapy are important aspects of speech therapy and need to be researched and evaluated with the same rigour as is now being applied to the treatment of the cognitive dimensions of aphasia. The point we would emphasise is that family therapy is not in any way at variance with the cognitive neuropsychological approach. On the contrary, the therapist who carries out good cognitive neuropsychological diagnoses is in a position to be a better family therapist. In addition, patients armed with an understanding of their own problems are in a better position to work out strategies for themselves. They can become active collaborators in the quest for improvements, not merely passive recipients of treatments dispensed by others.

## Case Management

Because the methodology of cognitive neuropsychology is so much more rigorous, it allows more informed decisions to be made about the day-to-day management of a patient's condition. Even the most common sense decisions about how the patient and those around them should maximise their communicative abilities should be based on a thorough knowledge of those communicative abilities.

Take, for example, the question of whether to advise a patient to attempt to write down words they are struggling to say. A thorough cognitive neuropsychological analysis will want to compare a patient's ability to comprehend and produce written words in reading and spelling with that patient' s ability to comprehend and produce spoken words. The Boston Diagnostic Aphasia Examination (Goodglass & Kaplan, 1972) is standardised with respect to the aphasic population. A therapist might administer the naming and writing subtests of the Boston and discover that the patient performs at an average level on the writing tests and one standard deviation below average on the test of spoken naming. This could be seriously misleading, however. Most aphasics are considerably worse at spoken than written naming, so the average for written naming is well below that for spoken naming. It is therefore possible for a patient to perform below average on spoken naming and above average on written naming, yet still to be more impaired at written than spoken naming.

A cognitive neuropsychological assessment would require the patient to name the same items in speech and writing, allowing a direct comparison to be made. If the spoken naming was done on one day and the written naming on another, there is a danger that an apparent difference would be found that was actually a consequence of day-to-day fluctuations in the patient's concentration, or could even be the result of a practice effect. If picture naming was being used as the basis for assessment, a better approach would be to begin by dividing the pictures into two balanced sets, A and B. In one testing session the patient would be asked to say the names of the set A pictures then write the names of the set B pictures. In a later session, the patient would write the names of set A then say the names of set B. That way, speaking and writing would be done in both sessions. The fact that speaking is done first in one session and writing first in the other would mean that changes due to practice or fatigue within testing sessions would not be mistaken for differences between the two language modalities. Such a method does not eliminate problems of interpretation, but it does try to anticipate, minimise and control spurious results. Confidence in any conclusions arising from discrepancies in performance either between sessions or between functions tested will be strengthened by demonstrating similar patterns in repetitions of the tests.

The therapist will also want to discover what specific things help a patient to understand or produce speech—things like phonemic or semantic cuing, lip reading, extra time or practice. Again, the cognitive neuropsychological approach requires that these matters be evaluated systematically. The ABBA design outlined here could again be used to compare a patient's success in naming pictures with or without semantic cues, or with or without lip movement cues. Good assessment feeds automatically into good management.

A detailed assessment may also reveal pockets of relatively preserved processing in a patient who otherwise has severe and multiple problems. These could serve as a basis for communication. The analysis by Howard and Orchard-Lisle (1984) of their global patient J.C.U. provides a case in point. We have noted that J.C.U.'s spontaneous speech was limited to "yes", "no", and a small selection of phrases like "flipping 'eck" and "cor blimey". Spontaneous object naming was minimal. Closer testing revealed that naming improved dramatically if she was given a (correct) phonemic cue—from 3% uncued to 49% cued. She also performed considerably better on tests of auditory word comprehension than would be expected of a global aphasic. Such observations based on careful assessment could form the basis of both advice to relatives and general management, as well as suggesting avenues for therapeutic intervention.

We noted at the outset of this chapter that the initial orientation of cognitive neuropsychology was towards discovering what we could learn about the normal structure and functioning of the mind from work with patients. If that was all that cognitive neuropsychology ever concerned itself with, then we believe that it would still have made a valuable and defensible contribution to knowledge. Nevertheless, as part of the growing maturity of cognitive neuropsychology, an increasing number of its practitioners are involving themselves in work on therapy.

The move to therapy is not unproblematic. Cognitive neuropsychologists disagree among themselves about the extent to which the approach can be expected to generate practical, clinical spin-offs (see Coltheart, this volume). As will become clear, we believe that cognitive neuropsychology has a considerable amount to contribute to the practical business of helping patients, though it also has limitations. We will discuss the contribution of cognitive neuropsychology to treatment under three headings—targeting treatments, devising treatments and evaluating treatments.

*Targeting treatments*

Because cognitive neuropsychology provides a more detailed diagnosis than conventional assessments, and hence more detailed information about the precise nature of the language deficit(s), it provides valuable cues to the therapists as to where therapy should be targeted.

Consider again the set of patients from the Franklin (1989) study. All had auditory word comprehension deficits, yet we saw that the locus of the breakdown was different in each case. Patient E.S. showed symptoms of word-sound deafness. Presumably he needs to devote time and energy to practising speech sound discrimination. The therapist will want to know if such patients benefit from lip reading cues. Patients of this type in the literature have frequently been shown to be assisted by speech movement cues (e.g. Albert & Bear, 1974; Saffran, Marin, & Yeni-Komshian, 1976). A patient studied by Auerbach et al. (1982) was so dependent on lip reading that he remarked, "If I go blind, I won't hear anything!". It turned out that E.S. was also helped by lip reading. Relatives and friends could be advised to make sure he had a clear view of their face when they were talking to him, and therapeutic exercises could be developed that exploited his intact processing of visible speech cues. E.S. also had what we would assume to be a separate semantic deficit evidenced by errors in a written version of the synonym judgements task. The therapist might want to work separately in such a case on improving semantic performance using written words or pictures.

Patient A.H. suffered from word-form deafness. He can no more understand spoken words than E.S. can, but his capacity to distinguish words from nonwords shows that he does not need to practice speech sound discrimination, but instead should focus on discriminating one word from another. As with E.S., errors in a written version of the synonym judgements task suggested an additional semantic deficit. Another patient in the Franklin (1989) study, M.K., who showed symptoms of word-form deafness was unimpaired at synonym judgements with written words. Hence it would be appropriate to do extra work with A.H. on semantic processing, but not with M.K.

Patient C.J. showed good phoneme discrimination and auditory lexical decision but poor semantic processing. He had comparable problems comprehending written words, and the deficit affected the comprehension of both concrete and abstract words. Thus, C.J. needs help on all manner of semantic tasks, but phoneme and word discrimination are unnecessary. Scott (1987) reports a treatment programme that had considerable success with a patient (A.B.) of this sort (see Byng et al., 1990, pp. 84-87). The programme was based on semantic processing tasks like categorisation and auditory word-picture matching, and progressed from requiring only very general semantic information (e.g. categorising objects as indoor or outdoor things) to more specific and precise information (e.g. categorising animals in terms of their natural habitat—land, sea or air). After three months of therapy involving three sessions per week, A.B.'s auditory comprehension had improved, but so had his naming. Although naming had not been included in the therapy programme, at the end of the programme A.B. could produce about 80% of words he had been taught to comprehend, whereas previously he could produce virtually none of them. This improvement had been predicted on the assumption that spoken word comprehension and naming utilise the same semantic representations, and on the assessment of A.B.'s problems as semantic in origin.

Patient D.I. from the Franklin (1989) study was diagnosed as having a central semantic deficit affecting both spoken and written words that was more marked for abstract than concrete nouns. Diagnosis here suggests the particular type of word that should be targeted in therapy. We will mention later the results of a successful intervention study involving a patient with a semantic deficit similar to D.I.'s.

Finally, Franklin's (1989) patient D.R.B. showed word-meaning deafness. His phoneme discrimination and lexical decision were both good, so those presumably do not need to be worked on in therapy. He was also good at written synonym judgements, so semantic tasks with written words and pictures may be inappropriate. A feature of D.R.B.'s performance that we have not mentioned thus far is that his word-meaning deafness was more profound for abstract than concrete nouns, so therapy should be targeted on the comprehension of heard abstract words.

Patient E.S.T of Kay and Ellis (1987) showed a marked frequency effect in naming. The therapist might then elect to target a set of words in the middle range of frequencies where he can access some of the words some of the time, but few of the words reliably. That might be a more productive set than very low frequency words. E.S.T did not show a length effect, so it would be as important to work on one-syllable words as words of three or four syllables .

### *Devising treatments*

Skilful cognitive neuropsychological assessment can yield quite detailed and specific aspects of dysfunction in need of treatment. It may specify the particular cognitive processes and the particular type of words that should be targeted for treatment. That is no mean achievement. Recent commentators have pointed out, however, that cognitive neuropsychology may be of less value when it comes to devising the precise treatments that might be tried. As Wilson and Patterson (1990) observe: "Some therapists would argue that neuropsychological theory plays no part in their treatment programmes, not because their knowledge of theory is lacking, but because theories about the nature of the deficit do not relate to questions that have to be asked in treatment or rehabilitation."

Part of the reason for this limitation is that cognitive neuropsychology has tended to stop at the point where it has identified *which* cognitive components are damaged; it rarely goes on to attempt any specification of the *nature* of the damage (Caramazza, 1989). In this sense a diagnosis of, say 'damage to the auditory input lexicon' is rather like a diagnosis of 'progressive renal failure'. Such a diagnosis alone would tell a doctor that treatment should be targeted on the kidneys but would not say what that treatment should be—whether drugs, dialysis, transplant or some other means. This limitation reflects the more general fact that cognitive models typically provide a functional specification, *not* a procedural specification of the underlying processes. We would note, though, that the problem is apparently not confined to cognitive neuropsychology, but seems to hold for more traditional approaches: Goodglass (1990, p. 94) writes: "I would be amazed if there are any trained clinicians who seriously look to their language assessment as providing a formula for a therapeutic approach."

In the meantime, the therapist must use a combination of experience, intuition and guesswork to think up tasks that might help improve a patient's performance. We would not in any way underestimate or devalue the contribution of clinical experience. If a therapist can demonstrate, using sound methodology, that a particular procedure helps ameliorate a given and well specified deficit, then the fact that the procedure was not deduced from theoretical first principles should not inhibit its application. Orthodox medicine is full of treatments that doctors know to work, though they do not know why they work. As Ellis, Kay and Franklin (1991) point out, bread poultices were successfully applied to wounds for many centuries before the secretions of the penicillium mould were discovered to be the active ingredient. Advances in knowledge should eventually help us to understand why treatments achieve the effects they do, and trying to discover why therapies work should help advance the underlying theory.

### *Evaluating treatments*

Cognitive neuropsychology comes back into its own when we consider the evaluation of treatments. Cognitive neuropsychologists have made important contributions in recent years to the development of methodologies for assessing the efficacy of therapy, particularly at the level of the single patient (Coltheart, 1983; Pring, 1986). In fact those contributions have arisen more out of the training that cognitive neuropsychologists receive in general experimental methodology and statistics than out of the cognitive theories they employ.

In the past, when questions about the effectiveness of therapy have been tackled, it has been at a range of levels. The highest (and perhaps the coarsest) level has involved asking whether therapy can help aphasics, where the nature of the therapy and of the aphasia are largely left unspecified. Sometimes the results of these large-scale studies have been disappointingly negative; other times more positive. Either way, the cognitive neuropsychologist regards them as conveying very little information of value. Howard and Hatfield (1987) liken this to asking, "Does therapy in general help aphasics in general?". It is rather like trying to ascertain whether doctoring improves the health of patients with bodily illness. Even if the answer is yes, questions about which particular treatments aid which particular conditions remain unanswered. Yet those are the very answers that are needed if rational decisions are to be made.

Between the very large-scale studies and the single case studies we shall come to shortly, lie a set of studies using smaller groups of aphasics chosen for the fact that they share certain language problems. Despite their prediliction for single-case research, cognitive neuropsychologists have been known to get involved in such studies. Patterson, Purrell, and Morton (1983), for example, studied the effects of different cues in facilitating naming in a group of patients identified as having word retrieval problems. They measured the ability of patients to name pictures that had earlier been either phonemically cued or simply repeated. They found that any effects of the phonemic cue disappeared in a matter of minutes. Although this might suggest that such cues are not the most effective way of achieving long-term effects, it remains possible that naming practice using phonemic cues or repetition might improve word finding if the task is repeated many times. And as we have pointed out, phonemic cuing may still be a useful *management* strategy, in terms of reducing the immediate frustration of being unable to find a word.

Howard et al. (1985a;b) contrasted tasks that required phonemic processing with ones that required semantic processing. Again they found that repetition only improved naming for a short time. The same effect was found for giving a word that rhymed with the word to be named, or for judging which of two words rhymed (one of the pair corresponding to the picture to be named). By contrast, tasks that required semantic processing improved naming for a much longer period: picture naming still showed benefits a day after some semantic task had been carried out using the word. The semantic tasks used were hearing the word and selecting the picture from an array of semantically related pictures (e.g. "dog" with pictured dog, cat, rabbit and mouse); the same task but with the word written down, and a semantic judgment task involving the target word (e.g. "does a dog bark?"). As in the cuing studies mentioned earlier, the task was only effective if it was lexically specific: pointing to a picture of an associated word did not facilitate naming.

Howard et al. (1985b) went on to look at the effect of practising the two types of therapy (semantic and phonological) on patients' naming. The patients, who had longstanding, stable aphasias with good word comprehension, were given two periods of either one or two weeks of daily therapy. Each period of therapy utilised a different set of words, and within each set half the words were given therapy (either three semantic therapies or three phonological therapies) and the other half were just given for naming practice. Another set of words was tested before and after the therapies. For the group of patients as a whole, both types of therapy were effective in improving naming, but the semantic therapies improved performance more quickly, and there was some generalisation to untreated items after semantic therapy, which was not true for phonological therapy.

Studies of this sort have made important contributions. They suggest, for example, that although phonemic cuing appears to be doing a lot of good when it helps a patient to name an object he/she was previously struggling to name, for the majority of patients with naming difficulties, therapy based on providing phonemic cues will have little or no long-term benefits. Cognitive neuropsychology is, however, having its greatest impact in the area of single case studies of remediation. Reflecting the historical emphasis in cognitive neuropsychology on reading, a number of those studies have been concerned with the treatment of patients with acquired dyslexia (Patterson, this volume). We have briefly mentioned some single case studies of naming and auditory word comprehension deficits earlier in this chapter. In what remains we should like to turn briefly to a single-case treatment study that incorporates many of the elements one would hope to see in efficacy research.

Byng (1989) and Byng and Coltheart (1986) report a successful treatment of a patient B.R.B. with a sentence comprehension disorder. B.R.B. suffered an extensive left hemisphere infarct at the age of 41. Conventional aphasia assessment diagnosed him as showing a moderate-to-severe expressive dysphasia and a mild receptive dysphasia. Tested four years post-stroke he was found to have difficulty comprehending abstract words but not more imageable, concrete words, and problems comprehending "reversible" declarative and locative sentences, whether heard or read. A reversible declarative sentence would be "The vicar shoots the doctor", where the reversed form "The doctor shoots the vicar" is no less plausible, and where only the grammatical structure of the sentence tells the listener who is shooting whom. A reversible locative sentence would be "The hook is above the switch", where again there is a plausible reversed variant ("The switch is above the hook").

Byng and Coltheart undertook a series of further investigations to discover more precisely the source of B.K.B.'s problem with reversible sentences. Analysis of B.R.B.'s spontaneous speech showed that much of his speech was made up of single words or phrases lacking verbs. B.R.B. was good at distinguishing grammatical from ungrammatical sentences, but performed poorly on a task in which he was asked to indicate which of two verbs matched a videoed action. Byng and Coltheart argued on the basis of these and other results that B.R.B. could parse sentences; that is, that he could compute descriptions of their surface form involving categories such as *subject, verb* and *object*. They also argued that he had a preserved grasp of underlying sentence meanings, where the relevant concepts are categories like *agent* (the person or object performing an action) and *theme* (the person or object acted upon). In the opinion of Byng and Coltheart, B.R.B.'s problem lay in an inability to map between semantic and syntactic structures.

This hypothesis guided the creation of a treatment programme focusing on B.R.B.'s comprehension of reversible sentences. Twenty reversible locative sentences involving four spatial prepositions (e.g. *in, above*) were selected for treatment. Each sentence was accompanied by two pictures, one depicting the sentence correctly, the other depicting the reversed form of the sentence. Various clues were used to indicate the meanings of the spatial prepositions used and the relationship between the words in the sentence and the objects in the pictures. B.R.B. practiced this task at home for two weeks, at the end of which he scored 20/20 on matching the treated sentences to the appropriate pictures. The improvement extended beyond the treated sentences in important ways. Treatment involved written, locative sentences, but performance on heard, non-locative passive sentences (e.g., "The soldier was pushed by the policeman") improved over the same period, as did comprehension of single verbs. B.R.B.'s spontaneous speech also improved, but not in a wholesale manner: structural aspects of B.R.B.'s speech such as the ratio of sentences to single words improved, but non-structural aspects such as the underuse of function words did not.

B.R.B.'s comprehension of abstract words also remained poor at the end of the treatment period, providing further evidence against any suggestion that these were nonspecific treatment effects. Six months after completing the sentence therapy, treatment of B.R.B.'s abstract word comprehension problem (which appears to have been similar to that of Franklin's, 1989, patient D.I.) was begun. In this case the treatment focused on picture-word matching and generating synonyms with the aid of a dictionary. As with the sentence therapy task, these were designed to be tasks that B.R.B. could practice at home. After four weeks of therapy, abstract word comprehension improved from 16% to 94%. Comprehension of reversible sentences continued to be 100%.

The work of Byng and Coltheart is appealing for a number of reasons, not least of which is the fact that improvement was achieved using therapy tasks that B.R.B. could practice at home, with only his usual weekly visits to the speech therapy clinic. The study illustrates what Coltheart (1983) calls a "crossover-treatment design". In order to use this design, one needs a patient who has deficits affecting two different cognitive functions, X and Y. Both are assessed before any treatment begins. One function, X, is then treated before both functions are reassessed. Y is then treated before both functions are reassessed for a third time. In B.R.B.'s case, X was the sentence comprehension (mapping) deficit and Y the abstract word comprehension deficit. Treating X improved X but not Y, then treating Y improved Y while X remained good. Such a pattern, when obtained, cannot be attributed to general treatment effects, improvement in health, practice, or whatever, but must be the result of targeted treatments having targeted effects.

## CONCLUSIONS

Studies of the efficacy of treatment motivated by cognitive neuropsychological concerns are still few and far between. If speech therapy is to be placed on a firm empirical footing we need many more. At the moment the contribution of cognitive neuropsychology is greatest in the areas of diagnosis, feedback and management, but the more therapists can build systematic efficacy evaluation into their routine work the better. Without evaluation, it is impossible to build up a systematic body of knowledge of which procedures are effective in the treatment of which deficits, yet such studies should provide the very foundations for the profession of speech therapy.

What we need now is a generation of single case studies of the effectiveness of specified therapies in the treatment of different forms of language disorder. We need studies in which patients are carefully profiled before receiving replicable treatments, so that we can relate patterns of success and failure to pre-treatment differences between patients. Fuller cognitive neuropsychological profiles of patients entering into treatment should help us to understand why some patients benefit more than others from particular treatments (Basso, 1989; Wilson & Patterson, 1990).

The phase of basic research in cognitive neuropsychology that is just coming to maturity has been made possible by collaborative efforts between academic neuropsychologists and sympathetic practitioners. What we need now is a second phase in which cognitive neuropsychologists and clinicians work together to explore both the potential and the limitations of cognitive neuropsychology as applied to cognitive rehabilitation. Only in that way will we gain the accumulated wisdom necessary to ensure the survival and future health of the enterprise of speech therapy.

## REFERENCES


Albert, M.L. & Bear, D. (1974). Time to understand: A case study of word deafness with reference to the role of time in auditory comprehension. *Brain, 97,* 373-384.

Auerbach, S.H., Allard, T., Naeser, M., Alexander, M.P., & Albert, M.L. (1982). Pure word deafness: An analysis of a case with bilateral lesions and a defect at the prephonemic level. *Brain, 105*, 271-300.

Basso, A. (1989). Spontaneous recovery and language rehabilitation. In X. Seron & G. Deloche (Eds.), *Cognitive approaches in neuropsychological rehabilitation*. Hillsdale, N.J.: Lawrence Erlbaum Associates Inc.

Benson, D.F. (1979). Neurologic correlates of anomia. In H. Whitaker & H.A. Whitaker (Eds.), *Studies in neurolinguistics*, Vol. 4. New York: Academic Press.

Bramwell, B. (1897). Illustrative cases of aphasia. *Lancet, 1,* 1256-1259. Reprinted as "A case of word meaning deafness". *Cognitive Neuropsychology,* 1984, *1,* 249-258.

Byng, S. (1989). Sentence processing deficits: Theory and therapy. *Cognitive Neuropsychology, 5*, 629-676.

Byng, S. & Coltheart, M. (1986). Aphasia therapy research: Methodological requirements and illustrative results. In E. Hjelmquist & L.-G. Nilsson (Eds.), *Communication and handicap. Aspects of psychological compensation and technical aids*. Amsterdam: Elsevier Science.

Byng, S., Kay, J., Edmundson, A., & Scott, C. (1990). Aphasia tests reconsidered. *Aphasiology, 4*, 67-91.

Caramazza, A. (1984). The logic of neuropsychological research and the problem of patient classification in aphasia. *Brain and Language, 21*, 9-20.

Caramazza, A. (1986). On drawing inferences about the structure of normal cognitive systems from the analysis of patterns of impaired performance: The case for single-patient studies. *Brain and Cognition, 5*, 41-66.

Caramazza, A. (1989). Cognitive neuropsychology and rehabilitation: An unfulfilled promise? In X. Seron & G. Deloche (Eds.), *Cognitive approaches in neuropsychological rehabilitation*. Hillsdale, N.J.: Lawrence Erlbaum Associates Inc.

Coltheart, M. (1983). Investigating the efficacy of speech therapy. In C. Code & D.J. Müller (Eds.), *Aphasia therapy*. London: Edward Arnold.

Coltheart, M. & Funnell, E. (1987). Reading and writing: One lexicon or two? In D.A. Allport, D.G. Mackay, W. Prinz & E. Scheerer (Eds.), *Language perception and production: Shared mechanisms in listening, speaking, reading and writing*. London: Academic Press .

Ellis, A.W. (1984). Introduction to Byrom Bramwell's (1897) case of word meaning deafness. *Cognitive Neuropsychology, 1*, 245-258.

Ellis, A.W. (1987). Intimations of modularity, Or, The modelarity of mind: Some problems and prospects for cognitive neuropsychology. In M. Coltheart, G. Sartori, & R. Job (Eds.), *The cognitive neuropsychology of language*. London: Lawrence Erlbaum Associates Ltd.

Ellis, A.W., Kay, J., & Franklin, S. (1992). Anomia: Differentiating between semantic and phonological deficits. In D.I. Margolin (Ed.), *Cognitive neuropsychology in clinical practice*. New York: Oxford University Press.

Ellis, A.W. & Young, A.W. (1988). *Human cognitive neuropsychology*. Hove: Lawrence Erlbaum Associates.

Franklin, S. (1989). Dissociations in auditory word comprehension: Evidence from nine fluent aphasics. *Aphasiology, 3*, 189-207.

Gainotti, G., Silveri, M.C., Villa. G., & Miceli, G. (1986). Anomia with and without lexical comprehension disorders. *Brain and Language, 29*, 18-33.

Garnham, A. (1985). *Psycholinguistics: Central topics*. London: Methuen

Garrett, M.F. (1982). Production of speech: Evidence from normal and pathological language use. In A.W. Ellis (Ed.), *Normality and pathology in cognitive functions*. London: Academic Press.

Goodglass, H. (1990). Cognitive psychology and clinical aphasiology. *Aphasiology, 4*, 93-95.

Goodglass, H. & Kaplan, E. (1972). *Assessment of aphasia and related disorders*. Philadelphia: Lea and Febinger.

Hirsh, K.W., Ellis, A.W., & McCloskey, M.E. (1990). *Naming and word frequency: Predicting success but not error type*. Paper presented to the Experimental Psychology Society, Oxford, 5-6 July 1990.

Howard, D. & Hatfield, F.M. (1987). *Aphasia therapy: Historical and contemporary issues*. London: Lawrence Erlbaum Associates Ltd.

Howard, D. & Orchard-Lisle, V.M. (1984). On the origin of semantic errors in naming: Evidence from the case of a global aphasic. *Cognitive Neuropsychology, 1*, 163-190.

Howard, D., Patterson, K.E., Franklin, S., Orchard-Lisle, V.M., & Morton, J. (1985a). The facilitation of picture naming in aphasia. *Cognitive Neuropsychology, 2*, 49-80.

Howard, D., Patterson, K.E., Franklin, S., Orchard-Lisle, V.M., & Morton, J. (1985b). The treatment of word retrieval deficits in aphasia: A comparison of two therapy methods. *Brain, 108*, 817-829.

Kay, J. & Ellis, A.W. (1987). A cognitive neuropsychological case study of anomia. *Brain, 110*, 613-629.

Kay, J., Lesser, R., & Coltheart, M. (1992). *Psycholinguistic assessments of language processing in aphasia (PALPA)*. Hove: Lawrence Erlbaum Associates Ltd.

Kohn, S., & Friedman, R. (1986). Word-meaning deafness: A phonological-semantic dissociation. *Cognitive Neuropsychology, 3*, 291-308.

Miceli, G., Giustolisi, L., & Caramazza, A. (1991). The interaction of lexical and non-lexical processing mechanisms: Evidence from aphasia. *Cortex, 27*, 57-80.

Miller, D. & Ellis, A.W. (1987). Speech and writing errors in neologistic jargonaphasia: A lexical activation hypothesis. In M. Coltheart, G. Sartori & R. Job (Eds.), *The cognitive neuropsychology of language*. London: Lawrence Erlbaum Associates Ltd.

Monsell, S. (1987). On the relation between lexical input and output pathways for speech. In D.A. Allport, D. MacKay, W. Prinz & E. Scheerer (Eds.), *Language perception and production: relationships between listening, speaking, reading and writing*. London: Academic Press.

Patterson, K.E., Purrell, C., & Morton, J. (1983). The facilitation of naming in aphasia. In C. Code & D.J. Müller (Eds), *Aphasia therapy*. London: Edward Arnold.

Pring, T.R. (1986). Evaluating the effects of speech therapy for aphasics: Developing the single case methodology. *British Journal of Disorders of Communication, 21*, 103-115.

Riddoch, M.J., Humphreys, G.W., Coltheart, M., & Funnell, E. (1988). Semantic system or systems? Neuropsychological evidence re-examined. *Cognitive Neuropsychology, 5*, 3-25.

Saffran, E.M. (1982). Neuropsychological approaches to the study of language. *British Journal of Psychology, 73*, 317-337.

Saffran, E., Marin, O.S.M., & Yeni-Komshian, G. (1976). An analysis of speech perception in word deafness. *Brain and Language, 3*, 209-228 .

Scott, C. (1987). *Cognitive neuropsychological remediation of acquired language disorders*. Unpublished M. Phil. Thesis, City University, London.

Shallice, T. (1988a). *From neuropsychology to mental structure*. Cambridge: Cambridge University Press.

Shallice, T. (1988b). Specialisation within the semantic system. *Cognitive Neuropsychology, 5*, 133-142.

Snodgrass, J.G. & Vanderwart, M. (1980). A standardized set of 260 pictures: Norms for name agreement, image agreement, familiarity, and visual complexity. *Journal of Experimental Psychology: Human Learning and Memory, 6*, 174-215.

Wilson, B. & Patterson, K.E. (1990). Rehabilitation for cognitive impairment: Does cognitive psychology apply? *Applied Cognitive Psychology, 4*, 247-260.

Zingeser, E.B. & Berndt, R.S. (1988). Grammatical class and context effects in a case of pure anomia: Implications for models of language production. *Cognitive Neuropsychology, 5*, 473-516.

CHAPTER FIFTEEN

# Verb Retrieval and Sentence Construction: Effects of Targeted Intervention

Charlotte C. Mitchum and Rita Sloan Berndt
*University of Maryland School of Medicine, Department of Neurology, Baltimore, Maryland, USA*

## INTRODUCTION

An inability to produce semantically appropriate and syntactically well formed spoken sentences is a symptom found very frequently in aphasia. Such an impairment can take many different forms, and can occur in conjunction with a variety of other symptoms. It is often the impairment that interferes most with patients' functional recovery, and it is a frequent residual symptom after single word retrieval and language comprehension have improved to functional levels. Despite the pervasiveness and seriousness of sentence production deficits in aphasia, there are relatively few treatment options available to address these impairments.

The most popular approach to treatment of sentence production problems is to focus on a single sentence type or syntactic element, and re-establish its use through repeated practice in its actual production. For example, Holland and Levy (1971) describe a highly programmed, multimodal stimulation treatment they used with seven aphasic patients to improve production of active declarative sentences. They found that treatment effects were limited in their generalisation to other syntactic structures, and had little influence on the production of structurally identical sentences that used untrained lexical items. Furthermore, some patients responded much better than others, for reasons that were unclear. Another approach (Kearns & Salmon, 1984) used a treatment program to address the frequently observed pattern of omission of a specific grammatical element (the auxiliary verb) in agrammatic Broca's aphasia. The treatment—again based on repeated production of target structures—retrained production of "is" in one grammatical context (as an auxiliary), then assessed generalisation of "is" in untreated grammatical contexts (as a copula). Two agrammatic patients who participated in the intervention successfully learned to use "is" as an auxiliary verb, and could integrate that structure with untrained lexical content. There was limited generalisation to use of "is" as a copula, and no generalisation to use of "is" in spontaneous speech.

Although studies of sentence production therapy consistently demonstrate that it is possible to effect change in patients' sentence production patterns, and that these changes may even have limited functional utility (see also Loverso, Prescott, & Selinger, 1988), we would argue that the basic approach underlying these types of interventions makes it difficult, if not impossible, to interpret the result of intervention. There are at least two problems that seriously complicate ongoing development of sentence production treatment strategies. The first of these relates to the assessment of patients' symptoms, i.e. to describing symptoms in terms that help to determine their functional source(s). Even the most cursory consideration of the operations necessary to transform thoughts, messages and intentions into an ordered string of words that comprises a sentence suggests that the timely accomplishment of a number of separate operations is required. Current widely available aphasia assessment instruments provide no information about which of these many operations has broken down to cause a patient's disordered production. A standard assessment thus provides little basis for the clinician to develop hypotheses about potential sources of symptoms that might yield to specific treatments. Moreover, failure to identify the functional deficits that potentially give rise to particular symptoms prevents the effective comparison of patients that is required for replication of treatment effects. Thus, failure to provide a detailed assessment of patients' language capacities may underlie the frequently-reported finding that a treatment technique that is successful with one patient is unsuccessful when used with a patient whose symptoms are superficially similar.

Another set of problems that have plagued efforts to develop effective treatment for sentence production impairments relates to predicting the generalisation of treatment effects, both from specific, treated lexical and structural content to untreated content, and from specific contexts of elicitation to sentence production in general. Generalisation of treatment effects to untreated instances is a critical element in the evaluation of treatment efficacy. In addition to the obvious practical benefits of maximizing the impact that the treatment has on a patient's communication, generalisation of treatment to untrained content and contexts suggests that a meaningful change in processing has been achieved, rather than just the rote learning of specific responses. Despite its importance, few studies of treatment effects have developed a rationale for predicting that specific types of generalisation will or will not occur (for an exception couched in behaviourist terms, see Kearns & Salmon, 1984).

Both types of issues—those relating to assessment of symptoms and to predicting generalisation of effects—can be linked to the fact that treatment approaches have not, in general, been built upon an understanding of how sentences are normally produced, nor of how the patient's symptoms might reflect a breakdown of normal functioning. The cognitive neuropsychological approach to treatment that is the topic of this volume provides a framework within which problems of assessment and generalisation can be approached systematically. Symptom assessment is individually tailored to describe the nature of the production impairment for a particular patient. Rather than comparing the pattern of production to other patterns of impairment, the assessment allows comparison of the disordered production with what is expected in normal production. This permits an analysis of possible underlying causes of the deficit from examination of how the impaired pattern deviates from normal. Once some hypotheses are formulated about the cause (or causes) of impaired production, treatment can focus on remediation of the suspected underlying problem. Further, if the intervention is carefully controlled, the effect of improvement within a single processing component can be interpreted from the context of what is known about normal processing. Working from the normal model thus provides a basis for predicting which untreated elements of the normal model might be affected by establishing a change in the treated component. In other words, generalisation of treatment effects can be systematically predicted and interpreted.

Despite its basic appeal, there are also problems with the cognitive neuropsychological approach to aphasia therapy. First, there are few well developed models of normal cognitive operations on which to base an assessment detailed enough for clinical intervention. Second, the extent to which the intervention might be affected by impairments of cognitive capacities such as attention and memory, which are not part of the language model, is unclear (see also Berndt and Mitchum, this volume). Nevertheless, initial attempts to apply the principles of cognitive neuropsychological assessment and intervention to sentence production impairments in aphasia have produced some encouraging results.

Several clinical interpretations of sentence production impairments have drawn upon the theory of normal sentence construction developed by Garrett (1975; 1980) and have focused on the sentence production impairments that are characteristic of agrammatism (Byng, 1988; Jones, 1986). Even though the details of normal production continue to be actively debated (see Berndt, 1991, for review), the application of Garrett's model has provided clinical researchers with a framework within which to interpret the deficits that arise in agrammatic sentence production. For example, frequently observed and long-recognised symptoms of production impairment such as the omission of free and bound grammatical morphemes, the relative inaccessibility of verbs, and the misordering of the nouns in sentences can be interpreted within the context of the Garrett model as resulting from specific processing failures (see Berndt, 1991; Schwartz, 1987).

The database on which Garrett's sentence production model was built did not come from the production errors of aphasic patients but from normal speakers' so-called "slips of the tongue". The important assumption underlying this and other similar models (Bock, 1987; Fromkin, 1973; Stemberger, 1985) is that normal speech errors reflect (momentary) breakdown in the formulation of a sentence that can indicate which processes were being executed when the slip occurred. By examining the relative frequency of various types of errors (e.g. errors involving meaning, or those involving sound) Garrett has identified five sequentially organised levels of representation that appear to be functionally independent of one another. What is not made clear from the normal speech error data (unfortunately for our purposes) is the nature of the processes that operate to transform one representational level into the next. This means that there are only minimal assumptions within the model concerning the temporal unfolding of the events that result in the construction of a new representational level. Garrett's model requires only that the five levels be roughly serial and that information flow be one-directional (i.e. with no backflow). Even these minimal constraints have recently been subjected to serious challenge (Bock, 1987; Dell, 1986). Nonetheless, Garrett's five representational levels have provided a useful framework within which a wide range of aphasic production disorders have been interpreted (Garrett, 1982; Kohn, Lorch, & Pearson, 1989; Pate, Saffran, & Martin, 1987; Schwartz 1987).

The first of Garrett's levels is the "message level", and here the representation is conceptual: a notion of what one wants to say, stimulated by an idea, by inferential processes, and/or by the experience of some non-linguistic, sensory information. At the next, "functional level", this somewhat amorphous "message" has yielded to the extraction of abstract lexical identities, i.e. discrete concepts for the people, things, actions and attributes that will ultimately be labelled with words. Part of the functional level representation also codes in some way the logical relationships among these abstract lexical entities—the identification of "who is doing what to whom".

At the next, "positional" level of representation, the phonological forms for the selected lexical items are specified, as are the phrasal level constituents (subject noun phrase, verb phrase, etc.), that will form the sentence. The ordering of these constituents, along with the generation of the set of grammatical morphemes that make up the constituents, creates a syntactic frame into which the phonologically coded lexical items are inserted. Evidence from normal slips of the tongue indicates that the grammatical elements in the syntactic frame are assigned in a step that is functionally separate from the insertion of the lexical elements themselves. Errors such as saying "it waits to pay" instead of "it pays to wait" indicate that grammatical inflections can be stranded in a rigid frame position when major lexical items (in this case, verbs) are exchanged (see Fromkin, 1973; Garrett, 1980), indicating considerable autonomy of inflections from their stems. The final representation made available at the positional level is thus a syntactically ordered, phonologically specified sentence to be spoken.

The output of the positional level is converted to a phonetic level representation that provides the articulators with the information needed to engage motor-speech level mechanisms. These final two levels, although of relevance for some forms of pathological speech/language production (cf. Schwartz, 1987), will not be considered further in this chapter.

Of particular interest for analysis of agrammatic production are the representations made available at the functional and positional levels. It is at these levels that lexical and syntactic information is specified and coordinated. As shown in Fig. 15.1, the description of a scene in which an adult male is shown lathering a sports car with soap (assumed to constitute the "message") requires that the lexical items to be used in the sentence be selected and matched to express the appropriate logical relationship. For example, if the verb "wash" is selected to describe the action, the noun "man" is identified as the agent of the action and the noun "car" is identified as the theme. The final representation available at the functional level is fairly specific (though

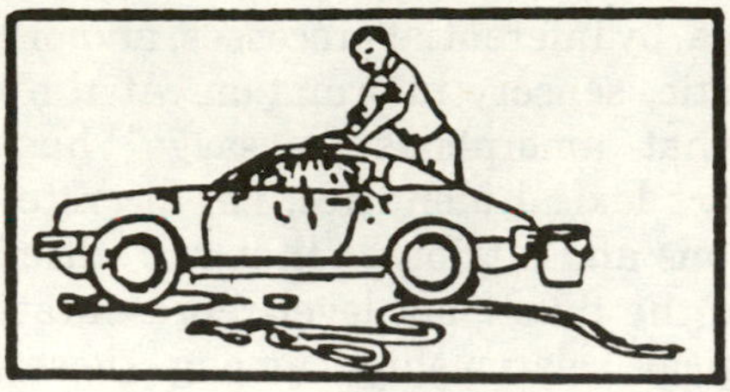

**FUNCTIONAL LEVEL REPRESENTATION**

(wash) (man) (car)

action: agent, recipient

action agent recipient
(wash) (man) (car)

***who is doing what to whom***

**POSITIONAL LEVEL REPRESENTATION**

/mæn/ /waʃ/ /kar/

SNP + VP + ONP

**the** man **is** wash **ing the** car

***"the man is washing the car"***

FIG. 15.1. An example of functional and positional level information obtained in the construction of a sentence to describe an action scene.

phonologically unspecified) information about the action, person and object to be described, as well as about "who is doing what to whom". All of this information must undergo further transformation to result in a positional level representation that combines phonologically specified content words with a properly constructed syntactic frame to convey the intended message, i.e. "The man is washing the car", "The car is washed by the man", etc.

It should be clear from the above summary of the model that many of the symptoms of aphasic sentence production impairments could be linked to failure at any one of a number of these early levels of the model. Traditional clinical approaches to sentence production have nonetheless focused only on the levels of the model that are closest to the act of production—on aspects of phonological specification, phonetic encoding and articulatory execution. Treatment has emphasised, for the most part, repeated practice saying particular words in particular grammatical structures. The model outlined above suggests that these efforts will succeed only if deficits at these levels are the primary causes of a patient's symptoms, i.e. that there are no more fundamental problems earlier in the sentence formulation process. However, there are strong indications that many patients do indeed fail to achieve fully-specified representations at the functional level. Such failures could result in poor sentence production even if phonological, phonetic and articulatory processes are unaffected.

Saffran, Schwartz, and Marin (1980) suggested some years ago that failure to specify the verb at the functional level may be a fundamental deficit in the sentence production of agrammatic patients who are found to produce nouns in the wrong order in semantically reversible sentences. Such a deficit could give rise to the symptom of inappropriate ordering of nouns in the sentence because it would be difficult to map the logical relationship of nouns to a poorly or incorrectly specified verb. Indeed, successful interventions have been directed at explicit identification of the main verb along with its logical relationship to the nouns in simple active sentences (Byng, 1988; Jones, 1986; Le Dorze, Jacob, & Coderre, 1991; Saffran, Schwartz, Fink, Myers, & Martin, 1992). Although each of these treatment studies adopted a different approach, all of them eschewed repeated practice in speaking as a treatment strategy. Instead, they focused on enlightening the patient, in a variety of ways, about the centrality of the predicate (preposition or verb), and the relationship of the nouns in sentences to that predicate. In each case, there was marked improvement in sentence production abilities despite the lack of explicit practice producing sentences.

The study reported here also focuses on these earlier representational levels and processes, i.e. on the operations needed to identify relevant lexical elements and to insert them into an appropriate syntactic frame. Unlike the studies cited above, however, we included explicit practice in the production of these elements as part of the treatment. The patient we will describe here, like "agrammatic" patients who participated in the treatments described, demonstrates impaired production of verbs and poor sentence construction skill, including misordering of nouns around the verb to reflect the appropriate logical relationship among constituents. However, this patient is fluent in his attempts at sentence production, and he produces a variety of grammatical morphemes in narrative speech. Despite his fluency and some retention of grammatical morphemes, his sentence construction impairment shares many characteristics of agrammatic sentence production, including poor verb retrieval. Thus, we were able to carry out two targeted interventions that focused separately on specific symptoms of agrammatic production, but in the unique context of fluent, easily articulated speech.

## CASE HISTORY

M.L. is a 54 year old right-handed male who suffered a massive left C.V.A. in 1983 at age 47. A C.T. scan at nine days post onset revealed a massive left fronto-parietal area infarction and possible infarction of the posterior aspect of the right internal capsule. The C.V.A. resulted in severe right hemiparesis, dysarthria and severe "mixed" (expressive/receptive) aphasia. Prior to onset, M.L. was well educated (18+ years) and practiced as an attorney. On the basis of his educational and occupational history, it was assumed that his premorbid language skills, including reading and writing, were at least within a normal range.

### Baseline Assessment

*Standard tests*

In the seven years since onset, M.L. had improved dramatically in language function. Speech therapy, which he attended regularly for about five years following the C.V.A., is said to have focused on improvement of functional skills including single word production and comprehension, whole word reading, writing and basic calculation. In our initial evaluation (carried out at 4½ years post-onset), M.L.'s spontaneous speech was fluent but marked by frequent phonemic paraphasias, poorly structured, fragmented utterances and impaired word retrieval. The Boston Diagnostic Aphasia Examination (Goodglass & Kaplan, 1983) revealed only a mild impairment in the comprehension of single words (80th percentile) but poor comprehension of more complex material (60th percentile) and verbal commands (10th percentile). Repetition of single words was good (70th percentile), but sentence repetition was very poor due mainly to the intrusion of phonemic paraphasias.

*Experimental tests of production of words and sentences*
An extensive evaluation of M.L.'s ability to produce single words and sentences is reported in Berndt and Mitchum (1991); only tasks that bear directly on the interventions will be described here.

*Narrative speech.* A sample of uninterrupted narrative speech was obtained by instructing M.L. to tell a familiar fairy tale in narrative style. A quantitative analysis of the sample was carried out using methods described by Saffran, Berndt, and Schwartz (1989). This analysis permitted quantification of specific morphological and structural aspects of M.L.'s narrative utterances. The results were compared to the mean values for the same measures obtained from groups of five agrammatic and five normal speakers (the patient and control group data reported by Saffran et al., 1989). The pattern of production that emerged from this comparison indicated that the overall proportion of closed class words M.L. produced (0.41) was low relative to the mean for normal speakers (0.56) and within the upper range (0.21-0.43) of agrammatic speakers. Closer examination of specific grammatical morphemes produced by M.L. revealed nearly normal inclusion of the determiner preceding a noun in contexts that required a determiner (0.85 for M.L. vs. a mean of 1.00 for normal and of 0.37 for agrammatic speakers).

In contrast, M.L.'s use of verb-relevant grammatical morphemes was comparable to the lower range of agrammatic speakers. M.L. produced an inflection for only a small proportion (0.28) of inflectable verbs compared to the mean for agrammatic speakers (0.36) and for normal speakers (0.98). M.L. never used auxiliary verbs in the narrative sample. Although the ratio of nouns-to-verbs produced was essentially within a normal range, a type/token analysis of the verbs used by M.L. relative to those used by a normal speaker (matched to M.L. in age and education) revealed a strong reliance on high frequency verbs with a broad range of meanings (e.g. "go", "take"). In a sample of about 200 narrative words, the proportion of verbs in total words was essentially the same for M.L. (0.13) and the normal speaker (0.17). However, seven verbs with a particularly high frequency of occurrence (range = 606 to 6,375; Francis & Kuçera, 1982 base frequencies) were used repeatedly and accounted for 0.85 of M.L.'s total of 27 verb usages, whereas these verbs accounted for only 0.36 of the 42 verb usages of the normal speaker ($z=3.98$, $P<0.0001$).

*Picture Naming.* M.L. was asked to name, with a single word, one set of thirty action pictures and two sets of thirty object pictures. One set of object pictures elicited target nouns matched to the base frequency of a verb, and a second set of object pictures was matched to the cumulative frequency of each verb 1.[1] For example, an action picture to elicit the target verb "sing" (cumulative/base frequency = 120/27) was matched by cumulative frequency to the target noun "ball" (123) and by base frequency to the target noun "fence" (30). Significantly better naming was obtained for object pictures (0.87 for both noun sets) relative to pictures of actions (0.67) ($z=2.24$, $P<0.006$).

*Picture Description.* Sixteen professional quality line-drawn pictures were used to elicit sentences describing action scenes. Each picture involved an animate agent engaged in a clearly depicted action that could be described using a transitive verb in a Subject-Verb-Object (S-V-O) construction. Sentences to describe each picture were elicited in two conditions. "Unconstrained" sentences were elicited by instructing M.L. to describe the picture in one sentence. In a "constrained" elicitation (on a different day), passive sentences to describe the same pictures were elicited by providing him with the non-agent noun and instructing him to start with that word. For example, in response to a picture of a boy eating an apple, an expected "unconstrained" response would be "the boy is eating the apple". In the elicitation of the passive, M.L. was instructed to begin his sentence with "the apple"; the expected response was "the apple is eaten by the boy". Several practice elicitations preceded the test trials. As M.L. produced many false starts and intrusions, the most complete attempt at a structured sentence was scored.

M.L. produced very similar sentence structures, and demonstrated consistent problems producing verbs, in both the unconstrained and the constrained versions of the task. The target verb (or an acceptable alternative) was produced in only 0.40 of the 32 sentences M.L. constructed. Errors included verbs that were semantically inaccurate (0.39 of errors, e.g. The woman is hugging the boy →"The grandmother was kissing the boy"); uses of a noun instead of a verb in verb position (0.28 of errors, e.g. The boy is touching the girl (on the shoulder) →"The girl was shoulder the boy"); and substitution of high frequency, semantically "empty" verbs (0.33 of errors, e.g. The boy is kicking the ball →"The young man was taking the soccer ball") . Another striking aspect of M.L.'s responses in this task was his repeated use of an S-V-O structure (0.62 of responses in each condition) which always included the verb inflection "-ing".

In the condition in which M.L. was constrained to begin his sentence with a noun that required production of a passive, the use of this structural form resulted in incorrect expression of the logical roles of sentence nouns. For example, constrained to begin his description of a picture showing a girl reading a book with "the book", M.L. said "The book is reading the girl". In addition, two responses in the unconstrained condition clearly reversed noun order (e.g. The man is pushing the woman →"The lady is shoving her boy"), suggesting that a fundamental difficulty in the assignment of logical roles to nouns constitutes one of M.L.'s underlying sentence production impairments. Alternatively, the inflexibility and repetition in the choice of grammatical morphemes constituting an S-V-O structural frame suggests lack of understanding of, or control over, the structural elements (word order and verb morphology) required for expression of sentence nouns' logical roles. Although it is not entirely clear that the problems with logical roles is not a reflection of the problems creating a structural frame, rather than an independent deficit, they will be treated as separate impairments.

To summarise: Baseline analysis of M.L.'s sentence production revealed three possible deficits:

1. poor verb retrieval in production of both single words and sentences;
2. limited and often incorrect use of verb-related grammatical morphemes (auxiliary verbs and inflections);
3. incorrect realisation of the logical relations between the verb and nouns in a sentence.

These deficits can be linked to several probable points of failure in the sentence production process. First, it is not clear that M.L. obtains an accurate functional level representation. The logical role reversals elicited in sentence production tasks suggest that he may not assign nouns correctly to their logical roles of agent and recipient, even in cases where the verb is produced correctly. Failure to retrieve the correct verb could also arise at the functional level if M.L. failed to extract a correct verb concept from the message level representation. An inability to distinguish the target verb from semantically similar alternatives could result in failure to obtain an abstract verb representation. Alternatively, verb selection could be achieved by M.L. at the functional level, but fail to be realised phonologically at the positional level. In either case, the symptom of an impaired positional level representation would emerge. Finally, in narrative speech, M.L. produces only some of the necessary grammatical elements that comprise a structural frame. Although a frame is produced in the picture description task, over-reliance on a single auxiliary verb and inflection suggest that this frame is not computed anew for each sentence, but is used inflexibly and repeatedly with new sets of lexical items.

Comparison of the characteristics of M.L.'s sentence production to the model of normal production emphasizes the important role of the verb. Failure to specify the verb at the functional level representation would undermine the mapping between the verb and its logical arguments. Verb retrieval failure at the positional level would interfere with creation of the positional level representation by failing to provide a phonological form to fill the verb slot. Thus, a summary of M.L.'s deficits suggests that impaired verb retrieval could be a primary deficit that consequently undermines the execution of related processes. This isolation of the verb retrieval impairment as a possible primary deficit provides a basis for the focus of treatment.

## EXPERIMENT 1: FACILITATION OF VERB RETRIEVAL

The hypothesis that impaired verb retrieval causes or at least contributes to M.L.'s poor sentence production motivated an intervention to facilitate verb retrieval (details of this intervention are described in Mitchum & Berndt, 1988, and are summarised here). Treatment was based on the rationale that facile and accurate production of verbs is a crucial prerequisite to successful sentence production.

### *Materials*

Eight transitive verbs were selected for training. Verb frequency, regularity of the past tense, phonological complexity and ease of depiction were controlled. In order to avoid repeated use of the same pictures in pre/post-therapy assessment and in training, eleven *different* depictions of each of the eight target actions were drawn (by a professional artist). For each verb, two different depictions of each action were used to elicit single verb production before and after therapy; another two depictions for each verb elicited full sentences before and after treatment. The remaining seven depictions, all showing the same verb but with various nouns, were used as training stimuli. An example of the stimuli used for the target verb "pour" are shown in Fig. 15.2.

### *Procedures*

Two verb targets were trained in each one-hour therapy session. Repeated naming of each action picture was practiced until M.L. could name all seven depictions of a target verb within three seconds of

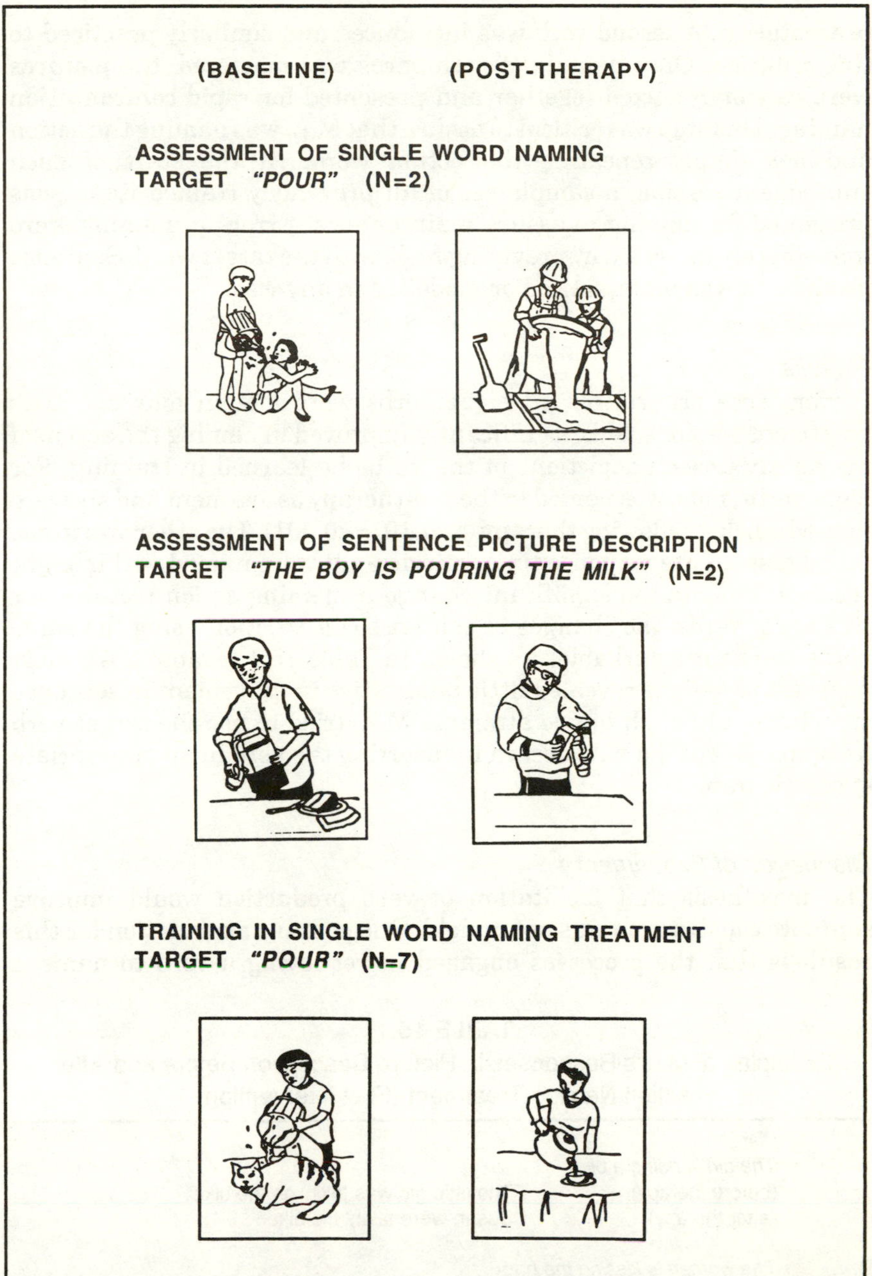


FIG. 15.2. Sample of picture stimuli used to elicit the target verb "pour" before and after first treatment in two assessment conditions and in naming training.

presentation. A second verb was introduced and similarly practiced to this criterion. Once naming of both verbs was mastered, the pictures were randomly mixed together and presented for rapid confrontation naming. This step was critical to assure that M.L. was naming the action and not simply repeating the action word. At the start of each subsequent session, a sample set of all previously trained items was presented for naming to assure maintenance. Errors in naming were immediately corrected by providing M.L. with the target word. Sentence production was not practiced or modelled in any way.

### *Results*

Performance criteria for all eight verbs were met in four one-hour treatment sessions. M.L. significantly improved in naming the action of previously unseen depictions of the verbs he learned in training. For eight verbs, none was named in the pre-therapy assessment and six were named quickly following therapy ($z=3.10$, $P<0.001$). The other two items failed to meet the response time criterion but were named within eight seconds. Despite the significant change in naming action pictures for this set of verbs, the changes in sentence construction using the same verbs were unremarkable. As shown in Table 15.1 (example A), most post-test responses revealed little qualitative improvement in sentence structures, although in two attempts M.L. tried to use the target verb (example B) but did not succeed in inserting the verb in an appropriate syntactic frame.

### *Discussion of Experiment 1*

The hypothesis that facilitation of verb production would improve sentence construction was not upheld. One possible explanation for this result is that the processes engaged in retrieving a verb to name a

TABLE 15.1
Examples of M.L.'s Responses in Picture Description Before and After Action Naming Treatment (First Intervention)

| | | |
|---|---|---|
| | (Target) | |
| A. | *The girl is riding a bike* | |
| | (before therapy) | "The little girl was takin' on the bike" |
| | (after therapy) | "Susan were takin' the bike" |
| B. | *The woman is kissing the baby* | |
| | (before therapy) | "My wife was very pretty because these a baby and the hairs" |
| | (after therapy) | "The mother and her baby are, the mother is very, the kiss" |

pictured action are functionally distinct from the processes needed to retrieve a verb to construct a sentence. In other words, although the action naming treatment itself was effective, it failed to generalise from single verb retrieval to verb retrieval in sentences. An alternative explanation is that untreated impairments in addition to a verb retrieval deficit continued to undermine the construction of sentences. In either case, continuation of the verb facilitation therapy was contraindicated by the preliminary outcome.

As discussed above, three deficits revealed in the baseline assessment of M.L.'s sentence production impairment included: 1. poor verb retrieval; 2. limited use of verb-related grammatical morphemes; and 3. poor surface structure realisation of the logical roles of the nouns in the sentence. The verb retrieval treatment focused on the first of these problems. The goal was to improve functional and positional level representations by requiring the identification of a nameable action from a pictured scene, as well as the phonological specification of that action name. Although these steps appear to be necessary in the construction of a sentence, they are clearly not sufficient. Specification of the morphological elements of the verb (the second problem noted above) is asserted by the model to occur independently of retrieval and phonological realisation of the main verb; this independence is supported by our results. That is, M.L.'s improved ability to retrieve a limited set of verbs had no effect on production of auxiliary verbs or verb inflections. The next logical step to address M.L.'s impairments therefore appeared to require explicit attention to specification of the morphological verb elements.

## EXPERIMENT 2: FACILITATION OF GRAMMATICAL "FRAME" CONSTRUCTION

A second intervention was carried out with M.L. to test the hypothesis that sentence construction was undermined by poor accessibility to the grammatical elements that form a verb phrase. In order to link the training of relatively abstract elements such as auxiliary verbs to a meaningful proposition, a treatment task was constructed to focus on the morphological elements associated with verb tense and aspect. Sequential pictures of an on-going, common activity provided contextual information to elicit a target verb before, during and after completion of the activity. These sequential picture stimuli were used to elicit sentences before and after treatment, and also formed the basis of the training exercises. An additional sentence elicitation procedure was developed that did not rely on picture description.

*Materials*

*Sequential Pictures.* Fourteen common activities were selected for which three points in the sequential time course of the activity (future, present and past) could be depicted clearly. For example, one set of pictures could readily elicit the descriptions "the man will wash the car/the man is washing the car/the man has washed the car". The verbs were selected on the basis of picturability, phonological complexity and regularity. The past participle form of half the verbs was regular (e.g. closed) and for half was irregular (e.g. eaten). Line drawings (8½" x 11") created by a professional artist were cut into thirds so that each frame of the sequence could be presented individually.

*Sentence formulation using a spoken target word.* Sentence production elicited with minimal constraint was obtained in a sentence formulation task that required M.L. to use a target word to construct an original sentence. As M.L.'s attempts to construct a sentence revealed sensitivity to the form-class of lexical items, a set of 54 words was selected from Frances and Kuçera (1982) to represent various degrees of form class ambiguity. "Unambiguous" nouns and verbs provided no alternative form class usage greater than 1 million. Two sets of 12 nouns were pairwise matched to the cumulative or to the base frequencies of a set of 12 verbs. Ambiguous words could function as either a noun or a verb. This category included six words for which noun and verb usages are about equal in the language (noun and verb frequencies differ by less than a log frequency of 0.2). Another six words were included for which the noun usage predominated (by more than a log frequency of 0.2), and six words were included for which the verb usage predominated using the same criterion. The task instructions were simply to make up a sentence using the target word somewhere in the sentence.

*Procedures*

Baseline samples of sentence production were obtained by asking M.L. to order the set of sequential pictures and then to describe each picture with a simple sentence. The sentence formulation task was used to obtain additional baseline samples of sentence production, but under conditions of minimal constraint and without pictures.

Training used six of the fourteen sequential picture triads; the remaining eight sets were reserved to test for generalisation to untreated but highly comparable stimuli. M.L. was instructed to describe each ordered sequential frame using the auxiliary verb and the appropriate inflection of the main verb to denote if "the action is *about to happen*", "the action is *right now*" or "the action is *already done*". These particular verbal instructions avoided inadvertent modelling of the target auxiliaries and inflections and were expected to provide M.L. with a self-cue technique that he could eventually initiate independently of the examiner. The actual grammatical targets that are most naturally elicited by the pictures are future tense (e.g. "will jump"), present progressive (e.g. "is jumping") and present perfect (e.g. "has jumped").

Cues to assist M.L. were presented systematically according to the type of error he committed. A "reminder" to select grammatical morphemes to express the temporal target was provided when necessary by preceding his description with the tense-indicative cue (i.e. "about to..."; "right now..." or "already..."). In cases where M.L. failed to name the action, the verb was provided. Increasingly detailed cues were included as needed by modelling larger and larger parts of the target sentence. Once M.L. could describe each frame of a triad without error on three consecutive trials, a randomised elicitation was obtained for the triad set. As many triad sets as possible were presented in each session. Thus, earlier sessions included presentation of only one or two sets, whereas later sessions used all six triad sets. M.L.'s description of each verb triad became increasingly facile throughout the ten two-hour treatment sessions it took to obtain error-free performance.

### Results

*Sequential pictures—treated and untreated.* M.L. ordered all 14 sequential triads correctly and without hesitation, indicating a well-preserved conceptual understanding of the temporal relationship among the pictures. In the verbal description of each picture, M.L.'s most complete response was scored for the presence of specific lexical and grammatical elements. Examples of M.L.'s responses to the training sets before and after treatment (shown in Table 15.2) illustrate the improvement that was apparent for the training stimuli.

Tabulation of M.L.'s post-treatment descriptions for the 14 sequential picture sets (see Table 15.3) revealed flawless production of auxiliary/inflection combinations for the six trained picture sets, as well as for the eight sets that were not used in training. M.L.'s pre-treatment tendency to overproduce the present progressive verb form was modified in response to the intervention to reflect accurate use of the variety of phrases introduced in training. Moreover, there was no need for special instruction regarding irregular verbs (e.g. "has eaten"), as M.L. produced them correctly in response to the standard cues.

*Sentence formulation using a spoken target word.* To assess the availability of structural elements in a less constrained sentence elicitation task, M.L. was again asked to construct original sentences using spoken target words. As described earlier, the target words around

TABLE 15.2
Examples of M.L.'s Responses Before and After Second Intervention (Using Sequential Pictures to Enhance Accurate Production of the Auxiliary Verb and Main Verb Inflection)

| | | |
|---|---|---|
| (Target Picture) | | |
| GIRL FIXING PLANE | | |
| *(Action)* | *(Before)* | *(After)* |
| about to ... | The girl fix the plane | The girl will fix the plane |
| right now | The girl is fixing | The girl is fixing the plane |
| already | The girl will fixing the plane | The girl has fixed the plane |
| GIRL RINGING BELL | | |
| *(Action)* | *(Before)* | *(After)* |
| about to ... | The girl will ring | The girl will ring the bell |
| right now | The girl will ringing | The girl is ringing the bell |
| already | The girl are ringing | The girl has rung the bell |

which a sentence was to be constructed were unambiguous nouns[2], unambiguous verbs, or could function in either grammatical class. The sentences produced before and after treatment were independently scored by three judges (the authors and a doctoral candidate in linguistics who was naive to the nature of the study). Separate judgements were made of whether each response was syntactically well-formed and semantically accurate/informative[3]. The rate of agreement was somewhat higher for the syntactic (0.97) than the semantic (0.88) judgments, but was assumed to indicate good agreement for both. For those cases where there were disagreements, scoring was based on the agreed judgments of two of the three scorers.

As shown in Table 15.4, post-treatment responses over all targets showed gains in both syntactic and semantic well-formedness relative to pre-treatment responses; the number of sentences M.L. produced that were acceptable in both respects was significantly greater after than before the treatment (chi-square with continuity correction=5.44, $P$= 0.01). The only target grammatical class showing a reliable change in syntactic well-formedness following treatment was the class of

TABLE 15.3
Production of Auxiliary Verbs and Main Verb Inflections by M.L. Before and After Second Intervention (in Proportion Correct)

| *auxiliary verb (n = 14)* | | | *inflection (n = 14)* | | |
|---|---|---|---|---|---|
| | (pre) | (post) | | (pre) | (post) |
| will | 0.36 | 1.00 | (null) | 0.57 | 1.00 |
| is | 0.71 | 1.00 | -ing | 1.00 | 1.00 |
| has | 0.00 | 1.00 | -ed (or irregular) | 0.00 | 1.00 |

TABLE 15.4
Syntactic and Semantic Well-formedness of Responses in Sentence Formulation Task Before and After Second Intervention
(in Proportion Judged to be Well-formed)

| | *Target Word* | | | | | | | |
|---|---|---|---|---|---|---|---|---|
| | *verb (N = 12)* | | *noun (N = 23)* | | *ambiguous (N = 18)* | | *all targets (N = 53)* | |
| | *pre* | *post* | *pre* | *post* | *pre* | *post* | *pre* | *post* |
| Syntactically well-formed | 0.58 | 0.75 | 0.87 | 0.78 | 0.55 | 0.94 | 0.70 | 0.83 |
| Semantically coherent/ informative | 0.75 | 0.83 | 0.39 | 0.69 | 0.44 | 0.67 | 0.43 | 0.72 |
| Both syntactically and semantically correct | 0.50 | 0.58 | 0.39 | 0.69 | 0.44 | 0.61 | 0.40 | 0.64 |

ambiguous targets (chi-square=5.33, P=0.02). Less impressive gains were made when the target was a verb, and M.L. produced slightly *fewer* well-formed sentences after treatment when the target was a noun. All categories of targets showed some improvement in terms of their semantic informativeness.

One possible effect of the intervention on M.L.'s performance of this task might relate to an improved appreciation of the centrality of the verb in sentence construction, or to some improvement in his knowledge of which words could actually serve as verbs in sentences. Pre-treatment responses in the sentence formulation task (Table 15.5) suggest some difficulty using verb targets as verbs in sentences, but no such difficulty with noun targets.

After treatment, all verb targets were used as verbs, but some noun targets were used in other grammatical classes. The largest shift in the

TABLE 15.5
Grammatical Class of Target Words in Responses to Sentence Formulation Task Before and After Second Intervention

| | *Grammatical Class of Target* | | | | | |
|---|---|---|---|---|---|---|
| *Grammatical class of target in response* | *Verb (N = 12)* | | *Noun (N = 23)* | | *Ambiguous (N = 18)* | |
| | *Pre* | *Post* | *Pre* | *Post* | *Pre* | *Post* |
| Verb | 0.67 | 1.00 | 0.00 | 0.00 | 0.28 | 0.78 |
| Noun | 0.08 | 0.00 | 1.00 | 0.91 | 0.61 | 0.22 |
| Other | 0.00 | 0.00 | 0.00 | 0.04 | 0.11 | 0.00 |
| Cannot be determined from context | 0.25 | 0.00 | 0.00 | 0.04 | 0.00 | 0.00 |

use of targets is apparent when these words could serve in either grammatical class. Prior to treatment, M.L. attempted to use few of the ambiguous words (0.28) as verbs; following treatment, he used most of them (0.78) as verbs (chi-square=7.1; $P$=0.007). These shifts suggest that the treatment resulted in some improvement in M.L.'s knowledge that a particular target word could function as a main verb in the sentence he was asked to construct. This change is also indicated by a marked decline following treatment in the use of very high frequency, general verbs ("have", "take", "get", etc.) as main verbs.

Even though the treatment was followed by a significant improvement in the production of well-formed and informative sentences, M.L.'s responses in this task were mostly syntactically well-formed even prior to treatment (see Table 15.4). An inspection of the verb forms used in these well-formed sentences reveals a major qualitative change in the type of structures employed. As shown in Table 15.6, well-formed sentences prior to treatment relied on untensed main verbs, especially the imperative form. Although these were most often structurally correct, they were often semantically empty uses of the target (e.g. "take a *drill*"; "get the *glass*"). After treatment, in contrast, most of the structurally correct sentences employed at least an auxiliary verb, and often included both an auxiliary and an inflected main verb. As might be expected, the auxiliaries and inflections employed in these responses were those that had been the target of the intervention, with a marked preference for the future tense (0.61 of all post-test responses employed "will"). As shown in Table 15.7, however, this tendency to use the trained grammatical frames was not accompanied by a tendency to use the main verbs that had been drilled in training. Some examples of these effects are presented in Table 15.8.

TABLE 15.6

Verb Structures Used in Syntactically Well-formed Responses in Sentence Formulation Task Before and After Second Intervention

| | *Proportion Well-formed Responses* | |
|---|---|---|
| *Verb Structure Used* | *Pre-Treatment* (N = 37) | *Post-Treatment* (N = 44) |
| Imperative | 0.43 | 0.09 |
| "Frozen" infinitive (e.g. "love to ...") | 0.05 | 0.00 |
| Main Verb | | |
| – untensed | 0.19 | 0.07 |
| – with inflection only | 0.05 | 0.00 |
| – with auxiliary only | 0.05 | 0.61 |
| – with both | 0.00 | 0.23 |
| "have", "is" only | 0.22 | 0.00 |

TABLE 15.7
Sentence Formulation Using Spoken Target Word: Proportion Syntactically and Semantically "Correct" Sentences and Proportion of Trained Elements Present in Each Response Before and After Second Intervention

| | *before treatment* (N = 53) | *after treatment* (N = 53) |
|---|---|---|
| Proportion "correct" | 0.40 | 0.64 |
| Proportion "trained" frame | 0.06 | 0.81 |
| Proportion "trained" verb | 0.00 | 0.20 |

TABLE 15.8
Examples of Change in Sentence Formulation Using Spoken Target Word Following Second Intervention (Target Word is Underlined)

| | | | |
|---|---|---|---|
| 1. | *Change to "correct"* | | |
| | pour (before) | : | He get the bucket where the pour |
| | (after) | : | The lady will pour the soup |
| | toast (before) | : | Take it in the toast |
| | (after) | : | The grandmother will eat the toast |
| 2. | *Use of "trained" grammatical frame* | | |
| | dial (before) | : | The dial is broken |
| | (after) | : | the lady has dialled the telephone |
| | drill (before) | : | Take a drill |
| | (after) | : | the mechanic will drill the tyres |
| 3. | *Use of "untrained" main verb* | | |
| | cannon (before) | : | We take it to the cannon |
| | (after) | : | The woman will fire the cannon |
| | kite (before) | : | We had the big kite |
| | (after) | : | The boy will find a kite |

### *Discussion of Experiment 2*

The results of the intervention to facilitate M.L.'s construction of a verb phrase indicate that an impairment of this ability was a major source of his difficulty in sentence production. Although the therapy exercises explicitly directed M.L.'s attention to the production of the grammatical elements and to their salience for tense and aspect, it was impossible to avoid practice in verb retrieval at the same time. In many therapy trials, M.L. isolated the action in the present-progressive frame (the only picture that showed the action actually happening) even when the target sentence was not the present progressive. This self-initiated strategy seemed to assist him in retrieving the verb and indicated that he had learned to focus attention on identification of the action *before* attempting to construct a sentence. The use of many relevant, untrained verbs in the two sentence production post-tests suggests that availability of the structural frame enhanced production of semantically specific verbs. This improvement may be related to M.L.'s strategy to identify explicitly the central action in the message. If so, then it is of interest that the learned strategy of isolating the action in pictures spontaneously generalised to the sentence formulation task, in which pictures were not provided.

Although the goal of the grammatical frame construction treatment was to improve the construction of a positional level sentence frame, its effects were probably not limited to improvement at that level. The explicit use of temporal information in the treatment may have provided a very early source of information about the aspects of the message level representations that were relevant for construction of the next level. More precise specification of the functional level verb representation may also have been achieved through M.L.'s strategy of deliberately extracting the central action from the message (in this case, from the pictures). In any case, better controlled use of main verb inflections and auxiliary verbs, as well as better production of main verbs, was evident after therapy. The generalisation of improved production to an untrained task of sentence formulation without pictures suggests that whatever the precise locus of improvement, the changes induced by the treatment are not bound to specific stimulus and elicitation types.

## REASSESSMENT OF ORIGINAL BASELINE TESTS

Baseline tasks used to obtain samples of narrative speech, picture description and noun/verb naming were repeated to assess generalisation to a variety of other contexts.

### *Naming*

Despite remarkably improved use of main verbs in the sentences M.L. produced following the second intervention, there was no change in his post-treatment confrontation naming of frequency-matched actions and objects (pre/post assessment for naming 30 action pictures=0.67/0.63; naming 60 object pictures=0.87/0.86).

### *Picture description*

Unconstrained description of the sixteen pictures used in the baseline assessment improved both in the production of an appropriate verb (from 0.31 to 0.69; $z=2.15$; $P<0.01$), and in the correct ordering of the noun phrases around the verb (from 0.63 to 1.00; $z=2.69$, $P<0.001$).

However, in the condition in which M.L. was constrained to produce a passive structure, little improvement was observed either in number of verbs produced (0.56 to 0.69; $z=0.76$, $P>0.15$) or in noun-phrase order (0.00 to 0.00). M.L.'s pre-treatment tendency to rely on a single S-V-O structure, and his difficulty expressing logical roles in passive voice sentences was, if anything, exacerbated by the treatment. Production of the auxiliary/inflection combination "is (verb)ing" accounted for over half (0.56) of responses in passive sentence construction before treatment and appeared in *all* post-therapy responses. This reliance on a single grammatical frame, in conjunction with the task constraint to begin the sentence with the theme rather than the agent noun, resulted in consistent reversal of noun order after treatment. Thus, post-treatment responses included many semantic oddities such as "the bike is riding the girl", which M.L. frequently indicated he knew were incorrect but could not correct. It would appear, then, that improved availability of some aspects of verb morphology (tense markers) did nothing to improve the use of the morphological elements needed to produce passive voice.

### *Narrative speech*

A post-treatment sample of M.L.'s narrative speech was obtained using the story telling procedure described in the baseline assessment. Table 15.9 compares the changes in various morphological and structural measures obtained in the pre- and post-treatment analyses. All changes were in the direction of normal performance. The magnitude of change in each of M.L.'s scores was compared to the standard deviation of the scores for five normal speakers reported by Saffran et al. (1989)[4]. M.L.'s use of verb inflections improved more than would be expected to occur as normal variability; however, a type-token analysis of the variety of verbs produced revealed no change. High frequency, semantically empty verbs continued to predominate, although there was a slight increase in the production of the irregular (uninflected) past tense form of these verbs. Improvement was most apparent in structural measures, including the length and well-formedness of sentences. Even so, none of these changes approached the striking improvements found for single sentence production in the more constrained tasks. Thus, the treatment appears to have had only minimal influence on M.L.'s ability to construct sentences in narrative context, despite remarkable improvement in the production of isolated sentences. Nevertheless, a trend in the direction of improvement, particularly in measures of structural completeness, was evident in post-treatment narrative production.

TABLE 15.9
Quantitative Indices of Sentence Formulation in Narrative Speech Before and After Intervention

| *Speech rate* | *Before treatment* | *After treatment* | *Before treatment – after treatment (S.D. for normal speakers)* |
|---|---|---|---|
| # words per minute | 79.90 | 93.00 | 13.10 (19.0) |
| *Morphological measures* | | | |
| closed class/total words | 0.41 | 0.40 | –0.01 (0.04) |
| noun/pronoun ratio | 3.25 | 3.31 | 0.06 (0.85) |
| noun/verb ratio | 1.68 | 1.52 | –0.16 (0.30) |
| determiner/noun ratio | 0.85 | 0.94 | 0.09 (0.00) (c) |
| verb inflection index | 0.28 | 0.38 | 0.10* (0.05) |
| *Structural measures* | | | |
| words in sentence/ narrative words | 0.53 | 0.61 | 0.08 (0.00) (c) |
| mean sentence length | 5.09 | 5.90 | 0.81* (0.20) |
| well formed sentences/ total sentences | 0.41 | 0.53 | 0.12* (0.05) |
| elaboration of subject noun phrase | 1.14 | 1.13 | –0.01 (0.05) |
| elaboration of verb phrase | 2.18 | 2.38 | 0.20 (0.19) |
| embedding index | 0.00 | 0.15 | 0.15 (0.33) |

* measures in which the change in M.L.'s scores after therapy exceeded the standard deviation obtained from a group of five normal speakers.
(c) indicates ceiling-level performance, and thus no variability, for normal speakers.

## DISCUSSION

The cognitive neuropsychological approach to rehabilitation mandates that treatment be motivated by a model of the normal system that is the focus of the intervention. The study reported here illustrates the utility of a normal model in planning and prioritising treatment, but at the same time it points out the types of difficulties that are encountered. It was argued in the Introduction that a model of normal function is required for a reasonable assessment of the patient's symptoms, and for predicting the effect of treatment on untreated components. The rationale for this argument is that the model provides a framework for interpreting the patient's symptoms as manifestations of particular functional impairments, and for linking those functional deficits to other processes that might be affected by treatment.

The model of sentence production that guided this study motivated an assessment of M.L.'s ability to formulate sentences under various conditions. It also suggested a basis for analysis of his responses in terms of several elements that, according to the model, occur relatively early in the course of sentence production. This assessment and subsequent analysis uncovered several symptoms that were not obvious from simply listening to the patient attempting to communicate, and that would not have been highlighted using standard clinical language tests. First, the assessment showed that within the general context of aphasic word-finding problems, M.L. had a disproportionate difficulty in producing verbs. This symptom was manifested differently under different conditions: in spontaneous narrative speech M.L. relied upon high frequency empty verbs such as "have", "get", and "take", which resulted in the production of sentences instead of fragments, but which nonetheless yielded structurally impoverished utterances and undermined the communication of content. In a picture description task, M.L. continued to rely to some extent on these very general verbs, but also substituted some semantically inappropriate verbs in constructing sentences to describe action pictures. This problem of retrieving and producing verbs was apparently not an artifact of word frequency because he demonstrated significantly poorer production of verbs in an action vs. object picture naming task in which the verb and noun targets were carefully matched.

The second symptom that emerged from the assessment was a relative lack of use of the bound and free-standing grammatical morphemes associated with verbs (auxiliary verbs and verb inflections), accompanied by normal production of the grammatical morphemes associated with nouns (pronouns and determiners). M.L. did not typically omit these elements in contexts where they were clearly required. Rather, he tended to rely on syntactic structures and main verb forms that did not require auxiliaries and inflections. In spontaneous speech, he produced a variety of irregular past tense forms such as "had", "was", "got", and few regular verbs that required an inflection. In picture description, he relied on a "frozen" progressive grammatical frame and used it for all of his N-V-N constructions.

The third symptom that was uncovered in the initial assessment was difficulty expressing the logical roles (agent, patient, theme) in reversible sentences. This problem was very clearly evident in picture description under conditions in which M.L. was constrained to begin the sentence with a non-agent noun, but it also occurred occasionally in active sentences. These "role reversal" errors are not easily detected in spontaneous speech, and may be masked by heuristic strategies patients adopt to begin sentences with the most salient noun (often the agent), using canonical word order (Saffran, Schwartz, & Marin, 1980). Moreover, the agrammatic patients who often exhibit this problem with order have great difficulty producing the morphological elements required for passive voice, complicating the interpretation of order errors. That is, it might be that the misordered nouns in an "agrammatic" sentence that looks like an active (e.g. "cat chase dog") is actually a passive sentence with the morphological elements omitted (see Caramazza & Berndt, 1985, for arguments along these lines). For M.L., in contrast, the order errors are unlikely to result from such omissions because he is capable of producing a wide range of grammatical morphemes and even produced two passive voice sentences in the unconstrained version of the picture description task.

The normal model had suggested that each of these symptoms could play a major role in M.L.'s difficulty producing well-formed and informative sentences. Unfortunately, the model provided little suggestion about the relationship among these symptoms, i.e. about whether more than one of them was likely to arise from the same underlying impairment. For example, a failure to lexicalise the verb correctly at the functional level would cause the verb retrieval symptom, and might also disrupt the assignment of logical roles to the nouns that are lexicalised at the same stage in the process. Such verb lexicalisation failure might also disrupt the specification of grammatical morphemes at the positional level by failing to provide the information needed to generate the phonological form of a verb (i.e. information to which the inflection, at least, must attach). Various other possible relations between the specific surface symptoms and their underlying functional deficit(s) could be postulated; the point is that the model does not provide the detail about the temporal course of these various operations, nor about their interactions, that would support the principled generation of hypotheses. Thus, our first intervention essentially followed the reasoning developed immediately above, and focused on enhancing the lexicalisation and production of a small set of verbs. The goal was to determine whether or not improvement in verb retrieval would affect the production of verbs in sentences, and of verb-relevant grammatical morphemes, resulting in grammatical structures. The results were clear: despite much improved ability to name action pictures using specific verb targets, M.L. was no better at producing full sentences to describe pictures using the same verb targets.

This lack of generalisation of a successful treatment effect might indicate that the retrieval of the verb is not as critical to sentence construction as the model had suggested. Alternatively, it could be that our treatment task of repeated picture naming did not engage the same processes that are responsible for lexicalising the verb at the functional level when a sentence is being produced. Another possibility is that additional impairments continued to impede M.L. from inserting the verb properly into a syntactic frame at the positional level, despite the enhanced availability of the treated verbs. The second intervention, therefore, focused explicitly on the production of verb morphology within the limited domain of tense/aspect markers, and succeeded in reinstating M.L.'s ability to use these elements productively.

This result appears to have had far-reaching effects on M.L.'s ability to formulate sentences. First, there was generalisation of the morphological elements that were the focus of treatment to untrained verbs, even some that had an irregular past participle. This finding is important as it suggests that M.L. had learned a general rule for the application of tense markers and could apply it to unpracticed lexical items. It also suggests that lexical forms that he never used prior to treatment had not been lost, but could be made available in the right circumstances. Generalisation was also observed in a novel elicitation context: M.L. was able to produce morphologically complete and semantically specific verb phrases in the sentence formulation task in which there was neither specific focus on temporal factors nor provision of a pictured action. This finding suggests that M.L. had internalised the information about temporal relationships and the identification of the action word that he had learned in treatment. This type of generalisation is particularly important because it represents a link between the changes established in very structured treatment contexts and the application of those changes to more natural discourse settings. There was, however, no improvement in the production of sentences in narrative speech (the story telling task) that was comparable to the marked improvement in tasks eliciting single sentences. In fact, M.L. appeared to revert to his old strategy of producing uninflected high frequency general verbs, although the structures he produced were somewhat longer and better formed. One additional requirement of the story telling task relative to the single-sentence tasks is recall of the details and sequence of the story. These demands, together with increased requirements for specific lexical items that were difficult for M.L. to retrieve, may have diverted processing resources away from structural and morphological processing.

The idea that aspects of performance may be attributable to shifts in the allocation of limited processing resources may also be invoked to explain what may be the most important effect of treatment: marked improvement in the ability to produce specific, relevant main verbs that had not been the focus of training. This effect was most clearly evident in M.L.'s post-treatment responses in the sentence formulation task using spoken target words. The guiding model provides little basis for accounting for this finding. One intriguing possibility is that the enhanced availability of the grammatical elements of the syntactic frame (at the positional level) freed up processing resources that could be devoted to retrieval of the main verb. Bock (1982) has offered a number of arguments supporting the interactive nature of lexical and syntactic processes as they compete for limited processing resources in the act of sentence formulation. Within this framework, virtually any intervention that makes some aspect of processing more automatic (i.e. less engaging of limited processing capacity) could enhance the operation of some other process.

Another way of looking at possible lexical/syntactic interactions is more positive: rather than competing for processing resources, the morphological verb elements available following treatment may have provided a kind of syntactic prime—indicating, for example, that a verb was required in the next slot in the frame. Such effects, in conjunction with semantic priming effects available from the nouns M.L. could more easily retrieve, may have succeeded in boosting activation of verb representations to threshold levels. Such syntactic and semantic effects on lexical access have been demonstrated for the retrieval of nouns in sentence completion contexts (Zingeser & Berndt, 1988), but have not been shown to enhance verb retrieval. This possibility is clinically significant, in that it suggests a variety of ways in which the pervasive lexical retrieval problems of aphasic patients might be approached using syntactic priming.

Two of the three symptoms uncovered in the initial assessment of M.L.'s sentence production impairment were thus improved following the second intervention. No comparable gains were registered in the third symptom: difficulty in the expression of logical roles for sentence nouns. The model provides little information about how logical roles are yoked to elements of surface structure during production, and in fact there are several possibilities (see Berndt, 1991, for discussion). As noted in the Introduction, several successful treatment programs have carried out explicit interventions directed at mapping between logical roles and surface syntax (Byng, 1988; Jones, 1986). Neither of these studies required patients to demonstrate production of passive voice, nor did they provide any test that forced the patient to produce structures using non-canonical word order. Thus, there are no available protocols for us to use in designing a treatment for M.L. directed at this aspect of the normal model. The current plan is first to attempt to re-establish M.L.'s ability to produce more reliably the surface syntax of passive voice. Once two different surface forms are available as options to express logical roles (active and passive), explicit attention to mapping these roles to subject and object noun phrases can be undertaken.

We are encouraged by data suggesting that surface structures, such as passive morphology, can be elicited under the behaviorally passive conditions of syntactic priming (Saffran & Martin, 1990), suggesting that a patient who does not spontaneously use them may nonetheless have such structures available. If such procedures can be adapted for intervention, it may be possible to establish greater proficiency in production of a range of syntactic structures without explicit attention to all of the lexical and syntactic factors involved. For M.L. it would be of theoretical and practical interest to determine if the availability of a wide range of structures would generalise to more accurate and elaborated conveyance of complex messages, for example in spontaneous speech.

The outcome of the two interventions described here, and considered together, have been interpreted as directly relevant to the clinical issues raised in the Introduction. As argued earlier, two issues that are central to planning and evaluating interventions in aphasia relate to the assessment of the patient's language impairment, and the ability to predict generalisation of a specific treatment to other processing functions and contexts. We would argue that it is virtually impossible to interpret the results of intervention that is based on standard clinical assessment (i.e. syndrome analysis) because such an assessment does not provide a means for determining the underlying functional impairment(s) or for predicting how various impairments may be related. The standard assessment of M.L.'s production impairment simply validated the obvious symptoms: fluent, well-articulated utterances with marked impairment of sentence structure and poor word finding. Based on descriptions such as these, it is remarkable that clinicians have been successful in bringing about changes in a processing system as complex as sentence production. Indeed, the apparent ease with which changes in sentence construction patterns can be induced in some patients is a clinically encouraging phenomenon. However, the purpose of aphasia rehabilitation is not to produce haphazard change, but to establish systematic improvement in language functions, and to do so in the most expeditious manner possible. Cognitive neuropsychological approaches to intervention promise to provide a means for identifying the treatment that is most suitable for a particular patient. Just as importantly, treatments that suggest the greatest potential for generalisation can be selected, and the different aspects of generalisation can be predicted and measured. This more detailed and motivated approach to the treatment of aphasia should serve as a basis for the development of a theory of therapy, built upon the cumulative results of theoretically oriented treatment studies.

## ACKNOWLEDGEMENT

This work was supported by grant R1-DC00262 from the National Institutes of Health. The authors are grateful to Anne N. Haendiges for assistance in many aspects of this project including task construction and testing, to Maryne C. Glowacki for careful typing of the manuscript and, above all, to M.L. for his dedicated participation in this project.

## NOTES

1. The two-way frequency matching of noun targets to both the higher and lower estimates of the verbs' frequencies was done to ensure that any differences obtained between noun and verb retrieval (in either direction) was not simply a frequency effect. Subsequent work using these stimuli including that reported here (see also Zingeser & Berndt, 1990) has found little difference in noun production for the two noun lists.
2. M.L. failed to incorporate one of the target nouns into his response, so all trials (pre- and post-treatment) using this target were eliminated from analysis yielding N=23 for noun targets.
3. The criteria on which these judgments were based were as follows: syntactic violations included sentence fragments; responses in which words were used in an incorrect form class context; subcategorisation violations; failures of noun/verb number agreement; other inflectional errors. Semantic violations included sentence fragments in which an underlying proposition could not be discerned; selectional restriction violations; errors of fact or sentences that did not make logical sense; sentences with little meaningful content. An operational definition of the last criterion was to score as lacking content all utterances in which a target word was used in a context in which a large number of other words could easily be inserted, and which contained no other word with a semantic relationship to the target. Thus, "I like CHEESE" would be scored as without semantic content, whereas "The mouse likes CHEESE" or "I eat CHEESE" would be scored as semantically informative.
4. The numbers yielded by this analysis system are generated using a variety of different calculations. The underlying distribution of these scores for a normal or for a patient population is unknown. We have thus chosen not to attempt statistical analysis of the changes in these scores following the intervention, but simply compare the magnitude of the change for descriptive purposes to rough estimates of expected normal variation.

## REFERENCES

Berndt, R.S. (1991). Sentence processing in aphasia. In M.T. Sarno (Ed.), *Acquired aphasia*, 2nd Edition. New York: Academic Press.

Berndt, R.S. & Mitchum, C.C. (1991). *Verb production impairments: Exploring the functional source of the deficit*. Paper presented at the Academy of Aphasia, Rome, Italy.

Bock, J.K. (1982). Toward a cognitive psychology of syntax: Information processing contributions to sentence formulation. *Psychological Review, 89*, 1-47.

Bock, J.K. (1987). Co-ordinating words and syntax in speech plans. In A. W. Ellis (Ed.), *Progress in the psychology of language*. London: Lawrence Erlbaum Associates Ltd.

Byng, S. (1988). Sentence processing deficits: Theory and therapy. *Cognitive Neuropsychology, 5*, 629-676.

Caramazza, A. & Berndt, R.S. (1985). A multicomponent deficit view of agrammatic Broca's aphasia. In M.L. Kean (Ed.), *Agrammatism*. Orlando, FL: Academic Press.

Dell, G. (1986). A spreading activation theory of retrieval in sentence production. *Psychological Review, 93*, 283-321.

Frances, W.N. & Kuçera, H. (1982). *Frequency analysis of English usage: Lexicon and grammar*. Boston: Houghton Mifflin Company.

Fromkin, V.A. (1973). *Speech errors as linguistic evidence*. Mouton: The Hague.

Garrett, M.F. (1975). The analysis of sentence production. In G.H. Bower (Ed.), *The psychology of learning and motivation*, *Vol. 9* (pp.133-177). New York: Academic Press.

Garrett, M.F. (1980). Levels of processing in sentence production. In B. Butterworth (Ed.), *Language production*, *Vol. 1*. New York: Academic Press.

Garrett, M.F. (1982). The organization of processing structure for language production: Applications to aphasic speech. In D. Caplan, A.R. Lecours, & A. Smith (Eds.), *Biological perspectives on language*. Cambridge, MA: MIT Press.

Goodglass, H. & Kaplan, E. (1983). *The Assessment of Aphasia and Related Disorders*, 2nd Edition. Philadelphia: Lea and Febiger.

Holland, A.L. & Levy, C. (1971). Syntactic generalisation in aphasia as a function of relearning an active declarative sentence. *Acta Symbolica, 2*, 34-41.

Jones, E.V. (1986). Building the foundations for sentence production in a non-fluent aphasic. *British Journal of Disorders of Communication, 21*, 63-82.

Kearns, K.P. & Salmon, S.J. (1984). An experimental analysis of auxiliary and copula verb generalisation in aphasia. *Journal of Speech and Hearing Disorders, 49*, 152-163.

Kohn, S.E., Lorch, M.P., & Pearson, D.M. (1989). Verb finding in aphasia. *Cortex, 25,* 57-69.

Le Dorze, G., Jacob, A., & Coderre L. (1991). Aphasia rehabilitation with a case of agrammatism: A partial replication. *Aphasiology, 5*(1), 63-85.

Loverso, F., Prescott, T., & Selinger, M. (1988). Cueing verbs: A treatment strategy for aphasic adults (CVT). *Journal of Rehabilitation Research and Development, 25(2),* 47-60.

Mitchum, C.C. & Berndt, R.S. (1988). *Verb retrieval and sentence production*. Paper presented at the Academy of Aphasia, Santa Fe, NM.

Pate, D.S., Saffran, E.M., & Martin, N. (1987). Specifying the nature of the production impairment in a conduction aphasic: A case study. *Language and Cognitive Processes, 2,* 43-84.

Saffran, E. M., Berndt, R.S., & Schwartz, M.F. (1989). The quantitative analysis of agrammatic production: Procedure and data. *Brain and Language, 37,* 440-479.

Saffran, E.M. & Martin, N. (1990). *Effects of syntactic priming on sentence production in an agrammatic aphasic.* Presented at the Academy of Aphasia 28th Annual Meeting, Baltimore, MD.

Saffran, E.M., Schwartz, M.F., & Marin, O.S.M. (1980). Evidence from aphasia: Isolating the components of a production model. In B. Butterworth (Ed.), *Language production, Vol. 1.* London: Academic Press.

Saffran, E.M., Schwartz, M.F., Fink, R., Myers, J., & Martin, N. (1992). Mapping therapy: An approach to remediating agrammatic sentence comprehension and production. In J.A. Cooper (Ed.), *Aphasia treatment: Current approaches and research opportunities.* U.S. Department of Health and Human Services, NIH Publication # 93-3424.

Schwartz, M.F. (1987). Patterns of speech production deficit within and across aphasia syndromes: Application of a psycholinguistic mode. In M. Coltheart, G. Sartori, & R. Job (Eds.), *The cognitive neuropsychology of language.* Hillsdale: NJ: Lawrence Erlbaum Associates Inc.

Stemberger, J.P. (1985). An interactive activation model of language production. In A. Ellis (Ed.), *Progress in the psychology of language, Vol. 1.* London: Lawrence Erlbaum Associates Ltd.

Zingeser, L. & Berndt, R.S. (1988). Grammatical class and context effects in a case of pure anomia: Implications for models of language production. *Cognitive Neuropsychology, 5,* 473-516.

Zingeser, L. & Berndt, R.S. (1990). Retrieval of nouns and verbs in agrammatism and anomia. *Brain and Language, 39,* 14-32.

CHAPTER SIXTEEN

# Application of Cognitive Models to Remediation in Cases of Developmental Dyslexia

Philip H.K. Seymour and Frances Bunce
*Department of Psychology, The University, Dundee, UK*

## ABSTRACT

The chapter is concerned with the remediation of reading and spelling disorders in cases of childhood dyslexia. Three theoretical approaches of possible relevance are: (1) a cognitive architecture representing the modular structure of the orthographic systems (Ellis & Young, 1988); (2) a developmental stage model (Frith, 1985); or (3) an account of the content and structural organisation of a developing orthographic framework (Seymour, 1990b). Two case studies of eight year old boys are reported. A cognitive assessment, using a word/nonword contrast, suggested different presenting patterns, with D.K. being a case of phonological (dysphonetic) dyslexia and R.C. of morphemic (dyseidetic, surface) dyslexia. The intervention was directed towards the establishment of an orthographic structure and involved standard pedagogic techniques with controls on cognitive focus (reading/spelling, lexical/nonlexical) and organisation (2D, 3D). The subjects differed in their response to the intervention, with R.C. retaining essentially the same processing pattern, while D.K. showed a resolution of his difficulties in spelling plus a strategic change in reading. Manipulation of aspects of the teaching approach did not produce clear effects. It was concluded that dyslexic cases may show distinctive patterns and may respond differently to instruction, but that they confront a common task of forming an orthographic framework. The critical remaining question appeared to be one of defining the content of this structure and the way in which an initial core system may be expanded.

## INTRODUCTION

There has been a large emphasis in cognitive neuropsychological approaches to rehabilitation on the re-establishment of cognitive functions that have been lost as a consequence of neurological damage. This chapter will discuss a related, though not identical, problem—that of creating a new function (here, basic literacy), which has failed to develop normally despite the usual parental and educational encouragements. The main argument will be that, although the question of *methodology* (i.e. the task of verifying whether or not an intervention has produced a beneficial effect) may be common to the rehabilitation of neurological disorders and the remediation of childhood disorders, the underlying cognitive *theory* by which practice can be guided and interpreted may be rather different.

## THEORETICAL OPTIONS

It may be helpful, as a first step, to consider three theoretical approaches that are potentially relevant to the design of procedures for the assessment and remediation of literacy disorders. Between them, the three approaches make suggestions about the structure of the *orthographic system* that underlies competent reading and spelling, the way in which this system emerges during development, and the format of the representations it contains.

### Modular Information Processing Model

Ellis and Young (1988) outlined a scheme that they derived from earlier statements of the 'cognitive architecture' of the reading and spelling systems by Morton (1980), Newcombe and Marshall (1980), Patterson and Shewell (1987), and others. The key proposal is that the orthographic system is subdivided into a number of components (modules), such that:

- input systems, required for reading, are distinct from output systems, involved in spelling;
- reading depends on two distinct processors, one required for recognition of lexical items (words, morphemes), and the other for nonlexical letter-sound conversion;
- spelling depends on an analogous structure, consisting of a lexicon of word-forms and a process of sound-letter translation.

In effect, the theory maintains that the orthographic system possesses a 2 × 2 modular structure (input/output × lexical/nonlexical), so that four component modules are identified, each vulnerable to neurological damage or to a developmental impairment.

*Implication for assessment.* The 2 × 2 modular structure suggests that a cognitive assessment should, at a minimum, include a probe for each of the four components. Cognitive neuropsychological research suggests that the appropriate tests are: (1) oral reading of words (lexical input); (2) oral reading of matched nonwords (nonlexical input); (3) writing dictated words (lexical output); and (4) writing dictated nonwords (nonlexical output). Contrasts between an individual's accuracy scores on the word and nonword lists and the results of normally developing children can be used to display the distribution of impairments across the four sub-systems. Error patterns, reaction times, and psycholinguistic effects provide additional information (Seymour, 1986).

*Implication for remediation.* The main contribution of the model lies in the mapping of impairments across the modular components of the orthographic system. This can provide a rationale for the direction of therapy towards the most impaired systems (treating the weakness) or towards the least impaired systems (exploiting the strengths) (see, for example, Boder, 1973). The procedures themselves are not specified but will arise out of assumptions about the *cognitive focus* of pedagogic tasks and about the information represented in each module (e.g. grapheme-phoneme associations for the nonlexical processes, frequency ordered word lists for the lexicons).

### Developmental Stage Model

Frith (1985) presented persuasive arguments for the view that the appropriate framework for discussion of *developmental disorders*, such as childhood dyslexia, is a developmental theory rather than a 'cognitive architecture'. She suggested that literacy development could be described in terms of the dominant strategy used by a child in dealing with print. Three main strategies were identified, referred to as: (1) logographic (recognition or storage of whole words); (2) alphabetic (letter-sound association); and (3) orthographic (combination of abstract letter structures corresponding to morphemes). Frith proposed that the strategies emerge in sequence and that earlier levels must be attained before later ones can be approached. The same sequence applies to reading and spelling but in an asynchronous form, with a logographic approach predominating in early reading and an alphabetic approach in early spelling. Across domain influences are proposed, e.g. an alphabetic approach to spelling eventually promotes the adoption of the same procedure in reading. Dyslexia is defined as a 'developmental arrest' (failure to advance from one stage to the next), with the shift from a logographic to an alphabetic approach being seen as the key to the problem.

Frith's scheme can be related to the information processing model by equating strategies with functions or modules (Morton, 1989; Seymour, 1987a; Seymour & MacGregor, 1984). If this approach is adopted a 'cognitive architecture' can be set out for each step in the developmental sequence. Working in this way, Seymour (1990b) concluded, on the basis of data from a longitudinal study of children beginning to learn to read (Seymour & Evans, 1992), that a modified version of Frith's model, allowing for concurrent development of the logographic and alphabetic processes, might be preferred. This scheme is shown in Fig. 16.1 and

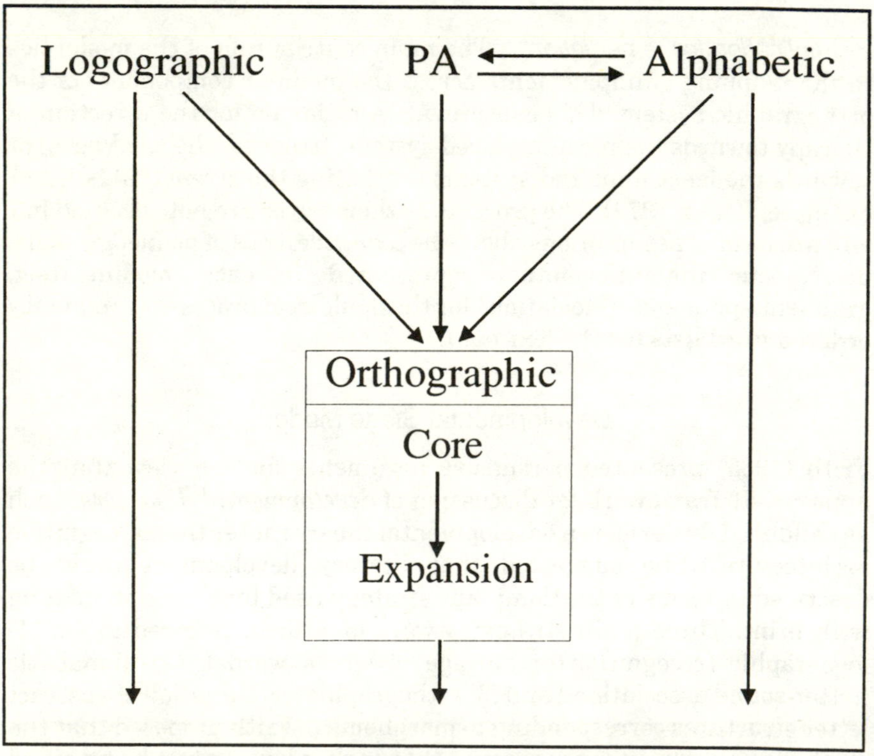


FIG. 16.1. Schematic representation of 'dual foundation' model of orthographic development. the formation and expansion of a 'core' structure is assisted by alphabetic (letter-sound) associations, a representation of syllabic structure (PA), and stored logographic forms.

may be referred to as a 'dual foundation' model of orthographic development. The main proposal is that the construction of an orthographic framework normally depends on contributions from: (1) an alphabetic knowledge of letter-sound associations; (2) structures represented in a logographically stored vocabulary; and (3) an overall organisational framework contributed by 'phonological awareness' (PA).

*Implications for assessment.* The developmental models include aspects of the dual-process assumptions of the cognitive architecture models, especially the contrast between logographic and alphabetic processes. The word/nonword method can be used to test for these functions. In general, availability of a logographic process but absence of an alphabetic process will be indexed by ability to read a proportion of words but inability to read nonwords. An alphabetic process will be shown by slow, length dependent reading of words and nonwords, possibly accompanied by sounding. A dual (logographic + alphabetic) process will be implied if words appear to be read by a fast direct process while nonwords are read by the slow length dependent process. The distinction between the orthographic process and the earlier procedures is more problematic. However, one possibility is that the availability of the framework allows words and nonwords to be translated via the same process, giving an approximation to direct reading for both classes of stimuli (see Seidenberg & McClelland, 1989; Seymour & Evans, 1992).

*Implications for remediation.* Frith's sequential stage model suggests that a child should be helped through the stage at which arrest has occurred. In the dual foundation model, the implication is that instruction might initially focus on the establishment of both logographic and alphabetic processes, although the main requirement remains the building up of the orthographic framework.

## Orthographic Framework Model

The orthographic framework model is a statement of the content of the system developed during the orthographic stage of the dual foundation model. The main suggestion is that phonological structure provides an organising principle for a framework in which orthographic elements are arrayed.

The framework might be viewed as a two-dimensional (2D) structure in which syllabic forms are defined by combinations of elements drawn from sets of initial consonants (onsets) and vowel + terminal consonants (rimes). Alternatively, one might envisage a three-dimensional (3D) structure defined by identities of initial consonant (IC), vowel (V) and terminal consonant (TC) structures (Seymour, 1987a; Seymour & MacGregor, 1984). According to this approach, the orthographic system codes syllabic forms within a combinatorial framework, which reflects possible levels of hierarchical structure in syllables. Lexical items are located within the framework, together with pointers to semantics and indications of deviations or inconsistencies in pronunciation. Seymour (1990b) has outlined a developmental version of the model. This suggests the existence of a "core" structure (simple initial and terminal consonants and short vowels), which is subsequently expanded to incorporate more complex forms (consonant clusters and lengthened vowels) (see also Seymour, Bruce, & Evans, 1992).

*Implications for assessment.* The theory suggests that assessment might be based on word and nonword lists that sample the orthographic elements defining the 2D or 3D representation. Separate lists might be constructed for the 'core' lexicon and for each of the postulated expansions. Results should indicate the level of orthographic development attained by an individual and also the location of gaps in the framework (structures that consistently attract errors).

*Implications for remediation.* The theory implies that remediation should initially focus on the establishment of the core structure, with emphasis on the *positions* of orthographic elements in a 2D (onset × rime) or 3D (IC × V × TC) structure, and the placement of known words within the structure. Once the core was available, indexed by competent reading or spelling of (almost) any word or nonword sampled from the structure, a move towards 'expansion' by introduction of more complex elements should become possible.

## HETEROGENEITY OF DYSLEXIA

A critical question for remediation is whether cases of disability are *heterogeneous* in ways that are likely to interact with the instructional approach adopted. This remains a controversial issue in the field of reading disability and dyslexia. Many investigators continue to study the disability via global comparisons between groups of dyslexic and normal readers, thus implicitly assuming that dyslexia is a homogeneous category that can be differentiated in some general way from the population of normal readers. Others take the view that dyslexia is divisible into a limited number of internally homogeneous sub-types. For example, Boder (1973) proposed a contrast between *dysphonetic dyslexia*, marked by a difficulty in using letter-sound correspondences (alphabetic, nonlexical processes), and *dyseidetic dyslexia*, marked by over-reliance on correspondences and a lack of lexical knowledge. However, an effective operational definition of these categories is lacking and it has not yet been demonstrated that they are in practice distinct. A current view, set out by Ellis (1985), is that the heterogeneity of cases of reading disability may reflect continuous variation within a space defined by a number of cognitive dimensions, two of which correspond to the lexical and nonlexical processes postulated in the information processing and developmental models.

No generally satisfactory way of dealing with "heterogeneity without clustering" has yet been identified. However, an approach that recommends itself in the interim may be simply to plot the scatter of cases on a two-dimensional surface defining the efficiency of the lexical process on the one hand, and of the nonlexical process on the other (e.g. performance on a word reading test on the ordinate vs. performance on a nonword reading test on the abscissa). When this is done the great majority of cases appear to fall below the diagonal representing equivalent error rates in words and nonwords. The scatter may, nonetheless, extend throughout the lower triangle of the graph, indicating that there are some subjects whose word and nonword reading appear roughly equivalent, but others who read nonwords dramatically less efficiently than words (Seymour, 1987b; 1990a; Seymour & Evans, in press ). The scatter of cases reveals the degree and form of heterogeneity within the sample. It is then possible to select individual cases who occupy particular regions of the two-dimensional space and to subject them to a more detailed analysis.

## Initial Assessment

In the present study, two cases will be reported, who are referred to by their initials, D.K. and R.C. They were originally part of a larger study, involving more than 100 subjects, including both dyslexic and normal readers, who were assessed on the word and nonword reading tasks. A detailed account of the sample is given by Seymour and Evans (in press). D.K. appeared to be an extreme example of an individual whose nonword reading was very much worse than his word reading (located at the lower right corner of the scattergraph). R.C., by contrast, had elevated error rates on both words and nonwords (located close to the diagonal). In view of the preceding discussion, it should be clear that the cases are not presented as representatives of sub-types (in Boder's categorial sense) but simply as examples of individuals who are drawn from distinct regions of the two-dimensional (lexical vs. nonlexical) space, and who might, therefore, be expected to show differing patterns, perhaps having differing implications for remediation.

## Psychometric Assessment

D.K. was aged eight years when initially seen. He presented with a history of language difficulty that had required treatment by a speech therapist. At seven years, a clinical report mentioned phonological delay, articulatory disorder, and difficulties with rhythm and timing and muscular control. He was considered bright and enthusiastic at school, with good progress in reading. The psychometric assessments summarised in Table 16.1 support this account, showing superior intelligence, especially on the performance scales, and reading which was at age in November 1987.

However, the re-assessment in November 1988 suggests that reading, and particularly spelling, had fallen well behind age. The recent assessment, following the intervention, indicates a considerable gain in spelling, though D.K. still performed below his age.

R.C. was also aged eight years when first assessed. His general intelligence appeared average. The results in Table 16.1 show that there was no advance in reading or spelling between February and November 1988. The gain in 1990, following the intervention, was more obvious for reading than for spelling but left him well behind his age in both. His mother mentioned an early hearing problem (not serious), early difficulty in look-and-say reading, and the possibility of dyslexia on his father's side.

TABLE 16.1

Details of I.Q. Scores (WISC-R) and Reading and Spelling Assessments (Schonell Graded Word Tests) for Subjects D.K. and R.C. Results of Literacy Assessments are Reported as a Reading Age (RA) and Spelling Age (SA). The Third Assessment was Carried Out After the Intervention

| *Subject* | *Intelligence* | | *Literacy assessments* | | |
|---|---|---|---|---|---|
| | VIQ | PIQ | CA | RA | SA |
| D.K. | 96 | 149 | 8.7 | 8.4 | 7.3 |
| | | | 9.6 | 8.8 | 7.2 |
| | | | 10.9 | 9.9 | 9.4 |
| R.C. | 94 | 102 | 8.4 | 7.1 | 7.0 |
| | | | 9.2 | 7.3 | 6.8 |
| | | | 10.6 | 8.9 | 7.5 |

## Cognitive Assessment

The assessment involved some visual and semantic tasks (Seymour, 1986) plus vocal reading and spelling to dictation of isolated words and nonwords. Edwards and Gibbon's (1973) lists of words used by children in early primary school provided the main source of items. The lists were stratified by frequency, length, and spelling-sound regularity. Regularity was defined in terms of three levels: (1) Regular (RG): pronunciation consistently derivable from letters considered individually, e.g. dog, tank, frost. (2) Rule-based (RL): pronunciation dependent on conventions regarding letter combinations, e.g. here, reach, bridge. (3) Irregular (I): containing low frequency or unique correspondences, e.g. ready, vase, yacht. Nonword sets were constructed to match the words in terms of orthographic components and lengths. Reading tests were presented via an Apple II microcomputer, using a voice switch for timing of vocal reactions. Items were dictated for spelling, accompanied by a context sentence in the case of the words. Sample lists appear in Seymour, Bunce, and Evans (1992).

Both subjects completed the assessment procedure twice before the intervention, and twice following the intervention, the two runs being separated by a period of about four weeks. Results for the initial assessment appear in Table 16.2 as error rates for the reading and spelling of word and nonword lists. It can be seen that D.K. exhibited a "phonological dyslexia" (specific difficulty in nonword reading) combined with a "phonological dysgraphia" (nonword spelling much worse than word spelling). These effects were not evident, in the case of

TABLE 16.2
Percent Error Scores for D.K. and R.C. in Reading and Spelling the Word and Nonword Lists Used in the Cognitive Assessment. The Table Also Shows the Total Number of Items Presented (N) and the Lexicality Effect (NW Error – W Error)

| | | *READING* | | | *SPELLING* | |
|---|---|---|---|---|---|---|
| | N | 1 | 2 | N | 1 | 2 |
| *Subject D.K.* | | | | | | |
| Word | 128 | 13 | 9 | 123 | 59 | 59 |
| Nonword | 128 | 95 | 94 | 60 | 92 | 98 |
| Difference | | 82 | 85 | | 33 | 39 |
| *Subject R.C.* | | | | | | |
| Word | 128 | 36 | 39 | 123 | 80 | 80 |
| Nonword | 128 | 59 | 48 | 60 | 53 | 48 |
| Difference | | 23 | 9 | | –27 | –32 |

R.C., who showed a smaller word/nonword difference in reading, and a reversal of the effect in spelling (a "lexical dysgraphia").

For purposes of statistical analysis, the word and nonword lists were partitioned into representative subsets of items (usually five sets of eight items, varying frequency and length, for each of the three regularity defined lists). Number of items correct in each subset was scored and the values were entered into a series of analyses of variance. For reading, the two cases (D.K. and R.C.) were treated as a "between" factor, and Lexicality (word vs. nonword) as a "within factor". A significant Cases × Lexicality interaction ($F(1,56)=91.51$, $P<0.001$) confirmed that D.K. and R.C. had different reading patterns. The analysis of spelling involved separate comparisons of nonwords with high and low frequency words, using four-item subsets. (This was because a reduced sample of items had been used in nonword spelling). The Cases × Lexicality interaction was significant in both analyses ($F(1,56)=69.4$ and 50.1, $P<0.001$). This confirms the existence of a "phonological" vs. "lexical" contrast between D.K. and R.C. in spelling.

## Process Analysis

In order to determine in more detail how D.K. and R.C. were reading and spelling some additional indicators were examined, including: (1) vocal reaction time in reading; (2) types of errors produced in reading and spelling; and (3) the impact of the psycholinguistic variations, especially word length and regularity.

*Reaction times.* Previous research (Seymour, 1986; 1987b) has suggested that the pattern of reaction times produced in word and nonword reading has some diagnostic significance. Cases of "phonological dyslexia" frequently produce discrepant patterns, with a predominance of fast times (below 2000ms) for words combined with a widely dispersed distribution for nonwords. The "morphemic" (surface dyslexic, dyseidetic) pattern, by contrast, is marked by a dispersed distribution in word reading that is closely matched in nonword reading. Table 16.3 provides information about the proportions of reaction times falling below 2000ms. R.C.'s distributions lacked a preponderance of fast times and showed approximately equivalent dispersed patterns for words and nonwords (test of difference gives $t(183)<1$). D.K.'s distributions consisted mainly of fast responses. Unlike other cases of phonological dyslexia this was true of nonwords as well as words. Seymour and Evans (in press) have described other examples of this fast "nonword" pattern.

TABLE 16.3
Summary of Reaction Time Data for D.K. and R.C. The Results are for Correct Responses Only, Except that D.K.'s Error Responses Were Used for the Nonword Reading Pre-test. The Table Gives the Mean and SD of the Reaction Time Distribution, the Percentage of Times Falling At or Below 2000ms, and a Processing Rate (ms/letter) Estimated by the Least Squares Procedure

| | | $\overline{X}$ *(ms)* | *sd (ms)* | *rate (ms/letter)* | *Per cent < 2000ms* |
|---|---|---|---|---|---|
| *PRE-TEST* | | | | | |
| D.K. | Words | 1202 | 422 | 6 | 93 |
| | Nonwords | 1661 | 701 | 49 | 85 |
| R.C. | Words | 3451 | 1923 | 664 | 17 |
| | Nonwords | 3631 | 1268 | 525 | 7 |
| *POST-TEST* | | | | | |
| D.K. | Words | 1193 | 549 | 61 | 93 |
| | Nonwords | 2756 | 1783 | 126 | 49 |
| R.C. | Words | 1671 | 1015 | 319 | 81 |
| | Nonwords | 2178 | 1252 | 612 | 75 |

*Length effects.* The earlier studies by Seymour (1986) suggested that a morphemic (word recognition) impairment was typically associated with serial reading, marked by a strong effect of word length on reading reaction time. Table 16.3 includes estimates of the slopes of the lines of best fit for the relation of reaction time to word/nonword length. In the case of R.C. these values were extremely large. Tests of linear trend were strongly significant. D.K.'s word reading, by contrast, showed little evidence of a length effect.

*Regularity effect.* According to Coltheart et al. (1983), the primary indicator of a word recognition disturbance (morphemic or surface dyslexia) is an effect of spelling-to-sound regularity. This occurs because words that cannot be recognised by the lexical system are processed via the nonlexical (grapheme-phoneme) system, which is liable to make errors on irregular forms. Table 16.4 gives error rates for the lists of Regular (RG), Rule-based (RL) and Irregular (I) words. It can be seen that R.C. has a high error rate (50% or more) on the irregular words. An analysis of variance, with Cases and Lists as factors, indicated a significant difference between Cases ($F(1,24)=35.5$, $P<0.001$), and a significant Cases × Regularity interaction ($F(2,24)=4.172$, $P<0.05$), which occurred because R.C. had particularly high error rates on the irregular word list.

TABLE 16.4
Error Rates (Per cent) on Lists of Regular, Rule and Irregular Words for D.K. and R.C. (Pre-test)

| | WORD LIST | | | | | |
|---|---|---|---|---|---|---|
| | *Regular* | | *Rule* | | *Irregular* | |
| Trial | 1 | 2 | 1 | 2 | 1 | 2 |
| D.K. | 8 | 3 | 15 | 13 | 17 | 10 |
| R.C. | 30 | 35 | 25 | 25 | 50 | 54 |

*Error pattern.* Two indicators of the availability of an alphabetic (grapheme-phoneme) process are: (1) the occurrence of nonword responses (including regularisations) in reading; and (2) the production of "phonetically plausible" error responses in spelling. Table 16.5 provides information about D.K. and R.C.'s error patterns together with some examples. R.C.'s errors suggest a reliance on letter-sound processing in the absence of word-specific knowledge. D.K.'s spelling errors, by contrast, were seriously dysphonetic. One unexpected feature was that reading errors on the nonword lists were frequently nonwords and not lexical substitutions as often occurs in phonological dyslexia. Inspection suggested that the errors often matched only the first letter of the target and that D.K. used a strategy of repetition of endings as a way of generating nonlexical forms.

## Conclusion

These analyses support the conclusion that a cognitive assessment method deriving from the dual-process model (Ellis & Young, 1988) is effective in revealing differences between cases of developmental dyslexia. D.K. possesses lexical word recognition and spelling processes but lacks the modules required for letter-sound translation. In Frith's (1985) terms, he appears to be a *logographic reader* whose alphabetic development has been blocked. The enormous word/nonword discrepancy is interpreted in the "dual foundation" model as an indication of the absence of a general purpose orthographic framework, attributable to a primary phonological disturbance. R.C., by contrast, seems not to possess efficient procedures for direct recognition of familiar words or storage and production of specific spellings. His results can be interpreted as reflecting the processing of both words and nonwords via a malformed orthographic framework, with a primary impairment of the logographic process being seen as the basis of the difficulty.

TABLE 16.5
Incidence of Word and Nonword Responses to Word or Nonword Targets in Reading by D.K. and R.C. Plus Numbers of Phonetic and Dysphonetic Spelling Responses to Words

| | | *READING* | | | *SPELLING* | | |
|---|---|---|---|---|---|---|---|
| | | Word | Nonword | Total | Phonetic | Dys-phonetic | Total |
| D.K. | Word | 33 | 7 | 40 | 3 | 150 | 153 |
| | Nonword | 69 | 253 | 322 | | | 115 |
| R.C. | Word | 46 | 70 | 116 | 120 | 143 | 263 |
| | Nonword | 30 | 45 | 75 | | | 58 |

*Examples of errors*

*Subject D.K.*

| Reading | Spelling |
|---|---|
| camel → "calm" | "crown" → kaig |
| began → "begin" | "frost" → forot |
| here → "hurt" | "special" → sental |
| | "control" → coladn |
| | "biscuit" → brish |
| | "sudden" → steeter |
| | "pillow" → pouul |
| haid → "had" | "breat" → bettn |
| poad → "pad" | "trut" → hotiner |
| gright → "rad" | "sep" → stnor |
| amicol → "hab" | "swamble" → wzit |
| raddot → "rab" | "bippot" → gozx |
| | "chidge" → goozxt |
| | "fough" → keet |

*Subject R.C.*

| Reading | Spelling |
|---|---|
| desk → "disk" | "thick" → fik |
| fright → "frajit" | "little" → litl |
| ribbon → "rebbon" | "fright" → frit |
| | "girl" → gurl |
| him → "heron" | "seach" → sech |
| sep → "seep" | "bamp" → bap |
| lotter → "loater" | "clise" → klis |
| pive → "pivvey" | |

## DESIGN OF THE INTERVENTION

The interpretation of the initial assessment has been that D.K. and R.C. share a common feature—the absence of a properly formed, general purpose orthographic framework—although the underlying causes differ, being hypothesised as a phonological disturbance in D.K. but as an impairment of logographic recognition processes in R.C. The dual foundation model suggests two main approaches to the design of a remedial programme for use with contrasting cases of this kind:

*1. Indirect approach—Treat the underlying causes.* On this view, instruction should be focused on the foundation processes. D.K. and R.C. would require different remedial programmes, with emphasis on sounds, letters and phonological structures for D.K. and on the rapid recognition of whole words for R.C.

*2. Direct approach—Treat the problem.* Here, instruction focuses on the establishment of the orthographic framework, starting with the Core and progressing towards the Expansions. A common set of procedures might be appropriate for D.K. and R.C.

Recent work has suggested that the indirect approach is mainly appropriate for children who are younger or more severely impaired than D.K. or R.C. (Reading Age<6.5–7.0yrs), where a basic knowledge of letter-sound associations and a minimal sight vocabulary may be absent. The study of D.K. and R.C., who already possessed these capabilities, was accordingly based on a direct attempt at construction of a framework.

Given this goal, the principal source of theoretical influence on the design of the programme was the model of the steps in the development of an orthographic framework (Seymour, 1990b; Seymour, Bunce, & Evans, 1992), especially the distinction between "core" and "expanded" structures and the ideas about 2D and 3D principles of organisation. This defined the levels and content of the instruction and the alternative structures that might be emphasised. At the same time an attempt was made to retain contact with the dual-process view contained in the modular information processing theories (Ellis & Young, 1988) and their developmental variants (Morton, 1989). These requirements resolved into three sets of constraints that were taken into account when the teaching materials were designed.

### 1. Orthographic Level

The content of instruction was determined by reference to the model of the developing orthographic lexicon (Seymour, 1990b; Seymour, Bunce, & Evans, 1992). This identifies a "core" structure (Level 1), which was treated as a starting point for instruction for both D.K. and R.C. The model identifies three further levels of expansion of the core. Only the first of these (Level 2—IC and TC clusters) was used in the study.

*Core structure.* The core structure was defined by the combination of a set of 24 simple initial consonants, the 5 simple vowels, and a set of 14 terminal consonants. The structure forms a 3D space of $24 \times 5 \times 14 = 1680$ cells, about 40 of which contain English words. The space was mapped as a set of five IC × TC matrices, one for each vowel, and the lexical entries were classified according to frequency of occurrence, length in letters, and regularity (whether or not the pronunciations assigned to the IC, V, and TC components conformed to the remainder of the matrix). Frequencies of the individual IC, V, and TC elements in the matrices were determined by summing across the word entries. Five lists of 28 words each were then selected, under the constraint that each list should reflect the distribution of word frequency and regularity within the matrix as a whole, and that all orthographic elements should occur in approximate proportion to their incidence in the words contained in the matrix. A second set of parallel nonword lists was formed by swapping IC and V+TC structures. This procedure yielded a sample of nonwords that are drawn from the 3D matrix and which correspond exactly to the words in their orthographic content. Instruction at the core level was carried out using items from one of the lists as exemplars. The full set of lists was used to monitor the effects of the intervention.

*First expansion.* The expanded structure was formed by adding two- and three-letter IC and TC structures (e.g. pr-, bl-, shr-; -nt, -sp, -nch, etc) to the core groups, yielding sets of 59 ICs and 29 TCs. The lengthened vowel 'ee' was added to the V set together with the -y vowels (y, ay, ey, oy, uy), which occur only with a null TC. The enlarged matrix was plotted, categorised according to frequency and regularity of lexical entries, and used as the basis for selection of a new set of five word lists, each containing 51 items. The words contained one or more complex structures and the content of the lists reflected the distributions of orthographic elements and word frequencies in the overall matrix. A parallel set of five nonword lists was formed by recombination of elements. These lists provided the teaching examples and tests for the second level intervention.

## 2. Organising Structure

A second feature of the instruction was the organising principle that was emphasised. This was considered to have three levels, depending on whether the lexicon was viewed as a simple list of unanalysed items (thought of as a unidimensional or 1D representation) or as a framework defined by two dimensions (onset × rime) or three dimensions (IC × V × TC). It can be noted that only the 2D and 3D structures satisfy the definition of an "orthographic framework" intended in this discussion.

*3D structure.* The IC × V × TC structure was emphasised by the division of the items used in instruction into three components, presented on separate cards and marked by a colour code (IC=blue, V=red, TC=green). The children also assembled a personal dictionary in which items were listed according to all three components. The activities employed in the teaching stressed the three positionally defined sets of units. For example, the child might be asked to solve anagrams in which IC, V, and TC structures were preserved (TRNKU, EESHP), or to produce words having the same IC, V or TC as a pair of targets (e.g. lamp and pump).

*2D structure.* The procedures paralleled those used for 3D, except that the division was into two parts, colour coded as Onset=blue and Rime=green. Thus, the child might be asked for rhymes or alliterations or to swap onset and rime components to produce new words.

*1D structure* Analysis into components was not stressed but exercises dealt with global features such as word length or word shape, using tasks of matching against boxes shaped to follow the pattern of ascenders and descenders or matching across upper and lower case.

## 3. Cognitive Focus

In order to test the possibility that impaired components might be treated selectively, an attempt was made to manipulate the *cognitive focus* of instruction.

*Input vs. Output.* Two versions of the procedures were prepared, one consisting of exercises that emphasised recognition processes at a visual, phonological or semantic level (input or Reading focus) whereas the second emphasised output, by requiring written responses, including the use of coloured pens to show the elements of the 2D or 3D organisational structures (output or Spelling focus).

*Lexical vs. Nonlexical.* The list of items providing the examples for instruction could consist of real words (lexical focus) or nonwords (nonlexical focus).

## Teaching Programmes

Given these three sets of distinctions and their incorporation into the teaching materials it became possible to set out the following definitions:

> A *teaching phase* is a period in which a particular combination of instructional variables remains in force, e.g. Reading focus, sub-lexical focus (nonword examples), directed at the core orthographic structure, with emphasis on 3D organisation.
> A *teaching programme* is a series of teaching phases.

The actual programmes undertaken by D.K. and R.C. are shown in Table 16.6.

Both subjects started with two teaching phases directed at the Core structure. A Nonlexical Focus was used for D.K. and a Lexical Focus for R.C., but the procedures were otherwise equivalent, involving Reading Focus followed by Spelling Focus, with emphasis on the 3D organisational framework. In the later period, when the Expansion was taught, a trial was made of a wider range of procedures, including 2D and 1D emphasis.

The instruction was carried out by F. Bunce, using standard pedagogic techniques that were developed within the constraints imposed by the definition of a teaching phase set out earlier. Further details are contained in Seymour, Bunce, and Evans (1992). The tuition was one-to-one and was given at the schools attended by the children in weekly one hour sessions. Table 16.6 shows the numbers of weeks devoted to the core and expanded structures.

TABLE 16.6
Summary of the Structure of the Intervention and Test Programme Applied to D.K. and R.C.

| | CORE | | | | | 1st EXPANSION | | | | | | | CORE |
|---|---|---|---|---|---|---|---|---|---|---|---|---|---|
| Test | 1 | | 2 | | 3 | 1 | | 2 | | 3 | | 4 | 4 |
| Teaching phase | | 1 | | 2 | | | 1 | | 2 | | 3 | | |
| Subject D.K. | | Read<br>NW<br>3D | | Spell<br>NW<br>3D | | | Read<br>W<br>3D | | Spell<br>W<br>1D | | Spell<br>NW<br>2D | | |
| Subject R.C. | | Read<br>W<br>3D | | Spell<br>W<br>3D | | | Read<br>W<br>3D | | Spell<br>W<br>1D | | Spell<br>W<br>2D | | |
| Duration | | | | | | | | | | | | | |
| hours | | 9 | | 7 | | | 9 | | 10 | | 11 | | |
| months | | | 4+ | | | | | | 11 | | | | |

## MONITORING THE INTERVENTION

The impact of the intervention was monitored by applying the complete set of five word lists and five nonword lists for reading and spelling before and after each instructional phase. Thus, for the Core, there was a pre-test, a post-test after Phase 1, and a post-test after Phase 2. The lists were also repeated at the end of the Expansion intervention (delayed post-test). The Expansion involved a pre-test and three post-tests, one following each teaching phase. Reading tests were applied by computer, and included both reaction time measurements in addition to accuracy measurements. Spelling lists involved the standard dictation procedure. The assessments were made by another research worker who was not involved in the instructional programme.

Table 16.7 shows the progress of word and nonword reading and spelling through the two periods of instruction for the two subjects.

The scores have been summed over the five word and five nonword lists and are given in the form of accuracy levels and gains following each teaching phase. For purposes of statistical analysis the lists were divided into subsets of items (seven sets of four items for the Core, seven sets of seven items for the Expansion) and each subset was given a score (number of items correct). The scores were then entered into a series of analyses of variance.

### *Subject D.K.*

The Core pre-test confirmed the presence of D.K.'s phonological dyslexia and dysgraphia (nonwords substantially worse than words). There were large gains in nonword reading and spelling following the two teaching phases. These were tested in a design with Lists (1-5) as a "between" factor and Tasks (Read, Spell) and Trials (1-3) as "within" factors. The Trials effect was significant ($F(2,60)=129.26$, $P<0.001$) but independent of Tasks ($F(2,60)<1$). This absence of an interaction implies that the manipulation of Input vs. Output Focus had no measurable effect on D.K.'s progress. Similarly, even though a nonlexical focus (nonword examples) was maintained across both phases, there were significant gains for *word* reading and spelling ($F(2,60)=27.29$, $P<0.001$). A comparison between Trial 3 and the delayed post-test indicated that the gains were stable ($F(1,60)=1.59$ and <1 for Reading and Spelling respectively). The changes were apparent in all five test lists, though there was some evidence of an advantage for the list used in teaching.

The Expansion results suggest that the word/nonword difference was larger for reading than for spelling but that the rate of gain was more marked for spelling than for reading. An overall analysis (Lists × Tasks × Words/Nonwords × Trials) confirmed that there was a significant

TABLE 16.7
Items Correct (Per cent) and Gain Relative to Previous Test for Reading and Spelling of Words and Nonwords at Core (N = 140) and at 1st Expansion (N = 255) by D.K. and R.C.

| | | *CORE* | | | *1st EXPANSION* | | | *CORE* |
|---|---|---|---|---|---|---|---|---|
| Test | 1 | 2 | 3 | 1 | 2 | 3 | 4 | 4 |
| *Subject D.K.* | | | | | | | | |
| READING | | | | | | | | |
| Words | | | | | | | | |
| Correct % | 88 | 95 | 98 | 80 | 77 | 89 | 92 | 95 |
| Gain % | | +7 | +3 | | −3 | +12 | +3 | −3 |
| Nonwords | | | | | | | | |
| Correct % | 29 | 60 | 80 | 53 | 59 | 67 | 70 | 89 |
| Gain % | | +31 | +20 | | +6 | +8 | +3 | +9 |
| SPELLING | | | | | | | | |
| Words | | | | | | | | |
| Correct % | 72 | 84 | 91 | 45 | 55 | 76 | 85 | 94 |
| Gain % | | +12 | +7 | | +10 | +11 | +9 | +3 |
| Nonwords | | | | | | | | |
| Correct % | 23 | 50 | 78 | 24 | 41 | 58 | 71 | 73 |
| Gain % | | +27 | +28 | | +17 | +17 | +13 | −5 |
| *Subject R.C.* | | | | | | | | |
| READING | | | | | | | | |
| Words | | | | | | | | |
| Correct % | 79 | 86 | 91 | 84 | 85 | 91 | 89 | 93 |
| Gain % | | +7 | +5 | | +1 | +6 | −2 | +2 |
| Nonwords | | | | | | | | |
| Correct % | 66 | 85 | 91 | 83 | 85 | 88 | 87 | 94 |
| Gain % | | +19 | +6 | | +2 | +3 | −1 | +3 |
| SPELLING | | | | | | | | |
| Words | | | | | | | | |
| Correct % | 53 | 63 | 81 | 41 | 44 | 64 | 54 | 84 |
| Gain % | | +10 | +18 | | +3 | +20 | −10 | +3 |
| Nonwords | | | | | | | | |
| Correct % | 70 | 81 | 84 | 68 | 71 | 81 | 83 | 83 |
| Gain % | | +11 | +3 | | +3 | +10 | +2 | −1 |

Trials effect ($F(3,180)=121.087$, $P<0.001$) which interacted with Tasks ($F(3,180)=27.21$, $P<0.001$). The interaction occurred because the rate of change was higher for spelling than for reading. Within each task the word/nonword difference remained approximately constant (Word/Nonword × Trials interaction, $F(3,180)=1.27$ and 1.101 for Reading and Spelling respectively). Thus, the effect of the intervention seems to have been to produce dramatic alterations in D.K.'s spelling while leaving the word/nonword gap in reading largely unaltered.

*Subject R.C.*
Table 16.7 presents the data for Subject R.C.. The pre-tests validated the lexical dysgraphia found in the cognitive assessment (word spelling much worse than nonword spelling).

At the Core the two periods of instruction were associated with general reductions in error rate and convergence of the word and nonword scores. The analysis of variance confirmed the trials effect (F(2,120)=62.12, *P*<0.001) and also the interaction with Word vs. Nonword (F(2,120)=3.94 for Reading and 7.49 for Spelling, *P*<0.05 and 0.01). Stability of the gain was suggested by the absence of a difference between Trial 3 and the delayed post-test (F(1,60)=1.6 and <1 for Reading and Spelling separately). The word/nonword difference in spelling was significant at the beginning of the instruction (F(1,60)=11.71, *P*<0.01) but had been eliminated by the end (F(1,60)<1).

The analysis of the Expansion results indicated an overall gain (F(3,180)=41.97, *P*<0.001). This was more substantial for spelling than for reading. There was no word/nonword difference in reading (F(1,60) <1). The lexical dysgraphia (word spelling worse than nonword spelling) persisted across the whole period of the intervention (F(1,60)=205.7, *P*<0.001) but interacted with trials, probably because of the large gain after teaching phase 2 (1D word spelling) and its reversal after phase 3.

## COGNITIVE REASSESSMENT

Following the intervention, the word and nonword lists used in the original assessment were re-run with both subjects on two occasions, separated by about four weeks. Table 16.8 gives a summary of the proportions of items correct and gains relative to the second trial of the pre-test. Analyses of variance confirmed that the difference between the pre- and post-tests was significant (*P*<0.001 in each case).

*Subject D.K.*
Following the intervention D.K.'s performance on the nonword lists was greatly improved, though the effect was more dramatic for spelling than for reading (F(1,12)=25.93, *P*<0.001 for Pre-/Post- × Tasks interaction). While nonword error levels were equivalent for reading and spelling at the pre-test (see Table 16.2), there was a difference in favour of spelling at the post-test (F(1,12)=25.9, P<0.001). The effect of this was to minimise the word/nonword difference in spelling (F(1,24)=1.61 for comparison between nonwords and lower frequency words). In reading,

TABLE 16.8
Incidence of Correct Responses (Number and Percent) in Reading and Spelling Words and Nonwords on Trials 1 and 2 of the Cognitive Reassessment by D.K. and R.C. The Gain Score on Trial 1 is Expressed Relative to the Second Trial of the Pre-test (Table 16.2)

| | *READING* | | | | *SPELLING* | | | |
|---|---|---|---|---|---|---|---|---|
| | *Words* | | *Nonwords* | | *Words* | | *Nonwords* | |
| Trial | 1 | 2 | 1 | 2 | 1 | 2 | 1 | 2 |
| N | 128 | 128 | 128 | 128 | 123 | 123 | 60 | 60 |
| *Subject D.K.* | | | | | | | | |
| Correct | 125 | 125 | 74 | 73 | 110 | 118 | 45 | 57 |
| % | 98 | 98 | 58 | 57 | 89 | 96 | 75 | 95 |
| Gain % | +8 | 0 | +52 | –1 | +48 | +7 | +73 | +20 |
| *Subject R.C.* | | | | | | | | |
| Correct | 108 | 112 | 84 | 99 | 58 | 71 | 44 | 51 |
| % | 83 | 88 | 66 | 77 | 47 | 58 | 73 | 85 |
| Gain % | +22 | +5 | +14 | +11 | +27 | +11 | +21 | +12 |

by contrast, the word/nonword difference remained substantial (F(1,24)=174.97, *P*<0.001). For words, there was a large reduction in the disadvantage of spelling relative to reading (F(1,24)=123.6, <0.001 for Tasks × Tests interaction) and the difference had been more or less eliminated by the second trial of the post-test.

In the initial assessment D.K. read familiar words by a fast accurate process, which was unaffected by spelling-to-sound regularity or word length. A pre- vs. post-test comparison confirmed that regularity was not a factor (F(2,24)=1.2) although there was a small gain in accuracy at the post-test (F(1,24)=14.4, *P*<0.01). Table 16.3 includes information on the distribution of reaction times (relative to the 2000ms divide) and also the processing rate per letter. Word reading seems to have involved essentially the same process at the pre- and post-tests. Nonword reading, by contrast, gives indications of a change of process. In the initial assessment nonwords were read rapidly but inaccurately. At the post-test, the gain in accuracy was accompanied by a slowing of response, producing a dispersed distribution including times above 2000ms. In order to determine when this change occurred reaction time distributions were plotted for each of the tests given during the intervention. It was clear that the word/nonword divergence emerged at the end of the second Core teaching phase and persisted thereafter. Sounding of letters, never observed in the original assessment, occurred on 23% of items in the first trial of the post-test and on 11% in the second.

*Subject R.C.*
For R.C. the change between the pre- and post-tests appeared mainly quantitative. Although general reductions in error rate occurred, the disadvantage of word spelling relative to nonword spelling and the small superiority of word reading over nonword reading persisted unaltered. This was confirmed by the analyses of variance. In spelling, there were main effects for Word vs. Nonword and for Pre-Test vs. Post-test but no interaction ($F(1,24)=1.2$ and $<1$ for the tests using the high and low frequency word sets). The same was true of reading, where there were effects of Pre- vs. Post- and Word vs. Nonword but no evidence of an interaction ($F(1,24)<1$ ).

In the original assessment R.C. was strongly affected by the regularity variable. An analysis of variance on scores for the word lists confirmed that this effect was significant ($F(2,24)=33.01$, $P<0.001$) and independent of the Pre- vs. Post-effect ($F(2.24)=1.03$ for Regularity × Tests interaction). The other main features noted in the pre-test were a strong dependence of reading reaction time on word length and the occurrence of equivalent, widely dispersed distributions of times for words and nonwords. Table 16.3 provides information on these indicators for the post-test. There was a marked speeding up of reaction time (with the main bulk of times falling below 2000ms). Responses to words were about 500ms faster than responses to nonwords ($F(400)=4.471$, $P<0.001$). Nonetheless, reaction time remained dependent on word length (rate= 319ms/letter, $F(1,217)=34.72$, $P<0.001$ for test of linear trend).

These results establish that the underlying character of R.C.'s reading process did not alter during the intervention.

## GENERAL DISCUSSION

The principal goal of this chapter has been to explore some implications of cognitive neuropsychology for the design and evaluation of programmes of remediation in cases of childhood dyslexia. The contributions that appeared relevant included:

- a cognitive assessment method (essentially the word vs. nonword procedure);
- a cognitive architecture (the modular structure of the reading and spelling systems); and
- theories of literacy development (order of emergence of systems, inter-dependencies, orthographic structure and content).

## Cognitive Assessment

The cognitive assessment served two distinct functions. One of these was *diagnostic* and concerned the question of the heterogeneity of the dyslexic population, especially the possibility that cases may differ in ways that are relevant to the task of choosing an appropriate method of intervention. The other was *evaluative* and involved an attempt to document cognitive changes associated with the intervention, including questions about the relative effectiveness of different methods in cases possessing differing characteristics. The study supports the conclusion that the cognitive method is a useful technique for identifying individual patterns of dyslexia. D.K. and R.C. presented with quite different sets of characteristics, which were interpretable as an impairment of the nonlexical processes in D.K. and as an impairment of word recognition and lexical spelling in R.C. Following the intervention, both subjects demonstrated gains in all systems. For R.C., this appeared to be a quantitative improvement imposed on a stable cognitive pattern (reading continued to be a serial letter-by-letter process, marked by special difficulty with irregular words; word spelling remained worse than nonword spelling). In D.K. there was more evidence of a quantitative improvement combined with some qualitative changes. There were dramatic gains in spelling, including the elimination of the earlier difficulty with nonwords. There was also a change of strategy in nonword reading, where gains in accuracy were combined with the introduction of slow, effortful processing and sounding.

## Cognitive Architecture

A first question is whether cognitive architectures, deriving from research in adult cognitive neuropsychology, provide a useful blueprint for studies of remediation of developmental disorders. The main contribution of such models lies in the assertion that the orthographic system possesses a 2 x 2 modular structure. As was noted by Frith (1985), a model of this kind allows for independent impairment of each module, creating the possibility of a large number of distinct patterns, depending on which component, or combination of components, is affected. A distinction may be made between this kind of *functional modularity* (independence of processes) and a related notion of *developmental modularity*. The latter concerns the question of whether or not a particular function can develop irrespective of the status of another function (see Seymour & Evans (1992) for further comment on this issue).

The results obtained from D.K. and R.C. provide somewhat conflicting messages. In the case of R.C., there was no strong evidence to support the ideas of either functional or developmental modularity. So far as processing is concerned, the close similarity of the reaction time patterns for word and nonword reading suggests the involvement of a single underlying process. Further, R.C. showed a lexical (surface, morphemic) pattern in spelling as well as in reading. This inter-dependency is in agreement with Boder's (1973) original view of dyslexia as a pattern affecting reading *and* spelling in the same way. Thus, R.C.'s results may be interpreted as a denial of the modularity of the lexical and nonlexical levels and of the input and output systems.

The implications of D.K.'s results are somewhat different. The initial presentation of a phonological dyslexia combined with a phonological dysgraphia might be taken as evidence of the developmental inter-dependency of the nonlexical systems (i.e. of Boder's "dysphonetic" pattern). However, this conclusion is not supported by the post-test results, which suggested elimination of the phonological dysgraphia combined with preservation of the phonological dyslexia. This differential response to the intervention is evidence of the developmental modularity of the nonlexical input and output systems. The more dramatic support for the modular position is, of course, provided by the word/nonword dissociation in reading. D.K. had developed an effective lexical input system *despite* the extreme impairment of the nonlexical grapheme-phoneme process. The position regarding spelling is slightly less clear. At the time of the pre-test D.K. had established a substantial store of word-forms even though the nonlexical (phoneme-grapheme) process was severely impaired. This suggests developmental modularity of the lexical spelling system. It was also true at that stage that spelling was much less effective than reading (i.e. there was a substantial set of words that D.K. could read but not spell). However, the elimination of this reading-spelling gap seemed to implicate concurrent changes in both nonlexical and lexical spelling (see results for the monitoring of the Expansion intervention). This could suggest that the lexical and nonlexical levels are not modular, at least in the later stages of development.

A main potential benefit of the modular architecture was that it appeared to offer guidance in directing the *focus* of remedial instruction. This prospect presupposes both the modularity of the underlying systems and the possibility of devising sets of instructions, which are selective or module-specific in their effects. The results of this study are not encouraging for this enterprise. Although attempts were made to set up teaching procedures that were directed at reading or at spelling, or at the lexical or nonlexical levels, there was little evidence of specific or selective effects. This could mean that the methods of achieving selectivity were inadequate. Or it may be that a narrow focus of this kind is not possible within the framework of a pedagogically viable programme. Alternatively, the results may imply that the orthographic system is nonmodular in its response to instructional input.

This discussion shows that the basic tenets of the architectural model—that impaired systems can be pinpointed and remedial instruction directed accordingly—may be uncertainly founded. The studies of D.K. and R.C. suggest that the indications of modularity may vary between individuals or developmental levels. Further, the idea of module-specific instruction may be an illusion.

## Developmental Models

The second possibility is that a developmental model provides a more appropriate framework for remediation than an architectural model. The study of D.K. provides good support for this position. At the time of the initial assessment he appeared to be a clear example of a logographic reader and speller whose alphabetic development had been blocked. The intervention involved an attempt to move him forward to an orthographic level. The observation that progress entailed the adoption of an alphabetic procedure, marked by sounding of letters and a dispersed nonword reaction time distribution, is in agreement with Frith's suggestion that the alphabetic stage is essential and cannot be skipped. Further, the post-test advantage for nonword spelling over nonword reading agrees with the contention that spelling is the pacemaker for the alphabetic stage.

The "dual foundation" model (Fig. 16.1) differs from Frith's scheme in the suggested parallelism of logographic and alphabetic development. D.K.'s results for reading support this position since the direct process used in word reading was not modified by the adoption a serial alphabetic process. Seymour and Evans (1992) have presented similar results for word and nonword reading by normally developing children. An implication is that Morton's (1989) assertion that alphabetic processes effectively replace early logographic processes may be incorrect.

A second point is that the "dual foundation" model defines the orthographic stage as the construction of a general purpose framework. If attainment of this stage is marked by similar processing of words and nonwords, it might be concluded that D.K. achieved an orthographic level in *spelling* but not in reading. This follows from the observation that words and nonwords were written with equal facility but read differently (by a direct process for words, but by a slow, error-prone procedure for nonwords). Such an outcome is contrary to Frith's contention that reading is the pacemaker for the orthographic stage. It could, however, indicate that a phonologically based structural reorganisation is more appropriate for the output lexicon than for the input lexicon.

R.C.'s results are less readily accommodated by Frith's scheme. This is because a primary logographic impairment combined with near normal alphabetic development is a violation of the principle of succession of stages (and also the idea that "classic" developmental dyslexia is attributable to alphabetic arrest). The striking feature was the equivalence of the reaction time patterns for words and nonwords. This was true of the pre- and post-tests and also of all eight tests applied during the intervention. According to the dual foundation model, an outcome of this kind reflects the availability of a *defective* orthographic framework. The suggestion is that simple alphabetic processing results in the formation of a rudimentary framework but that subsequent expansion is hampered by a paucity of stored logographic forms. R.C.'s results are, in some respects, consistent with the connectionist (PDP) models of the type described by Seidenberg and McClelland (1989). A feature of these models is the suggestion that word and nonword reading may be handled within a single network in which orthographic units are linked to phonemic units via a set of hidden units. The introduction of a "lesion" by reduction of the number of central hidden units produces a surface dyslexic pattern, that is, a reduced capacity to encode unusual (irregular) forms. There are arguments, cited by Seidenberg and McClelland, for viewing this as a "typical" form of reading disability. If this is correct, and if there is merit in the hypothesis that a logographic failure is the primary source of R.C.'s difficulties, then the widely held view that alphabetic/phonological problems lie at the heart of reading difficulty (Frith, 1985; Stanovich, 1988) may need to be reconsidered.

## Orthographic Framework

The discussion of D.K. and R.C. supports the conclusion that the decision to direct the intervention towards the establishment of an orthographic framework was probably justified. R.C. already possessed such a framework but additional work was needed to identify orthographic units and to accommodate deviant lexical forms . D.K. had not developed a framework but was able to establish an effective system for spelling when given help with the organising principles and relevant orthographic structures. It seems very possible that an orthographic approach of this kind will be appropriate for *all* dyslexic cases, providing only that foundation levels of sight vocabulary and letter-sound association are present.

The important question is: How can orthographic structure and content best be communicated? The failure to show differences due to reading vs. spelling emphasis, or real word vs. nonword examples, suggests that these aspects may be interchangeable. Some recent studies suggest that 2D (onset + rime) segmentation may have an advantage. The findings for D.K. and R.C. are equivocal on this issue. For the Core structure, the 2D matrix contained $5 \times 14 = 70$ rime structures. To teach these as independent elements without reference to the systematic variation indicated by the vowel seemed unwise. The Expansion included trials of all three structural approaches. However, there was little evidence of systematic effects, excepting possibly the gain in R.C.'s word spelling after Phase 2 (1D emphasis) and its reversal after Phase 3 (2D emphasis).

## CONCLUSION

Although this study represents no more than a preliminary trial of a cognitive intervention approach in the area of developmental dyslexia, it may be helpful in pointing a direction for future studies.

1. The study supports the conclusion that cases of developmental dyslexia may differ significantly one from another. These differences can be detected by the cognitive assessment method and represented in the terminology of a modular architecture.
2. When a pressure towards change is applied by a remedial teaching programme the resulting developmental changes may differ between cases, depending on their starting configurations.
3. The possibility of directing remediation towards specific modules (input/output, lexical/nonlexical) was not upheld.
4. The common feature of the two cases appeared to be the absence of a properly formed general purpose orthographic framework. The goal of remedial instruction was seen as one of bringing such a framework into existence.
5. The possibility that 2D and 3D structural emphases might differ in effectiveness was not supported (though the issue deserves further study).

A general conclusion is that cognitive architectures and developmental stage theories are useful primarily as schemes for describing the general pattern displayed by an individual before and after an intervention and for identifying the global character of change. The models do not carry strong implications for the design of the intervention programme itself. More relevant here is an account of the content of an orthographic framework and of the steps involved in its construction. If so, the important requirement is probably one of determining the optimal content of a core structure and its expansions. Future research might usefully focus on the more detailed mapping of the growth of an orthographic structure using the method of longitudinal investigation of individuals with differing presenting patterns which has been tried here.

## ACKNOWLEDGEMENT

The research reported in this chapter was conducted with the assistance of a grant from the Medical Research Council of the U.K. We are grateful to D.K. and R.C. for their participation in the study.

## REFERENCES

Boder, E.M. (1973). Developmental dyslexia: A diagnostic approach based on three atypical reading-spelling patterns. *Developmental Medicine and Child Neurology, 15*, 663-687.

Coltheart, M., Masterson, J., Byng, S., Prior, M., & Riddoch, J. (1983). Surface dyslexia. *Quarterly Journal of Experimental Psychology, 35A*, 469-495.

Edwards, R.P.A. & Gibbon, V. (1973). *Words your children use*. London: Burke Books.

Ellis, A.W. (1985). The cognitive neuropsychology of developmental (and acquired) dyslexia. *Cognitive Neuropsychology, 2,* 169-205.

Ellis, A.W. & Young, A.W. (1988). *Human cognitive neuropsychology*. London: Lawrence Erlbaum Associates Ltd.

Frith, U. (1985). Beneath the surface of developmental dyslexia. In K.Patterson, J.Marshall and M.Coltheart (Eds.), *Surface dyslexia: Neuropsychological and cognitive studies of phonological reading*. London: Lawrence Erlbaum Associates Ltd.

Morton, J. (1980). The logogen model and orthographic structure. In U.Frith (Ed.). *Cognitive processes in spelling*. London: Academic Press.

Morton, J. (1989). An information-processing account of reading acquisition. In A.M.Galaburda (Ed.). *From reading to neurons*. Cambridge, Mass: The MIT Press.

Newcombe, F. & Marshall, J.C. (1980). Transcoding and lexical stabilisation in deep dyslexia. In M.Coltheart, K.Patterson and J.C.Marshall (Eds.), *Deep dyslexia*. London: Routledge & Kegan Paul.

Olson, R.K., Kleigl, R., Davidson, B.J., & Foltz, G. (1985). Individual and developmental differences in reading disability. In G.E.McKinnon and T.G.Waller (Eds.), *Reading research: Advances in theory and practice*, Vol 4. Orlando, FL: Academic Press.

Patterson, K.E. & Shewell, C. (1987). Speak and spell: Dissociations and word class effects. In M.Coltheart, G.Sartori, and R.Job (Eds.), *The cognitive neuropsychology of language*. London: Lawrence Erlbaum Associates Ltd.

Seidenberg, M.S. & McClelland, J.L. (1989). A distributed developmental model of word recognition and naming. *Psychological Review, 96*, 523-568.

Seymour, P.H.K. (1986). *Cognitive analysis of dyslexia*. London: Routledge & Kegan Paul.

Seymour, P.H.K. (1987a). Developmental dyslexia: A cognitive experimental analysis. In M. Coltheart, G. Sartori, & R. Job (Eds.), *The cognitive neuropsychology of language*. London: Lawrence Erlbaum Associates Ltd.

Seymour, P.H.K. (1987b). Individual cognitive analysis of competent and impaired reading. *British Journal of Psychology, 78*, 483-506.

Seymour, P.H.K. (1990a). Cognitive descriptions of dyslexia. In G.Th.Pavlidis (Ed.), *Perspectives on dyslexia: Vol 2—Cognition, language and treatment*. Chichester: Wiley.

Seymour, P.H.K. (1990b). Developmental dyslexia. In M.W.Eysenck (Ed.), *Cognitive psychology: An international review*. Chichester: Wiley.

Seymour, P.H.K., Bunce, F., & Evans, H.M. (1992). A framework for orthographic assessment and remediation. In C. Stirling & C. Robson (Eds.), *Psychology, spelling and education*. Clevedon: Multilingual Matters.

Seymour, P.H.K. & Evans, H.M. (1992). Beginning reading without semantics: A cognitive study of hyperlexia. *Cognitive Neuropsychology, 9*, 89-122

Seymour, P.H.K. & Evans, H.M. (in press). The visual (orthographic) processor and developmental dyslexia. In D. Willows, R. Kruk, & E. Corcos (Eds.), *Visual processes in reading and writing disabilities*. Hillsdale, NJ: Lawrence Erlbaum Associates Inc.

Seymour, P.H.K. & MacGregor, C.J. (1984). Developmental dyslexia: A cognitive experimental analysis of phonological, morphemic and visual impairments. *Cognitive Neuropsychology, 1*, 43-82.

Stanovich, K.E. (1988). Explaining the differences between the dyslexic and the garden-variety poor reader: The phonological core variable difference model. *Journal of Learning Disabilities, 21*, 590-612.

CHAPTER SEVENTEEN

# Phonological Processing Deficits as the Basis of Developmental Dyslexia: Implications for Remediation

Linda S. Siegel
*Ontario Institute for Studies in Education, Toronto, Ontario, Canada*

## ABSTRACT

Stanovich (1988a; 1988b) has proposed that deficits in phonological processing are at the basis of developmental dyslexia. According to this theoretical approach, phonological processing constitutes a modular function that operates automatically and independently of general cognitive ability. In this chapter, I will provide evidence for the nature and extent of the phonological processing deficits in dyslexia and I will discuss these phonological processing skills in the context of dual route theories of reading. Evidence is offered that dyslexic children have deficits in a variety of phonological skills, including the reading and spelling of pseudowords, recognising the visual form of a pseudoword and a phonological-lexical task that involved recognising whether a pseudoword could be pronounced like an English word. In particular, their reading of pseudowords was significantly poorer than normal readers of the same chronological age and even reading age controls. In addition, evidence is presented to show that phonological processing skills is independent of general cognitive ability as measured by intelligence test scores.

Although phonological processing skills are relevant to reading by grapheme-phoneme conversion (GPC) rules, orthographic skills may be considered a measure of reading by the lexical, or visual, route. The performance of dyslexics and normal readers on two orthographic tasks will also be described. The orthographic tasks included detecting the spelling of a word when required to choose between the correct spelling and a pseudohomophone and recognising whether a pseudoword contained an orthographically illegal bigram. Whereas the dyslexic children matched on

reading grade with the normal reader, they lagged behind the normal readers on all the phonological tasks, the dyslexics were, in some cases, significantly more advanced than reading level matched controls in orthographic skills.
These results are interpreted to indicate that dyslexics have a significant impairment in the use of the phonological route but are less impaired in the direct lexical access, or visual route, and, in some cases, may be more sensitive to the orthographic features of words than normal readers.
These results suggest that extreme difficulties with phonics are characteristics of dyslexics and have some implications for the remediation of reading problems. Drill with phonics would seem to be relatively unproductive in the teaching of reading to dyslexics, although there obviously needs to be some exposure to grapheme-phoneme conversion rules. However, remediation capitalising on the strengths of the dyslexics in the visual route might prove to be more successful. In a test of this hypothesis, dyslexics were taught a sight word vocabulary using the Bridge Reading System, which uses icons as picture cues for words. After eight months of reading instruction with this method, the children who had been exposed to this program achieved significantly higher scores on tests of word reading and were able to read letters, individual words, and connected text more quickly than a control group of children who did not receive the special program.
Severe phonological processing deficits appear to be the fundamental problems of developmental dyslexia although orthographic processing is relatively intact. Early reading instruction for dyslexics which capitalises on the strength of the direct lexical access or visual route appears to be useful for the remediation of reading skills in dyslexic children.

## INTRODUCTION

Stanovich (1988a; 1988b) has proposed that deficits in phonological processing are at the basis of developmental dyslexia. According to this theoretical approach, phonological processing constitutes a modular function that operates automatically and independently of general cognitive ability. In this chapter, I will: (1) provide evidence for the nature and extent of the phonological deficits in dyslexia and the independence of phonological processing deficits from general cognitive ability; (2) examine the development of the understanding of the orthographic features of English in children with dyslexia; and (3) discuss the implications of the research on phonological and orthographic processing for the treatment of dyslexia.

### Dual Route Theories

I will present the research on the basic processes in dyslexia in the context of dual route theories of reading. These theories have a variety of manifestations but their basic premise is that there are two possible routes involved in gaining access to the meaning of print (e.g. Coltheart, 1978; Forster & Chambers, 1973; Meyer, Schvanevelt, & Ruddy, 1975).

One of these routes involves direct lexical access, that is, visually reading a word without any intermediate phonological processing. The orthographic configuration of a word is directly mapped onto an internal visual store in lexical memory. This process is often referred to as "whole word recognition". The other route, the phonological route, involves the use of grapheme-phoneme conversion rules to gain lexical access to a print stimulus. Spelling-sound correspondence rules are used to translate a graphemic code into a phonemic one. This route is referred to as nonlexical because the application of the rules does not rely on word specific spelling-to-sound pronunciations. Instead, grapheme-to-phoneme correspondence rules are presumed to be stored explicitly and used to determine a word's pronunciation. According to this model, pseudowords can only be read by means of a nonlexical route as, by definition, there cannot be a lexical representation of a pseudoword. It is appropriate to note that there have been some challenges to dual route theories. For example, the reading of nonwords is influenced by their similarity to a real word and regular words that have irregular orthographic neighbours are read more slowly than regular consistent ones, indicating reciprocal influences of these two routes. Also, multiple level models (e.g. Brown, 1987) and connectionist models (e.g. Seidenberg & McClelland, 1989) have been proposed that postulate a variety of units and processes but do not assume two distinct routes. (for an extended discussion of these issues, see also Besner, Twilley, McCann, & Seergobin, 1990; Glushko, 1979; Humphreys & Evett, 1985; Metsala & Siegel, 1992; Stanovich, 1991). However, in spite of these ambiguities, conceptualisations of reading in terms of dual route theory represent one way of examining the reading performance of dyslexic children. I will discuss tasks that measure both these kind of processing and the performance of dyslexic and normal readers on these types of tasks.

## PHONOLOGICAL PROCESSING AND DYSLEXIA

Dyslexics are hypothesised to have significant problems with reading by the phonological route, that is using grapheme- phoneme conversion rules. Perhaps, the best measure of understanding of grapheme-phoneme conversion rules is the reading of pseudowords, pronounceable combinations of letters that are not real words. While it may seem possible that these pseudowords can be read by analogy to a real word, in fact, it would not be possible to read a pseudoword correctly without doing some phonemic segmentation. For example, consider the pseudoword *shum*. It could be read by analogy to *shun*, but to be read correctly it would have to be segmented and there would have to awareness of the sound of *n* as compared to *m*. In addition, Siegel and Geva (1990) have shown that in the case of pseudowords that can be read either by analogy or by grapheme phoneme conversion rules, such as *fody*, that can be read with a long *o* or by analogy to *body* with a short *o*, normal readers typically read pseudowords using the grapheme phoneme conversion rules, that is, nonlexically, rather than reading by analogy, even if the corresponding analogous word is of high frequency.

There is ample evidence that children with dyslexia have a great deal of difficulty reading pseudowords. Studies such as those of Snowling (1980), Siegel and Ryan (1988) and Waters, Bruck, and Seidenberg (1985) have shown that dyslexics have more difficulty reading

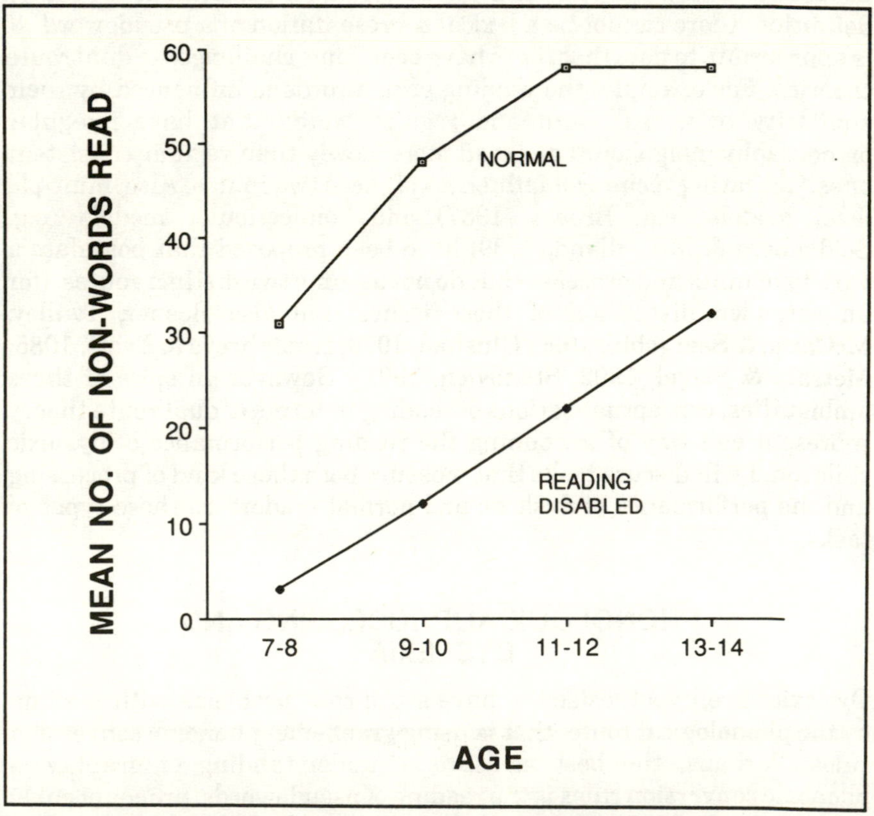


FIG. 17.1. Number of pseudowords read correctly (out of 60) by normal readers and dyslexics as a function of chronological age.

pseudowords than both chronological age and reading level matched normal readers. For example, Siegel and Ryan (1988) found that 13-14 year old dyslexics read pseudowords at the same level as 7-8 year old normal readers. These data are shown in Fig. 17.1. In addition, dyslexics matched on reading level with normal readers made significantly *more* errors than the normal readers in the reading of pseudowords. This comparison is shown in Fig. 17.2. This finding is a particularly striking one in light of the fact that dyslexics of the same reading level are considerably *older* than the normal readers.

Although we have evidence about the inadequate phonological skills of dyslexics, little is known about the manner in which the complex set of grapheme-phoneme conversion rules of the English language is acquired. The ascertainment of the order and nature of the acquisition

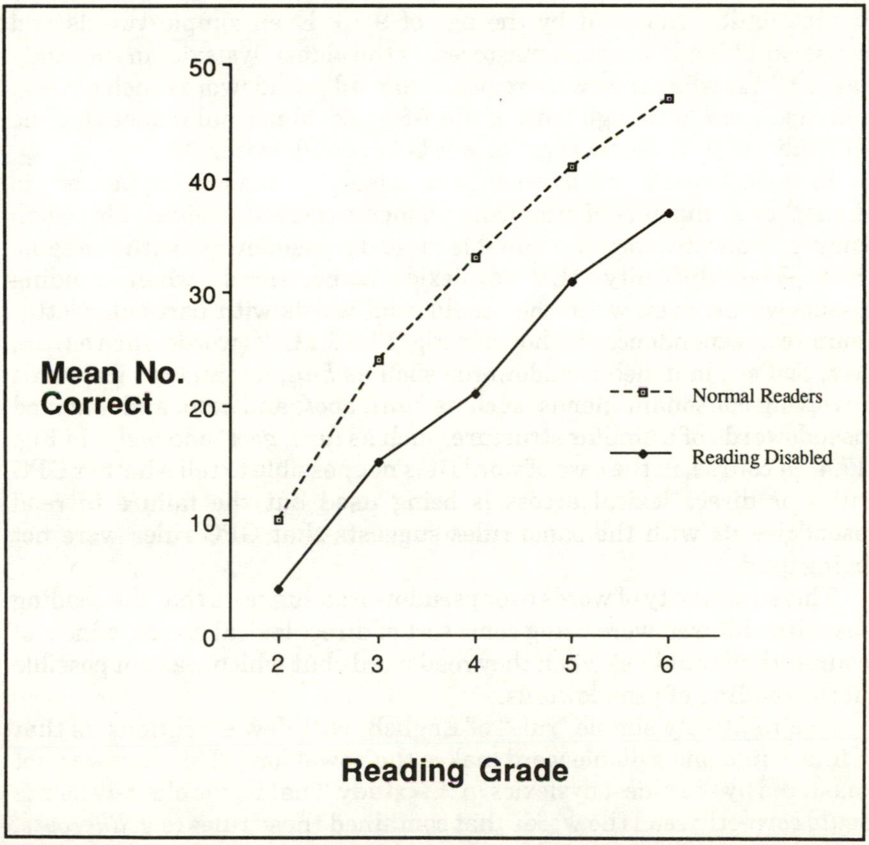


FIG. 17.2. Number of pseudowords read correctly (out of 60) by normal readers and dyslexics matched on reading grade level.

of these rules is an important first step in the understanding and treatment of dyslexia. A number of investigators have begun to work on the issue of the order of acquisition of these grapheme-phoneme conversion rules with the expectation that the rules are acquired in a relatively fixed and predictable order, in a manner similar to the way syntactic structures are in oral language (e.g. Guthrie & Seifert, 1979; Siegel & Faux, 1989; Snowling, 1980). To study these issues, we presented dyslexics and normal readers with words and pseudowords that involved a variety of grapheme-phoneme conversion rules, such as consonant blends, r-influenced vowels, inconsistent vowels, etc. (Siegel & Faux, 1989). We found that complexity, as measured by the number of syllables in a pseudoword, was a significant determinant of the difficulty of reading. Two syllable and multisyllable pseudowords were quite difficult for older dyslexics even though normal readers had become quite proficient by the age of 9-10. Even simple vowels and consonant blends were not mastered by the oldest dyslexics in the study (ages 11-14) when they were required to read pseudowords such as *mog*, *lun*, and *spad*, although most of the 7-8 year old normal readers had no difficulty with these features in words or pseudowords.

In most cases, even when the disabled readers appeared to demonstrate mastery of grapheme-phoneme correspondence rules when they read a word, they were unable to read a pseudoword with the same rule. The difficulty that dyslexics experienced when reading pseudowords, even when they could read words with particular letter sound correspondences is shown in Fig. 17.3 for CVC words, such as *ran*, *wet*, and *sit*, matched pseudowords such as *han*, *fet*, and *rit*, for words involving consonant blends, such as *hunt*, *spot*, and *help*, and matched pseudowords of a similar structure, such as *lunt*, *grot*, and *melp*, in Fig. 17.4. Of course, in the case of words it is not possible to tell whether GPC rules or direct lexical access is being used but the failure to read pseudowords with the same rules suggests that GPC rules were not being used.

This superiority of words over pseudowords suggests that the reading disabled children were using some sort of direct lexical access, which, of course, they could use when they read words but which was not possible in the reading of pseudowords.

One relatively simple "rule" of English, with few exceptions, is that a final *e* in a one syllable word makes the vowel long. This rule was not mastered by the oldest dyslexics in this study. That is, the older dyslexics could correctly read the words that contained these rules (e.g. *like*, *cute*, *nose*) but could not read the comparable pseudoword (e.g. *rike*, *fute*, *mose*). This difficulty is quite surprising as this rule is repeatedly stressed in reading instruction and is normally mastered very early in

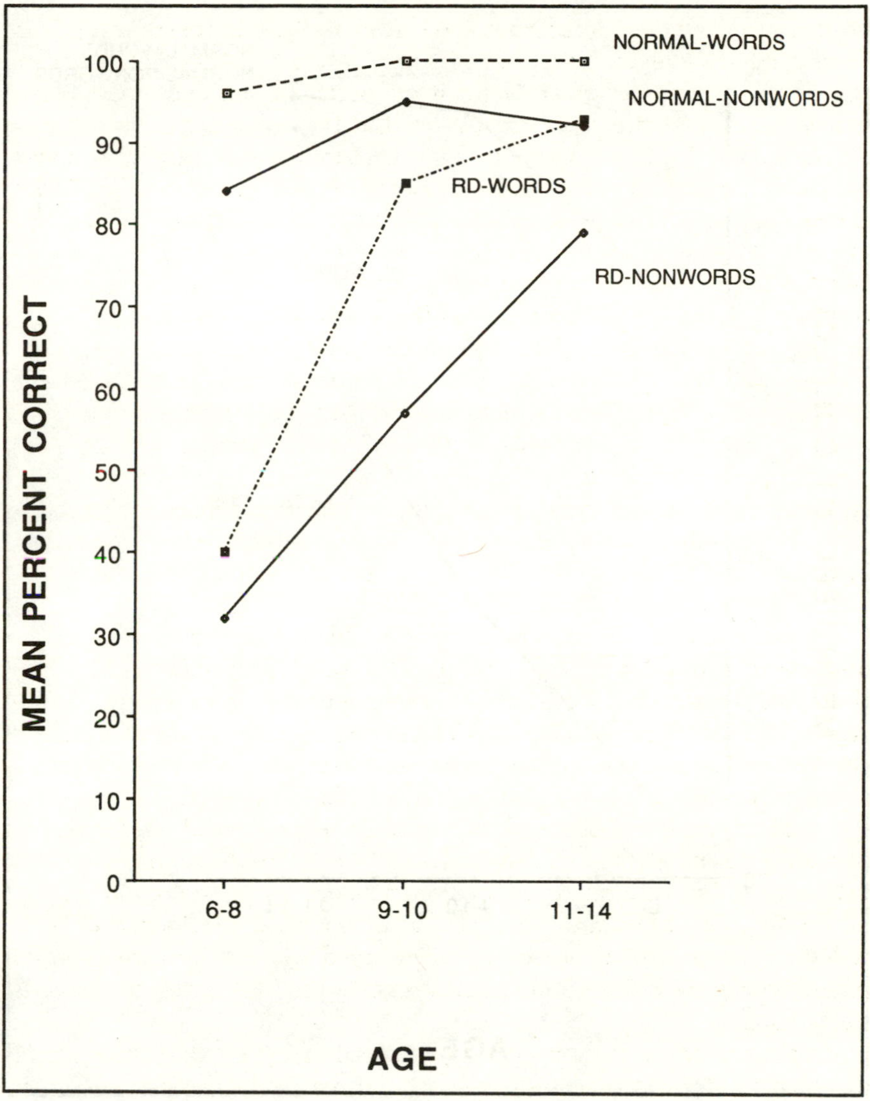


FIG. 17.3. Mean percentage of CVC trigrams read correctly by normal readers and dyslexics as a function of chronological age.

the development of reading skills. When the reading disabled and normal readers were matched on reading grade level, there were many instances in which the scores of the reading disabled were significantly lower than normal readers who were the reading age controls. For example, the normal readers attained significantly higher scores than

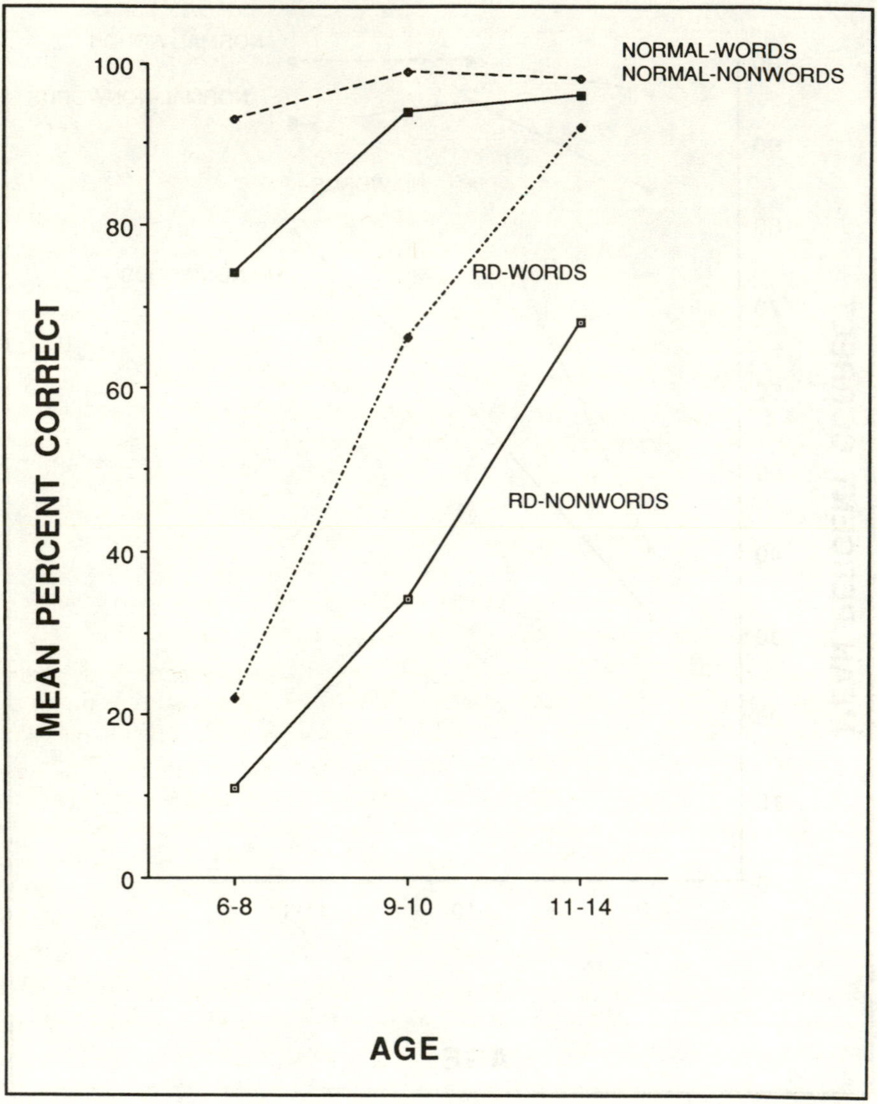


FIG. 17.4. Mean percentage of consonant blends read correctly by normal readers and dyslexics as a function of chronological age.

the disabled readers of the same reading age on the following tasks, reading one syllable pseudowords at grade level 3, two syllable pseudowords at grade 4-5, multisyllable pseudowords at grade 6, pseudowords with consonant blends at grade level 2, 3, and 6. There were some cases in which there were no differences between dyslexics and reading level matched normal readers; however, these instances were often ones in which there were floor or ceiling effects.

As words can obviously be read by some sort of direct visual access but pseudowords cannot be read without intermediate phonological processing, these data indicated that dyslexics have a severe deficit in phonological processing.

There is additional evidence that dyslexics have difficulty with the phonological route and use other processes to read words. In one study, we contrasted the reading of pseudowords that could be read by analogy or by grapheme-phoneme conversion rules, for example, *puscle*, *fody*, *risten* (Siegel & Geva, 1990). Dyslexics had a great deal of difficulty with these pseudowords and even when matched with normal readers of the same reading grade level, had significantly lower scores. When compared to normal readers on this pseudoword reading task, dyslexics were significantly less likely to use grapheme-phoneme conversion rules and to use an analogy strategy; responses of this type suggest a greater reliance on a visual reading route.

There are a number of other tasks that involve phonological processing and on which dyslexics have shown a poorer performance than normal readers. These tasks represent different aspects of phonological processing. One of these tasks is pseudoword spelling. Obviously, pseudowords can be spelled only by using phoneme-grapheme conversion strategies as no lexical entry exists. We have found that dyslexics had significantly lower scores on a task that involved the spelling of pseudowords, even when the dyslexics were at the same reading grade level as younger normal readers (Siegel & Ryan, 1988).

One type of evidence of phonological processing skills is the use of phonological recoding in short-term memory such that rhyming (confusable) stimuli are more difficult to remember than non-rhyming stimuli. A number of studies have found that younger dyslexics are less disrupted by rhyming stimuli (e.g. Byrne & Shea, 1979; Mann, Liberman, & Shankweiler, 1980; Shankweiler, Liberman, Mark, Fowler, & Fischer, 1979; Siegel & Linder, 1984). However, Johnston (1982) and Siegel and Linder (1983) have found that older dyslexic children do show phonetic confusability although their short-term memory for letters was significantly poorer than age match controls. Memory for rhyming or non-rhyming letters is also influenced by phonological coding, so it is not surprising that the dyslexics had significantly lower scores than normal reading on these tasks.

Phonemic awareness, the ability to recognise the basic phonemic segments of the language is obviously an important component of phonological processing. There is evidence that difficulties with phonemic awareness predict subsequent reading problems (e.g. Bradley & Bryant, 1983; Wallach & Wallach, 1976). In addition, poor readers also have deficits in phonological production tasks, for example, naming of objects represented by multisyllable words, and repetition of multisyllabic words and difficult phrases with alliteration. Pratt and Brady (1988) found differences between good and poor readers on the ability to segment words into phonemes, delete sounds from words, and the ability to judge the length of a word or pseudoword.

Dyslexics also have difficulty recognising the visual form of sounds (Siegel & Ryan, 1988). In the Gates McKillop test (Gates & McKillop, 1962) the children hear pseudowords such as *whiskate* and are asked to select the correct version of the word from among four printed choices: *iskate*, *wiskay*, *wiskate*, and *whestit*. Dyslexics had significantly lower scores on this task than normal readers. While this task involves skills that are relevant to spelling, aspects of it are relevant to phonological processing, including the segmentation involved in analysing the pseudoword and in decoding the alternatives.

One of the issues that has been raised in the study of dyslexia is whether these phonological processing deficits are characteristic of all dyslexics or only a subset of the population of dyslexics. It has been argued that there may be subtypes within the population of dyslexics (see Siegel & Heaven, 1986; Siegel, Levey, & Ferris, 1985; Siegel & Metsala, 1992, for a review of studies and methodological issues). However, there is no reliable evidence to support the concept of subtypes; clear subtypes have not been delineated. On the contrary, dyslexic children show a remarkable homogeneity in the profiles of their cognitive abilities (e.g. Siegel, 1993) and, in the cases where there is heterogeneity, it seems to be a result of the particular definition. Evidence indicates that the definition of dyslexia used in the study can influence the conclusions made about the heterogeneity of the population. For example, Siegel and Ryan (1989) have shown that if dyslexia is defined as a deficit in word reading skills, all the dyslexic children have deficits in phonological processing, working and short-term memory, and syntactic awareness. The pattern is similar if a deficit in pseudoword reading skills is used as the basis of the definition of dyslexia. On the other hand, if dyslexia is defined on the basis of a deficit in reading comprehension, then the group that emerges is heterogeneous and does not show deficits in phonological processing or syntactic skills, but does show deficits in working and short-term memory. Thus, subtypes, if and when they occur within the dyslexic population may be an artifact of the definition used. However, children who have a deficit in word recognition skills uniformly show phonological processing deficits.

## PHONOLOGICAL PROCESSING AND GENERAL COGNITIVE ABILITY

Recently, Stanovich (1988a; 1988b) has proposed that a deficit in phonological processing lies at the core of dyslexia. Phonological processing was characterised as a modular function that (Stanovich, 1988b, p. 158): "is not under the direction of higher level cognitive structures and is not supplemented by real world knowledge." Furthermore, according to Stanovich's model, phonological processing "may fail without disrupting the operations of central processes that do not depend on its output, and also that efficiently functioning central processes cannot remedy a module that is functioning inefficiently." (Stanovich, 1988b, p. 158). This theory would predict that: (1) a phonological processing deficit should be characteristic of all disabled readers; (2) phonological processing deficits should be independent of general cognitive ability. Regarding the first prediction, there is ample evidence, described earlier in this chapter, that difficulties with phonological processing are a pervasive characteristic of dyslexics. Regarding the second prediction, phonological processing should show a much stronger correlation with reading skills than general cognitive ability (operationalized as I.Q. test scores) and I.Q. scores should not contribute a significant amount of independent variance to the prediction of reading skills.

There is evidence from a number of sources that phonological processing skills are independent of general cognitive abilities. Reading disabled children at all I.Q. levels show equal difficulty with phonological processing tasks such as pseudoword reading, recognising the visual form of a pseudoword, pseudoword spelling, and a phonological lexical decision task with written words (e.g. distinguishing which of two pseudowords sounds like a real word, given stimuli such as *kake-dake*, and *joak-joap* (Siegel, 1988).

In addition, there were no differences between dyslexics, defined as children who had low reading scores (<25 centile) and whose reading scores were significantly (one standard deviation) below their I.Q. scores, and poor readers, who had low reading scores and whose reading scores were not below the level that would be predicted from their I.Q., on any of the phonological processing tasks described here (Siegel, 1992). Indeed, if the relative contributions of I.Q. and pseudoword reading are compared, then I.Q. contributes little independent variance to that contributed by pseudoword reading in the prediction of word reading and reading comprehension scores (Siegel, in press). Most of the variance is contributed by phonological processing as measured by pseudoword reading.

## Visual and Orthographic Processing

Phonological recoding is one route in reading. As described earlier, direct lexical access can also occur. Olson, Kliegl, Davidson, and Foltz (1985) have developed two tasks that provide a direct contrast between the visual and phonological processing routes. In the Phonological Task, the child has to specify which of two pseudowords, presented visually, sounds like a real word (e.g. *kake-dake*, *joap-joak*). In the Visual Task, the child is presented with a real word and a pseudoword (e.g. *rain-rane*, *boal-bowl*) and has to select the correct spelling. These tasks are designed so that only one process can operate in each task. That is, in the visual task both choices sound exactly the same, so that visual memory for the orthography of a word must be used; phonological processes are not helpful in this case because sounding out the words would produce the identical responses to each word. For the Phonological Task, recall of the visual pattern would not be useful because neither alternative is a correct visual pattern in the English lexicon. However, one of the alternatives, when sounded out, does produce an English word, although it is obviously not the correct orthographic form. These tasks were administered to dyslexic and normal readers, aged 7-16 years.

Not surprisingly, the reading disabled children performed more poorly on the Phonological Task than the normal readers and did not catch up to the normal readers until the age of 13. However, the reading disabled children also had difficulty with the Visual Task although visual processes are relatively less impaired than phonological ones. This Visual Task relies on memory for specific orthographic entries and, as spelling is typically a problem for dyslexics (e.g. Siegel & Ryan, 1988), this result is not surprising. The dyslexics performed more poorly on the Visual Task than normal readers at ages 7-12, although not at ages 13-16 or in adulthood (Shafrir & Siegel, 1991). These data are shown in Fig. 17.5. Therefore, both phonological and visual processing are impaired in dyslexics, but visual processing, as measured by this task, is relatively less impaired.

The picture is somewhat different when a reading grade level match was used. When dyslexic readers are compared to normal readers of the same reading age, so that dyslexic readers are matched with much younger normal readers, the dyslexic actually performed at a significantly *higher* level than the normal readers on the Visual Task at reading grade level 2. The dyslexics did not perform more poorly than normal readers of the same reading age on the Phonological Task. These data are shown in Fig. 17.6. It should be remembered that this Phonological Task merely requires the selection of one of two

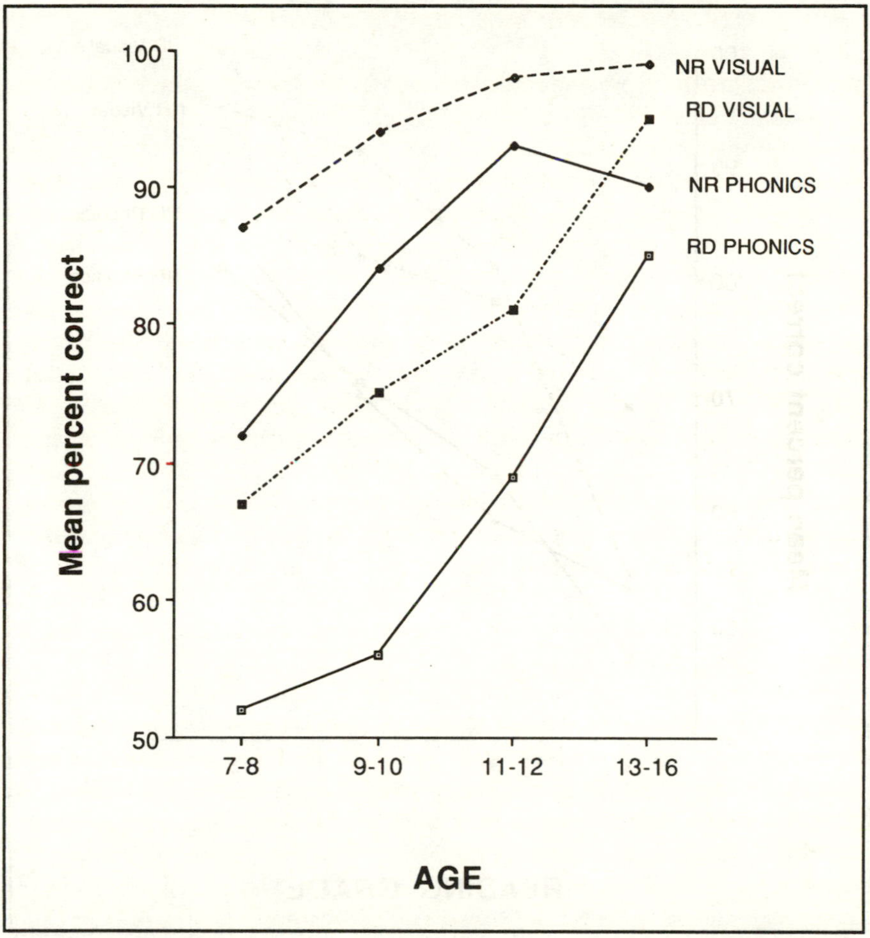


FIG. 17.5. Mean percentage correct responses on the Visual and Phonological Tasks for the normal readers (NR) and the dyslexics (RD) as a function of chronological age.

alternatives and it is not a production task, such as the pseudoword reading task, so that it may be considerably easier. This difference may explain why dyslexics of the same reading grade level as normal readers did not show the degree of deficit evidenced when reading pseudowords.

In order to study the awareness of orthographic structures, a task was developed (Siegel, Geva, & Share, 1990) in which the ability to recognise legal and illegal orthographic combinations of English letters was assessed. The task was a two choice one in which the children were presented with 18 pairs of pronounceable pseudowords, one of which

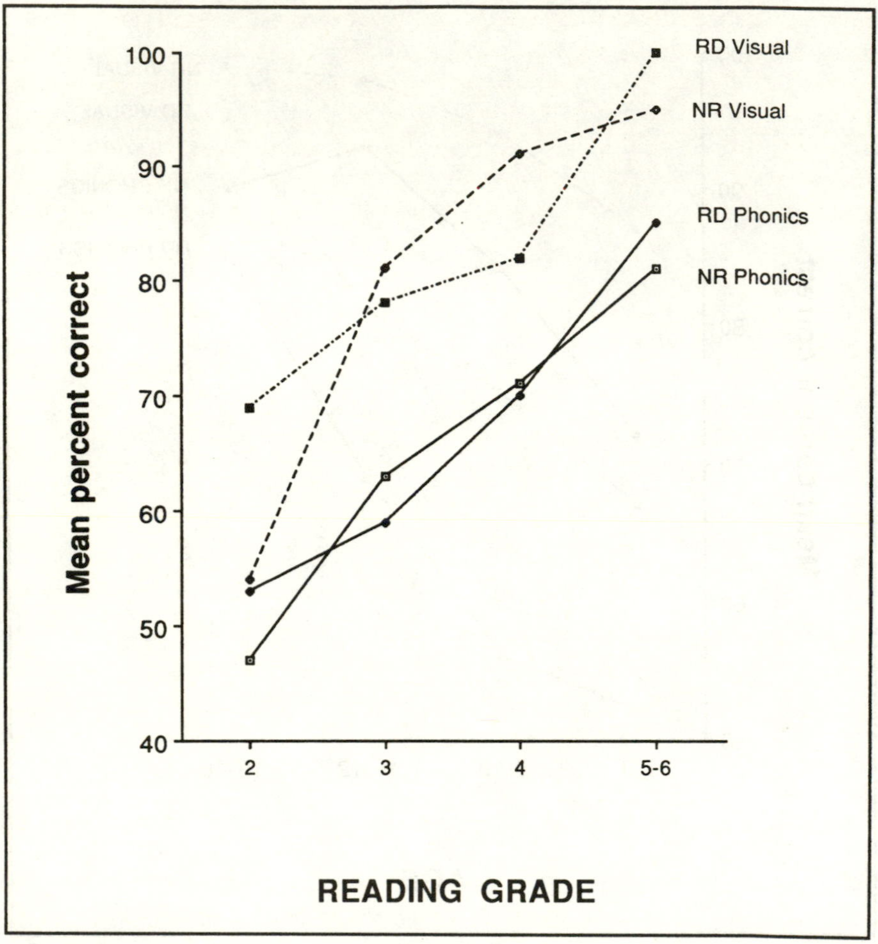


FIG. 17.6. Mean percentage correct responses on the Visual and Phonological Tasks for the normal readers (NR) and the dyslexics (RD) as a function of reading grade level.

contained a bigram that never occurs in an English word in a particular position and the other one that contained an orthographic string that occurs in English. Examples included *filv - filk, moke - moje, vism - visn,* and *powl - lowp*. The children were told that neither was a real word but their task was to specify which one could be a word. This task was administered to normal readers and dyslexics, aged 7-16 years.

Apart from the youngest ages (7-8 years) in which the dyslexics made significantly more errors than normal readers of the same chronological age, the performance of the normal readers and dyslexics did not differ.

These data are shown in Fig. 17.7. The dyslexic children did not perform more poorly than the normal readers at ages 9-16. However, when the normal and dyslexic readers were matched on reading level, the dyslexics performed at a level *higher* than the normal readers. These data are shown in Fig. 17.8. These data indicate that at the same level of reading skill, the dyslexics are better able to recognise the orthographic features of English. One possible mechanism by which this

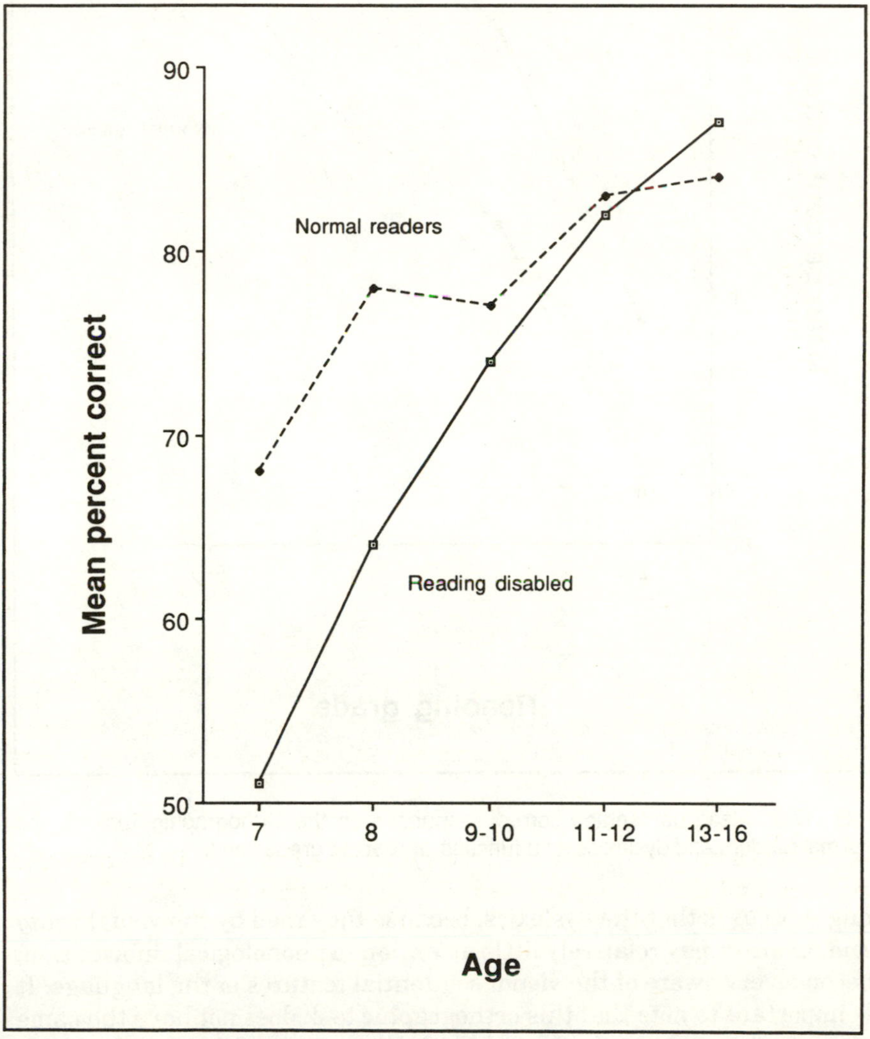


FIG. 17.7. Mean percentage correct responses on the Orthographic Task for the normal readers and dyslexics as a function of chronological age.

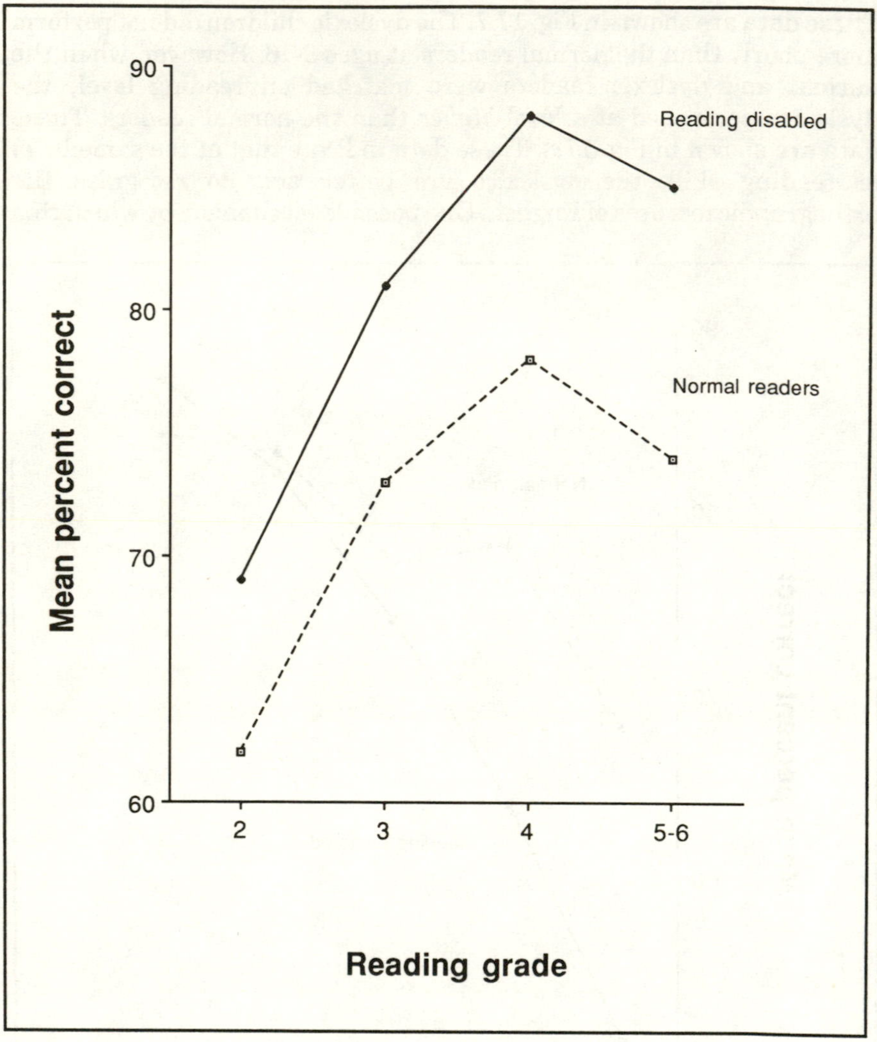


FIG. 17.8. Mean percentage correct responses on the Orthographic Task for the normal readers and dyslexics as a function of reading grade level.

might occur is that the dyslexics, because they read by the visual route and ignore or pay relatively little attention to phonological information, become very aware of the visual sequential features of the language. It is important to note that this orthographic task does not have the same memory demands as the Visual Task because the Orthographic Task requires the extraction of orthographic conventions but not memory for exact spellings of words as does the Visual Task.

### Implications

These findings have some implications for the treatment of dyslexia. Firstly, it is clear that the ability to use grapheme-phoneme conversion rules is a very late developing skill in dyslexic children. One extensive program to promote the awareness of grapheme-phoneme conversion rules in reading disabled children was not successful in improving their knowledge of GPC rules but did result in better word recognition skills (Lovett, Ransby, Hardwick, Johns, & Donaldson, 1989). Endless drill with phonics would seem to be a nonproductive approach with these children. Obviously, phonics cannot be ignored, but it would make more sense gradually to introduce an awareness of letter sound conversion rules. This gradual introduction of the grapheme-phoneme conversion rules should include capitalising on the regularities in English, for example, the regular consonants, e.g. *t, m, b, d,* etc. and introducing these regularities first. The dyslexics are able to understand regular GPC rules before complex irregular ones (Siegel & Faux, 1989). Short words with regular consonant-vowel combination and in "families" should be introduced early, e.g. *cat*, *hat*, *rat*, *sat*, *mat*, *bat*, *pat*, *fat*, or *hop*, *mop*, *top*, *pop*.This method encourages segmentation and makes use of the regularities of English.

The visual route seems less impaired in dyslexics. In some cases, the performance of the dyslexics was superior to the normal readers of the same reading grade level on tasks that would appear to be measuring some aspects of reading by the visual route. Considering the relative strengths that the dyslexics demonstrate in using this route, instruction should capitalise on this skill. That is, treating word reading as a picture recognition task, in this case the picture being the word, would seem to be more productive. Reading instruction and remedial teaching systems that make use of the visual route would seem to have the most potential for severe dyslexics.

## READING INSTRUCTION BASED ON THE VISUAL ROUTE

We have conducted a test of the theory that stressing the visual route may be an valuable approach to use with children with severe reading problems (Biemiller & Siegel, 1990). We developed an experimental curriculum based on the Bridge Reading Program (Dewsbury, Jennings, & Boyle, 1983). This program involves the use of icons (logographs) as picture cues for words. The underlying assumption of the program is that the icons or picture symbols can be linked to the child's lexicon more readily than print symbols. These icons are used to train the child to associate the correct printed word with them and then are gradually withdrawn as supports. These icons then serve to help the child learn the print symbols over a number of successful trials in reading and activity contexts. Very simplified text material is used, along with workbooks and games designed to facilitate the transition from icons to print. The goal of the program is to develop a sight vocabulary of approximately 150 words. Some icons are shown in Fig. 17.9.

The children selected for the study were at the beginning stages of reading instruction, that is grade 1 in the Canadian school system, and

FIG. 17.9. Examples of some of the icons used in the Bridge Reading Program.

were six and seven year old children, who were selected by their teachers and on their performance on a variety of pretests to be at risk for reading problems. Four classrooms received the Bridge program and seven received the normal reading program in use at the school, essentially "a whole language program" in which the child is encouraged to learn the meanings of words in context and most of the reading involves reading words in context. Very little, if any, drill with sight word recognition or phonics is used.

Our preliminary results have shown that at the end of grade 1, after approximately eight months of reading instruction, the children who had received the Bridge reading instruction had significantly higher scores on a word reading test, the Wide Range Achievement Test, than the children who were in the regular whole language program and showed improvements in speed reading individual words and connected text. The children who had experienced the Bridge program recognised the words on which they had been trained but also appeared to have acquired knowledge of words on which they had not been specifically trained. The children in the regular reading program did not make any significant gains. We do not know if the gains will continue to be apparent after the program has stopped but we believe that these results are suggestive of the efficacy of the remediation of dyslexia in concentrating on the visual, as opposed the phonological, route.

## SUMMARY

Severe phonological processing deficits appear to be the fundamental problem of dyslexia and there is evidence that phonological processing is a modular function that is relatively independent of general cognitive ability. In addition, it appears that orthographic processing is relatively intact in dyslexics, or, at least, they do not show the same degree of deficit in this area. These results also suggest that dual route theories of reading are more likely to be correct as both phonological and direct lexical access seem to be operating in the reading process. It would seem appropriate to use constructs from dual route theories in the treatment of developmental dyslexia.

## ACKNOWLEDGEMENT

The preparation of this chapter and the studies reported in it were supported by a grant from the Natural Sciences and Engineering Research Council of Canada. The author wishes to thank Letty Guirnela for secretarial assistance.

## REFERENCES

Biemiller, A. & Siegel, L. S. (1990). *A test of an experimental reading curriculum with a disadvantaged population*. Unpublished manuscript.

Besner, D., Twilley, L., McCann, R. S., & Seergobin, K. (1990). On the association between connectionism and data: Are a few words necessary? *Psychological Review*.

Bradley, L. & Bryant, P.E. (1983). Categorizing sounds and learning to read: A causal connection. *Nature, 301*, 419-421.

Brown, G. D. (1987). Resolving inconsistency: A computational model of word naming. *Journal of Memory and Language, 26*, 1-23.

Byrne, B. & Shea, P. (1979). Semantic and phonemic memory in beginning readers. *Memory and Cognition*, 333-341.

Coltheart, M. (1978). Lexical access in simple reading tasks. In G. Underwood (Ed.), *Strategies of information processing* (pp.151-216). London: Academic Press.

Dewsbury, A., Jennings, J., & Boyle, D. (1983). *Bridge reading*. Toronto, Ont.: OISE Press.

Forster, K.I. & Chambers, S. (1973). Lexical access and naming time. *Journal of Verbal Learning and Verbal Behaviour, 12*, 627-635.

Gates, A. I. & McKillop, A. S. (1962). *Gates-McKillop Reading Diagnostic Tests*. New York: Teachers College Press.

Glushko, R. J. (1979). The organization and activation of orthographic knowledge in reading aloud. *Journal of Experimental Psychology: Human Perception and Performance, 5*, 674-691.

Guthrie, J. T. & Seifert, M. (1979). Letter-sound complexity in learning to identify words. *Journal of Educational Psychology, 69*, 686-696.

Humphreys, G. W. & Evett, L. J. (1985). Are there independent lexical and nonlexical routes in word processing? An evaluation of the dual route theory of reading. *Behavioral and Brain Sciences, 8*, 689-739.

Johnston, R. (1982). Phonological coding in dyslexic readers. *British Journal of Psychology, 73*, 455-460.

Lovett, M. W., Ransby, M. J., Hardwick, N., Johns, M. S., & Donaldson, S. A. (1989). Can dyslexia be treated? Treatment-specific and generalized treatment effects in dyslexic children's response to remediation. *Brain and Language, 37*, 90-121.

Mann, V. A., Liberman, I. Y., & Shankweiler, D. (1980). Children's memory for sentences and word strings in relation to reading ability. *Memory and Cognition, 8*, 329-335.

Metsala, J. & Siegel, L. S. (1992). Developmental dyslexia and hyperlexia: Attributes and underlying reading processes. In S. Segalowitz & I. Rapin (Eds.), *Developmental neuropsychology, Vol 7* (pp. 187-210). Amsterdam: Elsevier.

Meyer, D.E., Schvanevelt, R. W., & Ruddy, M.G. (1974). Loci of contextual effects on word recognition. In P.M.A. Rabbitt & S. Dornic (Eds.), *Attention and performance, Vol. 5* (pp.98-118). New York: Academic Press.

Olson, R., Kliegl, R., Davidson, B. J., & Foltz, G. (1985). Individual and developmental differences in reading disability. In T. G. Waller (Ed.), *Reading research: Advances in theory and practice, Vol. 4* (pp.1-64). NY: Academic Press.

Pratt, A. C. & Brady, S. (1988). Relations of phonological awareness to reading disability in children and adults. *Journal of Educational Psychology, 8*, 319-323.

Seidenberg, M. S. & McClelland, J. L. (1980). A distributed, developmental model of word recognition and naming. *Psychological Review, 9*, 523-568.

Shafrir, U. & Siegel, L. S. (1991). *The cognitive processes of subtypes of adults with learning disabilities*. Unpublished manuscript.

Shankweiler, D., Liberman, I. Y., Mark, L. S., Fowler, C. A., & Fischer, F. W. (1979). The speech code and learning to read. *Journal of Experimental Psychology: Human Learning and Memory, 5*, 531-545.

Siegel, L. S. (1986). Phonological deficits in children with a reading disability. *Canadian Journal of Special Education, 2*, 45-54.

Siegel, L. S. (1988). Evidence that I.Q. scores are irrelevant to the definition and analysis of reading disability. *Canadian Journal of Psychology, 42*, 201-215.

Siegel, L. S. (1992). An evaluation of the discrepancy definition of dyslexia. *Journal of Learning Disabilities, 25,* 618-629.

Siegel, L. S. (1993). The cognitive basis of dyslexia. In R. Pasnak & M. L. Howe (Eds.), *Emerging themes in cognitive development*. (pp. 33–52). New York: Springer-Verlag.

Siegel, L. S. (in press). Phonological processing deficits as the basis of a reading disability. *Developmental Review.*

Siegel, L. S. & Faux, D. (1989). Acquisition of certain grapheme-phoneme correspondences in normally achieving and disabled readers. *Reading and Writing: An Interdisciplinary Journal, 1*, 37-52.

Siegel, L. S. & Geva, E. (1990). *Reading by analogy or rules: A comparison of poor and normal readers*. Unpublished manuscript.

Siegel, L. S., Geva, E., & Share, D. (1990). *The development of orthographic skills in normal and disabled readers*. Unpublished manuscript.

Siegel, L. S. & Heaven, R. (1986). Defining and categorizing learning disabilities. In S. Ceci (Ed.), *Handbook of cognitive, social, and neuropsychological aspects of learning disabilities, Vol. 1*. (pp. 95-121). Hillsdale, N.J.: Lawrence Erlbaum Associates Inc.

Siegel, L. S., Levey, P., & Ferris, H. (1985). Subtypes of developmental dyslexia: Do they exist? In F. J. Morrison, C. Lord, & D. P.Keating (Eds.), *Applied developmental psychology, Vol. 2*. (pp. 169-190). New York: Academic Press.

Siegel, L. S. & Linder, B. A. (1984). Short-term memory processes in children with reading and arithmetic learning disabilities. *Developmental Psychology, 20*, 200-207.

Siegel, L. S. & Metsala, J. (1992). An alternative to the food processor approach to subtypes of learning disabilities. In N. N. Singh & I. Beale (Eds.), *Current perspectives in learning disabilities: Nature, theory, and treatment* (pp. 44-60). NY: Springer Verlag.

Siegel, L. S. & Ryan, E. B. (1988). Development of grammatical sensitivity, phonological, and short-term memory skills in normally achieving and learning disabled children. *Developmental Psychology, 24*, 28-37.

Snowling, M. J. (1980). The development of grapheme-phoneme correspondence in normal and dyslexic readers. *Journal of Experimental Child Psychology, 29*, 294-305.

Stanovich, K. E. (1988a). Explaining the differences between the dyslexic and garden variety poor reader: The phonological-core variance-difference model. *Journal of Learning Disabilities, 21*, 590-604, 612.

Stanovich, K. E. (1988b). The right and wrong places to look for the cognitive locus of reading disability. *Annals of Dyslexia, 38*, 154-177.

Stanovich, K. E. (1991). Word recognition: Changing perspectives. In P. D. Pearson (Ed.), *Handbook of reading research, Vol. 2*.

Wallach, M. A. & Wallach, L. (1976). *Teaching all children to read.* Chicago: University of Chicago Press.

Waters, G. S., Bruck, M., & Seidenberg, M. (1985). Do children use similar processes to read and spell words? *Journal of Experimental Child Psychology, 39*, 511-530.

CHAPTER EIGHTEEN

# The Association between Reading Strategies in Poor Readers and their Visual and Phonological Segmentation Skills

Rhona S. Johnston, Marjorie Anderson, and Lynne G. Duncan
*Department of Psychology, University of St Andrews, UK*

## ABSTRACT

Poor readers' visual and phonological segmentation skills were assessed in order to see whether strengths and weaknesses on these tasks were associated with differing reading strategies. The most striking pattern of performance was found in the subgroup 1 poor readers, who had visual segmentation skills appropriate for their chronological age but whose phonological segmentation skills were appropriate for their reading age. These children showed a logographic approach to word reading, and their nonword naming skills were worse than would be expected for their level of phonological segmentation ability. However, they made a high proportion of phonetic spelling errors, indicating that it was only in reading that they were unable to use their phonological skills effectively. Subgroups 2 and 3 had impairments in both visual and phonological segmentation ability for their chronological age, the latter group being phonologically impaired even for reading age. These subgroups showed less distinctive patterns of reading performance, but both showed signs of attempting to use a phonological approach to reading in some of the tasks. Neither group showed signs of a logographic approach to reading, despite having visual segmentation skills similar to their reading age controls, who used both logographic and phonological approaches to reading. This suggests that logographic reading in poor readers is the product of a high level of visual segmentation skill coupled with much weaker phonological segmentation ability.

## INTRODUCTION

The study of developmental reading disorders has been of concern to researchers since at least the turn of the century, and there have been many theories about why children of normal intelligence and good socio-economic background, who have received a thorough education, still fail to learn to read at an appropriate level for their general ability or chronological age. Given that reading involves translating the printed word into sounds and meaning, it is not surprising that a great deal of the early work concentrated on the idea that poor readers suffer from problems in the visual aspects of reading. Hinshelwood (1917), a Scottish ophthalmologist, concluded that poor readers were impaired in their visual memory for words, and that they would only make progress if they were taught to read by phonetic rules rather than "look say". Orton (1937) argued that the problem with poor readers was that they failed to suppress visual images from the right hemisphere, which led to problems such as mirror handwriting. For the next thirty or so years, various versions of the "perceptual deficit" hypothesis were pursued.

Vellutino (1979) launched a devastating attack on visual perceptual deficit theories of developmental reading disorders. He concluded that much of the work in the area showed weaknesses in design and sampling. One area with which he found fault was a small body of experiments that showed poor readers to have deficient visual segmentation skills (Goetzinger, Dirks, & Baer, 1960; Lovell, Gray, & Oliver, 1964; Stuart, 1967). In these studies, poor readers were found to have difficulty in perceiving a shape embedded within a more complex visual configuration. Vellutino dismissed these studies as unconvincing. For example, with the Lovell et al. (1964) study, he challenged the idea that the embedded figures problem indicated a deficit in visual analysis because the problem was specific to that task, the poor readers performing normally on the WISC Block Design subtest, and tests of figure rotation and spatial orientation. However, it is not necessary to assume that if poor readers have a problem with the visual aspects of reading that this will manifest itself across the entire spectrum of visual analysis tasks, which may in fact tap a number of different visual functions. Indeed, such assumptions are not made when studying phonological deficits in poor readers.

Vernon (1979), in a wide-ranging review of the literature, concluded that no reliable evidence has been found that poor readers have problems in perceiving simple shapes, but suggests that poor readers may have problems in perceiving and analysing complex perceptual patterns, that is, problems with analysing both visual and phonemic structures. Treiman and Baron (1981) further argue that the development of speech segmentation skills may reflect the general development of analytical skills, visual as well as phonological.

There is impressive evidence that phonological skills are significantly correlated with reading ability (Calfee, Lindamood, & Lindamood 1973; Fox & Routh, 1975; Rosner & Simon, 1971). In particular, Bradley and Bryant (1983) found that four year olds' performance on sound categorisation tasks (where the child has to detect the odd word out in an auditorily presented sequence such as "bud, bun, bus, rug") accounted for around 10% of the variance in reading ability three years later. Furthermore, there is evidence that some poor readers are impaired even for their reading age on these sound categorisation tasks, implying that this might be what actually causes their reading problems (Bradley & Bryant, 1978). A number of studies have also found impairments in using phonological skills in reading; for example, Snowling (1981) found poor readers to be worse at naming nonwords than reading age controls. Similarly, a number of case studies have found phonological impairments in the reading of poor readers (Johnston, 1983; Temple & Marshall, 1983). It might be concluded from these studies that all poor readers suffer from a fundamental phonological weakness, and that the amelioration of this problem should be the main priority in remedial programmes.

However, there is evidence which suggests that attributing developmental reading disorders purely to a phonological dysfunction may be too simplistic a view. For example, Waters, Seidenberg, and Bruck (1984) found poor readers to read regular words better than irregular words, indicating a phonological approach to reading. Johnston, Rugg, and Scott, (1987; 1988) further found that poor readers misclassified pseudohomophones as real words to the same extent as their reading age controls, indicating a phonological approach to reading, and were as good as these controls at pronouncing nonwords. Beech and Harding (1984) and Treiman and Hirsh-Pasek (1985) were also unable to find evidence of a phonological deficit in such children. This suggests that some poor readers are not arrested at the initial "logographic" stage of reading proposed by Frith (1985), where words are recognised on the basis of salient graphic features such as risers and descenders. The evidence in fact suggests that many poor readers develop the alphabetical skills that characterise the next stage, where unfamiliar words can be decoded by converting graphemes into phonemes. However, all poor readers seem to fail to develop the orthographic skills of the final stage, where, according to Frith, recognition is carried out on the basis of morphemes and small words which together make up a syllabary. As far as some poor readers are concerned, therefore, it might be fruitful to examine whether they have a visual weakness underlying their reading problems.

Johnston, Anderson, Perrett, and Holligan (1990) were able to replicate the earlier studies that showed poor readers to be impaired in identifying shapes embedded within more complex visual configurations. Moreover, although the poor readers were found to perform like their reading age controls on this task, a close examination of the data showed that this result was due to the very poor performance of a subgroup of children. Eight out of the twenty poor readers performed more than two standard deviations below the mean of the chronological age controls. Interestingly, the same was true with the sound categorisation task (based on Bradley & Bryant's, 1978, odd word out task); seven out of the twenty poor readers performed more than two standard deviations below the mean of the chronological age controls. Performance on the visual segmentation and sound categorisation tasks correlated significantly even when the effects of reading age and chronological age were partialled out, a reflection, in part, of the fact that five of the poor readers were severely impaired on both tasks. It was also found that performance on the visual segmentation task correlated with reading ability in the poor reader group even when the effects of chronological age and I.Q. were partialled out.

Given that the impaired performance on the visual and phonological segmentation tasks found in group studies of poor readers probably reflects the influence of subgroups of children with severe deficits in these areas, there is clearly a need for a closer analysis of individual differences in performance on these tasks. Case studies have already provided important insights into the variations in the problems experienced by poor readers. However, case studies in this area have been very theoretically motivated, with children being identified as having developmental analogues of acquired dyslexia syndromes in order to support or clarify a particular reading model (e.g. Johnston, 1983; Temple & Marshall, 1983). The cases chosen show particularly pure patterns of deficits, and those who do not fit these syndromes tend to be excluded or criticised. For example, Coltheart et al. (1983) studied a developmental dyslexic who showed many of the features of acquired surface dyslexia, using for the most part a phonological approach to word reading. However, she was also very poor at nonword naming, which is problematical for the dual route model of reading, in which the same phonological route can be used for both word and nonword naming. It is therefore possible to argue that this subject does not show a truly surface dyslexic pattern of performance. Rather than rejecting such cases as being somehow contaminated, we need to know if these patterns of reading performance are common among developmental dyslexics, and then account for their reading in terms of a model that can cope with such seeming anomalies. We will gain a better understanding of reading disorders, and be able to offer informed advice on remediation, if we can make generalisations about subgroups of disorders based on larger numbers of poor readers.

An alternative way of investigating subgroups of reading disorders, which is not heavily influenced by prevailing models of word recognition, is to select children on the basis of their performance on non-reading tasks that are known to be related to success in reading. The rationale for this is that it is likely that reading development is founded in part on information processing skills that are not initially developed specifically for reading (Wilding, 1990), although it is evident that segmentation skills develop to a certain extent through learning to read (Kolinsky, Morais, Content, & Cary, 1987; Morais, Cary, Alegria, & Bertelson, 1979). In the present study, performance on both visual and phonological segmentation tasks was used to select subgroups of poor readers. In order to measure visual segmentation skills, the children were tested on the Children's Embedded Figures Test (Witkin, Oltman, Raskin, & Karp, 1971), where they were asked to detect a shape embedded within a more complex configuration (e.g. a triangle hidden inside a clown's face). A phonological deletion task was carried out in order to assess phonological segmentation ability, where the child had to say what sound was left, for example, if the "f" was taken away from "flat". It was hypothesised that poor readers with good visual segmentation skills but impaired phonological segmentation skills would show a visual approach to reading, and that those with the reverse pattern would show a phonological approach to reading.

## METHOD

### Subjects

A sample of 25 children aged 9-11 who were attending a reading unit were studied. All of these children were being taught to read via a primarily phonics approach, where they were systematically taught the relationship between letters or letter sequences and their sounds. Intelligence was assessed using the short form of the WISC (Maxwell, 1959), reading was measured using the British Ability Scales Word Reading Test (Elliott, Murray, & Pearson, 1977), and spelling was assessed by the Schonell spelling test (see Table 18.1 for means and standard deviations).

Normal levels of performance for 10 year old children on visual and phonological segmentation tasks was assessed by reference to another study where 43 children had carried out the same tasks (Duncan, 1991). The mean age of this sample was 10.7 years (s.d. 0.7), mean visual segmentation performance was 72.0% (s.d. 14.6) and mean phonological segmentation performance was 90.7% (s.d. 7.1).

Abnormal performance was said to have occurred for the poor readers in the present sample if the scores were more than two standard deviations below the means of Duncan's large sample of chronological age controls. Twelve of the children showed very poor performance on one or more of the segmentation tasks compared with the normal 10 year olds in Duncan's (1991) study, and were categorised into three subgroups (described later). Twenty six reading age controls were matched on the basis of reading age and I.Q., and twenty two chronological age controls were matched on age and I.Q., to the poor readers so that statistical tests could be carried out on the experimental tasks in order to establish normal performance for 8 and 10 year olds (see Table 18.1 for means and standard deviations). All the normal readers had also been taught to read via a primarily phonics approach.

The subgroup 1 poor readers (n=5) performed normally on the visual segmentation task for their chronological age but were impaired on the phonological segmentation task, performing similarly to their reading age controls (see Table 18.3). The other two subgroups had impaired visual segmentation skills for their chronological age. The subgroup 2 poor readers (n=3) performed like their reading age controls on both the visual and phonological segmentation tasks, performance on the latter task also being very similar to that of the subgroup 1 children (see Table 18.5). The subgroup 3 poor readers (n=4) performed similarly to their reading age controls on the visual segmentation task, but were very impaired on the phonological segmentation task for their reading age

TABLE 18.1
Mean Reading and Spelling Age, I.Q., and Visual and Phonological Segmentation Scores for Large Group of Poor Readers and their Reading and Chronological Age Controls

| | | | | | *% correct Segmentation Tasks* | |
|---|---|---|---|---|---|---|
| | Age | Reading Age | Spelling Age | I.Q. | Visual | Phonological |
| *Poor readers* (n = 25) | | | | | | |
| $\overline{X}$ | 10.7 | 7.9 | 7.9 | 108.4 | 56.8 | 64.1 |
| S.D. | 0.8 | 0.9 | 0.8 | 12.5 | 20.4 | 21.0 |
| *Reading age controls* (n = 26) | | | | | | |
| $\overline{X}$ | 8.0 | 8.1 | 8.1 | 107.0 | 36.8 | 68.3 |
| S.D. | 0.7 | 0.7 | 1.0 | 10.1 | 17.3 | 17.3 |
| *Chronological age controls* (n = 22) | | | | | | |
| $\overline{X}$ | 10.4 | 10.5 | 10.5 | 110.8 | 63.6 | 88.5 |
| S.D. | 0.7 | 0.9 | 0.9 | 12.1 | 17.7 | 7.1 |

(see Table 18.7). Children with normal phonological segmentation skills and impaired visual skills for their chronological age were not found in this sample, although it is of interest that four children with appropriate phonological segmentation skills for their chronological age were found. Having identified subgroups of poor readers showing markedly different patterns of performance on the segmentation tasks, we then tested them on a range of word and nonword reading and spelling tasks, and compared them with their reading and chronological age controls.

## MATERIALS AND PROCEDURE

### Segmentation tasks

*Phonological deletion.* This task was devised by Duncan (1991). Subjects were individually read out words and nonwords, and were asked to say what sound was left when a particular sound was left out. Segmentation of initial and final sounds was carried out, half of the items involving splitting up a consonant cluster. Thus there were six each of the following word types: (f)lat, mus(t), (w)ork, and slee(p), and six each of the following nonword types: (s)mab, nol(p), (n)ost, and sno(l).

*Visual segmentation.* Witkin et al.'s (1971) Children's Embedded Figures Test was used. The children were familiarised with a triangular shape and a house shape, and asked to detect and trace out the shapes within coloured pictures of varying complexity. Only accuracy is recorded in the children's version of the task.

### Reading and Spelling Tasks

A range of word and nonword reading tasks was selected to assess what approach to reading the children were taking.

*Regularity task.* This task was designed to assess the extent to which the children took a phonological approach to reading. The rationale, according to the dual route model of reading (Coltheart, 1978), is that if regular words (e.g. "best") are read better than irregular words (e.g. "gone") of matched frequency, then the advantage must arise from the functioning of the phonological route in addition to the visual route. Only irregular words which conformed to Waters et al.'s (1984) "exception" word criteria were used. The regular and irregular words were of either high or low word frequency, and were matched using the Grade 3 norms of Carroll, Davies, and Richman (1971). There were 14 items in each category. The mean word frequency of the irregular high frequency words was 504.4 (s.d. 421.7), and of the regular high frequency words was 507.6 (s.d 413.5). The mean word frequency of the irregular low frequency was 28.1 (s.d. 23.3), and of the regular low frequency words was 25.9 (s.d. 21.6). The mean number of letters was matched across all four categories.

For this task, and all the other reading tasks, the order of the words was randomised, with the restriction that no more than three items of the same type appeared in sequence. The words were presented to the children on the monitor of a microcomputer. Each item was presented, in large lower case letters, one at a time in the centre of the screen. The child was asked to name the item as quickly and carefully as possible, the item remaining on screen until the voice key was activated. The child's responses were tape recorded and later analysed for accuracy.

*Nonword naming (short and long nonwords).* This task was designed to assess the children's phonological reading skills by asking them to read nonwords, that is, letter strings that conform to English spelling rules, but which do not exist in the language. Such items cannot be read by the direct visual route, and must be read phonologically, according to the dual route model of reading (Coltheart, 1978). The short nonwords consisted of 20 three-letter one syllable nonwords (e.g. "mip"). The long nonwords consisted of 20 six-letter two syllable nonwords (e.g. "bosdin"). None of the items were pseudohomophones.

*Distinctive letter features task.* This task was included to assess the extent to which the children's reading was influenced by visual factors. Two types of words were contrasted, those with risers and descenders (e.g. "plate"), and those without (e.g. "cane"). Words were also presented in both lower (e.g. "cream") and alternating case (e.g. "cReAm"), in order to examine whether the poor readers were differentially affected by loss of external word shape cues and the disruption of internal letter features. It was hypothesised that children who read "logographically", i.e. who identified words by their salient graphic features (Seymour & Elder, 1986), would read the words with risers and descenders better than those without. There were 18 items in each category. The mean word frequency for the words with risers and descenders was 60.3 (s.d. 86.1), and was 59.3 (s.d. 75.1) for those without these features (Carroll et al., Grade 3 norms). The items were matched for number of letters, the mean being 4.6 for each list.

The order of the items was predetermined so that repeated items (in normal versus alternating case) were well separated. Half the words with risers and descenders appeared first in normal, and then in alternating case, and the words without risers and descenders were similarly counterbalanced.

*Spelling task.* In this task the children were asked to spell 24 words and 26 nonwords of matched length, half of which had high, and half of which had low numbers of orthographic neighbours. First of all the nonwords were read out to the children in a block, and then the words. Each item was read out twice, the words also being presented in a sentence context. The responses were analysed according to Morris and Perney's (1984) developmental scheme, which is compatible with the stages in spelling development observed by Read (1986). Errors were classified as pre-phonetic, e.g. motor → "bott", phonetic 1; e.g. wake → "wak"; and phonetic 2 ("transitional" in Morris and Perney's terminology), e.g. wake → "wacke", in order of increasing maturity. The final category shows an emerging awareness of how to represent sounds according to English orthography. This error category most closely resembles the "phonetic" spelling errors of previous researchers (e.g. Nelson & Warrington, 1974).

## RESULTS OF POOR READERS AND THEIR CONTROLS

*Regularity task.* A three-way repeated measures analysis of variance was carried out on the accuracy data (see Table 18.2). There was an interaction between groups and regularity, $F(2,70)=7.41$, $P<0.001$. Newman Keuls tests showed that both the reading age and chronological age controls showed a regularity effect, whereas the poor readers did not. There was also a groups-by-frequency interaction, $F(2,70)=18.22$, $P<0.0001$. A Scheffe test showed that all the groups read high frequency words better than low, but that the difference was larger for the reading age controls. There was also a two way interaction between regularity and frequency, $F(1,70)= 21.71$, $P<0.0001$. Newman Keuls tests showed that the children found the regular words easier to read than the irregular words when they were of low frequency. However, both sets of items were read equally well when they were of high frequency.

*Nonword naming task.* There was an interaction between groups and ability to name short versus long nonwords, $F(2,70)=12.91$, $P<0.0001$. Newman Keuls tests showed that the chronological age controls were better at reading long nonwords than the other two

TABLE 18.2

(a) Mean % Correct Performance on Regularity, Distinctive Letter Features and Nonword Naming Tasks, Large Group of Poor Readers and their Reading Age and Chronological Age Controls

| | *Reading* | | | | | | | | | |
|---|---|---|---|---|---|---|---|---|---|---|
| | *Regularity* | | | | *Distinctive letter features* | | | | *Nonwords* | |
| | *High frequency* | | *Low frequency* | | *Normal case* | | *Alternating* | | | |
| | *Irreg* | *Reg* | *Irreg* | *Reg* | *r/d* | *no r/d* | *r/d* | *no r/d** | *short* | *long* |
| *Poor Readers* | | | | | | | | | | |
| $\bar{X}$ | 73.3 | 69.4 | 57.1 | 58.8 | 67.1 | 57.8 | 64.0 | 52.4 | 65.9 | 28.3 |
| SD | 21.1 | 19.9 | 21.3 | 20.6 | 19.3 | 17.8 | 20.1 | 14.5 | 18.7 | 22.7 |
| *Reading age controls* | | | | | | | | | | |
| $\bar{X}$ | 86.0 | 91.2 | 53.4 | 73.6 | 78.4 | 68.8 | 71.4 | 61.5 | 79.9 | 43.7 |
| SD | 13.2 | 14.0 | 18.0 | 20.7 | 19.0 | 18.3 | 20.3 | 18.5 | 14.2 | 27.2 |
| *Chronological age controls* | | | | | | | | | | |
| $\bar{X}$ | 96.4 | 98.4 | 83.1 | 94.8 | 97.5 | 94.4 | 91.1 | 90.4 | 86.6 | 73.9 |
| SD | 4.8 | 3.8 | 12.4 | 6.7 | 2.9 | 5.7 | 5.6 | 9.4 | 13.2 | 20.9 |

*r/d indicates words with risers and descenders
no r/d indicates words without risers and descenders

(b) % Spelling Errors for Large Group of Poor Readers and their Spelling Age Controls

| | *Nonwords* | | | *Words* | | |
|---|---|---|---|---|---|---|
| | *pre-phonetic* | *phon 1* | *phon 2* | *pre-phonetic* | *phon 1* | *phon 2* |
| *Poor readers* | | | | | | |
| $\bar{X}$ | 40.3 | 27.0 | 32.7 | 26.5 | 14.9 | 58.6 |
| SD | 18.2 | 16.3 | 19.3 | 17.3 | 11.9 | 18.2 |
| *Spelling age controls* | | | | | | |
| $\bar{X}$ | 46.6 | 17.6 | 35.8 | 29.6 | 16.6 | 53.8 |
| SD | 24.1 | 18.1 | 22.9 | 25.7 | 13.4 | 23.0 |

subgroups, and that the reading age controls performed better than the poor readers. However, the poor readers read the short nonwords as well as their reading age controls, but performed worse than the chronological age controls.

*Distinctive letters features task.* A three-way analysis of variance with repeated measures was carried out. Groups and word type interacted, $F(2,70)=5.18$, $P<0.008$. Newman Keuls tests showed that the poor readers and reading age controls read words with risers and descenders better than those without, but that the 10 year olds were unaffected by this manipulation. There was also a main effect of alternating case, $F(1,70)=38.89$, $P<0.0001$, words being read better in normal typescript. This factor did not interact with groups, $F< 1$.

*Spelling task.* As the chronological age controls often made no spelling errors at all in some categories, it was only feasible to make a comparison between the poor readers and the reading age controls. There was no main effects of groups, $F(1,49)=1.95$, N.S. However, there was an interaction between words and nonwords, high and low orthographic neighbours, and spelling error types, $F(2,98)=3.91$, $P<0.023$. Newman Keuls tests showed that responses to words with low numbers of orthographic neighbours were more likely to be pre-phonetic, whereas errors to words with high numbers of orthographic neighbours were more likely to be of the phonetic 2 type.

## RESULTS FOR SUBGROUPS OF POOR READERS

### Subgroup 1

These poor readers had normal performance on the visual segmentation task for their chronological age, and performed like reading age controls on the phonological segmentation task (see Table 18.3).

*Regularity task.* These poor readers were better at reading irregular than regular words (see Table 18.4). This was in marked contrast to the reading age (and chronological age) controls, who showed an advantage for regular versus irregular words on the low frequency items.

*Nonword naming task.* The poor readers found nonword naming

TABLE 18.3
Mean Reading Age, Spelling Age, I.Q., and Visual and Phonological Segmentation Scores for Subgroup 1 Poor Readers and Controls

| | | | | | % correct Segmentation Tasks | |
|---|---|---|---|---|---|---|
| | *Age* | *RA* | *SA* | *I.Q.* | *Visual* | *Phonological* |
| *Subgroup 1 (n = 5)* | | | | | | |
| $\bar{X}$ | 10.9 | 8.5 | 8.5 | 110.4 | 72.0 | 69.7 |
| SD | 0.8 | 0.9 | 0.8 | 8.2 | 11.3 | 4.8 |
| *Subgroup 1 reading age controls (n = 5)* | | | | | | |
| $\bar{X}$ | 8.0 | 8.5 | 8.5 | 109.2 | 44.8 | 74.6 |
| SD | 1.0 | 1.2 | 1.7 | 9.3 | 17.3 | 17.8 |
| *Subgroup 1 chronological age controls (n = 5)* | | | | | | |
| $\bar{X}$ | 10.5 | 10.8 | 10.7 | 109.7 | 64.8 | 87.1 |
| SD | 0.8 | 0.5 | 1.1 | 10.3 | 8.2 | 6.8 |

TABLE 18.4
Mean % Correct Performance on Regularity, Distinctive Letter Features and Nonword Naming tasks, Subgroup 1 Poor Readers and Reading and Chronological Age Controls

| | *Regularity* | | | | *Distinctive letter features* | | | | *Nonwords* | |
|---|---|---|---|---|---|---|---|---|---|---|
| | *High frequency* | | *Low frequency* | | *Normal case* | | *Alternating* | | | |
| | *Irreg* | *Reg* | *Irreg* | *Reg* | *r/d* | *no r/d* | *r/d* | *no r/d** | *short* | *long* |
| *Subgroup 1* | | | | | | | | | | |
| $\overline{X}$ | 77.8 | 68.9 | 78.9 | 57.8 | 77.8 | 68.9 | 81.1 | 57.8 | 56.0 | 21.0 |
| SD | 14.2 | 16.0 | 12.0 | 11.5 | 14.2 | 16.0 | 11.5 | 11.5 | 15.2 | 22.2 |
| *Subgroup 1 reading age controls* | | | | | | | | | | |
| $\overline{X}$ | 85.7 | 84.3 | 48.6 | 72.9 | 82.2 | 76.7 | 76.7 | 62.2 | 84.0 | 52.3 |
| SD | 11.3 | 23.4 | 29.6 | 25.5 | 16.4 | 14.9 | 16.4 | 17.3 | 15.2 | 26.0 |
| *Subgroup 1 chronological age controls* | | | | | | | | | | |
| $\overline{X}$ | 95.7 | 100.0 | 82.9 | 94.3 | 96.6 | 94.4 | 92.2 | 90.0 | 90.0 | 76.0 |
| SD | 3.9 | 0.0 | 20.0 | 3.2 | 3.1 | 3.9 | 3.0 | 9.9 | 6.1 | 18.5 |

*r/d indicates words with risers/descenders
no r/d indicates words with no risers/descenders

difficult and were much worse at this task than their reading age controls, even with simple three letter nonwords.

*Distinctive letter features task.* Here the poor readers showed a consistent advantage for words with risers and descenders compared to words without these features, as did the reading age controls.

*Spelling task.* These poor readers spelt words much more accurately than nonwords. They were particularly good at spelling words in a phonetically acceptable way compared to spelling age controls, in that they produced a high proportion of phonetic 2 errors, but they produced a similar proportion of phonetically acceptable mis-spellings of nonwords as their controls (see Table 18.9).

## Subgroup 2

This group had impaired visual and phonological segmentation skills for their chronological age, performing similarly to the large group of reading age controls on these two tasks. Their performance on the phonological segmentation task was also very similar to that of the subgroup 1 poor readers (see Table 18.5).

TABLE 18.5
Mean Reading Age, Spelling Age, I.Q., Visual and Phonological Segmentation Scores for Subgroup 2 Poor Readers and Controls

| | | | | | % correct Segmentation Tasks | |
|---|---|---|---|---|---|---|
| | *Age* | *RA* | *SA* | *I.Q.* | *Visual* | *Phonological* |
| | *Subgroup 2 (n = 3)* | | | | | |
| $\overline{X}$ | 10.8 | 8.0 | 7.9 | 94.0 | 37.3 | 71.8 |
| SD | 0.2 | 0.4 | 0.5 | 3.5 | 4.6 | 8.2 |
| | *Subgroup 2 reading age controls (n = 3)* | | | | | |
| $\overline{X}$ | 8.3 | 8.1 | 8.1 | 96.3 | 24.0 | 66.6 |
| SD | 0.4 | 0.4 | 0.4 | 9.5 | 6.9 | 12.7 |
| | *Subgroup 2 chronological age controls (n = 3)* | | | | | |
| $\overline{X}$ | 10.6 | 10.5 | 10.7 | 96.8 | 81.3 | 94.5 |
| SD | 0.5 | 0.3 | 0.7 | 7.3 | 9.2 | 3.2 |

*Regularity task.* These children showed a small regularity effect, but only on the high frequency words (see Table 18.6), whereas their reading age controls showed a marked regularity effect on the low frequency words. It is interesting to note that the subgroup 1 poor readers had very similar phonological segmentation scores to these subgroup 2 children and to the reading age controls, and yet they showed a markedly different pattern of performance on this task.

TABLE 18.6
Mean % Correct Performance on Regularity, Distinctive Letter Features and Nonword Naming Tasks, Subgroup 2 Poor Readers and Reading and Chronological Age Controls

| | *Regularity* | | | | *Distinctive letter features* | | | | *Nonwords* | |
|---|---|---|---|---|---|---|---|---|---|---|
| | *High frequency* | | *Low frequency* | | *Normal case* | | *Alternating* | | | |
| | *Irreg* | *Reg* | *Irreg* | *Reg* | *r/d* | *no r/d* | *r/d* | *no r/d** | *short* | *long* |
| | *Subgroup 2* | | | | | | | | | |
| $\overline{X}$ | 81.0 | 90.5 | 64.3 | 66.7 | 66.7 | 70.4 | 72.2 | 51,8 | 69.5 | 58.9 |
| SD | 14.9 | 4.2 | 7.2 | 18.0 | 5.6 | 8.5 | 5.6 | 6.4 | 15.0 | 8.4 |
| | *Subgroup 2 reading age controls* | | | | | | | | | |
| $\overline{X}$ | 83.3 | 92.9 | 46.2 | 78.5 | 77.8 | 66.7 | 70.4 | 64.8 | 81.7 | 43.6 |
| SD | 10.9 | 12.4 | 9.7 | 18.9 | 24.2 | 5.6 | 22.4 | 6.4 | 10.4 | 33.0 |
| | *Subgroup 2 chronological age controls* | | | | | | | | | |
| $\overline{X}$ | 95.3 | 100.0 | 76.2 | 97.6 | 98.1 | 90.7 | 90.7 | 87.4 | 93.3 | 83.3 |
| SD | 4.1 | 0.0 | 4.2 | 4.1 | 3.2 | 6.4 | 6.4 | 8.6 | 2.9 | 2.9 |

*r/d indicates words with risers/descenders
no r/d indicates words with no risers/descenders

*Nonword naming task.* Despite having very similar phonological segmentation skills to the subgroup 1 children, the subgroup 2 children were much better at reading the long nonwords. Furthermore, they were also somewhat better than their reading age controls at reading long nonwords.

*Distinctive letter features task.* Unlike the reading age controls and the subgroup 1 poor readers, these poor readers' performance on the lower case items was slightly better when the words had no risers and descenders, suggesting that these children made little use of salient graphic features when reading.

*Spelling task.* These children spelt nonwords better than words, a pattern found in no other group. As far as spelling errors to words were concerned, they produced a lot of phonetic 2 errors, performing like the subgroup 1 children rather than their controls (see Table 18.9). However, they produced rather a lot of pre-phonetic errors when spelling nonwords compared to their controls.

## Subgroup 3

These children had visual segmentation skills like those of their reading age controls (and the subgroup 2 poor readers), but their phonological segmentation skills were very impaired for reading age (see Table 18.7).

*Regularity task.* Overall, these children showed a regularity effect similar to that of their reading age controls, although accuracy levels were much lower (see Table 18.8).

*Nonword naming task.* They performed similarly to the subgroup 2 children when reading short nonwords, despite their much poorer phonological segmentation skills and lower reading age. However, they were very poor at naming long nonwords. Interestingly, the subgroup 1 children were nearly as poor at naming long nonwords as these subgroup 3 poor readers, despite having much better phonological segmentation skills and being nearly a year and a half ahead on the BAS Word Recognition Test.

*Distinctive letter features task.* These children did not find words with risers and descenders easier to read than those without these features, and in this respect they were similar to the subgroup 2 children.

TABLE 18.7
Mean Reading Age, Spelling Age, I.Q., Visual and Phonological Segmentation Scores for Subgroup 3 Poor Readers and Controls

| | *Age* | *RA* | *SA* | *I.Q.* | *% correct Segmentation Tasks* *Visual* | *Phonological* |
|---|---|---|---|---|---|---|
| | *Subgroup 3 (n = 4)* | | | | | |
| $\overline{X}$ | 10.4 | 7.1 | 7.0 | 105.6 | 31.9 | 28.9 |
| SD | 0.6 | 0.4 | 0.6 | 12.0 | 10.8 | 20.3 |
| | *Subgroup 3 reading age controls (n = 4)* | | | | | |
| $\overline{X}$ | 7.1 | 7.3 | 7.1 | 102.9 | 25.0 | 63.6 |
| SD | 0.2 | 0.3 | 1.1 | 8.4 | 6.0 | 27.1 |
| | *Subgroup 3 chronological age controls (n = 4)* | | | | | |
| $\overline{X}$ | 10.6 | 10.7 | 10.7 | 109.5 | 73.0 | 87.0 |
| SD | 0.6 | 1.2 | 0.7 | 11.0 | 6.83 | 6.0 |

*Spelling task.* Their spelling accuracy for words was similar to that of their spelling age controls, although they were somewhat worse at nonword spelling. They had normal levels of phonetic mis-spellings on words, but produced far fewer than spelling age controls on nonwords.

TABLE 18.8
Mean % Correct Performance on Regularity, Distinctive Letter Features and Nonword Naming Tasks, Subgroup 3 Poor Readers and Controls

| | *Regularity* | | | | *Distinctive letter features* | | | | *Nonwords* | |
|---|---|---|---|---|---|---|---|---|---|---|
| | *High frequency* | | *Low frequency* | | *Normal case* | | *Alternating* | | | |
| | *Irreg* | *Reg* | *Irreg* | *Reg* | *r/d* | *no r/d* | *r/d* | *no r/d** | *short* | *long* |
| | *Subgroup 3* | | | | | | | | | |
| $\overline{X}$ | 58.9 | 67.3 | 32.2 | 48.2 | 37.5 | 37.5 | 37.5 | 40.3 | 65.0 | 16.3 |
| SD | 29.9 | 14.7 | 14.9 | 16.9 | 9.5 | 12.3 | 7.0 | 7.0 | 28.0 | 29.3 |
| | *Subgroup 3 reading age controls* | | | | | | | | | |
| $\overline{X}$ | 80.4 | 89.3 | 41.1 | 57.1 | 70.8 | 56.9 | 61.1 | 51.4 | 78.3 | 33.8 |
| SD | 22.1 | 17.0 | 21.3 | 31.4 | 22.4 | 22.8 | 21.8 | 18.3 | 11.8 | 28.4 |
| | *Subgroup 3 chronological age controls* | | | | | | | | | |
| $\overline{X}$ | 98.2 | 100.0 | 83.9 | 98.2 | 97.2 | 97.2 | 91.7 | 95.8 | 82.5 | 70.0 |
| SD | 3.6 | 0.0 | 14.7 | 3.6 | 3.2 | 3.2 | 3.2 | 5.3 | 18.9 | 26.8 |

*r/d indicates words with risers/descenders
no r/d indicates words with no risers/descenders

TABLE 18.9
Mean % Correct Spelling of Words and Nonwords, and Mean % of Pre-phonetic, Phonetic 1 and Phonetic 2 Errors for Subgroups 1, 2 and 3 and Spelling Age Controls (Standard Deviations in Brackets)

| | *Nonword* | | | | *Word* | | | |
|---|---|---|---|---|---|---|---|---|
| | *Total % correct* | *% errors pre-phon* | *phon1* | *phon2* | *Total % correct* | *% errors pre-phon* | *phon1* | *phon2* |
| Sub-group 1 | 60.8 (7.4) | 31.4 (13.6) | 33.6 (15.6) | 35.0 (22.8) | 70.8 (6.6) | 23.7 (16.3) | 9.0 (9.3) | 67.3 (21.9) |
| SA | 65.4 (11.2) | 57.1 (18.0) | 9.2 (14.6) | 33.8 (18.0) | 63.3 (21.9) | 49.6 (17.6) | 7.6 (8.2) | 32.8 (22.4) |
| Sub-group 2 | 61.5 (2.3) | 56.1 (13.7) | 11.3 (12.0) | 32.7 (25.6) | 44.5 (4.8) | 24.9 (9.7) | 10.1 (5.8) | 65.1 (14.4) |
| SA | 56.4 (8.0) | 35.3 (18.3) | 27.4 (21.9) | 37.3 (9.2) | 56.9 10.5 | 37.5 (40.2) | 14.3 (10.9) | 48.2 (33.6) |
| Sub-group 3 | 22.1 (11.9) | 61.1 (15.5) | 27.3 (14.5) | 11.6 (2.4) | 39.6 (21.9) | 39.6 (25.8) | 21.9 (9.6) | 38.5 (18.5) |
| SA | 32.7 (27.8) | 57.6 (30.3) | 9.5 (8.0) | 24.5 (21.4) | 40.6 (23.9) | 40.9 (29.7) | 14.5 (9.8) | 44.7 (22.5) |

## DISCUSSION

The rationale for this study was that by selecting poor readers having varying impairments on visual and phonological segmentation tasks it might be possible to find subgroups of children having patterns of reading and spelling performance that showed the influence of these non-reading skills.

The subgroup 1 children showed a particularly distinctive pattern of performance. These children had normal visual segmentation skills for their chronological age, but had deficient phonological segmentation skills, performing like their reading age controls on this task. If visual segmentation ability has no influence on how poor readers read, then this group of children might be expected to read like their reading age controls. In some respects this was the case. These poor readers found words with risers and descenders easier to read than those without, as did the reading age (but not chronological age) controls.

However, in other respects these children were quite unlike their reading age controls. They did not show the normal pattern of reading regular words better than irregular ones, which was found for both the chronological and reading age controls in the large group analysis. In fact, there was a strong pattern in the opposite direction, suggesting that the irregular words were more visually distinctive, despite there being no difference in the occurrence of risers and descenders in the two types of words. Another feature of the subgroup 1 children was that although they had similar levels of phonological segmentation ability to their reading age controls, they were much poorer at reading nonwords. This suggests that their strongly visual approach to reading led them to fail to use these phonological skills when it was appropriate to do so. This interpretation is also supported by the fact that they were worse at reading long nonwords than the subgroup 2 poor readers, who had similar levels of phonological segmentation skill but did not have their visual strengths. Overall, the subgroup 1 children seem to show the logographic approach to reading proposed by Frith (1985) as being characteristic of the "classic" developmental dyslexic, recognising words on the basis of salient graphic features. They were good at focusing on the parts within the wholes in the visual segmentation task, and this may have aided the detection of the salient graphic features in the words.

In terms of spelling ability, these children were relatively good at spelling words compared to controls, but did not show this advantage with nonwords, which suggests that they were good at using word specific information. They were, however, also good at producing phonetically plausible mis-spellings, especially where words were concerned, which indicates some knowledge of English orthography. This suggests that they are like Temple and Marshall's (1983) developmental case H.M., who showed signs of a phonological disorder in reading, but who spelt phonetically. In their spelling, therefore, there was evidence of these children being able to use their phonological skills.

The pattern of performance shown by these poor readers also bears some relation to the performance of Funnell and Davison's (1989) subject Louise. This adult read words well, but was very poor at reading and spelling nonwords. Not surprisingly, she was shown to perform very poorly on phonological segmentation tasks like the one used in the present study. However, Louise was found to be able to read and spell nonwords very much better when using the International Phonetic Alphabet. Funnell and Davison concluded that the subject's approach to novel stimuli presented in alphabetic script was a lexical one, which they described as 'lexical capture', leading to very impaired performance on nonwords. They suggested that Louise may have initially experienced success in reading by using a visual approach, and that although phonological skills must have developed later, she was unable to use these skills when reading. One possibility suggested by the present study is that Louise had extremely good visual skills, and that she capitalised on this strength when learning to read. This is analogous to the subgroup 1 poor readers in the present study, who had phonological segmentation skills that they were unable to use effectively when pronouncing long nonwords, apparently because they had an overwhelmingly logographic approach to reading.

The subgroup 2 poor readers showed a less clear pattern of performance than the subgroup 1 children. They had similar visual and phonological segmentation skills to their reading age controls, and similar phonological skills to the subgroup 1 poor readers, but in several respects their performance was dissimilar to both groups. Their pattern of performance suggests a mostly phonological approach to reading and spelling, which was shown most clearly in nonword naming and spelling. Thus they were better at reading long nonwords than the subgroup 1 children and the reading age controls, and they also showed, if anything, a slight advantage for regular over irregular words. However, they exhibited no advantage for words with risers and descenders in the lower case condition, despite having similar levels of visual segmentation ability to their reading age controls. This suggests that it is the relative strengths and weaknesses of visual and phonological segmentation skills that are associated with how poor readers approach reading tasks, in addition to the absolute level of skill. In terms of spelling, this was the only subgroup that showed better spelling of nonwords than words, which may also indicate the use of a phonological approach. Their nonword spelling accuracy was appropriate for their spelling age, but the spelling of words was rather poor. However, they produced a lot of phonetically acceptable mis-spellings of words, performing similarly to the subgroup 1 children. They may have been better able to use their phonological skills in some of these tasks than the subgroup 1 children because they did not have strong visual skills predisposing them towards a visual approach to reading. Additionally, like all the poor readers reported here, these children were receiving a rigorous phonics-orientated remedial programme, which may have biased them towards a phonological approach.

The subgroup 3 children performed similarly to the reading age controls and the subgroup 2 poor readers on the visual segmentation task; however, they were poorer than both of these groups on the phonological segmentation task. Most of the children were virtually unable to read long nonwords, and it is interesting to note that their performance levels were very similar to those found in subgroup 1, despite the fact that the latter group had superior phonological segmentation skills and word reading ability. Despite this, they showed a regularity effect of similar magnitude to their reading age controls. Such a result might seem problematic for the dual route model of reading, where use of the grapheme to phoneme conversion route is thought to account for the regular word advantage as well as for nonword naming skill. The explanation of the regular word advantage is that these items are read by both the visual and the phonological route, whereas irregular words can only be read by the visual route. However, when a child sounds out a word this often seems to activate a weak word recognition unit. For example, children can be heard to sound out words like "laugh" and still generate the correct pronunciation. However, nonwords do not have recognition units, weak or otherwise, so accurate naming must depend more heavily on phonological skill, an area in which these children were particularly poor.

In spelling, their overall accuracy levels were like those of their spelling age controls as far as words were concerned, and they were reasonably good at producing phonologically acceptable mis-spellings of these items. However, they were poor at spelling nonwords, and their errors tended to be less mature than those of the spelling age controls.

Overall, these children showed evidence of being able to use a phonological approach to word reading appropriate for their reading age, but were unable to use this approach as effectively in nonword reading and spelling; this may be because these two tasks are particularly demanding in terms of phonological skill. In many respects, these poor readers are like the large group of 8 year old poor readers (who had a mean reading age of 7 years) studied by Holligan and Johnston (1988), who also showed regularity effects in word reading, but impaired nonword reading for reading age. Furthermore, another study of this same group (Holligan & Johnston, 1991) showed a developmental shift towards less phonetically accurate spelling errors, similar to the one observed in the subgroup 3 children.

Given that all of these children seem to fail to reach the orthographic stage of reading proposed by Frith (1985), it may be appropriate for them to be taught to read by an approach that develops orthographic skills. Despite its name, phonics is in fact a multisensory teaching method, which does not merely teach children how to convert graphemes into phonemes. Children are also taught how to segment words at various levels, including onset-rime, by showing them that visual spelling patterns such as "cake", "make", "bake" have consistent pronunciations. Seymour and Bunce (this volume) have devised a theoretically motivated phonics remediation programme to teach two boys with differing problems, one showing a surface or morphemic dyslexic pattern of reading, and the other having phonological dyslexic problems. This type of approach was efficacious for both boys in some respects, the effects of the intervention generalising between reading and spelling, and between word and nonword naming. Additionally, making orthographic segments visually salient seems to be very helpful in teaching reading

(Gattegno, 1969), and this may be a particularly beneficial approach for the subgroup 2 and 3 poor readers in the present study, who had very weak visual segmentation skills. Where some poor readers have a particularly marked strength, such as the subgroup 1 children's logographic skills, this could be capitalised on by trying to develop these skills further by encouraging them to recognise the visually salient features of words. However, in view of their well developed phonetic spelling skills, it would be unwise to conclude that phonics tuition is not useful for such children.

These visual and phonological segmentation deficits may not directly cause reading disorders. We know that there is variability in the reading strategies of normal readers (Baron 1979, Bryant & Impey, 1986), which may also be ultimately accounted for in terms of varying patterns of underlying cognitive skills. Strengths and weaknesses in visual and phonological segmentation skills may simply influence how poor readers approach reading given that they have a fundamental problem in learning to remember new words. When trying to pronounce unfamiliar words, poor readers may be forced to concentrate on those particular features of the words that they are able to use to aid recognition. In general, normal 8 year old readers seem to be able to use both a phonological and a logographic approach to recognising words, whereas many of the poor readers studied here seem to have only one of these options open to them. A further issue that needs to be addressed is how these segmentation skills arise, given that they are known to improve as children get older. There is evidence that learning to read aids the development of both phoneme deletion and visual embedded figures skills (Kolinsky et al., 1987; Morais et al., 1979). Furthermore, the methods we use to teach reading to both poor and normal readers may have an impact on the development of these skills. All of these factors may interact, and we need to tease them apart in order to come to a fuller understanding of reading disorders and normal reading development. These questions cannot be answered here, and will require further research.

## ACKNOWLEDGEMENT

This study was supported by grant number G8804473N from the Medical Research Council.

## REFERENCES

Baron, J. (1979). Orthographic and word-specific mechanisms in children's reading of words. *Child Development, 50*, 60-72.

Beech, J.R., & Harding, L.M. (1984). Phonemic processing and the poor reader from a developmental lag viewpoint. *Reading Research Quarterly, 19,* 357-366.

Bradley, L., & Bryant, P.E. (1978). Difficulties in auditory organisation as a possible cause of reading backwardness. *Nature, 271,* 746-747.

Bradley, L., & Bryant, P.E. (1983). Categorizing sounds and learning to read - a causal connection. *Nature, 301,* 419-421.

Bryant, P., & Impey, L. (1986). The similarities between normal readers and developmental and acquired dyslexics. *Cognition, 24,* 121-137.

Calfee, R.C., Lindamood, P., & Lindamood, C. (1973). Acoustic-phonetic skills and reading—kindergarten through twelfth grade. *Journal of Educational Psychology, 64,* 293-298.

Carroll, J.B., Davies, P., & Richman, B. (1971). *The Word Frequency Book.* New York: American Heritage.

Coltheart, M. (1978). Lexical access in simple reading tasks. G Underwood. (Ed.). *Strategies of Information Processing,* London: Academic Press.

Coltheart, M., Masterson, J., Byng, S., Prior, M., & Riddoch, J. (1983). Surface dyslexia. *Quarterly Journal of Experimental Psychology, 35A,* 469-495.

Duncan, L. (1991). *Cognitive and perceptual impairments in poor readers.* Unpublished Ph.D thesis, University of St Andrews.

Elliott, C.D., Murray, D.J., & Pearson, L.S. (1977). *The British Ability Scales.* Windsor: NFER Nelson.

Fox, B., & Routh, D.K. (1975). Analysing spoken language into words. *Journal of Psycholinguistic Research, 4,* 331-342.

Frith, U. (1985). Beneath the surface of developmental dyslexia. In K. Patterson, J. Marshall, & M. Coltheart (Eds.), *Surface dyslexia.* London: Lawrence Erlbaum Associates Ltd.

Funnell, E., & Davison, M. (1989). Lexical capture: A developmental disorder of reading and spelling. *Quarterly Journal of Experimental Psychology, 41A,* 471-487.

Gattegno, C. (1969). *Reading words in colour.* Reading: Educational Explorers Ltd.

Goetzinger, C.P., Dirks, D.D., & Baer, C.J. (1960). Auditory discrimination and visual perception in good and poor readers. *Annals of Otolaryngology, Rhinology and Laryngology, 67,* 121-136.

Hinshelwood, J. (1917). *Congenital Word Blindness.* London: Lewis.

Holligan, C., & Johnston, R.S. (1988). The use of phonological information by good and poor readers in memory and reading tasks. *Memory and Cognition, 16,* 522-532.

Holligan, C., & Johnston, R.S. (1991). Spelling errors and phonemic segmentation ability: the nature of the relationship. *Journal of Research in Reading, 14,* 21-32.

Johnston, R.S. (1983). Developmental deep dyslexia? *Cortex, 19,* 133-139.

Johnston, R.S., Rugg, M.D., & Scott, T. (1987). The influence of phonology on good and poor readers when reading for meaning. *Journal of Memory and Language, 26,* 57-68.

Johnston, R.S., Rugg, M.D., & Scott, T. (1988). Pseudohomophone effects in 8 and 11 year old good and poor readers. *Journal of Research in Reading, 11,* 110-119.

Johnston, R.S., Anderson, M., Perrett, D.I., & Holligan, C. (1990). Perceptual dysfunction in poor readers: evidence for visual and auditory segmentation problems in a sub-group of poor readers. *British Journal of Educational Psychology, 60,* 212-219.

Kolinsky, R., Morais, J., Content, A., & Cary, L. (1987). Finding parts within figures: A developmental study. *Perception, 16,* 399-407.

Lovell, K., Gray, E.A., & Oliver, D.E A. (1964). A further study of some cognitive and other disabilities in backward readers of average non-verbal reading scores. *British Journal of Educational Psychology, 34,* 275-279.

Maxwell, A.E. (1959). A factor analysis of the Wechsler Intelligence Scale for Children. *British Journal of Educational Psychology, 29,* 237-241.

Morais, J., Cary, L., Alegria, J., & Bertelson, P. (1979). Does awareness of speech as a sequence of phonemes arise spontaneously? *Cognition, 7,* 323-331.

Morris, D., & Perney, J. (1984). Developmental spelling as a predictor of first grade reading achievement. *The Elementary School Journal, 84,* 441-457.

Nelson, H.E. & Warrington, E.K. (1974). Developmental spelling retardation and its relation to other cognitive abilities. *British Journal of Psychology, 65,* 265-274.

Orton, S. T. (1937). *Reading, Writing and Speech Problems in Children.* New York: Norton.

Nelson, H.E. & Warrington, E.K. (1974). Developmental spelling retardation and its relation to other cognitive abilities. *British Journal of Psychology, 65,* 265-274.

Read, C. (1986). *Children's creative spelling.* Routledge & Kegan Paul: London.

Rosner, J., & Simon, D.P. (1971). The auditory analysis test: An initial report. *Journal of Learning Disabilities, 4,* 40-48.

Seymour, P.H.K. & Bunce, F. (this volume). Application of cognitive models to remediation in cases of developmental dyslexia.

Seymour, P.H.K., & Elder, L. (1986). Beginning reading without phonology. *Cognitive Neuropsychology, 1,* 43-82.

Snowling, M.J. (1981). Phonemic deficits in developmental dyslexia. *Psychological Research, 43,* 219-234.

Stuart, I.R. (1967). Perceptual style and reading ability. *Perceptual and Motor Skills, 24,* 135-138.

Temple, C.M., & Marshall, J.C. (1983). A case study of developmental phonological dyslexia. *British Journal of Psychology, 74,* 517-533.

Treiman, R., & Baron, J. (1981). Segmental analysis ability: Development and relation to reading ability. In J.G. Waller & G.E. MacKinnon (Eds.), *Reading research: Advances in theory and practice, 2,* 159-198.

Treiman, R., & Hirsh-Pasek, K. (1985). Are there qualitative differences in reading behaviour between dyslexics and normal readers? *Memory & Cognition, 13,* 357-364.

Vellutino, F.R. (1979). *Dyslexia: Theory and research.* Cambridge, Mass: MIT.

Vernon, M.D. (1979). Variability in reading retardation. *British Journal of Psychology, 70,* 7-16.

Waters, G.S., Seidenberg, M.S., & Bruck, M. (1984). Children's and adults' use of spelling-sound information in three reading tasks. *Memory & Cognition, 12,* 293-305.

Wilding, J. (1990). Developmental Dyslexics do not Fit into Boxes: Evidence from six new case studies. *European Journal of Cognitive Psychology, 2,* 97-131.
Witkin, H.A., Oltman, P.K., Raskin, E., & Karp, S.A. (1971). *Children's Embedded Figures Test.* Palo Alto: Consulting Psychologists Press Inc.

# PART SIX

## Written Language

CHAPTER NINETEEN

# Reading, Writing, and Rehabilitation: A Reckoning

Karalyn Patterson
*MRC Applied Psychology Unit, Cambridge, UK*

## INTRODUCTION

In the late 1980s and early 1990s, a number of books and even a new journal have appeared documenting research in neuropsychological rehabilitation. One possible reaction to this is to revise the gloomy assessment made by Beauvois and Derouesne (1982, p.167): "Rapports entre recherche et reeducation—ce qui n'existe pas". On the other hand, unbridled optimism may be premature. The arrival of *Neuropsychological Rehabilitation* and the recent books does not necessarily reflect significant integration between theory and therapy. An equally plausible hypothesis is that the current major increase in rehabilitation research is occurring in parallel with, but for the most part independently of, cognitive neuropsychology. In other words, even if theoretical and applied cognitive neuropsychology are both thriving, they may as yet be failing fully to communicate. It is worth briefly considering why this might be.

If applied neuropsychologists (i.e. people whose primary concern is the rehabilitation of cognitive deficits) are unenthusiastic about theoretical neuropsychology, this is probably because they do not perceive it as offering any genuine applicability. In a recent debate as to whether cognitive theory is pertinent to treatment, it was suggested on the negative side by Wilson and Patterson (1990, p.248) that "... theories about the nature of the deficit do not relate to questions that have to be asked in treatment or rehabilitation". Cognitive neuropsychology is *about* the nature of various deficits and what they imply for our understanding of cognitive mechanisms. If this is of no use in rehabilitation, then perhaps the field of rehabilitation research *ought* to proceed more or less independently of theoretical neuropsychology. There is, however, an opposing point of view (expressed hesitantly by Howard & Patterson, 1989; rather more forcefully by Mitchum & Berndt, 1990; and on the positive side of their debate by Wilson & Patterson, 1990) suggesting that treatment could in principle be guided by cognitive theory, even if this rarely occurs in practice.

On the other side of the non-communicating artery, why might theoretical neuropsychologists be failing to engage in or attend to rehabilitation research? One reason may be simply the daunting prospect of properly designed and executed cognitive rehabilitation research. The rare examples of this (e.g. Byng, 1988; De Partz, 1986) demonstrate that the enterprise requires everything in a good cognitive neuropsychology study (the background assessments, the deficit analysis, etc.) plus all the added work and complications of the treatment programme itself, the necessarily longitudinal nature of the research, the need to rule out explanations other than the treatment for any obtained effects, etc. It is hard work. A second possible reason is that the potential to learn something of real theoretical significance from the outcome of treatment may not be apparent (or convincing) to many neuropsychologists. Howard and Patterson (1989) argued that treatment studies may offer insights into cognitive architecture that are not (or at least not so easily) obtained from more standard experimental neuropsychology; but this view may not be widely shared.

As the issue of what theory and therapy have to offer one another is clearly a matter of both opinion and degree, it is time to turn to something more concrete and less speculative: a review of some current rehabilitation research. The studies included here were selected by the intersection of three defining features: (1) they involved treatment for acquired disorders of written language processing, either reading or writing; (2) whether or not the choice of treatment technique was genuinely guided by cognitive theory, most of these studies were conducted in a framework and spirit of cognitive neuropsychology; (3) they worked—i.e. the patient's performance improved as a result of the treatment.

## ACQUIRED DISORDERS OF READING

Figure 19.1 shows a very simplified (and despite its simplicity, speculative and probably controversial) sketch of the processes involved in recognising, pronouncing and comprehending written words. The implication of such a scheme is firstly that all and only these components

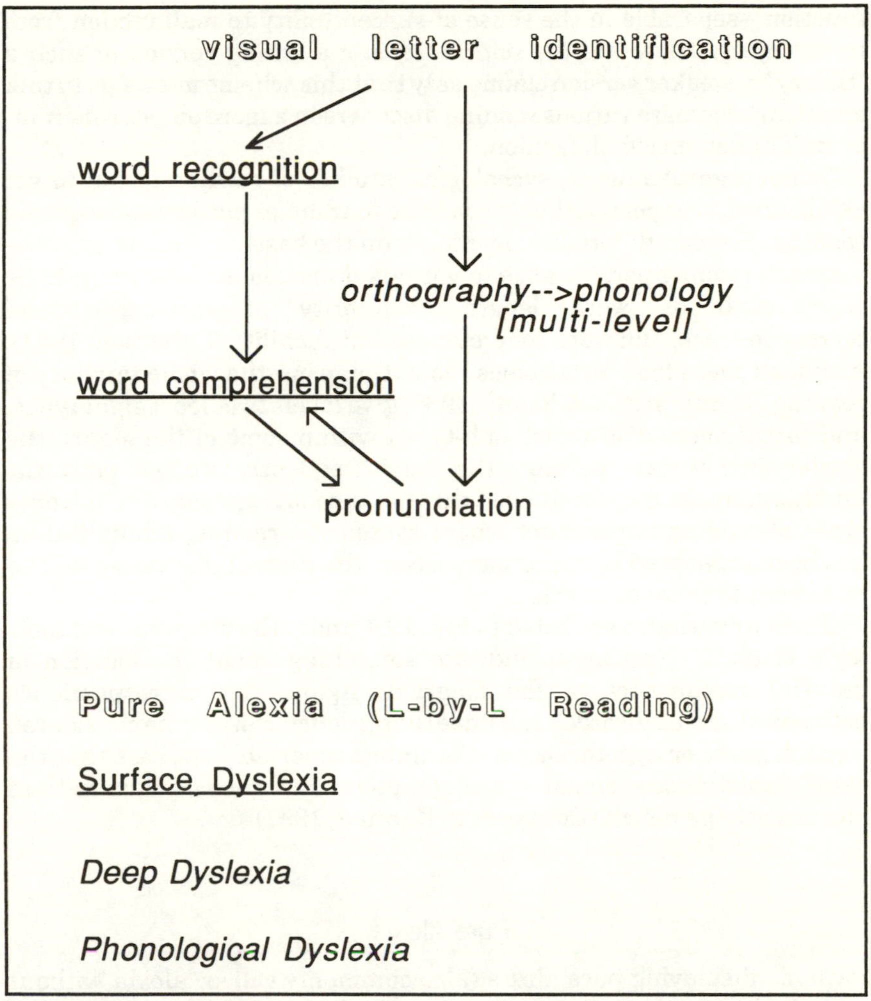


FIG. 19.1. A simplified descriptive scheme for the processes involved in recognising, comprehending and pronouncing a written word, with an indication of the disorders of reading likely to arise from selective impairments to these processes.

(and pathways of communication between them) are necessary to account for the performance of normal adult readers (of English) when they succeed in pronouncing or comprehending a written word, and secondly that each process and/or pathway is—though not independent of the other parts of the system in its normal activity and function—separable in the sense of susceptibility to malfunction from brain injury. These are the implications of a strong version of such a "theory"; a weaker version claims only that this scheme allows us to talk about and compare various reading disorders in a more or less coherent, even if under-specified, fashion.

When cognitive neuropsychological studies of reading began to get established, it appeared that there were four major patterns of acquired reading disorder, differentiable mainly on the basis of sensitivity of the patient's reading performance to various dimensions of the word to be read, such as word length, regularity of spelling-to-sound correspondence, and word concreteness/imageability (Patterson, 1981). Although these four "syndromes" do not map out the whole territory of reading disorders (Ellis & Young, 1988, give labels to at least eight types, and furthermore distinguish sub-types within some of the eight), the earlier four remain perhaps the most frequently studied patterns. Furthermore, as they (or at least three of the four) appear to be the only types of reading impairment where systematic reading rehabilitation has been attempted in one or more cases, the current discussion will be restricted to these patterns.

The four varieties are listed in Fig. 19.1 under the diagram, and their style of print is meant to indicate something about the location of putative impairment in the diagram. Again, this correspondence between observed disorder and underlying deficit can only be considered a rough guide or hypothesis, as it is almost invariably the case that the same symptom or even pattern of symptoms can arise from more than one underlying deficit (Coltheart & Funnell, 1987).

## Pure Alexia

Patients displaying pure alexia (also commonly called "alexia without agraphia" in the neurological literature and "letter-by-letter reading" in the neuropsychological literature) are poor at identifying written words, where poor always means slow—with word-naming speed a monotonic function of word length, hence the sobriquet letter-by-letter reading—and often inaccurate as well. By contrast, these patients typically show excellent performance at recognising words spelled aloud to them. This combination of features is compatible with the suggestion by various authors (e.g. Farah & Wallace, 1991; Howard, 1991; Price, 1990) and in Fig. 19.1 (indicated by shadowed print) that pure alexia may be attributable to a deficit in visual letter identification (or perhaps the transmission of information from letter identification to word recognition).

## Surface Dyslexia

Three prominent features of reading performance in patients displaying surface dyslexia are:

1. A major advantage in word naming (and sometimes in other tasks, such as lexical decision, as well) for words with a regular or typical spelling-sound correspondence (e.g. MINT) as compared to 'exception' words (like PINT).
2. A high probability that the patient's errors in naming exception words will be to regularise them, that is to assign the more typical phonological correspondences.
3. Many surface dyslexic patients have severe comprehension deficits for both written and spoken words (e.g. Bub, Cancelliere, & Kertesz, 1985). For those who do not, reading comprehension is often determined by phonological rather than orthographic characteristics of the word. This feature has several symptomatic consequences, including frequent errors in comprehending both exception words (BEAR might be defined as an alcoholic drink) and homophones (VAIN might be defined as something like an artery).

These three features suggest, as indicated by underlining in Fig. 19.1, that surface dyslexia usually arises from a deficit somewhere in the set of processes from letters to pronunciation via word recognition and comprehension. Written words must therefore be processed by direct computation of phonology from orthography, a procedure that is sensitive to the spelling-sound regularities of English.

## Deep and Phonological Dyslexia

Patients with these two patterns of reading disorder show severe or even total impairments in the ability to assign pronunciation to unfamiliar letter strings (e.g. nonwords such as RINT), and their accuracy in real word naming is unaffected by spelling-sound characteristics of the word. As suggested by use of italic print in Fig. 19.1, the procedure that translates directly from orthography to phonology is disrupted in both phonological and deep dyslexia, and the patients can only deal with letter strings that have meaning.

The differentiation between these two patterns of reading impairment, at least in the scheme of Fig. 19.1, comes from the status of the word recognition/comprehension routine. This appears to be relatively intact in phonological dyslexic patients, hence they can correctly name most real words (although many patients classified as phonological dyslexics do in fact make some errors in word naming, most notably when given function words and/or morphologically complex words). Deep dyslexic patients, on the other hand, typically make many errors in naming real words (including semantic errors such as GUILTY → "judge"), and are especially disadvantaged with abstract words. Some researchers have therefore concluded that, in addition to complete malfunction of the direct computation of phonology from orthography, the computation of meaning from orthography and/or pronunciation from meaning is also partially disrupted in deep dyslexia (see Coltheart, Patterson, & Marshall, 1987, for discussion).

## ACQUIRED DISORDERS OF WRITING

Although the skills involved in written language as a receptive task (reading) and as a productive task (writing) differ in undoubted and important ways, they also of course have significant similarities. In particular, it seems probable that the competent writer develops several different procedures or routines for computing an orthographic representation for a spoken word, parallel to those illustrated in Fig. 19.1 for computing a pronunciation for a written word. This view is supported by patterns of break-down observed in writing or spelling tasks, following brain injury in a previously literate adult. As with reading, the most basic distinction in disorders of writing is whether the patient is either forced to rely too heavily, or unable to rely sufficiently, on general knowledge governing the translation between phonology and orthography, independently of specific word recognition and comprehension. The former pattern, borrowing its designation from the domain of reading, is often referred to as surface dysgraphia, or sometimes lexical dysgraphia (Beauvois & Derouesne, 1981) or phonological writing (Hatfield & Patterson, 1983). Loss of the ability to write phonologically is (again, as with reading) typically subdivided into phonological dysgraphia (Shallice, 1981) and deep dysgraphia (Bub & Kertesz, 1982), depending on the degree of intactness of real-word writing and its sensitivity to variables such as word concreteness.

As in most aspects of research on reading and writing, studies of rehabilitation for impairments of writing are less common than those of reading; only three could be found in the literature that fitted the general approach of this review chapter.

## STUDIES OF TREATMENT FOR ACQUIRED DISORDERS OF READING AND WRITING

### Pure Alexia

Gonzalez-Rothi and Moss (1989) devised a treatment technique for a pure alexic patient on the basis of three theoretical assumptions or principles. Firstly, these authors hypothesised that, at least for some patients with this reading disorder, the deficit is not one of visual letter identification *per se*, but rather of the ability to match perceived letters to stored word knowledge. Secondly, given demonstrations for several pure alexic patients of above-chance performance on word comprehension tasks with stimulus presentation too brief to allow explicit word identification (e.g. Coslett & Saffran, 1989; Shallice & Saffran, 1986), Gonzalez-Rothi and Moss assumed that some word comprehension can be achieved without the word recognition stage of Fig. 19.1, that is, direct from an incompletely specified letter array to meaning. Finally, they suggested (along with Landis, Regard, & Serrat, 1980) that the explicit letter-by-letter (L-by-L) strategy of such patients may in fact inhibit word comprehension activated directly from the letter-array stage. The treatment devised by Gonzalez-Rothi and Moss was designed to disengage the patient's L-by-L strategy and to encourage his direct (even if partial) word comprehension.

The technique involved brief tachistoscopic presentation of letter strings, followed by one of three types of yes-no judgements. In the first task, the presented item was always a homophonic word (e.g. REIGN); the patient was subsequently given a spoken sentence (e.g. "It will rain today"), and asked to judge whether the written and spoken homophones were the same or different. In task 2, the patient was asked to judge whether a printed word (e.g. HORSE) was an instance of a subsequently named category ("Is it an animal?"). In task 3, the letter string was either a word or a nonword (e.g. BLIKE), and the patient was asked to make a lexical decision.

The exposure duration for each task was initially set to yield a maximum of 75% accuracy. The goal of the therapy was both to improve accuracy and to reduce exposure duration. The initially selected duration for each task was reduced during treatment in 50ms steps if the patient's accuracy improved to 90% on three consecutive sessions. Treatment consisted of 20 sessions (2/day, 10/week for 2 weeks).

Table 19.1 shows the patient's accuracy and exposure duration for the three tasks at session 1 and session 20. Accuracy increased in all three tasks, though only in task 2 was the improvement large and stable enough to permit a reduction of exposure duration.

TABLE 19.1
Results of Treatment by Gonzalez-Rothi and Moss (1989) for a Pure Alexic Disorder

| | *Task* | | |
|---|---|---|---|
| | *1* | *2* | *3* |
| Accuracy | | | |
| Pre-treatment | 72% | 71% | 57% |
| Session 20 | 100 | 90 | 90 |
| Exposure Duration | | | |
| Pre-treatment | 450ms | 500ms | 500ms |
| Session 20 | 450 | 400 | 500 |

Examples from the three yes/no judgement tasks:
TASK 1: Visually presented REIGN: Same word as in spoken sentence "It will rain today"?
TASK 2: Visually presented HORSE: Is it an animal?
TASK 3: Visually presented BLIKE: Is it a word?

How did Gonzalez-Rothi and Moss evaluate the more general effects of their treatment on the patient's reading ability? Pre-treatment, his word naming had been accurate but very slow; for example, he required two minutes to name a list of 10 words. Post-treatment, they were able to show that his word-naming speed had improved by an average of 21%. This sounds like a significant gain, and is certainly a major step in the right direction. It is however difficult to evaluate therapeutic effectiveness in clinical terms (usefulness to the patient). Moody (1988) makes this point in assessing the improvement of reading speed (measured in syllables/second in oral reading of text) in a pure alexic patient whom she treated with a technique developed by Moyer (1979). At the beginning of treatment, the patient was given a novel text (passage 1) for timed oral reading. He then practised reading this same text aloud at home for 20 minutes each day. At the end of a week, the patient was timed in reading both passage 1 (practised) and passage 2 (novel); this procedure carried on for 15 weeks, with one old and one new text being assessed each week. Although the patient's speed on both measures improved from the beginning to the end of treatment (see Table 19.2), Moody concluded that this improvement was more

TABLE 19.2
Results of Treatment by Moody (1988) for a Pure Alexic Disorder, using the Moyer Technique of Practised Text Reading

| | *Speed in syllables/second* | |
|---|---|---|
| | *Novel* | *Practised* |
| Text 1 | 0.18 | 0.25 |
| Text 15 | 0.52 | 0.74 |

statistically than clinically significant (my own very informal measurements suggest that a normal reader manages about 5 syllables/sec on novel text, a far cry from the patient's speed even on practised text).

To the extent that one can generalise from two cases of treatment, it appears that pure alexic patients who are slow (though not particularly inaccurate) in recognising letters and words can, via two quite different forms of treatment, achieve a measurable improvement in speed. It is unclear whether, when Gonzalez-Rothi and Moss (1989) and Moody (1988) stopped treating their patients, the improvements obtained amounted to the improvements obtainable, or whether further treatment might eventually have achieved reading speeds approaching normal.

One final set of observations about more severely alexic patients suggests that the 'trajectory' of improvement following treatment is not always what one might expect. Wilson (1987) treated two alexic patients who were certainly not typical L-by-L readers because their letter recognition skills were too poor to support L-by-L reading. These patients were trained on letter recognition, in one case by re-teaching the sounds of letters (this patient is also discussed in Wilson & Patterson, 1990), in the other case by a combination of visual discrimination and letter sounding. As these two patients improved enough to begin to read some words, both turned out to be (or turned into) surface dyslexic readers. This point will be mentioned again in the discussion.

## Surface Dyslexia and Dysgraphia

The treatment of a surface dyslexic patient by Coltheart and Byng (1989) probably represents the most thorough, and also the most explicitly cognitive, rehabilitation study in the area of written language skills. This is because, before deciding on a treatment technique, the authors took several other steps. First, they identified three different stages in a cognitive model at which abnormality of function might give rise to a surface dyslexic pattern of reading. In the terms of Fig. 19.1, these stages are word recognition, word comprehension, and the retrieval of phonological word forms (pronunciation). Coltheart and Byng then carried out tests specifically designed to determine which of these alternative deficits was responsible for this particular patient's surface dyslexia.

A phonological form deficit? No. Although the patient (E.E.) did have problems with retrieving spoken word forms in tasks other than oral reading (e.g. object naming), the authors argued that this could not be the main source of his surface dyslexia, for the following reason: it was rarely the case that E.E. understood a written word but failed to name it correctly; if he misnamed a written word, usually he also misunderstood it.

A comprehension deficit? No. E.E. had adequate comprehension of spoken words, and on the (rather standard) assumption that spoken and written words are merely two different forms of input to a common semantic system, this would seem to rule out a comprehension deficit as the primary source of E.E.'s surface dyslexia.

A written word recognition deficit? Yes. Coltheart and Byng drew this conclusion not just because it was the sole remaining alternative, but also due to E.E.'s frequent errors in comprehension of a particular kind of written word, namely homophones. Suppose that a patient defines the written word TAIL as a story and/or the written word TALE as the thing at the back of an animal (as E.E. was prone to do). Then, according to Coltheart and Byng, it is clear that the patient is comprehending those words by the following stages in Fig. 19.1: letter identification, translation of orthography to phonology, pronunciation, word comprehension. The source of impairment, then, must be in written word recognition (or perhaps access from it to word comprehension).

Coltheart and Byng thus concluded that any attempt to improve E.E.'s reading should be specifically targeted at the stage of visual word recognition, and their chosen technique paired written words with pictures and various other mnemonics that would enable E.E. to associate a particular orthographic form with the correct meaning. Table 19.3 shows the results of two (of several) studies based on this procedure. The first study focused on words such as BOUGH, ROUGH, COUGH, THROUGH, etc; the spelling pattern -OUGH is one of the most inconsistent in the English orthography, and surface dyslexic patients are predictably stumped by it. Twenty four words containing this spelling pattern were selected and, following a test to assess E.E.'s pre-treatment naming of these words, were divided into two sets. In the first treatment phase, E.E. was trained on group-1 words only; Table 19.3 demonstrates that two weeks of this therapy resulted in perfect performance on the treated words and also noticeable improvement on the untreated -OUGH words. In the second phase, group-2 words were treated and, by the end of that phase, E.E. named all 24 -OUGH words correctly. Furthermore, when re-assessed a year later, this perfect performance had been maintained.

The other treatment study summarised in Table 19.3 was not restricted to a particular spelling pattern causing difficulty for E.E. but simply included all of the items that he had previously misnamed from a list of words with frequencies of occurrence between 100 and 200 per

TABLE 19.3
Results of Treatment by Coltheart and Byng (1989) for a Surface Dyslexic Disorder

*Study 1* (24 -OUGH words): Number correct

| | *Pre-test* | *Group 1 words treated* | | *Group 2 words treated* | |
|---|---|---|---|---|---|
| | *Week 1* | *Week 2* | *Week 3* | *Week 4* | *Week 5* |
| Group 1 words | 4/11 | 7/11 | 12/12 | 11/12 | 12/12 |
| Group 2 words | 1/12 | 3/12 | 7/12 | 9/12 | 12/12 |

*Study 3* (101 mis-named words in frequency range 100-200/million): Proportion correct

| | *Pre-treatment* | | *Post-treatment* | |
|---|---|---|---|---|
| | *Test 1* | *Test 2* | *Test 1* | *Test 2* |
| Treated words | 0.45 | 0.63 | 1.00 | 0.96 |
| Untreated words | 0.48 | 0.52 | 0.78 | 0.70 |

million. The outcome was identical to study 1 in two respects: (a) performance on treated words became virtually error-free; (b) the benefits of treatment generalised to untreated words: performance on these, although not as good as on the treated words, was significantly altered as a result of therapy. The issue of generalisation will be taken up further in the discussion.

The strategy of identifying a patient's specific underlying impairment in the context of a cognitive model and then attempting to direct treatment at that specific processing function is, of course, the hallmark of the cognitive neuropsychological approach to rehabilitation. This approach is often advocated (e.g. Howard & Patterson, 1989; Mitchum & Berndt, 1990), but there are as yet few actual examples of it in the literature. Thus Coltheart and Byng's (1989) study is cognitive neuropsychological rehabilitation at its (existing) best. Even better (though, at least to my knowledge, not presently existing) would be the following strategy: having hypothesised that surface dyslexia can arise from deficits at each of three 'locations', Coltheart and Byng might have specified what treatment technique would be most appropriate to each of the three alternatives. Then, despite their conclusion that E.E.'s deficit was at the level of word recognition, they might have treated him (with three different sets of materials) using each of these techniques. If the one putatively directed at the stage of word recognition produced the most benefit, we would have some convincing support for the author's analysis either of E.E.'s deficit or of the link between it and the treatment (or both). When it is such hard work to evaluate the effects of even one technique, we should scarcely be surprised not to see such treatment-comparison studies. However, the link between deficit and treatment is often rather loose, and almost always intuitive; for example, in what sense can Coltheart and Byng's technique of indicating meaning for written words be said to affect word recognition as opposed to word comprehension? Eventually, therefore, treatment comparisons will be needed to achieve progress beyond the intuitive stage.

Another study of treatment for surface dyslexia, by Scott and Byng (1989), tackled the patient's problem with comprehension of homophones. Like E.E. (Coltheart & Byng), J.B. (Scott & Byng) frequently misunderstood a homophonic word as its mate; for example, she defined the written word VAIN as "veins and arteries", LYNX as "in your clothes ... jewellery as well", and FINED as "we went all over to find her". The treatment devised by Scott and Byng required J.B. to select the correct (homophonic) orthographic form, from one of six alternatives, to complete 136 sentences. For the sentence THE LADIES SERVED CREAM— , the six randomly ordered alternatives consisted of the correct word (TEAS), its homophonic word mate (TEASE), a homophonic nonword (TEEZE) and three orthographically similar word foils (TENS, TEAM, TENSE). Treatment took place over 29 sessions, during which J.B. was given feedback about the correctness of each of her choices. During treatment, J.B.'s accuracy in the completion task climbed steadily from about 70% correct choices to nearly perfect; furthermore, the time required for her to perform the task dropped steadily from a very slow speed of about 20 seconds/sentence at the beginning of therapy to around 3 seconds at the end.

J.B.'s overall performance, before and after the therapy programme, was assessed by a sentence sorting task: each of 270 homophonic words (135 pairs, half assigned to the treated set and half assigned to the control set) was embedded in both an appropriate sentence and an inappropriate sentence (e.g. *The angry child bawled at the top of her voice; The man with no hair is bawled)*, and J.B. was requested to sort these 540 sentences into correct and incorrect sets. From pre- to post-therapy, there was a highly significant improvement in her performance on the sentences containing treated words, and also a significant (though numerically smaller) improvement on the untreated items. Although significant generalisation occurred across items, Scott and Byng did not find generalisation from the reading domain to the spelling domain. As a surface dysgraphic as well as a surface dyslexic, J.B. made many errors in writing homophonic words to dictation (of course these were disambiguated for her by a sentence context); following therapy, her error rate on the homophonic writing assessment had not changed significantly, even on those words that had been amongst the set treated for reading comprehension.

Behrmann (1987), in a study paralleling the treatments just described for surface dyslexia, trained a surface dysgraphic patient C.C.M. on the written production of homophonic words like RIGHT - WRITE - RITE. Being surface dysgraphic, C.C.M. had no problem in producing a plausible spelling for the phonological form /rait/ but rather in achieving the particular spelling appropriate to a given lexical/semantic context. Therefore Behrmann used various techniques, including picture matching and sentence completion, to help C.C.M. to link specific homophonic words to their meanings. Behrmann selected 25 pairs of homophones (e.g. BREAK/BRAKE, BY/BUY, etc.) from a set of 69 pairs on which C.C.M. was originally tested; in the pre-treatment testing, C.C.M. had incorrectly spelled either both or at least one of the members of each of these 25 pairs. Training was administered on the homophones as pairs, to focus C.C.M.'s attention on the difference between the precise spelling patterns of BREAK and BRAKE, FOR and FOUR, and so on.

This procedure produced a significant improvement in C.C.M.'s writing of homophonic words, from 49% of the whole set of 138 words (69 pairs) pretreatment to 67% post-therapy. Two other features of the effects of C.C.M.'s therapy warrant comment. Firstly, as well as an improvement in accuracy, Behrmann found a change in the pattern of C.C.M.'s errors after the treatment programme: whereas pre-treatment the patient had produced many phonologically plausible nonword spellings as well as (the largest error category) productions of the opposite member of the homophone pair, post-treatment C.C.M.'s errors were almost exclusively homophonic words rather than nonwords. Secondly, unlike the results discussed above from the treatments for surface dyslexia by Coltheart and Byng (1989) and Scott and Byng (1989), Behrmann did not find significant item generalisation: C.C.M.'s writing performance on the untreated homophones did not improve from pre- to post-therapy. Somewhat puzzlingly however, the patient's writing of 75 words with an irregular correspondence between phonology and orthography (e.g. COMB, DOUBT, etc) was significantly better after than before the homophone therapy. This study therefore yields a mixed picture regarding the issue of generalisation across items, though Behrmann emphasises that homophones appear to require word-specific remediation.

## Deep Dyslexia and Dysgraphia

As indicated earlier in the brief summary on various patterns of acquired reading disorder, deep dyslexic patients appear to have lost the ability to translate directly from orthography to phonology. In her treatment programme, De Partz (1986) set out to re-teach this knowledge, in the form of associations between graphemes and phonemes, to the deep dyslexic patient S.P. It would come as no surprise to many researchers concerned with reading acquisition (e.g. Morais,

Cary, Alegria, & Bertelson, 1979) that, in order to accomplish manipulations involving individual phonemes, S.P. had to re-learn certain basic skills often summarised under the term "phonological awareness". Thus, after establishing a standard link word for each written letter of the alphabet (e.g. A → "Allo", B → "Bebe", C → "Carole", etc.), De Partz taught S.P. to segment the initial phoneme from each spoken link word. The sequence from the letter A to the spoken word "Allo" and thence to the single phoneme /a/ should (and did, in S.P.'s case) eventually enable the direct association A → /a/. After S.P. had mastered grapheme-phoneme correspondences for individual letters, De Partz trained him to blend individual phonemes into simple words and nonwords. Finally she tackled the problem that single phonemes sometimes correspond to letter sequences rather than single letters, by use of various mnemonics: for example, S.P. was taught to associate the letter sequence AU with the meaningful word "eau". At the end of these four stages of treatment, requiring nine months of intensive work, S.P.'s word naming had improved significantly on all word classes (see Table 19.4).

It is interesting to note the almost perfect parallel between the rehabilitation devised by De Partz for deep dyslexia in an alphabetic writing system and a rehabilitation programme devised by Monoi and Sasanuma (see Sasanuma, 1980) for acquired disorders in reading the Japanese syllabic/phonetic script, kana. It seems likely that this programme should be even more efficacious for Japanese kana than for the French or English alphabet, because individual characters of written kana correspond to morae of spoken Japanese (roughly speaking, morae are syllables, almost all CV or plain V). Therefore the crucial stage of the therapy programme where the patient must re-learn to segment words into component sounds only requires segmentation at the level of the syllable; and syllables form an easier unit for segmentation than

TABLE 19.4
Results of Treatment by De Partz (1986) for a Deep Dyslexic Disorder

| | % correct | |
|---|---|---|
| | *Pre* | *Post* |
| *Part of Speech* (N = 10 each) | | |
| Nouns | 50 | 90 |
| Adjectives | 20 | 80 |
| Verbs (infinitive) | 10 | 100 |
| Verbs (conjugated) | 0 | 40 |
| Adverbs | 10 | 70 |
| Prepositions | 0 | 100 |
| Pronouns | 0 | 80 |
| Nonwords (N = 20) | 0 | 90 |

phonemes (e.g. Mann, 1986). Furthermore kana, with its highly predictable print-sound relationships, does not suffer from the complications of the French and English writing system, namely the frequent irregularities and context sensitivities of print-sound correspondences.

The force of these complexities can be seen in the fact that, as a result of the treatment described above, S.P. became a surface dyslexic reader; in any writing system with one-to-many mappings between letters and sounds, a *successful* training programme based on one-to-one mappings is virtually guaranteed to produce this outcome. In French (as in English), C is pronounced /k/ if it is followed by the vowel A or O but /s/ if the succeeding vowel is E; thus the function word CELLE has the pronunciation /sel/. Before his treatment, the deep dyslexic patient S.P. was unable to produce any oral reading response to the word CELLE; after therapy in which he learned the sequence C → "Carole" → /k/, the surface dyslexic patient S.P. named the word CELLE as /kel/. Thus De Partz had to extend S.P.'s basic four stages of treatment with instruction about the context-sensitive pronunciations of certain letters, a technique appropriate for surface dyslexia.

In a research field as young as cognitive rehabilitation, attempts at replication are rare; but they are of course important, mainly for the standard scientific goal of establishing a body of reliable phenomena, but also for another reason. As emphasised repeatedly in recent literature on cognitive neuropsychology, the relationship of deficits to symptoms in patients (like that of graphemes to phonemes in English) is not a one-to-one mapping. The ways in which reading can be symptomatically impaired are rather limited (at least when considered in some summarised, coherent form rather than a complete listing of each patient's responses); but the possible underlying impairments giving rise to these symptoms are more numerous and graded. For example, patients A and B may be described as deep dyslexics because both fail in nonword naming and make semantic errors in real-word naming; but their anatomical and functional lesions may well be different. Thus it is by no means guaranteed that the same rehabilitation techniques will be effective for both (Wilson, 1987). If the technique shown to help patient A is applied to patient B, successful replication increases one's confidence in the usefulness of the treatment; but a failure to replicate may also be theoretically informative in highlighting differences in impairment between the superficially similar cases.

This point is well illustrated in an application of the De Partz (1986) rehabilitation programme to a study of a deep dyslexic patient by Nickels (1992). Before treatment, T.C. was unable to name any novel words (nonwords) and, despite showing the imageability effect in word reading characteristic of all deep dyslexic patients, was actually rather more impaired at naming high imageability words than S.P. (see Table 19.5). In therapy, he mastered the first two stages of De Partz's programme successfully; then, despite all efforts on the therapist's part, T.C. failed totally at stage 3, phoneme blending. If a patient can produce the individual phonemes for a simple nonword but cannot blend them into a single spoken syllable, then his nonword naming score will remain zero (as shown post-therapy for T.C. in Table 19.5).

Why then did the treatment lead to a marked increase in T.C.'s naming of high imageability words? The answer is that initial-phoneme cuing helped T.C.'s word naming, and as a result of stages 1 and 2 of his rehabilitation programme, he was able to produce his *own* initial phoneme cues in reading. The same cuing phenomenon (combined with the fact that T.C. was significantly better at producing written than spoken names for objects or pictures) accounts for the beneficial effect of the therapy on his spoken picture naming: given a picture to name aloud, he could often (internally) produce its written name, then use the technique learned in therapy to provide himself with the initial phoneme that could serve as a phonemic cue to oral naming.

In summary, when the therapy technique that had worked well with S.P. (De Partz, 1986) was administered to T.C. (Nickels, 1992), in one sense it failed completely (no improvement in T.C.'s ability to name novel words) due to a difference between the two patients in basic impairments. In another sense, the treatment worked well for T.C. (a significant improvement in word naming); but even the benefit experienced by the two patients requires different accounts. Further discussion of the efficacy of this rehabilitation programme can be found in the chapter by Mitchum and Berndt in this volume.

TABLE 19.5
Results of Treatment by Nickels (1992) for a Deep Dyslexic Disorder

| | *Proportion Correct* | | |
|---|---|---|---|
| | *Pre [12/88]* | *Post 1 [4/89]* | *Post 2 [9/89]* |
| Word Reading | | | |
| Hi Imag | 0.28 | 0.70 | 0.55 |
| Lo Imag | 0.00 | 0.05 | 0.13 |
| Nonword Reading | 0.00 | 0.00 | 0.00 |
| Picture Naming | | | |
| Spoken | 0.12 | 0.62 | 0.58 |
| Written | 0.65 | 0.78 | 0.78 |

Hatfield (1982; 1983) utilised a rather different approach to ameliorating some of the deficits in three patients with deep dyslexia/dysgraphia. Her technique, which she applied particularly in the writing domain, bears more resemblance to stage 4 of De Partz' programme than to stages 1-3: that is, Hatfield tried to exploit some of the patients' retained knowledge rather than re-teaching impaired procedures. As is typical in deep dyslexia/dysgraphia, Hatfield's patients had a particularly severe deficit in producing function words like prepositions and auxiliary verbs. Recall that in stage 4, De Partz used S.P.'s knowledge of the word EAU as a link to the pronunciation of the letter combination AU. Similarly, Hatfield used her deep dysgraphic patients' retained knowledge of the spelling of certain content words (e.g. INN and BEAN) as a strategy to help them produce the orthographically similar function words IN and BEEN. Function words were selected for treatment on the basis of one or both of two criteria: (1) words that seemed particularly useful to the patients (locative prepositions such as IN and ON, pronouns such as HIM, etc.), and (2) function words such as BEEN with an obvious content-word mate (BEAN) to serve as the link word. Link words were chosen individually for, and in consultation with, each patient.

Following establishment of the link words, therapy sessions consisted of the patients first writing the content link word, and then attempting to produce the corresponding function word (from dictation of a sentence containing the function word). In the third "direct" stage, the patients were not required (though they were always encouraged, if it helped) to engage in explicit use of the link words on the way to writing the target function words. These therapeutic procedures yielded somewhat variable results across the three deep dysgraphic patients; best results, for patient B.B., showed an improvement from 34% to 64% correct for a set of 18 function words. For patients with severe and multi-modality agrammatism, as Hatfield comments (1983, p.166), "Improvement, rather than mastery, would be a more realistic aim". Although this rehabilitation study is perhaps not the most rigorous in terms of some of the features that later research has incorporated (e.g. comparing treated vs. untreated items and/or tasks), it deserves mention here because Hatfield was one of the pioneers of this approach to treatment; a number of subsequent rehabilitation studies acknowledge her influence (e.g. De Partz, 1986). A sophisticated use of the link-word (or "lexical relay") technique can be found in the treatment of an Italian patient with a severe dysgraphia (Carlomagno & Parlato, 1989).

## CONCLUDING REMARKS

Given the infancy of cognitive neuropsychological rehabilitation, this review could not hope to be more than an interim reckoning: we will need many more individual studies, followed by attempts to find key recurring features across the individual studies, before we can begin to reckon up the practical benefits of this sort of rehabilitation and the theoretical benefits of this sort of rehabilitation research. Even at this early stage, however, it could be argued that a few general points are emerging from the specific findings. With regard to practical benefits, one can at least point to a number of significant (and in some cases, long-lasting) changes for the better in the treated patients' performance. A number of the effective treatment methods mentioned in this review took place many years after the patient's brain insult, years during which the patient had often received considerable amounts of therapy of one sort or another. Although rigorous comparisons of different therapy techniques are virtually non-existent, the success of treatment inspired by cognitive analysis in the absence of significant change consequent upon other techniques at least suggests that cognitive neuropsychological rehabilitation may be on to something.

With regard to theoretical implications, I would like to conclude with three points of a somewhat more speculative nature.

1. Table 19.6 lists instances, from the studies reviewed above, of both positive and negative answers to two questions about generalisation of treatment effects: Namely, is there generalisation across items (from treated to untreated words) and is there generalisation across tasks (from reading to writing or vice versa)? Whether one observes these two types of generalisation is of some consequence. This is of course true in a practical sense, because the therapist always hopes that the benefit of treatment will extend beyond the necessarily limited set of items practised in therapy (although, as was pointed out in discussion at the meeting of the book, such generalised benefit is not a pre-requisite for considering the treatment a success: if the therapist selects to-be-treated items that are of particular utility to the patient, improved performance restricted to those items may be well worth achieving). It is also true in a theoretical sense. Very different predictions about generalisation across words are made by theories that assume that individual words have discrete, local representations in the brain and by theories which contrastingly assume that words are represented by interconnected micro-features shared by many different words (for further discussion of this point, see Coltheart & Byng, 1989; Hinton, McClelland & Rumelhart, 1986; Patterson, 1990; Wilson & Patterson,

TABLE 19.6
Generalisation of Treatment Effects

| | | |
|---|---|---|
| 1. | *From treated to untreated items (words): relevant to issue of localist vs. distributed representations* | |
| | YES | Coltheart & Byng, 1989 |
| | | Scott & Byng, 1989 |
| | NO | Behrmann, 1987 |
| 2. | *From treated to untreated task (reading to writing or vice versa): relevant to issue of shared vs. separate procedures for reading/writing* | |
| | YES | Carlomagno & Parlato (1989) |
| | NO | Scott & Byng (1989) |

1990). Likewise, predictions about generalisation between reading and writing will depend on whether one's theory assumes, for example, that the orthographic representations underlying word recognition in reading and word production in writing are different or the same. Table 19.6 is not meant to offer a conclusion about either of these generalisation issues; indeed it could not do, given the small number of studies, not to mention differences amongst them in both procedure and outcome. Table 19.6 is included merely to highlight one way in which rehabilitation studies can make a unique contribution to theoretical issues.

2. Table 19.7 lists my summary of various issues or controversies that have recently characterised research on reading, both normal and impaired. There has been no attempt to make this list exhaustive, nor do I claim that it presents a clear or balanced view of this research field. The aim of Table 19.7 is merely to convey some of the detailed complexities exercising the minds of reading researchers. Compare this with Table 19.8, which lists my summary of the main types of treatment that have been applied to disorders of reading. There is, of course, an element of comparing chalk and cheese here; but I suggest that some of the lack of integration between theory and therapy (to which I drew attention in the introduction of this chapter) may derive from the startling difference in the questions addressed by typical theoretical and therapeutic research. If a theorist is doing experiments to inquire about inter-letter redundancies and a therapist is doing experiments where patients practise judging that a horse is an animal, perhaps it is not surprising if the common ground between them tends to appear meagre (Wilson & Patterson, 1990).

By the way, this contrast is not necessarily meant to favour the theoreticians. The treatment techniques in Table 19.8 may tend to look rather simplistic; but it is quite possible that Table 19.7 with all its complexity represents theorists' brains reflecting on reading processes

TABLE 19.7
A Sample of Theoretical Controversies Regarding the Nature of Processes and Representations Underlying Reading Skills

*Early Processing in Reading*
- How are letters recognised?
- Does word recognition require (complete) letter identification?
- Does word recognition use word shape?
- Does word recognition use inter-letter redundancies?

*Lexical Access*
- Is lexical access:
  - active/passive?
  - serial/parallel?
- Is there a discrete stage best characterised as lexical access?
- Do representations correspond to words or morphemes?
- Are representations localised or distributed?

*Orthography → Phonology*
- Is there a separate non-lexical routine?
  - If so, what size (or sizes) of unit does it operate on?
- Is there a separate lexical non-semantic routine?

*Orthography → Semantics*
- Is word comprehension ever/always mediated by phonology?
- Are there separate semantic systems for:
  - objects vs. words?
  - concrete vs. abstract words?
  - perceptual vs. conceptual information?

TABLE 19.8
Types of Treatment Utilised in Studies Reviewed in this Chapter

*Letter → Sound*
- Wilson (1987)
- De Partz (1986)
- Nickels (1992)

*Word → Meaning*
- Gonzalez-Rothi & Moss (1989)
- Coltheart & Byng (1989)
- Scott & Byng (1989)
- Behrmann (1987)

*Word via Other Word*
- Hatfield (1982; 1983)
- Carlomagno & Parlato (1989)

*General Practice*
- Wilson (1987)
- Moody (1988)

rather better than it represents readers' brains computing these processes. One of the most important potentials of computational models that learn to perform their computations is that they may reveal complex patterns of performance emerging from simple learning algorithms.

3. Finally, ending on a lighter note, it sometimes seems as if all paths lead to surface dyslexia and dysgraphia. For example, (1) as I commented earlier, patients treated for various other forms of acquired reading disorder sometimes evolve into surface dyslexics (e.g. De Partz, 1986; Wilson, 1987). (2) Patients with severe comprehension disorders typically become surface dyslexic and dysgraphic (e.g. Bub, Cancelliere, & Kertesz, 1985; McCarthy & Warrington, 1986). (3) Perfectly normal children learning to read and write make errors typical of surface dyslexia and dysgraphia. A 6-year-old child of my acquaintance has already learned a lot about writing but displays imperfect grasp of the context sensitivities of English (e.g. the fact that the sound /k/ must be represented by the letter K rather than the letter C in certain contexts); thus, in a letter where he wanted to express affection for someone, he wrote I LICE YOU. This spelling error is perhaps just a more amusing reminder than the other observations mentioned above that, even in a "quasi-regular" (Seidenberg & McClelland, 1989) alphabetic system like English, statistical regularities are powerful and always lurking in the background.

## REFERENCES


Beauvois, M. F., & Derouesne, J. (1981). Lexical or orthographic agraphia. *Brain, 104*, 21-49.

Beauvois, M. F., & Derouesne, J. (1982). Recherche en neuropsychologie et reeducation: Quels rapports? In X. Seron & C. Laterre (Eds.), *Reeduquer le Cerveau*. Brussels: Mardaga.

Behrmann, M. (1987). The rites of righting writing: homophone remediation in acquired dysgraphia. *Cognitive Neuropsychology, 4*, 365-384.

Bub, D, Cancelliere, A., & Kertesz, A. (1985). Whole-word and analytic translation of spelling to sound in a non-semantic reader. In K. E. Patterson, J. C. Marshall & M. Coltheart (Eds.), *Surface dyslexia*. London: Lawrence Erlbaum Associates Ltd.

Bub, D., & Kertesz, A. (1982). Deep agraphia. *Brain and Language, 17*, 146-165.

Byng, S. (1988). Sentence processing deficits in aphasia: theory and therapy. *Cognitive Neuropsychology, 5*, 629-676.

Carlomagno, S., & Parlato, V. (1989). Writing rehabilitation in brain-damaged adult patients: a cognitive approach. In X. Seron, & S. Deloche (Eds.), *Cognitive approaches in neuropsychological rehabilitation*. Hillsdale, N.J.: Lawrence Erlbaum Associates Inc.

Coltheart, M., & Byng, S. (1989). A treatment for surface dyslexia. In X. Seron & G. Deloche (Eds.), *Cognitive approaches in neuropsychological rehabilitation*. Hillsdale, N.J.: Lawrence Erlbaum Associates Inc.

Coltheart, M., & Funnell, E. (1987). Reading and writing: One lexicon or two? In D. A. Allport, D. G. MacKay, W. Prinz, & E. Scheerer (Eds.), *Language Perception and Production: Shared Mechanisms in listening, reading and writing*. London: Academic Press.

Coltheart, M., Patterson, K., & Marshall, J. C. (1987). Deep dyslexia since 1980. In M. Coltheart, K. Patterson & J. C. Marshall (Eds.). *Deep dyslexia*, (2nd edition). London: Routledge and Kegan Paul.

Coslett, H. B., & Saffran, E. M. (1989). Evidence for preserved reading in 'pure alexia'. *Brain, 112,* 327-359.

De Partz, M. (1986). Reeducation of a deep dyslexic patient: Rationale of the method and results. *Cognitive Neuropsychology, 3,* 149-177.

Ellis, A. W., & Young, A. W. (1988). *Human cognitive neuropsychology*. London: Lawrence Erlbaum Associates Ltd.

Farah, M. J., & Wallace, M. A. (1991). Pure alexia as a visual impairment: A reconsideration. *Cognitive Neuropsychology, 8,* 313-334.

Gonzalez-Rothi, L. J., & Moss, S. (1989). *Alexia without agraphia: A model driven therapy*. Paper presented at the Academy of Aphasia. Santa Fe, New Mexico, October 1989.

Hatfield, F. M., (1982). Diverses forms de desintegration du langage écrit et implications pour la reeducation. In X. Seron & C. Laterre (Eds.), *Reeduquer le Cerveau*. Brussels: Mardaga.

Hatfield, F. M. (1983). Aspects of acquired dysgraphia and implications for reeducation. In C. Code & D. J. Müller (Eds.), *Aphasia therapy*. London: Edward Arnold.

Hatfield, F. M., & Patterson, K. (1983). Phonological spelling. *Quarterly Journal of Experimental Psychology, 35A,* 451-468.

Hinton, G. E., McClelland, J. L., & Rumelhart, D. E. (1986). Distributed representations. In D. E. Rumelhart & J. L. McClelland (Eds.), *Parallel distributed processing,* Vol 1. Cambridge, Mass: MIT Press.

Howard, D. (1991). Letter-by-letter reading: evidence for parallel processing. In D. Besner & G. W. Humphreys (Eds.), *Basic processes in reading: Visual word recognition*. Hillsdale, N.J.: Lawrence Erlbaum Associates Inc.

Howard, D., & Patterson, K. (1989). Models for therapy. In X. Seron & G. Deloche (Eds.), *Cognitive approaches in neuropsychological rehabilitation*. Hillsdale, N.J.: Lawrence Erlbaum Associates Inc.

Landis, T., Regard, M., & Serrat, A. (1980). Iconic reading in a case of alexia without agraphia caused by a brain tumor: A tachistoscopic study. *Brain & Language, 11,* 45-53.

McCarthy, R., & Warrington, E. K. (1986). Phonological reading: phenomena and paradoxes. *Cortex, 22,* 359-380.

Mann, V. A. (1986). Phonological awareness: The role of reading experience. *Cognition, 24,* 65-92.

Mitchum, C. C., & Berndt, R. S. (1988). Aphasia rehabilitation: an approach to diagnosis and treatment of disorders of language production. In M. G. Eisenberg (Ed.), *Advances in clinical rehabilitation*. New York: Springer.

Moody, S. (1988). The Moyer reading technique re-evaluated. *Cortex, 24,* 473-476.

Morais, J., Cary, L., Alegria, J., & Bertelson, P. (1979). Does awareness of speech as a sequence of phones arise spontaneously? *Cognition, 7,* 323-331.

Moyer, S. B. (1979). Rehabilitation of alexia: A case study. *Cortex, 15,* 139-144.

Nickels, L. (1992). The autocue? Self-generated phonemic cues in the treatment of a disorder of reading and naming. *Cognitive Neuropsychology, 9,* 155-182.

Patterson, K. (1981). Neuropsychological approaches to the study of reading. *British Journal of Psychology, 72,* 151-174.

Patterson, K. (1990). Alexia and neural nets. *Japanese Journal of Neuropsychology, 6,* 90-99.

Price, C. J. (1990). *Simultanagnosia, letter-by-letter reading and attentional deficits in reading.* Unpublished PhD thesis, University of London.

Sasanuma, S. (1980). A therapy program for impairment of the use of the kana-syllabary of Japanese aphasic patients. In M. Taylor Sarno & O. Hook (Eds.), *Aphasia: Assessment and treatment.* Stockholm: Almqvist & Wiksell.

Scott, C., & Byng, S. (1989). Computer assisted remediation of a homophone comprehension disorder in surface dyslexia. *Aphasiology, 3,* 301-320.

Seidenberg, M. S., & McClelland, J. L. (1989). A distributed, developmental model of word recognition and naming. *Psychological Review, 96,* 523-568.

Shallice, T. (1981). Phonological agraphia and the lexical route in writing. *Brain, 104,* 413-429.

Shallice, T., & Saffran, E. (1986). Lexical processing in the absence of explicit word identification: Evidence from a letter-by-letter reader. *Cognitive Neuropsychology, 3,* 429-458.

Wilson, B. A. (1987). *Rehabilitation of memory.* New York: Guilford.

Wilson, B. A., & Patterson, K. (1990). Rehabilitation for cognitive impairment: Does cognitive psychology apply? *Applied Cognitive Psychology, 4,* 247-260.

CHAPTER TWENTY

# Theories of Lexical Processing and Rehabilitation of Lexical Deficits

Argye E. Hillis and Alfonso Caramazza
*Cognitive Science Center, Johns Hopkins University, Baltimore, Maryland, USA*

## ABSTRACT

A series of single-subject studies of brain-damaged patients who each make semantic errors in naming is presented. A cognitive analysis of performance in each case provides evidence for proposing relatively selective impairment to one or more components of lexical processing. Studies of the effectiveness of treatment for these patients indicate that some patients with the same putative locus of impairment require different treatments, and some patients with different loci of impairment respond to the same treatment. Three forms of the "diagnosis"/treatment relationship are illustrated: (1) two very different treatment approaches are equally appropriate with respect to a given locus of damage, but individual patients respond differentially to the two approaches; (2) a given treatment strategy is equally appropriate for multiple levels of disruption, although different components of the treatment may affect separate levels of processing; and (3) one strategy is appropriate for one level of damage, and a different strategy is required for a different level of damage. The first two cases are illustrated with multiple baseline (across behaviours) studies to measure the effects of intervention on treated and untreated naming tasks. Each therapy was sequentially applied to various tasks or to various sets of stimuli, for two patients using the same stimuli and procedures. We use the contrasting results of therapy for patients who presumably had the same loci of damage as a basis for addressing recent claims about the role of cognitive neuropsychological theories in developing and evaluating treatment strategies. Specifically, we examine models of lexical tasks with respect to predictions regarding the effects of particular interventions that follow from postulating a specific locus of disruption, and we consider the extent to which results of treatment for a given patient bear out predictions concerning whether or not the intervention will facilitate performance of other individuals with the same hypothesised impairment. We conclude by discussing the potential relevance of cognitive neuropsychological theories for the development and/or evaluation of a theory of rehabilitation—i.e. how cognitive processes are altered in response to specific interventions.

## INTRODUCTION

An issue that has received considerable attention in the past several years is the relationship between cognitive theory and rehabilitation of acquired disorders of cognition. Encouraged by cognitive neuropsychology's progress in explaining various forms of cognitive pathology in terms of relatively detailed models of cognitive functioning, various investigators have begun to explore the potential contribution of the results and methods of cognitive neuropsychology for a theoretically-informed therapeutic practice in the neuropsychology clinic (e.g. Behrmann & Herdan, 1987; Byng & Coltheart, 1986; Howard, Patterson, Franklin, Orchard-Lisle, & Morton, 1985b; Mitchum & Berndt, 1988; see also papers in Seron & Deloche, 1989).

This effort has led to the development of "cognitively-oriented" therapeutic interventions which, supposedly, may be distinguished from other forms of therapeutic practice by the fact that the former but not the latter, according to Seron and Deloche (1989, p.1), "... are explicitly based on a model describing the organization of the cognitive apparatus viewed as a complex architecture of at least partially autonomous functional units". Although these are welcome developments, some of the conclusions reached on the basis of these investigations may be premature (see Basso, 1989; Caramazza, 1989; Wilson & Patterson, in press[1], for critical assessments). In fact, Caramazza (1989) has argued that there is no indication in the putative cases of cognitive rehabilitation that the specific therapeutic interventions proposed for a particular patient were constrained to any significant extent by the specific content of the cognitive model used to analyse the patient's deficits. More generally, it is further argued that there is nothing about the structure or content of models of cognitive functioning, and related hypotheses about the nature of cognitive dysfunction in specific patients, which *alone* could serve to motivate specific therapeutic interventions.[2] For the latter purpose, we would need not only a theory of the cognitive mechanisms that subserve a specific cognitive function, and how these may be affected by brain damage, but also, and more importantly, a theory of how a damaged system may be affected by specific therapeutic procedures. The force of these claims may be made explicit by considering the following question in the specific context of remediation strategies for lexical processing deficits: What do we need to know about the structure of lexical processing and the specific form of impairment to the lexical system in a patient in order to plan effective therapy?

It is not obvious to us that there is a clear answer to this question. Suppose that we had a relatively detailed model of lexical processing that specified the identity and arrangement of major components of lexical tasks (such as reading, spelling, and naming). That is, suppose we have a model of the type schematically represented in Fig. 20.1. Let us further suppose that we can pinpoint a patient's impairment as resulting from a single component of this process, say, the phonological output lexicon. What will this knowledge allow us to do? Will it allow us to plan an effective remediation strategy? Surely not. We do not even have reason for supposing that the damaged component can recover function again, once damaged. In fact, we do not even know that "damage to the phonological output lexicon" is a sufficiently detailed characterisation to capture the nature of the impairment. Certainly, damage to the output lexicon might take a variety of forms affecting different aspects of the complex information computed by this component of the process and might occur across a variety of "severity" levels (e.g. from damage affecting only very low frequency lexical representations or only specific categories of representations, to damage affecting all lexical representations). Will the effects of therapy vary as a function of any one of these variables? Will different forms of impairment to the phonological output lexicon require different therapy approaches?

It is important to appreciate that the noted limitations in the role of models of cognitive processing in determining therapeutic practice are not merely the result of limitations of current models of lexical processing. That is, the situation would not be improved if we had more detailed theories of lexical processing. For even if we were to assume that we had the latter theories, we would still have to deal with the independent issue of whether and how the damaged components can recover. Answers to these questions do not depend only on a theory of lexical processing—they depend crucially on complex considerations about the possible changes that a damaged neural system may undergo as a function of stimulation. The latter considerations are outside the scope of cognitive theory. In short, a model of cognitive theory may be a *necessary* component of a theory of rehabilitation but it is not *sufficient*: Information about the functional locus of damage in a cognitive model does not exhaust what needs to be known in order to develop

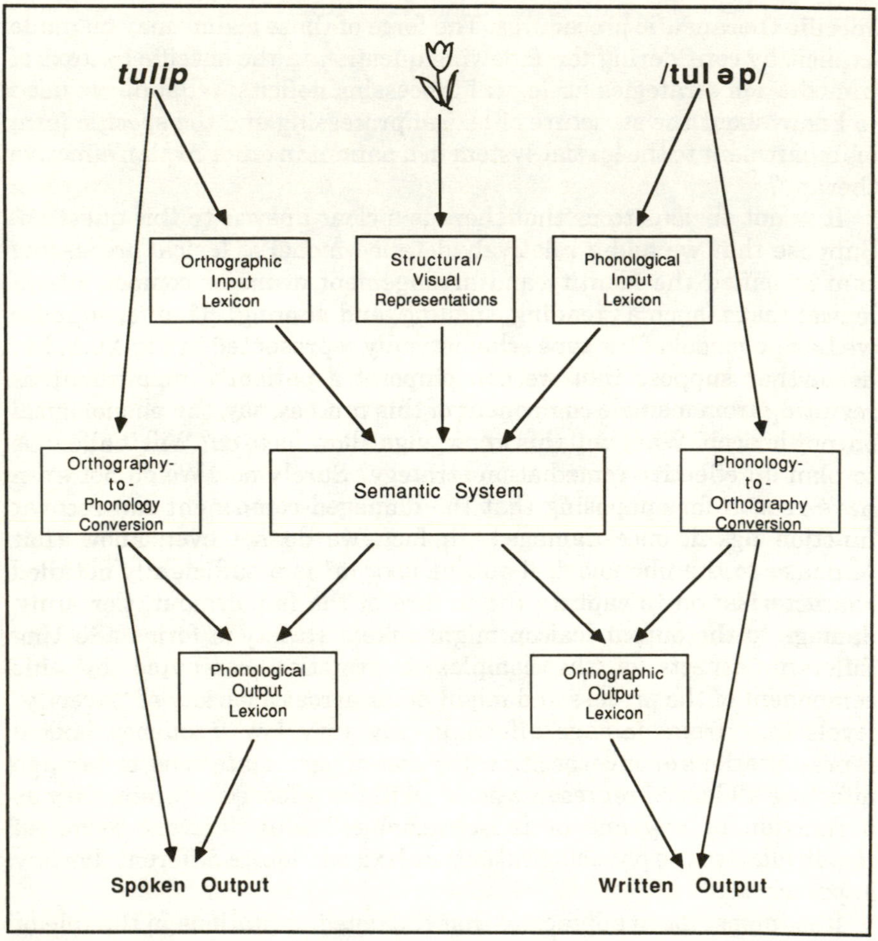


FIG. 20.1. A schematic representation of the cognitive processes involved in lexical tasks.

theoretically motivated therapeutic interventions for cognitively impaired patients.

Although we do not have a theory of rehabilitation, we can discuss the sorts of information that might be important for the development of a rational, model-based treatment of lexical impairments. To begin with, we would need a clear idea of what it is that we are to treat. In this sense, models of normal cognitive functioning play an important role in therapeutic practice. For instance, we would need to know what representations are computed and what transformations take place in the course of a specific lexical task and which of these mechanisms or representations are impaired in the individual patient. But, we would also need to know whether or not the damaged components of the process are subject to remediation. On the unsubstantiated, but probably uncontroversial, view that a given component of the lexical system may be recoverable in one patient but not in another, we would need to know the factors that influence the potential for recovery of that particular component. Such factors might include premorbid characteristics of the patient (e.g. education, intelligence, age), medical history (e.g. type of stroke, time post-onset, concurrent medical problems, previous neurological disease, and possibly site of brain damage), and less easily measurable variables such as motivation, discipline, opportunity for practice and/or training and so on. Moreover, if we were to base treatment for a particular patient on some approach that had been demonstrated to be effective for another patient with damage putatively to the same component of lexical processing, we would need to know what constitutes the "same" impairment. Qualitative or quantitative differences among patients in the form of damage to a particular cognitive mechanism, and variations with respect to the extent of damage to other, untreated mechanisms (i.e. residual skills) might play a role in determining treatment effects. However, many of these factors may turn out to be irrelevant to recovery of a specific skill, and other variables not considered here may turn out to have a marked influence on recovery.

Perhaps even more importantly, we would need to know what therapy *does* to a cognitive system. Does it stimulate a particular region of the brain that is associated with some specific cognitive mechanism? Does therapy lead to the acquisition of new procedures—sequences of transformations of representations that are different from those that take place in non brain-damaged subjects (sometimes referred to as "reorganisation" of a process)? Does it stimulate a region of the brain to "take over" a cognitive process that region did not previously carry out (one form of so-called "re-establishment" of a process)? Not only are we unable to answer these questions, but we also do not know which of the questions are, in fact, crucial to the patient's potential for recovering the impaired lexical processing component with facilitation by specific interventions.

As a starting point for discussing in greater detail the role of cognitive theory in rehabilitation practice, we present as an example a series of patients studied in our laboratory who made semantic errors in naming tasks. We provide evidence that the semantic errors by each patient resulted from impairment to different component(s) of the lexical system, and we present results of treatment strategies that were found to be effective (or ineffective) for each patient. These cases illustrate the following points concerning the potential relationships between "diagnosis" (in terms of a level of disruption) and treatment approaches:

(1) contrasting treatment approaches can be equally appropriate with respect to a given locus of damage (but individual patients respond differentially to the two approaches); (2) a given treatment strategy can be equally appropriate for damage to different components of the lexical system; and (3) in some cases, different strategies are differentially effective for different levels of damage in the naming process. We use these results as a basis for discussing the extent to which treatment results allow predictions concerning whether or not the intervention will facilitate performance on the same task by other patients with the same hypothesised locus of impairment. We conclude that results from the type of study we report cannot serve as the basis for strong predictions concerning the efficacy of treatment for specific cognitive deficits. The goal of presenting these case studies is not to cast doubt on the usefulness of cognitive neuropsychology (or more specifically, a cognitive analysis of the patient's performance) to the practice of rehabilitation. It is more to illustrate that there is not a *simple* relationship between the hypothesised locus of impairment and the intervention that will ultimately prove to be beneficial to the patient. The first set of studies demonstrate that differences between patients (whether in their residual skills, form or severity of functional deficit, etc.) and/or differences with respect to the effect of therapy on the individual's system (say, "reorganisation" vs. "re-establishment") critically influenced the effectiveness of treatment. Unfortunately, the observed patterns of performance (our only source of evidence) cannot serve as the basis for determining which of the many factors were the crucial variables. The last study, however, shows that despite the existence of individual differences and the uncertainties of "how therapy works", in some cases a cognitive analysis can be helpful in guiding the selection of one approach over another to treating a particular symptom.

Following discussion of our own cases, we consider whether or not previous treatment studies in the cognitive neuropsychology literature allow stronger conclusions than our study. We conclude by discussing some of the desired features of a theory of rehabilitation and the potential role of cognitive neuropsychology in developing and evaluating such a theory.

## STUDIES OF THERAPY TO REDUCE SEMANTIC PARAPHASIAS

In this section we present three studies of different treatment strategies for a single patient, H.W. In each study we compare effectiveness of treatment in her case to effectiveness of the same treatment for a patient (or patients) with similar symptoms—semantic errors in naming tasks.

In the first study, results for H.W. are compared to those obtained for two other patients with similar loci of impairment in lexical processing, as indicated by detailed analyses of performance across lexical tasks. In the next two studies, her performance is compared to performance by patients whose semantic errors can be explained by proposing damage to a different cognitive mechanism. In each case, we briefly summarise the analyses of each patient's pattern of performance across lexical tasks, which were used to infer hypotheses about the locus of impairment assumed to be responsible for the patients' errors. The therapeutic strategies that were attempted did not follow *directly* from our model of lexical processing, but followed *intuitively* from the proposed level of disruption as characterized in the model. In each case, an attempt was made either to re-teach components of the process that were not functional (e.g. phonology-to-orthography conversion; POC) or to elicit the functioning of a component on a more consistent basis (e.g. increase consistency of activating particular phonological representations for production of correct names). The techniques are standard for all sorts of therapy: Giving the patient as much help as needed until they produce the target behaviour, and fading assistance until the desired behaviour is produced independently.

## Study 1:
## Contrasting Treatments for Lexical Output Deficits

### *Subjects*

H.W. is a right-handed, 64 year-old female with 1 year of college education, who sustained left parietal and occipital strokes two and a half years before the study. S.J.D. is a 44 year-old, right-handed female, who suffered a left fronto-parietal lobe infarct four years prior to treatment. Both patients have fluent, meaningful and usually grammatical speech (with normal phrase length, intonation and variation in syntactic forms), although both subjects make morphological errors in speech tasks, and H.W. makes many semantic paraphasias. S.J.D. made frequent semantic (and morphological) errors in spontaneous writing (see Badecker & Caramazza, 1991, for detailed discussion of this aspect of the patient's performance). Her written narrative is legible and coherent except for omissions or substitutions of verbs and functions. The responsiveness of these patients to treatment is contrasted briefly with that of P.M. P.M. is a 50 year-old, left-handed, retired college administrator who earned a Ph.D. in English literature. She suffered a left fronto-temporal-parietal and basal ganglia stroke nearly two years before the reported therapy program. Her speech was usually grammatical, but hesitant and slightly slurred. All three of these patients had normal comprehension of single words, but had difficulty with auditory comprehension of syntactically complex sentences only when semantic/pragmatic cues did not support syntactic interpretation (such as semantically reversible sentences like: *The boy was hit by the girl.*)

*Identifying the loci of functional damage*
Initial assessment included administration of the Johns Hopkins University Dyslexia and Dysgraphia Batteries (Goodman & Caramazza, 1986), which revealed that H.W.'s oral reading performance and S.J.D.'s writing-to-dictation were significantly affected by grammatical word class and frequency, but not by regularity. On a longer list of 68 nouns and 68 verbs matched for frequency and length, H.W. correctly read aloud 38% of the nouns, compared to 18% of the verbs ($X_1^2$=7.158; $P$<0.01); S.J.D. correctly spelled to dictation 100% of the nouns and 79% of the verbs ($X_1^2$=13.457; $P$=.0002). Nearly all of H.W.'s errors in reading were semantic errors or omissions (she also had some articulatory difficulties, but these were not penalised if the response was recognisable as the target—see Caramazza & Hillis, 1990a, for detailed discussion of this case); and most of S.J.D.'s errors in writing were semantic (and/or morphological) errors or omissions.

Lexical processing in the other modality in each patient (writing by H.W. and reading by S.J.D.) was not significantly influenced by frequency or grammatical word class. H.W. produced all types of words relatively well in writing—her written responses were nearly all legible, although she made many spelling errors (but no semantic paragraphias; see examples of spellings in Appendix A). S.J.D. made no semantic errors in reading; her relatively infrequent errors in reading were morphological (e.g. suffix insertions, deletions or substitutions) or phonological. She correctly read 11% of both the nouns and the verbs on the Dyslexia Battery. Results of the batteries also showed that both patients had severe difficulties reading and spelling pseudowords: H.W. failed to read or write correctly any nonhomophonic nonwords and S.J.D. read incorrectly 72% of nonhomophonic nonwords and misspelled 93% of these nonwords.

Additional tasks that were used to evaluate the hypothesis that these patients had disproportionately impaired performance on verbs compared to nouns are reported in Caramazza and Hillis (1991). To briefly summarize, performance was tested on the following tasks: (1) oral and written naming of pictures corresponding to nouns and verbs matched for frequency and length; (2) oral reading and dictation of the items presented for naming tasks; (3) oral reading and dictation of homonyms embedded in sentences, once as a noun form and once as a verb form; and (4) verbal and written picture description. H.W. was significantly poorer in producing verbs compared to nouns in all tasks requiring *oral* output (30% vs. 61% correct performance for verbs and nouns, respectively), and S.J.D. was significantly poorer in producing verbs compared to nouns in all tasks requiring written output (76% vs. 99% correct performance for verbs and nouns, respectively). In the impaired modality, each patient produced the same phonological/orthographic form (one word of a pair of homonyms—e.g. crack) significantly more accurately when it was used as a noun than when it was used as a verb in the sentence context ($X^2_1$=21.665; $P$=0.0001 for S.J.D.; $X^2_1$=19.946; $P$<0.0001 for H.W.)—a result that was observed even for a subset of words in which the verb occurs more frequently than the noun (Table 20.1).

Results from these tasks indicate that both H.W. and S.J.D. had two primary deficits that interfered with performance of lexical tasks: (1) damage at the level of one modality-specific output lexicon[3] (the phonological output lexicon for H.W. and the orthographic output lexicon for S.J.D.) affecting verb more than noun production, and (2) damage to sublexical procedures for converting print to sound and sound to print. For neither patient can the deficit in verb naming be attributed to disruption at the semantic level of representation, because the patients had unimpaired comprehension of verbs (as demonstrated by performance on the Peabody Picture Vocabulary Test; Dunn & Dunn, 1981) and had intact naming of the same verbs in a different modality.[4] A more peripheral production deficit (such as impaired motor or

TABLE 20.1
Number (and %) of Correctly Produced Homonyms in Sentences

| | *Reading* | *Spelling to Dictation* |
|---|---|---|
| Performance by H.W. | | |
| *All stimuli* | | |
| Nouns | 44/50 (88) | 99/100 (99) |
| Verbs | 23/50 (46) | 98/100 (98) |
| *Subset in which verb form is more frequent than noun form* | | |
| Nouns | 19/20 (95) | 19/20 (95) |
| Verbs | 8/20 (40) | 19/20 (95) |
| Performance by S.J.D. | | |
| *All stimuli* | | |
| Nouns | 50/50 (100) | 99/100 (99) |
| Verbs | 50/50 (100) | 78/100 (78) |
| *Subset in which verb form is more frequent than noun form* | | |
| Nouns | 20/20 (100) | 20/20 (100) |
| Verbs | 20/20 (100) | 17/20 (85) |

planning skills for writing or articulation) was ruled out as the source of disproportionate verb errors in each patient, because such an impairment should equally affect nouns and should not lead to the predominant error type on verbs—semantic paraphasias or paragraphias. Hence, results suggest that both patients produced semantically related words when they were unable to access the target phonological or orthographic representation for output.

In a previous study it was reported that semantic errors in spontaneous writing (by a patient who had good comprehension of the words that elicited semantic errors) decreased when she improved in her ability to use POC procedures (Hillis Trupe, 1986). It was assumed that the basis for this outcome was that intact ability to convert sublexical phonology to orthography would "block" semantic paragraphias when the phonological representation was intact. It was also hypothesised that the ability to convert even part of the phonological representation to appropriate graphemes might cue access to the orthographic representation for output (e.g. by providing additional activation of the target orthographic representation). Thus, it was hypothesised that therapy directed to improve performance in the impaired modality of naming by H.W. and S.J.D. would be effective if it accomplished: (1) compensation for impaired retrieval, by converting successfully retrieved verbs in the unimpaired output modality to the impaired modality using procedures for translating phonemic strings to graphemes or vice versa; or (2) direct improvement in access to affected lexical output representations (particularly verbs) in the impaired modality.

### *Effective treatment for S.J.D.*

The paragraphs S.J.D. wrote each day in a journal contained sentences that were complete and grammatical except that most verbs were omitted or replaced by semantic errors. However, she correctly produced the verbs when she read the paragraphs aloud (Appendix B). Because S.J.D. was able to retrieve the phonological representation of the verb, she was taught to use this more intact oral naming to self-cue written naming by teaching her to convert the phonological form to an orthographic form. Thus, therapy for S.J.D. consisted of teaching her POC rules.

First, S.J.D. was taught to convert each of 30 phonemes, with relatively unambiguous graphemic correspondences, to letters using the cuing hierarchy in Table 20.2. This treatment approach entailed teaching her to associate each phoneme with a key word that she could spell (see Hillis Trupe, 1986 for further details). Retrieving the spelling of the key word amounted to retrieving the appropriate grapheme—the first letter of the key word.

TABLE 20.2
Cuing Hierarchy for Teaching POC

| | |
|---|---|
| 1. | Point to the letter that makes the sound /phoneme/. |
| 2. | Think of a word that starts with /phoneme/. |
| 3. | A word that starts with /phoneme/ is (*key word*). Point to the letter that makes the first sound of (*key word*). |
| 4. | Write (*key word*). Point to the letter that makes the first sound of (*key word*). |
| 5. | (*Target letter*) makes the first sound of (*key word*). /Phoneme/ is the first sound of (*key word*). (*Target letter*) makes the sound /phoneme/. Point to (*target letter*). (*Example: B* makes the first sound of *baby*. /b/ is the first sound of *baby*. *B* makes the sound /b/. Point to *b*.) |

Three sets of 10 phonemes each were sequentially trained for phonology to orthography translation. Baseline measures were collected for each set by asking S.J.D. to write a letter or letters (e.g. *th*) associated with each target phoneme in the set, with no feedback. After three baseline sessions, errors in response to phonemes in Set 1 were followed by the hierarchy of cues, until she wrote the correct letter(s). Then, previous cues were repeated, in reverse order, until she wrote the letter(s) correctly in response to the phoneme only. Only her response to the first stimulus (before cues) was scored. When performance was 100% correct for Set 1, the remaining sets were sequentially trained to criterion of 100% correct.

Figure 20.2 shows that S.J.D. learned POC rules for each of the three trained sets of phonemes when treatment was introduced for each set. This skill allowed her to convert the first sound of a successfully retrieved oral name to the initial letter(s). The initial letter(s) of the verb, in turn, often served to cue retrieval of the complete orthographic representation. Thus, following successful acquisition of POC rules, she learned to: (1) self-monitor semantic paragraphias (e.g. "listen" → hear) and (2) self-cue retrieval of the orthographic representation of verbs she would otherwise have omitted.

Progress was documented by scoring paragraphs that she wrote each day, about her daily activities or newspaper articles she read, according to the following measures: number of verbs; number of verbs per sentence (indicated by punctuation); percent correct verbs (i.e. number of appropriate and accurately spelled verbs divided by the total number of obligatory verb contexts, and multiplied by 100); number of affixes per sentence; and percent correct affixes. Affixes were scored separately, for a control measure, because S.J.D. made suffix and prefix errors in oral reading and spontaneous speech as well as in writing. Thus, if her writing improved as a function of translating phonological forms to

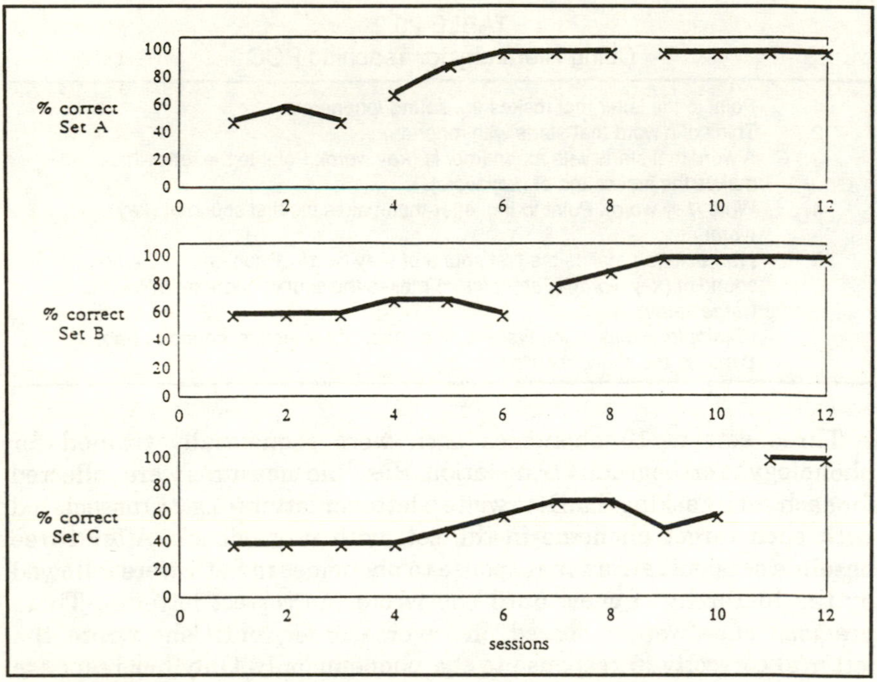


FIG. 20.2. S.J.D.'s improvement in phonology-to-orthography conversion that occurred with introduction of a cuing hierarchy. Each abscissa represents consecutive therapy sessions, and each ordinate represents the level of performance on the specified set of phonemes (before trreeatment was undertaken, if treatment was undertaken at all, that session). Sets A, B, and C were sets of phonemes that were treated separately. Baseline measures for sets B and C continued when treatment was initiated for set A, to show that improvement was faster for treated items than for untreated items that were practiced as frequently (thus demonstrating an effect of treatment beyond the effect of practice). Breaks in the graphs represent a change in phase, from baseline to treatment, or from treatment to maintenance (during which no treatment was carried out).

orthographic forms of the words, performance on affixes should not change since, presumably, these were not independently recoverable in the spoken modality.

During each session, after scoring her paragraph, S.J.D. was instructed to read aloud her intended wording and to evoke POC rules to self-monitor and facilitate verb writing. Treatment was associated with increases in all measures of verb production, while morphological errors in writing remained stable (Fig. 20.3). She was unable to correct suffix errors by reading them aloud and monitoring the phonology-orthography correspondence, because she also made morphological errors (but not verb errors) in oral reading. Subsequently, simple practice in writing suffixed words to dictation (indicated by the double arrows in Fig. 20.3) resulted in increased number and accuracy of affixes in written output.

### *Effective treatment for H.W.*

In contrast to the success obtained by S.J.D., H.W. was unable to exploit her more proficient written naming to increase oral production, because she was unable to learn effective orthography-to-phonology conversion procedures (OPC) or to blend those phonemes that she did translate. That is, even though she did learn to translate some (8/30) individual letters or letter combinations (e.g. *th*) to phonemes, the phonemes thus produced did not cue her retrieval of the phonological representation, neither could she assemble them to an appropriate phonological form. However, pinpointing H.W.'s naming deficit did provide an alternative idea for remediation—direct treatment toward facilitating retrieval of phonological forms of verbs. As retrieval of phonological representations is often thought to be a function of the resting threshold of activation for that particular representation, any technique that would lower the threshold of activation for specific representations might result in item-specific improvement in naming. One possibility for lowering the resting threshold of activation for a particular representation might be to increase massively the frequency of production of specific items over a period of time. If this were to be so, any technique that increases production of verbs over time, such as simple, daily practice in oral *reading* of verbs, should facilitate oral *naming* of the same verbs. Hence, trial treatment of oral naming focused on increasing the frequency of producing, over several weeks, a set of common verbs in oral reading tasks.

During baseline, 40 pictures depicting transitive verbs were presented for oral naming with no feedback. Then, the 20 items randomly assigned to Set A were presented for oral reading, with phonemic cuing or modelling as needed until the correct response was elicited. Each subsequent session began with an oral naming probe (no feedback), before presenting trained items in random order for cued oral reading. When H.W. reached 100% accuracy on Set A, Set B was treated in the same manner. Figure 20.4 shows that the cued oral reading treatment was associated with improved oral naming when it was applied to each set in turn. There was no generalisation of improvement to untrained words, indicating that oral reading influenced access only to those phonological representations that were activated in treatment (perhaps by lowering the threshold of activation of these words).

A comparable treatment for spelling-to-dictation was not tested for S.J.D., because her learned strategy for self-cuing resulted in improved

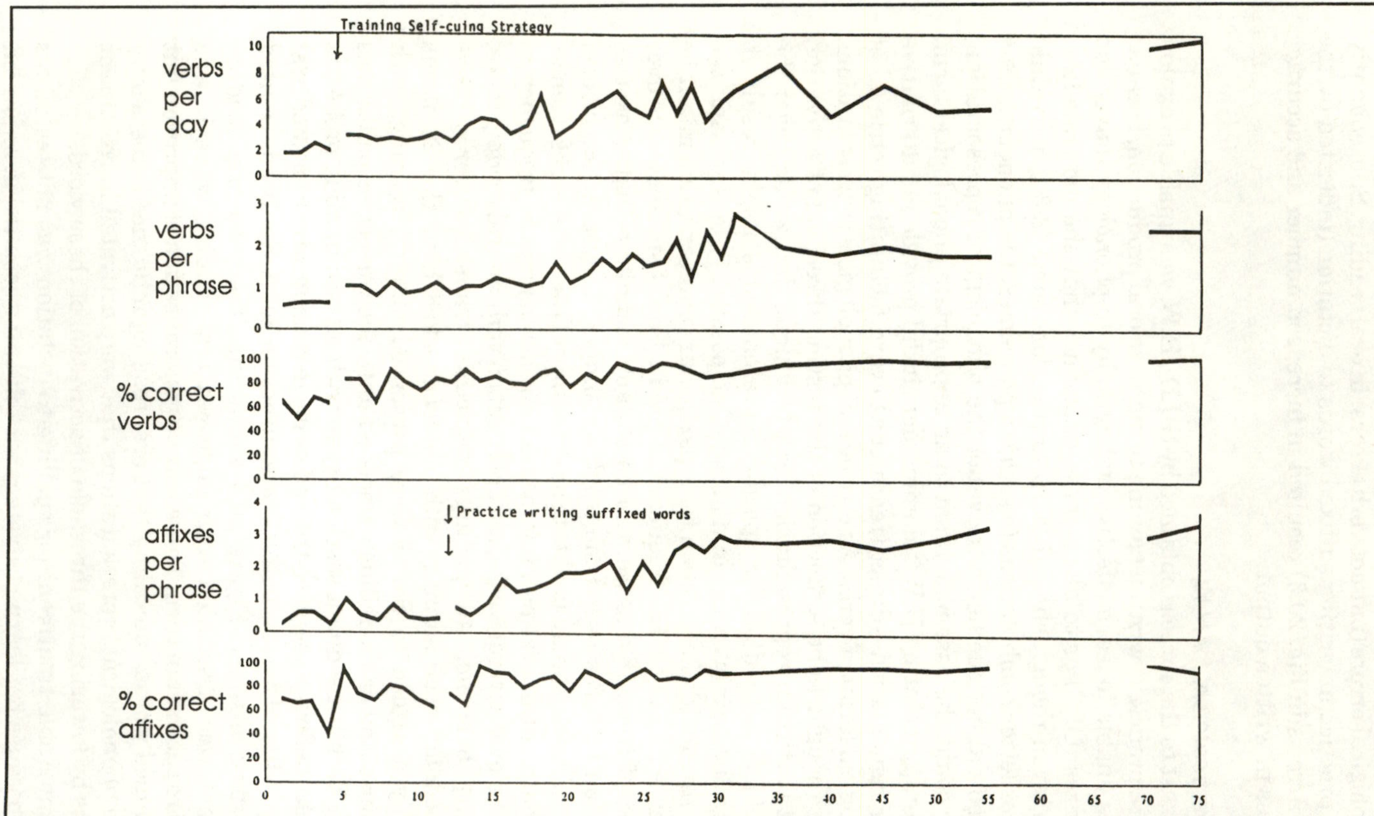


FIG. 20.3 SJD's improvement in various measures of verb production that occurred with improvement in, and training in use of, POC mechanisms. Each abscissa represents consecutive therapy sessions, and each ordinate represents the level of performance on the specified dimension of writing (with no treatment or before treatment was undertaken that session). Vertical arrows and breaks under the vertical arrows indicate the sessions in which treatment that influenced the specified dimension of writing was initiated.

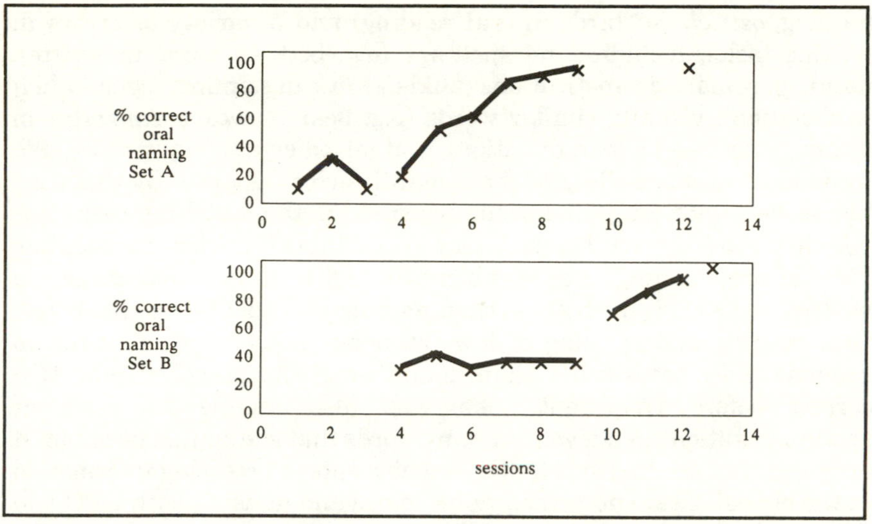


FIG. 20.4. H.W.'s improvement in oral naming of treated items associated with introduction of the oral reading strategy. Breaks in the graphs represent a change in phase, from baseline to treatment, or from treatment to maintenance (during which no treatment carried out). Sets A and B were word lists that were treated separately to distinguish the effects of treatment from the effects of repeated practice.

performance on *all* words (whereas the lexical strategy that helped H.W. did so for only a set of trained words).

The contrasting results obtained for the two patients with putatively comparable deficits (but with lexical output deficits in different modalities) illustrate that identifying the locus of impairment is not sufficient for identifying the approach to treatment. There are many possible reasons why H.W. was unable to achieve success in learning OPC procedures, whereas S.J.D. learned POC rules rather quickly. To begin with, the nature of damage to the output lexicons may be different in the two patients. Secondly, it is conceivable that POC rules are somehow easier to learn than OPC rules. However, performance by a third patient, P.M., shows that the latter possibility is not (or at least not always) the case.

*Contrasting results for P.M.*

P.M. was not tested as extensively as H.W. or S.J.D. on all classes of words. However, she was tested in tasks of oral reading, oral naming, written naming, writing to dictation, and spoken word/picture matching, using the same 144 items (picturable nouns). Performance revealed frequent semantic errors in all oral tasks (*cow* → "tiger" in oral naming, *ostrich* → "bird" in oral reading) and a variety of errors in writing tasks, including misspellings (e.g. belt → *brom* in written naming), semantic substitutions (ankle → *foot* in naming; tiger → *lion* in dictation), visually similar words (e.g. bean → *beat/bear/bead* in naming, tooth → *tools* in dictation), and mixed errors (e.g. wrist → *elb* in naming—a misspelling of the semantic error "elbow"). By this time her spoken word comprehension (measured in the matching task) was very high, 95% correct. Her accuracy in oral tasks (76% for oral reading; 75% for oral naming) was significantly higher than her accuracy in written tasks (11% for both written naming and spelling to dictation). Oral reading and spelling of low frequency nouns and of words in grammatical classes other than nouns were consistently below 10% correct before treatment. She was also unable to read or spell-to-dictation pseudowords or any words that she could not name. It appeared that she had substantial impairments in accessing information in the phonological and orthographic lexica and in using both OPC and POC mechanisms. As her oral skills were much less impaired than her written skills, the initial treatment focused on helping P.M. produce at least plausible spellings of words that she named orally.

Using the methods described as effective for S.J.D., an effort was made to train POC procedures, so that she might be able to convert her successfully retrieved oral names to writing. Unfortunately, P.M. never exceeded 60% accuracy on the trained set in five sessions, and decided to give up. It was not that she was incapable of improving in spelling, however; she did improve in spelling specifically trained sets of verbs (using a cuing hierarchy), as illustrated in Fig. 20.5. Writing remained virtually nonfunctional for untrained words.

P.M.'s failure to learn/recover POC procedures contrasts with the success of S.J.D., who had the same loci of deficits in lexical processing (although not necessarily the same type or severity of deficits at those levels of processing). Furthermore, the methods that were not effective in improving H.W.'s OPC performance, were effective for improving P.M.'s OPC performance (Fig. 20.6). P.M. was also able to use her improved OPC skill to produce phonemes in response to the written words, which cued accurate oral reading of the words. Thus, she improved significantly in oral reading performance, while oral naming remained unchanged: Her oral reading of the 144 (untrained) items tested before treatment improved from 76% to 89% correct (whereas on the same items, oral naming actually deteriorated insignificantly, from 75% to 69% correct). Unfortunately, P.M.'s newly recovered skill did not facilitate her oral naming under most circumstances, because she could rarely independently retrieve the spellings of words that she could not name orally.

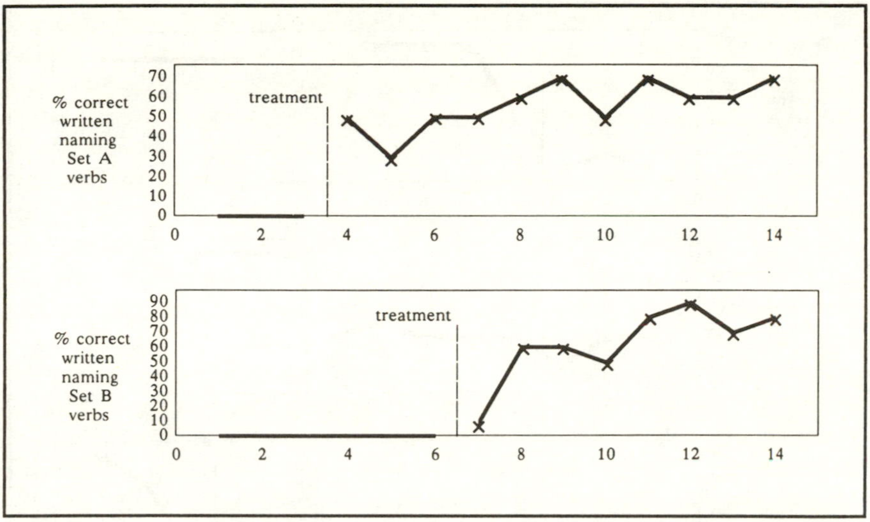


FIG. 20.5. P.M.'s improvement in written naming of treated verbs associated with introduction of a cuing hierarchy. Vertical arrows indicate the sessions in which treatment was initiated for each set. Sets A and B were word lists that were treated separately to distinguish the effects of treatment from the effects of repeated practice.

Why did S.J.D. achieve improvement in the use of POC procedures, whereas P.M. did not, when the same methods were applied in response to damage presumably to this component of the spelling process? Likewise, why did P.M. improve in the use of OPC procedures, whereas H.W. did not, when the same methods were applied in response to damage presumably to this component of the reading process? Perhaps the contrasting results reflect differences in the levels of severity or nature of damage to sublexical conversion mechanisms, or different combinations of deficits to other cognitive mechanisms that interfered to varying degrees with the patients' ability to learn these types of tasks. To illustrate the first possibility, translating a speech sound to a letter(s) (or vice versa) is a multicomponent task, requiring, among other things, segmenting auditory or visual input (attending to the stimulus to the exclusion of other inputs), categorising the allophone (a phonetic form, with specific pitch, volume, and duration) or allograph (a letter shape with specific case, style, etc.) as a particular phoneme or grapheme, mapping the abstract phoneme or grapheme to a particular grapheme or phoneme from amongst the set corresponding to the stimulus, and so on. Thus, impaired POC or OPC procedures might reflect a deficit to any one, or combination, of these components, which might be differentially remediable by the strategies attempted.

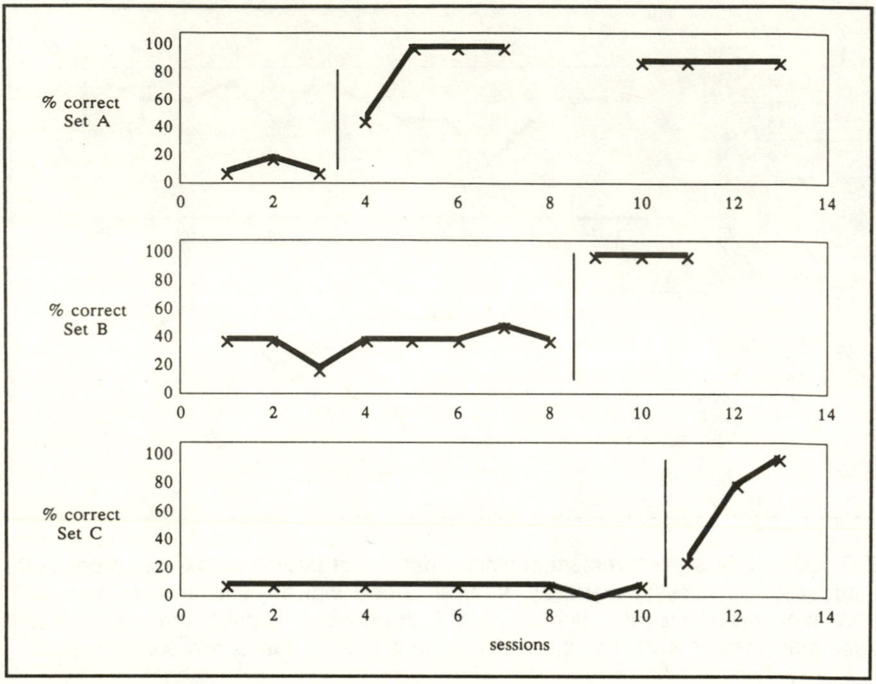


FIG. 20.6. P.M.'s improvement in orthography-to-phonology conversion associated with introduction of a cuing hierarchy. Sets A, B, and C were sets of phonemes that were treated separately. The vertical lines indicate the sessions in which treatment was initiated for each set. The break in the top graph represents a change from the treatment phase to a maintenance phase (during which no treatment carried out.)

## Study 2: The Same Treatment for Contrasting Deficits in Lexical Processing

*Subjects (and their respective loci impairment)*

H.W.'s responsiveness to a different treatment strategy, using a cuing hierarchy, was compared to responsiveness to the same treatment by K.E., a 51 year-old right-handed, college-educated male who suffered a left fronto-parietal infarct six months prior to this study. In a previous report, K.E.'s identical pattern of performance across lexical tasks was interpreted as evidence for selective impairment within lexical processing to the Semantic System, as represented in Fig. 20.1 (Hillis, Rapp, Romani, & Caramazza, 1990). The results are briefly summarised here; in particular, performance is contrasted to that of H.W. on the same tasks with the same stimuli (see Caramazza & Hillis, 1990a, for further details of H.W.'s performance on this set).

The set of 144 items presented to P.M. was presented to H.W. and K.E. for oral picture naming, written picture naming, writing to dictation, oral reading, auditory word/picture matching, and written word/picture matching. Stimuli were presented in blocks, in counterbalanced order, so that a given item was presented in only one task per session.

Except for some articulatory errors and omissions, all of H.W.'s errors in the oral tasks with these stimuli could be broadly classified as "semantic" errors (e.g. *table* → "chair"; *chicken* → "egg"; *bus* → "for going to school"). Her patterns of performance in oral reading and in oral naming were essentially identical to one another. In contrast to her frequent semantic errors in these tasks, most (266/288) of her responses in writing tasks were recognised as the target word by a naive judge (e.g. *jacket* → jack_t), and none resembled semantic errors. Thus, performance was consistent with the conclusion from the previously reported tasks that she was able to access the correct orthographic representation of an item, even when she was unable to access correctly the phonological representation of the same word (but activated instead the phonological representation of a related word). Additional evidence that her semantic errors resulted from damage at the level of the output lexicon was provided by her accurate performance on word/picture matching tasks with semantic distractors.

K.E.'s pattern of performance on these tasks was very different from that of H.W. In *all* tasks, the majority of K.E.'s incorrect responses were semantic errors. There were no significant differences in semantic error rates across tasks or total error rates across tasks.

It is extremely unlikely that a series of deficits across a number of lexical components would have affected word/picture matching, reading, writing, and naming (which do not involve the same input or output systems) to the same degree, and result in the same type of error. It was concluded, therefore, that K.E.'s semantic errors were attributable to a single component common to all of the lexical tasks evaluated—the semantic system[5].

*Treatment*

H.W. and K.E. presented with very different underlying deficits. Nonetheless, both patients were able to produce target names with very high reliability in response to various cues (e.g. the initial phoneme of the word). In the preceding study it was found that H.W.'s oral naming of a set of words improved when oral production of those names was elicited in oral reading tasks. One plausible explanation of these results is that increasing the frequency of production of a word lowers its activation threshold in the output lexicon in the trained modality. In this case, treatment should be equally effective for H.W. if the stimuli used to elicit the names are pictures rather than printed words. Oral names of pictures could be elicited in the same way as in the previous study (with phonemic cues) or by other cues (e.g. sentence completion cues, such as "Do you take cream or ...")—the type of cue should not matter, as long as it successfully elicits production of the name.

Eliciting the production of the name in response to the picture (by whatever cues are effective) *might* also improve naming when the disruption lies in the semantic system, because correct performance might involve activating semantic knowledge about what distinguishes related words from one another. Therefore, we evaluated the effects of various cues to elicit correct names for both H.W. and K.E.

A set of 50 drawings of familiar objects and 10 drawings of familiar actions was presented for consecutive sessions for oral naming (and written naming by K.E.), without feedback, until the patient showed a stable baseline of oral naming performance on a subset of 10 object pictures designated as the trained set. Then, presentation of each of item from the trained set was followed by a hierarchy of cues, including a sentence completion cue, an initial phoneme cue, and (if needed) the spoken word as a model, until the patient produced a correct response. After a correct response, each of the cues was presented again in reverse order, until the patient produced the name independently in response to the picture alone. Measures of oral naming (and written naming by K.E.) on the remaining stimuli continued without feedback. When the patient produced 90% correct performance on the trained set of nouns for two sessions, naming of the set of verbs was facilitated in the same manner.

H.W. again showed improved performance on oral naming of items that were elicited in treatment, but did not show generalisation to untrained words (Fig. 20.7). In contrast, for K.E., treatment using the same cuing hierarchy resulted in improved naming of trained *and* untrained items in the same semantic categories (Fig. 20.8). It appeared that his recovery of naming, say, *DOG* facilitated naming of related items, say, *CAT* (perhaps by reducing his incorrect production of trained words in response to the related pictures). Also, consistent with the hypothesis that a single deficit is responsible for K.E.'s errors in oral and written naming, his spoken and written naming performance improved when treatment involved only facilitation of spoken names (also, his oral and written naming performance improved when only written naming was treated, whereas H.W.'s oral naming was unaffected by treatment of written naming; see Hillis, 1989). The difference in results in terms of generalisation across items and across

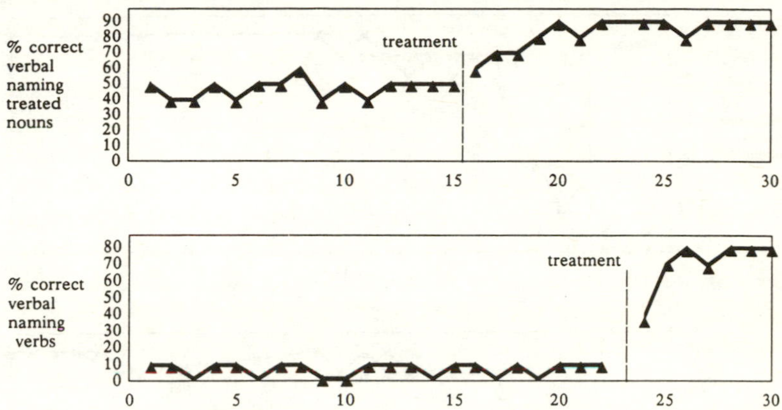


FIG. 20.7. H.W.'s improvement in oral naming of treated items associated with introduction of a cuing hierarchy.

output modalities were attributed to treatment effects on distinct levels of processing—the phonological output lexicon for H.W. and the semantic system for K.E.

It should be noted, however, that the treatment had several components, which individually might have had different effects for the two patients. Perhaps, for example, the production of the word was the important aspect for H.W., whereas the semantic information provided in the sentence completion cues was the important aspect of the treatment for K.E. However, for both patients, naming of the trained item was most frequently elicited by providing an initial phoneme cue. In each case, the phonemic cue might have provided additional activation of the target phonological representation (to the exclusion of other, semantically related, phonological representations)—which could have made the phonological representation available for further processing whether the impaired activation of the representation was due to damage at the semantic level or within the lexicon itself (see Hillis & Caramazza, 1992a, for discussion). This reasoning follows from the assumption that a semantic representation activates in parallel a number of phonological representations for semantically related words, corresponding to its component semantic features.

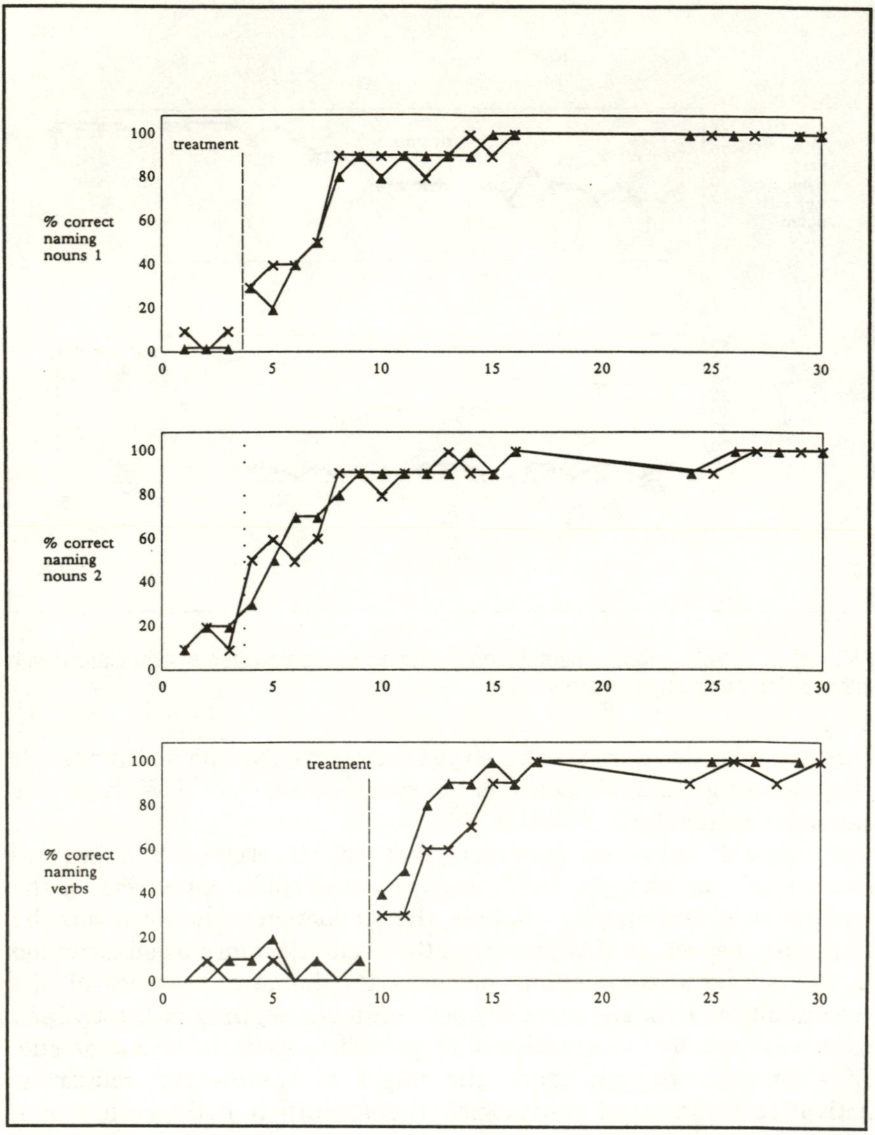


FIG. 20.8. K.E.'s improvement in oral and written naming of treated categories associated with introduction of a cuing hierarchy for oral naming. Triangles represent performance on oral naming; x's represent performance on written naming (which was not treated in this study). The vertical dashed lines on the top and bottom graphs indicate when treatment was initiated for the specified set of stimuli. The vertical dots in the middle graph indicate when treatment was initiated for set 1 nouns, which included stimuli in the same semantic categories as set 2 nouns (the latter of which was never directly treated).

## Study 3: Contrasting effects of different treatment approaches for patients with different loci of impairment

### *Subjects*

In the final study, H.W.'s responsiveness to two different treatment strategies was compared to responsiveness to the same strategies by J.J., who (like K.E.) showed selective damage to the semantic component in lexical processing. J.J. is a 67 year-old, right-handed retired corporate executive with two years of college education, who sustained a left temporal and basal ganglia stroke nine months before treatment began. J.J.'s striking accuracy in naming pictures of animals relative to other categories of words and details of his reading performance are reported elsewhere (Hillis & Caramazza, 1991a, b), and will thus be only briefly summarised here. On the lexical tasks presented to H.W. and K.E., as described above, J.J. showed frequent semantic errors on oral and written naming and word/picture tasks in all categories of words except animals. The similarity of his performance across tasks can be explained by assuming selective damage to the semantic component, that selectively spared semantic representations of animals. His oral reading and writing-to-dictation were more accurate than naming (for non-animal categories)—a result that can be attributed to his intact ability to use sublexical OPC and POC mechanisms to produce a plausible response (see Hillis & Caramazza, 1991a for detailed account of accurate reading of irregular words on the basis of partial semantic information in addition to partial phonological information).

### *Method and results*

For each patient, we compared changes in oral naming performance associated with two separate treatments (cued oral reading and word/picture matching). Intuitively, these treatments were not equally reasonable for the two patients. H.W. was already able to perform word/picture matching flawlessly, and J.J. was already relatively accurate in oral reading. So, it would seem unlikely that practicing tasks that are intact would have any substantial effect on language performance. However, Howard et al. (1985a) have claimed that, however counter-intuitive it may seem, all patients with naming deficits respond to treatment that involves word/picture matching. We tested the alternative hypothesis that word/picture matching treatment would help only the patient with a semantic impairment—J.J. In addition, the effects of oral reading treatment were measured to test the hypothesis that repeated production of oral names (irrespective of the context of their production) increases the probability of producing these names as appropriate responses. If such effects were found for J.J., whose accurate oral reading does not depend on intact semantic representations, it would undermine our conclusion from the study of K.E. that treatment of oral naming errors due to semantic deficits need in some way affect the semantic system.

Results of the two treatment approaches for the two patients were measured in the following manner. Each printed word in a set of 40 was randomly assigned during each session to one of two treatments (cued oral reading or written word/picture matching). Items that were assigned to the oral reading treatment for that session were presented in the form of printed words, and a correct oral reading response was elicited five times (with intervening items), using phonemic cues. Items that were assigned to the word/picture matching treatment for that session were presented in the form of a written word, and the patient was instructed to select the corresponding picture from a field consisting of all 40 stimulus pictures. Items that were initially incorrect were corrected and then repeated after intervening items, until a correct picture match was selected once by the patient. Lasting facilitation provided by each method was measured by probing accuracy of naming pictures corresponding to treated words the next session before treatment. Results indicated that cued oral reading practice improved the subsequent naming performance by H.W., and printed/word matching treatment improved the subsequent naming by J.J. The mean lasting facilitation of the treatments differed significantly, in opposite directions for the two subjects; $P<0.0001$ and $P<0.02$, by 2-tailed $t$-tests for H.W. and J.J., respectively. For J.J., of the 20 pictures that were matched to printed words with the clinician's assistance in a given session, an average of one to two pictures that were misnamed before the treatment were correctly named in the session following treatment. In contrast, mean change in picture naming performance as a result of the oral reading treatment was negative; thus, there was no cumulative facilitation[6] of picture naming provided by oral reading over the 13 sessions of testing. The opposite effects were shown by H.W. Over the 20 sessions of testing, there was no cumulative facilitation of picture naming provided by the word/picture matching treatment, but there was a substantial cumulative facilitation provided by oral reading (Fig. 20.9). Of the 20 items that were read aloud with clinician's assistance in a given session, an average of one to two of the corresponding pictures that were misnamed before the treatment were correctly named in the session following treatment.

H.W., whose production of semantic errors in naming were attributed to damage at the level of the phonological output lexicon, again showed

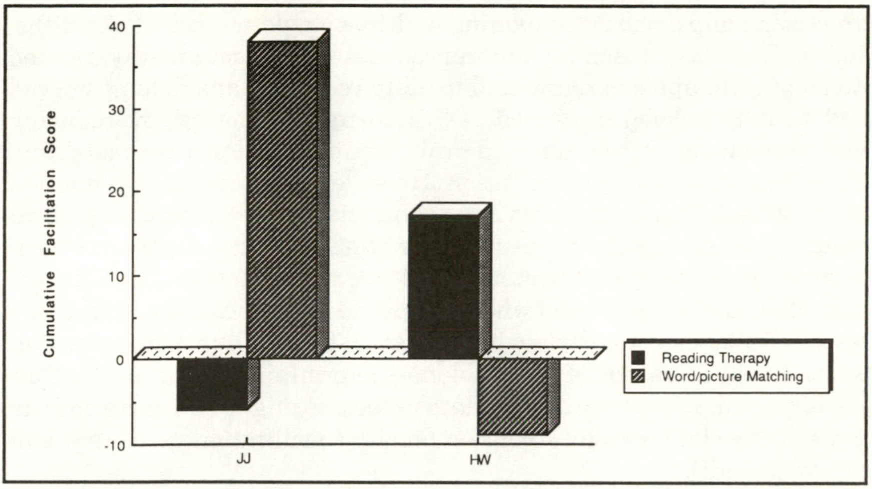


FIG. 20.9. Cumulative facilitation of picture naming (based on changes in accuracy the following session) provided by oral reading and word/picture matching strategies for J.J. vs. H.W.

improved spoken naming of trained items when treatment involved phonemic cuing to elicit oral reading of the stimulus names. It was hypothesised that this treatment, like the cuing hierarchy, resulted in improved oral naming of trained items by lowering the threshold of activation of their phonological representations. The same cued oral reading did not improve performance by J.J., whose semantic errors were attributed to selective damage to the semantic component in lexical processing. Instead, J.J.'s oral naming of the stimulus set improved when treatment involved reinforcing correct matching of printed words to pictures. This treatment might facilitate naming by teaching distinctions (or activating features that distinguish) among semantically related items. The results obtained in this study are consistent with the hypothesis that word/picture matching tasks can be used to improve naming of patients whose naming errors arise at the level of the semantic system, and facilitated practice of oral production of names (in oral reading, and perhaps in any other oral task) can facilitate oral naming when it is disrupted at the level of the phonological output lexicon.

Of course, many patients may benefit from both types of intervention, because many individuals have impairments at both levels of the naming process. Indeed, in an earlier study it was found that the two approaches of cued oral reading and teaching semantic distinctions with word/picture matching differentially affected distinct levels of processing impairments in naming within a single subject, H.G. (Hillis, 1990). Explicitly teaching differences between semantically related items (e.g. an apple is round and usually red; a banana is long, curved and usually yellow) increased H.G.'s correct responses (by reducing semantic errors) in written and oral naming, word/picture matching, repetition, and writing to dictation. However, *accurate* oral production of the stimuli improved only when pronunciation was corrected (in oral reading tasks). Again, the results are not surprising—she improved in aspects of naming performance that were emphasised, facilitated, corrected, and/or reinforced when she produced names. However, these results make the point that an important feature of clinical intervention is the detailed analysis of the problem—determining the processes that are impaired, so that the appropriate processes might be selected as the focus of the clinician's intervention (such as facilitation, teaching, and reinforcement).

Finally, it should be pointed out that the results reported for H.W. contrast with the conclusion reached by Patterson, Purrell, and Morton (1983) and by Howard et al. (1985a) that phonemic cues do not have any lasting effects on oral production of picture names: H.W. did show lasting effects of phonemic cues on oral production of picture names.

## DISCUSSION

From the treatment effects discussed here, we have only been able to illustrate a fairly limited role for cognitive neuropsychological theory in the practice of rehabilitation—in identifying what the problem is that needs to be treated. This role is not, however, trivial. The examples have shown that it is often possible to devise interventions that prove to be helpful to patients simply on the basis of a clear hypothesis about what component of the affected language task is impaired, along with speculation about how the patient might circumvent that component *or* observation of interventions that allow that component to function (such as a cue that elicits activation of the target phonological representation).

However, even this limited role of cognitive neuropsychological analysis in therapeutic practice should be tempered by the observation that generalisation from successfully treated cases to "similar" cases is not unproblematic. Thus to the extent that the functional deficit in two patients are "identical", we might expect that they will respond to the same treatment strategy. However, the results observed for treatment of S.J.D. as compared to P.M. (and for H.W. vs. P.M.) gave indication that present means of identifying the functional lesion of patients may not be adequate for this type of generalisation across patients. Recall that

S.J.D. and P.M. both showed chronic (lasting >2 years) impairments at the level of the orthographic output lexicon (and the phonological output lexicon, to a lesser extent), and at the level of sublexical mechanisms for converting print to sound and sound to print. Yet, S.J.D. was able to recover POC mechanisms to aid her written naming, whereas P.M. was not. Can we be satisfied that the functional lesions in the two patients were identical, yet showed discrepant recovery patterns in the two cases? Or, should we conclude instead that our methods of "diagnosis" of the problems in these patients were not sufficient to uncover critical differences in the nature of the impairment that influenced the probability of recovery of POC mechanisms? For example, were the discrepant results due to differences in residual skills of the two patients? The same questions can be asked regarding P.M.'s *success* in recovering OPC mechanisms contrasted to H.W.'s *failure* to do so. Unfortunately, it is not clear that we have any way of determining whether the differential effects of treatment were due to differences in the functional lesions, differences in the brain lesion, or differences with respect to premorbid variables that might influence recovery of the impaired mechanism (e.g. age, education, I.Q., etc.). We simply do not have sufficiently detailed theories about what constitutes a functional lesion, about the relationship between neural mechanisms and cognitive mechanisms, or about the factors related to recovery of *specific* cognitive mechanisms to formulate reasonable hypotheses on this issue.

In addition, we should note that the therapeutic strategies that were implemented are not novel; they are, in fact, very similar or identical to strategies that have been applied by clinicians and teachers for many decades. However, it is not obvious that the specific strategies would have been attempted without some idea of the patient's locus of impairment in each case. For example, efforts to improve H.W.'s oral naming by cuing her repeatedly to read aloud words corresponding to the picture name only makes sense if it is hypothesised that the same underlying deficit results in her errors in oral naming and oral reading (and, consequently, both correct oral naming and correct oral reading result from facilitated functioning of the impaired mechanism).

Thus, the most plausible conclusion to be drawn from the series of cases discussed is that a cognitive analysis of each patient's pattern of performance across lexical tasks can serve as a stimulus for calling upon the intuitions and experience of the therapist to develop appropriate treatment. This rather limited conclusion contrasts with much stronger claims drawn from previous reports of therapy for lexical deficits that are purportedly based on cognitive neuropsychological theory (see Byng & Coltheart, 1986; De Partz, 1986; Howard & Hatfield, 1987; Patterson, Purrell, & Morton, 1983).

Now we discuss just one of these reports to illustrate our concerns regarding strong claims about the contribution of cognitive neuropsychological analyses to clinical intervention. The study we have selected to discuss is among the clearest of efforts in applying a cognitive analysis to patient treatment. The point of this analysis is not to criticise such efforts, nor the specifics of this (or any other) treatment method, but to evaluate critically the types of claims that have been made regarding treatment effects in the cognitive neuropsychology literature.

## Stronger Claims about the Role of Neuropsychology in Rehabilitation: An Example

The central claim in many studies of the cognitive neuropsychological approach to treatment is that therapy techniques are motivated by the functional deficit hypothesised on the basis of a cognitive analysis of performance. For example, a study of treatment for dysgraphia was reported by Behrmann and Herdan (1987, p.8) that was "motivated by a fine-grained analysis of the subject's presenting deficits". They described a patient, C.C.M., who showed good performance on comprehension and reading tasks, but a clear pattern of impairment in spelling. Characteristics of her spelling performance included: (1) substantially better spelling of regular words and nonwords than irregular words, (2) higher accuracy on high frequency as compared to low frequency words, and (3) phonologically plausible misspellings (e.g. *ocean* → "owshin"). These features of spelling can be explained by proposing reliance on POC mechanisms in the face of damage to the orthographic output lexicon (or access to it). Thus we can consider how each of the treatment methods undertaken in C.C.M.'s case relates to the proposed functional deficit at the level of the orthographic output lexicon. The following interventions were undertaken:

1. C.C.M. was presented with the target word with its definition and/or corresponding picture. Given that C.C.M.'s reading comprehension is intact, the information represented in the definition and the picture should be redundant with semantic information available to C.C.M. from the written word. It is far from obvious to us that simple exposure to the written word or the semantic information should have any effect at the level of the orthographic output lexicon.

2. C.C.M. copied the correct spellings several times. Copying might be accomplished either by accessing the word in the output lexicon or by applying nonlexical mechanisms used to copy pseudowords and objects. Reliance on the latter would circumvent any effect on the orthographic output lexicon.

3. C.C.M. spelled aloud the word. Practice across several modalities (including copying) was reportedly undertaken to "strengthen the relationship between the word and its spelling". However, because oral spelling of a word should engage the lexical route of spelling in the same manner as would written spelling of the word (the two diverge only after the lexical-orthographic representation is accessed), it is unclear that this task should provide additional effect over written spelling.

4. The patient wrote the word to dictation, and errors were highlighted with coloured pens. Writing the word to dictation amounts to practising the task on which the patient is impaired—a method that may indeed be helpful (as suggested by the studies of our own cases), but that is explicitly rejected by the authors. Perhaps highlighting the errors differentiates the task from practice, but it is difficult to see how this intervention is motivated by assuming damage to the orthographic output lexicon. It *might* call attention to the errors and make them less likely to occur on future attempts, irrespective of the locus of damage in the spelling system.

5. C.C.M. practiced copying and word/picture matching at home. As noted, these tasks might be accomplished using spared skills (intact orthographic input lexicon and semantic system or nonlexical processing), making the tasks unlikely to affect the level of impairment.

6. C.C.M. selected the correct spelling in a multiple choice task. This task might also rely on the orthographic input lexicon (presumably intact). The expected effect on the orthographic output lexicon is not described.

Of the above therapy tasks, it would seem that only practice in written (or oral) spelling, with correction of errors, would be likely to stimulate, re-establish or otherwise affect processing at the proposed level of damage. However, corrected practice, or "rote learning", is hardly a new method that follows directly from the hypothesised impairment; it has long been used in remediation (and new learning) of spelling performance. Furthermore, Behrmann and Herdan explicitly claim that improvement attained by C.C.M. was *not* due to rote learning or practice, but was due to improvement in the lexical route of spelling. This disavowal leads to examination of a second type of claim made in remediation reports in the cognitive neuropsychology literature.

It has been asserted that appeal to cognitive neuropsychology allows one to determine how therapy effects change in performance (e.g. via re-organisation vs. re-establishment or practice vs. improved processing). Continuing with the same representative remediation study, we can examine whether or not the outcome of treatment can be, in the authors' words, "unequivocally interpreted". More specifically, did the reported results in the case of C.C.M. support the conclusion of improvement in the lexical route over and above a practice effect or rote learning of specific words? The authors draw this conclusion on the basis of presumably improved spelling of untrained words. However, the "improvement" was indicated by post-therapy testing of a subset of words in the pre-test—only those words that were incorrectly spelled. Thus, post-test performance was compared to 0% correct. However, without more complete testing, any change could be attributed to inconsistent performance on specific words across sessions. In fact, her post-test performance on untreated words (35/42; 83%) was no better than her pre-test performance for the whole set (123/150; 82%).

A practice effect was never evaluated in C.C.M.'s case. Baseline measures on spelling to dictation were taken, but involved three different sets of words (and improved somewhat across the three sessions). The effect of testing the same set of words over repeated sessions was not measured. Hence, the influence of the interventions, over and above repeated testing, cannot be evaluated. Thus, interpretation of how C.C.M.'s spelling performance improved as treatment was provided remains obscure (of course, even if we were to attribute the change to a practice effect, this "explanation" would not provide insight as to how the spelling process was modified).

Although many remediation studies that purport to follow a cognitive neuropsychological approach *do* demonstrate positive effects of treatment beyond a practice effect (e.g. Behrmann, 1987), this accomplishment is not linked to a cognitive analysis of the subject's performance but to the measurement design. Many more studies outside the realm of cognitive neuropsychology employ similar measurement designs with at least as much validity in demonstrating a functional relationship between an intervention and change in the subject's performance (e.g. Connell & Thompson, 1986; Simmons, 1984).

In short, effective treatment methods have been reported for individuals with relatively selective deficits identified through a cognitive analysis of performance across lexical tasks. Such treatment is clearly worthwhile (at least to the patient!). However, it is not clear that the role of cognitive neuropsychology in such treatment studies has been greater than that reported in our cases—identifying the component of lexical processing that is impaired, to guide the clinician's intuitions about what methods might affect processing at that level.

Wilson and Patterson (in press), in discussing treatment and cognitive neuropsychology have also noted that methods used in so-called cognitive neuropsychological rehabilitation are frequently the same as those employed by other schools of rehabilitation. They, too, have argued that models of cognitive processes do not provide the basis for developing treatment approaches. However, Wilson and Patterson find greater hope in parallel distributed processing (PDP) models in providing a foundation for treatment. This hope is founded on the fact that PDP models have, as an explicit component, features of learning. However, simply having a model of acquisition (even if it were an adequate model of acquisition) is far from having a theory about how a normal cognitive system can be modified once damaged. One would need not only a model of how a particular cognitive system acquires its functions, but also the nature of the damage to this system, the extent to which a damaged cognitive system with the particular sort of damage incurred is subject to recovery, and the methods that allow this recovery to take place. In the following discussion of the particular features of PDP models identified by the authors as relevant to rehabilitation, we fail to see such necessary components of a theory of rehabilitation.

Wilson and Patterson identify a single feature of PDP models, i.e. distributed representations, as offering promise to therapists in terms of guidance for rehabilitation. Two aspects of distributed representations are discussed as particularly germane to rehabilitation: partial loss of function and re-learning/generalisation. However, it should be pointed out that both of these features of impairment and recovery can be equally accounted for by competing models of cognitive processing[7]. For example, on the assumption that lexical representations (whether phonological, semantic, or orthographic) have a componential structure, traditional information processing models can account for partial loss of function by assuming that one or more of features of a representation is (are) damaged. Such an incomplete representation would then activate subsequent representations corresponding to its spared features, resulting in inconsistent incorrect and correct responses. Such models can also account for generalisation of recovery across trained and untrained items by assuming that treatment might affect particular features common to a set of representations (consisting of both trained and untrained items). Although such a notion is vague and speculative, the notion of "changing weights of hidden features" is no less so. In summary, it is unclear that PDP models offer any greater hope than the competing models presented in the cognitive neuropsychology literature for guiding therapeutic practice.

In conclusion, although it is not obvious that cognitive neuropsychology *alone* can provide the basis for better or more effective treatment methods, it can provide a more solid framework for investigating the relationship between rehabilitation and cognitive function. Progress toward understanding the recovery of specific cognitive mechanisms might then guide more efficient selection of treatment strategies. However, the usefulness of cognitive theory for clinicians involved in rehabilitation need not await a fully fledged theory of rehabilitation. We have noted that a rational approach to alleviating a problem requires an informed hypothesis about what the problem is. And, in this context, cognitive neuropsychological analyses will certainly be useful. Perhaps a more important message to clinicians is that patterns of recovery interpreted in light of a well-articulated model of the cognitive processes involved in the recovery will constitute a crucial component in the development of any forthcoming theory of rehabilitation (Caramazza, 1989). Toward this goal, cognitive neuropsychology has provided an indispensable framework for interpreting patterns of impaired performance and the changes in patterns of performance that result from clinical intervention.

## NOTES

1. From a similar analysis to that of Caramazza, Wilson, and Patterson reach additional conclusions about the type of theory that they consider most appropriate to characterize cognitive mechanisms. The basis for our disagreement with the latter conclusions is developed in the Discussion section.
2. This is not to say that the cognitive model was not useful in determining which process(es) needed to be improved upon, but simply that the model did not clearly constrain the choice of a particular therapy to improve those processes.
3. By proposing "damage at the level of the output lexicon", we are not making specific claims about whether the damage is to mechanisms for accessing lexical representations or to the representations themselves. To do so, we would have to give substance to such notions as "access" and "representation". Our current theories of lexical processing are not sufficiently detailed to enable us to distinguish between an impairment that, for example, takes the form of "raised thresholds of activation" of specific lexical representations and one that takes the form of impaired access procedures to the same representations (see Rapp & Caramazza, in press for detailed discussion).
4. Additional evidence that H.W.'s comprehension was intact for words that elicited semantic errors was provided by her flawless performance on word/picture matching tasks with pictures that she misnamed and by accurate definitions of printed words that she misread as semantically related words (see Caramazza & Hillis, 1990a, for details).
5. K.E. also demonstrated inability to read or spell to dictation nonwords; so it was also assumed that an impairment in sublexical POC and OPC mechanisms precluded reading and spelling nonlexically.
6. By "lasting facilitation" provided by each treatment we mean the change, from before treatment to the session following treatment, in oral naming performance for items subjected to that treatment. Cumulative facilitation refers to the sum of those positive or negative changes. See Appendix C for a summary of the measurement design.

7. Furthermore, the fact that PDP models predict *only* partial loss and not sudden, complete loss of function or abolition of certain items presents a problem for PDP models, because both patterns of performance do in fact occur in some brain damaged subjects. Also, generalisation of improvement across trained and untrained items only occurs in some cases; often, only trained items improve (e.g. Thompson & Kearns, 1981).

## ACKNOWLEDGEMENTS

The research reported here was supported in part by NIH grant NS22201 and by a grant from the McDonnell/Pew Program in Cognitive Neuroscience. This support is gratefully acknowledged. We are also grateful to H.W., K.E., S.J.D., P.M., and J.J. for their cheerful participation in the studies discussed. We thank Jane Riddoch, Glyn Humphreys, and an anonymous referee for helpful comments on an earlier version of this chapter.

## REFERENCES

Badecker, W., & Caramazza, A. (1991). Morphological composition in the lexical output system. *Cognitive Neuropsychology, 8,* 335-367.

Basso, A. (1989). Spontaneous recovery and language rehabilitation. In X. Seron & G. Deloche (Eds.), *Cognitive approaches in neuropsychological rehabilitation.* Hillsdale, N.J.: Lawrence Erlbaum Associates Inc.

Behrmann, M. (1987). The rites of righting writing: Homophone remediation in acquired dysgraphia. *Cognitive Neuropsychology, 4,* 365-384.

Behrmann, M., & Herdan, S. (1987). The case for cognitive neuropsychological remediation. *South African Journal of Communication Disorders, 34,* 3-9.

Byng, S., & Coltheart, M. (1986). Aphasia therapy and research: Methodological requirements and illustrative results. In E. Hjelmquist & L. G. Nilsson (Eds.), *Communication and handicap: Aspects of psychological compensation and technical aids.* North-Holland: Elsevier Science Publishers, B.V.

Caramazza, A. (1989). Cognitive Neuropsychology and rehabilitation: An unfulfilled promise? In X. Seron and G. DeLoche (Eds.), *Cognitive approaches in neuropsychological rehabilitation.* Hillsdale, N.J.: Lawrence Erlbaum Associates Inc.

Caramazza, A., & Hillis, A. E. (1990a). Where do semantic errors come from? *Cortex, 26,* 95-122.

Caramazza, A. & Hillis, A.E. (1990b). Levels of representation, coordinate frames, and unilateral neglect. *Cognitive Neuropsychology, 7,* 391-445.

Caramazza, A., & Hillis, A. E. (1991). Lexical organization of nouns and verbs in the brain. *Nature, 349,* 778-790.

Connell, P., & Thompson, C. (1986). Flexibility of single-subject experimental designs. Part III: Using flexibility to design or modify experiments. *Journal of Speech and Hearing Disorders. 51,* 214-225.

De Partz, M. P. (1986). Re-education of a deep dyslexic patient: Rationale of the method and results. *Cognitive Neuropsychology, 3,* 149-177.

Dunn, L. M., & Dunn, L. M. (1981). *Peabody picture vocabulary test-revised.* Circle Pines, MN.: American Guidance Service.

Goodman, R. A., & Caramazza, A. (1986). *The Johns Hopkins University Dyslexia and Dysgraphia Batteries.* Unpublished.

Hatfield, F. M. (1983). Aspects of Acquired dysgraphia and implications for re-education. In C. Code & D.J. Müller (Eds.), *Aphasia therapy.* London: Edward Arnold Ltd.

Hillis Trupe, A. E. (1986). Effectiveness of retraining phoneme to grapheme conversion. In R.H. Brookshire (Ed.), *Clinical aphasiology 1986.* Minneapolis: BRK Publishers.

Hillis, A. E. (1989). Efficacy and generalisation of treatment for aphasic naming errors. *Archives of Physical Medicine and Rehabilitation, 70,* 632-636.

Hillis, A. E. (1990). Effects of a separate treatments for distinct impairments within the naming process. In T. Prescott (Ed.), *Clinical aphasiology 1989.* Austin, TX: Pro-Ed.

Hillis, A. E., & Caramazza, A. (1991a). Mechanisms for accessing lexical representations for output: Evidence from a category-specific semantic deficit. *Brain and Language, 40,* 106-144.

Hillis, A. E., & Caramazza, A. (1991b). Category-specific naming and comprehension impairment: A double dissociation. *Brain, 114,* 2081-2094.

Hillis, A.E. & Caramazza, A. (1992). The reading process and its disorders. In D. Margolin (Ed.), *Cognitive neuropsychology in clinical practice.* New York: Oxford University Press.

Hillis, A. E., Rapp, B. C., Romani, C., & Caramazza, A. (1990). Selective impairment of semantics in lexical processing. *Cognitive Neuropsychology, 7,* 191-244.

Howard, D., & Hatfield, F. (1987). *Aphasia therapy: Historical and contemporary issues.* Hillsdale, N.J.: Lawrence Erlbaum Associates Inc.

Howard, D., Patterson, K., Franklin, S., Orchard-Lisle, V., & Morton, J. (1985a). The facilitation of picture naming in aphasia. *Cognitive Neuropsychology, 2,* 42-80.

Howard, D., Patterson, K., Franklin, S., Orchard-Lisle, V., & Morton, J. (1985b). Treatment of word retrieval deficits in aphasia: A comparison of two therapy methods. *Brain, 108,* 817-829.

Mitchum, C. C., & Berndt, R. (1988). Aphasia rehabilitation: An approach to diagnosis and treatment of disorders of language production. In M.G. Eisenberg (Ed.), *Advances in clinical rehabilitation.* New York: Springer.

Patterson, K. E., Purrell, C., & Morton, J. (1983). The facilitation of word retrieval in aphasia. In C. Code & D.J. Müller (Eds.), *Aphasia therapy.* London: Arnold.

Rapp, B., & Caramazza, A. (in press). On the distinction between deficits of access and deficits of storage. In H.A. Whitaker & A. Caramazza (Eds.), *Methodological and theoretical issues in cognitive neuropsychology.* New York: Springer-Verlag.

Seron, X., & Deloche, G. (1989) *Cognitive approaches in neuropsychological rehabilitation.* Hillsdale, N.J.: Lawrence Erlbaum Associates Inc.

Simmons, N. (1984). Experimental analysis of a treatment program for alexia without agraphia. In R. Brookshire (Ed.), *Clinical aphasiology 1984.* Minneapolis: BRK Publishers.

Thompson, C., & Kearns, K. (1981). Experimental analysis of acquisition, generalisation, and naming behaviours in a patient with anomia. In R.H. Brookshire (Ed.), *Clinical aphasiology 1981.* Minneapolis: BRK Publishers.
Wilson, B., & Patterson, K. (in press). Rehabilitation for cognitive impairment: Does cognitive psychology apply? *Applied Cognitive Psychology.*

## APPENDIX A: EXAMPLES OF H.W.'S RESPONSES TO NOUNS AND VERBS

*Oral Reading*

| *Responses to Nouns* | *Responses to Verbs* |
|---|---|
| nature → + | become → "finish" |
| church → + | preach → "church" |
| street → + | starve → "hungry" |

*Spelling to Dictation*

| *Responses to Nouns* | *Responses to Verbs* |
|---|---|
| engine → engrne | suffer → + |
| summer → summr | follow → follo |
| woman → womat | listen → lislen |
| sky → + | ask → + |
| bird → + | send → + |
| river → rivre | argue → augre |

## APPENDIX B: EXAMPLES OF S.J.D.'S NARRATIVE WRITING

*March 30.*
*Winter will ——— to Baltimore this week. Andy —— to Virginia for eleven weeks.*
Read as: "Winter will return to Baltimore this week. Andy went to Virginia for eleven weeks."

*April 6.*
*When I opened the shade, the snow has —— on the yard. I hate snow in April. I —— flowers inside, not outside.*
Read as: "When I opened the shade, the snow had fallen on the yard. I hate snow in April. I want flowers inside, not outside."

*April 13.*
*Milt —— his neck.*
Read as: "Milt hurt his neck."

## APPENDIX C: SUMMARY OF TREATMENT DESIGN FOR H.W. AND J.J.

*Session 1*

| | | | |
|---|---|---|---|
| Naming Probe #1 | | Random assignment to treatment groups **A – K ...** | Treatment of oral reading for items **A, C, D, F, K ...** |
| | | | Treatment of printed word/picture matching for items **B, E, G, I, J ...** |

*Session 2*

| | | | |
|---|---|---|---|
| Naming Probe #2 | Compare accuracy of naming in Probes 1 & 2 for items **A, C, D, F, K, ...** Change = facilitation score for oral reading treatment | Random assignment to treatment groups **A – K** ... | Treatment of oral reading for items **B, D, E, F, H, K** ... |
| | Compare accuracy of naming in Probes 1 & 2 for items **B, E, G, H, I, J ...** Change = facilitation score for word/picture matching treatment | | Treatment of word/picture matching for items **A, C, G, I, J ...** |

*Session 3*

| | | | |
|---|---|---|---|
| Naming Probe #3 | Compare accuracy of naming in Probes 2 & 3 for items **B, D, E, F, H, K**, ... Change = facilitation score for oral reading treatment | Random assignment to treatment groups **A – K ...** | Treatment of oral reading for items C, F, G, H, J ... |
| | Compare accuracy of naming in Probes 2 & 3 for items **A, C, G, I, J ...** Change = facilitation score for word/picture matching treatment | | Treatment of word/picture matching for items A, B, D, I, K ... |

CHAPTER TWENTY-ONE

# Cognitive Approaches to Writing Rehabilitation: From Single Case to Group Studies

**Sergio Carlomagno, Alessandro Iavarone, and Anna Colombo**
*Istituto di Scienze Neurologiche, Università di Napoli;*
*Centro Ricerche Clinica Santa Lucia, Roma, Italy*

## ABSTRACT

Two rehabilitation programs were devised for aphasics' writing disturbances according to current dual route model(s) of writing function. The phonological treatment stimulated writing by means of nonlexical phoneme to grapheme conversion procedures whereas the visual-semantic one re-trained patients in writing by practising whole word forms. Six aphasic patients received both treatment programs in a cross-over design. Overall results showed that the effects of both treatment procedures were significant and that learning transferred to untreated items. Furthermore, following tests provided evidence that patients retained what they had learned. However, when single case improvement was taken into account, almost all patients were found to respond only to one treatment. The results are consistent with a view that the effectiveness of a writing rehabilitation procedure relies on (partially) spared components of writing system to which the procedure itself proposes to affect.

## INTRODUCTION

It is widely accepted in the neuropsychological literature that single case studies carried out within the framework of current models of normal cognitive functions can offer important contributions to the analysis of neuropsychological deficits. Furthermore, in recent years, a few single case studies have attempted to demonstrate that a similar approach can be used to devise specific rehabilitation programs. We will offer here an example of the most recent possibility concerning some aspects of writing rehabilitation in aphasics. Our work brought into focus the dissociation in the writing rehabilitation literature between the prodigious effects of therapies in single cases and the less encouraging results of group studies (see also Coltheart, this volume, for discussion of the contrast between single case and group studies of aphasia). The dissociation is so marked that it is at present even difficult to conclude whether writing rehabilitation is suitable for aphasic patients. Such a state of affairs led us to develop two cognitively oriented rehabilitation programs and to test their effectiveness on a small sample of patients. Results of our experience will be discussed in the framework of the present debate on the validity of the cognitive approach to neuropsychological rehabilitation.

## THE STATE OF THE ART

In 1976 Hatfield and Weddel presented data concerning the effects of different methods on the re-training of writing in severely aphasic patients. One of the treatments, the "visual-kinaesthetic" method, consisted of a step by step procedure from simple copying from memory and, finally, to writing from dictation. The therapy aimed to restore, by "visuo-kinaesthetic memorising", writing of items of practical importance in order to replace impaired oral language. Two patients suffering from severe expressive aphasia were treated. The results showed a significant improvement in one patient. When retested one month after therapy completion there was little retention of treated items but there was some learning indicated by partial knowledge about spelling (e.g. of initial letter, approximate word length and consonant-vowel structure). Such an observation led the authors to conclude that a visual (visuo-kinaesthetic) approach seemed useful for re-training writing in less severe aphasic patients.

In the second treatment, based on Luria, Naydin, Tveskova, and Virnarskaya's (1969) suggestion that writing involves a segmental transformation of phonological strings into their graphemic counterparts, Hatfield and Weddel (1976) treated two patients by practising auditory-phonemic analysis of words and some phoneme-grapheme correspondences. The first patient, case S4, showed improvement on phonemic analysis but he was unable to set up phoneme-grapheme correspondences. The second patient appeared to be more sensitive to this kind of training. Unfortunately, she was an Austrian lady and improvement could not be demonstrated because of intrusions of German phoneme-grapheme correspondences.

The study of Hatfield and Weddel (1976) does not encourage belief that writing rehabilitation can play a role when treating aphasic disturbances. However, some points of the paper deserve further consideration. It was stressed that spelling in normal adults does not solely reflect phonemic analysis and segmental translation of phonemes into graphemes but also visually based strategies. It was thus suggested that two different strategies, phonological and visual, tied to the strategies used by normal spellers, could be used in writing rehabilitation. Indeed, visual strategies could explain some features of residual writing abilities in the aphasics. For instance, when attempting to write 'glass', "Patient S4 wrote the first two letters, left a gap, then the two s's and, finally, she inserted the 'a' into the gap" (for a notable description of such strategies see Hatfield & Weddell, 1976, p. 74; Hatfield, 1985). This suggests the possibility that writing of patient S4, which did not improve by practising phoneme-grapheme correspondences, would have improved if a visual strategy had been used.

In the light of this suggestion, consider treatment of writing problems in a group of aphasic patients reported by Seron, Deloche, Moulard, and Rouselle (1980). They presented data concerning the retraining of aphasic patients by means of a computer-aided technique (typewriting from dictation). The program focused on the choice and serial ordering of letters when patients were given visual cues: The number of letters belonging to the target word, the relative position of a letter in the string and so on. Progression was assured by fading out the cues and by increasing the orthographic complexity of the stimuli. Furthermore, in order to evaluate whether learning generalised across items (learning transfer) a separate list of stimuli was used at test. Generalisation across learning context was tested by requiring patients to write by hand. An initial post-test showed a significant improvement in all subjects in terms of the percentage of words correctly written, the total number of errors and the similarity between responses and target items. At a second post-test, six weeks later, the improvement was not retained except in the case of one patient whose improvement, according to the authors, could have been due to spontaneous recovery. Seron et al.'s data (1980) suggest that, when submitted to structured experimental testing, writing rehabilitation on a group of aphasics again seems unsuccessful. However, an analysis of patients' writing errors showed a marked tendency to write by using phoneme-grapheme correspondences (e.g. there was a high rate of plausible phonemic errors). Furthermore, the orthographic complexity of target items was found to be an important source of errors, because performance on words that contained as many letters as phonemes was significantly better than with other words.

Possibly the technique, which was intended to implement writing by means of visual strategies, was in conflict with patients' spontaneous tendency to write by audiographic correspondences.

Further insight into patients' spontaneous compensatory strategies in writing rehabilitation was provided by a study of Hatfield (1984). According to the models of writing function put forward by Ellis (1982), Hatfield and Patterson (1984), Morton (1980), and Shallice (1981), writing, like reading (see Coltheart this volume), involves two primary routes. The first entails the direct retrieval of a word's spelling stored in the orthographic output lexicon (the direct or lexical route). The second (nonlexical) route uses segmental translation from phonology to orthography (phoneme-grapheme conversion).

Hatfield worked with deep dysgraphic patients, who, amongst other symptoms, are better able to write content words (e.g. nouns) than function words (e.g. *at*, *then, by*) and are unable to write nonwords. The latter symptom is typically taken to imply that nonlexical route for writing is impaired. Hatfield tried to build on their relatively good performance with content words, which presumably arises from a partially spared lexical route. It was observed that one patient, B.B., when attempting to write the function word "in", spontaneously spelled the homophonic word "inn". Hatfield hypothesised that instructing the patient to use such a "lexical" strategy might influence his writing of function words. For instance, to write the word "on", the patient was instructed to write the Christian name "Ron" and then to delete the "*r*", the aim being to bypass the impaired access to the spelling of the word "on". The results of this training program were very positive (patient B.B.'s score on function words improved from 34% to 63.5%). It was suggested that writing processes can be rehabilitated by using the less impaired component (in this case the lexical route) in the writing system. Note also that B.B. had been trained to write function words by practising phoneme-grapheme correspondences, but no improvement could be noticed.

More recently Carlomagno and Parlato (1989) have presented results on the rehabilitation of writing disturbances where an attempt was made to reorganise writing by phoneme to grapheme correspondences. The patient was mildly dyslexic and severely dysgraphic. The writing disorder was stable over a period of 15 months despite having received 3 months extensive writing training intended to reteach whole word forms for a few items, and sound-to-letter correspondences. However, the patient was shown to exhibit an interesting dissociation in reading. For instance, he regularised stress and was confused by non-homographic homophones (e.g. "know" and "no", in English) suggesting that his reading was supported by grapheme to phoneme conversion procedures (see Coltheart, Masterson, Byng, Prior, & Riddoch, 1983). However, although word reading was about 80% correct, nonword reading was only 30%. To explain such a dissociation, it was suggested that word-reading took advantage of a spontaneous lexical strategy, which enabled him to access grapheme-phoneme correspondences. In other words his reading probably consisted of segmenting a letter string into syllabic or subsyllabic units. In this way a phonological counterpart was obtained for each unit. Finally, the resulting phonological units were matched with the phonological structure of a real word (lexical relay) to produce an oral response. Our hypothesis was confirmed by 80% correct reading of non-words homophonic with a word (e.g. pseudohomopones such as "nale" in English).

Our therapeutic program for writing was to instruct the patient to apply an analogous strategy of lexical relay between phonologically coded syllables and graphemic forms using code-names. As the correspondence between the written syllable "ca" and its phonological counterpart /ka/ was available, in reading, only when embedded in a word, the graphemic counterpart of a dictated /ka/ would be available for writing when using a very familiar word containing that syllable in the first position. A detailed description of the therapy stages, which share similarities with the program devised by De Partz (1986) for a deep dyslexic patient, is available in Carlomagno and Parlato (1989). Briefly, the patient was trained to segment orally a dictated stimulus, to link each syllabic unit to a code-name (usually a name of an Italian town) and, finally, to write the syllabic unit. The results indicated that the strategy could be used efficiently. For instance, upon completion of the treatment program, he scored 83% correct on writing words and 80% correct on non-words and, during therapy stages, a continuous transfer of learning to untreated syllables was observed. Furthermore, learning transfer was also found in nonword reading as he scored 80% correct upon completion of the therapy program. Thus, both the quantitative and qualitative results supported the hypothesis that a lexical strategy, analogous to that the patient used in word reading, could facilitate access to spared phoneme-grapheme (or grapheme-phoneme) correspondences which could then be used in writing and in nonword reading.

On the whole, our data and those of Hatfield (1984) suggest that it is possible to devise efficient treatment procedures for aphasics' writing disturbances. Moreover, the effectiveness of a treatment depends on our knowledge of both defective and intact components of a processing system. Selective stimulation of spontaneous residual strategies, which probably correspond to the functioning of (partially) spared components of the writing system, is critical for obtaining positive effects of treatment programs (Carlomagno & Parlato, 1989; Hatfield, 1984).

Failure to demonstrate positive effects of writing rehabilitation programs on groups of aphasics is thus likely due to: (1) individual variability of damaged and spared components of the writing system, and (2) the possibility that treatment did not preferentially stimulate (partially) spared components of the damaged system.

Our present work aimed at testing such an hypothesis by submitting a group of unselected aphasic patients to each of two treatment programs intended to stimulate writing by using either phoneme-grapheme conversion procedures or visual (lexical) strategies. Our main prediction was that both the rehabilitation strategies would have improved whole group performance since the two strategies stimulated residual activity of the two writing routines. However, given the individual variability of these residual skills, single cases, or at least some of them, would have shown selective response to one of the two.

## PATIENTS

Eight aphasic patients were chosen as having a stable language deficit, ranging from mild to moderate severity. They were at least eight months post-onset of a single hemispheric stroke and repeated assessments on reading and writing subsets of a standard aphasia test (Pizzamiglio, Mammuccari, & Razzano, 1985), did not show significant improvement. Two of them, however, dropped the treatment program at the end of the first treatment: One died, the other, who was right hemisphere damaged patient, became depressed and refused to continue. Clinical and epidemiological data concerning the six patients who completed the entire program of two treatments are reported in Table 21.1.

### Assessment

The writing abilities of the six patients during the study period were evaluated by means of a shortened version of the "Batteria per la valutazione dei disturbi di lettura e scrittura in soggetti cerebrolesi di lingua italiana" (Burani, Laudanna, Miceli, & Caramazza, 1984). The original form of the battery includes different tasks to investigate writing abilities including: matching letters printed in upper and lower case, copying, writing of words and pronounceable nonsense strings both to dictation, and written naming. It also includes tasks to evaluate phoneme discrimination and single word and nonword repetition skills. Reading and lexical decision tasks included in the battery, were also

TABLE 21.1

(a) Epidemiological Features of the Six Patients who Participated in the Study

| | SUBJECTS | | | | | |
|---|---|---|---|---|---|---|
| | *1* | *2* | *3* | *4* | *5* | *6* |
| Age | 43 | 30 | 59 | 45 | 63 | 66 |
| Sex | M | F | M | M | F | M |
| Education (years) | 18 | 13 | 18 | 13 | 11 | 9 |
| Lesion (CT scan) | F-P | F-T-P | F-T-P | F-T-P | P-O | P-T |
| Etiology | MAV | CVA | MAV | CVA | CVA | CVA |
| Months post onset | 15 | 8 | 9 | 66 | 72 | 35 |

F = frontal, T = temporal, P = parietal, O = occipital
MAV = artero-venous malformation surgically treated, CVA = cerebrovascular accident

(b) Language Disturbances on Aphasia Test (Pizzamiglio et al., 1985)

| | | | | | | |
|---|---|---|---|---|---|---|
| Fluency | ± | ± | ± | + | – | – |
| Dysarthria | + | ± | + | – | – | – |
| Word Finding | + | + | ± | + | + | ± |
| Repetition | + | + | ± | ± | + | ± |
| Paraphasia | Ph | Ph | Ph | S | Ph | – |
| Comprehension (oral) | – | – | – | – | ± | – |
| Reading | – | – | – | – | – | – |
| Written Naming | + | + | + | + | + | + |
| Writing to Dictation | + | + | + | + | + | + |

+ = severe deficit; ± = mild deficit; – = no deficit
Ph = phonemic paraphasia; S = semantic paraphasia

performed. However, as far as this paper is concerned, we shall focus on written naming and the word and nonword writing to dictation tasks.

The written naming task consists of 40 stimuli chosen from the Snodgrass and Vanderwart (1980) list so that the corresponding Italian names are controlled for frequency, orthographic complexity and length (ranging from four to nine letters). It should be stressed that written Italian is usually considered a transparent language as one-to-one phoneme to grapheme correspondences mostly apply. There are only a few occasions where one phoneme is translated into two or three graphemes or one phoneme can be converted into two different alternatives (e.g. /k/ → "c" or "ch") depending on the following context, see Coltheart, (1984). Following these orthographic peculiarities of written Italian, half the stimuli contained only one-to-one phoneme to grapheme correspondences, half contained at least one single phoneme to multigraphemic string correspondence. To the original object naming list we added 40 items to test naming of actions. The items were chosen from a larger sample so that there was 90% name agreement by 12 normal controls. Action names were matched to object names for length (third person form), orthographic complexity and frequency. Patients were requested to write the infinitive or the third person form of the verb.

The nonword and word lists of the original battery, 147 and 249 stimuli respectively, were reduced to 80 stimuli and the resulting lists of words and nonwords were matched for length and orthographic complexity to that of written naming. Moreover, in the case of words, care was taken to maintain grammatical class, frequency and concreteness dimensions used in the original battery.

## TREATMENT PROCEDURES

Each treatment program was structured in order to ensure that:

1. It would stimulate, as much as possible, only one of the two writing routines assumed by current dual route models of writing. For instance, to stimulate the nonlexical writing routine the patients were trained to write pronounceable nonsense letter strings (phonological treatment). On the other hand, written naming with visual and semantic cues was used in order to stimulate the lexical writing routine (visual-semantic treatment).
2. It encompassed all possible stages involved in each writing routine (see Table 21.2). For instance, according to Hatfield and Patterson (1984), phoneme-grapheme conversion entails (at least) that the stimulus is divided into phonological segments; those segments, in turn, have to be translated into their orthographic counterparts; then, graphemic segments have to be assembled in the written form of the target. The phonological treatment was structured so that each stage of the phoneme to grapheme conversion procedure could be contemplated as a particular step in the treatment itself. It was supposed that visual-semantic treatment would stimulate the patient to use residual semantic information and residual knowledge of the whole word form including the number of letters, the relative positions of letters in the string or the presence of a relevant orthographic group. Partial information on the whole word form has been described even in the case of

severely dysgraphic patients (Hatfield, 1985; Hatfield & Weddel, 1976; Seron et al., 1980). Therefore, the visual-semantic treatment was structured as a crossword puzzle (see Table 21.2), which is a task where partial semantic and visual information may normally be used to retrieve whole word form spellings. For instance, see Fig. 21.1, it was assumed that visual cues (the number of letters, the word contour and

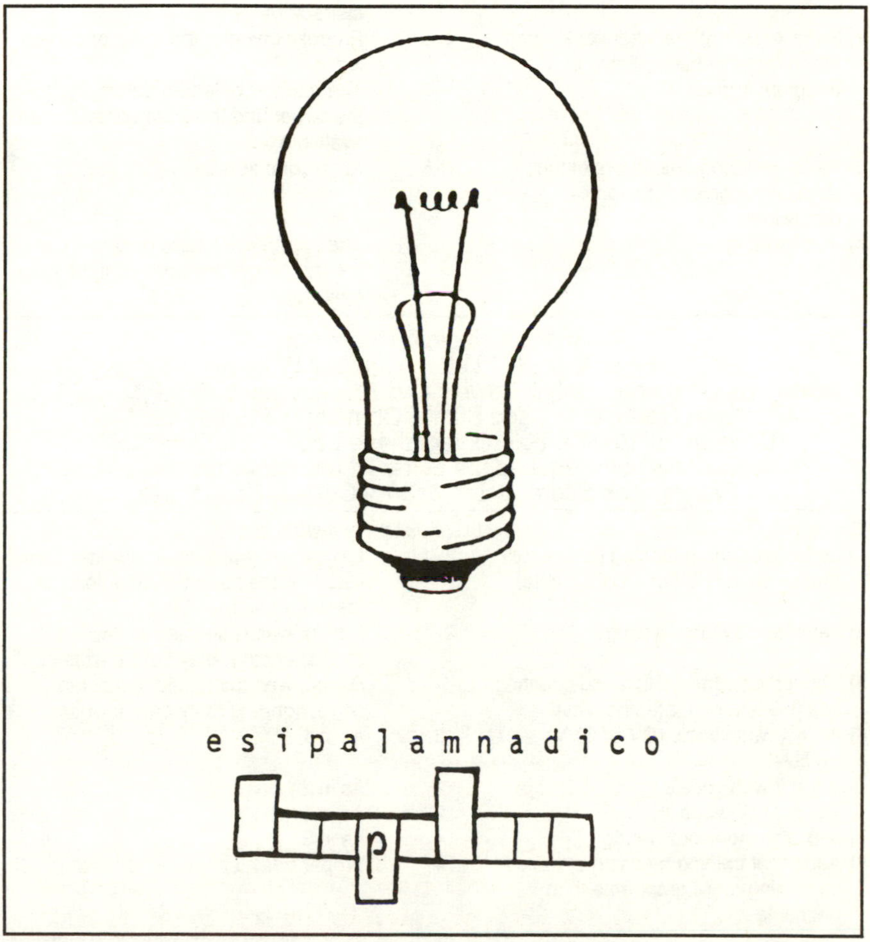


FIG. 21.1 An example of the training condition of the visual-semantic treatment: Step 3, target item = "lampadina". The patient was told the number of letters belonging to the target word and its visual contour. The correct letters were provided along with 2 or 3 distractors in an anagram format. Prepositioning of a central letter by the clinician served as a visual cue.

TABLE 21.2

(a) Visual-semantic Treatment

Final Task = Written Naming of Objects (4 x 10 Items) or Actions (4 x 10 Items)
Progression: Groups of 10 Items Per Session Were Alternated in Each Treatment Condition. To Move from a Condition to the Next, the Patient had to Obtain a Score of 80% Correct Responses on the Items of the Session

| *Conditions* | *N. Sessions* | *Available cue* |
|---|---|---|
| 1) Copy and delayed copy | 4–8 | Prior to copying, patients had to point to the targets presented with distractors |
| 2) Serial ordering: the letters belonging to the target were available in anagram format | 4–8 | Prepositioning of the initial or central letter<br>The number of letters belonging to the target and the word contour were available |
| 3) Serial ordering: the letters of the target were given with some distractors | 4–8 | As in condition 2 |
| 4) Handwriting | 4 | The number of letters belonging to the target and the word contour were available |

(b) Phonological Treatment

Final Task: 4–7 Letter Nonword Writing.
Nonwords Contained Only 5 Vowels and 7 Consonants (R,T,P,M,C,S,V).
Additional Treatments Used Stimuli Containing Phonemes Which Correspond to a Combination of these Letters, i.e.: /s/ - "sci".
or which Required the Letter H, i.e.: /ki/ = "chi".
Progression Score: Score of 80% Correct Responses

| *Conditions* | *N. Sessions* | *Available cue* |
|---|---|---|
| 1) Letter to sound matching (phoneme presented in a CV or CCV syllable) | 2–4 | Lexical relay available in written form, i.e.: /k/ = the patient had to point to the written name "Carlo" |
| 2) Letter and syllable writing | 2–4 | Patient was requested to say the corresponding relay before writing |
| 3) Phoneme segmentation and counting in a 3–5 letter dictated nonword | 4 | Patient was requested to say the corresponding relay before writing |
| 4) As in 1 with vocals (CV or CVV syllable) | 2 | As in 1 |
| 5) As in 2 with vocals | 2 | As in 2 |
| 6) As in 3 with vocals | 2 | As in 3 |
| 7) 4–8 letter nonword writing | 4 | As in 3 |
| 8) Additional training by using syllables containing more grapheme than phoneme | 4 | Proper relay, i.e.: /ki/ = "Chiara" |

the relative position of letter "p") and semantic cues ("it is an electrical thing"; "it is an object to let light into a room when switched on") could facilitate access to the whole word form "lampadina" (bulb).

3. It should follow a progression rate through appropriate levels of difficulty until a predetermined level was reached.
4. It avoided overtraining on a few stimuli by alternating practising items.
5. It should permit tests of learning transfer (see Discussion).

Accordingly, practice lists, containing items different from those of the assessment, were used. For instance, visual-semantic treatment used a list of 40 picturable objects and 40 picturable actions whose names were, as much as possible, matched to those of the assessment items for length, frequency and orthographic complexity. Transfer of the phonological treatment was assessed using, as practice items, nonwords composed only of seven selected consonants and the five vowels of the Italian alphabet, while the nonwords of the assessment lists contained all the twenty one letters of the written Italian.

Finally, the dual route model of writing predicts that each treatment program would give significant improvement only in those tasks where lexical or nonlexical writing strategies could be successfully applied. For instance, the visual-semantic treatment should not produce significant improvement in nonword writing and, conversely, the phonological treatment should not produce improvement in written naming (except for those items which were named orally). Thus, we had the chance to evaluate the specific effect of each therapy as each would produce a specific pattern of improvement.

## Design

We used a multiple baseline, crossover, ABCB design, where A and C refer to the two experimental treatments and B refers to other communication oriented therapies. In particular each patient received an initial 20-24 sessions writing treatment followed by 18-20 sessions of PACE therapy (Carlomagno, Emanuelli, Casadio, & Losanno, 1990; Davis & Wilcox, 1985, see also note 1). There were subsequently 20-24 sessions of the second writing rehabilitation program, and finally 18-20 sessions of another language therapy, not involving writing abilities.

Three patients, namely cases 2, 3 and 6, received the visual-semantic treatment first, cases 1, 4 and 5 received the phonological treatment first.

Writing abilities were assessed in a pre-test and on completion of each writing treatment (the post-test), and also about 50 days after the end of the writing rehabilitation program (delayed control test). The pre-test of the second treatment course was the delayed control for the first.

## RESULTS

The number of correct responses out of the 240 target items obtained by each patient in the five testing sessions (with the results of the three writing tasks pooled together) are reported in Table 21.3.

The results were analysed by means of an ANOVA, which showed significant variation of whole group performance through the five testing sessions ($F=20.15$, $df=4$, $P < 0.001$). Post-hoc comparisons (Newmann-Keuls) failed to show significant differences between each post-therapy evaluation and the respective delayed control. All other comparisons were significant ($P < 0.05$). On the whole, the results indicated that writing improvement could be confidently attributed to the two treatment programs because there was no improvement during the time where the other (non-writing) aphasia therapies were administered. Furthermore, according to our experimental design, the results of delayed control tests showed that patients retained what they had learned.

A second three-way (pre/post evaluation x type of treatment x task) ANOVA was performed to compare the relative effectiveness of the two therapy programs. We found a significant effect of pre- vs. post-evaluation ($F=112.46$, $df= 1$, $P < 0.001$) and of writing task ($F=24.81$, $df= 2$, $P < 0.001$) but neither an effect of the type of treatment nor any interactions. Although there was no main effect of the type of treatment, it is possible that whole group performance obscured individual patterns. Consequently, single case results were analysed by means of $x^2$ test. It was found that for the majority of the patients only one treatment was effective. For patients 2, 4 and 5 the phonological

TABLE 21.3
Results Based on Number of Total Correct Responses out of the 240 Items (80 x 3 Writing Tasks) Before (Pre) and on Completion (Post) of Each Treatment and 40–50 Days Later (Delayed Control)

| | *Treatment 1* | | | | *Treatment 2* | | | | *delayed* |
|---|---|---|---|---|---|---|---|---|---|
| | *pre* | | *post* | | *pre* | | *post* | | *control* |
| Patient | | | | | | | | | |
| 1 | 122 | ± | 144* | | 165 | + | 193 | | 209 |
| 2 | 41 | | 45 | | 48 | + | 116* | | 140 |
| 3 | 95 | + | 167 | | 177 | | 185* | | 192 |
| 4 | 127 | + | 162* | | 150 | | 168 | | 176 |
| 5 | 44 | + | 94* | | 114 | | 119 | | 115 |
| 6 | 111 | + | 173 | | 167 | ± | 189* | | 181 |
| $\overline{X}$ | 90 | + | 130.8 | = | 136.8 | + | 161.7 | = | 168.8 |

* = phonological treatment
+ = $P < 0.01$, $X^2$ test or $P < 0.05$ (Newmann-Keuls)
± = $0.02 < P < 0.05$, $X^2$ test

treatment significantly improved performance ($P<0.001$) whereas the visual-semantic did not. The reverse pattern (effect of the visual-semantic, $P<0.001$) was found in the case of patient 3. For patients 1 and 6 there were significant effects of both treatments ($P<0.001$ for the visual-semantic treatment, $P<0.05$ for the phonological). Thus, four out of the six patients involved in the present study showed a positive response only to one treatment. It might be argued that, in carrying out the single case analyses by means of $x^2$ test, the large number of unconstrained tests made possible a type 1 error. However, it should be stressed that: (1) when an effect of a particular treatment was found, the effect reached a high level of significance; and (2) our main focus was to demonstrate that in some cases patients did not improve following one of the two treatments. Furthermore, the possibility that a ceiling effect would have biased these results is explored in the Discussion section.

According to our experimental design, the relative effectiveness of the two therapeutic strategies can also be analysed by assessing the patterns of improvement on the three different writing materials. This was done by single case analyses using $x^2$ tests. Table 21.4 gives the scores for the individual patients on each test type and the effect of the phonological treatment spread over the three tasks.

Improving the phoneme to grapheme writing routines could result in a better performance in written naming task if patients used a self-dictation strategy. This pattern was clearly shown by two out of the three patients whose writing performance improved only as a result of phonological treatment (patients 2 and 5). The third patient who had shown selective response to the phonological treatment overall (patient 4) exhibited an abnormal pattern in that his written naming alone showed a significant improvement. However, it should be noted that the extent of his general improvement was limited. Such a limited improvement could have obscured effects of the phonological treatment on word and nonword writing. Patient 1, who improved following both treatments, exhibited a better performance only on writing words and nonwords to dictation.

In contrast, the visual-semantic treatment appeared to affect performance mostly in written naming and word writing. Such a pattern was clearly exhibited by patient 3 and, to a lesser extent, by patient 1 (improvement on his word writing was obscured by a ceiling effect). However, unexpectedly, patient 6 showed improved performance on nonword writing, as well as on written naming and word writing. It should be stressed that the last finding, and that involving patient 4 (see earlier), were the only exceptions we found to the predicted patterns of improvement.

TABLE 21.4
Results Based on the Number of Correct Responses (out of 80) on the 3 Writing Tasks Before (Pre) and on Completion (Post) of Each Type of Treatment

| | *Written Naming* | | | *Word Writing* | | | *Nonword Writing* | | | *Total effect* |
|---|---|---|---|---|---|---|---|---|---|---|
| | Pre | | Post | Pre | | Post | Pre | | Post | |
| **(a) Visual-semantic Treatment** | | | | | | | | | | |
| *Patient* | | | | | | | | | | |
| 1 | 53 | + | 76 | 72 | | 73 | 40 | | 44 | + |
| 2 | 22 | | 24 | 13 | | 17 | 6 | | 4 | – |
| 3 | 29 | + | 57 | 25 | + | 65 | 41 | | 45 | + |
| 4 | 42 | | 50 | 68 | | 66 | 40 | | 52 | + |
| 5 | 46 | | 52 | 44 | | 43 | 24 | | 24 | – |
| 6 | 32 | + | 65 | 53 | + | 66 | 26 | + | 42 | + |
| $\bar{X}$ | 37.3 | | 54 | 45.8 | | 55 | 28.6 | | 34.6 | |
| **(b) Phonological Treatment** | | | | | | | | | | |
| *Patient* | | | | | | | | | | |
| 1 | 50 | | 42 | 46 | + | 62 | 26 | + | 40 | ± |
| 2 | 22 | + | 38 | 20 | + | 60 | 6 | + | 18 | + |
| 3 | 62 | | 62 | 69 | | 69 | 46 | | 54 | – |
| 4 | 34 | + | 50 | 51 | | 62 | 42 | | 50 | + |
| 5 | 14 | + | 38 | 24 | + | 40 | 6 | ± | 16 | + |
| 6 | 56 | | 64 | 63 | | 67 | 48 | | 58 | ± |
| $\bar{X}$ | 39.7 | | 49 | 45.5 | | 60 | 29 | | 39.3 | |

Total Effect = significant effect of treatment on the whole performance, ($x^2$ test), see Table 21.2
+ = $p < 0.02$, $x^2$ test; ± = $p < 0.05$, $x^2$ test

## DISCUSSION

The first problem our work addressed concerned the effectiveness of the two "theoretically driven" rehabilitation programs for writing disturbances in aphasia. That there were real effects is supported by a number of constraints in the experimental design. First, we chose patients who were neurologically stable, according to the criteria that they were at least eight months post-onset of a single left hemisphere stroke and, despite language therapy, no writing improvement could be noticed on aphasia testing. Second, the ABCB paradigm indicated that the improvement could be confidently assigned to the experimental treatment programs. Finally, there was learning transfer to untreated items, (see later). Indeed, the clinical relevance of our treatment is indicated by the retention of what patients had learned 40-50 days after completion of both therapy programs. With reference to this, we should like to underline the fact that, when therapy stopped, some patients spontaneously practiced writing in daily life. For instance, cases 1 and

2 maintained a personal diary, and case 3 wrote captions to illustrations in advertising magazines in which he was interested. That would probably account for the further slight writing improvement that was observed at the delayed control in their case, (see Table 21.2).

On the whole, our results were quite different from those of Hatfield and Weddel (1976) and Seron et al. (1980) whose studies did not succeed in showing any stable effect of writing rehabilitation procedures over time. Hatfield and Weddel's (1976) study involved severe aphasic patients. Their failure to maintain performance suggests that the relative gravity of aphasic disturbances may be important. However, this is unlikely to be the only contrast with respect to Seron et al.'s (1980) study, where an effect of therapy was found at the first post-test. One difference is that Seron et al. did not take into account the relative effectiveness of the two (lexical and nonlexical) writing routines nor the variability of patients' compensatory behaviour. We propose that Seron et al.'s study could have been biased by conflict between patients' spontaneous strategies and the rehabilitation techniques so that any training effect was not stable. This hypothesis was supported by our finding that the majority of cases (patients 2, 3, 4, and 5) improved by means of only one treatment. That was clearly observed in the case of patients 2 and 5 where only the second treatment produced significant effects. For patients 3 and 4, who did not show improvement from the second treatment, it might be argued that there was a ceiling effect. Against this, patient 3 did not show improvement in nonword writing following the phonological treatment and, conversely, written naming of patient 4 did not improve with the visual-semantic treatment (see Table 21.4). In both cases, we should have observed a significant effect in at least these two tasks.

We also suggested that each therapeutic program might stimulate (partially) spared components of one of the two writing routines. This was also supported by the two observed patterns of improvement: i.e. word and nonword writing improved following the phonological treatment; written naming and word writing improved following the visual-semantic treatment. It should also be noted that we found only two exceptions to these predictions out of the 12 therapeutic attempts. One exceptional case is patient 4, where the limited general improvement could have obscured the predicted improvement in word and nonword writing. The second exception, patient 6, had improved performance in nonword writing by means of the visual-semantic treatment. In this case, there was a positive response also to the phonological treatment. This may indicate the relative efficiency of partially spared components of the phonological writing routine. Thus, this particular finding would not contradict the general impression that each of the two therapies selectively stimulated only one of the two writing routines. We argue that a selective stimulation of one (better preserved) writing mechanism would account for the finding that therapy effects were stable over time.

As a final consideration, it should be pointed out that our work involved unselected aphasic patients without taking into account the initial pattern of dysgraphia. From this point of view our work was different from those studies where a single malfunctioning component of a cognitive model was identified and the subsequent therapeutic program focused on restoration of the impaired aspect, see for instance remediation of homophone writing following damage to the lexical writing routine (Behrmann, 1987). Our therapeutic hypotheses assumed that in all patients both writing routines were damaged but residual knowledge of whole word form spelling (Hatfield, 1985) or residual phoneme to grapheme conversion abilities (Carlomagno & Parlato, 1989) could be present. Therefore, our therapeutic programs were structured so that patients could be enabled to use such residual writing skills. The significant learning transfer to untreated items, which was observed following both the visual-semantic and the phonological treatment, was consistent with our hypotheses. Consider, in fact, the writing improvement of patient 3. He had been trained to write the word "lampadina" by semantic and visual cues (see Treatment Procedures earlier). Following the visual-semantic treatment the patient became able to spell correctly the untreated item "cartolina" (postcard). As his nonlexical writing abilities did not improve it is likely that he was able to access the whole word form "cartolina", which was unavailable before. We argue that, to do this, patient 3 used his residual knowledge about word spelling (it contains 9 letters, there is one letter "t" in the fourth position) and word meaning (it is usually sent by travellers to their friends, it needs a stamp) as *self-generated* visual and semantic cues. Similarly, learning generalised across untreated items (the seven untreated consonants) in the case of the phonological treatment. We argue that patient 2, for instance, following the treatment, became able to self-generate code-names (key-words) for the seven untreated consonants and to use it efficiently when attempting phoneme to grapheme conversion of a phonological unit.

On the whole our data support the hypothesis that cognitive models can provide a rationale for planning treatments for aphasic disturbances. For instance, when language stimulation ceases to produce significant improvement, specific therapeutic programs can be provided for obviating selective features of an aphasic deficit. Moreover, these programs, as in the present work, should be tied down to a sufficiently clear representation of cognitive processes, which produce normal function (Seron, 1984) and to plausible hypotheses aimed at identifying residual knowledge that the treatment itself would stimulate (Carlomagno & Parlato, 1989; Hatfield, 1984). With reference to this, it should be stressed that both treatments and their relative patterns of improvement could be predicted by the dual route model(s) of writing functions.

## NOTE

1. The Promoting Aphasics' Communicative Effectiveness (PACE) is an aphasia treatment technique that is, according to Davis and Wilcox (1985) "...intended to reshape structured interaction between clinician and aphasic clients into a form resembling face to face conversation" (p.89). The six patients also participated in a PACE treatment program in order to improve their referential communication abilities in face to face conversation by using nonverbal communication strategies (Carlomagno et al., 1991).

## ACKNOWLEDGEMENTS

This work has been supported by a grant from Centro Ricerche Clinica Santa Lucia, Roma. The authors are deeply grateful to P. Casadio, S. Emanuelli and C. Razzano from the clinical staff of Centro Ricerche Clinica Santa Lucia. G. Deloche (INSERM, Paris) provided helpful suggestions on the structure of visual-semantic treatment.

## REFERENCES

Behrmann, M. (1987). The rites of righting writing: Homophone remediation in acquired dysgraphia. *Cognitive Neuropsychology, 4,* 365-384.

Burani, C., Laudanna, A., Miceli, G., & Caramazza, A., (1984). *Una batteria per la valutazione dei disturbi di lettura e scrittura in soggetti cerebrolesi di lingua italiana.* Unpublished.

Carlomagno S., Emanuelli S., Casadio P., & Losanno N. (1991). Expressive language recovery or improved communicative skills: Effects of PACE therapy on aphasics' referential communication and story retelling. *Aphasiology, 5(4-5),* 419-424.

Carlomagno S., & Parlato V. (1989). Writing rehabilitation in brain damaged adult patients: A cognitive approach. In X. Seron & G. Deloche (Eds.), *Cognitive approaches in neuropsychological rehabilitation.* Hillsdale, N.J.: Lawrence Erlbaum Associates Inc.

Coltheart, M. (1984). Writing systems and reading disorders. In L. Henderson (Ed.), *Orthographies and reading.* Hillsdale, N.J.: Lawrence Erlbaum Associates Inc.

Coltheart, M., Masterson, J., Byng, S., Prior, M., & Riddoch, J. (1983). Surface dyslexia. *Quarterly Journal of Experimental Psychology, 35A,* 469-495.

Davis, A., & Wilcox, M.J. (1985). *Adult aphasia rehabilitation: Applied Pragmatics.* San Diego, C.A.: College Hill Press.

De Partz, M.P. (1986). Reeducation of a deep dyslexic patient: Rationale of the method and results. *Cognitive Neuropsychology, 3,* 149-177.

Ellis, A.W. (1982). Spelling and writing (and reading and speaking). In A.W. Ellis (Ed.), *Normality and pathology of cognitive functions.* London: Academic Press.

Hatfield, M.F. (1984). Aspect of acquired dysgraphia and implication for re-education. In C. Code, & D.J. Müller (Eds.), *Aphasia therapy.* London: Edward Arnold Publisher.

Hatfield, M.F. (1985). Visual and phonological factors in acquired dysgraphia. *Neuropsychologica, 23(1),* 13-29.

Hatfield. M.F., & Patterson, K.E. (1984). Interpretation of spelling disorders in aphasia: Impact of recent developments in cognitive psychology. In F.C. Rose (Ed.), *Advances in neurology, Vol. 42: Progress in aphasiology.* New York: Raven Press.

Hatfield, M.F., & Weddel R. (1976). Re-training in writing in severe aphasia. In Y. Lebrun & R. Hoops (Eds.), *Recovery in aphasics.* Amsterdam: Swets and Zeitlinger.

Luria, A.R., Naydin, V.L., Tveskova, L.S., & Virnarskaya, E.N. (1969). Restoration of higher cortical function following local brain damage. In P. Vinken & G.N. Bruyn (Eds.), *Handbook of clinical neurology, Vol. 3.* Amsterdam: North Holland.

Morton, J. (1980). The logogen model and the orthographic structure. In U. Frith (Ed.), *Cognitive processes in spelling.* London: Academic Press.

Pizzamiglio, L., Mammuccari, A., & Razzano, C. (1985). Evidence for sex differences in brain organization from recovery in aphasia. *Brain and Language, 25,* 213-223.

Seron, X. (1984). Reeducation strategies in neuropsychology: Cognitive and pragmatic approaches. In F.C. Rose (Ed.), *Advances in neurology, Vol 42: Progress in aphasiology.* New York: Raven Press.

Seron, X., Deloche, G., Moulard, G., & Rousselle, M. (1980). A computer based therapy for the treatment of aphasic subjects with writing disorders. *Journal of Speech and Hearing Disorders, 45,* 45-58.

Shallice, T. (1981). Phonological agraphia and the lexical route in writing. *Brain, 104,* 413-429.

Snodgrass, J.G., & Vanderwart, M. (1980). A standardised set of 260 pictures: Norms for name agreement, image agreement, familiarity and visual complexity. *Journal of Experimental Psychology: Human Learning and Memory, 6,* 174 - 215.

CHAPTER TWENTY-TWO

# Approaches to the Rehabilitation of "Phonological Assembly": Elaborating the Model of Nonlexical Reading

Rita Sloan Berndt and Charlotte C. Mitchum
*University of Maryland School of Medicine, Baltimore, Maryland, USA*

## INTRODUCTION

There are a variety of ways that models of normal cognition can be applied to rehabilitation of patients with cognitive deficits, and many of them are illustrated in this volume. This chapter concerns a somewhat different type of application. It focuses on the contribution that attempting to carry out a treatment study can make to the development and expansion of the models themselves. We will try to demonstrate, using the outcome of an attempt to teach a severely aphasic/dyslexic patient to "sound out" print, that thinking about how to improve patients' deficits forces one to consider carefully a set of issues that are often ignored or downplayed in cognitive neuropsychology. In order to design a set of therapy tasks directed at specific components of a cognitive model, it is essential to have some idea about the answers to the following questions:

1. What sorts of representations and processes does the model postulate? If the model is schematised using the typical boxes and arrows format, this question asks that details about the contents of the boxes and the nature of the arrows be specified.
2. Can the components of the model (i.e. the boxes and arrows) be analysed with respect to their potential recovery through treatment?

3. How do isolated components of a specific model (the boxes) interact with or exploit other *specific* cognitive processes from other domains?
4. To what extent do isolated components of specific models require that more *general* cognitive capacities are intact?

An example might clarify these somewhat vague questions. Figure 22.1 represents a fairly standard dual-route model of reading, adapted from Newcombe and Marshall (1984). Several of the recent applications of cognitive models to rehabilitation have begun with a model such as this one, and have focused on the remediation of discrete processing components within the model. For example, successful interventions have been reported that focused: (1) on the left side of this model, resulting in improvement in direct lexical access from printed words (Coltheart & Byng, 1989); (2) on the right side of the model, re-establishing the procedures for generating sound from print nonlexically (DePartz, 1986). In these examples, the therapy focused on the explicit teaching of a limited body of information that was postulated by the normal model to be required for the successful accomplishment of a specific cognitive activity.

One aspect of these kinds of cognitive models, made evident by attempting to design a treatment based on them, is that there are very different types of information in the different boxes. It may be that our tendency to think about cognition in terms of boxes and arrows, though without doubt useful, has obscured the fact that the content of the boxes, let alone the nature of what is represented by the arrows, differs qualitatively from box to box, arrow to arrow. On the left, lexical side of the model, there are several boxes that are apparently assumed to hold a set of representations—a sort of listing, organised in some fashion, of letters, orthographic word forms, phonological word forms etc. We can refer to these types of boxes as CONTENT boxes, because we assume that they represent some describable set of discrete entities—some content. Other boxes on this model do not represent content, but what we might call OPERATIONS. On the right, nonlexical side of the model, *grapheme parsing* presumably refers to some sort of segmentation operation that readers must carry out to divide an input letter string into pronounceable units. *Phoneme blending* presumably refers to a combinatorial operation that allows individual sounds to be expressed as syllables and other, larger phonologically specified patterns.

If we begin to think this way about the differences between these boxes, question 2, posed earlier, can be addressed: Will some types of deficit be more tractable targets for treatment than will others? Loss of content, or loss of accessibility to content, can be addressed in a number of ways. For example, Coltheart and Byng (1989) taught a surface

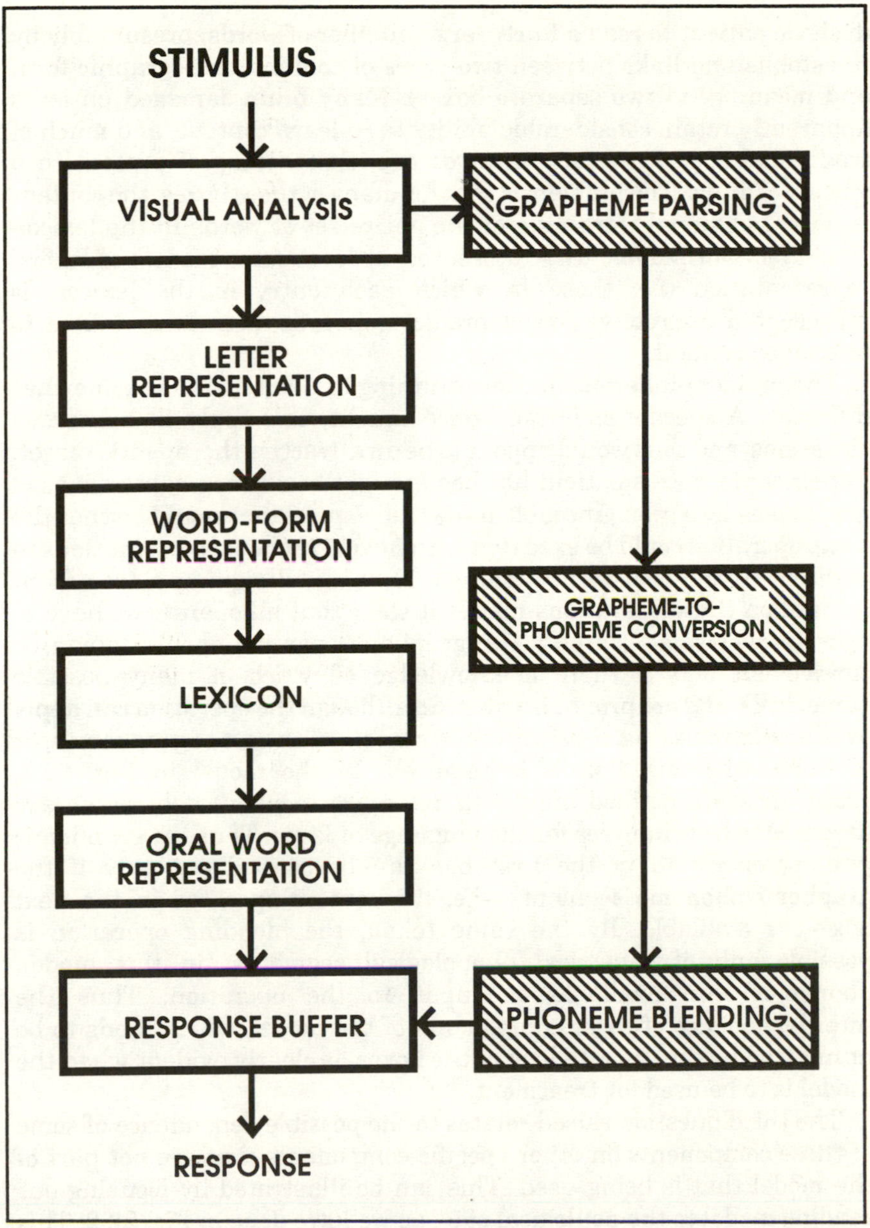


FIG. 22.1. Dual route model of normal reading (adapted from Newcombe & Marshall, 1984). Left, (unshaded) components are implicated in "addressed" or lexical reading; right (shaded) components are hypothesised for "assembled" or non-lexical reading.

dyslexic patient to read a fairly large number of words, presumably by re-establishing links between two types of content: orthographic form and meaning (in two separate boxes). Many brain-damaged patients apparently retain considerable ability to re-learn content, and much of traditional speech therapy involves explicit teaching of content in a variety of areas. The problem is that for many of these boxes, the content is vast: Individual retraining of the entire set of words in the lexicon would be a formidable task. Moreover, at least some models of lexical representation (i.e. those in which each entry in the lexicon is represented discretely) do not predict generalisation from trained to untrained content.

The problem inherent in the retraining of OPERATIONS is somewhat different. A specific operation, once taught, can apply in numerous situations, and thus would appear to be an attractive therapeutic target. For example, once a patient has been taught how to segment strings of graphemes into pronounceable units, the expectation would be that the same operation could be executed with novel grapheme combinations in addition to those explicitly trained. Even so, designing a treatment focused on these operations makes it clear that all operations have to operate over some content: The graphemic parsing operation can be carried out only if there is knowledge of which of many possible sublexical units are pronounceable. So although the operation can apply over any input string, a listing of the content of the set of graphemes, or of some other sized unit, is required. In the model in Fig. 22.1, graphemes are defined only with reference to phonemes, which are assumed to be primitives for the language at issue. Thus the graphemic parsing operation in the first box can be carried out only if the grapheme/phoneme segments—i.e. the content specified in the next box—are available. By the same token, the blending operation is possible only if sublexical phonological segments (in this model, phonemes) are available as input to the operation. Thus the interdependence of these components of the model, which tends to be minimized by the discrete look of the boxes, is clearly evident when the model is to be used for treatment.

The third question raised relates to the possible dependence of some of these components on other specific components that are not part of the model that is being used. This can be illustrated by focusing our reading model to the nonlexical side, as we have done in Fig. 22.2. This figure represents the assumed output of each of the components, which indicates that some type of phonological processing must occur during nonlexical reading, both to provide sublexical phonological segments for association with graphemes, and to ensure that the combination of these segments during the blending stage adheres to phonological rules. These

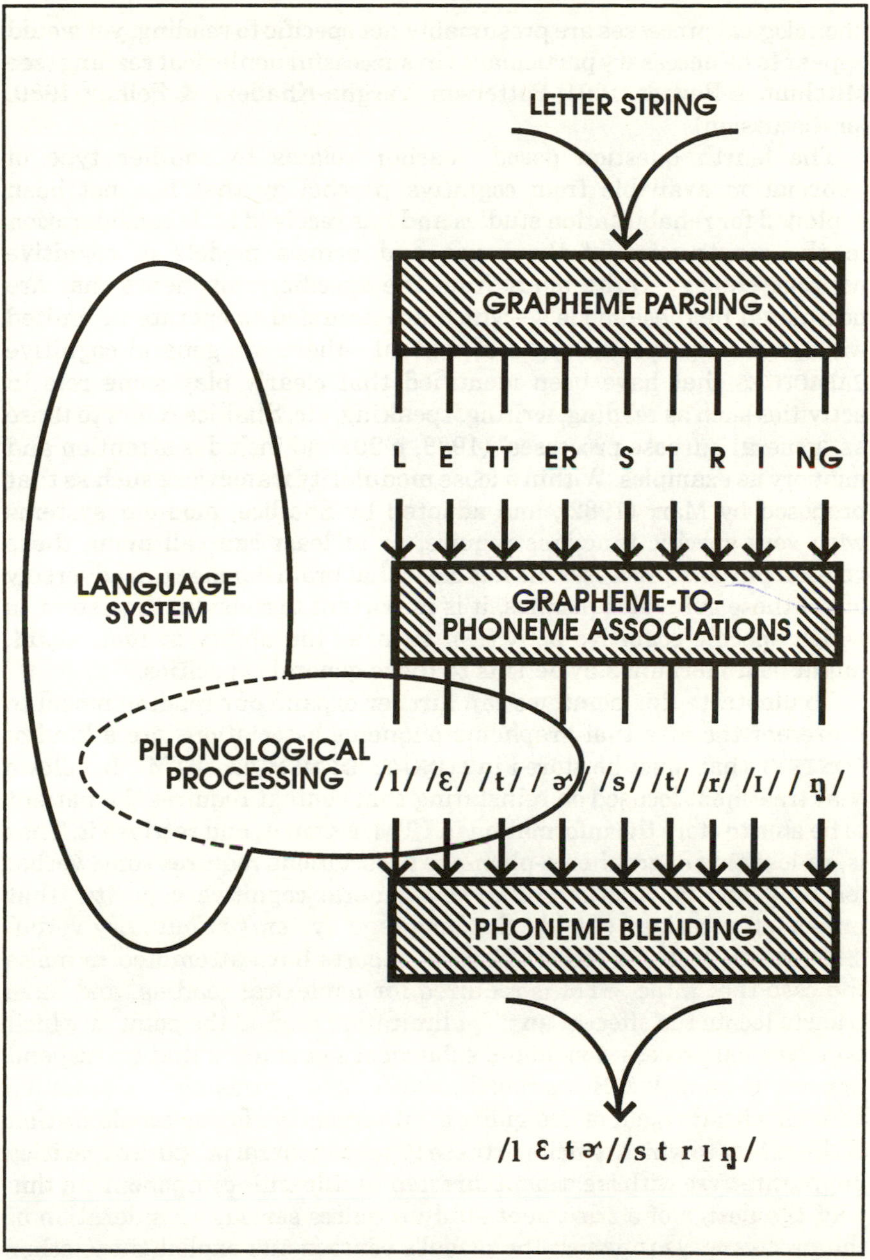


FIG. 22.2. Expansion model of nonlexical reading (shaded route in Fig. 22.1) showing more detailed input/output and possible involvement of a component from the general language system.

phonological processes are presumably not specific to reading, yet would appear to be necessary participants in successful nonlexical reading (see Mitchum & Berndt, 1991; Patterson, Vargha-Khadem, & Polkey, 1989, for discussion).

The fourth question posed earlier relates to another type of information available from cognitive psychology that has not been exploited for rehabilitation studies and has received little consideration in the construction of the boxes and arrows models of cognitive neuropsychology. Quite apart from the specific components that are postulated by these models—which are assumed to operate in limited ways over very specific types of content—there are general cognitive CAPACITIES that have been identified that clearly play some role in activities such as reading, writing, speaking, etc. Shallice refers to these as "general purpose processes" (1988, p.20) and includes attention and memory as examples. Within a loose modularity framework such as that proposed by Marr (1982), and adapted by Shallice, modular systems with very specific functions require, or at least can call upon, these general purpose processes. As it is clear that brain damage can adversely affect these general capacities, it is important to consider the extent to which specific cognitive activities, such as the ability to read aloud, might be undermined by deficits to these general capacities.

To illustrate this point, we can further expand our reading model to represent the idea that grapheme-phoneme associations are a kind of CONTENT that must be stored in LONG-TERM MEMORY (LTM). It follows that treatment focused on reinstating that content requires the patient to be able to store the information in LTM, retain it, and retrieve it. That is, re-learning of grapheme-phoneme associations requires some verbal learning ability. Another relatively general cognitive capacity (that presumably resides outside the language system) is auditory-verbal SHORT-TERM MEMORY (STM). Several reports have attempted to make the case that intact STM is required for nonlexical reading, and have tried to locate the effect of an STM limitation around the point at which phonological processes yield the sublexical sound units that correspond to print (Campbell & Butterworth, 1985). Again, focusing on a patient's deficits with the goal of designing an intervention forces consideration of the extent to which deficits to these types of general purpose capacities might interfere with treatment directed at a specific component. In this way, the design of a treatment study requires serious consideration of the precise ways in which the model's components exploit these other cognitive processes.

A further, related issue that to date has not generated much discussion is the likelihood that these qualitatively distinct levels of possible deficit—specific content and operations within a particular

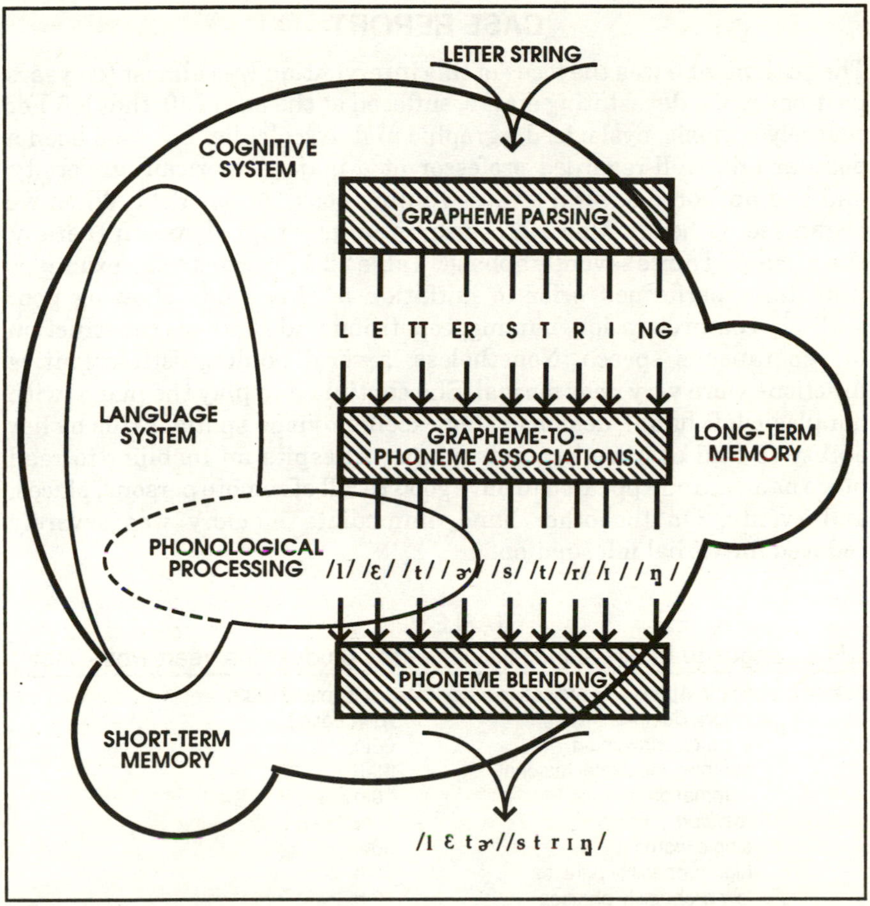


FIG. 22.3 Further expansion of model of nonlexical reading suggesting two possible interfaces with general purpose cognitive capacities (memory).

domain such as oral reading; specific processes and representations that are shared across several domains such as reading and speaking; and "general purpose" cognitive capacities such as attention and memory—are quite distinct in their potential for remediation. Although there are a variety of means available for addressing deficits to specific CONTENT and OPERATIONS, few useful ideas have been proposed to improve or circumvent deficits to general cognitive capacities. It is not clear, for example, that diminished capacity in short-term memory can be improved by clinical intervention. We will return to this point—which we believe is crucial when applying cognitive models to rehabilitation—when we have presented some results of our intervention study.

## CASE REPORT

The patient who was the focus of this intervention was almost ten years post-onset of a devastating stroke, suffered at the age of 50, that left her severely aphasic, dyslexic, dysgraphic and dyscalculic. L.R. had been a popular and well-regarded professor at a major American university, and had authored several award-winning books in her field. When we began seeing her in May 1987, despite uninterrupted speech therapy, she remained quite severely aphasic. Table 22.1 provides some examples from tests performed prior to initiation of this study showing poor auditory comprehension, naming, repetition and sentence construction in spontaneous speech. Nonetheless, several nonlinguistic cognitive functions were very near normal. She continued to play the piano (with nonplegic left hand), demonstrated excellent visuo-spatial skills by her ability to find obscure locations on maps despite an inability to read place names, and appeared to have good recall of remote persons, places, and events. On the other hand, immediate memory was severely reduced for verbal information.

TABLE 22.1

L.R.'s Language Profile at the Initiation of the Study (Nine Years Post-Onset)

| | | |
|---|---|---|
| Boston Diagnostic Aphasia Examination (Goodglass & Kaplan, 1983) | | |
| *Auditory Comprehension* | *(percentile)* | |
| word discrimination | 60th | |
| complex ideational material | 30th | |
| commands | 10th | |
| *Repetition* | | |
| single words | 50th | |
| high probability phrases | 50th | |
| low probability phrases | 40th | |
| Naming | | |
| *Boston Naming Test (Kaplan, Goodglass, & Weintraub, 1978)* | *31/60* | *(65% semantic errors)* |
| naming objects | 19/20 | |
| naming actions | 4/20 | |
| Sentence production in narrative speech (Saffran, Berndt, & Schwartz, 1990) | | |
| – slow speech rate | | |
| – few verbs, function words | | |
| – spared bound morphemes | | |
| – many single word utterances | | |
| – many sentence fragments | | |
| Memory | | |
| LTM: | apparently near normal | |
| STM: | digit span = 2 | |
| | 4-word probe recognition—poor with severe "no" response bias | |

## MOTIVATING THE SPECIFIC INTERVENTION

Despite the severity of L.R.'s deficits, several factors influenced us to begin working to improve her reading ability. The first is that she herself was obsessed with regaining the ability to read—she maintains that reading is the most important thing in her life. Her motivation and premorbid capacities in this area were clear. Second, despite severe aphasia, she had been able to achieve some improvement in her reading, and regularly attempted to write words with some success. A third factor that motivated us to proceed was that the pattern of her reading abilities was quite similar to the initial pattern reported for the French-speaking patient S.P., whose reading had been very successfully treated in a cognitive neuropsychological study carried out by DePartz (1986). As shown in Table 22.2, both L.R. and S.P. could be characterised as deep dyslexics, with poor non-word reading, better reading of high than low imageable words, and no regularity effect[1]. Both patients produced some semantic errors.

De Partz's treatment had focused on the re-education of nonlexical reading, using a technique of having the patient sound out each letter of the target word by generating a cue word that began with that letter, then segmenting off the initial phoneme of that word and pronouncing it in isolation (DePartz, 1986; see also Bachy-Langedock & DePartz, 1989). S.P. had great difficulty learning to associate isolated letters with cue words (requiring fifty-two sessions on this phase of the treatment). Nonetheless, once letters and words were associated, S.P. learned to perform the operation needed to segment the initial sound from the cue word, and required no special treatment of the blending operation.

TABLE 22.2
Proportion Correct, Pre-treatment Oral Reading, L.R. and S.P. (De Partz, 1986)

| | | *L.R.* | *S.P.* (Tables 9, 10 and 13, p.165) | |
|---|---|---|---|---|
| *Imageability* | | | | |
| High | (N=18) | 0.56 | 0.60 | (N=20) |
| Low | (N=18) | 0.28 | 0.00 | (N=20) |
| *Regularity* | | | | |
| Regular | (N=18) | 0.28 | 0.33 | (N=15) |
| Irregular | (N=18) | 0.28 | 0.26 | (N=15) |
| *Form Class* | | | | |
| Uninflected nouns | (N=10) | 0.60 | 0.50 | (N=10) |
| Uninflected verbs | (N=10) | 0.70 | 0.10 | (N=10) |
| Functors | (N=47) | 0.53 | 0.00 | (N=20) |
| 3-Letter nonwords | (N=15) | 0.08 | 0.07 | (N=30) |
| *Error Distribution (proportion of errors, all real words)* | | | | |
| Semantic | | 0.10 | 0.12 | |
| Visual/Phonologic | | 0.60 | 0.08 | |
| Other | | 0.30 | 0.80 (0.42 "no response") | |

The goal of this kind of treatment—and this was our primary motivation in thinking about L.R.—is not to turn the patient into a surface dyslexic who must sound out every word encountered, but to place some constraints on the operation of the lexical reading processes on which these patients rely. The idea is that some knowledge of grapheme/phoneme associations will result in a decline in the number of semantic errors, as the patient will know, for example, that the word "pixie" cannot be the word "gnome" because it must start with a /p/. Visual errors might also be expected to decline with improved knowledge of letter/sound correspondences, if the patient can be induced to check for sound correspondences at both the beginnings *and* ends of words. For example, 60% of L.R.'s paralexic errors shared visual and/or phonological information with the target, with the mismatch limited to the ends of words (e.g. MILE→MILK; SWIM→SWING). On the basis of these considerations, we decided to focus on nonlexical reading, or in Patterson's (1982) terminology, on the assembly of phonology from print, and to use as a guiding model the skeletal framework presented in Fig. 22.1 and elaborated in Figs. 22.2 and 22.3.

## LOCATING THE DEFICIT ON THE MODEL

The three components that have been argued to comprise the phonological assembly process (see Fig. 22.1, shaded boxes) have been the focus of a number of cognitive neuropsychological studies that have attempted to explain a patient's inability to read non-words as arising from a deficit to one of the components (see Coltheart, 1985; Shallice, 1988, for reviews). Thus, patients have been identified whose inability to read non-words has been argued to result from a deficit of the graphemic parsing operation (Beauvois & Derouesne, 1979; Newcombe & Marshall, 1985), from an impairment of the ability to link graphemes and phonemes (e.g. Funnell, 1983), and from an inability to combine the phonemes that are successfully recovered into a unified syllabic representation (Derouesne & Beauvois, 1985).

Testing before initiation of the treatment (see Table 22.3) indicated that L.R. had some problems with all three of the model's components. Graphemic parsing was intact for lexical units (she was able to find and circle a word in a larger non-word and to place a line between lexical stems and their inflections), but she was not able to divide printed words into syllables. We could not test L.R.'s ability to segment letter strings into graphemes because, as discussed later, we could not demonstrate that she had any concept of phonemes. We should also point out that many other purported attempts to test the graphemic parsing

TABLE 22.3
Pre-treatment Assessment of Three Components of Phonological Assembly

| | | |
|---|---|---|
| *Graphemic parsing* | | |
| circling words embedded in nonwords (e.g. fa*pen*lep) | | 15/19 |
| placing a line between stems/inflections | | 17/18 |
| placing a line between syllables in words | | 2/10 |
| *Grapheme/phoneme associations* | | |
| letter sounding | ($\bar{X}$ RT = 16sec.) | 9/26 |
| pointing to letter from sound (3 distractors) | | 18/26 |
| *Blending* | | |
| lexical (saying a single compound word after hearing its two parts spoken, 2sec. apart) | | 18/18 |
| sublexical (saying a 3-phoneme word after hearing the 3 phonemes spoken separately at 2sec. intervals) | | 3/7 |

component have failed to test patients' appreciation of graphemes, but have relied for evidence of intact graphemic segmentation on patients' ability to identify lexical segments embedded in nonlexical strings, (e.g. Funnell, 1983). Though we could not document that L.R. understood that both single letters and multiple letters could function as a single unit for pronunciation, she at least demonstrated no difficulty with the idea that printed letter strings were analysable into smaller parts.

Tests of grapheme/phoneme associations, finally completed after considerable training and orientation to the tasks used, uncovered some ability to produce phonemes from isolated letters (letter sounding, Table 22.3), and considerable ability to map from spoken phonemes to graphemes (pointing to the correct letter in a field of four). Tests of the blending component revealed great difficulty blending aurally presented phonemes into words, although blending small lexical segments into a new, larger word (i.e. a compound word) was intact.

As suggested by our discussions of Fig. 22.2, models of oral reading have tended to neglect specification of the phonological processes that are presumably required to generate the sublexical segments to which graphemes must be mapped, and that govern the combination of sublexical segments at the blending stage. Although only a few studies of acquired dyslexia have considered these phonological operations, research on the *development* of reading has emphasised them. The current thinking on the relationship between phonological operations such as phonological segmentation and the development of reading seems to be that the two develop in tandem and are mutually reinforcing: The ability to perform segmentation operations enhances the learning of sublexical print-to-sound correspondences, and learning to read enhances the ability to perform phonological tasks (especially those requiring phonemic-level, as opposed to simply phonetic, decisions) (Coltheart & Stuart, 1988). De Partz's patient S.P. had little problem performing the segmentation operations, and in fact, was able to perform phonological segmentation and manipulation at a normal level if printed words were not involved. The situation for L.R. was quite different: At the initiation of treatment, L.R. demonstrated no appreciation of the fact that spoken words could be analysed into component sounds. She was unable even to segment two-syllable compound words into two parts.

## TREATMENTS 1 AND 2: PHONOLOGICAL SEGMENTATION; GRAPHEME/PHONEME ASSOCIATIONS

The pre-treatment diagnostic assessment had uncovered a number of deficits, but did not indicate which was primary, nor which should be addressed first. We reasoned as follows: Although both the operations of graphemic parsing and phonological blending showed evidence of impairment, the latter quite severe, real tests of the extent of those impairments were impossible to carry out without some evidence that the patient was able to generate and maintain phonemes or some other sublexical segments. Thus, the ability to link graphemes to phonemes appeared to be the place to start in terms of the three-component model on the nonlexical side of Fig. 22.1. This starting point seemed to require some preliminary work on the phonological processes (Fig. 22.2) that would allow L.R. to segment whole, spoken words (which she could produce without much difficulty) into their component phonemes (which she showed no indication of being able to produce).

Treatment 1 was thus directed at phonological segmentation, and used colour-coded tokens to represent discrete sound segments that could be added, deleted and re-ordered (see Mitchum & Berndt, 1991, for details). For example, three segmented sounds would be spoken and three corresponding coloured tokens would be presented with those sounds. For example, /p/ /p/ /I/ would be presented with (perhaps) two blue, and one yellow token. The exercises focused on manipulating the sounds and their corresponding colours; e.g. L.R. would be asked to move the tokens to represent /p/ /I/ /p/. The idea was to proceed gradually to a situation in which vowels and consonants were spoken as a blended segment, e.g. /pIp/, but continued to be represented as three separate sounds by the coloured tokens. This treatment did not proceed in quite the way we had planned: L.R. resisted the idea that spoken, blended words and non-words could be decomposed, although she performed quite well when the component phonemes were spoken separately.

After many sessions we abandoned our attempt to separate the treatment of phonological segmentation from treatment of grapheme/phoneme associations, and we introduced written letters. Re-testing of letter sounding at this time showed, to our surprise, a marked improvement (from a zero baseline to 35% correct). Although the exercise in phonological segmentation had to be abandoned, it seemed to establish an appreciation for the general concept of sublexical sound pattern, that L.R. used when attempting to sound out letters. After working with written letters for a few sessions, L.R. was able to segment the initial sounds from spoken words without difficulty. Despite her complete inability to produce any sublexical segments prior to intervention, she could now produce the sound /kə/, without effort, when hearing the spoken word CAT. We interpret these findings as support for the reciprocal relationship between phonological segmentation and letter sounding that has emerged from the developmental literature (Coltheart & Stuart, 1988). That is, practice in manipulating sound segments appeared to enhance letter sounding; practice with letter sounds and their combinations enhanced auditory segmentation.

We introduced immediately a second treatment program designed to reinstate grapheme/phoneme correspondences for 18 very predictable consonant graphemes (including two two-letter graphemes), and for the most probable correspondences for the five vowels (Berndt, Reggia, & Mitchum, 1987). We used De Partz's basic technique: Associating each grapheme with a cue word, then segmenting its initial phoneme and pronouncing it in isolation. After 17 one-hour sessions, the cue words were no longer required, and L.R. was able to produce isolated phonemes relatively quickly and, most often, accurately in response to presented graphemes (69% sounded within three seconds). Thus, we succeeded to some extent in reinstating grapheme/phoneme correspondences, at least for the most predictable associations. Re-testing fifteen three-phoneme nonwords after this treatment showed that, indeed, L.R. correctly produced more of the component sounds of the nonwords after (0.53) than before (0.27) this treatment ($z=2.5$, $P=0.006$). Nonetheless, her success in producing the entire three-sound segment of the nonwords was unchanged (1/15 vs. 2/15). It was clear from this and other post-tests conducted at this point that an inability to blend the phonemes she could generate was at least one of the factors undermining her ability to read non-words, as we had suspected it might be from our preliminary testing. Now that we had established that L.R. could produce consistently a limited number of phonemes in response to graphemes, it was possible to attempt to work on the blending component. Before proceeding, however, we carried out further assessment of L.R.'s auditory processing and memory, which we knew to be faulty.

## DIAGNOSTIC ASSESSMENTS PRIOR TO BLENDING TREATMENT

It is clear from Table 22.4 that L.R.'s ability to make fine discriminations between minimal pairs of aurally presented stimuli was intact, and was even quite good when a two-second unfilled delay was interposed between the two stimuli during discrimination judgments. We used this two-second delay because we thought it would take about that long for L.R. to generate the phonemes from print if she were reading, and we were attempting to determine whether or not her STM could support that operation.

The situation was quite different when L.R. was required to *produce* sublexical segments after a delay, as shown in Table 22.4. Although she was able to repeat fairly well the three-phoneme nonwords that she had been unable to blend in the nonword reading post-test, she had some difficulty repeating even a single phoneme following a delay, and was very poor at repeating two phonemes presented with a two second delay between items. Most errors in these two-item repetition tasks involved failure to repeat the first phoneme.

These data appear to confirm that L.R. has a very serious short-term memory limitation, most likely originating in the articulatory loop (output) component of the working memory system (Baddeley, 1986). Nonetheless, it is not clear that this deficit, though severe, should *preclude* the blending of phonemes into larger phonological patterns; in the reading task, memory can be continually refreshed by re-generation of phonemes from print. This possibility, in addition to L.R.'s ability to learn grapheme/phoneme associations, encouraged us to attempt to reinstate the blending operation.

TABLE 22.4
Results of Assessments Preliminary to Initiation of Blending Treatment

| | |
|---|---|
| *Auditory Discrimination:* | |
| Words (minimal contrasts, e.g. seal/zeal) | 47/48 |
| Nonwords (minimal contrasts on vowels or final consonant, e.g. /tep/ /teb/) | 40/40 |
| Phonemes (minimal contrasts) | |
| no delay between items | 35/36 |
| 2sec. delay, unfilled | 34/36 |
| *Sublexical Repetition:* | |
| 3-phoneme nonwords | 17/21 |
| Single phoneme, 2sec. delay before responding | 22/30 |
| Two consonants, 2sec. delay between elements | 6/20 |
| Consonant, vowel (unblended) | |
| 2sec. delay between | 0/12 |
| 1sec. delay between | 4/12 |

## TREATMENT 3: PHONEME BLENDING

Treatment of the blending component focused on two-phoneme combinations of the grapheme/phoneme correspondences that L.R. had already successfully learned. Consonant plus vowel (C+V) combinations were introduced first; L.R. was encouraged to sound the individual graphemes (which she generally did with relative ease) and then to "say them together with no pause". Six sessions included exercises in which the consonant varied but the vowel remained constant in blends that combined C+V; another six sessions focused on items in which the vowel varied, while the consonant remained unchanged. For each condition, four combinations of C+V were used in training and four were retained as untrained. When L.R. had successfully blended two-thirds of the trials within a training session, these untrained items were presented. If L.R. succeeded in blending all four untrained pairs, a new condition (i.e. a new constant) was introduced. If L.R. failed any of the untrained items, the exercise continued in the same condition. Thus, the precise number of times L.R. practised blending specific items was quite varied. At the conclusion of the sessions—she had now demonstrated good blending of all the untrained items—we re-administered a set of C-V-C non-words that combined all of the trained and untrained C+V and vowel plus consonant (V+C) combinations (with those yielding words excluded). Her ability to blend three items after this extensive blending treatment (+16/54) was no different from her ability to blend them before treatment (+14/54).

In an attempt to account for this disappointing result, we analysed L.R.'s responses during the treatment trials with the two-phoneme (C+V and V+C) blends. She had been quite successful in her attempts to blend consonant plus vowel: 71% of blending attempts with C+V were correct without any cue. Most C+V blending errors involved difficulty deleting the *schwa* sound from the consonant before blending with the vowel. The situation was quite different for the vowel plus consonant blends: Only 42% were successfully blended on the first attempt during training. Almost half (43%) of the V+C errors involved the phonetic feature of voice-onset time: She substituted almost randomly among voicing cognates if they occurred in post-vocalic position.

For each consonant in V+C attempts, we analysed separately L.R.'s success realising the phonetic features involving place, manner and mode of articulation. That is, each attempt (or the first two attempts in what was often a rather long series) was scored as to whether it was correct in terms of its place of articulation, (labial, bilabial, velar, etc.), manner of articulation (fricative, affricate, stop, etc.), and mode (voiced or voiceless). This scoring was carried out separately for the attempts that led, ultimately, to successful blending, and those that never resulted in success. As shown in Table 22.5, even when L.R. finally succeeded in producing a correct blend, she showed evidence of having lacked control over the voice feature 17% of the time; in attempts that did not lead to success she started out with a voicing problem almost half the time.

Understanding the direction of this effect is complicated by the fact that when L.R. made a voicing error when sounding consonants in isolation, or in blending C+V, she frequently (0.76) produced the voiceless cognate. That is, she was much more likely to read /DA/ as /TA/ than vice versa. When blending V+C, on the other hand, her responses were randomly distributed between the voiced and voiceless variants. Thus, it would appear that the glottal pulsing (phonation) that was initiated by pronunciation of the vowel somewhat diminished L.R.'s tendency to de-voice voiced cognates, but could not overcome it altogether. One of the factors that most seriously undermined her ability to blend phonemes would seem to be, then, some fairly consistent effects involving the realisation of the phonetic feature of voice onset time. A contributing factor was L.R.'s memory impairment: An analysis of the cues used during treatment showed that she required re-orientation to the element *that remained constant* fully 35% of the time.

Although our attempt to retrain L.R. to assemble phonology from print uncovered some unpredicted and theoretically interesting deficits, it brought about no improvement in her ability to read non-words. Of more practical interest is the question of whether or not improved knowledge of grapheme/phoneme correspondences led to improvement in L.R.'s reading of words. We had predicted that grapheme/phoneme knowledge, even if not accompanied by an ability to perform the blending operation, might place phonological constraints on the lexical route and result in a decrease in the number of semantic and visual/phonologic errors. To assess this possibility, we readministered the subsets of the words manipulating imageability and orthographic regularity that L.R. had read in the baseline assessment. As shown in Table 22.6, there was an overall (non-significant) improvement in the reading of these words. As might be expected given the nature of the

TABLE 22.5
Proportion Correct Realisation of Phonetic Feature in Initial Attempts, (Vowel + Consonant Blending)

| | *Feature* | | |
|---|---|---|---|
| | *Place* | *Manner* | *Mode* |
| Target eventually correct (N=55) | 0.94 | 0.94 | 0.83 |
| Target never correct (N=75) | 0.82 | 0.86 | 0.56 |

TABLE 22.6
Proportion Correct Oral Reading Before and After Treatments

| *Word Type* | *Pre-treatment Baseline* | *Post-treatment Re-test* |
|---|---|---|
| Regular (N = 18) | 0.22 | 0.44 |
| Irregular (N = 18) | 0.28 | 0.17 |
| High imageability (N = 18) | 0.56 | 0.89 |
| Low imageability (N = 18) | 0.28 | 0.33 |
| Total (N = 72) | 0.33 | 0.46 |
| Proportion errors | (N = 47 errors) | (N = 39 errors) |
| Semantic | 0.11 | 0.03 |
| Visual | 0.38 | 0.56 |

interventions carried out, performance with orthographically regular words improved, whereas performance with irregular words declined[2]. Less clear is the basis for the marked improvement reading words high in imageability, an effect that approached significance (chi-square=3.46, $P$=0.06), with no comparable improvement reading words low in imageability. Semantic errors declined, as predicted, but errors with visual and/or phonological similarity to the target actually increased following treatment. These results suggest that L.R. was attempting to use sublexical information when reading words, but that the effect of such attempts on her word reading was considerably more complicated than had been predicted.

## DISCUSSION

We interpret the results of these interventions as constraining in several ways the evolving model of nonlexical reading. First, the results suggest some specific and previously undescribed ways in which failures of phonetic control can affect oral reading, effects that appear to reflect an impairment within the short-term memory system. Second, the results when compared with findings from another patient suggest that impairments of STM may take several quite different forms, with different effects on patients' performance. Third, the results provide some indications about the ways in which components of the reading model interact with specific components of the language system and with general cognitive capacities. Finally, these results allow some consideration of which of these various aspects of the cognitive system are most likely to yield to intervention.

The primary finding emerging from our attempts to retrain L.R. to blend phonemes that she could generate from print was that the phonetic feature of voice onset time (VOT) was disproportionately difficult to control relative to other features. This finding mirrors results that have been available for some years concerning the phonetic impairments of patients classified as Broca's aphasics (Blumstein et al., 1980; Gandour & Dardarananda, 1984) or of patients with "apraxia of speech" (Freeman, Sands, & Harris, 1978; Hoit-Dalgaard, Murry, & Kopp, 1983). Control of the voicing feature is frequently poor in patients who fall into these classifications, even when other articulatory features are realised correctly. The current hypothesis concerning the underlying basis of this deficit (Blumstein, 1991) is that it reflects an impairment of the coordination of the timing relationship between two independent articulatory features: phonation and upper airway constriction and release. These two features can be implemented separately without difficulty, suggesting that the impairment is not at the level of strictly motor speech programming. Rather, the deficit appears to relate to higher level processes that regulate the timing characteristics of the separate features that contribute to a particular sound segment.

One interesting aspect of L.R.'s deficit in this regard—and it is unclear whether or not it is also true for the patients in the group studies referred to above—is that the voicing deficit does not appear to emerge in *lexical* production tasks such as naming, or even in reading that is accomplished via the lexical route. One might argue that our failure to detect voicing errors on *words* is more of a perceptual than a production effect. That is, one would be unlikely to judge that a patient was saying /paesket/ when naming a *basket* unless the expected voicing lead were realised as a *very* clear voicing lag. Such "listener bias" cannot, however, explain the lack of voicing errors in L.R.'s *nonword* repetition responses. Despite clear difficulty repeating multisyllabic words and multimorphemic strings of any kind, L.R. was able to repeat with considerable success the isolated non-words that she could not read or blend aurally (see Table 22.4). Of four errors committed in a 21-item non-word repetition task, only one involved the feature of voice onset time.

L.R.'s relatively good performance repeating non-words, and the difference in error patterns for repetition vs. reading and blending, distinguishes her from a similar patient (M.V.) described by Bub, Black, Howell, and Kertesz (1987). M.V. showed very similar types of errors when repeating and reading nonwords, but was able to read and repeat real words with considerable success. The account given of M.V.'s deficit stresses these similarities and differences, and describes the impairment as one in which there is abnormal "noise" or interference within a response buffer that is shared across all production tasks. The argument is made that this interference is exacerbated when *unfamiliar* sequences are stored in the buffer; hence all performance with nonwords is degraded similarly. This account does not accommodate L.R.'s data, whose performance is particularly poor not with nonwords across all tasks, but with multi-segment stimuli (lexical or nonlexical) across all tasks. Thus it may be that L.R.'s impairment within the output buffer is not one in which there is abnormal interference that undermines retention of unfamiliar sequences, but a limited capacity, or abnormal item-specific decay rate, that precludes simultaneous storage of several distinct items. A blended, syllabic nonword, presented in isolation as a single unit, can be retained well enough, or long enough, to support repetition. A word or nonword presented in three segments cannot apparently be maintained well enough, or long enough to carry out the blending operation.

Although it appears that the nature of the impairment to L.R.'s short-term memory differs from the memory impairment suffered by M.V., it is by no means clear how L.R.'s memory deficit should be characterised. The results indicate that the impairment is to an output component of the STM system, and that the number of separate elements that must be stored, and/or the length of the interval over which they must be stored, predicts loss from memory. These findings are compatible with a number of possible types of deficit. L.R.'s buffer may be severely limited in its absolute capacity, with newly arriving items displacing those already in storage. Alternatively, an abnormally fast decay rate might affect each element independently. Phoneme repetition data (Table 22.4) do not clearly distinguish these possibilities. Some decay for a single phoneme apparently occurred over a two-second unfilled delay, but performance was much worse when two elements were to be stored.

Whatever the precise mechanism responsible for the loss from memory, its effects are particularly apparent when the phonetic realisation of a segment requires the temporal coordination of two independent articulatory gestures, i.e. when it involves control of voice onset time. The exacerbation of problems when maintaining voicing cognates may reflect the increased number of discrete elements that must be held in memory to control VOT, even though these are not normally experienced as separate during the act of speaking. This would suggest that the memory impairment is a primary source of L.R.'s blending problems—the phonetic effects are manifested only when multiple elements (i.e. segmented stimuli) must be stored.

In addition to suggesting these possible interactions of phonological processes with memory, there are several ways in which the results of this intervention study can be related to the question of the "treatability" of the model's components. First, it is clear that even severely impaired patients can be taught *content*, even when that content involves sublexical elements. This successful re-learning of content would seem to require relatively intact verbal learning ability—the ability to put new information into long term memory. Although the learning of new information is compromised by some forms of brain damage, it was apparently spared in our severely impaired aphasic, dyslexic patient. This sparing is evident in the face of a seriously limited short-term memory—another piece of neuropsychological evidence for the functional independence of short-term memory and verbal learning (cf. Shallice, 1988). By the same token, reduced short-term memory did not appear to interfere with L.R.'s ability to perform the phonological operations needed to yield the sublexical segments used in training.

However, what did emerge in addition to these positive findings were several intractable deficits that undermined the blending stage of phonological assembly. The phonetic deficits that especially interfered with V+C blending may originate in the language system; their potential for remediation is currently unknown. One consideration that we did not raise earlier concerns the "learnability" of various components of cognitive models, and this involvement of the language system is a case in point. The ability to read is obviously a learnable task that does not emerge in individuals who are not provided with some opportunity to learn how to do it. Many aspects of language, including the ability to articulate the types of phonetic distinctions that were difficult for L.R., clearly emerge without specific training as a result of a hard-wired capacity within the genetically determined language system. These same distinctions are much harder to learn later in life (as when normal adults attempt to learn new phonemes in a foreign language), perhaps because brain maturation has moved beyond a critical period for their emergence. Moreover, it may be that operations such as these—acquired easily by normal children but difficult to learn through explicit instruction—are linked to specific neural tissue that must be intact for successful execution. It is not clear to what extent such emergent properties can be retrained after brain damage, but there are reasons to be pessimistic.

The more general cognitive capacities present another level of difficulty. L.R.'s short-term memory problem does not interfere with all aspects of her functioning, but exercises its effects quite selectively. When it interferes, however, its effects are devastating. It may be that more detailed understanding of the nature of memory impairments will provide some suggestions for treatment. As we have noted here, for example, one type of memory deficit may involve "noise" that degrades the memory trace selectively as items are less familiar (Bub, et al., 1987). Treatment strategies could focus in such cases on improving the distinctiveness and identifiability of items to be stored. Our patient, in contrast, was not apparently subject to such noise but was limited in terms of the number of separate items that could be stored. Here the therapeutic focus could centre on training that allows larger single segments to be stored in lieu of smaller, separate segments. That is, the limits of patients' verbal learning capacities could be stretched to accommodate this type of memory impairment by attempting to reinstate larger chunks of content that can be stored as fewer units. To test this possibility, a treatment study with L.R. is currently under way in which she is asked to blend initial consonants with "word bodies" (e.g. UNK, AKE), learned as units.

Both these suggested approaches to the treatment of short-term memory impairments differ in an important regard from the types of interventions reviewed above that focus on re-establishing content or re-training operations. These suggested STM interventions, even if successful, would presumably not alter the affected component, but would simply provide a means of accommodating the deficit. Nonetheless, the clear lesson that emerges from this study for therapists is that a thorough investigation of patients' short-term memory capacities (as well as other general purpose cognitive capacities such as verbal learning) should be an early step in the planning of the rehabilitation of phonological assembly.

Another finding with clear clinical relevance involves the apparent effects of these interventions on L.R.'s attempts to read *words*. Prior to treatment, L.R. appeared to rely exclusively on the lexical route when reading, producing errors on words and non-words that indicated interference from, or confusion with, other words. After learning some grapheme-phoneme correspondences, she was considerably less likely to make a semantic error, but more likely to make a visual/phonologic error. This result appears to reflect both residual imperfections in the operation of the nonlexical mapping procedures, and failure to use lexical and nonlexical information in a manner that is mutually constraining. Her newly acquired knowledge of grapheme-phoneme correspondences seems to have provided her with enough information to allow rejection of responses bearing no phonological relationship to the target, but not with all the information and operations needed to read entire targets using nonlexical procedures. Thus, the treatment resulted in a decline in errors such as MIND→"think"; EFFORT→"difficult" (pre-treatment responses) and an increase in errors such as MIND→"minute"; EFFORT→"ford" (post-treatment responses).

The important unanswered question is why the two routines (lexical and nonlexical) do not appear to work together for L.R. These post-treatment examples illustrate that when attempting to use nonlexical procedures to read words, L.R. appeared not to use lexical/semantic knowledge. The model guiding these investigations offers little insight into the ways in which lexical and nonlexical procedures might interact during reading, but details of this interaction are crucial to determining whether or not re-training of phonological assembly will be of practical value to dyslexic patients. Clearly, the clinical goal is not simply to establish change but to establish functionally relevant change. One intriguing result in this regard that merits follow-up is the unpredicted, marked improvement following intervention in L.R.'s ability to read words high in imageability. Knowledge of grapheme-phoneme correspondences seems to have improved L.R.'s ability to read highly imageable words, which were the easiest category for her to read even before treatment. One possibility is that the limited phonological information that was made available by the nonlexical procedures was sufficient to increase activation to threshold for words already close to threshold. Further study is needed to probe the limits of these types of effects. For example, it might be possible for some patients to learn to combine lexical and nonlexical procedures explicitly when attempting to read words. Furthermore, such efforts to train patients to use both types of information when reading might uncover important principles about the normal interaction between lexical and nonlexical reading.

## NOTES

1. The composition of the word lists used in the baseline assessment was limited by the extensiveness of L.R.'s deficit. To determine the effects of the factors of interest, it was necessary to administer items that she had some hope of reading. Higher-frequency word pairs were selected from Coltheart's (unpublished) lists for the comparison based on orthographic regularity. For the imageability contrast, eight high-frequency pairs from Coltheart's lists were combined with ten additional high-frequency (>125/million; Francis & Kuçera, 1982) pairs selected to be either high (4-7) or low (1-3) in imageability (Paivio, Yuille, & Madigan, 1968). Nouns and verbs were unambiguous for form class (Frances & Kuçera, 1982) and picturable in a line drawing format. Functors were pronouns, conjunctions and prepositions, all very high in frequency.
2. The entire set of frequency-matched regular and irregular words (Coltheart, unpublished) was administered to L.R. as a post-test. Although she read more regular (21/39) than irregular (13/39) words, the effect was not significant (chi-square=2.56, $P$=0.11).

## ACKNOWLEDGEMENTS

This work was supported by grant R01-DC-00699 from the National Institutes of Health. The authors are grateful to Anne N. Haendiges for assistance in data analysis and to Maryne C. Glowacki for careful typing of the manuscript. Address correspondence and reprint requests to Department of Neurology, University of Maryland School of Medicine, 22 S. Greene Street, Baltimore, Maryland 21201.

## REFERENCES

Bachy-Langedock, N. & De Partz, M.P. (1989). Coordination of two reorganization therapies in a deep dyslexic patient with oral naming disorder. In X. Seron & G. Deloche (Eds.), *Cognitive approaches in neuropsychological rehabilitation.* Hillsdale, N.J.: Lawrence Erlbaum Associates Inc.

Baddeley, A. (1986). *Working memory.* Oxford: Clarendon Press.

Beauvois, M.F. & Derouesne, J. (1979). Phonological alexia: Three dissociations, *Journal of Neurology, Neurosurgery, and Psychiatry, 42,* 1115-1124.

Berndt, R.S., Reggia, J.A., & Mitchum, C.C. (1987). Empirically derived probabilities for grapheme-to-phoneme correspondences in English. *Behaviour Research Methods, Instruments, and Computers, 19* (1), 1-9.

Blumstein, S. (1991). Phonological aspects of aphasia. In M.T. Sarno (Ed.), *Acquired aphasia,* 2nd Edition. New York: Academic Press.

Blumstein, S.E., Cooper, W.E., Goodglass, H., Statlender, S., & Gottlieb, J. (1980). Production deficits in aphasia: A voice-onset time analysis. *Brain and Language, 9,* 153-170.

Bub, D., Black, S., Howell, J. & Kertesz, A. (1987). Speech output processes and reading. In M. Coltheart, G. Sartori & R. Job (Eds.), *The cognitive neuropsychology of language* (pp. 79-110). London: Lawrence Erlbaum Associates Ltd.

Campbell, R. & Butterworth, B. (1985). Phonological dyslexia and dysgraphia in a highly literate subject: A developmental case with associated deficits of phonemic processing and awareness. *Quarterly Journal of Experimental Psychology, 37A,* 43-75.

Coltheart, M. (1985). Cognitive neuropsychology and the study of reading. In M. I. Posner & O.S.M. Marin (Eds.), *Attention and performance, XI* (pp. 3-37). Hillsdale, N.J.: Lawrence Erlbaum Associates Inc.

Coltheart, M. & Byng, S. (1989). A treatment for surface dyslexia. In X. Seron & G. Deloche (Eds.), *Cognitive approaches in neuropsychological rehabilitation.* Hillsdale, N.J.: Lawrence Erlbaum Associates Inc.

Coltheart, M. & Stuart, M. (1988). Does reading develop in a series of stages? *Cognition, 30*(2), 139-181.

De Partz, M.P. (1986). Re-education of a deep dyslexic patient: rationale of the method and results. *Cognitive Neuropsychology, 3* (2), 149-177.

Derouesne, J. & Beauvois, M.-F. (1985). The "phonemic" stage in the nonlexical reading process: Evidence from a case of phonological alexia. In K. E. Patterson, J.C. Marshall, & M. Coltheart (Eds.), *Surface dyslexia: Neuropsychological and cognitive studies of phonological reading* (pp. 339-457). London: Lawrence Erlbaum Associates Ltd.

Frances, W.N. & Kuçera, H. (1982). *Frequency analysis of English usage: Lexicon and grammar.* Boston: Houghton-Mifflin.

Freeman, F.J., Sands, E.S., & Harris, K.S. (1978). Temporal coordination of phonation and articulation in a case of verbal apraxia: A voice onset time study. *Brain and Language, 6*, 106-111.

Funnell, E. (1983). Phonological processes in reading: New evidence in acquired dyslexia. *British Journal of Psychology, 74*, 159-180.

Gandour, J. & Dardarananda, R. (1984). Voice onset time in aphasia: Thai II. Production. *Brain and Language, 23*, 177-205.

Goodglass, H. & Kaplan, E. (1983). *The assessment of aphasia and related disorders.* (Second Edition). Philadelphia: Lea and Febiger.

Hoit-Dalgaard, J., Murry, T., & Kopp, H.G. (1983). Voice onset time production and perception in apraxic subjects. *Brain and Language, 20*, 329-339.

Kaplan, E., Goodglass, J., & Weintraub, B. (1978). *The Boston Naming Test.* Philadelphia: Lee and Febiger.

Marr, D. (1982). *Vision.* San Francisco: Freeman.

Mitchum, C.C. & Berndt, R.S. (1991). Diagnosis and treatment of "phonological assembly" in acquired dyslexia: An illustration of the cognitive neuropsychological approach. *Journal of Neurolinguistics, 6*(2), 103-137.

Newcombe, F. & Marshall, J. (1984). Varieties of acquired dyslexia: A linguistic approach. *Seminars in Neurology, 4*, 181-195.

Newcombe, F. & Marshall, J. (1985). Reading and writing by letter sounds. In K. Patterson, J.C. Marshall, & M. Coltheart (Eds.), *Surface dyslexia: Neuropsychological and cognitive studies of phonological reading* (pp. 35-51). London: Lawrence Erlbaum Associates Ltd.

Paivio, A., Yuille, J.C., & Madigan, S.A. (1968). Concreteness, imagery, and meaningfulness values for 925 nouns. *Journal of Experimental Psychology, Monograph Supplement, 76*, 1-25.

Patterson, K. (1982). The relation between reading and phonological coding: Further neuropsychological observations. In A.W. Ellis (Ed.), *Normality and pathology in cognitive functions* (pp. 77-111). London: Academic Press.

Patterson, K., Vargha-Khadem, F., & Polkey, C.E. (1989). Reading with one hemisphere. *Brain, 12*, 39-63.

Saffran, E.M., Berndt, R.S., & Schwartz, M.F. (1990). The quantitative analysis of agrammatic production: Procedure and data. *Brain and Language, 27*, 440-479.

Shallice, T. (1988). *From neuropsychology to mental structure.* Cambridge: Cambridge University Press.

# PART SEVEN

## Memory

CHAPTER TWENTY-THREE

# Domain-specific Learning and Remediation of Memory Disorders

Elizabeth L. Glisky, Daniel L. Schacter*, and Meryl A. Butters
*Department of Psychology, University of Arizona, USA*

## ABSTRACT

This chapter describes the domain-specific learning approach to the remediation of memory disorders. Based on empirical findings of preserved memory functions in amnesic patients, this approach attempts to exploit such intact processes in order to teach patients complex knowledge and tasks relevant in everyday life. Several studies are outlined that illustrate the capability of memory-impaired patients to acquire complex, domain-specific knowledge, using their preserved ability to respond normally to partial cues. Successful acquisition by amnesic patients of new vocabulary, of computer operations, and of data-entry procedures are described. Issues of specificity of learning and problems in transfer are considered empirically and in the context of relevant theoretical ideas. Failures of transfer are shown not to be a consequence of the extensive repetition and overlearning that is required for patients to acquire new information initially. Speculations concerning the characteristics of the memory system or systems that may support learning in amnesic patients are introduced. Finally, implications of the findings for rehabilitation programs are discussed.

*Dan Schacter is now at Harvard University.

## INTRODUCTION

The study of human memory is one of the most active research areas in neuropsychology and cognitive psychology. Hundreds of experimental studies are published in scientific journals each year, and hypotheses, ideas, and explanations of all manner are put forward in an attempt to account for the observed data. The list of topics addressed by memory researchers is virtually limitless, and includes such phenomena and ideas as context effects, depth of processing, dual process theory, encoding specificity principle, flashbulb memories, forgetting curves, generation effects, implicit memory, metamemory, massed vs. spaced repetition, mood and emotion, proactive interference, reality monitoring, reminding, retrograde amnesia, schemas, state-dependent retrieval, working memory, and many others (for reviews, see Baddeley, 1990; Ellis & Hunt, 1989; Schacter, 1989). Relevant literature dates back at least to the pioneering experimental studies of Ebbinghaus (1885) and clinical observations of Ribot (1882), although the bulk of research and theory has been published during the past 25-30 years.

The pertinent question for the present purposes concerns the relation between this rather formidable body of knowledge about human memory and clinical investigations of memory remediation: Has basic memory research informed or advanced the development of remedial interventions? On the one hand, it is possible to cite a number of instances in the published literature where the design of an intervention was motivated directly by a set of findings from the experimental memory literature. For example, research that has attempted to teach memory-impaired patients to use various mnemonic strategies, such as imagery (e.g. Gade, this volume: Jones, 1974; Wilson, 1987), elaboration (e.g. Gianutsos & Gianutsos, 1979; Kovner, Mattis, & Pass, 1985), and rehearsal (e.g. Schacter, Rich, & Stampp, 1985), was based on prior findings indicating that these strategies improve the memory performance of normal subjects (e.g. Bower, 1972; Craik & Tulving, 1975; Landauer & Bjork, 1978). In addition, our own studies on domain-specific learning, which will be discussed at some length later in the chapter, were motivated directly by findings and theories about preserved learning in amnesic patients (Glisky & Schacter, 1989b; Schacter & Glisky, 1986).

On the other hand, it has been pointed out repeatedly in recent review articles and chapters that the day-to-day clinical practice of memory remediation in hospital and rehabilitation settings is little influenced by basic memory research (cf. Grafman, 1984; O'Connor & Cermak, 1987; Schacter & Glisky, 1986; Van der Linden & Van der Kaa, 1989). This relatively atheoretical orientation is perhaps reflected in the fact that many rehabilitation workers subscribe to outdated and even misleading notions about memory, such as the idea that memory is like a muscle whose function can be improved in some global sense by exercise (Harris & Sunderland, 1981).

It is hardly controversial to suggest that the practice of memory remediation would benefit from greater attention to, and utilisation of, data and theory concerning normal memory. Indeed, van der Linden and Van der Kaa (1989) have recently provided a useful tutorial discussion of basic models of memory for the rehabilitation specialist, and the reader interested in a broad overview of contemporary theories of memory in relation to rehabilitation is referred to their presentation. In the present chapter, we will also examine the ways in which data and theory concerning memory function can inform rehabilitation, but with a rather more restricted focus. Specifically, we will summarise the rationale for an approach to memory remediation that we have developed, referred to as *domain-specific learning*, that has been greatly influenced by neuropsychological models of memory function. The basic idea underlying this approach is that memory processes and systems that are spared by brain damage can be exploited in order to teach patients complex tasks that are useful in everyday life. We will describe briefly several studies that illustrate the domain-specific approach, and then focus on issues of *specificity* and *transfer* of learning. We believe that these are crucial problems for the domain-specific and any other approach to memory remediation, and we consider them in light of relevant theoretical ideas.

## DOMAIN-SPECIFIC LEARNING: RATIONALE AND EVIDENCE

### Spared Implicit Memory in Amnesic Patients

Considerable research has demonstrated that the memory impairment associated with various kinds of brain damage is not global but is instead selective: Some forms of memory are lost while others are spared. For example, amnesic patients are able to acquire normally a variety of motor, perceptual and cognitive skills such as rotor pursuit, mirror-reading, puzzle-solving, and mathematical rule-learning, although they have no memory for the learning occasions (e.g. Brooks & Baddeley, 1976; Charness, Milberg, & Alexander, 1988; Cohen & Squire, 1980; Milner, Corkin, & Teuber, 1968; Nissen & Bullemer, 1987). These findings have led to rather general agreement that procedural learning is preserved in amnesia although the ability to recollect specific past events is impaired. Memory-disordered patients also exhibit normal repetition priming effects; that is, they are as likely as normal subjects to produce previously studied words on tests of word completion, free association, and perceptual identification, even though they are unable to remember the prior study episode (e.g. Cermak, Talbot, Chandler, & Wolbarst, 1985; Diamond & Rozin, 1984; Graf, Squire, & Mandler, 1984; Schacter & Graf, 1986; Shimamura & Squire, 1984; Warrington & Weiskrantz, 1968; 1974). In addition, amnesic patients show intact priming of various kinds of nonverbal information, including melodies (Johnson, Kim, & Risse, 1985), dot patterns (Gabrieli, Milberg, Keane, & Corkin, 1990), and novel three-dimensional objects (Schacter, Cooper, Tharan, & Rubens, 1991) .

Findings such as these have prompted theorists to propose that memory is not a unitary entity, but consists instead of different processes and/or systems, some of which are damaged in amnesia and others of which are preserved (e.g. Johnson, 1991; Schacter, 1990; Squire & Cohen, 1984; Tulving, 1985; for reviews, see Richardson-Klavehn & Bjork, 1988; Schacter, 1987). Considerable effort has been devoted to exploring functional and statistical dissociations between different memory measures in an attempt to characterise different memory systems and processes. The intact performance of amnesic patients, and the documentation of conditions under which their performance is normal or impaired relative to control subjects, has been of key theoretical importance in these endeavours.

## Method of Vanishing Cues

From a rehabilitation perspective, knowledge of preserved learning and memory functions can have important implications for the development of remedial interventions: As it appears that some aspects of memory are intact in amnesic patients, it ought to be possible to make use of them in rehabilitation (O'Connor & Cermak, 1987; Salmon & Butters, 1987; Schacter & Glisky, 1986). Our approach to memory rehabilitation has been to attempt to make use of amnesic patients' spared abilities to overcome some of the problems of daily living that have resulted from a loss of explicit memory function. The approach is based specifically on two previously mentioned empirical findings: (1) amnesic patients are capable of acquiring new skills and procedures and therefore retain some learning abilities, and (2) they respond normally to partial cues under implicit memory conditions. This latter finding has been illustrated by patients' normal responses to word-fragment cues (e.g. WIN ) when asked to say the first thing that comes to mind. Under these instructions, patients are as likely as control subjects to produce previously-studied words (e.g. WINDOW) rather than items that had not occurred previously (e.g. WINTER) (Graf et al., 1984; Schacter & Graf, 1986; Warrington & Weiskrantz, 1968; 1974).

We proposed to teach amnesic patients real-world knowledge and skills by using their preserved ability to respond to fragment cues. The learning of new knowledge or factual information had not been demonstrated in amnesic patients to any significant degree. Although studies had shown that patients were able to acquire a few pieces of new knowledge such as the names of one or two people in their environment (e.g. Dolan & Norton, 1977; Jaffe & Katz, 1975; Wilson, 1982), the failure to acquire factual information was considered to be the defining characteristic of the amnesic deficit. Our goal was to try to use patients' intact priming abilities to help them acquire new knowledge and skills, relevant to their everyday functioning.

To facilitate what we have called the domain-specific learning process, we developed a training technique designed to tap into patients' preserved ability to use fragment cues. This technique, which we have termed the *method of vanishing cues*, provides sufficient cue information on every learning trial, in the form of initial letters of target words, to enable a patient to produce a correct response. Across learning trials, cue information is gradually withdrawn until eventually responses are required in the absence of partial cues. In view of the fact that patients show normal repetition priming effects, we expected that they would be able to produce correct responses in the presence of partial letter information. We were more interested, however, in whether or not repeated priming of a response could enable a more durable form of learning that could be accessed in the absence of cues. In addition to tapping into preserved priming processes, the vanishing cues procedure also allows for gradual "shaping" of target responses in a manner similar to that of Skinner's (1958) teaching machines.

## Vocabulary Learning

An initial study explored whether four memory-impaired patients could acquire and retain the vocabulary associated with the use of a microcomputer (Glisky, Schacter, & Tulving, 1986b). Previous attempts to teach new vocabulary to amnesic patients had failed (Gabrieli, Cohen, & Corkin, 1983). However, using the method of vanishing cues, patients in this study were able to acquire 10-15 items of new vocabulary and retain them over a six-week interval. On each trial, patients were presented with a definition, for example, *to store a program*, and were required to produce the correct response (i.e. SAVE). They were given as many letters of the word as they needed in order to make the correct response (e.g. SAV_). As training progressed, letters were gradually withdrawn (e.g. SA__, S___, ____) until subjects produced the answers without letter cues. Although patients were able to acquire many new items of vocabulary in this way, their learning was not normal. They required many more trials to learn the vocabulary items than normal subjects and their newly-acquired knowledge appeared to be *hyper-specific*: Patients were much less likely than control subjects to produce the target responses to altered definitional cues on a transfer test.

The results of this study raised two interesting theoretical questions. First, why was the method of vanishing cues more effective than a traditional anticipation approach for memory-impaired patients but not for normal subjects, and second, what might account for the differences in transfer between amnesic patients and control subjects? We speculated that the vanishing cues procedure may have allowed patients to make use of the same intact memory system or processes that underlie priming, whereas control subjects relied on their normal explicit memory. To the extent that memories achieved in these different systems have different characteristics and organisational structures, transfer of learning to new materials or contexts might be expected to differ. Patients may have learned the vocabulary through the establishment of simple stimulus-response bonds, a type of learning that may be possible via a system or systems involved in implicit memory (see Graf & Schacter, 1985; Schacter & Graf, 1986). Normal subjects, on the other hand, by using explicit memory processes, may have been able to form more elaborate representations that supported higher levels of transfer. To explore these issues further, we developed a series of experiments to investigate the acquisition of more complex forms of computer knowledge, which would seem to require something more than simple stimulus-response associations.

## Computer Learning

Using the same vanishing cues procedure, we attempted to teach eight amnesic patients how to perform the basic functions required for the operation of a microcomputer (Glisky, Schacter, & Tulving, 1986a). All patients were able to learn to display and erase information from the computer screen, to perform disk storage and retrieval operations, and to write and edit simple computer programs. Furthermore, they retained this knowledge over delays of up to 9 months (Glisky & Schacter, 1988).

Patients' learning, however, was again characterised by "hyper-specificity". When asked to answer general or open-ended questions about what they had learned or questions in which the wording was altered from that used during training, patients exhibited poor performance. Control subjects, on the other hand, had no problem with such questions. We proposed that knowledge acquired by patients, even though complex, may be represented differently from that acquired by control subjects, perhaps in a sequential or stimulus-response fashion rather than in a more elaborate branching structure (cf. Wickelgren, 1979). If newly acquired information is not linked to other pre-existing knowledge structures, access may be limited and require re-presentation of original learning cues.

Shimamura and Squire (1988) have suggested that the knowledge acquired by patients in these computer learning studies may have been largely procedural. There is no doubt that learning included a substantial procedural component. However, patients were able to respond to some questions about what they had learned, so that their knowledge seemed to be at least partly declarative. They also did not acquire the knowledge at a normal rate, as has often been found with procedural learning. Perhaps as Shimamura and Squire (1988) have suggested, the learning of computer skills is partly declarative and partly procedural. Knowledge is acquired slowly by virtue of a damaged declarative memory system, but gradually becomes proceduralised (Anderson, 1987). Because procedural memory is thought to be domain-specific, it is relatively inflexible and only narrowly accessible (Squire, 1987). Although this explanation might account for the results of the computer learning studies, it is less satisfactory in accounting for vocabulary learning, which seems unlikely to be represented in procedural form.

The results of these experiments still remain somewhat of a theoretical puzzle. One barrier to straightforward interpretation is that tasks as complex as the ones that we have used are likely to draw on a variety of memory systems and processes. It is therefore difficult to make direct mappings from theoretical notions about specific memory systems to the processes responsible for complex learning. Nonetheless, the fact that we were successful in teaching amnesic patients new information and skills illustrates the importance of basing interventions on data and theory derived from careful cognitive and neuropsychological research. Many remedial procedures currently in use (e.g. drill therapies) lack theoretical and empirical rationale, and perhaps for this reason have failed to produce positive or significant outcomes. The present studies also demonstrate that research with an applied focus, in this case on rehabilitation of memory disorders, can inform and challenge mainstream psychological theory.

## REAL-WORLD APPLICATIONS OF DOMAIN-SPECIFIC LEARNING

Although the computer learning experiments demonstrated that patients with memory disorders are capable of acquiring complex domain-specific knowledge, the apparent hyperspecificity of patients' learning suggested that transfer from the laboratory to the real-world might be problematic. Our next studies, therefore, were designed to test whether learning acquired in the laboratory could be applied in an important domain of everyday life—the workplace.

### Computer Data-Entry: A Case Study

Because we were sensitive to the inflexibility of learning acquired by memory-impaired patients, we wanted to select a job for training that would minimize transfer problems. A computer data-entry task seemed to possess the necessary characteristics. It consists of a set of procedures that remain relatively invariant over time and materials. Although this particular job was quite complex, it could be broken down into simple components so that each step could be taught explicitly and directly; the need for inferences and on-line problem-solving would thus be minimized. In addition, the job could be closely simulated in the laboratory so that there would be few differences between the laboratory version of the task and the actual job itself.

Our initial vocational training study (Glisky & Schacter, 1987), focused on patient H.D., a 32-year old woman who had become severely amnesic as a result of herpes simplex encephalitis. On the Wechsler Memory Scale, H.D. obtained a score of 65 and was unable to recall any of the stories, drawings, or word-paired associates after a 30 minute delay. She had previously been employed in a secretarial position, but following her illness was unable to continue in that capacity and had been assigned to a low-level clerical position. We were able to identify a data-entry job within the corporation that seemed appropriate.

The data-entry task was carefully analysed and simulated in the laboratory as closely as possible. The job required H.D. to learn how to extract information from company documents called "meter cards" and enter it into a coded computer display. All cards were similar in appearance and relevant information appeared in the same location across cards. To perform the task successfully, H.D. had to learn considerable amounts of factual information: general terminology, meanings of various codes, location of critical information on the cards, and mappings between the cards and the display.

In the first phase of training—the knowledge acquisition phase—28 incomplete sentences were presented on the computer screen and H.D.'s task was to type the correct completion for each sentence on the keyboard. The missing words comprised the key facts needed to understand and perform the data-entry task. To exploit her preserved learning abilities as much as possible, the training technique was the method of vanishing cues.

On the first trial, H.D. needed 60 letter hints and took 56 minutes to complete the 28 sentences. However, by the end of 27 trials over 6 sessions, she was performing perfectly without hints and needed only 10 minutes to complete a trial. She then entered the skill acquisition phase of training in which she received extensive practice in the actual data-entry procedures. She showed steady improvement over a period of 5 weeks increasing her data-entry speed from 63 seconds per card to 13 seconds, a time that was comparable to that of experienced data-entry clerks.

During the final phase of training, we accompanied H.D. to the workplace where her performance was monitored over several days. She rapidly adjusted to the work environment, making few errors, and by the second day she was performing as quickly as in the laboratory. Thus, despite H.D.'s initial difficulty with this complex task, she was eventually able to learn to perform it in the real world as efficiently as full-time employees.

Because the meter-card job provided the patient with only part-time employment, we undertook a further training study (Glisky & Schacter, 1989a) that, if successful, would enable H.D. to return to work full-time. The job in question was an extension of the data-entry task just described but was considerably more complex. The expanded task required the entry of information from 11 different document types with varied exemplars, the learning of approximately 250 discrete items of new information concerning rules and procedures for the job, and the transfer of learning to documents never encountered before. The teaching technique was again the method of vanishing cues.

In the first phase of training, H.D. was taught the discriminating features of each of the 11 document types and the two-letter codes associated with them. She was then required to learn a set of rules and procedures for recognising and locating information on the documents and entering it into the computer display. Basic rules and procedures were first taught using a fixed set of 40 documents. The job was broken down into a series of component steps, each of which was taught explicitly and directly. As each successive step of the procedure was learned, it was linked to the immediately prior component and training on the combined steps was provided. Training continued in the laboratory daily for three months until H.D. was able to perform without error the complete sequence of data-entry operations for all 40 test documents.

The real-world job included an infinite variety of exemplars of each document type, and it was necessary for H.D. to be able to handle all these documents regardless of variations in content or form. In an attempt to facilitate flexible application of the learned rules, we then exposed H.D. to an additional 240 actual company documents, representing multiple versions of the 11 document types. She received extensive data-entry practice on these documents for a period of two months under conditions that closely simulated the actual job situation. She then entered the workplace accompanied by a laboratory assistant, who ensured that the job was executed correctly. Although H.D.'s performance slowed considerably when she transferred to the work environment, she nevertheless managed to accomplish the task with minimal help, and within four to five weeks on the job, she had exceeded laboratory levels of performance. Since that time, she has continued to work independently as a full-time employee.

These two vocational training studies demonstrate that a severely amnesic patient is capable of acquiring substantial amounts of complex knowledge and skills in the laboratory and of applying them in a real-world domain. Although learning was slow, there was evidence of considerable transfer even in the more complex task. When H.D. encountered novel documents, her entry times slowed relative to times for familiar documents. Nevertheless, she handled the new documents with few errors, applying learned rules and procedures, and gradually gaining speed with continued practice.

Successful performance by H.D. was almost certainly achieved as a result of the large numbers of exemplars that were used during training and the many, many hours of data-entry practice that were provided. Under such conditions, learning may have become highly proceduralised and domain-specific (Anderson, 1987). According to Singley and Anderson (1989), when a task becomes proceduralised, knowledge becomes encapsulated in the procedures and may be inaccessible in other contexts. To the extent that the same procedures are required across materials, transfer should be good. However, independent access to the knowledge incorporated in the skill may be difficult. The fact that H.D. was unable to describe details of the data-entry task although she was able to perform it effectively suggests that her knowledge may have been almost totally procedural. Such an interpretation is consistent with other findings of preserved procedural memory in amnesic patients. However, H.D. was also able to acquire large amounts of factual information, although not at a normal rate. The processes underlying this kind of learning by amnesic patients are still unclear.

## HYPERSPECIFICITY AND TRANSFER

The problems that memory-impaired patients experience in applying newly acquired knowledge in novel situations are well-known to rehabilitation professionals. In the studies reported above, we have demonstrated that information acquired by amnesic subjects is often hyperspecific—tightly bound to learning context and not readily accessible to changed cues. We have also shown, however, that patient H.D. was capable of considerable transfer in the data-entry task and that this may have been attributable to extensive practice with varied exemplars.

These findings invite some interesting theoretical speculations concerning the characteristics of the memory system or systems that may support learning in amnesic patients. Tulving (1985; Hayman & Tulving, 1989) has suggested that there may be a memory system that is preserved in amnesia, which is neither procedural nor declarative (episodic or semantic), and which is responsible for priming effects. Evidence discussed by Schacter (1990; Schacter, Cooper, & Delaney, 1990) indicates that the system involved in priming likely operates at a pre-semantic, perceptual level, and thus has been referred to as a *perceptual representation system*, which is composed of several domain-specific subsystems (see also Tulving & Schacter, 1990).

In studies with normal subjects, Hayman and Tulving (1989) found that performance on two successive word-fragment completion tests was independent when the word-fragment was changed. In other words, the completion of an initial word fragment (e.g. A—D—RK) did not facilitate subsequent completion of a different fragment of the same word (e.g. -AR-VA—). These specific transfer effects are reminiscent of the hyperspecificity exhibited by amnesic patients in the vocabulary and computer learning tasks. Specificity effects in priming have also been observed in a variety of other situations (e.g. Graf & Ryan, 1990; Jacoby & Hayman, 1987; Roediger & Blaxton, 1987), although such effects are not always observed (e.g. Carr, Brown, & Charalambous, 1989). If learning by amnesic patients is achieved through the same system that purportedly mediates priming effects, then failures of transfer across changes in the wording of cues should be expected. On the other hand, if patients are able to achieve more abstract knowledge representations, such as those associated with a declarative or semantic memory system, then transfer across surface changes in materials should occur.

We have attempted to explore the issues of hyperspecificity and transfer in two further rehabilitation-oriented experiments. The first experiment explores transfer in the context of a real-world task with a strong procedural component (data-entry), and the second study investigates some of the variables that might contribute to the hyperspecificity of declarative learning.

## Transfer of Procedural Learning

The vocational case studies, described above, demonstrated that a severely amnesic patient, H.D., was able to learn a computer data-entry job and perform it successfully in a competitive work environment. An important question, from a rehabilitation perspective, concerns whether other brain-damaged patients can learn the data-entry task. Although H.D.'s memory impairment is severe and her IQ is relatively low, she retains excellent attentional capabilities that may have contributed to her success. Many brain-injured patients, as a result of frontal lobe damage, have attentional deficits that might cause problems in complex learning tasks. To test the generality of our findings with other brain-damaged patients and examine issues concerning transfer of learning, we constructed an analog of the laboratory training segment of the meter card task to be administered to patients with a range of cognitive deficits. The exact procedures of the prior study were replicated; the only difference was that the documents used were laboratory imitations rather than real meter cards (Glisky, 1982).

Ten patients with memory disorders of varying severity and of various etiologies along with five control subjects participated in the study. All patients were at least one-year post-trauma and had memory deficits disproportional to any intellectual impairments. All but two of the patients also showed signs of frontal lobe pathology.

The results of the knowledge acquisition phase of training, which required the learning of 28 facts, indicated that all patients, even those with the most severe cognitive deficits, were able to acquire the factual information associated with the data-entry job (see Table 23.1). On the average, the patient group learned the task more slowly than the control group (84.6 trials compared to 19 trials) and required more time to complete a perfect trial (10.9 mins compared to 6.6 mins). Note, however, that patients with the mildest memory impairments (i.e., C.C., V.R., and D.L.) performed as well or better than normal control subjects on all measures (see Gade, this volume for a similar finding). In the subsequent skill acquisition phase of training, where subjects actually performed the data-entry task, results indicated steady improvement by patients over trials, with speed of performance increasing from an

TABLE 23.1
Results of the Knowledge Acquisition Phase of the Computer Data-entry Task

| *Patients* | *Diagnosis** | *Trials to Criterion* | *Range of Hints* | *Range of Times (min)* |
|---|---|---|---|---|
| C.C. | CHI | 15 | 42–0 | 41.4–11.6 |
| V.R. | CHI | 9 | 41–0 | 18.6– 6.4 |
| M.R. | CHI | 50 | 106–0 | 114.4–25.7 |
| M.C. | CHI | 61 | 167–0 | 50.0– 9.3 |
| J.L. | CHI | 114 | 101–0 | 70.3–10.6 |
| W.D | ACAA | 79 | 107–1 | 79.0–10.1 |
| B.R. | ACAA | 125 | 92–0 | 62.0– 7.2 |
| D.L. | ENCEPH | 15 | 56–0 | 19.9– 5.9 |
| C.W. | ANOXIA | 180 | 153–0 | 87.7– 9.1 |
| D.H. | ACAA | 198 | 118–0 | 69.7–13.5 |
| *Mean* | | *84.6* | *98.3–0* | *61.3–10.9* |
| H.D.† | ENCEPH | 27 | 60–0 | 55.5– 9.9 |
| *Controls* | | | | |
| J.N. | — | 20 | 79–0 | 50.4– 7.8 |
| J.U. | — | 15 | 66–0 | 23.8– 5.3 |
| J.S. | — | 17 | 97–0 | 19.8– 7.4 |
| D.C. | — | 19 | 106–0 | 20.3– 6.3 |
| B.Y. | — | 24 | 94–0 | 32.4– 6.0 |
| *Mean* | | *19* | *88.4–0* | *29.3– 6.6* |

*CHI = closed head injury; ACAA = anterior communicating artery aneurysm; ENCEPH = encephalitis.

†H.D. is the patient from the original case study, shown here for comparison purposes.

initial mean of 131 seconds per card to 50 seconds per card after 45 trials. Although patients were generally slower than control subjects, the pattern of skill learning was similar in all cases.

The final part of this experiment differed from the case study in that we explored the extent to which learning would transfer across relatively minor changes in materials—the kinds of changes that might reasonably be expected in a real-world job. Two different transfer tasks were devised: In Task A, two of the descriptive headings were omitted from the meter cards; in Task B, in addition to the omitted headings, the location of two pieces of information was reversed on the cards. Subjects were informed of the nature of the changes and were instructed to proceed with the data-entry task as before. Patients showed no significant increases in errors on either of the transfer tasks although performance slowed significantly in both cases (50.8 to 58.5 secs in Task A; 49.0 to 67.4 secs in Task B). More importantly, from a rehabilitation perspective, after one trial, speeds returned to close to baseline levels (see Table 23.2). These results suggest that transfer across minor changes in materials can be accomplished by memory-impaired patients under some conditions; some degree of hyperspecificity is still evident, however, in the greater slowing of patients' performance relative to control subjects.

TABLE 23.2
Mean Data-entry Times Per Card (in secs) in Transfer Tasks A and B, Compared to Baseline Entry Times

| | *Transfer Task A* | | | *Transfer Task B* | | |
|---|---|---|---|---|---|---|
| | *Baseline* | *Transfer* | | *Baseline* | *Transfer* | |
| | | *1* | *2* | | *1* | *2* |
| Patients | 50.8 | 58.5 | 53.2 | 49.0 | 67.4 | 57.2 |
| Controls | 21.3 | 24.1 | 24.0 | 21.8 | 27.1 | 26.0 |

Interestingly, Charness et al. (1988), in a mathematical rule learning task, found that a Korsakoff patient showed less specificity in a transfer test than normal subjects. The patient was able to solve new problems, according to a learned algorithm, as quickly as problems that he had practised for several days. Normal subjects, on the other hand, were faster at solving old problems (see Cohen & Squire, 1980, for a related finding). Charness et al. suggested that proceduralisation, which should result in highly specific representations of problem-solving operations, had not occurred normally for the amnesic patient. Alternatively, the performance of normal subjects may have been affected by explicit memory for prior problems and solutions.

The results of our studies with the computer data-entry task as well as those of Charness et al. suggest that procedural knowledge or skill acquired after many repetitions will be relatively insensitive to changes in materials given that little or no alteration in procedures is required. From an applied point of view, these findings suggest that jobs that consist of a set of invariant procedures will be most appropriate for memory-impaired patients and that minor variations in materials will have little impact on job performance.

## Transfer of Declarative Learning

The next study attempted to explore some of the variables that may have contributed to findings of hyperspecificity in our earlier experiments on vocabulary and computer learning. As suggested previously, if learning by amnesic patients is accomplished primarily by means of a perceptual representation system that is involved in priming, then transfer across surface changes in materials will often be poor. Shimamura and Squire (1988) have also suggested that hyperspecificity may occur when the knowledge acquired by amnesic patients relies more on priming or procedural memory than does the knowledge acquired by normal subjects. These authors speculated that the extensive repetition and overlearning experienced by patients in our studies may have produced an inflexible procedural memory representation, which could not support good transfer.

In an experiment to investigate whether or not declarative memories attained by amnesic patients are similarly hyperspecific or differ qualitatively from those acquired by normal subjects, Shimamura and Squire gave subjects just four study trials to learn sentence completions. Subjects studied 20 sentences describing common everyday events and were later tested for recall of the final word in each sentence. Recall testing was either direct, in which the original sentence frame was re-presented, or indirect, in which a paraphrase of the original sentence was presented. The investigators found no evidence of hyperspecificity in this task. When direct recall was equated for the two groups (normal subjects were tested after a one to two week delay, patients after a one-hour delay), amnesic patients were as likely as control subjects to complete the paraphrased sentences correctly. Shimamura and Squire concluded that, in these tasks, the memory representations of amnesic patients were not qualitatively different from those of delayed control subjects and were therefore likely dependent on residual declarative memory.

As Shimamura and Squire noted, a possible key difference between their experiment and ours was the degree of original learning. The extensive repetition required by amnesic patients for learning in our studies may have produced an inflexible representation that could not be easily accessed in other contexts. If this were the case, then the rehabilitation potential of our methods would be called into question.

Our next study (Butters, Glisky, & Schacter, 1993) was designed to investigate the effects of degree of original learning on transfer. We proposed to compare the effects on transfer of underlearning (50% of material learned), learning to one perfect trial, and overlearning (10 trials beyond one perfect trial), for both amnesic patients and control subjects. The Shimamura and Squire results suggest that transfer might be best in the underlearning condition. Evidence from some classical paired-associate learning experiments predicts a similar outcome (Martin, 1965). Cognitive theory, on the other hand, might predict a different result (e.g. Craik & Tulving, 1975; Jacoby & Craik, 1979; Klein & Saltz, 1976). When given greater amounts of study time as in the overlearning condition, subjects may be able to achieve more elaborate encodings that would support better transfer. Finally, if amnesic patients' learning depends solely on the perceptual representation system, transfer should be poor in all conditions.

Six memory-impaired patients and six matched control subjects participated in the study. The stimulus materials consisted of sentences that defined a series of business-related forms and functions. The subject's task was to learn the final word in each sentence, which was always the name of a defined document. Using the method of vanishing cues, subjects learned three 16-item lists, one to each of the three learning criteria: 50%, 100%, and 100% plus 10 trials. In each case, when the criterion was reached, subjects were immediately given a transfer test. Transfer sentences were constructed by substituting synonyms for key content words and reversing the voice (active to passive or vice versa); meaning was retained. For example: "When employees suffer physical harm on-the-job, they are required to file a form called a(n) ACCIDENT REPORT" was changed to, "When an injury is suffered while at work, employees are required to file a form called a(n) ACCIDENT REPORT".

The results of this study indicated that patients achieved surprisingly good transfer performance in this task, recalling an average of 80% of the originally learned items to the changed sentence cues. Nevertheless, transfer was poorer for patients than for control subjects, who produced 94% of the items on the transfer test. The results, however, did not support the hypothesis that greater amounts of overlearning contributed to the hyperspecificity of patients' learning. Both groups showed highest levels of transfer performance following overlearning and lowest levels in the underlearning condition. Furthermore, an interaction between group and learning condition indicated that patients' transfer performance was particularly impaired relative to controls in the underlearning condition. As shown in Table 23.3, patients were able to produce only 56% of the words that they learned in this condition compared to 87% for control subjects. Both groups performed well in the other two conditions (89% and 95% after one perfect trial; 95% and 100% after overlearning for patients and controls respectively). There was thus no indication in this experiment that extensive repetition and overlearning contribute to hyperspecificity. On the contrary, overlearning appeared to facilitate transfer.

The advantage for overlearning is consistent with the view that, with repeated opportunities for study, memory records become more elaborated, and thus support better transfer (Bransford, Franks, Morris, & Stein, 1979). Amnesic patients may have difficulty forming well-elaborated representations of new information, particularly early

TABLE 23.3
Proportion of Originally Learned Words Produced on the First Transfer Trial as a Function of Degree of Original Learning

| | *Learning Criterion* | | |
|---|---|---|---|
| *Group* | *Underlearning (50% correct)* | *One Perfect Trial* | *Overlearning (Perfect + 10)* |
| Patients | 0.56 | 0.89 | 0.95 |
| Controls | 0.87 | 0.95 | 1.00 |

in the learning process (e.g. Cermak, 1979), and for this reason show deficits relative to control subjects on transfer tests. However, with repeated presentations, they may be able to elaborate the material more thoroughly with a corresponding improvement in transfer.

Note also that the good transfer performance by amnesic patients is inconsistent with the notion that learning is occurring solely within a perceptual representation system. Although patients may rely on priming during the initial stages of learning, with sufficient repetition they seem able to establish representations in declarative or semantic memory. This latter observation is hardly surprising with respect to the sentence task that we used, which almost surely involves some semantic elaborative processing beyond a perceptual level.

The Butters et al. experiment confirms the importance of degree of original learning for transfer, but cannot account for the differences in transfer between Shimamura and Squire's experiments and those of Glisky et al. (1989a;b). We suggest that the important variable may be the amount of prior knowledge that subjects possess about the materials to be learned. To the extent that materials are familiar, they may fit rather easily into existing knowledge structures. For example, the sentences in the Shimamura and Squire study, which described common everyday events, might fall into this category. Patients may be able to process these materials as elaboratively as normal subjects and thus show equivalent transfer. On the other hand, new computer vocabulary about which subjects have little or no knowledge may be rather difficult to elaborate, and patients may be unable to forge connections to existing knowledge. Under these conditions, they may rely more on a perceptually-based system. Transfer then will be more difficult. Sentences such as those in the Butters et al. study, which related to business procedures, might fall somewhere between these extremes. In this case, patients are likely to have some prior knowledge about the materials, but not enough to make elaboration easy or effortless. Early in the learning process, patients may expend all of their cognitive resources on trying to establish simple stimulus-response connections. However, as learning proceeds and memory demands are reduced, processing resources may become available for more cognitively demanding activities such as elaboration, and transfer thereby improves.

## APPLIED IMPLICATIONS

What are the implications of these findings for rehabilitation? First, they suggest that training programs should attempt to capitalise on patients' prior knowledge. Training patients for tasks about which they already have some knowledge is likely to be more successful than training for a completely new job. Second, to maximize possibilities for transfer, all training programs should allow for extensive amounts of overlearning. Third, learning materials should be well-elaborated and patients should be encouraged and helped to establish links between information that they are attempting to learn and pre-existing knowledge. Elaborations of unfamiliar materials may have to be taught explicitly and directly. However, although more elaborated encodings will produce better transfer, they are likely to be extremely difficult for amnesic patients to learn. Thus, there may well be a trade-off between learning and transfer. When patients can rely largely on the output of the pre-semantic, perceptually based system that seems to be involved in various priming effects, learning will proceed relatively rapidly, but transfer may be poor. On the other hand, when elaborations are required or encouraged, as is probably necessary in semantically complex task domains, amnesic patients may have a great deal of difficulty with initial learning, but transfer may be improved. Future studies of memory rehabilitation that explore this issue could provide important practical information concerning the ecological validity of training procedures and, at the same time, shed light on the nature of and relations between human memory systems.

## ACKNOWLEDGEMENTS

Preparation of this manuscript was supported by the Social and Behaviourial Sciences Research Institute of the University of Arizona and by the McDonnell-Pew Cognitive Neuroscience Foundation.

## REFERENCES

Anderson, J. R. (1987). Skill acquisition: Compilation of weak-method problem solutions. *Psychological Review, 94,* 192-210.

Baddeley, A. (1990). *Human memory.* Boston, MA: Allyn and Bacon.

Bower, G. H. (1972). Mental imagery and associative learning. In L. W. Gregg (Ed.), *Cognition in learning and memory.* New York: Wiley.

Bransford, J. D., Franks, J. J., Morris, C. D., & Stein, B. S. (1979). Some general constraints on learning and memory research. In L. S. Cermak & F. I. M. Craik (Eds.), *Levels of processing in human memory* (pp. 331-354). Hillsdale, N.J.: Lawrence Erlbaum Associates Inc.

Brooks, D. N., & Baddeley, A. D. (1976). What can amnesic patients learn? *Neuropsychologia, 14,* 111-122.

Butters, M. A., Glisky, E. L., & Schacter. D. L. (1993). Transfer of new learning in memory-impaired patients. *Journal of Clinical and Experimental Neuropsychology, 15.*

Carr, T. H., Brown, J. S., & Charalambous, A. (1989). Repetition and reading: Perceptual encoding mechanisms are very abstract but not very interactive. *Journal of Experimental Psychology: Learning, Memory, and Cognition, 15,* 763-778.

Cermak, L. S. (1979). Amnesic patients' level of processing. In L. S. Cermak & F. I. M. Craik (Eds.), *Levels of processing in human memory* (pp. 119-139). Hillsdale, N.J.: Lawrence Erlbaum Associates Inc.

Cermak, L. S., Talbot, N., Chandler, K., & Wolbarst, L. R. (1985). The perceptual priming phenomenon in amnesia. *Neuropsychologia, 23,* 615-622.

Charness, N., Milberg, W., & Alexander, M.P. (1988). Teaching an amnesic a complex cognitive skill. *Brain and Cognition, 8,* 253-272.

Cohen, N. J., & Squire, L. R. (1980). Preserved learning and retention of pattern-analyzing skill in amnesia: Dissociation of "knowing how" and "knowing that". *Science, 210,* 207-209.

Craik, F. I. M., & Tulving, E. (1975). Depth of processing and the retention of words in episodic memory. *Journal of Experimental Psychology: General, 104,* 268-294.

Diamond, R., & Rozin, P. (1984). Activation of existing memories in the amnesic syndrome. *Journal of Abnormal Psychology, 93,* 98-105.

Dolan, M. P., & Norton, J. C. (1977). A programmed training technique that uses reinforcement to facilitate acquisition and retention in brain-damaged patients. *Journal of Clinical Psychology, 33,* 495-501.

Ebbinghaus, H. (1885). *Über das Gedachtnis.* Leipzig: Duncker and Humblot.

Ellis, H. C., & Hunt, R. R. (1989). *Fundamentals of human memory and cognition.* Dubuque, IA: Wm C. Brown.

Gabrieli, J. D. E., Cohen, N. J., & Corkin, S. (1983). The acquisition of lexical and semantic knowledge in amnesia. *Society for Neuroscience Abstracts, 9,* 238.

Gabrieli, J. D. E., Milberg, W., Keane, M. M., & Corkin, S. (1990). Intact priming of patterns despite impaired memory. *Neuropsychologia, 28,* 417-428.

Gianutsos, R., & Gianutsos, J. (1979). Rehabilitating the verbal recall of brain-damaged patients by mnemonic training: An experimental demonstration using single-case methodology. *Journal of Clinical Neuropsychology, 1,* 117-135.

Glisky, E.L. (1992). Acquisition and transfer of declarative and procedural knowledge by memory-impaired patients: A computer data-entry task. *Neuropsychologia, 30,* 899-910.

Glisky, E. L., & Schacter, D. L. (1987). Acquisition of domain-specific knowledge in organic amnesia: Training for computer-related work. *Neuropsychologia, 25,* 893-906.

Glisky, E. L., & Schacter, D. L. (1988). Long-term retention of computer learning by patients with memory disorders. *Neuropsychologia, 26,* 173-178.

Glisky, E. L., & Schacter, D. L. (1989a). Extending the limits of complex learning in organic amnesia: Computer training in a vocational domain. *Neuropsychologia, 27,* 107-120.

Glisky, E. L., & Schacter, D. L. (1989b). Models and methods of memory rehabilitation. In F. Boller & J. Grafman (Eds.), *Handbook of neuropsychology* (Vol. 3, pp. 233-246). Amsterdam: Elsevier.

Glisky, E. L., Schacter, D. L., & Tulving, E. (1986a). Computer learning by memory-impaired patients: Acquisition and retention of complex knowledge. *Neuropsychologia, 24,* 313-328.

Glisky, E. L., Schacter, D. L., & Tulving, E. (1986b). Learning and retention of computer-related vocabulary in amnesic patients: Method of vanishing cues. *Journal of Clinical and Experimental Neuropsychology, 8,* 292-312.

Graf, P., & Ryan, L. (1990). Transfer-appropriate processing for implicit and explicit memory. *Journal of Experimental Psychology: Learning, Memory, and Cognition, 16,* 978-992.

Graf, P., & Schacter, D. L. (1985). Implicit and explicit memory for new associations in normal and amnesic patients. *Journal of Experimental Psychology: Learning, Memory, and Cognition, 11,* 501-518.

Graf, P., Squire, L. S, & Mandler, G. (1984). The information that amnesic patients do not forget. *Journal of Experimental Psychology: Learning Memory and Cognition, 10,* 164-178.

Grafman, J. (1984). Memory assessment and remediation in brain-injured patients: From theory to practice. In B. A. Edelstein & E. T. Couture (Eds.), *Behaviourial assessment and rehabilitation of the traumatically brain-injured* (pp. 151-189). New York: Plenum.

Harris, J. E., & Sunderland, A. (1981). A brief survey of the management of memory disorders in rehabilitation units in Britain. *International Rehabilitation Medicine, 3,* 206-209.

Hayman, C. A. G., & Tulving, E. (1989). Is priming in fragment completion based on a "traceless" memory system? *Journal of Experimental Psychology: Learning, Memory, and Cognition, 15,* 941-956.

Jacoby, L. L., & Craik, F. I. M. (1979). Effects of elaboration of processing at encoding and retrieval: Trace distinctiveness and recovery of initial context. In L. S. Cermak & F. I. M. Craik (Eds.), *Levels of processing in human memory* (pp. 1-21). Hillsdale, N.J.: Lawrence Erlbaum Associates Inc.

Jacoby, L. L., & Hayman, C. A. G. (1987). Specificity of visual transfer in word identification. *Journal of Experimental Psychology: Learning, Memory, and Cognition, 13,* 456-463.

Jaffe, P. G., & Katz, A. N. (1975). Attenuating anterograde amnesia in Korsakoff's psychosis. *Journal of Abnormal Psychology, 34,* 559-562.

Johnson, M. K. (1991). Reality monitoring: Evidence from confabulation in organic brain disease patients. In G. P. Prigatano & D. L. Schacter (Eds.), *Awareness of deficit after brain injury: Clinical and theoretical issues* (pp. 176-197). New York: Oxford University Press.

Johnson, M. K., Kim, J. K., & Risse, G. (1985). Do alcoholic Korsakoff's syndrome patients acquire affective reactions? *Journal of Experimental Psychology: Learning, Memory, and Cognition, 11,* 27-36.

Jones, M. K. (1974). Imagery as a mnemonic aid after left temporal lobectomy: Contrast between material specific and generalized memory disorders. *Neuropsychologia, 12,* 21-30.

Klein, K. & Saltz, E. (1976). Specifying the mechanisms in a levels-of-processing approach to memory. *Journal of Experimental Psychology: Human Learning and Memory, 2,* 671-679.

Kovner, R., Mattis, S., & Pass, R. (1985). Some amnesic patients can freely recall large amounts of information in new contexts. *Journal of Clinical and Experimental Neuropsychology, 7,* 395-411.

Landauer, T. K., & Bjork, R. A. (1978). Optimum rehearsal patterns and name learning. In M. M. Gruneberg, P. E. Morris, & R. N. Sykes (Eds.), *Practical aspects of memory* (pp. 625-632). London: Academic Press.

Martin, E. (1965). Transfer of verbal paired associates. *Psychological Review, 72,* 327-343.

Milner, B., Corkin, S., & Teuber, H. L. (1968). Further analysis of the hippocampal amnesic syndrome: 14 year follow-up study of H.M. *Neuropsychologia, 6,* 215-234.

Nissen, M. J., & Bullemer, P. (1987). Attentional requirements of learning: Evidence from performance measures. *Cognitive Psychology, 19,* 1-32

O'Connor, M., & Cermak, L. S. (1987). Rehabilitation of organic memory disorders. In M. J. Meier, A. L. Benton, & L. Diller (Eds.), *Neuropsychological rehabilitation* (pp. 260-279). New York: Guilford.

Ribot, T. A. (1882). *Diseases of memory.* New York: D. Appleton.

Richardson-Klavehn, A., & Bjork, R. A. (1988). Measures of memory. *Annual Review of Psychology 39,* 475-543.

Roediger, H. L., & Blaxton, T. A. (1987). Effects of varying modality, surface features, and retention interval on priming in word fragment completion. *Memory & Cognition, 15,* 379-388.

Salmon, D. P., & Butters, N. (1987). Recent developments in learning and memory: Implications for the rehabilitation of the amnesic patient. In M. J. Meier, A. L. Benton, & L. Diller (Eds.), *Neuropsychological rehabilitation* (pp. 280-293). New York: Guilford.

Schacter, D. L. (1987). Implicit memory: History and current status. *Journal of Experimental Psychology: Learning, Memory, and Cognition, 13,* 501-518.

Schacter, D. L. (1989). Memory. In M. I. Posner (Ed.), *Foundations of cognitive science.* Cambridge, MA: MIT Press, A Bradford Book.

Schacter, D. L. (1990). Perceptual representation systems and implicit memory: Toward a resolution of the multiple memory systems debate. In A. Diamond (Ed.), *Developmental and neural bases of higher cognition. Annals of the New York Academy of Sciences, 608,* 543-571.

Schacter, D. L., Cooper, L. A., & Delaney, S. M. (1990). Implicit memory for unfamiliar objects depends on access to structural descriptions. *Journal of Experimental Psychology: General, 119,* 5-24.

Schacter, D. L., Cooper, L. A., Tharan, M., & Rubens, A. R. (1991). Preserved priming of novel objects in patients with memory disorders. *Journal of Cognitive Neuroscience.*

Schacter, D. L., & Glisky, E. L. (1986). Memory remediation: Restoration, alleviation, and the acquisition of domain-specific knowledge. In B. Uzzell & Y. Gross (Eds.), *Clinical neuropsychology of intervention* (pp. 257-282). Boston: Nijhoff.

Schacter, D. L., & Graf, P. (1986). Preserved learning in amnesic patients: Perspectives from research on direct priming. *Journal of Clinical and Experimental Neuropsychology, 8,* 727-743.

Schacter, D. L., Rich, S. A., & Stampp, M. S. (1985). Remediation of memory disorders: Experimental evaluation of the spaced-retrieval technique. *Journal of Clinical and Experimental Neuropsychology, 7,* 79-96.

Shimamura, A. P., & Squire, L. R. (1984). Paired-associate learning and priming effects in amnesia: A neuropsychological study. *Journal of Experimental Psychology: General, 11,* 556-570.

Shimamura, A. P. , & Squire, L. R. (1988). Long-term memory in amnesia: Cued recall, recognition memory, and confidence ratings. *Journal of Experimental Psychology: Learning, Memory, and Cognition, 14,* 763-770.

Singley, M. K., & Anderson, J. R. (1989). *The transfer of cognitive skill.* Cambridge, MA: Harvard University Press.

Skinner, B. F. (1958). Teaching machines. *Science, 128,* 969-977.

Squire, L. R. (1987). *Memory and brain.* New York: Oxford University Press.

Squire, L. R., & Cohen, N. J. (1984). Human memory and amnesia. In G. Lynch, J. L. McGaugh, & N. M. Weinberger (Eds.), *The neurobiology of learning and memory* (pp. 3-64). New York: Guilford Press.

Tulving, E. (1985). How many memory systems are there? *American Psychologist, 40,* 385-398.

Tulving, E., & Schacter, D. L. (1990). Priming and human memory systems. *Science, 247,* 301-306.

Van der Linden, M., & Van der Kaa, M. (1989). Reorganization therapy for memory impairments. In X. Seron & G. Deloche (Eds.), *Cognitive approaches in neuropsychological rehabilitation* (pp. 105-158). Hillsdale, N.J.: Lawrence Erlbaum Associates Inc.

Warrington, E. K., & Weiskrantz, L. (1968). New method of testing long-term retention with special reference to amnesic patients. *Nature, 217,* 972-974.

Warrington, E. K., & Weiskrantz, L. (1974). The effect of prior learning on subsequent retention in amnesic patients. *Neuropsychologia, 12,* 419-428.

Wickelgren, W. A. (1979). Chunking and consolidation: A theoretical synthesis of semantic networks, configuring in conditioning, S-R versus cognitive learning, normal forgetting, the amnesic syndrome, and the hippocampal arousal system. *Psychological Review, 86,* 44-60.

Wilson, B. (1982). Success and failure in memory training following a cerebral vascular accident. *Cortex, 18,* 581-594.

Wilson, B. (1987). *Rehabilitation of memory.* New York: Guilford.

CHAPTER TWENTY-FOUR

# The Flexibility of Implicit Memory: An Exploration Using Discrimination Learning

Alan D. Pickering
*Department of Psychology, St. George's Hospital Medical School, London , UK*

## ABSTRACT

This chapter addresses the notion of implicit memory (IM) from a number of perspectives: the basic phenomenon; the interpretative problems it poses; its use as a vehicle for memory rehabilitation; the proposal that it is an inflexible form of memory performance typified by access to information from a highly specific set of cues only; and, finally, its relationship to the relational/isolational processing distinction emerging from work on animal discrimination learning. Relational processing involves the encoding of relations between multiple stimuli and their responses and was considered to be a flexible, cognitive form of processing of considerable relevance to explicit memory (EM). Isolational processing, conversely, deals with each stimulus-response (S-R) link in isolation, and was considered an inflexible, noncognitive form of processing which may be subserving IM performance. As such the IM of amnesic patients should, qualitatively, be isolational in nature.

A preliminary exploration of visual discrimination learning is presented with data from a single amnesic case and controls. The patient learned the task very well (only 16/23 controls managed this). His performance was considered to be implicit on operational grounds and because he displayed no EM for the materials used in the task. Qualitatively, his performance appeared relational in nature, contrary to predictions. Eleven out of twenty three controls displayed evidence of relational processing. Amnesics' IM may therefore be less inflexible than was previously supposed (at least for some cases), giving grounds for greater optimism about the usefulness of rehabilitative methods, which utilise this preserved capacity.

## INTRODUCTION

Across the whole of scientific endeavour, a common complaint is that there is a serious communication gap between theoretical scientists and the practitioners (e.g. clinicians) seeking to implement their ideas. In many fields, this may be because the scientists are too theoretical and too abstract to provide practically useful information. In contrast, this chapter will argue that, in the neuropsychology of memory, a part of this problem stems from too little rather than too much theory. Theories must eventually become more than re-descriptions of the data-base and must be couched precisely enough to allow experimental refutation. The present chapter will attempt to integrate a relatively precise theoretical account of the function of the hippocampal system, based upon animal experiments, with the literature on the characteristics of some preserved memory functions in amnesics, the latter having been a source of recent advances in the area of rehabilitation (Glisky, Schacter, & Butters, this volume).

## IMPLICIT MEMORY: DATA AND DIFFICULTIES

Domains of preserved function within a neuropsychological syndrome are extremely important in elucidating normal brain mechanisms. They are additionally of prime importance for rehabilitation, offering potential routes through which impaired functions may be redirected and regained. This is undoubtedly why the finding of normal implicit memory (IM) in amnesic patients has produced so much interest and experimentation. Indeed IM research has led more or less directly to the use of "vanishing cues" in rehabilitation (see Glisky et al., this volume). The outcomes of the early treatment studies, which were validated in real world settings, were several orders of magnitude more successful than previous attempts at memory rehabilitation (see Glisky & Schacter, 1987; 1989). This chapter will, however, contend that the considerable IM research energy generated has so far been suboptimally employed, for reasons which stem from the ontogeny of IM research.

Before discussing the above notion in detail, the term IM must be clarified. A standard experimental task will serve as an illustration. Consider a word stem, STA—-, which may begin many common English words. On being asked to complete this stem to yield the first legitimate word which comes to mind (*stem completion*), there is a small probability that a specific completion (e.g. STATION) will be produced. This probability can be considerably increased if the word STATION has been presented to the subjects some time prior to the stem completion task. Thus the experimenter infers, from the change in the subjects' behaviour, that there is a 'memory' for the previous exposure to the word STATION. Explicit reference to a (to-be-) remembered event is made by neither subject nor experimenter. In this chapter, IM will be used to refer to any memory of this kind. Note that the stem completion task is superficially identical to cued recall ("which word beginning with STA did you see earlier?") except for the experimental instructions. Cued recall is an example of an explicit memory (EM) task.

Many researchers have argued that the processes underlying IM and EM performance are distinct and separable, perhaps reflecting the operation of separable memory systems (e.g. Tulving & Schacter, 1990). Two major pieces of evidence have been cited in support of such thinking. Firstly, amnesic patients, who by definition show extremely poor EM performance, often show normal IM performance on various tasks such as stem completion (e.g. Graf, Squire, & Mandler, 1984). Secondly, when either amnesic or normal subjects are tested twice on the same items, once implicitly and once explicitly, it is often found that the size of the IM effect is the same when calculated separately for explicitly remembered and non-remembered items (e.g. Tulving, Schacter, & Stark, 1982). That is, IM and EM can be stochastically independent (uncorrelated).

In order to see IM in proper historical context, it is critical to remember that these interesting findings originally emerged from EM experiments using cued recall (e.g. Warrington & Weiskrantz, 1968; 1970). On some occasions, with partial cues such as stems, amnesics seemed able to demonstrate normal cued recall. Later, these results were reinterpreted as evidence of preserved amnesic IM performance, which researchers had accidentally invoked during a test normally construed as an index of EM performance. Thus IM research inherited a dominant task (stem completion) and the concept was used to explain an existing and adventitious finding, rather than emerging from considerations of possible mechanisms. These historical factors have, I suggest, been somewhat detrimental to the scientific development of ideas about IM.

On the surface, stem completion differs from cued recall only in the instructions given to the subjects. Therefore, dissociations between these tasks may be extremely labile depending on the extent to which subjects follow instructions (*vide* early cued recall experiments now being considered as examples of IM). This leads to the highly unsatisfactory state of affairs wherein contradictory findings can be dismissed on the grounds that IM (or EM) performance may not have been selectively reflected in the particular experimental tasks used. For example, when Graf and Schacter (1985) found cued recall and completion performance to be stochastically dependent (correlated), they suggested that EM might have been contributing to both tasks. This circular argument has appeared in many of the sizeable number of experiments failing to show stochastic independence between EM and IM. In passing, it is worth noting that other major conceptualisations in cognitive psychology have suffered similar logical problems (see, for example, Allport, 1980, on 'automaticity' - the idea that certain types of information processing require few general mental resources and can be performed effortlessly). Such difficulties inevitably arise when an independent means of assessing the entity in question is lacking (here, the implicitness or explicitness of the memory performance being measured).

In terms of theoretical mechanisms, IM research is also unsatisfactory. Proponents of the 'separate memory systems' view argue that existing mental representations are transiently activated when stimuli corresponding to these representations are perceived. This activation facilitates, or primes, later processing of those stimuli. Hence, some forms of IM are often referred to as priming. It is recommended here and elsewhere (e.g. Richardson-Klavehn & Bjork, 1988) that a theoretically laden name, such as priming, should be avoided. Priming mechanisms cannot easily explain any of the following: IM in normal or amnesic subjects for novel material which has no pre-existing mental representation (e.g. Johnson, Kim, & Risse, 1985; Kunst-Wilson & Zajonc, 1980); the influence of recently learned associates on stem completion (e.g. Graf & Schacter, 1985); and IM effects that have been reported to last for days or weeks (see Richardson-Klavehn & Bjork, 1988, for a review).

The alternative major view (e.g. Jacoby, 1983) does not invoke separate memory systems for IM and EM, rather IM and EM are considered to differ in the aspects of an information-processing episode on which they depend. IM is conceived as being highly dependent upon data-driven processing (because the subject focuses on perceptual data such as word stems) and EM upon conceptually-driven processing (because the subject focuses on semantic, and other, associations between mental events).

This view also falls short in the face of the evidence. IM performance on some tasks can be substantially improved by instructing the subject to engage in conceptual processing (Graf & Schacter, 1985; Pickering, Mayes, & Shoqeirat, 1988). This contrasts with the pattern obtained for stem completion (e.g. Graf, Mandler, & Haden, 1982). Furthermore, a recent study (Hunt & Toth, 1990) reported improved free-recall (EM) and completion (IM) performance in orthographically distinct, as compared with orthographically common, words (a manipulation primarily affecting data-driven processing). It is interesting to note that proponents of the separate systems view of the IM/EM distinction also argue for a perceptual emphasis in IM performance (Tulving & Schacter, 1990). The difficulties posed above are avoided by unparsimoniously distinguishing separate kinds of IM, for example: perceptual vs. conceptual priming (Tulving & Schacter, 1990). In such a scheme, conceptual priming is viewed as an implicit modification of semantic memory.

In light of such difficulties, it is therefore suggested that IM research makes a fresh start; not that we should forget the valuable data that have been gathered, but that we should now proceed in proper scientific fashion by deriving hypotheses as to what IM is, and by seeking to interrogate these ideas experimentally. This will necessitate the design and use of new experimental procedures and, commensurately, will place less emphasis on stem completion. Although such a move essentially represents a theoretical enterprise, potential practical benefits may ultimately ensue, particularly in rehabilitation (Glisky et al., this volume). If IM offers a viable route for cognitive rehabilitation of some amnesics, then to optimise its application necessitates as complete an understanding of IM mechanisms as possible. Considerable though Glisky and Schacter's (1987; 1989) rehabilitation successes have been, their methods were extremely time-consuming; more rapid acquisition via IM could perhaps be achieved if its characteristics were better understood. In the remainder of this chapter I will outline one attempt to advance our understanding of IM.

## IMPLICIT MEMORY, COGNITION, AND FLEXIBILITY

Tulving and Schacter emphasise that IM—perceptual priming, in their nomenclature—(1990, p. 301) "involves cognitive representations and expresses itself in cognition rather than behaviour". Even ignoring any philosophical arguments about the separateness of cognition and behaviour, the statement is highly controversial. Firstly, our present position would seem at odds with the latter part of the statement. We have already argued that IM can only be inferred from a change in behaviour. EM, on the other hand, appears quintessentially cognitive; reflecting, as it does, the subject's introspection about past experiences ("Have I seen this word before in the experiment?").

Secondly, Tulving and Schacter, in elaborating the properties of IM, comment upon the inflexibility (or hyperspecificity) of access to the information on which it is based (see also Glisky et al., this volume). If an essential part of cognitive activity is the creation of informational structures, which allow flexibility in mental activity, then the inflexibility of IM would tend to locate it at least partially outside the cognitive domain.

'Flexible informational structures' begins to sound like impenetrable jargon; I shall make this point more concretely in relation to the ideas of Eichenbaum and his colleagues (Eichenbaum, Fagan, Mathews, & Cohen, 1988; Eichenbaum, Mathews, & Cohen, 1989), which are closely related to those of several other theorists (e.g. Wickelgren, 1979). Specifically, Eichenbaum et al. propose that limbic system structures carry out *relational* processing, which they define as "the encoding of relations among multiple stimuli" (Eichenbaum et al., 1988, p. 331). Thus, the memory representations that are the product of such processing, contrast with those arising from "adaptations to particular stimuli encoded individually". This latter mode of memory will be denoted *isolational* as each stimulus or stimulus element is assigned a response in isolation, that is, independently of other stimulus-response (S-R) relationships.

An anecdote may best illustrate both the nature of this distinction and the powerful relational processing tendencies with which we humans, I believe, approach many situations. A distinguished psychologist sought me out after attending a departmental visitor's day during which he had failed to solve the computerised learning task that I had displayed.

Basically, this required the subject to learn which four of eight coloured locations concealed targets. The colours changed their spatial locations from trial to trial but it was always the same four, arbitrarily designated, which concealed the targets. It was the arbitrariness that made this task so difficult. My colleague said that he had unsuccessfully explored various hypotheses: Were the targets concealed by the primary colours? or were they at the locations to the left of the screen? etc. etc. So powerful was his need to construct an overarching structure, or rule, that he could not learn four simple, but arbitrary, S-R connections. He approached the problem with a relational processing strategy incompatible with the isolational structure of the task.

Does this make isolational processing inflexible? After a little thought one can see that this must obviously be the case. Imagine someone being told two facts: "John is Stephen's father"; "Stephen is Clare's brother". Individuals processing this information relationally or isolationally would be able to respond equally well to the questions: "Who is Stephen's father?" "Who is Clare's brother?" However, only relational processing allows one to answer questions such as "Who is Clare's father?" Thus, information access is inflexible after isolational processing, that is, it can be elicited only by highly specific cues. Interestingly, this kind of issue is beginning to move centre-stage in contemporary computer models of memory (see Hinton, 1989).

We have thus generated a hypothesis that EM is essentially a product of cognition, supported by relational processing, with flexible access to the relevant memory traces. By contrast, IM is a non-cognitive product, supported by isolational processing and characterised by inflexible, hyperspecific access to the relevant memory traces. The experiment presented below is a preliminary test of such a proposal in an amnesic subject. Performance in this patient should be largely based on IM and therefore display isolational processing. The experiment employed a human analogue of the tasks used by Eichenbaum and colleagues with rats.

## EICHENBAUM'S EXPERIMENTS

Eichenbaum et al. used a variety of odour discrimination tasks. In one of these, the discriminanda were odours A and B puffed simultaneously into the experimental chamber one from the left and the other from the right. Both spatial permutations of the odours were used. For one of these permutations the rats had to learn to make a nose-poke into the left "sniff port" in order to receive water reward, for the other pairing the required response was into the right port. In other words, reward was always associated with one of the odours (e.g. A). These spatially distributed pairs of odours will be denoted Ab and bA, with the upper-case letter representing the odour associated with reward; that is, the odour presented on the side to which the correct response should be made.

It is possible for rats to configure and solve this task in at least three qualitatively distinct ways. The first solution is relational and involves perceiving the relationship between the Ab and bA pairings, namely that they require (spatially) complementary responses. The efficiency of such solutions lies in the fact that they allow information-processing to become more selective. After initially engaging in extensive comparative processing, between and within odour pairs, the relational processor can eventually respond largely to the A odour alone (in the above example), as it always occurs on the side to which a response is required.

The second, contrasting, solution is isolational. Here, the odour pairing as a whole functions as the stimulus (rather than one of its two constituent odours), and these require that two unconnected S-R relationships be forged (e.g. AB—go left; BA—go right; the upper/lower-case notation is not relevant here). This reveals another reason why relational processing is more efficient than isolational: Learning the responses to the Ab and bA pairings occurs together, which is not necessarily the case for an isolational solution. The third kind of solution will be described later.

Eichenbaum et al. (1988; 1989) compared fornix-lesioned rats with sham-operated controls. The fornical lesions were intended as a crude model of human bi-temporal amnesia. Eichenbaum et al. (1989) reported that in their fornix-lesioned animals there was an almost complete lack of acetylcholinesterase staining in the hippocampal formation and inferred that cholinergic input to the hippocampus had been eliminated. Although fornix lesions in primates may not be a particularly good model of bi-temporal amnesia (e.g. Squire & Zola-Morgan, 1983), the extreme deprivation of cholinergic input to, and subsequent functional disruption of, the hippocampal formation in Eichenbaum's rats gives considerable credibility to the model in rodents.

Fornix lesions severely disrupted acquisition of the particular class of discrimination problem described above. Eichenbaum and colleagues interpreted this finding as evidence for the lack of relational processing abilities in the fornical rats. This interpretation was consistent with the finding that the fornix rats were actually superior to the control animals on very similar odour discrimination tasks in which the odours were presented centrally and separately and only one odour (A but not B) required a central nose-poke response (formally a successive discrimination problem in contrast to the simultaneous discriminations at which the fornical animals were impaired). Relational processing was argued to confer no advantage in the successive discrimination problems.

Despite severe overall deficits, some fornix-lesioned animals did, however, learn about a quarter of the series of simultaneous discrimination problems on which they were tested. Eichenbaum et al. were interested in the qualitative aspects of these occasional sucesses. They argued that they may have arisen from isolational solutions of the kind described above, or by a third kind of solution which they termed *guidance-based* (following O'Keefe & Conway, 1980).

It is possible that guidance solutions may allow similar results to those achieved by relational strategies without the need for an appreciation of the relationships built into the structure of the task. In more detail, the rat may make an initial lateralised response by chance (e.g. a nose-poke to the left port) and, depending on reinforcement (receipt of water or not), this may set up approach or avoidance tendencies towards the odour present in the port. Correct responses on subsequent trials, even when the odour is in the other port, could thus be acquired without relational processing and would lead to a similar selective reduction in processing demands.

In their later study, (Eichenbaum et al., 1989) these workers investigated whether the fornix rats were limited to isolational solutions. They reasoned, as I have done above, that relational, in contrast with isolational, processing allows (p. 1208) "the *flexible* use of prior specific experiences in new contexts" (emphasis added). They tested this idea directly. Fornix rats were trained until they reached a 90% criterion on two out of ten standard simultaneous discriminations of the kind described above. These will be referred to as Ab/bA and Cd/dC. They were then matched to sham-operated controls, which had solved the same two problems and testing continued for just the two problems randomly interleaved within sessions. Probe trials were mixed in, with low probability, amongst standard trials in this post-criterion testing. These probe trials consisted of the previously unused, crossover odour pairs Ad, dA, Cb, and bC with consistency in the response relationships between standard and probe trials (i.e. Ab and Cd are combined to give Ad and not aD etc.).

Using isolational processing alone, the probe trials effectively represent new discriminanda for which responses have to be acquired as they cannot be related to previous experience. Hence, responding should be error-prone. However, one should note that the simplification of the task afforded by relational or guidance strategies, can effectively solve the probe trials using the learning acquired from the original standard Ab/bA and Cd/dC problems. Consider such strategies in relation to Ad or dA probes; the correct response is still to be made to the side of odour A and not to the side of odour d, as in the standard trials.

Eichenbaum and colleagues (1989) found that the fornix-lesioned animals performed poorly on the probe trials, initially at a chance level, as if they had never experienced the constituent stimuli. It should be stressed that this was found for probes derived from standard problems on which the experimental and control animals achieved comparable levels of success. This outcome is in keeping with the idea that the lesioned animals were utilising isolational processing only. By contrast, sham-operated rats performed as well on the probe trials as they did on standard trials, even initially.

Eichenbaum et al. also came to the conclusion that the control animals were using relational rather than guidance strategies. Why did they reach such a view as neither would produce difficulties on the probe trials? Their case was based on a detailed comparison of response latencies between the different groups. For reasons beyond the scope of the present chapter, it was felt that this particular test of relational processing may not apply to the human experiment conducted here, and so, as we shall see, the outcome of probe testing was utilised as the primary test of relational processing. To do this, it was therefore necessary to eliminate the possibility of guidance solutions; the method by which this was achieved will also be explained.

I have devoted a considerable amount of detailed analysis to the Eichenbaum studies because they are complex and central to the understanding of the present experiment. It is to this that I now turn.

## AN OVERVIEW OF THE ANALOGOUS HUMAN DISCRIMINATION TASK

The experiment to be reported employed a computerised visual pattern discrimination task closely modelled on Eichenbaum et al.'s (1989) olfactory procedure with rats. Before proceeding further, it is important to note that while the human task is conceptually analogous to that used with rats, the different presentation and response modalities will cause considerable differences between such tasks. Nonetheless, it is predicted that these will not mask the commonalities between species in the solution strategies adopted and the way that these are manifested in behaviour. General concerns about S-R learning in animals as opposed to cognitive learning in humans are not an issue either, as Eichenbaum's analysis suggests that the control rats are solving the simultaneous discriminations in a cognitive (i.e. relational) rather than an S-R (i.e. isolational) manner.

The human subjects were presented, on a microcomputer, with pairs of distinct visual patterns to which they had to respond by making left-, or right-, handed responses on horizontally arranged response buttons (on the computer's mouse). If the discrimination stimuli had been arranged horizontally it was felt that guidance strategies would have been possible. It will be recalled that guidance strategies for rats could arise because the responses consisted in approach (or avoidance) to the stimuli themselves; in the present task it seemed possible that a stimulus on one side of the computer screen might attract attention to that side of space and thus favour a response on that side of the horizontal (mouse) response configuration. In order to eliminate guidance strategies it was therefore decided to change to a vertical (above-below) arrangement of the paired visual pattern stimuli.

Each subject saw four stimuli (A to D) in standard trials and the stimulus pairings and required responses are illustrated in Fig. 24.1. As in the Eichenbaum et al. (1989) study, the stimuli were paired to give two randomly interleaved simultaneous discrimination problems which were trained to a criterion with probe trials intermixed during post-criterion testing. In the text, AB will refer to a stimulus pairing in which pattern A appears above pattern B and vice versa for BA. The required responses (L or R button) will be additionally designated thus: (AB)-L; (BA)-R etc. The standard trials used were: (AB)-L; (BA)-R; (CD)-L; (DC)-R. As we consider how different solution styles affect

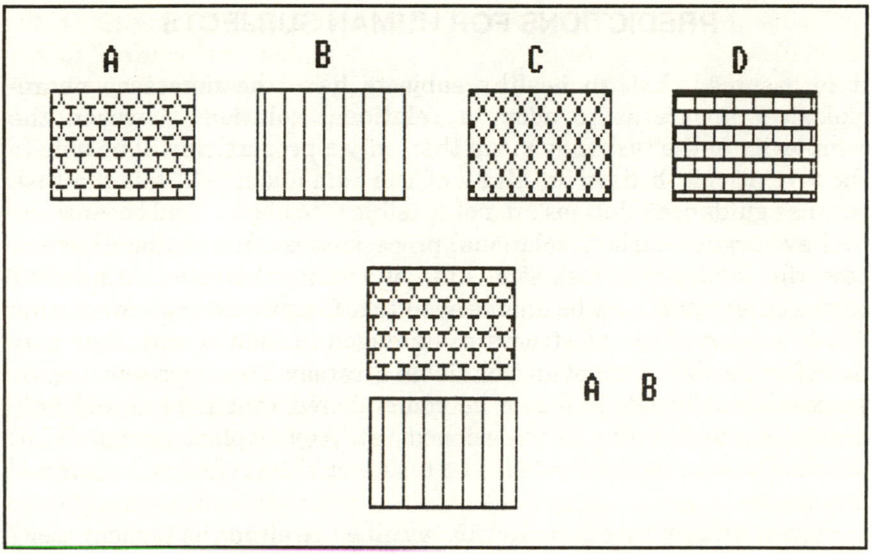


FIG. 24.1. The four patterns assigned to the stimulus 'roles' A–D for a particular subject. The stimulus pairing AB (pattern A above pattern B) is also illustrated.

performance on this task, we shall see that the use of vertically arranged discrimination stimuli and horizontally arranged responses necessitated the use of a greater variety of probe trials than those employed in the animal task. In fact, all other combinations of stimuli were tested and these constituted the probe trials (see Table 24.1).

TABLE 24.1
The Full Range of Stimuli, the Number of Each Kind Used in Post-criterial Testing and their Correct Responses (L or R hand) - see Fig. 24.1

| *Stimulus Pair* | *N* | *Type* | *Correct Response* |
|---|---|---|---|
| AB | 15 | Standard | L |
| BA | 15 | Standard | R |
| CD | 15 | Standard | L |
| DC | 15 | Standard | R |
| AD | 2 | Probe | L |
| DA | 1 | Probe | R |
| BC | 2 | Probe | R |
| CB | 1 | Probe | L |
| CA | 2 | Probe | L |
| AC | 1 | Probe | R |
| DB | 2 | Probe | R |
| BD | 1 | Probe | L |

## PREDICTIONS FOR HUMAN SUBJECTS

It is assumed that all healthy subjects have the necessary neurobiological apparatus to adopt a relational solution. However, the complexity of the task may mean that only a proportion will be able to show relational behaviour. Many of the remainder will fail the task because guidance solutions are not feasible (see above), and because, as we have argued earlier, isolational processing is often inhibited by the powerful tendency to seek some kind of relational strategy. Amnesics, on the other hand, may be unable even to attempt relational processing if it is subserved by the structures damaged in their brains; they may therefore be able to adopt an isolational strategy. This approach may be successful, although it should be remembered that it produced only limited success in the fornix-lesioned rat. Any implicit memory (IM) which amnesics demonstrate in the task would therefore be isolational in nature.

How would relational behaviour manifest itself in the present task? The spatial compatibility between stimuli and responses, which was present in the animal task, led to a natural simplification of processing demands as a result of relational processing (effectively subjects come to respond to the side on which odour A was found etc.). The absence of a natural spatial mapping between stimuli and responses in the present task leads to a much greater variety of outcomes produced by relational processing strategies. For example, rather than focusing selectively upon a particular pattern element (e.g. A in AB and BA trials, as in the animal task), subjects might also appreciate, via relational processing, that it is a valid strategy to focus on a particular stimulus position (e.g. the upper pattern).

Even if one were to concentrate only on subjects using element-focused strategies one can easily see the complexities inherent in making detailed predictions for behaviour on probe trials. For example, such subjects are likely to concentrate on the element they perceive as the more salient within each pairing. Salience is likely to differ from subject to subject, but assume for one subject that A and C are the more salient elements from the standard stimuli AB/BA and CD/DC respectively. The probe trials, which contain neither of these elements (BD and DB in our example), will be difficult for this subject (and perhaps also the probe trials which contain both of them: AC; CA), but AD and DA probes will not be difficult (check this prediction using Table 24.1). The picture would be completely different if elements A and D were the most salient.

In summary, it is possible to say, however, that the relational processor should, having mastered the standard problems, make high levels of errors on no more than two of the four probe types used. For the reasons given earlier we cannot know, in advance, which probe types are going to be difficult for relational processors; we know that there are likely to be some. That is why all four probe types needed to be included in the present experiment (rather than only two in the original animal experiments). Therefore, if we rank the four probe types in terms of errors there should be a single marked discontinuity for relational processors between the probe types which can and cannot be solved on the basis of the solutions to the standard problems.

To an isolational processor, all probe types effectively constitute a new problem, and are therefore learned *de novo* with high numbers of errors. There should no clear discontinuity across the four probe types in terms of error rate (i.e. all should be equally difficult).

From the standpoint of flexibility, another of our present themes, one could derive equivalent predictions. One would argue that more flexible learning achieved on the standard problems would be transferred more easily to, and to a wider range of, related probe trials. Flexible learning has been equated earlier with relational processing. In conclusion therefore, if amnesics are limited to isolational, inflexible, implicit learning on the present task, then they should show none of the features of relational processing outlined above.

## METHOD

### Subjects

An amnesic patient (G.S.) was tested on this task. When seen, at age 32 years, he was an in-patient of the Regional Neurological Rehabilitation Unit (RNRU), at the Homerton Hospital in East London. He is a former flying instructor who suffered CO poisoning as a result of an abortive suicide attempt in February 1990. G.S. is severely amnesic. Tested immediately, he remembered only two items from each of two prose passages on the WMS (each containing more than 20 items). After a ten-minute delay he recalled nothing. He is consistently unable to remember the names of those testing him for longer than a few seconds, and once turned up for a testing session at the time noted in his timetable, having no recollection that the session had been moved forward, and had finished an hour earlier. There are signs of reductions in other cognitive functions from the level expected given his previous occupation, but these are not as marked as his memory problems. His current Wechsler Adult Intelligence Scale (Revised) full-scale IQ of 76, and Mill Hill Vocabulary IQ of 87, both reflect this decline; there is less sign of deterioration in his National Adult Reading Test (NART) IQ, currently 101. His Wechsler Memory Quotient (62) is an order of magnitude worse.

The patient was compared with 23 healthy controls, recruited from a local unemployment centre and from non-academic staff of St. George's Hospital. Their mean age was 36.0 years and they had a mean NART IQ of 115.7.

### Procedure

Six distinct patterns (e.g. thick vertical stripes, thin oblique stripes, brickwork, etc.) were generated. For each subject, at random, four were selected and randomly assigned to the standard AB, BA, CD and DC pairings described earlier (see also Fig. 24.1). In these pairs, the two patterns (2.5cm x 3.0cm) were presented one directly above the other in the centre of the computer screen. They remained there until the subject pressed either the left or right response button. On responding, subjects were given feedback via high or low tones, and by the words "correct" or "wrong" appearing below the discriminanda. It is important to note that the subjects were not instructed in how to configure the task but were simply told that they should press one of the two buttons in response to what appeared on the screen and that they would be given feedback about their responses. They were told that they would have to use trial and error at the beginning.

The two simultaneous discriminations, AB and CD, were randomly interleaved, and errors and response latencies were recorded. Subjects were trained to a criterion of four correct responses out of the last five on both problems simultaneously, with training terminating if they did not achieve this criterion in 72 trials. Those achieving the criterion proceeded without a break to 72 further trials containing 12 previously unseen probe pairs. The probe stimuli, along with their required responses (left or right hand), are shown in Table 24.1.

For those subjects who reached criterion in the first stage, the second stage (with probes) was followed by a cued recognition test (EM) for the pattern pairings that had been presented. Here, each pattern element (A to D), in each of its two positions (up/down), was shown in a fixed random order. For each, the subject had to recognise the pattern(s) that had occupied the accompanying (now blank) screen location. Subjects were told that there may have been more than one accompanying pattern, and chose from six possible patterns (A to F; E,F having never previously appeared), displayed on the computer screen. For each of the eight cues (A to D, each in two locations) there were actually three accompanying patterns, giving a maximum score of 24 (100%). For each false positive (selection of E or F) a point was deducted, giving the possibility of negative scores down to a minimum of -16 (-67%).

## RESULTS AND DISCUSSION

The response buttons were quite sensitive and, very occasionally, subjects pressed them unintentionally. If a response latency was recorded on such an occasion it was detectable (very rapid, <0.2 secs). Such responses were discounted in the following analyses which were therefore based on reduced numbers of trials. The criterion used (see earlier) was quite lax and subjects could pass it by chance. Thus, importance was placed upon the performance (percentage correct) on post-criterion standard trials (PCSTs). Two of the twenty three controls failed to reach criterion in 72 trials and a further five showed less than 75% correct on PCSTs for one or both of the two problems. These seven subjects were excluded leaving 16 whose data are reported henceforth.

The controls' mean percentage correct on PCSTs, averaged across both problems, was 92.8% (range 83.3-100). The first point to note is that G.S., despite his inferior intelligence, was able to perform very creditably, acquiring the discrimination as rapidly as the best control subject and averaging 93.1% correct on PCSTs (89.7% AB/BA problem; 96.5% CD/DC problem). Moreover, finding an amnesic who could learn the task did not require testing of many patients—G.S. was only the second amnesic patient to be tested on the task (see later).

Was the successful learning, achieved by G.S. implicit in nature? It would qualify as such from the standpoint of the operational definition of IM offered at the start of this chapter. Subjects were never requested to introspect on the remembering aspect of the discriminations, but merely responded to the patterns seen. Moreover, G.S.'s discrimination learning seems to be dissociated from his EM for the patterns involved. Consider EM performance on the cued recognition task. Control subjects showed excellent EM with a mean score of 75.0% correct. G.S., in stark contrast, actually achieved a negative score ( 20.8%). This means that G.S. showed no ability to recall the patterns seen, even the standard pairings that had occurred many times each. This lack of EM lends considerable weight to the suggestion that G.S.'s discrimination learning is an example of IM.

It is important to sound a cautionary note along with the preceding interpretation. It is conceivable that, between the end of the discrimination trials and the start of the cued recognition task, G.S.'s EM for the patterns could have decayed very rapidly. Thus, processes related to EM performance could have been supporting G.S.'s discrimination learning even though the task is operationally one measuring performance implicitly. This does not seem very likely given the enormous degree of exposure to each of the standard patterns but is clearly an issue for further exploration.

The primary purpose of the experiment was to evaluate the qualitative nature of any discrimination learning achieved. We have already seen that isolational processing is relatively unlikely to solve this kind of problem in rata. Nonetheless, we must look for evidence as to whether G.S. solved the task using relational or isolational processing.

The characteristics of relational processing relate to error rates across the four probe types (AC/CA; AD/DA; BC/CB; BD/DB). For each subject, probes were ranked in terms of their error rates (errors per three probes). Figure 24.2 shows the results of this process for G.S. and the sixteen controls who showed good levels of learning. It is clear that G.S. shows the features that were argued to be characteristic of subjects using a relational strategy: (a) at least two probe types which do not

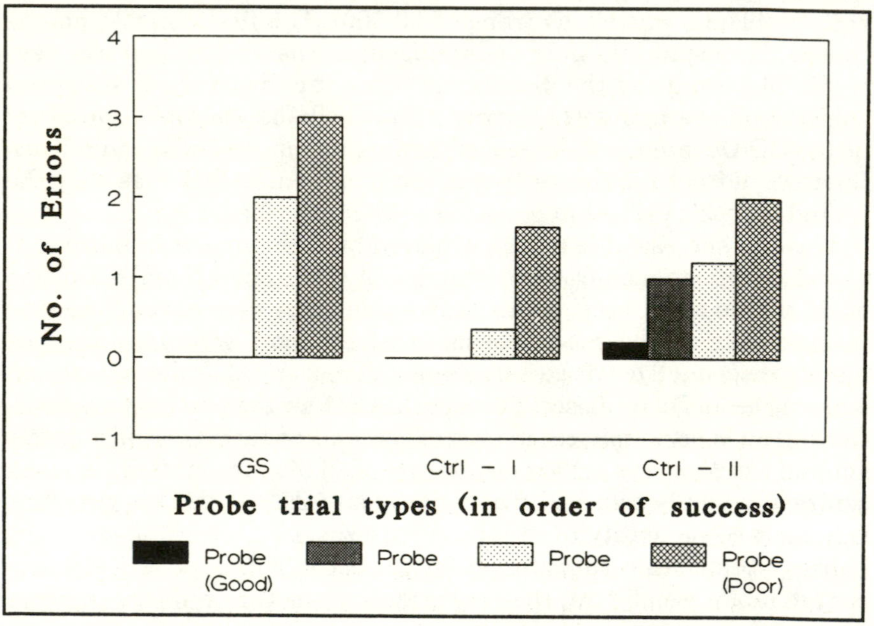


FIG. 24.2. Number of errors made on probe trials during post-criterial testing by amnesic G.S. and two subgroups of control subjects. Ctrl-I (N=11) show evidence of relational processing (0 errors on 2 or more probe types); Ctrl-II (N=5) do not show clear evidence of relational processing (1 or more errors on 3 or more probe types). Performance is broken down by probe types and is shown in the figure in order of decreasing success (i.e. increasing errors from left to right).

present difficulties (0 errors); and (b) a single marked discontinuity in error rates across probe types. Eleven of the sixteen controls responded to two or more probe types without error and are thus likely to be using relational strategies. In Fig. 24.2 these subjects (controls-I) are presented separately from the other five (controls-II) in whom the evidence of the use of relational processing is less clear.

On these criteria, G.S. showed the characteristics of relational processing, and to a greater degree than a number of controls who were reasonably successful in learning the task. In alternative terms, we might conclude that G.S.'s discrimination learning showed a similar degree of flexibility to that of many subjects whose EM performance (relating to the elements of the discrimination task) was far superior to his own. This flexibility means that G.S. could transfer his learning successfully from well-learned (standard) problems to novel related problems (some of the probes) immediately and without difficulty. We shall now consider the implications of these data, for theory and rehabilitation, in more detail.

## THEORETICAL IMPLICATIONS

The basic model that was tested in the present experiment seems to be refuted by these data. First, the idea that all amnesics are incapable of relational processing cannot be maintained. One attempt to defend the model could be to suggest that the amnesics who cannot perform relational processing are those with medial temporal, rather than other (e.g. diencephalic) damage, as the animal data are relevant to medial temporal amnesia exclusively. The present data do not speak to this issue directly, as we have no prima facie evidence as to the location of G.S.'s pathology. His CT scan was unhelpful: it revealed "no significant lesion". Nonetheless, for many years it has been widely held that the neuropathological locus of anoxic-ischemic amnesia (and G.S.'s CO-induced amnesia is likely to have been of this kind) lies in medial temporal structures such as the hippocampus (e.g. see Adams, Brierley, Connor, & Treip, 1966).

If one accepts the arguments that the discrimination learning shown by G.S. was a form of IM, then these data also refute the idea that IM is necessarily isolational and inflexible. For certain patients, therefore, IM may be less limited than was suspected, and can be influenced by higher-order structure present in the material to be learned—a conclusion with important ramifications for rehabilitation (see later). Furthermore, as G.S.'s EM performance was at chance levels, then relational processing would appear *not* to be a *sufficient* condition for successful EM. However, this is not to deny its usefulness for EM.

When the EM performance of the two control subgroups (I and II, see Fig. 24.2) was compared, subgroup I showed significantly higher levels of EM than subgroup II ($F_{1,14}$=5.2, $P < 0.05$ ), and the difference would have been very highly significant but for the presence of one subject with poor EM in subgroup I (33.3% c.f. mean 87.1% and s.d. 13.1, for the other 10 subjects). Subgroup I, it will be recalled, contained the controls who showed clearest evidence of relational processing.

Finally, there remains the interesting question as to whether G.S. could have explicitly stated the rules he was using to solve the task. This may seem a strange question to ask given that we have already argued that G.S.'s performance on the task was implicit and that many researchers view IM as being memory without awareness (see Richardson-Klavehn & Bjork, 1988). Nonetheless, it is possible that performance could be guided by rules that can be stated more or less explicitly without an ability to recollect (i.e. without subjective awareness of) the specific episodes that allowed the rules to be extracted. Many examples of procedural (skill) memory may be like this: one only has to think of driving a car. Based on an observation made during another computerised discrimination task, we may speculate that G.S. may have had explicit access to his performance strategy. In this task the discriminanda were pairs of words, one living and one non-living in each pair. The correct response on each occasion was to type the living word on the keyboard. G.S. failed to learn this task, but stated several relational hypotheses aloud (including the correct one, not pursued further) whilst puzzling over his strategy.

## IMPLICATIONS FOR REHABILITATION

What may the current experiment suggest for clinical practice? If IM is to be pursued as a primary route for the rehabilitation of memory disorders then the present result is quite encouraging. Some kinds of IM in some patients may be more flexible than previously supposed. For what proportion of amnesics this assertion is true remains an empirical question. One might suspect that case G.S. was atypical. Certainly Glisky, Schacter, and Butters (this volume) describe hyperspecificity (inflexibility) in the IM performance acquired using vanishing cues by their amnesics, and imply that it was fairly universal. Nonetheless, it is important to note that G.S.'s success on the task is made all the more impressive by the fact that he can, in no sense, be regarded as a pure amnesic. Despite quite marked cognitive difficulties outside the domain of memory he was still able to show relational processing. Theoretically interesting results are often derived from rare pure cases and the utility of the findings for rehabilitation is undermined by the fact that the common presentation of amnesia to the therapist is as one component of a broader cognitive decline. The present finding is made stronger by the fact that it came from an impure case.

One might screen for cases capable of relational processing by tasks such as the one discussed here and then the rehabilitation targets set for such patients could be commensurately higher. If one is teaching skills of everyday living, one could tailor the client's program more appropriately in light of their ability to encode "the relations amongst multiple stimuli" and flexibly to generalise their learning to new contexts. In terms of concrete examples, a patient who can achieve relational processing could be expected to progress rapidly from learning how to make buttered toast to learning how to prepare a variety of dishes based around toast. Such a patient could also be expected to learn to use public transport more flexibly and not remain limited to a few set routes.

The idea of general purpose procedures becomes more appropriate for the relational processor by dint of their ability to generalise any learning achieved. Purer cases of amnesia may not need retraining in basic life skills but may need to be drilled in a number of habitual checking procedures to avoid serious dangers (e.g. are electrical appliances switched off?). The patient capable of relational processing will find it much easier to use such procedures in a wide range of related contexts (e.g. kettles, irons, electric cookers etc.).

It is important to stress that subjects not capable of relational processing may be able to achieve similar results via alternative routes such as guidance strategies (if available). G.S. was the second amnesic tested on the present task. The first case also came from the RNRU at the Homerton Hospital. N.B., a severe post-encephalitic amnesic, failed to learn the task on three separate occasions. We therefore tested her using an analogous test with horizontally arranged discrimination stimuli, as in the original experiment by Eichenbaum and his colleagues. On two out of four occasions she learned the task successfully: For post-criterion standard trials she attained an average (across the Ab/bA, Cd/dC problems) of 87.1% and 85% correct respectively. Critically, however, N.B. was untroubled by the Ad/dA and bC/Cb probe trials. She achieved a similar level of success (87.5% correct) on these problems.

I have already argued that the horizontally arranged discrimination task would allow guidance solutions specifically excluded in the vertical version and these, as for relational solutions, would allow successful solution of probe trials. This is, I suspect, how N.B. achieved her successes on the horizontal task. From the standpoint of rehabilitation, her success teaches us a valuable lesson. A simple manipulation (a 90 degree rotation) of stimulus materials, for this particular patient, transformed the task from something unlearnable into a problem that was (often) soluble. The powerful effects of stimulus-response compatibility (i.e. left-sided responses to the left-hand element of the stimulus pair etc.) may have enabled appropriate approach/avoidance behaviours to be set up, thereby bypassing N.B.'s inability to utilise cognitively the task's inherent structure.

In attempts at rehabilitation with N.B., we may have observed her preserved ability to develop approach behaviour. She was specifically trained to use a notebook as an appointments diary for therapy sessions and for general orientation. In a video-taped session she repeatedly failed to give the correct day and date but was then asked how she might find out this information. While saying that she had no idea (she had been trained over many hours that the information was in the notebook kept in her handbag), she was observed reaching for her handbag and beginning to inspect its contents in a rather automatic and habitual way. One might be tempted to speculate that this was evidence of a primitive, implicit form of S-R approach behaviour, which may ultimately provide the basis for successful diary use.

## ACKNOWLEDGEMENTS

The ideas on relational processing discussed here were developed whilst the author was supported by the Wellcome Trust, and later by the Medical Research Council of the UK. Thanks are due to: Dr. Richard Greenwood for allowing testing of patients in his care; Prof. Mort Mishkin, the editors and an anonymous reviewer for detailed comments on versions of this chapter; Sharon Abrahams and Dr. Jane Powell for research assistance and comments on the text.

## REFERENCES

Adams, J. H., Brierley, J. B., Connor, R. C. R., & Treip, C. S. (1966). The effects of systemic hypotension upon the human brain: Clinical and neuropathological observations in 11 cases. *Brain, 89,* 235-268.

Allport, D. A. (1980). Attention and performance. In G. Claxton (Ed.), *Cognitive psychology* (pp. 112-153). London: Routledge Kegan Paul.

Eichenbaum, H., Fagan, A., Mathews, P., & Cohen, N. J. (1988). Hippocampal system dysfunction and odour discrimination learning in rats: Impairment or facilitation depending on representational demands. *Behavioral Neuroscience, 102,* 331-339.

Eichenbaum, H., Mathews, P., & Cohen, N. J. (1989). Further studies of hippocampal representation during odour discrimination learning. *Behavioral Neuroscience, 103,* 1207-1216.

Glisky, E., & Schacter, D. L. (1987). Acquisition of domain-specific knowledge in organic amnesia: Training for computer-related work. *Neuropsychologia, 25,* 893-906.

Glisky, E., & Schacter, D. L. (1989). Extending the limits of complex learning in organic amnesia: Computer training in a vocational domain. *Neuropsychologia, 27,* 107-120.

Graf, P., Mandler, G., & Haden, P. E. (1982). Simulating amnesic symptoms in normals. *Science, 218,* 1243-1244.

Graf, P., & Schacter, D. L. (1985). Implicit and explicit memory for new associations in normal and amnesic subjects. *Journal of Experimental Psychology: Learning, Memory, and Cognition, 11,* 501-518.

Graf, P., Squire, L. R., & Mandler, G. (1984). The information that amnesic patients do not forget. *Journal of Experimental Psychology: Learning, Memory, and Cognition, 10,* 164-178.

Hinton, G. E. (1989). Learning distributed representations of concepts. In R. G. M. Morris (Ed.), *Parallel distributed processing: Implications for psychology and neurobiology* (pp. 46-61). Oxford: Clarendon Press.

Hunt, R. R., & Toth J. P. (1990). Perceptual identification, fragment completion and free recall: Concepts and data. *Journal of Experimental Psychology: Learning, Memory, and Cognition, 16,* 282-290.

Jacoby, L. L. (1983). Perceptual enhancement: Persistent effects of an experience. *Journal of Experimental Psychology: Learning, Memory, and Cognition, 9,* 21-38.

Johnson, M. K., Kim, J. K., & Risse, G. (1985). Do alcoholic Korsakoff's syndrome patients acquire affective reactions? *Journal of Experimental Psychology: Learning, Memory, and Cognition, 11,* 22-36.

Kunst-Wilson, U. R., & Zajonc, R. B. (1980). Affective discrimination of stimuli that are not recognised. *Science, 207,* 557-558.

O'Keefe, J., & Conway, D. H. (1980). On the trail of the hippocampal engram. *Physiological Psychology, 2,* 229-238.

Pickering, A. D., Mayes, A. R., & Shoqeirat, M. (1988). Priming tasks in normal subjects: What do they reveal about amnesia? In M. M. Gruneberg, P. E. Morris, & R. N. Sykes (Eds.), *Practical aspects of memory. Vol 1. Clinical and educational implications* (pp. 58-63). Chichester: Wiley.

Richardson-Klavehn, A., & Bjork, R. A. (1988). Measures of memory. *Annual Review of Psychology, 39,* 475-543.

Squire, L. R., & Zola-Morgan, S. (1983). The neurology of memory: The case for the correspondence between the findings for human and nonhuman primate. In J. A. Deutsch (Ed.), *The physiological basis of memory* (2nd Edn, pp. 199-268). New York: Academic Press.

Tulving, E., & Schacter, D. L. (1990). Priming and human memory systems. *Science, 247,* 301-306.

Tulving, E., Schacter, D. L., & Stark, H. (1982). Priming effects in word-fragment completion are independent of recognition memory. *Journal of Experimental Psychology: Human Learning and Memory, 8,* 336-342.

Warrington, E. K., & Weiskrantz, L. (1968). New method of testing long-term retention with special reference to amnesic patients. *Nature, 217,* 972-974.

Warrington, E. K., & Weiskrantz, L. (1970). Amnesic syndrome: Consolidation or retrieval? *Nature, 228,* 628-630.

Wickelgren, U. A. (1979). Chunking and consolidation: A theoretical synthesis of semantic networks, configuring in conditioning, S-R versus cognitive learning, normal forgetting, the amnesic syndrome and the hippocampal arousal system. *Psychological Review, 86,* 44-60.

CHAPTER TWENTY-FIVE

# Imagery as a Mnemonic Aid in Amnesia Patients: Effects of Amnesia Subtype and Severity

Anders Gade

*Psychological Laboratory, Copenhagen University, and Department of Neurology, Rigshospitalet, Copenhagen, Denmark*

## ABSTRACT

Thirty five amnesic patients, in four subgroups, were studied using the paired associate task introduced by Jones (1974). Three lists of concrete noun pairs were presented and tested in three learning trials and retention one hour later. The first list was presented under standard conditions, i.e. without requests of any specific strategy. The second list was presented with imagery instructions and illustrative pictures. For the third list the patients were requested to generate their own images.

Improvement under imagery conditions was seen in all subgroups. However, severely amnesic patients benefited minimally from imagery. Patients with moderate deficits improved considerably from illustrative pictures, but less so with self-generated imagery. Mildly amnesic patients improved greatly, and the improvement was maintained with self-generated images.

These results indicate that severity of amnesia may be decisive in determining whether imagery instructions aid amnesics, and this could explain why previous studies have produced conflicting results.

Versions of a dual code hypothesis attributing a dominant role to the right hemisphere in the visual imagery effect are not supported by the results.

## INTRODUCTION

Use of imagery was central to the ancient art of memory, which was still taught and used in the middle ages (Patten, 1990). The art may have lost favour with the greater availability of ink and paper during the renaissance, but imagery as a human faculty continued to fascinate, and to Wundt, founder of the first psychological laboratory, images were the constituent elements of ideas, or of consciousness. Other psychologists of the time sought to relate individual differences in recall to vividness of imagery, based on Galton's (1883) observations. Both of these research strategies relied on introspective data, and neither survived the criticisms of the Würzburg school of psychology and behaviourism (Kosslyn, 1980). Imagery itself, derided as "the figment of the psychologist's terminology" (Watson, 1928, p. 76), became a subject largely ignored by psychologists.

When interest in imagery was reawakened, it was at first mainly as an aid to remembering (Miller, Galanter, & Pribram, 1960). Behaviourist approaches to verbal learning were increasingly regarded as too restrictive, and during the 1960s a flurry of studies, summarised by Paivio (1969) and Bower (1972), demonstrated the superior recall when subjects were instructed to use imagery. Both free recall and paired associate (PA) learning were commonly used, but in this paper I shall concern myself only with the latter. In a typical PA task, the subject is presented with a list of word pairs, usually unrelated nouns, and at recall the first word serves as a cue for report of the second word. Subjects may be left to their own devices for remembering, or they might be told before presentation to imagine a visual scene or mentally to picture the two objects interacting in some way. The difference in recall in these two conditions can be quite dramatic in normal subjects, provided lists are sufficiently long to avoid ceiling effects. Although some subjects spontaneously use imagery under standard conditions, a doubling of percentage recalled may be seen with imagery instructions (Bower, 1972).

To account for these and related findings Paivio (1969) assumed that images and verbal processes function as alternative coding systems, or modes of symbolic representation. Imagery improves recall because in this situation the words are doubly coded, and sensory images evoked at recall may serve as mediators to the verbal system. It may be relevant to distinguish between two aspects of Paivio's dual code theory, termed by Marschark and Hunt (1989) dual processing and dual memory. Dual processing refers to separate representations in short-term memory, largely consistent with Baddeley's (1986) working memory slave systems, the visuo-spatial sketchpad and the articulatory loop. This aspect of the theory has been broadly accepted. Dual memory, on the other hand, refers to modality-specific representations in long-term memory. This aspect of the theory has been controversial (Marschark, Richman, Yuille, & Hunt, 1987). Nevertheless, in most of the literature of the imagery effect in learning tasks, Paivio's dual code theory has been generally accepted without consideration of the distinction between the two aspects.

A strong version of dual code theory, linking images and image-mediated verbal learning with the right hemisphere, has also been invoked to explain findings in neurological patients with unilateral lesions (Jones, 1974; Jones-Gotman & Milner, 1978; Patten, 1990). Given the large and well-documented effects of imagery on normal learning, it is natural that clinicians have looked to this technique with some hope for helping their patients with memory deficits. Patten (1972), himself a mnemonist, appears to have been the first to report on its efficacy. He taught the ancient peg-word system to seven patients, reporting good results in four patients with left hemisphere lesions. The three patients who failed to respond were severely amnesic without awareness of their memory defect, and hence uninterested in improving it. Patten's results were based on clinical observation, but replicated by Jones (1974) in a controlled PA study. Patients with removals from the left temporal lobe could benefit from imagery instructions to approximately the same extent as normal controls. Contrary to expectations, however, patients with right temporal lobectomies also improved in the imagery condition. Jones included in her study two amnesic subjects (one of whom was H.M.), who performed at zero level throughout.

The capacity of amnesic patients to improve their verbal learning with imagery in PA tasks has been evaluated in several subsequent studies, with conflicting results. Jones (1974) noted that the failure of her two amnesic patients was not due to a failure to generate images, and Kapur (1978) also demonstrated in Korsakoff patients that generation and inspection of visual images were unproblematic. Yet in two studies (Baddeley & Warrington, 1973; Cutting, 1978) imagery failed completely to improve verbal learning, and Baddeley (1982) has referred to an unpublished study, conducted in association with Brooks, in which amnesic patients sketched on paper generated images to word pairs, yet could not use this to improve retention. Cermak (1975) did find a statistically significant improvement from imagery in six Korsakoff amnesic patients, but later (1980) characterised the effect as fleeting and of doubtful therapeutic value (p.163): "The patients had to be reminded constantly of the specific mnemonic they were using or, for that matter, that a mnemonic had been used at all" . Howes (1983) also obtained a significant effect in Korsakoff patients, although with self-generated imagery the effect was quite modest, and indeed smaller than with experimenter-supplied images, and for neither of the two imagery conditions were any carry-over effects to the succeeding baseline phase evident. Only Leng and Parkin (1988) have reported unambiguously positive findings, using this demonstration of imagery effect to argue against (a strong version of) the cognitive mediation hypothesis (Warrington & Weiskrantz, 1982). Leng and Parkin compared PA learning under standard (no strategy) conditions with both imagery and verbal mediation conditions. No improvement was seen with verbal mediation, whereas images, whether provided by the experimenter or self-generated, gave significantly fewer errors than either standard condition or verbal mediation. The results were similar in two subgroups, one consisting of six patients with bilateral mesial temporal lobe lesions, the other seven Korsakoff patients.

How can we account for or resolve these discrepancies in reported effects of imagery on verbal learning in amnesic patients? One possible explanation was suggested by Leng and Parkin (1988). These authors noted that Baddeley and Warrington (1973) had used an imagery procedure that possibly was too complex, and that Cutting's (1978) similarly negative results could be due to floor effects, with Korsakoff scores being virtually zero under all conditions. A recent review (Glisky & Schacter, 1989) pointed to another factor, suggesting that possibly mild-to-moderately amnesic patients can benefit from imagery techniques whereas those with more severe amnesia cannot. This idea is compatible with Wilson's (1987) observations from both group and single case studies of the effects of imagery in various memory deficient patient categories. The reported data on severity in the reviewed studies do not allow any systematic comparison, but it may be noted that the two amnesics in one negative study (Jones, 1974) had a mean IQ-MQ discrepancy of 46 points, whereas IQ-MQ discrepancies in two positive studies (Howes, 1983; Leng & Parkin, 1988) were 14 and 25, respectively. Furthermore, Weiskrantz (1985) has argued that amnesics studied in London (Baddeley & Warrington, 1973—negative results) were generally more severely amnesic than Korsakoff patients studied in Boston (Cermak, 1975—positive results). Both Baddeley and Warrington's, and Cutting's patients were described as being completely disoriented in time and place. None of the studies, however, has provided within-study comparisons of the imagery effect in moderately and severely amnesic patients, nor correlations between individual severity measures and imagery effects.

The present study was initially designed to explore the effect of visual imagery on verbal learning in patients with amnesia following surgery of aneurysms of the anterior communicating artery, compared to patients with amnesia of other etiologies. The data indicate that etiology is not a significant factor, whereas indeed severity is.

# METHODS

## Patients

Subjects for this study were recruited during a period of seven years (1983-1990) from nine different hospitals. Criteria for inclusion were clinically obvious amnesia and neuropsychological confirmation of memory impairment as either the only cognitive impairment or disproportionately severe relative to other impairments. Clinical data are provided in Table 25.1. The patients were divided into four groups according to etiology.

*Patients with amnesic syndrome after surgery for aneurysms of the anterior communicating artery (ACoA).* In this group of fifteen patients, five had been identified in a prospective study (Gade, 1982), and the present data were collected when these patients were seen for the third time about six years after amnesia onset. Some of the other test data had been collected two years postoperatively, but all five patients were unchanged in amnesia severity. The other ten patients in this group were seen after the prospective study and tested at varying times after amnesia onset, ranging from three weeks in one case to two years. The patients ranged in age from 23 to 58 years, mean 44.5 years. Like the other groups, their mean educational level was somewhat above average. Only three patients were unskilled.

TABLE 25.1
Background Variables and Background Test Scores[1]
in 4 Groups of Amnesic Patients

| | *ACoA* | *DIENCEPHAL.* | *BITEMP.* | *MIX.* |
|---|---|---|---|---|
| N | 15 | 7 | 6 | 7 |
| Age | 44.5 ± 12.1 | 45.6 ± 11.7 | 47.3 ± 10.1 | 33.7 ± 12.8 |
| Education | 12.7 ± 2.6 | 12.8 ± 2.3 | 13.6 ± 2.3 | 12.0 ± 1.7 |
| Male/female ratio | 9/6 | 4/2 | 5/1 | 4/3 |
| DVIQ | 106.1 ± 15.2 | 110.5 ± 8.9 | 112.8 ± 12.7 | 100.0 ± 8.8 |
| Dart | 26.6 ± 10.3 | 32.7 ± 3.3 | 31.8 ± 8.4 | 23.0 ± 7.5 |
| Orientation | 11.7 ± 3.0 | 9.9 ± 4.2 | 12.3 ± 2.0 | 11.3 ± 2.2 |
| Amnesia rating | 32.1 ± 9.2 | 29.2 ± 7.3 | 38.8 ± 12.2 | 30.1 ± 12.5 |
| Independent PA task (15 word pairs: No. correct at criterion of 40 errors) | 4.2 ± 3.4 | 3.1 ± 3.1 | 5.0 ± 3.0 | 4.9 ± 5.1 |
| Buschke selective reminding | 45.1 ± 12.6 | 42.0 ± 11.2 | 38.5 ± 11.4 | 38.4 ± 20.2 |
| 50 words recogn. | 35.7 ± 7.8 | 35.3 ± 3.2 | 38.3 ± 7.4 | 35.4 ± 3.6 |
| 50 faces recogn. | 39.2 ± 8.2 | 36.5 ± 6.0 | 37.0 ± 9.3 | 35.2 ± 5.9 |
| Rey 3 min. recall | 4.1 ± 4.6 | 4.5 ± 7.1 | 8.0 ± 5.2 | 6.3 ± 6.6 |

[1] Higher scores indicate better performance in all tasks except Buschke.

*Patients with amnesia associated with diencephalic lesions (Dienceph.).* Seven patients, six with Korsakoff amnesia and one patient amnesic after removal of a third ventricle tumour. The demographic characteristics of the group were virtually identical to that of the ACoA group.

*Patients with amnesia associated with bilateral lesions of the mesial temporal lobes (Bitemp.).* Four of these patients were amnesic secondary to an anoxic episode; two secondary to herpes simplex encephalitis. These patients tended to be slightly better educated than those in the other groups, and by various test criteria (Table 25.1) they were less severely amnesic. In this respect the group was very heterogeneous, however, as it also included the most severely amnesic patient of the study.

*Patients with amnesia associated with various other etioloqies (Mix.)* Seven patients, including one closed head injury case, one patient amnesic following removal of a pineal body tumour, two patients amnesic after surgery of aneurysms of an internal carotid artery, and three patients amnesic following an encephalitis of unknown type. These patients tended to be younger and slightly less educated compared with the other groups.

One indication of amnesia severity is working capacity. Of the 35 patients included in this study, two patients had been able to maintain employment in their previous jobs, and one recovered after the study to resume previous employment. Five patients had secured employment at lower job levels. Twenty seven patients were either in sheltered employment or unemployed with disablement pension. Only three were in nursing homes at the time of testing or subsequently.

## PROCEDURE

### Paired Associate Learning Task with Imagery

This task is in all essential details identical to that used by Jones (1974). Three lists of each 10 word pairs were prepared (listed in appendix 1). In each list, seven pairs consisted of concrete, high imagery words, and three pairs were abstract and presumably difficult to image visually. The stimuli were common nouns, and the lists were matched on number of words with a frequency of at least 16 per million (11 or 12 of the 20 words in each list were included in the Maegaard and Ruus (1981) word frequency count). For use with the concrete pairs of the second list, a set of cards with colored, cartoon-like illustrations were prepared. The illustrations were clearly drawn, and very simple, showing the two items of each pair in interaction. The words for the three abstract pairs were printed on cards. Examples of the drawings and printed words were shown by Jones (1974, Fig. 1).

The first list provided a baseline of associate learning ability. The second list was a demonstration or teaching list, where the patient was introduced to the idea of visual images as a memory aid and, by the example, was shown how to use it. In the third list the patient was requested to use this method with self-generated images. The following conditions were common for all three lists. Each list was presented in three learning trials, each followed by a test. The first presentation of each list was at a rate of one pair every 10sec.; the second and third readings were at a rate of one pair every 5sec. Immediately following each reading, cued recall was tested by providing the first word of each pair to the patient, who was to respond with the second word. If the patient failed to respond within 15sec. or gave a wrong response, he was told the correct word. On each presentation and each recall trial a different order of presentation was used. This order was the same in each of the three lists. A minimum of four items separated presentation and recall of the same word pairs.

The first list was presented to the patients with standard PA instructions, i.e. as pairs of words to be remembered together, with an explanation of the recall procedure, but without any indication of how remembering could be achieved. List II was presented in trial 1 together with the drawn pictures, preceded by imagery instructions (see appendix 2). The abstract word-pairs were presented in a similar manner, with the explanation that these words had been too difficult to draw, and therefore had been written instead. The cards with pictures or words were shown only during the first reading, but the patients were reminded of the images before the second and third reading, and asked to recreate the images during presentation. Before each recall, the patients were again reminded to use the images for recall.

List III presentation was preceded by an instruction to the patients to generate their own images of each pair of words in interaction, stressing the importance of pictorial vividness. They were not asked to describe their images, but after presentation they were briefly asked to indicate the approximate number of images formed. Between trials they were again reminded to recreate or use the images.

A delayed recall of all three lists was obtained without warning approximately one hour after termination of the learning trials. In the delay period the patients were engaged in unrelated nonverbal tests.

Correct responses to the concrete and abstract word pairs were tallied separately, but to simplify data presentation scores have been collapsed over the three learning trials and delayed recall to yield just one score for each of the three lists for concrete (maximum 28) and abstract (maximum 12) word pairs respectively.

## Other Tests

All patients were administered a range of other memory and general cognitive tests—the latter to ensure the specificity of memory deficits.

Results from a separate, independent paired associate learning test (Andersen, 1976) served as a basis for separating the patients into severity groups. The test consisted of fifteen word pairs, eight unrelated and seven with some semantic relationship between cue and response words. The word pairs were printed on cards, cue word on one side, response word on the other. Cards were presented (and turned over for a view of both sides) at a rate of 6sec. per card, followed immediately by several corrected test trials until all cue words had been responded to correctly (at which time that card was removed from the stack), or until a criterion of 40 failed responses. The measure used in this study was the number of correct responses.

Other reported test measures include a prorated verbal IQ (Gade & Mortensen, 1990), the DART reading test of vocabulary (Danish version of NART), and Warrington's (1985) Recognition Memory Test. As two further illustrations of verbal and figural memory in our patients we selected number of errors in a Buschke learning test (10-word list over 10 trials with selective reminding), and retention of the Rey figure 3min. after completion of copying the figure. An orientation score is based on 14 questions concerning knowledge of time, place and personal data, and the scores of four other mental status tests (Strub & Black, 1985) were added to that of orientation to yield an amnesia rating. These other tests were: recall at delays of 10 and 30min. of three words (6 points), and of three hidden objects and their location (12 points), immediate story recall (12 points), and category-cued recall of 30 named pictures (30 points). The maximum score was 74. In a previous study (Gade & Mortensen, 1990) the normal control group (N:28) scored a mean of 54.8 $\pm$ 5.4.

## RESULTS

*Etiology groups—amnesia severity.* Mean performances of the four amnesia groups on measures of severity are shown in Table 25.1. Amnesic patients with bilateral mesial temporal lobe lesions tended to be less impaired than patients in the other three groups, but none of the differences between groups in measures reported in Table 25.1 reached statistical significance in analyses of variance.

*Etiology groups—imagery tasks.* Mean performances of the four amnesia groups on the abstract word pairs of the three lists are provided in Table 25.2. Performance was very poor in all four groups, and there is obviously no difference between conditions in any of the groups. Comparable values from the three subject groups in Jones' (1974, Fig. 3) study over the three conditions were: normal controls 4.7, 4.6, 7.0; left temporal lobe removals 2.4, 2.3, 3.9; and right temporal lobe removals 6.5, 7.0, 7.8.

The data from the concrete word pairs over the three conditions are shown in Table 25.3. Multivariate analysis of variance (MANOVA) did not indicate any significant intergroup differences ($F(9,93)=0.51$). The condition main effect was highly significant ($F(2,30)=24.0$, $P < 0.0001$),

TABLE 25.2
Mean Performance of the Four Amnesic Patient Groups on the Three Abstract Word Pairs
(Three Learning Trials + Delayed Recall; Maximum Score 12)

| *Group* | *Condition* | | |
|---|---|---|---|
| | *I* | *II* | *III* |
| ACoA | 1.4 ± 2.1 | 1.0 ± 1.3 | 1.3 ± 2.5 |
| DIENCEPH. | 0.4 ± 1.2 | 0.4 ± 0.8 | 0.4 ± 1.2 |
| BITEMP. | 1.5 ± 1.8 | 1.8 ± 2.6 | 2.2 ± 3.9 |
| MIX. | 1.1 ± 1.9 | 1.0 ± 1.5 | 2.3 ± 2.9 |

TABLE 25.3
Mean Performance of the Four Amnesic Patient Groups on the Seven Concrete Word Pairs
(3 Learning Trials + Delayed Recall; Maximum Score 28)

| *Group* | *Condition* | | |
|---|---|---|---|
| | *I* | *II* | *III* |
| ACoA | 4.9 ± 5.7 | 11.7 ± 8.3 | 10.1 ± 9.3 |
| DIENCEPH. | 1.1 ± 1.1 | 8.6 ± 5.7 | 6.1 ± 5.9 |
| BITEMP. | 5.5 ± 6.4 | 14.5 ± 11.3 | 13.8 ± 10.8 |
| MIX. | 5.0 ± 5.5 | 11.4 ± 8.5 | 10.1 ± 8.3 |

but there was no significant group x condition interaction ($F(6,62)=0.31$).

The amnesic patients here performed at much lower levels than Jones' control subjects (who obtained means of 23, 27, and 27 out of 28 possible in the three conditions) and patients with right and left temporal lobe removals (with means of 18, 27, and 26, and of 14, 24, and 21, respectively, in the three conditions). In spite of these lower levels of performance, the gain of the four amnesic groups in scores from standard to imagery conditions were roughly similar to that of Jones' subjects.

*Severity groups—amnesia severity.* Based on the amnesia patients' performance in the independent paired associate task, a division into three groups of approximately equal size was made. Patients with zero or one correct response were designated severely amnesic, patients with two-five correct responses moderately severely amnesic, and patients with six or more correct responses mildly amnesic. These severity designations are intended to characterise the patients' paired associate learning ability only. The mean performances of these severity groups on other memory measures are listed in Table 25.4. Severely amnesic patients are indeed severely impaired on all other memory tasks, but the division between moderate and mild amnesia is not general. Mildly amnesic patients score higher than moderately amnesic patients in the amnesia rating, but the two groups do not differ in orientation,

TABLE 25.4
Mean Performance Levels and Approximate Number of Standard Deviations Below Normal Mean on Memory Measures of the Three Severity Groups

| | | | | *No. of SD's below normal mean* | | |
|---|---|---|---|---|---|---|
| | *Severe* | *Mod.* | *Mild* | *severe* | *mod.* | *mild* |
| Orientation (max. 14) | 10.4 (2.5) | 12.3 (1.3) | 11.6 (3.8) | | | |
| Amnesia rating | 24.9 (4.9) | 32.0 (8.4) | 38.8 (10.3) | 6 | 5 | 3 |
| Word recognition (max. 50) | 32.9 (3.9) | 36.9 (5.9) | 38.1 (7.0) | 4 | 2 | 3 |
| Face recognition (max. 50) | 35.3 (5.1) | 39.8 (6.0) | 38.0 (9.2) | 3 | 1 | 2 |
| Buschke errors | 47.5 (5.9) | 38.8 (16.2) | 39.4 (16.0) | 4 | 3 | 3 |
| Rey 3 min. ret. (max. 36) | 1.3 (2.8) | 7.1 (6.3) | 8.2 (5.1) | 2 | 1 | 1 |

recognition memory, or the Buschke or Rey tasks. Following Weiskrantz's (1985) suggestion, Table 25.4 also lists the approximate mean number of standard deviations below normal values on these memory measures of the three groups.

*Severity groups—imagery task.* Mean performances of the three severity groups on the abstract word pairs on lists I, II and III were: Severe amnesia 0.1, 0.3, 0.0; Moderately severe amnesia 1.7, 0.5, 0.8; and mild amnesia 1.9, 2.1, 3.1.

Results from the concrete word pairs are provided in Table 25.5 for both individual patients and group means. All differences between group means are significant ($P < 0.05$) except between severely and moderately severely amnesic patients in condition I. In MANOVA the main effect of condition is highly significant ($F(3,30)=40.10$, $P <0.0001$), and, most importantly, the group x condition interaction is also significant ($F(6,62)=4.52$, $P < 0.001$). Relative to baseline performance, all three groups improved under imagery instructions. In terms of absolute number of correct responses, the gain with imagery is minimal and clinically insignificant in severely amnesic patients. In moderate and mild amnesia the gain is greater, about 8 and 10 points, respectively, which is comparable to the gain reported by Jones (1974) in patients with unilateral left temporal lobe removals. With self-generated images (list III) patients with moderate amnesia tend to regress towards baseline performance, whereas mildly amnesic patients tend to maintain the imagery gain.

The division into severity groups was based on the patients' performance in a paired associates task, which was different from the dependent measures, yet closely related in its demands on memory functioning. To examine the generality of the effect of amnesia severity for the effectiveness of imagery, a series of MANOVAS were computed with severity defined by each of the six other memory tasks listed in Table 25.1. In each case, the group of amnesic patients was divided into one half with the lowest scores and one half with the highest scores. In MANOVA, the interaction between conditions and severity was not significant with severity defined by errors in the Buschke task ($F(2,32)=1.23$) or orientation ($F=3.04$, $P=0.06$), but did reach significance with severity defined by amnesia rating ($F=7.41$, $P < 0.01$), face recognition ($F=4.29$, $P < 0.05$), word recognition ($F=3.34$, $P < 0.05$) and the Rey task ($F=5.43$, $P < 0.01$).

TABLE 25.5
Individual Results of Patients in the Three Severity Groups on the Independent PA Task (PA) and the Three Conditions of the Imagery Task

| | *Severe* | | | | | *Moderately severe* | | | | | *Mild* | | | |
|---|---|---|---|---|---|---|---|---|---|---|---|---|---|---|
| *Pt. No.* | *PA* | *I* | *II* | *III* | *Pt. No.* | *PA* | *I* | *II* | *III* | *Pt. No.* | *PA* | *I* | *II* | *III* |
| M 28 | 0 | 0 | 0 | 2 | M 23 | 2 | 9 | 12 | 9 | M 20 | 6 | 0 | 13 | 12 |
| A 22 | 0 | 2 | 11 | 3 | A 27 | 2 | 1 | 13 | 5 | A 17 | 6 | 9 | 17 | 22 |
| A 24 | 0 | 0 | 0 | 1 | B 30 | 2 | 2 | 1 | 1 | A 25 | 6 | 0 | 7 | 5 |
| A 33 | 0 | 0 | 6 | 0 | M 9 | 3 | 1 | 14 | 4 | A 16 | 6 | 11 | 20 | 22 |
| D 22 | 0 | 0 | 8 | 6 | D 41 | 3 | 2 | 18 | 13 | D 43 | 6 | 0 | 5 | 1 |
| D 36 | 0 | 1 | 9 | 2 | A 23 | 4 | 5 | 13 | 16 | B 42 | 6 | 2 | 23 | 21 |
| M 27 | 1 | 2 | 0 | 2 | A 30 | 5 | 10 | 20 | 16 | M 40 | 7 | 10 | 20 | 21 |
| A 15 | 1 | 1 | 2 | 1 | B 39 | 5 | 3 | 16 | 15 | A 19 | 7 | 3 | 19 | 19 |
| A 31 | 1 | 1 | 1 | 0 | D 47 | 5 | 0 | 0 | 0 | D 29 | 7 | 2 | 13 | 6 |
| D 32 | 1 | 3 | 7 | 15 | | | | | | B 44 | 7 | 9 | 21 | 21 |
| B 33 | 1 | 0 | 0 | 0 | | | | | | A 34 | 9 | 12 | 25 | 18 |
| A 35 | 1 | 0 | 2 | 1 | | | | | | B 37 | 9 | 17 | 26 | 25 |
| | | | | | | | | | | A 28 | 10 | 18 | 20 | 23 |
| | | | | | | | | | | M 35 | 15 | 13 | 21 | 21 |
| $\bar{x}$ | | 0.8 | 3.8 | 2.8 | | | 3.7 | 11.9 | 8.8 | | | 7.6 | 17.9 | 17.0 |
| SD | | 1.0 | 4.1 | 4.2 | | | 3.6 | 7.0 | 6.5 | | | 6.3 | 6.3 | 7.7 |

Abbreviations in pt. numbers: A = ACoA; D = diencephalic; B = bilateral temporal lobe; M = mix

## DISCUSSION

There were considerable individual differences among amnesia patients in their ability to utilise imagery as a mnemonic aid. Part of this variability is related to amnesia severity, and I propose that this has been the main factor underlying previous contradictory findings of imagery effects in amnesia. Wilson (1987) also used Jones' (1974) task in a study of 36 patients with memory impairment, most of them after head injury. Although these patients were not classified as amnesics, and generally performed at a higher level than the amnesic patients in this study, Wilson's results were very similar to those obtained in the present study. Her severely impaired group was as poor on list III (self-generated imagery) as they were when they had no strategy at all. Her moderately impaired group did benefit from self-generated imagery, but modestly and not to the same extent as they were able to benefit from pictures. Mildly impaired patients found pictures and self-generated images equally beneficial.

The present results, like those of Leng and Parkin (1988), indicate that the etiology, and hence lesion localisation, of the amnesic syndrome play little role for the imagery effect in verbal learning. Considering my and Wilson's (1987) results together, this conclusion seems further strengthened. The potential role of other factors, over and above severity, may be informally explored by considering characteristics of cases that are exceptions to the severity group tendencies indicated in Table 25.5. Among severely amnesic patients, the only truly exceptional case was patient D 32, who gave 15 correct responses (out of 28 possible) with self-generated imagery. D 32 was a 42 year old male Korsakoff patient, who was disoriented and severely amnesic across the board, and yet gave a good response to imagery. There is no ready explanation for this. Among moderately amnesic patients, a good response was seen in patients D 41, A 23, and B 39. Case D 41 and A 23 have in common relatively preserved pictorial memory. Their 3min. retention of the Rey figure was 20 and 10 points, respectively, and in both cases face recognition was better than word recognition (42 and 41 correct on faces; 30 and 31 on words).

To check the generality of this finding, I identified three more patients with a significant (at least 10 point) superiority of face recognition over word recognition (Cases A 15, A 28, and M 28) . These patients did not benefit from imagery instructions. It may also be noted (Table 25.4) that face recognition and 3min. retention of the Rey figure do not differentiate in general between moderate and mild amnesia. Relatively preserved pictorial memory thus does not seem to predict a good imagery response. The third good responder in the moderately amnesic group was B 39, a 50 year old patient amnesic after cardiac arrest. This patient, although severely impaired in both verbal and pictorial learning and recall tasks, displayed completely intact recognition memory. Five other patients were identified with intact performance on face and word recognition tests (Patients A 16, A 17, A 19, B 37, and A 30). By a number of criteria, these patients could all be characterised as among the most mildly amnesic of those included in the study, and they all responded well to imagery (averaging 9.8, 16.4, and 20.8 correct responses in the three lists). This analysis indicates that intact recognition memory may be a factor of some importance. Non-responders in the moderately and mildly amnesic groups, such as cases D 47, A 25, D 43, and D 29, were—in spite of at least five correct responses on the independent PA task—uniformly rather severely amnesic, and also displayed very poor recognition memory.[1]

Fifteen of the present patients had amnesia following surgery of aneurysms of the anterior communicating artery (ACoA). These patients are presumed to have lesions in midline portions of the basal forebrain (Gade, 1982; Phillips, Sangalang, & Sterns, 1987). Based on single case or small group studies, several unique features of the amnesia with this lesion location have been proposed, but so far no systematic differences from amnesic patients with other etiologies have been verified in large group studies (Corkin et al., 1985; Gade & Mortensen, 1986; 1990). In the present study, the patients with basal forebrain amnesia (the ACoA group) did not differ from the other amnesia groups in their ability to utilise imagery as a mnemonic aid in the experimental situation. Among others, Weiskrantz (1985) has argued for a basic similarity in core deficits of all amnesic patients, irrespective of etiology. Others (e.g. Lhermitte & Signoret, 1972; Parkin & Leng, 1988) have demonstrated differences between amnesic patients with diencephalic lesions and bilateral lesions of the mesial temporal lobes, and taken these differences to reflect qualitatively different syndromes. Whatever differences may exist between groups of amnesic patients of different etiologies, an ability to use imagery with benefit seems not to be one of them.

More intuitively surprising, may seem the fact that the moderately amnesic patients, though functioning at a generally lower level, appeared to benefit as much from imagery as did Jones' (1974) patients with unilateral left temporal removals. Yet it should be recalled that Jones' right temporal lobectomy patients also improved with imagery. Jones (1974) had not expected this result, and in a subsequent study Jones-Gotman and Milner (1978), with a more difficult concrete paired associates task with imagery instructions, purported to show that right temporal lobectomy patients were impaired. In this latter study the patients did perform significantly below the normal control group, but the difference was not large, and considerably smaller than between right and left temporal lobectomy groups.[2] This issue has been discussed at greater length by Richardson (1990), who draws the strong conclusion from these data (p.358) "that the neuroanatomical basis of mental imagery is not contained within the structures of the right temporal lobe". The amnesic patients may forget the images they formed, or even forget to use imagery at all, but the mechanism subserving the imagery effect in verbal memory is, it seems from the present data, intact, and hence distinct from the mechanisms of memory itself. Goldenberg, Podreka, Steiner, and Willmes, (1987) attempted to study this directly by measurements of regional cerebral blood flow in normal volunteers during learning of lists of concrete nouns, with and without imagery instructions. Additional control tasks involved the learning of meaningless words and abstract nouns. Performance in all memory tasks was associated with increased blood flow in the hippocampal and inferior temporal regions of both hemispheres, but during the learning of concrete nouns greater activation was seen in occipital regions on both sides as well. The explicit instruction to use imagery led to a leftward shift of hemispheric activity, although at the same time more right hemispheric regions were also activated than without the imagery instruction. Goldenberg et al. interpreted these results as a clear contradiction of the assumption of a right hemisphere specialisation for visual imagery. Farah (1984; 1989) has shown, based on analyses of various components of the imagery ability of patients with localised lesions, that at least the process of generating images seems to depend mainly on a region in the posterior left hemisphere.

This mounting evidence suggests a refutation of strong versions of dual code theory linking the imagery effect in verbal learning to either the right hemisphere specifically or to dual long-term memory (cf. Marschark & Hunt, 1989) . Weak versions of dual code theory, linking the imagery effect with processes in working memory, do not seem to be in conflict with any of the data. Visual working memory may to a large extent be subserved by the same neural structures as visual perception (Farah, 1989), and both these processes and the occipital brain regions are generally intact in amnesic patients.

So, amnesic patients may benefit from visual imagery in a verbal learning task in the laboratory. Does the method also have clinical utility? Can the patients, or some of the patients, improve their functional memory capacity in daily life with imagery? This study did not attempt to answer these questions, and to my knowledge no relevant hard data exist. I did attempt to teach two of the good responders in this study how to apply imagery in daily memory situations. One of these patients elected not to follow my advice, having developed on his own highly efficient, elaborate external memory aids. The other patient was greatly inconvenienced by his inability to learn the names of fellow clients in his day-centre, and successfully learned and used an imagery face-name association technique (Wilson, 1987).

Like Richardson, Cermak, Blackford, and O'Connor (1987), I am sceptical of the real life efficacy of imagery mnemonics in the large majority of amnesic or other patients with brain damage. Wilson (1987) also commented on the disappointingly little spontaneous use of imagery in her memory impaired patients after otherwise successful training of the method in face-name associations. Yet, there seems to be no reason why mild-moderately amnesic patients without other cognitive deficits and with preserved drive should not potentially benefit to the same extent as other patients, and apart from external memory aids other mnemonic techniques seem unattractive. Imagery effect in a PA task, as here, may be a necessary but not sufficient condition for real life efficacy. It is suggested that future attempts to explore the clinical value of imagery techniques, whether in group or single case studies, include Jones' test before the idea of imagery mnemonics is explained and taught to the patients. Common use of this as a screening test may facilitate the research process of identifying the characteristics of those patients, if any, who may be expected to benefit from imagery mnemonics also outside the laboratory, and hence should receive instruction.

## NOTES

1. Ideally factors of predictive significance should be identified using regression analysis, but this would require a considerably larger group of patients than the 35 included in this study to provide robust findings.
2. Milner, Taylor, and Jones-Gotman (1990) have reported an interesting and important study, which came to my attention after completion of the manuscript. They tested eight commissurotomy patients with presumed complete section of the interhemispheric commissures with the original Jones (1974) task. The commissurotomy group performed poorly overall on the learning task, but derived as much benefit as other patient groups from instructions to use imagery. The authors reasoned: "The findings that the disconnected left hemisphere responds normally to imagery instructions was contrary to our prediction, but, in retrospect, it seems that the prediction was based on a failure to analyse the requirements of our learning task. The use of an imagery mnemonic imposes no constraints as to the accuracy or wealth of detail in the image evoked, but only that it function as an adequate mediator between words. There is no evidence that the evocation of such images is critically dependent upon the right hemisphere..." (p.301). These authors' interpretation is thus no longer in disagreement with the interpretation offered in this chapter.

## ACKNOWLEDGEMENTS

This study was supported by a grant from the Danish Medical Research Council. Erik Lykke Mortensen assisted in data analysis, and Elisabeth Glisky and the editors provided helpful comments. Lisbeth Nymann typed the manuscript.

## REFERENCES

Andersen, R. (1976). Verbal and visuo-spatial memory. Two clinical tests administered to a group of normal subjects. *Scandinavian Journal of Psychology, 17,* 198-204.

Baddeley, A.D. (1982). Amnesia: A minimal model and an interpretation. In L.S. Cermak (Ed.), *Human memory and amnesia* (pp. 305-336). Hillsdale, NJ: Lawrence Erlbaum Associates Inc.

Baddeley, A.D. (1986). *Working memory.* Oxford: Clarendon Press.

Baddeley, A.D., & Warrington, E.K. (1973). Memory coding and amnesia. *Neuropsychologia, 11,* 159-165.

Bower, G.H. (1972). Mental imagery and associative learning. In L.W. Gregg (Ed.), *Cognition in learning and memory* (pp. 51-88). New York: Wiley.

Cermak, L. S. (1975). Imagery as an aid to retrieval for Korsakoff patients. *Cortex, II,* 163-169.

Cermak, L. S. (1980). Improving retention in alcoholic Korsakoff patients. *Journal of Studies on Alcohol, 41,* 159-169.

Corkin, S., Cohen, N.J., Sullivan, E.V., Clegg, R.A., Rosen, T.J. & Ackerman, R.H. (1985). Analyses of global memory impairments of different etiologies. *Annals of the New York Academy of Sciences, 444,* 10-40.

Cutting, J. (1978). A cognitive approach to Korsakoff's syndrome. *Cortex, 14,* 485-495.

Farah, M.J. (1984). The neurological basis of mental imagery: A componential analysis. *Cognition, 18,* 245-272.

Farah, M.J. (1989). The neuropsychology of mental imagery. In F. Boller & J. Grafman (Eds.), *Handbook of neuropsychology,* Vol. 2 (pp. 395-413). Amsterdam: Elsevier.

Gade, A. (1982). Amnesia after operations on aneurysms of the anterior communicating artery. *Surgical Neurology, 18,* 46-49.

Gade, A., & Mortensen, E.L. (1986). *A comparison of memory deficits in amnesia associated with aneurysms of the anterior communicating artery and amnesia with other etiologies.* Presented at the Third Nordic Meeting in Neuropsychology. Bergen, Norway, 13-15 August, 1986.

Gade, A., & Mortensen, E.L. (1990). Temporal gradient in the remote memory impairment of amnesic patients with lesions in the basal forebrain. *Neuropsychologia, 28,* 985-1001.

Galton, F. (1883). *Inquiries into human faculty and its development.* London: MacMillan.

Glisky, E.L., & Schacter, D.L. (1989). Models and methods of memory rehabilitation. In F. Boller & J. Grafman (Eds.), *Handbook of neuropsychology,* Vol. 3. Amsterdam: Elsevier.

Goldenberg, G., Podreka, I, Steiner, M., & Willmes, K. (1987). Patterns of regional cerebral blood flow related to memorizing of high and low imagery words—an emission computer tomography study. *Neuropsychologia, 25,* 473-485.

Howes, J. (1983). Effects of experimenter and self-generated imagery on the Korsakoff patient's memory performance. *Neuropsychologia, 21,* 341-349.

Jones, M.K. (1974). Imagery as a mnemonic aid after left temporal lobectomy: Contrast between material-specific and generalized memory disorders. *Neuropsychologia. 12,* 21-30.

Jones-Gotman, M. & Milner, B. (1978). Right temporal-lobe contribution to image-mediated verbal learning. *Neuropsychologia, 16,* 61-71.

Kapur, N. (1978). Visual imagery capacity of alcoholic Korsakoff patients. *Neuropsychologia. 16,* 517-519.

Kosslyn, S.M. (1980). *Image and mind.* Cambridge: Harvard University Press.

Leng, N.R.C., & Parkin, A.J. (1988). Amnesic patients can benefit from instructions to use imagery: Evidence against the cognitive mediation hypothesis. *Cortex. 24,* 33-39.

Lhermitte, F., & Signoret, J.L. (1972). Analyse neuropsychologique et différenciation des syndromes amnésiques. *Revue Neurologique, 126,* 161-178.

Maegaard, B., & Ruus, H. (1981). *Hyppige ord i danske romaner.* Copenhagen: Gyldeldal.

Marschark, M., & Hunt, R.R. (1989). A reexamination of the role of imagery in learning and memory. *Journal of Experimental Psychology: Learning, Memory, and Cognition. 15,* 710-720.

Marschark, M., Richman, C.L., Yuille, J.C., & Hunt, R.R. (1987). The role of imagery in memory: On shared and distinctive information. *Psychological Bulletin, 102,* 28-41.

Miller, G.A., Galanter, E., & Pribram, K.H. (1960). *Plans and the structure of behaviour.* New York: Holt, Rinehart and Winston.

Paivio, A. (1969). Mental imagery in associative learning and memory. *Psychological Review, 76,* 241-263.

Parkin, A.J., & Leng, N.R.C. (1988). Comparative studies of human amnesia: Syndrome or syndromes? In H. Maskowitsch (Ed.), *Information processing and the brain* (pp. 107-123). Toronto: Hans Huber.

Patten, B.M. (1972). The ancient art of memory. Usefulness in treatment. *Archives of Neurology, 26,* 25-31.

Patten, B.M. (1990). The history of memory arts. *Neurology, 40,* 346-352.

Phillips, S., Sangalang, V., & Sterns, G. (1987). Basal forebrain infarction. A clinicopathological correlation. *Archives of Neurology, 44,* 1134-1138.

Richardson, J.T.E. (1990). Imagery and memory in brain-damaged patients. In P.J. Hampson, D.F. Marks & J.T.E. Richardson (Eds.), *Imagery. Current developments.* London: Routledge.

Richardson, J.T.E., Cermak, L.S., Blackford, S.P., & O'Connor, M. (1987). The efficacy of imagery mnemonics following brain damage. In M.A. McDaniel & M. Pressley (Eds.), *Imaginal and related mnemonic processes* (pp. 303-328). New York: Springer Verlag.

Strub, R.L., & Black, F.W. (1985). *The mental status examination in neurology.* Philadelphia: F.A. Davis Co.

Warrington, E.K. (1985). *Recognition Memory Test.* Windsor: NFER-Nelson.

Warrington, E.K., & Weiskrantz, L. (1982). Amnesia: A disconnection syndrome? *Neuropsychologia. 20,* 233-242.
Watson, J.B. (1928). *The ways of behaviourism.* New York: Harper and Brothers.
Weiskrantz, L. (1985). Issues and theories in the study of the amnesic syndrome. In N.M. Weinberger, J.L. McGaugh & G. Lynch (Eds.), *Memory systems of the brain* (pp. 380-415). New York: Guilford Press.
Wilson, B.A. (1987). *Rehabilitation of memory.* New York: Guilford Press.

## APPENDIX 1

### Word pair lists* used for the three conditions

| *List I* | | *List II* | | *List III* | |
|---|---|---|---|---|---|
| pilot | – magazine | bouquet | – elephant | strawberry | – Chinese |
| rain | – glass | prison | – frog | fire | – soldier |
| rat | – bush | snake | – stone | belt | – goat |
| farm | – lion | mushroom | – rooster | saw | – sledge |
| blackbird | – bookcase | wagon | – globe | star | – man |
| match | – doormat | sun | – girl | anchor | – lorry |
| chair | – fork | mill | – axe | drinking bar | – giraffe |
| conversation | – happiness | truth | – amount | pain | – lecture |
| benefit | – song | error | – moment | shout | – work |
| correction | – boredom | lesson | – flight | belief | – goal |

*Some of the words have slightly different connotations in Danish. Word-pair order was not fixed.

## APPENDIX 2

### Imagery instructions

"Now I will read another list to you, much like the first, but this time—while reading the word-pairs—I will show you a method which you are to use to remember them better. You are to imagine the two things in some kind of interaction, and you are to see this as a picture in your "mind's eye". To show you how literally I mean this, I will—while reading each word pair—at the same time show you a picture of the two things. Later, at recall, I want you to use this image to recall the second word, when I tell you the first".

# Author Index

# Subject Index